BARRON'S

HOW TO PREPARE FOR THE

LSAT®

LAW SCHOOL ADMISSION TEST

10TH EDITION

JERRY BOBROW, Ph.D.
Executive Director, Bobrow Test Preparation Services
Programs at major universities, colleges, and law schools throughout California
Lecturer, consultant, author of over 20 nationally known test preparation books
Dr. Bobrow personally instructs over 2,000 LSAT test takers each year

Contributing Authors and Consultants

WILLIAM A. COVINO, Ph.D.
Chairman, Department of English
Florida Atlantic University, Florida

BRIAN N. SIEGEL, J.D.
Bar Review Specialist
Author/Legal Study Aids

MERRITT L. WEISINGER, J.D.
Attorney at Law, Lecturer
Weisinger and Associates

DAVID A. KAY, M.S.
Chairman, Math Department
Moorpark College, California

DANIEL C. SPENCER, M.S.
Management Services Officer
University of California at Los Angeles (UCLA)

ALLAN CASSON, Ph.D.
Former Chairman, Department of English
University of Southern California (USC)

BENARD V. ZANDY, M.S.
Chairman, Math Department
Fullerton College, California

BARRON'S

All inquiries should be addressed to:
Barron's Educational Series, Inc.
250 Wireless Boulevard
Hauppauge, New York 11788
http://www.barronseduc.com

Paper Edition
International Standard Book No. (book only) 0-7641-1665-7
International Standard Book No. (with CD-ROM) 0-7641-7452-5
International Standard Serial No. 1066-5803

PRINTED IN THE UNITED STATES OF AMERICA
987654

Contents

PART TWO ANALYSIS
Understanding the Sections and the Key Strategies 35

Part Three **PRACTICE**
Mastering Problem Types and Time Pressures 239

PREFACE

The LSAT is a difficult exam and we want to give you every possible advantage!

In this book we have gathered the expertise and materials developed in over 28 years of successful LSAT, GMAT, GRE, NTE, CBEST, MSAT, ELM, and SAT preparation courses that are currently offered at over 25 universities, colleges, and law schools.

So how are we going to give you every possible advantage?

By thoroughly analyzing each of the sections of the LSAT and reviewing the thinking processes and the skills necessary for top performance, this text aims at complete preparation. It is up to date with the most recent forms of the latest test. The staff of writers and consultants includes specialists in problem solving, reading, writing, logic, law, and test psychology. All these authors and consultants have been teaching prelaw students in LSAT preparation programs for many, many years.

An introductory mini-exam will both acquaint you with the format of the LSAT and help you spot any of your test-taking weaknesses. Then, a series of insightful chapters on the most recent sections of the test will carefully analyze each question type, pinpoint specific test-taking strategies, and give additional practice. Six full-length practice tests will allow you to get the feel of the real thing while you begin applying new skills and techniques. Your answer sheet will resemble the machine-graded LSAT answer sheet, and an analysis chart will enable you to assess your strengths and weaknesses. The answers to each practice test are fully explained.

Will this be effective?

Complete analysis, thorough instruction, extensive practice, up-to-date examples, and the most successful overall systems of objective test taking are described in detail in this book to give you invaluable insight into the LSAT. The test-taking strategies and approaches we've included have been proven effective for over 2,000,000 graduate and undergraduate students and teachers whom we've assisted in preparing for these important exams.

All right, let's get down to business and start with a brief overview of How to Prepare.

Preparing for the LSAT: A Five-Step Approach

Preparing to take the LSAT is no easy task; it takes a well thought-out, focused study plan. This plan should follow these five basic steps:

1. Awareness
2. Knowing the Basic Skills
3. Understanding the Thinking Processes
4. Applying Strategies and Techniques
5. Practice, Practice, Practice

Awareness

Before taking the LSAT, you should know everything possible about the test from the length of each section to the specific types of questions. Be an expert on the structure and construction of the exam.

The LSAT consists of five 35-minute multiple-choice sections. Four sections count toward your LSAT score; one experimental section is a repeat of the other sections and does not count toward your score. An unscored essay is also included. The types of questions are: Reading Comprehension (one section), Analytical Reasoning (one section), and Logical Reasoning (two sections).

Reading Comprehension—one section that includes four fairly sophisticated passages, each ranging from about 400 to 600 words with 5 to 8 questions per passage for a total of about 26 to 28 questions. The passages can be from the fields of science, philosophy, economy, history, law, and so on, but the questions must be answered from the actual passages given, not from your general or specific knowledge of a subject.

Analytical Reasoning—one section that includes four sets of conditions, statements, or rules. You are required to see the relationships among the items being described and discussed. Constructing a simple display or diagram using the information given is an important part of attacking this question type. Each set is followed by 4 to 7 questions for a total of 22 to 24 questions. This section appears to be the most difficult for most test takers, but it also appears to be the most preparable.

Logical Reasoning—two sections that include short passages, statements, arguments, or discussions, each followed by 1 or 2 questions asking about the reasoning involved. Each section contains between 24 and 26 questions. This question type requires good reading and reasoning skills and accounts for 50 percent of your LSAT score. You will have two sections of Logical Reasoning, about 50 of the 100 questions that count toward your score. A course in formal logic is not necessary but could be helpful, as would any course that requires critical reading and reasoning.

These sections total from 96 to 104 questions and are scaled to a scoring range of 120 to 180 with an average score about 150 or 151. Approximately 60 percent correct is necessary to obtain an average score. There is no penalty for guessing on the LSAT, so never leave a question without at least taking a guess.

Unscored Essay—the multiple-choice sections of the LSAT are followed by a 30-minute unscored essay. This essay is written on a special sheet of paper with about 25 lines and is written in ink (a pen is provided). Scratch paper is given so that you can organize your essay before writing. A copy of your essay is sent to each law school to which you apply. The law schools may use the essay in a number of ways—as a tie-breaker between two applicants, as a measure for admittance, and so on. Test takers who have not seen a sample topic are often worried about the essay topic. You should review a few sample topics and try writing a few essays. The topics typically involve a selection that needs to be made between two people, items, techniques, places, and so on. There is no right or wrong answer. Simply make your selection and support it by using the criteria and information given.

Knowing the Basic Skills

You should know the basic skills necessary to do well on the LSAT. Because the LSAT is designed to measure skills necessary to do well your first year in law school (and not what kind of an attorney you are going to be), it is important to focus your study and some review on these skills. These skills include reading comprehension skills, critical reading skills, analytical skills, and reasoning skills. Notice that the test is reading and reasoning based.

Understanding the Thinking Processes

The LSAT, unlike many other standardized exams, is not content oriented, but is reasoning oriented. Therefore, it is vital to understand the thinking processes involved in obtaining the correct/credited response. You should not memorize information, but focus your preparation on understanding the reasoning involved. Carefully analyzing each question type, the credited response, and the common mistakes will help you understand the thinking processes. You should understand that the correct answer to each question is facing you on the page and that the incorrect answers are called "distracters." An incorrect answer that looks good or is close is often called an "attractive distracter." Learn to avoid the attractive distracters by analyzing the choices and understanding the thinking processes.

Applying Strategies and Techniques

There are many strategies and techniques that you can and should learn before taking your LSAT. The general strategies include how and when to skip problems, eliminate answers, and circle important words. The specific strategies should include how to draw diagrams or simple displays for Analytical Reasoning, how to actively read Reading Comprehension passages and how to preread questions and focus on Logical Reasoning questions. You should also be very familiar with the many types of questions you could be asked in each section. You should take the test only after reviewing and practicing many specific strategies for the question types.

Practice, Practice, Practice

As with other standardized exams, becoming a proficient LSAT test taker takes lots of practice. This practice helps you get acclimated to working under time pressure as well as dealing with the fatigue factor. When you practice, try to replicate testing conditions. Don't use scratch paper, do your work in the test booklet, and transfer your answers to an answer sheet. Don't practice on a large tabletop, as in most cases you will be taking your test in a classroom with fairly small desktops. When you practice, you should give yourself only 30 minutes to complete a section, even though the time allotted is actually 35 minutes. Shorting yourself on time will force you to work faster and should increase your speed. Another reason for extended practice is to identify the types of mistakes you make when you're tired, that is, dealing with the fatigue factor. Practice taking three 35-minute sections (giving yourself 30 minutes for each section) back to back to back with only about a five second break between each one. Then, take a short break of about ten minutes and try another two sections. When you complete your practice tests, carefully analyze each section and watch for any consistent types of errors. On your next practice session, focus on eliminating those errors.

The LSAT is an important, difficult exam, but you can prepare for it, and you owe it to yourself to be prepared. Read and review this book carefully. You'll be glad you did.

Good Luck!!!
Jerry Bobrow, Ph.D.

Jerry Bobrow, Ph.D., author of *Barron's How to Prepare for the LSAT* and many other national best-selling preparation books, has been teaching and directing preparation programs for most of the California State universities for the past 28 years. He personally lectures and teaches over 2,000 LSAT test takers each year.

ACKNOWLEDGMENTS

I gratefully acknowledge the following sources for granting permission to use materials from their publications:

Pages 22, 51, 56, 243, 305, 359, 382, 475, 533, 535, 556: Dean Seymour Greitzer, Law Reviews from Glendale University College of Law.

Pages 37, 42, 50, 443: George E. Riggs, publisher; news articles and editorials from *The Herald News*, Fontana, California.

Page 53: Angela Roddey Holder and John Thomas Roddey Holder, *The Meaning of the Constitution*, 3rd Ed., Barron's Educational Series, Inc., Hauppauge, N.Y., 1997.

Pages 180, 183: Dr. Albert Upton, *Design for Thinking*, Stanford University Press, Stanford, Calif.

Page 245: Herbert Marder, *Feminism & Art: A Study of Virginia Woolf.* Chicago: University of Chicago Press, 1995.

Page 247: C. Vann Woodward, *The Future of the Past.* New York: Oxford University Press, 1991.

Page 307: Roy Sieber and Arnold Rubin, *Sculpture of Black Africa: The Paul Tishman Collection.* Los Angeles: Los Angeles County Museum of Art, 1981. By permission of the copyright holder.

Page 310: John Kenneth Galbraith, *American Capitalism.* Sentry edition. Boston: Houghton Mifflin, 1962.

Page 312: Steve Jones, *The Language of Genes: Unraveling Mysteries of Human Genetics.* New York: Doubleday (Anchor Books), 1995.

Page 327: Law Reviews from the University of California at Los Angeles (UCLA) Law School—Comment, "United States Tax Treaty Policy Toward Developing Countries: The China Example," 35 UCLA L. Rev. 369 (1987).

Page 329: Spiro Kostof, *A History of Architecture.* New York: Oxford University Press, 1995.

Page 332: Robert A. Nisbet, *The Present Age: Progress and Anarchy in Modern America.* New York: Harper & Row, 1988. Reprinted by permission of HarperCollins.

Page 335: Gabrielle I. Edwards, *Biology the Easy Way*, 3rd Ed., Barron's Educational Series, Inc., 2000.

Page 361: Fred Kaplan, *Dickens: A Biography.* New York: William Morrow & Company, 1988.

Page 364: Robert H. Wiebe, *The Segmented Society: An Historical Preface to the Meaning of America.* New York: Oxford University Press, 1983.

Page 387: Paul Veyne, ed., & Arthur Goldhammer, translator, *A History of Private Life: Volume I—From Pagan Rome to Byzantium.* Philippe Aries and Georges Duby, series general editors. Cambridge, Massachusetts: The Belknap Press of Harvard University Press, 1987. Copyright 1987 by the President and Fellows of Harvard College.

Page 389: Joachim Ekrutt, *Stars and Planets*, 2nd Ed. (Consulting Ed. Clint Hatchett), Barron's Educational Series, Inc., Hauppauge, N.Y., 2000.

Pages 439, 554: Roger-Gerard Schwartzenberg, *The Superstar Show of Government*, © 1980 by Barron's Educational Series, Inc., Hauppauge, N.Y. © Flammarion, 1977, solely with respect to the French language edition.

Page 441: Adapted from Arthur Bell, Donald W. Heiney, and Lenthiel H. Downs, *American Literature: 1930 to the Present*, © 1994 by Barron's Educational Series, Inc., Hauppauge, N.Y.

Page 473: Ernst B. Schultz, *Democracy*, 2nd ed., © 1977 by Barron's Educational Series, Inc., Hauppauge, N.Y.

Page 477: Adapted from Arthur Bell, Donald W. Heiney, and Lenthiel H. Downs, *English Literature: 1900 to the Present*, © 1994 by Barron's Educational Series, Inc., Hauppauge, N.Y.

Pages 479, 558: Nicholas Horvath, *Essentials of Philosophy*, © 1974 by Barron's Educational Series, Inc., Hauppauge, N.Y.

Pages 531, 537: Ann Fagan Ginger, *The Law, the Supreme Court and the People's Rights*, © 1977 by Barron's Educational Series, Inc., Hauppauge, N.Y.

Page 560: Mark Willner et al., *Let's Review: Global History and Geography*, 3rd Ed., Barron's Educational Series, Inc., Hauppauge, N.Y., 2000.

Page 580: *Barron's Guide to Law Schools*, © 2002 by Barron's Educational Series, Inc., Hauppauge, N.Y.

(Note: Some of the Law Reviews have been edited, including changes in names, places, and dates).

My thanks to James Zinger, President, Hypmovation, for the use of excerpts from his writings; to Jean Eggenschwiler, writer and editor, for her contributions; to Stacey Baum, Joy Mondragon, and Kristen Fest-Tennison, Deena Mondragon, for their assistance in assembling the manuscript; to Lynn Turner, Dana Lind, Brenda Clodfelter, and Jennifer Johnson for typing the manuscript; and to Linda Turner for manuscript editing and final preparation.

And finally thanks to my wife, Susan Bobrow, for critical analysis and moral support; and to my three children, Jennifer Lynn, 24, Adam Michael, 21, and Jonathan Matthew, 17, for comic relief.

PART ONE

INTRODUCTION

Getting Acquainted with the Test

INTRODUCTION TO THE LSAT

Answers to Some Commonly Asked Questions

What does the LSAT measure?

The LSAT is designed to measure a range of mental abilities related to the study of law; therefore, it is used by most law schools to evaluate their applicants.

Will any special knowledge of the law raise my score on the LSAT?

The LSAT is designed so that candidates from a particular academic background are given no advantage. The questions measure reading comprehension, logical reasoning, and analytical reasoning, drawing from a variety of verbal and analytical material.

Does a high score on the LSAT predict success in law school or in the practice of law?

Success on the LSAT demonstrates your ability to read with understanding and to reason clearly under pressure; surely these strengths are important to both the study and the practice of law, as is the ability to write well, measured by the LSAT Writing Sample. To say that success on the LSAT *predicts* success in law school may overstate the case, however, because success in law school also involves skills that are not measured by the LSAT.

When is the LSAT administered?

The regular administration of the test occurs nationwide four times each year, around the beginning of the fall, winter, spring, and summer seasons. Except for the summer month, the test is usually administered on a Saturday morning from 8:30 A.M. to about 1:00 P.M. For the past few years, the *summer exam* has been given on a Monday afternoon. Dates are announced annually by the Law School Admission Council (LSAC) in Newtown, PA.

What if I cannot take the test on a Saturday?

Some special arrangements are possible: Check the Law School Admission Services (LSAS) General Information Booklet in your registration packet. Those who must take the exam at a time when the regular administration occurs on Saturday, but who cannot participate on Saturday for religious reasons, may arrange for a special Monday administration.

How early should I register?

Regular registration closes about one month before the exam date. Late registration is available up to three weeks prior to the exam date. There is an additional fee for late registration.

How do I register for the LSAT?

You can register for the LSAT three different ways: online, by telephone, or by mail. **To register online,** use: www.LSAC.org. **To register by telephone,** call (215) 968-1001 (Be sure to complete the worksheet in the *Registration/Information Book* before calling.) **To register by mail,** complete the appropriate sections in the *LSAT &*

LSDAS Registration/Information Book and mail with payment to Law Services in the preaddressed return envelope.

Is walk-in registration available?

No. The Law School Admission Council will not permit walk-ins on the day of the test. Be sure to read carefully the LSAT & LSDAS Registration/Information Book section on registering to take the LSAT.

What is the LSDAS?

The LSDAS (Law School Data Assembly Service) compiles a report about each subscribing applicant. The report contains LSAT results, a summary of the applicant's academic work, and copies of college transcripts. A report is sent to each law school that the applicant designates. Thus, if you register for the LSDAS, you will not need to mail a separate transcript to each of your prospective law schools. Reminder: You should review information regarding the Candidate Referral Service in your *LSAT & LSDAS Registration/Information Book*.

How is the LSAT used?

Your LSAT score is one common denominator by which a law school compares you to other applicants. Other factors also determine your acceptance to law school: a law school may consider your personal qualities, grade-point average, extracurricular achievements, and letters of recommendation. Requirements for admission vary widely from school to school, so you are wise to contact the law school of your choice for specific information.

How do I obtain registration forms and registration information?

The registration forms covering the LSAT and LSDAS are available in the *LSAT & LSDAS Registration/Information Book*. Copies of the book are available at the admissions offices of most law schools and testing offices at most undergraduate universities and colleges. You may also obtain the book and more information by writing to Law Services, Box 2000, 661 Penn Street, Newtown, PA 18940-0998; by Internet using www.LSAC.org; by fax at (215) 968-1119; by e-mail at Lsacinfor@LSAC.org, or by telephone at (215) 968-1001.

What is the structure of the LSAT?

The LSAT contains five 35-minute multiple-choice sections followed by a 30-minute Writing Sample. The Writing Sample does not count as part of your LSAT score. The common question types that do count toward your score are Logical Reasoning (two sections), Analytical Reasoning (one section), and Reading Comprehension (one section). In addition to these four sections, one experimental or pretest section will appear. This experimental or pretest section, which will probably be a repeat of one of the common question types, will not count in your score.

How is the LSAT scored?

The score for the objective portion of the test ranges from 120 to 180, and there is no penalty for wrong answers. The Writing Sample is unscored, but copies are sent to the law schools of your choice for evaluation.

What about question structure and value?

All LSAT questions, apart from the Writing Sample, are multiple-choice with five choices. All questions within a section are of equal value, regardless of difficulty.

Should I guess?

There is no penalty for guessing on the LSAT. Therefore, before you move on to the next question, at least take a guess. You should fill in guess answers for those you have left blank or did not get to, before time is called for that section. If you can eliminate one or more choices as incorrect, your chances for a correct guess increase.

How often can I take the LSAT?

You may take the LSAT more than once if you wish. But keep in mind that any report sent to you or to law schools will contain scores for any exams taken over about the past five years, along with an average score for those exams. The law school receiving your scores will decide which score is the best estimate of your ability; many law schools rely on the average score as a reliable figure. Normally, you may not take the test more than three times in a two-year period.

Is it possible to cancel my LSAT scores?

You may cancel your score at the test center or within nine calendar days after taking the test.

How early should I arrive at the test center and what should I bring?

Arrive at the test center 20 to 30 minutes before the time designated on your admission ticket. Bring three or four sharpened No. 2 pencils, an eraser, and a noiseless watch (no alarm, calculator, or beeping), as well as your LSAT Admission Ticket and proper identification as described in the *LSAT & LSDAS Registration/Information Book*. **Note:** You may use only a No. 2 pencil or highlighter pen to underline passages in the test book. Ink or ballpoint pens are not permitted.

Are there accommodations for persons with disabilities?

Persons with documented disabilities may have special accommodations available. Candidates who need accommodations are urged to register and submit all required documentation well in advance of the registration deadlines.

Can I prepare for the LSAT?

Yes. Reading skills and test-taking strategies should be the focus of your preparation for the test as a whole. Success on the more specialized analytical sections of the test depends on your thorough familiarity with the types of problems you are likely to encounter and the reasoning process involved. For maximum preparation, work through this book and practice the strategies and techniques outlined in each section.

Basic Format of the LSAT and Scoring

THE *ORDER* OF THE FOLLOWING MULTIPLE-CHOICE SECTIONS *WILL* VARY. The Experimental Section is not necessarily the last section.

Section	Number of Questions	Minutes
I. Logical Reasoning	24–26	35
II. Analytical Reasoning	22–24 (4 sets)	35
III. Reading Comprehension	26–28 (4 passages)	35
IV. Logical Reasoning	24–26	35
V. Experimental Section	varies	35
Writing Sample	1 essay	30
TOTALS	118–132 questions (only 96–104 count toward your score)	205 minutes or 3 hours 25 minutes

NOTE: For your convenience, this Barron's text labels each section of the diagnostic test (e.g., Reading Comprehension, Logical Reasoning, etc.). In contrast, sections of the actual LSAT exam are not usually labeled.

The LSAT is scored on a 120 to 180 scale.

The following simple chart will give you a very general approximation of the LSAT scoring system. It shows the approximate percentage of right answers necessary on the LSAT to be in a certain score range.

Approximate % of right answers	Approximate Score Range
Between 75% and 100%	160–180
Between 50% and 75%	145–159
Between 25% and 50%	130–144
Between 0% and 25%	120–129

Note that this chart is meant to give you an *approximate* score range.

A Closer Look at the Timing— What It Really Means

Although the LSAT comprises five 35-minute multiple-choice sections and a 30-minute unscored essay, it is important to understand the timing breakdown and what it means. The test is actually broken down as follows:

105 minutes {
Section I 35 minutes
Section II 35 minutes
Section III 35 minutes

Short break—usually 10–15 minutes

70 minutes {
Section IV 35 minutes
Section V 35 minutes

Very, very short break—usually 1 or 2 minutes

30 minutes { Writing Sample (Essay)—30 minutes

Notice that you are given three multiple-choice sections with no breaks in between. When they say "stop" at the end of 35 minutes they will immediately say something like, "Turn to the next section, make sure that you are in the right section, ready, begin." So, in essence, you are working three sections back to back to back. This means that when you practice you should be sure to practice testing for 1 hour and 45 minutes without a break.

After the short break, when you may get up, get a drink, and go to the restroom, you are back for two more back-to-back multiple-choice sections.

For the final 30-minute writing sample you will be given a pen and scratch paper to do your prewriting or outlining.

Keep in mind that there will be some time taken before the exam and after the exam for clerical-type paperwork—distributing and picking up paperwork, filling out test forms, and so on.

Important Reminders

- At least half of your test will contain Logical Reasoning questions; prepare accordingly. Make sure that you are good at Logical Reasoning!
- The experimental or pretest section will usually repeat other sections and can appear in different places on the exam. At the time of the exam, you will not know which section is experimental. Take the test as if all of the sections count.
- Scoring will be from 120 to 180. This is the score, and the percentile rank that goes with it is what the law schools look at and are referring to in their discussions.
- All questions in a section are of equal value, so do not get stuck on any one question. The scores are determined by totaling all of your right answers on the test and then scaling.
- There is NO PENALTY for guessing, so at least take a guess before you move to the next question.
- The 30-minute Writing Sample will not be scored, but copies will be forwarded to the law schools to which you apply. Scratch paper and a pen will be provided for the Writing Sample only.
- Keep in mind that regardless of the format of your exam, two sections of Logical Reasoning, one section of Analytical Reasoning, and one section of Reading Comprehension always count toward your score.

Some Words to the Wise

Ask a Few Questions

Before you actually start your study plan there are four basic questions that you should ask the law schools to which you are applying:

1. Considering my GPA and other qualifications, what score do you think I need to get into your law school?
2. When do you need to get my score reports? Or, When should I take the test to meet your deadlines?
3. What do you do if I take the LSAT more than once? Remember that when the law school receives your score report it will see a score for each time you've taken the test *and* an average of the scores. It is up to the law schools and their governing bodies as to what score(s) they will consider. Try to do your best on the first try and take the LSAT only once, if possible.
4. What do you do with my Writing Sample? Is it used as a tiebreaker? Do you score it yourself? Is it just another piece of the process?

Knowing the answers to most of these questions before you start your study will help you understand what is expected and will help you get mentally ready for the task ahead.

An Effective Study Program

A Five-Week LSAT Study Plan

Many students don't even bother to read the LSAT bulletin, let alone do any thorough preparation for the test. You, however, should begin your LSAT preparation by reading the LSAT bulletin (book) carefully; information about how to obtain one is on page 4. The bulletin is filled with information about registration and score reporting. Also provided in the registration book is an "official" practice test. You should also send for copies of old exams (good practice).

With the preliminaries out of the way, begin working through this book. If you have the time, the following study plan is ideal and is used in many LSAT preparation programs at major universities and colleges. However, if you have a shorter time to prepare, simply adjust the following five-week plan to meet your needs (remember, lots of *practice* and *analysis*). You will find the techniques, strategies, practice, and analyses in this book invaluable to your preparation, either with the ideal five-week plan or with the shorter study plan.

Most people can keep up with the following study sequence by devoting about 7 to 10 hours a week. It is most important that you review and practice *daily*, for about an hour or two each day. Don't "save up" your practice for one long session each week. Shorter, regular practice sessions will allow you to assimilate skills and strategies more effectively and efficiently.

Always spend some extra time reviewing "why" you made your mistakes. Watch for repeated or consistent errors. These errors are often the easiest to correct. As you review, focus on the thinking process involved in reaching the credited response, and note specifically where you made the error.

If you have reviewed an explanation, and still do not understand where you made an error, mark the problem in your book and go on. Return to review this problem later, after you have had an opportunity to review other problems that use similar thinking processes. Don't get stuck on reviewing one problem.

Week 1

- Read the section "Answers to Some Commonly Asked Questions" (p. 2).
- Complete, correct, and analyze the Diagnostic Mini-Exam (p. 15).
- Read carefully "Before You Begin" (p. 9), paying special attention to the "One-Check, Two-Check System" and the "Elimination Strategy." Applying these techniques confidently should make quite a difference in your test taking.
- Read carefully the chapters on Reading Comprehension, Logical Reasoning, Analytical Reasoning, and the Writing Sample.
- Spend some extra time reviewing the chapter on Logical Reasoning. Remember: Logical Reasoning will comprise two of the four scored sections of your exam.

Week 2

- Review the chapter on Reading Comprehension. Do the Reading Comprehension problems in the chapter, the ones in the LSAT sample test, and those in Model Test One (p. 243). Correct and analyze your performance.

    Note: Do not time yourself on these practice tests. Your task at present is to familiarize yourself with strategies and techniques, a task that is best done slowly, working back and forth between the introductory chapter and the practice problems. You may get an uncomfortable number of problems wrong at this stage, but, instead of being discouraged, you should attempt to understand clearly the reasons for your errors. Such understanding will become a plus in the future.

- Review the chapter on the Writing Sample, and write an essay about one of the given topics. Ask a friend with good writing skills to read your essay and offer constructive criticism.
- Review the chapter on Logical Reasoning. Do the Logical Reasoning problems in the chapter, those in the LSAT practice test, and the ones in Model Test One (pp. 256 and 268). Correct and analyze your performance.

Week 3

- Review the chapter on Analytical Reasoning. Do the Analytical Reasoning problems in the chapter, those in the LSAT practice test, and those in Model Test One (pp. 252 and 264). Correct and analyze your performance.
    Note: At this point you have introduced yourself to the whole test, and have tried some effective strategies. Now you should begin timing each of your practice tests.
- Do the Reading Comprehension problems in Model Test Two (pp. 305 and 327), and the Logical Reasoning problems in Model Test Two (pp. 297 and 319). Correct and analyze your performance.
- Do the Analytical Reasoning problems in Model Test Two (p. 315). Correct and analyze your performance.
- Write another essay about one of the topics given in the Writing Sample chapter, and have a friend read and respond to your effort.

Week 4

- Do all of Model Test Three; practice and review two or three sections each day. For each section, time yourself (always short yourself on time during practice by about 10 to 15 percent), then correct and analyze your performance.
- Do all of Model Test Four. Start with the first three sections. After a sufficient break, correct and analyze your performance. On the next day, take the next three sections (two multiple-choice sections and the Writing Sample) in one sitting. Correct and analyze your performance. Have a friend read and respond to your Writing Sample.
    Note: This long practice testing will familiarize you with some of the difficulties you will encounter on the actual test—maintaining focus and concentration, dealing with fatigue, pacing, etc. It will also help you build your endurance. Remember, as you analyze your mistakes, to watch for repeated errors. Sometimes these are the easiest to eliminate.

Week 5

- Early in the week, do all of Model Test Five; practice and review three sections each day. For each section, time yourself, then correct and analyze your performance. Again, have a friend read and respond to your efforts on the Writing Sample.
- If you have time early in the week, you may wish to do Model Test Six for extra practice. You can follow the procedure used for Model Test Five, or simply take and review individual sections as needed.
- A few days before your exam, review some of the problems you have already completed—focus on the thinking processes. You may wish to reread chapters that gave you the most difficulty.

- Finally, carefully read the review of test-taking strategies at the end of the book (p. 576). It will recap the highlights of the book, and supply a variety of tips for putting yourself into an effective state of mind before the LSAT.

Before You Begin

The Main Focus

Understanding the Thinking Processes

One of the key factors in your success on the LSAT is your mastery of the LSAT "thinking processes." There is no question that this will take lots of time working practice problems, but it will also take a carefully focused analysis of that practice.

As you read each introductory chapter, keep in mind the thinking process involved as it is explained. You are not trying to learn or memorize any actual problem; rather, you are trying to learn the process behind solving each problem type so that you will be able to apply that process to new problems.

Notice that each section is designed to analyze this thinking process and to help you understand what the test maker had in mind when constructing the question. Learn to understand the reasoning behind the construction of each question.

If you focus on this reasoning as you prepare, the techniques carefully explained in each chapter will be easier to apply and will become even more effective. Remember that it is the mastery of this thinking process within the time constraints that will yield success on the LSAT.

Some General Strategies

The One-Check, Two-Check System

Many people score lower than they should on the LSAT simply because they do not get to many of the easier problems. They puzzle over difficult questions and use up the time that could be spent answering easy ones. In fact, the easy questions are worth exactly the same as the difficult ones, so it makes sense not to do the hard problems until you have answered all the easy ones.

To maximize your correct answers by focusing on the easier problems, use the following system:

1. Attempt the first question. If it is answerable quickly and easily, work the problem, circle the answer in the question booklet, and then mark that answer on the answer sheet. The mark on the answer sheet should be a complete mark, not merely a dot, because you may not be given time at the end of the test to darken marks.
2. If a question seems impossible, place two checks (✔✔) on or next to the question number in the question booklet and mark the answer you guess on the answer sheet. Again, the mark on the answer sheet should be a complete mark, not merely a dot.
3. If you're in the midst of a question that seems to be taking too much time, or if you immediately spot that a question is answerable but time-consuming (that is, it will require more than two minutes

to answer), place one check (✔) next to the question number, mark an answer you guess on the answer sheet, and continue with the next question.

NOTE THAT NO QUESTIONS ARE LEFT BLANK. AN ANSWER CHOICE IS *ALWAYS* FILLED IN BEFORE LEAVING THAT QUESTION.

4. When all the problems in a section have been attempted in this manner, there may still be time left. If so, return to the single-check (✔) questions, working as many as possible, changing each guessed answer to a worked-out answer, if necessary.

5. If time remains after all the single-check (✔) questions are completed, you can choose between

   a. attempting those "impossible" double-check (✔✔) questions (sometimes a question later on in the test may trigger one's memory to allow once-impossible questions to be solved);

   or

   b. spending time checking and reworking the easier questions to eliminate any careless errors.

6. Remember: use *all* the allotted time as effectively as possible.

You should use this system as you work through the practice tests in this book; such practice will allow you to make "one-check, two-check" judgments quickly when you actually take the LSAT. As our extensive research has shown, use of this system results in less wasted time on the LSAT.

The Elimination Strategy

Faced with five answer choices, you will work more efficiently and effectively if you *eliminate unreasonable or irrelevant answers immediately*. In most cases, two or three choices in every set will stand out as obviously incorrect. Many test takers don't perceive this because they painstakingly analyze every choice, even the obviously ridiculous ones.

Consider the following Logical Reasoning problem:

According to the theory of aerodynamics, the bumblebee is unable to fly. This is because the size, weight, and shape of its body in relationship to the total wingspan make flying impossible. The bumblebee, being ignorant of this "scientific truth," flies anyway.

The author's statement would be strengthened by pointing out that

(A) the theory of aerodynamics may be readily tested

(B) the bumblebee does not actually fly but glides instead

(C) bumblebees cannot fly in strong winds

(D) bumblebees are ignorant of other things but can't do all of them

(E) nothing is impossible

A student who does not immediately eliminate the unreasonable choices here, and instead tries to analyze every choice, will find herself becoming confused and anxious as she tries to decide how even silly choices might be correct. Her thinking goes something like this: "I wonder if bumblebees do glide; I've never looked that closely—maybe the test has me on this one . . . come to think of it, I've never seen a bumblebee in a strong wind; (C) is tricky, but it just might be right . . . I can't understand (D); it seems irrelevant but that just might be a trick . . ."

On and on she goes, becoming more and more uncertain.

Using the elimination strategy, a confident test taker proceeds as follows:

?(A) Possible choice.
(B) Ridiculous. Both false and irrelevant. Cross it out.
(C) Another ridiculous, irrelevant one. Cross it out.
(D) Incomprehensible! Eliminate it.
?(E) Too *general* to be the best choice.

This test taker, aware that most answer choices can be easily eliminated, does so without complicating the process by considering unreasonable possibilities.

To summarize the elimination strategy:

* Look for unreasonable or incorrect answer choices first. Expect to find at least two or three of these with every problem.
* When a choice seems wrong, cross it out in your test booklet *immediately*, so that you will not be tempted to reconsider it.

Eliminating choices in this fashion will lead you to correct answers more quickly, and will increase your overall confidence.

Marking in the Test Booklet

Many test takers don't take full advantage of opportunities to mark key words and draw diagrams in the test booklet. Remember that, in the Reading Comprehension and Logical Reasoning sections, *marking key words and phrases will significantly increase your comprehension and lead you to a correct answer.* Marking also helps to keep you focused and alert. In the Analytical Reasoning section, *drawing diagrams is absolutely essential.*

Further, more specific hints about marking are given in the introductory chapters that follow. The important general point to stress here is that active, successful test taking entails marking and drawing, and that passive, weak test takers make little use of this technique.

Guessing

Because there is no penalty for guessing, you should *never leave a question without taking a guess*. And because there is no penalty for guessing, when you have about 3 minutes left, place your finger on where you are on your answer sheet (or make a light mark in your question booklet); then take your favorite letter and fill in the remaining answers on your answer sheet for that section. That is, if there are 26 questions in a section, you should fill in 26 answers. Once you have taken your ending guesses, go back and continue working where you left off and change your answers on the answer sheet. That way, if the proctor says "Stop, time is up!" you will at least have gotten all your guesses in.

The "Multiple-Multiple-Choice" Item
(Not appeared recently)

Although the "Multiple-Multiple-Choice" Item has not appeared in the last nine or ten years, we have included a few samples with some excellent strategies in the event that any do reappear on a future exam.

EXAMPLE

According to the theory of aerodynamics, the bumblebee should be unable to fly. But it flies anyway.

Which of the following can be logically inferred from the above statement?

I. The bumblebee's behavior contradicts scientific theory.
II. The bumblebee is not really able to fly.
III. Some theories don't hold true in all cases.
(A) I only   (B) II only   (C) I and II only   (D) I and III only
(E) I, II, and III

Analysis

When faced with a problem of this structure, first try to quickly answer each of the roman numerals as true or false and label them accordingly. They would therefore be labeled as follows:

T I. The bumblebee's behavior contradicts scientific theory.
F II. The bumblebee is not really able to fly.
T III. Some theories don't hold true in all cases.
(A) I only   (B) II only   (C) I and II only   (D) I and III only   (E) I, II, and III

Therefore, since I and III are true, the answer is (D).

Quite frequently, however, determining each of the roman numerals as true or false is not a quick or easy proposition. In such a case it may be effective (and possibly less time consuming) to skip the difficult roman numerals, solve the easy ones, and then eliminate the final choices, as follows:

?   I. The bumblebee's behavior contradicts scientific theory.
F   II. The bumblebee is not really able to fly.
T   III. Some theories don't hold true in all cases.
   (A) I only   (B) II only   (C) I and II only   (D) I and III only   (E) I, II, and III

Notice that, since II is false, any choice containing a false II may be eliminated. Thus, (B), (C), and (E) should be crossed out. Continuing, since III is true, any remaining choice must contain a true III for it to be correct. Thus, choice (A) may be eliminated as it does not contain a true III. This leaves only choice (D) as the correct answer.

In some cases you will be able to eliminate all but the correct answer, as above. In other cases you may find several possible choices remaining, and thus have a more educated guess.

Becoming familiar with this technique will often save you time and allow you to take better educated guesses in those cases when you have partial information, when parts of the problem appear too difficult, or when the question itself does not appear to give enough direction.

Pitfalls—What to Watch Out For

The Common Mistake—The Misread

The most common mistake for many test takers is the MISREAD. The MISREAD occurs when you read the question incorrectly. For example, "Which of the following *must* be true?" is often read as "Which of the following *could* be true?" and "All of the following must be true EXCEPT" often loses the word "except."

If you MISREAD the question, you will be looking for the wrong answer.

To help eliminate the MISREAD, always underline or circle what you are looking for in the question. This will also help you focus on the main point of the question.

By the way, the MISREAD also occurs while reading answer choices. You may wish to underline or circle key words in the answers to help you avoid the MISREAD.

Distracters and "Attractive" Distracters

When the test makers put together the LSAT they spend a great deal of time and effort not only making sure that "credited response" is the best answer given, but also that the wrong answer choices (distracters) are good possibilities.

Distracters, as the word indicates, are meant to distract you away from the right answer. Some distracters are easily eliminated as they are just "wrong"—they are irrelevant, contradict something, or bring in items that are not addressed. Some distracters are too general, too specific or narrow, or use a word or words that miss the mark or point of the question. Some distracters are very close to the best or right answer. We refer to the wrong answers that are close as "attractive distracters." The choice looked good but was wrong. When you have narrowed your choices down to two, let's say (A) or (B), keep in mind that one is probably an "attractive distracter."

As you prepare for the LSAT it is important that you focus on the difference (in some cases a very fine difference) between the correct answer and the attractive distracter(s). When you analyze your practice tests, focus on what constitutes a right answer and on spotting the differences.

Analyzing Your LSAT Score: A Broad Range Score Approximator

The chart that follows is designed to give you a general approximation of the number of questions you need to get right to fall into a general score range and percentile rank on your LSAT. It should help you see if you are in the "ballpark" of the score you need. This range approximator is *not* designed to give you an exact score or to predict your LSAT score. The actual LSAT will have questions that are similar to the ones encountered in this book, but some questions may be either easier or more difficult. The variance in difficulty levels and testing conditions can affect your score range.

Obtaining Your Approximate Score Range

Although the LSAT uses a very precise formula to convert raw scores to scaled scores, for the purpose of this broad range approximation simply total the number of questions you answered correctly. Next, divide the total number of correct answers by the total number of questions on the sample test. This will give you the percent correct. Now look at the following chart to see the approximate percent you need to get right to get into your score range. Remember, on the actual test one of the sections is experimental and, therefore, doesn't count toward your score.

Approximate Scaled Score Range	Approx. % of Correct Answers Necessary	Approx. Score Percentile for 94–95 Test takers (Est. % below)
171–180	95 and up	99–99.9%
161–170	80–94%	88–98%
151–160	65–79%	53–85%
141–150	45–64%	17–48%
131–140	30–44%	3–15%
121–130	20–29%	0–2%

On the actual LSAT, the percent of correct answers to get certain scores will vary slightly from test to test, depending on the number of problems and the level of difficulty of that particular exam.

An average score is approximately 151.

If you are not in the range that you wish to achieve, check the approximate percent of correct answers that you need to achieve that range. Carefully analyze the types of errors you are making and continue practicing and analyzing. Remember, in trying to approximate a score range, you must take the complete sample test under strict time and test conditions.

Chapter 1
A DIAGNOSTIC MINI-EXAM

The purpose of this mini-exam is to familiarize you with the common areas on the LSAT by giving you a sampling of typical problems. It is designed to introduce the testing areas. The chapters to follow on each exam area will give you a much more complete range of the problem types and difficulties.

This mini-exam should be taken under strict test conditions with each section timed as follows:

Section	Description	Number of Questions	Time Allowed
I.	Logical Reasoning	9	10 minutes
II.	Reading Comprehension	7	10 minutes
III.	Analytical Reasoning	7	10 minutes
IV.	Logical Reasoning	9	10 minutes
	Writing Sample		30 minutes
TOTALS:		32	70 minutes

The actual LSAT contains five 35-minute sections plus a 30-minute Writing Sample for a total of almost 3½ hours of testing. Note that one section will be experimental and will be a duplication of one of the above sections. Also note that it may appear anywhere in the test. Thus, only four sections will count toward your score—two Logical Reasonings, one Analytical Reasoning, and one Reading Comprehension.

After correcting the mini-exam and assessing your strengths and weaknesses, you should start your area analysis with Chapters 2 through 5.

Now tear out your answer sheet from this book, turn to the next page, and begin the mini-exam.

Answer Sheet—

Practice Mini-Exam Law School Admission Test (LSAT)

Note: The actual LSAT has five sections, plus a Writing Sample. Section titles are not given.

Section 1	Section 2	Section 3	Section 4
Logical Reasoning	Reading Comprehension	Analytical Reasoning	Logical Reasoning

Section 1
Logical Reasoning

1. Ⓐ Ⓑ Ⓒ Ⓓ Ⓔ
2. Ⓐ Ⓑ Ⓒ Ⓓ Ⓔ
3. Ⓐ Ⓑ Ⓒ Ⓓ Ⓔ
4. Ⓐ Ⓑ Ⓒ Ⓓ Ⓔ
5. Ⓐ Ⓑ Ⓒ Ⓓ Ⓔ
6. Ⓐ Ⓑ Ⓒ Ⓓ Ⓔ
7. Ⓐ Ⓑ Ⓒ Ⓓ Ⓔ
8. Ⓐ Ⓑ Ⓒ Ⓓ Ⓔ
9. Ⓐ Ⓑ Ⓒ Ⓓ Ⓔ

Section 2
Reading Comprehension

1. Ⓐ Ⓑ Ⓒ Ⓓ Ⓔ
2. Ⓐ Ⓑ Ⓒ Ⓓ Ⓔ
3. Ⓐ Ⓑ Ⓒ Ⓓ Ⓔ
4. Ⓐ Ⓑ Ⓒ Ⓓ Ⓔ
5. Ⓐ Ⓑ Ⓒ Ⓓ Ⓔ
6. Ⓐ Ⓑ Ⓒ Ⓓ Ⓔ
7. Ⓐ Ⓑ Ⓒ Ⓓ Ⓔ

Section 3
Analytical Reasoning

1. Ⓐ Ⓑ Ⓒ Ⓓ Ⓔ
2. Ⓐ Ⓑ Ⓒ Ⓓ Ⓔ
3. Ⓐ Ⓑ Ⓒ Ⓓ Ⓔ
4. Ⓐ Ⓑ Ⓒ Ⓓ Ⓔ
5. Ⓐ Ⓑ Ⓒ Ⓓ Ⓔ
6. Ⓐ Ⓑ Ⓒ Ⓓ Ⓔ
7. Ⓐ Ⓑ Ⓒ Ⓓ Ⓔ

Section 4
Logical Reasoning

1. Ⓐ Ⓑ Ⓒ Ⓓ Ⓔ
2. Ⓐ Ⓑ Ⓒ Ⓓ Ⓔ
3. Ⓐ Ⓑ Ⓒ Ⓓ Ⓔ
4. Ⓐ Ⓑ Ⓒ Ⓓ Ⓔ
5. Ⓐ Ⓑ Ⓒ Ⓓ Ⓔ
6. Ⓐ Ⓑ Ⓒ Ⓓ Ⓔ
7. Ⓐ Ⓑ Ⓒ Ⓓ Ⓔ
8. Ⓐ Ⓑ Ⓒ Ⓓ Ⓔ
9. Ⓐ Ⓑ Ⓒ Ⓓ Ⓔ

✂ To remove, cut along dotted rule.

1   1   1   1   1

SECTION I
TIME — 10 MINUTES
9 QUESTIONS

<u>Directions:</u> In this section you will be given brief statements or passages and will be required to evaluate the reasoning involved. In some instances, more than one choice will appear to be a possible answer. You are to choose the *best* answer. Use common sense and reasonableness in making your selection; then mark the proper space on the answer sheet.

1. The theory that the subconscious is simply the unsymbolized suggests the desirability of adequate verbalization at the earliest possible stage of emotional development. It is the nameless fears and frustrations that defy analysis.

   The author of this passage would most likely agree that

   (A) there is nothing to fear but fear itself
   (B) emotional development starts at birth
   (C) verbalization is the key to complete emotional development
   (D) unsymbolized thoughts and emotions cannot be analyzed
   (E) the subconscious initiates only nameless fears and frustrations

2. *Article:* Many studies have demonstrated that cardiovascular health is greatly improved by regular exercise. As little as a half-hour's walk three times a week is sufficient to strengthen the heart and to help control weight. Even men and women in their 50s and 60s who have not exercised regularly for many years show beneficial effects almost at once. But there may be a slight disadvantage.

   Which one of the following most logically completes this paragraph?

   (A) Their hearts will never be as strong as those of men and women who have exercised regularly throughout their lives.
   (B) The half-hour's walk can be gradually extended to increase the cardiovascular benefit.
   (C) Other exercises to increase lung and upper-body strength are also recommended.
   (D) Weight control should combine moderate exercise with a carefully planned diet.
   (E) Older people are likely to suffer from muscle aches, especially in the first few months of a new exercise program.

GO ON TO THE NEXT PAGE ➤

1   **1**   **1**   **1**   **1**

3. The most serious threat to modern man, it would seem, is not physical annihilation but the alleged meaninglessness of life. This latent vacuum becomes manifest in a state of boredom. Automation will lead to more and more free time and many will not know how to use their leisure hours. This is evidenced today by what Dr. Frankl refers to as Sunday Neurosis, the depression that afflicts people who become conscious of the lack of content in their lives when the rush of the busy week stops. Nothing in the world helps man to keep healthy so much as the knowledge of a life task. Nietzsche wisely said, "He who knows a Why of living surmounts every How."

Which one of the following is the best refutation of the above argument?

(A) The availability of free time does not afford people more opportunity to enjoy their blessings.
(B) Nuclear annihilation would vastly transcend the issue of personal meaningfulness.
(C) Automation may actually result in more people working in such fields as computer science and technology.
(D) The problem of personal meaning has existed since the beginning of modern times.
(E) Most people actually enjoy their weekends when their work week ends on Friday.

4. Reading is an activity involving the use of the visual apparatus by means of which printed words are recognized.

The above definition would be weakened most by pointing out that

(A) a "nonreader" can recognize words
(B) skimming is a form of reading
(C) some printed words can be difficult to interpret
(D) seeing is necessary for reading
(E) lengthy printed words are not easily recognized

Questions 5–6

Juan said, "It takes a good swing to be a good golfer. It takes practice to develop a good swing. Thus, it takes practice to be a good golfer."

5. Which of the following most closely parallels the logic of this statement?

(A) Betsy can bake a good cake if she wants to. Betsy baked a good cake. Thus, she must have wanted to bake a good cake.
(B) A vote for Senator Cobb is a vote for peace. I voted for Senator Cobb. Thus, I want peace.
(C) You must work to earn money. You need money to pay the rent. Thus, you must work to pay the rent.
(D) It costs $200 to buy the TV. It costs $50 to buy the radio. Thus, the TV costs more than the radio.
(E) It is important to be alert when you take an exam. If you take a cold shower, you will be alert. Thus, you should take a cold shower before you take your exam.

6. Which of the following would weaken Juan's argument the most?

(A) It takes more than a good swing to be a good golfer.
(B) Some good golfers have average swings.
(C) Some people are born with a good golf swing.
(D) It takes strong forearms to have a good golf swing.
(E) Many good golfers lift weights.

GO ON TO THE NEXT PAGE ➤

1　　　**1**　　　**1**　　　**1**　　　**1**

Questions 7–8

A leading discount chain store recently held a large nationwide sale of reproductions of masterpieces of the past and present. In every city, by far the largest sales were of nineteenth-century realistic landscapes, while hardly any paintings by cubist and abstract artists of the twentieth century found buyers. Since all the paintings were inexpensive and of approximately the same size, it is clear that popular tastes have not caught up with the last hundred years in the development of painting. Attendance figures suggest that modern audiences are equally behind the times in their response to classical music and ballet.

7. If the statements above are true, which one of the following is also most likely to be true?

   (A) At auctions, original paintings by leading artists of the twentieth century will sell for lower prices than nineteenth-century landscapes.
   (B) Summer outdoor concerts of classical music attract larger crowds for programs of nineteenth-century music than for concerts of works by contemporary composers.
   (C) The size of the audience for ballet and the number of professional ballet companies has declined in the years between 1950 and 1990.
   (D) Most interior decorators choose a painting for the suitability of its colors to the room in which it will be placed.
   (E) There is rarely any clear relationship between the painting and the music of a particular era.

8. Upon which one of the following assumptions does this passage rely?

   (A) A person who dislikes modern art will also dislike modern music.
   (B) The rise in the cost of tickets does not explain the changing attendance patterns of ballet and opera.
   (C) The decline in interest in serious art and music coincides with the rise in the popularity of television.
   (D) The audience for art and music in the nineteenth century was more discriminating than the twentieth-century audience.
   (E) Chain store sales are an adequate indicator of popular taste in art.

9. X: The federal and the state governments are violating the Constitution. The Constitution guarantees my right to bear arms. The new federal law that requires a three-day waiting period when I buy a gun is an illegal infringement of my Constitutional rights. So is the state requirement that I register each time I buy ammunition.

   Y: Because the Constitution guarantees the right of assembly does not mean that a group may gather to plan to disrupt the services of a religious sect.

   The method Y uses to attack X's argument is to

   (A) define a term more carefully
   (B) distinguish a fact from an opinion
   (C) expose a false assumption
   (D) employ an analogy
   (E) question an unproven premise

STOP

IF YOU FINISH BEFORE TIME IS UP, CHECK YOUR WORK ON THIS SECTION OF THE TEST ONLY.
DO NOT GO ON TO THE NEXT SECTION OF THE TEST UNTIL TIME IS UP FOR THIS SECTION.

2   **2**   **2**   **2**   **2**

SECTION II
TIME — 10 MINUTES
7 QUESTIONS

<u>Directions:</u> Read the passages and answer the questions following each passage by blackening the appropriate space on the answer sheet. You may refer back to the passages when answering the questions. Answer all questions on the basis of what is stated or implied.

In 1957, Congress passed the Price-Anderson Act, which provides a current limitation of $665 million on the
line liability of nuclear power companies in
(5) the event of a "nuclear incident." The dual purpose of the Act is to "protect the public and encourage the development of the atomic energy industry." While the objective of
(10) encouraging the development of atomic energy has been achieved, it is not yet known if Price-Anderson would fully compensate the public in the event of a serious nuclear accident.
(15) In the event that a major accident does occur in this country, would the victims be adequately compensated for their injuries? The nuclear industry is promoted under Price-Anderson by
(20) having a limit on potential liability even if the accident was the result of gross negligence or willful misconduct. Victims are protected by having an asset pool of at least $665 million in which to
(25) recover for damages. This amount will undoubtedly be raised when Price-Anderson is renewed. Victims are also protected if an accident is deemed to be an "extraordinary nuclear occurrence"
(30) by the requirement that certain defenses be waived by the utility company. However, the victims would still substantially bear the risk because of the uncertainty of recovery for
(35) radiation injuries. This is contrary to the tort (wrongful act) concept that "he who breaks must pay."
The Price-Anderson Act does not disturb the common law rule of
(40) causation. A person injured in a nuclear incident has the burden of proving a causal relationship between the incident and his alleged injury. While the plaintiff does not have to show that
(45) the conduct of the defendant was the sole cause of the injury, the plaintiff must prove that it is more likely than

not that the conduct of the defendant was a substantial factor in bringing
(50) about the injury. The plaintiff has the burden of showing that there is a high probability (i.e., 51 percent or more) that the defendant's conduct caused his alleged injury. A mere possibility of
(55) such causation is not enough; and when the matter remains one of pure speculation or conjecture, or the probabilities are at least evenly balanced, it becomes the duty of the
(60) court to direct a verdict for the defendant. In the event of a nuclear incident involving a large release of radioactive material, such as Chernobyl, it would probably not be difficult for
(65) immediate victims to demonstrate a causal link between the accident and their injuries. Scientists are able to detect approximately how much radiation was released into the
(70) atmosphere, and how surrounding areas are affected by it.
An argument in favor of Price-Anderson is that it ensures that claimants have an asset pool of at least
(75) $665 million in which to recover for damages. Without Price-Anderson, the possibility is very real that the utility company would be unable to pay claims arising out of a major accident. If the
(80) claims were sufficiently large or numerous, a private company could well choose bankruptcy over paying the claims. For example, the Planex Corporation, a defendant in
(85) thousands of asbestos cases, filed for reorganization under Chapter 11 of the Bankruptcy Code in 1982.

GO ON TO THE NEXT PAGE ➤

2   **2**   **2**   **2**   **2**

1. The primary purpose of the passage is to

   (A) describe the Price-Anderson Act
   (B) criticize the Price-Anderson Act
   (C) support the Price-Anderson Act
   (D) analyze and then condemn the Price-Anderson Act
   (E) present the advantages and disadvantages of the Price-Anderson Act

2. The advantages to the nuclear industry in the United States of the Price-Anderson Act include all of the following EXCEPT

   (A) the limitation of the liability to $665 million
   (B) some injuries may not be apparent until after the statute of limitations has expired
   (C) the potential liability far exceeds the limit fixed
   (D) the plaintiff must show the high probability that the defendant's conduct caused the injury
   (E) the ceiling on liability will probably be raised when Price-Anderson is renewed

3. If there were a major nuclear accident in the United States equal in size to the Chernobyl incident, we can infer that under the rules of the Price-Anderson Act

   (A) there would be difficulty in proving causation
   (B) the asset pool would be exhausted
   (C) victims with latent injuries would be able to collect damages
   (D) the liability would not apply if the accident was caused by provable negligence
   (E) the concept of "he who breaks must pay" would be applied

4. Which one of the following is an advantage of the Price-Anderson Act to the general public?

   (A) The liability pool of $665 million would pay many victims of a nuclear accident.
   (B) A utility company responsible for a nuclear accident would not need to file for bankruptcy if the claim exceeded the $665 million in the asset pool.
   (C) A claim against a company responsible for a nuclear accident could be filed under relaxed common law rules of causation.
   (D) Injuries caused by nuclear exposure might not be apparent for many years.
   (E) Victims of an accident could collect punitive damages if an accident is caused by industry negligence.

5. Under the terms of Price-Anderson, in the case of a minor nuclear accident a successful plaintiff would have to show that the defendant's conduct was the

   (A) sole cause of his injury
   (B) probable cause of his injury
   (C) possible cause of his injury
   (D) contributing cause of his injury
   (E) cause of his injury through negligence

6. According to the passage, the Planex Corporation (line 84) filed for bankruptcy

   (A) after paying damages in a nuclear accident case
   (B) after paying damages in a toxic waste case
   (C) after paying damages in an asbestos case
   (D) to avoid paying damages in a toxic waste case
   (E) to avoid paying damages in an asbestos case

GO ON TO THE NEXT PAGE ➤

2   **2**   **2**   **2**   **2**

7. With which one of the following statements would the author of the passage be most likely to disagree?

(A) Attitudes toward nuclear energy have changed dramatically since the incidents at Three Mile Island and Chernobyl.

(B) The radioactive contamination from Chernobyl may result in thousands of cancer deaths in the next 50 years.

(C) Congress should disallow any expansion of the nuclear power industry.

(D) The size of the asset pool under Price-Anderson should be increased.

(E) The 20-year statute of limitations under Price-Anderson is too short.

STOP

IF YOU FINISH BEFORE TIME IS UP, CHECK YOUR WORK ON THIS SECTION OF THE TEST ONLY.
DO NOT GO ON TO THE NEXT SECTION OF THE TEST UNTIL TIME IS UP FOR THIS SECTION.

3   **3**   **3**   **3**   **3**

SECTION III
TIME — 10 MINUTES
7 QUESTIONS

<u>Directions:</u> In this section you will be given a group of questions based on a specific set of conditions. Drawing a simple diagram may be helpful in answering some of the questions. You are to choose the best answer and mark the corresponding space on your answer sheet.

Eight students—A, B, C, D, E, F, G, and H—are standing in a straight line waiting to have their pictures taken. Although the actual order of the students is not known, the following is known:

The first and last people in line are the two tallest.
The 4th, 5th, and 6th students in line are the only girls.
C is always third in line.
E is always next to F, and they are not girls.
H is a boy.
A and D are sisters, but will not stand next to each other.

1. If G is a girl, then which one of the following must be true?

(A) D is in the 4th place.
(B) A is next to C.
(C) D is in the 5th place.
(D) G is in the 5th place.
(E) G is next to C.

2. If H is one of the two tallest, then H could be next to

(A) F   (B) B   (C) C   (D) D   (E) E

3. If G is a girl and H is last in line, then

(A) E must be the other tallest student.
(B) E may be next to a girl.
(C) D must be next to C.
(D) G may be next to C.
(E) B must be next to H.

4. If F is 2nd in line, which one of the following must be true?

(A) E is the shortest.
(B) B is either 7th or 8th in line.
(C) H is either 7th or 8th in line.
(D) C is 4th in line.
(E) F is one of the two tallest.

5. If E and B are the two tallest students, then which one of the following is a possible order of the students?

(A)	E	F	C	D	H	A	G	B
(B)	E	H	C	A	G	D	F	B
(C)	B	H	C	A	G	D	F	E
(D)	B	G	C	D	H	A	F	E
(E)	E	F	C	G	A	D	H	B

6. If H is last in line, which one of the following could be true?

(A) E is one of the tallest.
(B) G is next to C.
(C) B is one of the tallest.
(D) D is one of the tallest.
(E) B is next to G.

7. If E and G are the two tallest students, then which one of the following is a possible order of the students?

(A)	G	F	C	A	B	D	H	E
(B)	G	B	C	A	H	D	F	E
(C)	E	H	C	D	B	A	F	G
(D)	E	F	C	D	B	A	H	G
(E)	E	F	C	D	H	A	B	G

STOP

IF YOU FINISH BEFORE TIME IS UP, CHECK YOUR WORK ON THIS SECTION OF THE TEST ONLY.
DO NOT GO ON TO THE NEXT SECTION OF THE TEST UNTIL TIME IS UP FOR THIS SECTION.

| 4 | 4 | 4 | 4 | 4 |

SECTION IV
TIME — 10 MINUTES
9 QUESTIONS

<u>Directions:</u> In this section you will be given brief statements or passages and will be required to evaluate the reasoning involved. In some instances, more than one choice will appear to be a possible answer. You are to choose the *best* answer. Use common sense and reasonableness in making your selection; then mark the proper space on the answer sheet.

1. Although man is thinking constantly during the course of every day, he is usually not aware of his thoughts. Just walking a few steps entails a number of mental choices and activities that are performed more or less unconsciously. To become conscious of everything going on in the mind would be immobilizing.

Which one of the following best supports the passage above?

(A) Researchers have concluded that driving an automobile for only one minute entails over one thousand separate unconscious decisions.
(B) Thinking is such a complex process that it cannot be adequately defined.
(C) People have difficulty remembering more than three diverse concepts.
(D) Most individuals can perform more than one task simultaneously.
(E) The unconscious mind is still a mystery even to most psychologists.

2. During the last 50 years, the majority of individuals receiving awards for their humanitarian works have been blonde. Therefore, having blonde hair is the cause of humanitarianism.

Each of the following, if true, *weakens* the preceding conclusion EXCEPT

(A) these people who received such honors are not representative of all humanitarians
(B) a physical condition not caused by having blonde hair, but more prevalent among blondes than among others, causes humanitarian behavior
(C) during the last 100 years fewer blondes than others received humanitarian honors
(D) the total population contains a higher percentage of blondes than others at any given time
(E) the total population contains a far smaller percentage of blondes than does the subpopulation consisting of those individuals having received honors for humanitarian endeavors

GO ON TO THE NEXT PAGE ➤

4   4   4   4   4

Questions 3–4

Editorialist: Lotteries are a socially expensive form of generating revenues. They attract those least able to afford it, and thus, become a form of regressive taxation. A six-month study conducted in 1979 in New Castle County, Delaware, found that poor persons bet three times as much on a regular basis as did those from upper-middle income areas. In fact, most lottery machines were located in the poorest areas of the county, areas where unemployment is highest and the standard of living lowest. By contrast, not a single lottery machine was located in the high-income neighborhood of the county. Maryland's instant lottery came under such severe criticism that it was soaking the poor that the government finally scrapped it several weeks ago.

3. Which one of the following facts would be most useful in judging the effectiveness of the details offered to support the author's criticism of lotteries?

    (A) the name of the group that conducted the six-month survey
    (B) a comparison of the amounts bet by the poor, the middle class, and the upper class
    (C) a discussion of the gambling activity of upper-class citizens
    (D) the rationale for locating the lottery machines in poor neighborhoods
    (E) a discussion of the revenue-generating programs that preceded the lottery in Delaware

4. Which one of the following, if true, would be the best refutation of the argument above?

    (A) Many of the poor have enjoyed the opportunity to gamble.
    (B) The high-income neighborhood is exclusively residential.
    (C) Money from the lottery is generated more from the middle-class areas.
    (D) The study conducted in New Castle has been duplicated elsewhere, but other lotteries continue to operate.
    (E) The upper-class citizens shoulder 10 percent of the tax burden.

5. Every movie star I have read about lives in an expensive home. They must all live in such places.

    Which one of the following most nearly parallels the logic of the foregoing argument?

    (A) All movie producers must be demanding, probably because of the stresses placed upon them.
    (B) This piece of matter must be a rock, since it does not fit any other description in the textbook.
    (C) All the paintings by Visson in the library are bright. Every one of his works must be bright.
    (D) All paint has noxious odor. This liquid has such an odor and, therefore, must be paint.
    (E) Inasmuch as all pine trees are evergreen and this tree has not lost its needles, it is likely to be a pine.

6. Smith, Klingle, and Smith, a well-known national polling firm, surveyed one thousand registered voters in Kentucky to determine their positions on the No-Fault Insurance Initiative, Ballot Proposition No. 106. Their survey included the following results regarding Proposition No. 106:

Strongly support	43%
Support	18%
Oppose	21%
Strongly oppose	11%
Undecided	7%

    Which one of the conclusions below can be best supported by the results of the survey above?

    (A) Most Kentucky voters strongly oppose Ballot Proposition No. 106.
    (B) Most Kentucky voters are not well aware of Ballot Proposition No. 106.
    (C) A majority of Kentucky voters are not in favor of Ballot Proposition No. 106.
    (D) A majority of Kentucky voters will probably vote for the Ballot Proposition No. 106.
    (E) The Kentucky voters who are undecided will change the outcome of the vote.

GO ON TO THE NEXT PAGE ➤

7. All medications are habit forming.
Everything habit forming soothes pain.
Nothing nonaddictive soothes pain.

Given that the foregoing are true, which
one of the following must be FALSE?

(A) All medications soothe pain.
(B) Some medications are nonaddictive.
(C) Aspirins are habit forming and
addictive.
(D) Addictive medications soothe pain.
(E) No medications are not habit
forming.

Questions 8–9

With so many opportunities for true reform
that would save the taxpayers' money, there
is reason to look askance at proposals by
legislators that would make life easier for
them with public funds. Only last year, the
Assembly, after a considerable public
outcry, finally ruled out a bill whereby only
25 percent of campaign spending reports
filed by legislative candidates would be
audited instead of 50 percent under current
law.

8. Which one of the following is the most
logical continuation of this passage?

(A) Clearly, it is through increased
auditing of campaign spending that
we will secure honest
representation.
(B) Must we consider every "gift" the
legislator offers us as a Trojan
horse, filled with traitors bent on
destroying the state?
(C) Who are they trying to kid?
(D) We must bemoan the fact that there
are no opportunities for true reform,
only for white-collar fraud.
(E) Is it any wonder, then, that citizens
should be as wary of legislators
bearing election reforms as the
adage warns one to be of Greeks
bearing gifts?

9. The author is arguing that

(A) legislators often act in their own
best interests
(B) public outcry is more effective than
the ballot box
(C) more than half of campaign
expenditures are unwarranted
(D) legislators are not aware of
opportunities for true reform
(E) this year, reform is more possible
than it was last year

STOP

END OF MULTIPLE-CHOICE EXAMINATION.

IF YOU FINISH BEFORE TIME IS UP, CHECK YOUR WORK ON THIS SECTION OF THE TEST ONLY.
DO NOT GO BACK TO ANY OTHER SECTION OF THE EXAMINATION.

Writing Sample
TIME — 30 MINUTES

<u>Directions:</u> You have 30 minutes to write an essay in response to a given topic. Take a few minutes to plan your work before you begin writing. DO NOT WRITE ON A TOPIC OF YOUR OWN CHOICE. ESSAYS THAT DO NOT ADDRESS THE GIVEN TOPIC ARE UNACCEPTABLE.

The quality of your writing is more important than the length of your response or the content. Pay attention to organization, appropriate diction, and correct usage. You will not be expected to display any specialized knowledge in your response, nor will you be expected to write a "perfect" essay; law schools understand that you are writing under a time constraint, and will allow for the minor lapses in writing ability that might occur under this circumstance.

Only the lined area in your booklet will be reproduced for the law schools, so do not write outside this space. *Do not* skip lines or use wide margins. These precautions, along with careful planning and legible handwriting that is not unduly large, will keep you within the allowed space.

Sample Topic

Read the following descriptions of Bergquist and Kretchmer, applicants for the job of Assistant Director on a major motion picture. *Then, in the space provided, write an argument for hiring either Bergquist or Kretchmer.* The following criteria are relevant to your decision:

- In addition to working closely with and advising the Director on creative decisions, the Assistant Director must work with all types of individuals—from stars to Teamster truck drivers—and elicit the best from every cast and crew member for the good of the motion picture.
- The Assistant Director is responsible for all the planning and organization—including paperwork, travel itinerary, and meals, of the entire film project. He/she lays the groundwork for a successful "shoot."

BERGQUIST began her career in films as an Administrative Assistant to the president of a major film studio. As such, she often accompanied her employer in his wining and dining of stars, or to the set when problems arose. She double-checked contracts, shooting schedules, cast and crew checks, and kept a close eye on the budget of several multimillion-dollar films. When her boss was subsequently fired due to a poor season of films, Bergquist was able to secure a position as Assistant Editor at the studio, helping several highly respected film editors "cut" feature films. It was here that she learned about the creative end of the business, and soon after became the chief editor of an hour-long studio documentary, which won several awards. After two years, Bergquist was accepted into the Assistant Directors Training Program, and is presently a candidate for Assistant Director of this new $15,000,000 motion picture.

KRETCHMER was a principal/teacher for 12 years before embarking on a film career. She taught math at the New York School for the Creative Arts, and also worked with parents in the community, the board of education, and local government representatives in securing financing for the $20,000,000 school building. As Chairperson of the New Building Committee, she worked closely with architects, townspeople, contractors, and even children to understand their needs for the building. Today the building stands as a model for such schools everywhere. Eight years ago, Kretchmer came to Hollywood and, through persistence and charm, secured a studio position and worked her way up to Chief Auditor, where she oversaw budgets on several multimillion-dollar films. She enrolled in the Assistant Directors Training Program, which she recently completed, and is now a candidate for the position of Assistant Director of this new film.

Answer Key

Section I: Logical Reasoning

1. **D**	3. **B**	5. **C**	7. **B**	9. **D**
2. **E**	4. **A**	6. **B**	8. **E**	

Section II: Reading Comprehension

1. **E**	3. **B**	5. **B**	7. **C**
2. **E**	4. **A**	6. **E**	

Section III: Analytical Reasoning

1. **D**	3. **E**	5. **C**	7. **D**
2. **B**	4. **C**	6. **A**	

Section IV: Logical Reasoning

1. **A**	3. **B**	5. **C**	7. **B**	9. **A**
2. **E**	4. **C**	6. **D**	8. **E**	

Mini-Exam Analysis

Section	Total Number of Questions	Number Correct	Number Incorrect	Number Unanswered*
I: Logical Reasoning	9			
II: Reading Comprehension	7			
III: Analytical Reasoning	7			
IV: Logical Reasoning	9			
TOTAL:	32			

*Since there is no penalty for incorrect answers on the LSAT, you should leave no question unanswered. Even if you don't have time to answer a question, at least fill in the answer space with a guess.

Explanation of Answers

Section I

1. **D** The passage states that nameless fears and frustrations defy analysis and implies that unsymbolized thoughts and emotions constitute nameless fears and frustrations. (C) and (E) are close, but note the absolute words "complete" and "only" in each.

2. **E** The final sentence is introduced by "But" and notice of a "slight disadvantage." The best example of a "slight disadvantage" in the five choices is the "muscle aches" of (B).

3. **B** The consequences of nuclear annihilation—namely the end of human life—would include the disappearance of all other human questions. Thus, the author's contention that the most serious threat to modern man may be the alleged meaninglessness of life is seriously challenged by the magnitude of nuclear annihilation.

4. **A** If a "nonreader" (one who cannot read) can recognize words, then reading cannot be defined as the act of recognizing words.

5. **C** Good swing implies good golfer and practice implies good swing; therefore practice implies good golfer. (*X* implies *Y* and *Y* implies *Z*; therefore *X* implies *Z*.) This is most closely paralleled by (C), even though the terms are in slightly different order, or not exactly parallel. (B) is wrong since voting for peace and wanting peace are two different things. Betsy may have baked a good cake (A) even if she did not want to. (E), although in proper form, brings in excess subjectivity.

6. **B** This is the only answer that refutes the premise that you need a good swing. (A) talks about what else you need, and (C) says nothing about the need for a good swing.

7. **B** The passage is dealing with the "popular tastes" in art and music, with the people who purchase paintings at discount stores rather than at auctions of original leading artists (A). The larger attendance figures for concerts of nineteenth-century music is a logical corollary. For (C) to be relevant, we would have to know what ballets were performed. (D) may be true, but it has no bearing on this passage. (E) contradicts the implications of this passage.

8. **E** The passage endorses the position of (A), but offers evidence to support the idea ("attendance figures") rather than assuming it to be true. E is an assumption of the writer who concludes from the sales ("it is clear") that popular tastes have fallen behind. The other options may or may not be true; they are not assumptions underlying this paragraph.

9. **D** The method used is an analogy, a comparison citing another case where an apparent Constitutional guarantee is qualified.

Section II

1. **E** Though the author has reservations about the Price-Anderson Act, the passage presents both the advantages and suggestions to rectify what the author sees as disadvantages.

2. **E** All of the first four items are advantageous financially to the industry. The rise in the ceiling on liability will raise the potential costs to the industry in the event of an "incident."

3. **B** The number of deaths, injuries, and damages caused by the accident at Chernobyl would surely cost more than $665 million in the asset pool. The other four answers are false.

4. **A** Only (A) is true and an advantage to the public. (B) is an advantage to the company, not to the public. (C) and (E) are untrue. (D) is true, but because the injuries might be slow to be recognized, the victim might not be able to qualify for reparations before the statute of limitations expired.

5. **B** The plaintiff under common law rules of causation would have to show a probability of 51 percent or more.

6. **E** The passage asserts that Planex declared bankruptcy to avoid the damages in a large number of suits involving asbestos.

7. **C** Though the author points to faults in Price-Anderson, he never suggests that the nuclear power industry's growth should be restricted. All of the other statements are either factual or opinions specifically supported in the passage.

Section III

From the information given, a "position" diagram may be drawn as follows:

$$\underset{\underset{\text{tallest}}{1}}{\_\_}\ \underset{2}{\_\_}\ \underset{3}{C}\ \underset{\underset{\text{girl}}{4}}{A/D}\ \underset{\underset{\text{girl}}{5}}{\_\_}\ \underset{\underset{\text{girl}}{6}}{D/A}\ \underset{7}{\_\_}\ \underset{\underset{\text{tallest}}{8}}{\_\_}$$

Now notice that, since E and F are always adjacent, they may be in positions 1 and 2, or in positions 7 and 8. And, for instance, if they are in 7 and 8, then H (a boy) must be in 1 or 2 (and vice versa).

1. **D** If G is a girl, then she must be in 5th place, since the sisters (A and D) will not stand next to each other.

2. **B** If H is one of the two tallest, then H will be on one end. Thus, at the other end must be E and F. Therefore, H could be next to either B or G, depending upon who is the boy.

3. **E** If G is a girl, and H is last in line, your diagram must look like this:

$$\underset{}{E/F}\ \underset{}{F/E}\ \underset{}{C}\ \underset{}{A/D}\ \underset{}{G}\ \underset{}{D/A}\ \underset{}{B}\ \underset{}{H}$$

Thus, the only true statement is (E), B must be next to H.

4. **C** If F is second in line, then your diagram should look like this:

$$\underset{}{E}\ \underset{}{F}\ \underset{}{C}\ \underset{}{A/D}\ \underset{}{\_\_}\ \underset{}{D/A}\ \underset{}{H?}\ \underset{}{H?}$$

From the diagram, H is 7th or 8th in line. Notice that B could possibly be 5th in line, so (B) is not true.

5. **C** If E and B are the two tallest, then two diagrams are possible:

$$\underset{}{E}\ \underset{}{F}\ \underset{}{C}\ \underset{}{A/D}\ \underset{}{G}\ \underset{}{D/A}\ \underset{}{H}\ \underset{}{B}$$
and
$$\underset{}{B}\ \underset{}{H}\ \underset{}{C}\ \underset{}{A/D}\ \underset{}{G}\ \underset{}{D/A}\ \underset{}{F}\ \underset{}{E}$$

Notice that (A) and (D) are incorrect because H, a boy, cannot be in the 5th place. (B) is incorrect because E and F must be adjacent. Finally, (E) is incorrect because A and D will not stand next to each other in line.

6. **A** If H is last in line, then your diagram should look like this:

$$\underset{}{E/F}\ \underset{}{F/E}\ \underset{}{C}\ \underset{}{A/D}\ \underset{}{\_\_}\ \underset{}{D/A}\ \underset{}{\_\_}\ \underset{}{H}$$

Notice that B and G must go in the 5th and 7th spots, but we cannot tell which one goes where. Therefore, the only statement that may possibly be true is (A): E is one of the tallest.

7. **D** If E and G are the two tallest, your diagram is either

$$\underset{}{E}\ \underset{}{F}\ \underset{}{C}\ \underset{}{A/D}\ \underset{}{B}\ \underset{}{D/A}\ \underset{}{H}\ \underset{}{G}$$
or
$$\underset{}{G}\ \underset{}{H}\ \underset{}{C}\ \underset{}{A/D}\ \underset{}{B}\ \underset{}{D/A}\ \underset{}{F}\ \underset{}{E}$$

Notice that, since H is a boy, he must be next to G. Therefore, (D) is the only possible correct order of the students.

Section IV

1. **A**   This statement lends even more support to the passage that normal activities are conducted through constant thought processes, many of which are done more or less unconsciously.

2. **E**   (E) may be restated: "The group consisting of humanitarians who received honors contains a much higher proportion of blondes than that which exists in the total population." Such a condition increases the credibility of the conclusion. (A), (B), (C), and (D) all reduce the probability of the conclusion.

3. **B**   The author's criticism of lotteries is based on the contention that poor persons are spending more than they can afford. However, the details he offers in support of this contention mention the frequency of betting without specifying the amount gambled. The effectiveness of the *frequency* detail could be better judged if the *amount* were given. None of the other choices is closely related to the author's central criticism, the costliness of the lotteries.

4. **C**   This fact severely weakens the author's contention that most of the revenue from the lottery comes from the lower class or poor.

5. **C**   The given argument may be reduced to:
<u>Some</u> stars (those the speaker has read about) <u>have</u> expensive homes.
<u>All</u> <u>stars</u> (they) <u>have</u> expensive homes (such places).

   (C) is the only choice that both parallels the faulty logic of the original and retains the pattern, specific to general:

   <u>Some</u> movie stars → <u>All</u> movie stars.
   Note the structure of (C):
   <u>Some</u> paintings (those in the library) <u>are</u> bright.
   <u>All</u> paintings (every one) <u>are</u> bright.

6. **D**   Because 43 percent strongly support the ballot and 18 percent support the ballot, a total of 61 percent are in favor of the ballot and will probably vote for it. This is the only conclusion of the five given that can be plausibly supported.

7. **B**   Since all medications are habit forming and everything habit forming soothes pain, then all medications make one feel better; therefore, (A) is true. Since nothing nonaddictive soothes pain and all medications soothe pain, then no medications can be nonaddictive; therefore, (B) is false.

8. **E**   (A) is a *non sequitur;* the passage does not align honestly with auditing. (B) is weaker than (E) because it mentions destroying the state, an extreme not expressed or implied in the passage. (C) is too vague. (D) introduces a new subject, fraud.

9. **A**   The author explicitly opposes legislative proposals that would "make life easier for them [the legislators]."

PART TWO

ANALYSIS

Understanding the Sections
and the Key Strategies

## Chapter 2

READING COMPREHENSION

Introduction to Question Type

The entire LSAT is, generally speaking, a test of reading comprehension. However, the Reading Comprehension section itself is a test of general reading skills rather than the more particular analytical skills stressed in the Analytical Reasoning section.

Each Reading Comprehension section consists of four passages that range in length from 400 to 600 words. Each passage is followed by six to eight questions relating to the passage. These 26 to 28 questions are to be answered in 35 minutes.

The four passages are drawn from the humanities, the natural sciences, the social sciences, and law. No specialized knowledge is necessary to answer any of the questions. All of the questions can be answered by referring to the passage.

Some of the common types of Reading Comprehension questions that follow a passage include questions about:

- the main point of the passage or the passage's primary purpose;
- the meaning or function of specific words or phrases in the context of the passage;
- information that is explicitly stated in the passage;
- inferences and implications related to the passage;
- the author's tone or attitude;
- the function of a paragraph within the passage as a whole;
- the organization of the passage.

Active Reading

The Reading Comprehension section presents long passages demanding your steady concentration. Because such passages are complex, you must approach them actively, focusing on a specific plan of attack.

Suppose that midway through the first paragraph of a passage you encounter a sentence like this:

> Ordinarily, of course, we are invited only to criticize the current neglect of government programs; politicians cling to their own fringe benefits while the strife in our inner cities is only nominally contained with a plethora of half-baked local projects whose actual effect is the gradual erosion of trust in the beneficence of the republic.

Different students may respond in different ways:

"What? Let me read that again" (and again and again).

"I used to know what beneficence meant; uh. . . ."

"Boy, am I tired."

"I should have eaten a better breakfast; my head aches."

"I wonder what I'll do tonight. . . ."

"This writer is screwy; I was a senator's aide and I know he's wrong."

"How can I read this!? It's written so poorly; that word *plethora* is a terrible choice."

These typical responses—getting stuck, getting distracted, getting angry—all work against your purpose: understanding the information given in the passage to answer the questions that follow. The techniques described below should help you avoid some common reading test pitfalls.

Essentially, active reading consists of marking as you read. But the marking you do must be strategic and efficient. To present some effective active reading techniques, we will consider seven typical LSAT questions and a sample reading passage that is shorter and less complex than those in the exam.

EXAMPLE

With the possible exception of equal rights, perhaps the most controversial issue across the United States today is the death penalty. Many argue that it is an effective deterrent to murder, while others maintain there is no conclusive

(5) evidence that the death penalty reduces the number of murders, and go on to contend that it is cruel and inhuman punishment, that it is the mark of a brutal society, and finally, that it is of questionable effectiveness as a deterrent to crime anyway.

(10) But, the death penalty is a necessary evil. Throughout recorded history there have always been those extreme individuals who were capable of terribly violent crimes such as murder. But some are more extreme, more diabolical than others. It is one thing to take the life of another in a momen-

(15) tary fit of blind rage, but quite another to coldly plot and carry out the murder of one or more people in the style of an executioner. Thus, murder, like all other crimes, is a matter of relative degree. While it could be argued with some conviction that the criminal in the first instance should be merely

(20) isolated from society, such should not be the fate of the latter type murderer. To quote Moshe Dayan, "Unfortunately, we must kill them." The value of the death penalty as a deterrent to crime may be open to debate, but there remains one irrefutable fact: Gary Gilmore will never commit another

(25) murder. Charles Manson and his followers, were they to escape, or—God forbid—be paroled, very well might.

The overwhelming majority of citizens believe that the death penalty protects them. Their belief is reinforced by evidence that shows that the death penalty deters murder. For

(30) example, the Attorney General points out that from 1954 to

1963, when the death penalty was consistently imposed in California, the murder rate remained between three and four murders for each 100,000 population. Since 1964 the death penalty has been imposed only once (in 1967), and the mur-
(35) der rate has skyrocketed to 10.4 murders for each 100,000 population. The sharp climb in the state's murder rate, which commenced when executions stopped, is no coincidence. It is convincing evidence that the death penalty does deter many murderers. If the governor were to veto a bill reestab-
(40) lishing the death penalty, an initiative would surely follow. However, an initiative cannot restore the death penalty for six months. In the interim, innocent people will be murdered—some whose lives may have been saved if the death penalty were in effect.

1. The primary purpose of the passage is to

   (A) criticize the governor
   (B) argue for the value of the death penalty
   (C) initiate a veto
   (D) speak for the majority
   (E) impose a six-month moratorium on the death penalty

2. The passage attempts to establish a relationship between

   (A) Gary Gilmore and Charles Manson
   (B) the importance of both equal rights and the death penalty
   (C) the murder rate and the imposition of the death penalty
   (D) executions and murders
   (E) the effects of parole and the effects of isolation

3. It can be inferred that the author assumes which one of the following about a governor's veto of the death penalty legislation?

   (A) It might be upheld.
   (B) It will certainly be overridden.
   (C) It represents consultation with a majority of citizens.
   (D) The veto is important, but not crucial.
   (E) It is based on the principle of equal protection for accused murderers.

4. The author's response to those who urge the death penalty for all degrees of murder would most likely be

   (A) strongly supportive
   (B) noncommittal
   (C) negative
   (D) supportive
   (E) uncomprehending

5. In the passage the author is primarily concerned with

   (A) supporting a position
   (B) describing an occurrence
   (C) citing authorities
   (D) analyzing a problem objectively
   (E) settling a dispute

6. In lines 40–41 "initiative" refers to

   (A) a demonstration against the governor's action
   (B) a rise in the murder rate
   (C) a more vocal response by the majority of citizens
   (D) the introduction of legislation to reinstate the death penalty
   (E) overriding the governor's veto

7. The passage provides answers to all of the following questions EXCEPT

   (A) Are all murders equally diabolical?
   (B) Does the public believe the death penalty deters murder?
   (C) What happened to Gary Gilmore?
   (D) Will Charles Manson be paroled?
   (E) Should the governor support the death penalty?

Four-Step Approach

Step One: Skim the Questions

Before reading the passage, spend a short time familiarizing yourself with the questions. You should preread or "skim" the questions for two reasons: (1) to learn what *types* of questions are being asked; and (2) to learn what specific *information* to look for when you do read the passage. In order to skim efficiently and effectively, you should read over only the portion of each question that *precedes* the multiple choices, and you should mark *key words* as you do so.

A *key word* or phrase is any segment that suggests what you should look for when you read the passage. Marking these key words will help you remember them as you read (luckily, the questions will be printed directly below and alongside the passage, so that as you read the passage you will be able to glance at the questions and remind yourself about what you've marked). In order to further explain and clarify these tips on skimming, let's examine the questions that follow the preceding passage.

The key words for each of them are circled.

1. The primary purpose of the passage is to. . . .

This is a "main idea" or "primary purpose" question; most LSAT reading passages are followed by at least one of these. You are asked what the passage is trying to *do* or *express*, as a whole. Here is a list of possible purposes that may be embodied in a reading passage:

to inform	to criticize	to show
to persuade	to argue for or against	to question
to analyze	to illustrate	to explain
to change	to represent	to prove
to restore	to parody	to describe

This list is by no means exhaustive; the possible purposes are almost endless, and you might try thinking of some yourself.

The main idea or primary purpose of a passage is usually stated or implied in the *thesis sentence* of one or more of the paragraphs. A thesis sentence tells what the paragraph as a whole is about; it states a main idea or primary purpose. For example, the second sentence of paragraph 3 in the passage is the thesis sentence; it sums up the evidence of that paragraph into a single statement.

A primary purpose or main idea question should direct your attention to the thesis sentences in the passage, that is, the *general statements* that sum up the specific details.

2. The passage attempts to establish a relationship between. . . .

This question requires that you locate *explicit* (established) *information* in the passage, information that defines a relationship. The question allows you to anticipate the mention of at least one relationship in the passage, and warns you through its wording that the relationship is not "hidden," but is instead one that the author deliberately attempts to establish.

3. It can be inferred that the author assumes which of the following about the veto of a governor's death penalty legislation?

This question requires that you locate *implicit*, rather than explicit, information; you are asked to draw an *inference* (a conclusion based on reasoning), not just to locate obvious material. It is more difficult than question 2. When you read about the governor's veto in the passage, you should take mental note of any unstated assumptions that seem to lie behind the author's commentary.

4. The author's response to those who urge the death penalty for all degrees of murder would most likely be. . . .

This question type, usually more difficult than the types previously discussed, requires you to *apply* the information in the passage itself. As you read the passage, you should pay special attention to the author's attitude toward types, or degrees, of murder; applying this attitude to the situation described in the question should lead to the answer.

5. In the passage the author is primarily concerned with. . . .

This is another variety of the "primary purpose" or "main idea" question.

6. In lines 40–41, "initiative" refers to. . . .

The question requires you to focus on specific language in the passage and define it in context. Such a question is relatively easy insofar as it specifies just where to look for an answer; its difficulty varies according to the difficulty of the word or phrase you are asked to consider.

7. The passage provides answers to all of the following questions EXCEPT. . . .

Although many questions that you skim will lead you to useful information in the passage, some like this one, do not. It is still important, however, to circle key words in the question to avoid the <u>misread</u>.

In general, spend only a few seconds skimming the questions. Read each question, mark key words, and move on.
DO NOT:

- dwell on a question and analyze it extensively.
- be concerned with whether you are marking the "right" words (trust your intuition).
- read the multiple choices (this wastes time).

Step Two (Optional): Skim the Passage

Some students find skimming the passage helpful. Skimming the passage consists of quickly reading the first sentence of each paragraph, and marking key words and phrases. This will give you an idea of what the paragraph as a whole is about. The first sentence is often a general statement or thesis sentence that gives the gist of the paragraph.

Consider the passage given above. Reading the first sentence of each paragraph, we mark the key words and phrases, and may draw the following conclusions:

Paragraph 1: "With the possible exception of equal rights, perhaps the most controversial issue across the United States today is the death penalty." This sentence suggests that the passage will be about the death penalty, and the word "controversial" suggests that the author is about to take a stand on the controversy.

". . . that it is cruel and inhuman punishment, that it is the mark of a brutal society, and finally that it is of questionable effectiveness as a deterrent to crime anyway." This sentence presents opposition arguments, and because those arguments are presented as the views of others, not the views of the author, we begin to suspect that he does not align himself with the opposition.

Paragraph 2: "But, the death penalty is a necessary evil." This confirms our suspicion; the author is beginning an argument *in favor* of the death penalty.

"For example, it is one thing to take the life of another in a momentary fit of blind rage but quite another to coldly plot and carry out the murder of one or more people in the style of an executioner." Here the author is distinguishing between *degrees* of murder, and you may at this point recall question 4; this information seems relevant to that question.

"The value of the death penalty as a deterrent to crime may be open to debate, but there remains one irrefutable fact: Gary Gilmore will never commit another murder." The most significant feature of this sentence is that the author's tone is so absolute, indicating his strong belief in his own position.

Paragraph 3: "The overwhelming majority of citizens believe that the death penalty protects them." This sentence points toward statistical evidence in favor of the author's view.

"If the governor were to veto a bill reestablishing the death penalty, an initiative will surely follow." Coincidentally with the author's faith in the will of the majority, here he suggests that the death penalty will be upheld one way or another, by overriding a veto or through initiative.

Do not expect your own skimming of the passage to necessarily yield a series of conclusions such as those expressed above. Most of the knowledge you gather as you skim will "happen" without a deliberate effort on your part to translate your intuitions into sentences. Just read and mark the sentences, without slowing yourself down by analyzing each sentence. The preceding analysis suggests some possible conclusions that may occur to a reader, but drawing such full conclusions from sentence clues will take both practice and a relaxed attitude; don't push yourself to make sense out of everything and don't reread sentences (skimming the passage should take only a few seconds). Some sentences you read may be too difficult to make sense of immediately; just leave these alone and move along. Remember that getting stuck wastes time and raises anxiety.

Step Three: Read and Mark the Passage

Now you are ready to read the entire passage. To read quickly, carefully, and efficiently, you must be *marking* important words and phrases while you read. At least such marking will keep you alert and focused. At most it will locate the answers to many questions.

Skimming the questions will have helped you decide what to mark. If a question refers to a specific line, sentence, or quotation from the passage, you will want to mark this reference and pay special attention to it. Whenever a key word from a question corresponds with a spot in the passage, mark the spot. In the scheme for marking a passage, these spots are called, simply, ANSWER SPOTS. There are two other kinds of "spots" that you should mark as you read: REPEAT SPOTS and INTUITION SPOTS. Repeat spots are sections of the passage in which the same type of information is repeated.

Consider the following excerpt from a passage:

Proposed cutbacks in the Human Resources Agency are scheduled for hearing 9 A.M. on the 17th. Included in possible program reductions are cutbacks in the veterans' affairs program, including closure of the local office; in potential support for the county's Commission on the Status of Women; and in payments provided by the county for foster home care, which are not being adjusted for cost-of-living increases this year.

Programs in the Environmental Improvement Agency will be examined by the board beginning 9 A.M. Friday, August 18. The milk and dairy inspection program has been recommended by County Administrative Officer Fred Higgins for transfer to state administration. In addition, budget recommendations do not include funds for numerous community general plans which have been discussed previously by the board of supervisors. Such areas as Joshua Tree, Crestline, Lytle Creek, and Yucaipa are not included in the Planning Department's program for the upcoming year.

A special session to discuss proposed budget cuts in the county's General Services Agency will be conducted at 9 A.M. Saturday, August 19. A number of county branch libraries have been proposed for closure next year, including the Adelanto, Bloomington, Crestline, Joshua Tree, Mentone, Morongo, Muscoy, and Running Springs locations. A rollback in hours of operation will also be considered. Branches now open 60 hours a week will be cut to 52 hours. Other 50-hour-a-week branches will be reduced to 32 hours a week. Testimony will be heard on cutbacks in various agricultural service programs, including the county trapper program in the Yucaipa region and support for 4-H activities.

Generally, this excerpt stresses information about times, dates, and locations; we are conscious of repeated numbers and repeated place names. Marking the spots in which such information is found will help you to sort out the information, and also to answer more efficiently a question that addresses such information, a question such as "Which of the following cities are (is) *not* included in the Planning Department's program and *are* (is) liable to lose a branch library?" Having marked the REPEAT SPOTS that contain location names, you may be better able to focus on the appropriate information quickly.

INTUITION SPOTS are any spots that strike you as significant, for whatever reason. As we read, we tend to pay special attention to certain information; marking those spots that your intuition perceives as important will help increase your comprehension and will therefore contribute to correct answers.

You may notice that ANSWER SPOTS, REPEAT SPOTS, and INTUITION SPOTS are not necessarily different spots. An answer spot may also be a spot that contains repeat information AND appeals to your intuition.

Don't overmark. Some students, fearing that they will miss an important point, underline everything. Such misplaced thoroughness makes it impossible to find any specific word or phrase. Just mark the main idea of each paragraph and several important words or phrases. And vary your marks. You may want to underline main ideas, use circles or brackets or stars to indicate other important spots, and jot some notes to yourself in the margin. Here is how you might mark the death penalty passage:

With the possible exception of equal rights, perhaps the most (controversial issue) across the United States today is the (death penalty.) Many argue that it is an effective deterrent to murder, while others maintain there is no conclusive
(5) evidence that the death penalty reduces the number of murders, and go on to contend that it is cruel and inhuman punishment, that it is the mark of a brutal society, and finally that it is of questionable effectiveness as a deterrent to crime anyway.

*Contrast
opposition
points*

(10) (But, the death penalty is a necessary evil.) Throughout recorded history there have always been those extreme individuals who were capable of terribly violent crimes such as murder. But some are more extreme, more diabolical than others. It is one thing to take the life of another in a momen-
(15) tary fit of blind rage, but quite another to coldly plot and carry out the murder of one or more people in the style of an executioner. Thus, murder, like all other crimes, is a matter of (relative degree.) While it could be argued with some conviction that the criminal in the first instance should be merely
(20) isolated from society, such should not be the fate of the latter type murderer. To quote Moshe Dayan, "Unfortunately, we must kill them." The value of the death penalty as a deterrent to crime may be open to debate, but there remains one <u>irrefutable fact</u>: Gary Gilmore will never commit another
(25) murder. Charles Manson and his followers, were they to escape, or—God forbid—be paroled, very well might.

*degrees
of
murder*

penalty

STATS

[The overwhelming majority of citizens believe that the death penalty protects them.] Their belief is reinforced by evidence that shows that the death penalty deters murder. For
(30) example, the Attorney General points out that from 1954 to 1963, when the death penalty was consistently imposed in California, the murder rate remained between three and four murders for each 100,000 population. Since 1964 the death penalty has been imposed only once (in 1967), and the mur-
(35) der rate has skyrocketed to 10.4 murders for each 100,000 population. The sharp climb in the state's murder rate, which commenced when executions stopped, is no coincidence. It is convincing evidence that the death penalty does deter many murderers. (If the governor were to veto) a bill reestab-
(40) lishing the death penalty, an initiative would surely follow. However, an initiative cannot restore the death penalty for six months. In the interim, innocent people will be murdered—some whose lives may have been saved if the death penalty were in effect.

*veto
effects*

Your marking method should be active, playful, and personal. While you are marking, don't worry about whether you are doing it correctly. You may notice that, in the discussion of skimming the passage, some sentences are marked differently than they are here, in order to stress that there is no single, "correct" method.

Remember not to react subjectively to the passage, or add to it. Your own background may have you disagreeing with the passage, or you may be tempted to supply information from your own experience in order to answer a question. You must use only the information you are given, and you must accept it as true.

Avoid wasting time with very difficult or technical sentences. Concentrating on the sentences and ideas you do understand will often supply you with enough material to answer the questions. Rereading difficult sentences takes time, and usually does not bring greater clarity.

Step Four: Answer the Questions

As you attempt to answer each question, follow these steps:

1. assess the level of difficulty, and skip the question if necessary;
2. eliminate unreasonable and incorrect answer choices;
3. make certain that information in the passage supports your answer.

We will follow this procedure, using the questions on the "death penalty" passage as examples.

Question 1

The primary purpose of the passage is to

(A) criticize the governor
(B) argue for the value of the death penalty
(C) initiate a veto
(D) speak for the majority
(E) impose a six-month moratorium on the death penalty

Analysis
The correct answer is B. Remember that this sort of question asks for the *primary* purpose, not a subsidiary purpose. Often the incorrect answer choices will express minor or subsidiary purposes; this is true of (A) and (D). Another type of incorrect answer choice *contradicts* the information in the passage. So it is with (C) and (E). Both contradict the author's expressed support of the death penalty. Having marked thesis sentences in the passage, you should be aware of the author's repeated arguments for the value of the death penalty, and choose (B).

Question 2

The passage attempts to establish a relationship between

(A) Gary Gilmore and Charles Manson
(B) the importance of both equal rights and the death penalty
(C) the murder rate and the imposition of the death penalty
(D) executions and murders
(E) the effects of parole and the effects of isolation

Analysis

The correct answer is C. "Equal rights" is mentioned only in passing, and a relationship between parole and isolation is scarcely even implied; therefore (B) and (E) should be eliminated. (A) is not a good answer because, strictly speaking, Gary Gilmore and Charles Manson are not compared; their *sentences* are. (D) is a true answer, but not the best one because it is more vague and general than the best choice, (C); paragraph 3 makes this specific comparison.

Question 3

It can be inferred that the author assumes which of the following about a governor's veto of the death penalty legislation?

(A) It might be upheld.
(B) It will certainly be overridden.
(C) It represents consultation with a majority of citizens.
(D) The veto is important, but not crucial.
(E) It is based on the principle of equal protection for accused murderers.

Analysis

The correct answer is A. We are looking for information that is (1) assumed but not explicit, and (2) relevant to the governor's veto. Having marked the appropriate section of the passage, you are able to return immediately to the final two paragraphs, which discuss the veto. (B), (C), and (D) contradict passage information. (C) contradicts the author's earlier explanations that most citizens approve of the death penalty, and (D) contradicts the author's final statement. (B) contradicts the author's assumption that the veto might be upheld. (E) is irrelevant to the veto issue. (A) is correct because the assumption that the veto might be upheld would certainly underlie an argument against it.

Question 4

The author's response to those who urge the death penalty for all degrees of murder would most likely be

(A) strongly supportive
(B) noncommittal
(C) negative
(D) supportive
(E) uncomprehending

Analysis

The correct answer is C. Having marked the section that refers to different degrees of murder, you are once again able to focus on the appropriate section. In paragraph 2 the author argues that unpremeditated murder may not warrant the death penalty. This argument suggests his negative attitude toward someone who urges the death penalty for all murderers.

Question 5

In the passage the author is primarily concerned with

(A) supporting a position
(B) describing an occurrence
(C) citing authorities
(D) analyzing a problem objectively
(E) settling a dispute

Analysis

The correct answer is A. With your general knowledge of the passage, you should immediately eliminate (B) and (D), because the author is *argumentative* throughout, never merely descriptive or objective. Citing authorities (C) is a *subsidiary* rather than a primary concern; the author does so in paragraph 3. (E) is incorrect because it is the author himself who is *creating* a dispute over the death penalty. A review of the thesis sentences alone shows that the author is consistently supporting a position; (A) is certainly the best answer.

Question 6

In lines 40–41 "initiative" refers to

(A) a demonstration against the governor's action
(B) a rise in the murder rate
(C) a more vocal response by the majority of citizens
(D) the introduction of legislation to reinstate the death penalty
(E) overriding the governor's veto

Analysis

The correct answer is D. Skimming this question has allowed you to pay special attention to "initiative" as you read the passage. The sentence suggests that the initiative is a response to a governor's veto of the death penalty; and it is a *certain* response, as indicated by "surely." It is also an action that can eventually restore the death penalty; this fact especially signals (D) as the answer. (B) states information mentioned apart from the initiative; the murder rate will rise "in the interim." Demonstrations (A) or vocal responses (C) are not suggested as possibilities anywhere. (E) is eliminated because the last sentence of the passage urges an override, thus distinguishing this action from an initiative.

Question 7

The passage provides answers to all of the following questions
EXCEPT

(A) Are all murders equally diabolical?
(B) Does the public believe the death penalty deters murder?
(C) What happened to Gary Gilmore?
(D) Will Charles Manson be paroled?
(E) Should the governor support the death penalty?

Analysis
The correct answer is D. The passage answers all of these questions except the question of Manson's parole, which remains a possibility.

Active Reading, A Summary Chart

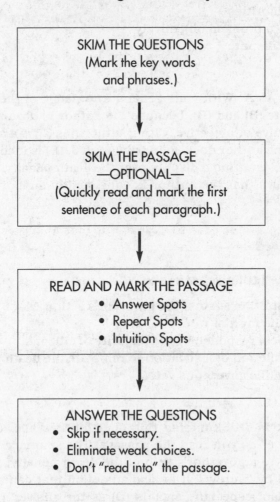

SKIM THE QUESTIONS
(Mark the key words
and phrases.)

SKIM THE PASSAGE
—OPTIONAL—
(Quickly read and mark the first
sentence of each paragraph.)

READ AND MARK THE PASSAGE
- Answer Spots
- Repeat Spots
- Intuition Spots

ANSWER THE QUESTIONS
- Skip if necessary.
- Eliminate weak choices.
- Don't "read into" the passage.

An Alternative General Approach

Some students, regardless of how much they review, analyze, and practice, cannot seem to finish the Reading Comprehension section. They simply cannot work fast enough and continue to maintain a high level of comprehension. If you find that you consistently have a problem getting to or into the fourth passage, you may wish to try this alternative approach: Focus your time on three of the four passages. That is, try to do well on the three passages and the questions that follow, and simply guess at the questions for the remaining passage. You can skip a passage and still receive a good score. The idea is to significantly raise your percentage of correct answers on the passages and questions you <u>are</u> completing. Remember, this is an alternative approach that you may wish to try if you are having a real problem getting to all four passages and maintaining a good level of comprehension.

Basic Training: Extra, Effective Practice

The following procedure, *practiced daily*, should strengthen precisely the kinds of skills that you will need for the Reading Comprehension section of the LSAT:

1. Locate the editorial page in your daily newspaper. There you will probably find three or four editorials on different subjects.
2. Read several editorials at your normal reading speed, marking them, if possible.
3. Set the editorials aside, and try to write a summary sentence describing each editorial. Make your summary as precise as possible. Do not write, "This editorial was about the economy." Instead, try to write something like this: "This editorial argued against the value of supply-side economics by referring to rising unemployment and interest rates."

   You may not be able to write so precise a summary right away, but after a few days of practicing this technique, you will find yourself better able to spot and remember main ideas and specific details, and to anticipate and understand the author's point of view.

   It is most important that you *write down* your summary statements. This takes more time and effort than silently "telling" yourself what the editorial means, but the time and effort pay off.
4. Every few days, create some of your own multiple-choice questions about an editorial. What would you ask if you were a test maker? Putting yourself in the test maker's shoes can be very instructive. You will realize, for instance, how weak or incorrect answer choices are constructed, and that realization will help you to eliminate such choices when you take the LSAT.

Extra Practice: Reading Comprehension

<u>Directions:</u> Read the passages and answer the questions following each passage by blackening the appropriate space on the answer sheet. You may refer back to the passages when answering the questions. Answer all questions on the basis of what is stated or implied.

Use the answer sheet found on page 63.

Passage 1 (Written in 1982)

A recent Harris Survey revealed that a majority of Americans say the price of gasoline would have to go to $1.50 a gallon before they would cut back on
(5) the use of their automobiles for pleasure driving. The survey, conducted among 1,517 adults nationwide, also found that gasoline prices would have to go to $1.85 per gallon before adults
(10) would cease to use their own cars to go to work and would turn to public transportation and car pooling.

In fact, the price of gasoline is presently going *down* rather than up.
(15) Major oil companies have announced plans to reduce wholesale prices by as much as eight cents a gallon. As a result, those drivers who insisted that only rising gasoline costs would cut
(20) their consumption will now probably begin to drive more rather than less. Already, according to the Highway Patrol, highways are becoming more crowded with cars carrying only one
(25) passenger, and with gas-guzzling recreational vehicles.

These results are interesting when one considers that we are presently at the height of the smog season. As most
(30) of us know by now, the majority of our smog problem is caused by exhaust emissions from cars. Yet how many of us have actually made an effort to drive less? In fact, how many of us have even
(35) made an effort to drive more slowly to help conserve gasoline? Unfortunately, the answer to both questions is: not very many. Even though we all are aware—or certainly should be by now—
(40) that there is a desperate need both to conserve fuel and to clean up our air, far too few of us are willing to make even a small sacrifice to help.

Recently, we read that a small group
(45) of botanists is busily attempting to develop a strain of pine tree that can resist the smog. It seems that as the smog has gotten worse each year it has taken an increasingly greater toll on the
(50) pines in mountain areas. Now the situation is becoming critical, either we develop a hardier tree or they will all die. It's sad to think that in a country which professes so much love for
(55) nature, and where so much natural beauty abounds, we have to develop a breed of "supertrees" which can cope with the polluted air we create.

The solution to our smog problem
(60) lies not in eliminating the steel industry's coke oven emissions, or any other industrial emissions, but in convincing the millions of people who traverse our freeways daily to try at least
(65) to drive less. Obviously, it's necessary to drive in order to get to and from work, but if each of us could at least reduce the pleasure driving a little, drive the speed limit, and have our automobile
(70) engines tuned regularly, the improvement would be immediately noticeable. If we make these small sacrifices we won't have to worry about eventually paying $1.85 per gallon for
(75) gasoline. The reduced consumption will keep prices low because there will be enough for everyone without having to increase prices to "force" us to use less.

1. The primary purpose of this passage is to

(A) convince smog producers to reduce emissions
(B) convince drivers to reduce smog
(C) convince drivers to drive less
(D) describe an instance of the supply/demand phenomenon
(E) argue against higher gasoline prices

2. The author puts the blame for air pollution on

(A) individuals
(B) institutions
(C) corporations
(D) botanists
(E) pollsters

3. With which one of the following statements about the effects of smog would the author be most likely to agree?

   (A) A greater number of vans and campers at our national parks threatens the parks' beauty.
   (B) Smog encourages the survival of hardy vegetation.
   (C) The price of gasoline may rise in the future.
   (D) People who drive alone have no respect for nature.
   (E) Smog will gradually become something we can live with.

4. Who of the following would be most likely to object to the author's argument?

   (A) an industrialist
   (B) an auto mechanic
   (C) a botanist
   (D) a Highway Patrol officer
   (E) a manufacturer of recreational vehicles

5. The author implies which one of the following in his argument?

   (A) Industrial emissions are uncontrollable.
   (B) Reduced driving will occur even if drivers do not follow his advice.
   (C) Reduced driving will not inconvenience drivers.
   (D) The diminishing supply of fuel is not a problem.
   (E) Gasoline prices should not go down.

6. The author's tone in this passage is

   (A) cynical
   (B) analytical
   (C) satirical
   (D) urgent
   (E) objective

7. To accept the author's argument, we must assume which one of the following about the Harris Survey?

   (A) The people conducting the survey were opposed to pleasure driving.
   (B) The people conducting the survey were not drivers.
   (C) The survey was conducted recently.
   (D) The 1,517 adults actually represent a majority of Americans.
   (E) The people conducting the survey were not employed by the steel industry.

Passage 2

A recent study surveyed 3,576 trials in two reporting samples. Over 500 judges cooperated in the study. The survey was conducted using judges as (5) reporters for jury trials. Two major questions were explored in the survey, "First, what is the magnitude and direction of the disagreement between judge and jury? And, second, what are (10) the sources and explanations of such disagreement?"

The study found that judges and juries agree (would decide the same case the same way) in 75.4 percent of (15) the cases. If cases in which the jury hung are eliminated, the overall agreement rate rises to 78 percent. Thus at the outset, whatever the defects of the jury system, it can be seen that the (20) jury at least arrives at the same result as the judge in over three-fourths of the cases.

The direction of disagreement is clearly toward a more lenient jury than (25) judge. The trend was not isolated to any particular type of offense but was spread throughout crime categories. Additionally, the pattern found was that in convictions, juries tended to be more (30) lenient as far as counts, degrees, and sentencing.

For civil cases the percentage of agreement and disagreement was about the same except that there did not (35) appear to be any strong sentiment in favor of plaintiff over defendant (or vice versa) by the jury.

In cases decided differently because the judge had facts the jury did not, (40) generally, these facts related to suppressed evidence, personal knowledge of the defendant's prior record, etc. The factors that made the difference between judge and jury in (45) these cases, then, were all facts that we as a society purposefully keep from juries because the information is irrelevant or because it is highly prejudicial. From the study it can be (50) assumed that the judge, hearing the information, did not disregard it but, quite the contrary, used it in reaching his (harsher) judgment.

The overwhelming number of cases in (55) which judge and jury agree argue for the jury's understanding of the evidence because it is not to be expected that a jury deciding cases it does not understand and a judge deciding cases

(60) he does understand (we presume) would
not agree in their results so often. Also,
judges themselves generally did not
identify "jury misunderstood the facts"
as the reason for disagreement.

(65)   The level of sympathy that the jury
had with the defendant did make some
difference. Although generally the jury
was neutral, in about 36 percent of the
cases the jury had some reaction
(70) (positive or negative) because of the
personal characteristics, occupation,
family, or court appearance. These
factors affected juries differently
depending on the age, race, or sex of the
(75) defendant. Through various statistical
evaluations the study is able to state
that "the sympathetic defendant causes
disagreement in . . . 4 percent of all
cases." Similar figures apply for the
(80) unsympathetic defendant.

8. This passage was probably written in
   response to an argument for

   (A) the appointment rather than the
       election of judges
   (B) the election rather than the
       appointment of judges
   (C) the wider use of the trial by jury
   (D) the reduced use of the trial by jury
   (E) the increased use of statistics in the
       courts

9. According to the passage, judge and jury
   are likely to reach the same verdict in

   (A) criminal cases rather than in civil
       cases
   (B) civil cases rather than in criminal
       cases
   (C) cases where the judge has facts
       denied to the jury
   (D) cases in which the jury hung
   (E) roughly three-quarters of the cases

10. The results of this study suggest that,
    when there is disagreement between a
    judge and a jury, the judgments of the
    judge are

    (A) harsher than those of juries
    (B) less harsh than those of juries
    (C) very nearly the same as those of
        juries
    (D) less likely to be influenced by
        irrelevant or prejudicial information
    (E) less harsh than those of juries in
        criminal cases only

11. From the results of the study we can
    infer that withholding from a jury
    information that is irrelevant or
    prejudicial to a defendant

    (A) has no significant effect on the
        results of a trial
    (B) works to the disadvantage of most
        defendants
    (C) works to the advantage of most
        defendants
    (D) works to increase the objectivity of
        the judge
    (E) works to decrease the objectivity of
        the jury

12. The author's argument for the jury's
    understanding of the evidence presented
    in trial is based upon

    (A) his assumption that the judge
        understands the evidence
    (B) his assumption that evidence too
        complex for the jury to understand
        would not be admitted
    (C) the fact that evidence is rarely
        complex
    (D) the fact that juries are able to reach
        verdicts
    (E) the fact that no judges have accused
        juries of misunderstanding

13. With which one of the following
    statements would the author be most
    likely to disagree?

    (A) Juries are likely to be influenced by
        the personal characteristics,
        occupation, family, or court
        appearance of defendants.
    (B) Juries are influenced by the age,
        race, or sex of the defendant.
    (C) The judge's misunderstanding the
        evidence is not a likely cause of
        judge-jury disagreements.
    (D) The jury's misunderstanding the
        evidence is not a likely cause of
        judge-jury disagreements.
    (E) The jury's sympathy with a
        defendant is a major cause of judge-
        jury disagreements.

14. By including the information in the final paragraph about the effect of sympathy with the defendant upon the jury, the author of the passage

(A) unfairly denigrates the opposing argument
(B) undermines the case he has presented
(C) suggests that his arguments are objective
(D) conceals a weakness in his case
(E) underscores the lack of objectivity in judges

15. The author includes statistical information in the passage chiefly in order to

(A) demonstrate his familiarity with social science research methods
(B) support his case for the use of juries
(C) make what is really a hypothesis appear to be factual
(D) give an appearance of objectivity to a subjective view
(E) support a case against the use of juries

Passage 3

The last twenty years of the 19th century were to become the pinnacle of success for big business. The legal climate was most conducive to
(5) enterprise. The courts of that time interpreted the 14th Amendment demand for "due process of law" in state action to include corporations as "citizens" and hence made them virtually immune
(10) to state regulation. Cases involving business occupied the Supreme Court continuously. The states had never had the power to regulate interstate railroads, although they frequently tried
(15) to do so, and the Interstate Commerce Act of 1887 attempted to do so. The income tax law of 1894 and the Sherman Antitrust Act of 1890 were Congressional attempts to moderate the
(20) abuses of the new industrial giants, but the Court continued to favor business interest and eviscerated all of the acts.
The 1872 *Slaughterhouse* case was the first blow to federal regulation of
(25) business. The Louisiana legislature had given a monopoly on slaughtering animals in New Orleans to one company and hundreds of butchers found themselves without facilities. They
(30) asked the federal courts to interpret the "privileges and immunities" clause of the 14th Amendment to incorporate a new federally protected right to make a living, which in turn would declare the
(35) monopoly unconstitutional. However, the Supreme Court held that the clause did not add any rights, it merely protected pre-existing federal ones, such as the right of interstate travel;
(40) therefore the monopoly was a valid use of state power.
In 1876 in *Munn vs. Illinois*, the Supreme Court upheld a state's right of regulation. Chicago was the hub of the
(45) grain storage industry, since grain was stored there upon receipt from the Midwest's farmers until it could be distributed through the East. Munn and other warehousemen made agreements
(50) with railroads to get a monopoly on each line's incoming shipments and then fixed prices. This was most damaging to the grain merchants, who pressured the Illinois legislature into
(55) legislating against these practices in 1871. Warehouse owners claimed that these regulations deprived them of their property rights without due process of law. The Supreme Court decision was
(60) rendered by Chief Justice Morrison Waite, who had been appointed by President Grant. He announced that although railroads were interstate commerce, grain storage was not and
(65) therefore the state regulations were valid. This was the last case in which the Supreme Court upheld any state regulation of business until 1937.
In addition to business cases, there
(70) were other problems as well. After Reconstruction officials left the South, the states began passing laws directed at the removal of the political rights the blacks had gained. For the first decade
(75) after the war, there were few "Jim Crow" laws requiring segregation, and integration was at least tolerated. However, persistent denials of the right to vote alarmed Congress and in 1875
(80) the Civil Rights Act was enacted, which protected the franchise and prohibited segregation in places of public accommodation. Several cases involving blacks who had been denied access to
(85) theaters and restaurants in New York City and other areas were decided by the Supreme Court in the *Civil Rights* cases of 1883. The Court (delaying as long as possible) did not hear a case of
(90) this type during the 1870s. The Court held that the 14th Amendment, providing

that "no state shall deny to any citizen the equal protection of the laws" applied only to state action and therefore,
(95) although official discrimination was prohibited, attempts to regulate private discrimination, as in restaurants, were unconstitutional. The results of this decision were the immediate
(100) segregation laws passed by every Southern state. Since political parties were not state organizations, the "white primary," in which the political party became a private club, was invented.

16. Based on the passage, which one of the following is an accurate statement about the Interstate Commerce Act of 1887?

    (A) The act was not supported by a majority in Congress.
    (B) The act was intended to increase the states' regulatory powers.
    (C) The act was intended to support the growth of interstate railroads.
    (D) The act favored federal regulation over state regulation.
    (E) The act was ruled unconstitutional.

17. In the 1872 *Slaughterhouse* case, the Supreme Court's decision achieved all of the following EXCEPT

    (A) helping big business
    (B) allowing a monopoly
    (C) upholding states' rights
    (D) narrowly interpreting a clause of the 14th Amendment
    (E) protecting Congress's right to regulate industry

18. According to the passage, the Supreme Court's decision in *Munn vs. Illinois* was based on

    (A) a state's right to regulate business.
    (B) a person's federally protected right to make a living.
    (C) a company's right to fix prices.
    (D) the federal government's right to regulate interstate commerce.
    (E) the negative effect of regulation on grain merchants.

19. Which one of the following interpretations can we infer was most important in the Supreme Court's pro-business decisions?

    (A) Corporations were to be viewed as "citizens" and given the same rights and privileges.
    (B) "Due process" was to be applied only to state actions.
    (C) All rights not specified in the Constitution were reserved for the individual states.
    (D) "Privileges and immunities" were to include the right to make a living.
    (E) Regulation was to be limited to interstate commerce.

20. The Supreme Court's ruling in the *Civil Rights* cases of 1883 can best be characterized as

    (A) the result of intimidation by the South.
    (B) progressive for its time.
    (C) the result of compromise.
    (D) the inevitable result of an all-white Court.
    (E) a victory for segregationists.

21. According to the passage, the "white primary" was introduced in the South to

    (A) defy the Supreme Court's authority.
    (B) prevent the election of African-Americans to state offices.
    (C) provide a way around the prohibition of official discrimination.
    (D) return authority for election procedures to individual states.
    (E) redefine the 14th Amendment to exclude certain rights.

22. The main purpose of the first three paragraphs of the passage is to

    (A) show that corruption of the Supreme Court in the late 19th century had far-reaching effects.
    (B) illustrate how Supreme Court decisions generally favored big business in the late 19th century.
    (C) analyze the pros and cons of two important Supreme Court decisions relating to big business.
    (D) explain why no regulatory legislation was passed during the late 19th century.
    (E) argue against the Supreme Court's decisions in the late 19th century.

23. The author's attitude expressed in this passage can best be described as
    (A) bitterly cynical.
    (B) thoughtfully positive.
    (C) mildly judgmental.
    (D) strictly objective.
    (E) harshly negative.

Passage 4

No sooner had the British forces in June 1944 carried out their part in the Allied invasion of Germany than they were faced with the fact that among the
(5) prisoners of war captured there were Russians in German uniforms. By the time the war in Europe ended, between two and three million Soviet citizens had passed through Allied hands. This
(10) extraordinary situation, certainly never before known in the history of war, was the consequence of the policy of both the Soviet and the German regimes. On the Soviet side, the very existence of
(15) prisoners of war was not recognized: the Soviet government refused to adhere to the Geneva Convention, and washed its hands of the millions who fell into German power.
(20) The Germans, in turn, treated their Soviet prisoners with such callous brutality that only a relatively small number of them survived. For a Soviet prisoner in German hands to enlist in
(25) the German armed forces was about the only way open to him of saving his life. There were also Soviet citizens whose hatred of the Communist regime was so strong that they were prepared to fight
(30) alongside the Germans in order to overthrow Stalin: nominally headed by General Andrey Vlasov, they saw little combat until the end of the war, largely because of Hitler's suspicion of Vlasov's
(35) claims to maintain his political independence of the National Socialist regime even as a prisoner of war. There were also some other combat units composed of Russians, some of them
(40) noted for their savagery. Then there were hordes of civilians in German hands—some compulsorily swept into the German labor mobilization drive, many more borne along the wave of the
(45) German retreat from Russia and thereafter drafted for labor duties. These civilians included many women and children.
The problem facing the British
(50) government from the outset was what policy to adopt toward this mass of humanity that did not fall into any of the accepted categories thrown up by war. Quite apart from the logistic
(55) problems, there existed a well-established tradition in Britain which refused to repatriate against their will people who found themselves in British hands and the nature of whose
(60) reception by their own government was, to say the least, dubious. The first inclination of the Cabinet—to send all captured Russians back to the Soviet Union—was challenged by the minister
(65) of economic warfare, Lord Selborne, who was moved by the fact that the Russians in British hands had only volunteered to serve in German uniforms as an alternative to certain
(70) death; and that it would therefore be inhuman to send them back to be shot or to suffer long periods of forced labor. Winston Churchill was also swayed by this argument.

24. The primary purpose of this passage is to
    (A) explain one of the problems facing British forces near the end of World War II
    (B) reveal the savagery of both the German and the Russian forces
    (C) stress America's noninvolvement
    (D) detail a "war within a war"
    (E) give evidence for Churchill's position

25. "Repatriate" in paragraph 3 means to
    (A) send back to the country of birth
    (B) send back to the country of allegiance
    (C) send back to the victorious country
    (D) reinstill patriotism
    (E) reinstill British patriotism

26. The author's position is
    (A) pro-Russian
    (B) anti-Russian
    (C) anti-British
    (D) pro-German
    (E) neutral

27. The problem in World War II concerning the disposition of Soviet prisoners of war was very similar to

    (A) the plight of Armenian refugees
    (B) Hitler's own loss of identity after 1944
    (C) the plight of British prisoners of war
    (D) no previous situation
    (E) several instances in the history of war

28. Lord Selborne's opinion disregards which of the following facts?

    (A) The Soviet Union posed a nuclear threat to the United States.
    (B) Traditionally, repatriation was not imposed by Great Britain.
    (C) Certain Soviet citizens wanted to overthrow Stalin.
    (D) General Andrey Vlasov was politically independent.
    (E) Soviet prisoners were treated brutally.

29. The German labor mobilization drive consisted partly of

    (A) women and children
    (B) retreating German soldiers
    (C) followers of General Andrey Vlasov
    (D) savage combat units
    (E) those born during the retreat

30. The Soviet policy toward their prisoners of war was one of

    (A) nonrecognition
    (B) nonaggression
    (C) nonproliferation
    (D) noncontempt
    (E) nonadherence

Passage 5

The right to an unbiased jury is an inseparable part of the right to trial by jury as guaranteed by the Seventh Amendment of the United States
(5) Constitution. This right guarantees that twelve impartial jurors will hear and "truly try" the cause before them.

In September 1982, the California Supreme Court upheld a lower court's
(10) $9.2 million verdict against Ford Motor Company despite the fact that three jurors had been working crossword puzzles and one juror had been reading a novel during the presentation of
(15) testimony. Four of the twelve jurors hearing the case were admittedly participating in the activities charged and were clearly guilty of misconduct, yet the California Supreme Court found
(20) no resultant prejudice against Ford's position.

In the United States, citizens are called upon by the government to serve as jurors. Only under extraordinary
(25) circumstances may a citizen be excused from such service. Juries are therefore not necessarily composed of willing volunteers, but instead, are sometimes made up of individuals who are serving
(30) against their will, and justice is adversely affected when citizens are "forced" to serve on juries. In "Reflections of a Juror," the author, who served as a juror himself, recognized
(35) two distinct perspectives shared among jurors. Some jurors have a very positive attitude about their being asked to serve on a jury. Their perspective is that of rendering a public service by fulfilling
(40) their jury duties. On the other hand, some jurors view their obligation as just that, a burdensome obligation, and nothing more. Their attitude is one of getting through with the ordeal as soon
(45) as possible, a let's-get-out-of-here-by-this-afternoon approach.

A study conducted with mock juries, concerned specifically with the issue of juror prejudgment, revealed that 25
(50) percent of the jurors polled reached their decision early in the trial. The jurors in the study who admitted to having made up their minds before having heard all the evidence also stated
(55) that they generally held to their first-impression assessments. By prejudging the outcome of the case the jurors had, in effect, breached their sworn duty.

From a reading of the California
(60) Supreme Court's opinion, it appears that the Court itself has committed the one form of conduct universally prohibited, that of prejudgment. Ford's battle was lost before it had even begun
(65) to present its case. In the first place, Ford is a multibillion-dollar international corporation with "pockets" deeper than most. Secondly, Ford had experienced a great deal of
(70) negative publicity resulting from recent jury verdicts awarding large sums of money to victims of Pinto automobile accidents wherein it was determined that Ford had defectively designed the
(75) Pinto's gasoline tank so that it was prone to explode upon rear end impacts. Finally, the plaintiff was a nineteen-year-old college freshman whose pursuit of a

(80) medical career was abruptly ended when he suffered extensive brain damage after the brakes on his 1966 Lincoln failed, causing him to crash into a fountain after careening down a steeply curving hillside street. Ford presented a

(85) considerable amount of evidence in an attempt to prove that the cause of the accident was driver error and faulty maintenance and not defective design. The Supreme Court responded to Ford's

(90) arguments by stating that the jury was responsible for judging the credibility of witnesses and it would be wholly improper for the Court to usurp that function by reweighing the evidence.

(95) How ironic that the Court should so gallantly refuse to upset the decision of the jury, a jury wherein four members admittedly were engaging in extraneous activities when they were supposed to

(100) be "judging the credibility of witnesses." It would appear from the misconduct of the jury and the conclusionary statements of the California Supreme Court that Ford's liability was indeed a

(105) predetermined, prejudged fact.

If the decision has any impact upon our present system of justice, it will regretfully be a negative one. The California Supreme Court has, in effect,

(110) approved a standard of jury conduct so unconscionable as to, in the words of dissenting Justice Richardson, "countenance such a complete erosion of a constitutional command," namely,

(115) the right to a fair and impartial jury trial.

31. Which one of the following best states the central idea of the passage?

(A) By not questioning the decision in the Ford case, the California Supreme Court, like the jury, was guilty of prejudgment.

(B) There are serious defects in the system of trial by jury.

(C) The jury in the Ford case was guilty of prejudging the case.

(D) The Supreme Court's handling of the Ford case may lead to an erosion of the constitutional right to a fair and impartial jury trial.

(E) Studies suggest that a large number of the men and women serving on juries fail to "truly try" the cases they hear.

32. All of the following data from the passage could be used to argue against the jury system EXCEPT

(A) in the Ford case, three jurors were working crossword puzzles and one was reading a novel during the presentation of testimony

(B) juries are likely to include individuals who are serving against their will

(C) in a study of mock jurors, 25 percent reached a decision early in the trial

(D) pretrial publicity about Ford Pintos resulting in large jury verdicts to victims influenced the Supreme Court's decision

(E) some jurors view their service as an ordeal to be ended as quickly as possible

33. The author's belief that Ford was denied a fair trial in the lower court is best supported by the fact that

(A) the jury was unduly sympathetic to the nineteen-year-old accident victim who suffered extensive brain damage

(B) the jury was influenced by unfavorable publicity about the defective gas tanks on the Ford Pinto

(C) three of the jurors were admittedly working crossword puzzles during the testimony

(D) the California Supreme Court refused to reverse the decision of the jury

(E) the California Supreme Court refused to judge the credibility of the witnesses

34. An argument in favor of the Supreme Court decision in the Ford case might include all of the following EXCEPT

    (A) if the case were retried, the jury would probably include jurors who were serving against their will
    (B) it is probable that the jurors working puzzles and reading were also paying attention to the testimony
    (C) if the case were retried, some members of the jury are likely to come to a decision early in the trial
    (D) if the case were retried, those jurors who made up their minds early would be unlikely to alter their verdicts later in the trial
    (E) the jury at the original trial is in a better position to judge the credibility of the witnesses than the Supreme Court

35. The author suggests that the California Supreme Court reached its decision in the Ford case for all of the following reasons EXCEPT

    (A) a prejudice against Ford because of its wealth
    (B) a prejudice against Ford because of recent negative publicity
    (C) an agreement with the lower court's evaluation of the credibility of the witnesses
    (D) a bias in favor of the young accident victim
    (E) a refusal to find fault with deplorable jury conduct

36. In the next to last paragraph of the passage, the author uses irony when he writes

    (A) "Ford's battle was lost before it had even begun to present its case."
    (B) "Ford is a multibillion-dollar international corporation with 'pockets' deeper than most."
    (C) The plaintiff's "pursuit of a medical career was abruptly ended when he suffered extensive brain damage . . ."
    (D) ". . . the Court should so gallantly refuse to upset the decision of the jury. . . ."
    (E) ". . . Ford's liability was indeed a predetermined, prejudged fact."

37. From information given in lines 106–116, it is clear that the Supreme Court decision

    (A) was unanimous
    (B) was not unanimous
    (C) will have a significant impact on the justice system
    (D) reverses that of the lower court
    (E) will be appealed

Answers and Explanations

Passage 1

1. **C** This purpose is stated most explicitly in paragraph 5, although there are several other points in the passage where the author urges drivers to drive less. (A) is weak because it is too general and inclusive; (B) is vague about the means of reducing smog; (D) and (E) are very minor points.

2. **A** This is stated explicitly in paragraph 5, where the author blames individual drivers rather than industry.

3. **A** The second paragraph implies that recreational vehicles create more smog, and the fourth paragraph describes smog's effects on nature; therefore, we may conclude that gas-guzzling vacation vehicles help to damage the natural beauty of vacation spots. The author *might* also agree with (D), but the evidence in the passage itself points more substantially to (A).

4. **E** The author criticizes the increased use of recreational vehicles (see explanation for question 3).

5. **B** The final sentence in the passage implies that we will be "forced" to conserve if we do not do so voluntarily. (A) is neither stated nor implied; the author does imply that industrial emissions *should not be controlled*, but this is not the same as suggesting that they are *uncontrollable*.

6. **D** The author is almost pleading that drivers make immediate changes in their habits; the urgency of his purpose coincides with the urgency of his tone.

7. **D** The author begins the passage by claiming that the Harris Survey represents a "majority of Americans"; we must share that assumption in order to accept the importance of his argument. All other choices are irrelevant.

Passage 2

8. **D** The passage is part of a longer essay written to refute the arguments of Judge Jerome Frank, who holds that a judge alone is likely to be more reliable than a jury.

9. **E** The second paragraph says that judges and juries agree in 75.4 percent of the cases, according to the study.

10. **A** The third paragraph discusses the greater harshness of judges in all categories of crime—in counts, degrees, and sentencing.

11. **C** Because the effect of this information upon judges is to make their judgments harsher, we can infer it would have the same effect on juries and the withholding of this information is, predictably, to the defendant's advantage.

12. **A** The author assumes the judge understands the evidence and because the juries agree with the judge so often, he argues the juries must also have understood the evidence to come to the same conclusion as the judge.

13. **E** The passage supports each of the first four statements, but the jury's sympathy with a defendant according to the last paragraph leads to judge-jury differences in only 4 percent of all the cases studied and so could not be called a "major" cause of disagreement.

14. **C** By admitting frankly that juries are not always fully objective the author demonstrates a willingness to discuss facts that may not advance his case. All of the four other options are false.

15. **B** The statistics are used to support the author's case for the use of juries. Because the statistics are the result of other writers' research, and are based upon a large sample, they give more than an "appearance" of objectivity.

Passage 3

16. **B** According to Paragraph 1, the states had never had the power to regulate interstate railroads, and the Interstate Commerce Act was an attempt to change this situation. (A) is an inference not supported by the passage, and although the passage says the Court "eviscerated" regulatory acts, it does not state or imply that this act was ruled unconstitutional (E). Both (D) and (C) are factually incorrect; the act was designed to provide state (not federal) regulation, and its purpose was to regulate railroads, not support their growth.

17. **E** The decision did not protect Congress's right to regulate industry. All of the other answers are true; the *Slaughterhouse* decision gave the state power (C) to give a monopoly to one company, (A, B). By refusing to extend the "privileges and immunities" clause of the 14th amendment to add the right to make a living, the Court was narrowly interpreting the clause (D).

18. **A** The Court found for Illinois, thereby confirming a state's right to regulate business. (B) was not considered in this decision. (D) is incorrect because the Court ruled that grain storage was not interstate commerce and therefore not under federal jurisdiction. Whereas grain merchants would be helped by Illinois regulating warehousemen, this fact did not serve as the basis for the Court's decision (E). Because the Court ruled for the state, (C) is simply incorrect.

19. **A** This is the best answer. By giving corporations the same rights and privileges as citizens, the Court made it almost impossible for states to regulate them. (B) was an important interpretation for cases involving private discrimination but not for cases involving regulation of business. (D) is incorrect; the Court ruled that the "privileges and immunities" clause did not include the right to make a living. (C) would not support business (and is not addressed in the passage), and the Court did not issue the ruling stated in (E).

20. **E** The ruling in the *Civil Rights* cases aided segregationists by limiting the 14th Amendment's application to state actions, thereby allowing private discrimination. There is no evidence that the ruling was the result of compromise (C), although it may have been, and it was definitely not a progressive decision, since official discrimination was already forbidden by the 14th Amendment (B). No evidence supports (A), and although the Justices may have all been white, that fact does not make the ruling "inevitable" (D).

21. **C** By making political parties private clubs, Southerners were able to circumvent the prohibition of official discrimination. Rather than defying the Court (A), they took advantage of its ruling on private discrimination. Although the "white primary" would prevent the election of African-Americans, that was not the reason it was created (B). (D) is irrelevant; the authority for election procedures was not in question. (E) is both vague and incorrect.

22. **B** The first three paragraphs illustrate by citing examples that the Court's decisions generally favored big business. The pros and cons of the decisions are neither addressed nor analyzed (C). The author does not suggest corruption in the Court nor does he describe "far-reaching effects" of any of the decisions (A). (D) is inaccurate; some regulatory legislation was passed during this period. (Beware of words like "no," "none," "never," etc.) The passage does not argue a point of view (E).

23. **C** Certain phrases indicate that the author is mildly judgmental; see lines 9, 20, 54, 70, and 88. (D) is a possible answer except for the use of the word "strictly." Connotations of words chosen by the author indicate some degree of judgment. Both (A) and (E) overstate the author's slightly judgmental attitude; he is neither cynical nor "harshly" negative. Nothing in the passage suggests (B).

Passage 4

24. **A** The passage discusses the past and present facts contributing to the British problem with captured Russians.

25. **A** The final paragraph discusses at length the question of whether to send Russians back to Russia despite their lack of allegiance to Russia. This is the repatriation question and is consistent with the dictionary definition of *repatriate*—to send back to the country of birth.

26. **E** The author does not himself argue for or against a particular position or nationality. He simply presents facts and the arguments of others. His comments in paragraph 2 might be called anti-German, but this attitude is not one of the choices.

27. **D** Paragraph 1 states, "This extraordinary situation [was] . . . never before known in the history of war."

28. **C** Selborne argued that Russians served the Germans only "as an alternative to certain death" (paragraph 3). But paragraph 2 states that some Russians fought with the Germans "in order to overthrow Stalin."

29. **A** Paragraph 2 says that "the German labor mobilization drive . . . included many women and children."

30. **A** Paragraph 1 states, "On the Soviet side, the very existence of prisoners of war was not recognized."

Passage 5

31. **A** The author wishes to criticize both the jury, which was inattentive, and the Supreme Court, which allowed the jury's decision to stand. Some of the other options are stated or implied ideas of the passage but not its central idea.

32. **D** (D) is relevant to the Supreme Court decision but not to the jury system. (A), (B), (C), and (E) all expose deficiencies in the jury system.

33. **C** The inattentiveness of four jurors is explicit support for a charge that Ford's case was not fairly heard. We don't know for certain if (A) or (B) is true. (D) and (E) are true but do not support the author's belief in the unfairness of the trial.

34. **B** The limitations of all juries discussed in the passage would apply as well to the jury retrying the case as to the jury who reached a decision already. The Supreme Court's argument that the original jury was in a better position to judge the credibility of the witnesses is surely correct; the Supreme Court did not see the witnesses who testified. Though (B) is remotely possible, it is not a point one would wish to use in support of the Supreme Court decision.

35. **C** Though the Supreme Court agreed with the lower court jury, it specifically asserted the impropriety of its attempting to reweigh the evidence and the credibility of the witnesses.

36. **D** A case could be made that (B), an understatement, is ironic, but a clearer instance is the sarcasm of "gallantly"; the author does not believe the Supreme Court acted gallantly.

37. **B** Because Justice Richardson dissented, the decision cannot have been unanimous.

Answer Sheet
Extra Practice:
Reading Comprehension

1. Ⓐ Ⓑ Ⓒ Ⓓ Ⓔ	14. Ⓐ Ⓑ Ⓒ Ⓓ Ⓔ	26. Ⓐ Ⓑ Ⓒ Ⓓ Ⓔ
2. Ⓐ Ⓑ Ⓒ Ⓓ Ⓔ	15. Ⓐ Ⓑ Ⓒ Ⓓ Ⓔ	27. Ⓐ Ⓑ Ⓒ Ⓓ Ⓔ
3. Ⓐ Ⓑ Ⓒ Ⓓ Ⓔ	16. Ⓐ Ⓑ Ⓒ Ⓓ Ⓔ	28. Ⓐ Ⓑ Ⓒ Ⓓ Ⓔ
4. Ⓐ Ⓑ Ⓒ Ⓓ Ⓔ	17. Ⓐ Ⓑ Ⓒ Ⓓ Ⓔ	29. Ⓐ Ⓑ Ⓒ Ⓓ Ⓔ
5. Ⓐ Ⓑ Ⓒ Ⓓ Ⓔ	18. Ⓐ Ⓑ Ⓒ Ⓓ Ⓔ	30. Ⓐ Ⓑ Ⓒ Ⓓ Ⓔ
6. Ⓐ Ⓑ Ⓒ Ⓓ Ⓔ	19. Ⓐ Ⓑ Ⓒ Ⓓ Ⓔ	31. Ⓐ Ⓑ Ⓒ Ⓓ Ⓔ
7. Ⓐ Ⓑ Ⓒ Ⓓ Ⓔ	20. Ⓐ Ⓑ Ⓒ Ⓓ Ⓔ	32. Ⓐ Ⓑ Ⓒ Ⓓ Ⓔ
8. Ⓐ Ⓑ Ⓒ Ⓓ Ⓔ	21. Ⓐ Ⓑ Ⓒ Ⓓ Ⓔ	33. Ⓐ Ⓑ Ⓒ Ⓓ Ⓔ
9. Ⓐ Ⓑ Ⓒ Ⓓ Ⓔ	22. Ⓐ Ⓑ Ⓒ Ⓓ Ⓔ	34. Ⓐ Ⓑ Ⓒ Ⓓ Ⓔ
10. Ⓐ Ⓑ Ⓒ Ⓓ Ⓔ	23. Ⓐ Ⓑ Ⓒ Ⓓ Ⓔ	35. Ⓐ Ⓑ Ⓒ Ⓓ Ⓔ
11. Ⓐ Ⓑ Ⓒ Ⓓ Ⓔ	24. Ⓐ Ⓑ Ⓒ Ⓓ Ⓔ	36. Ⓐ Ⓑ Ⓒ Ⓓ Ⓔ
12. Ⓐ Ⓑ Ⓒ Ⓓ Ⓔ	25. Ⓐ Ⓑ Ⓒ Ⓓ Ⓔ	37. Ⓐ Ⓑ Ⓒ Ⓓ Ⓔ
13. Ⓐ Ⓑ Ⓒ Ⓓ Ⓔ		

To remove, cut along dotted rule.

Chapter 3
ANALYTICAL REASONING

Introduction to Question Type

The Analytical Reasoning section is designed to measure your ability to analyze, understand, and draw conclusions from a group of conditions and relationships. This section is 35 minutes long and contains from 22 to 24 questions (usually four sets of conditions, statements, or rules). Each set is followed by four to seven questions.

The Analytical Reasoning type of question first appeared officially on the LSAT in June 1982, but a similar form of Analytical Reasoning has been used on the Graduate Record Exam since 1977.

Analytical Reasoning situations can take many forms, but you should be aware of some general things before reviewing the problem types.

When You Start a Set, Focus On:

Reading the Conditions

1. Read each statement carefully and actively, marking important words.
2. As you read, learn to flow with the information given, looking for relationships between items.
3. Remember that making simple charts, diagrams, or simply displaying information is essential on most sets, so read the conditions as though they are describing a display or diagram.
4. If you wish to read through all of the conditions of a set before starting a diagram, begin your diagram on the second reading.
5. If no diagram seems apparent or conducive to the information given, look at a few questions. Sometimes the questions can give you some good hints on how to display the information.

Marking the Conditions

1. Because you will probably be drawing some sort of diagram or display, place a check mark next to each statement or condition as you read it or use it in the diagram. This will help you avoid skipping a statement or condition as you work back and forth in setting up your diagram.
2. Put a star or an asterisk next to big, general, and important statements. Sometimes these statements will affect a group, category, or placement. (Examples are, "No two people of the same sex are sitting in adjacent seats," and "All of the members of a department cannot take the same day off." Two other examples might include: "At least two graduate students must be on the team," and "People with pets with them must stay in hotel room 1 or 8.")

3. Put a star or an asterisk by statements that are difficult to understand. Try to rephrase these statements to yourself for better understanding.

When You Start Drawing Your Display, Focus On:

Finding Key Items

1. Look for a simple way to display the information. Don't complicate the issue.
2. Look for the setup, frame, or framework. Sometimes this is given in the first statement, but in other cases you may need to read a number of conditions before constructing the type of drawing that will be most effective.
3. If you discover the frame or framework, fill in as much of the diagram as possible, but do not spend a great deal of time trying to complete it. This may not be possible or necessary to answer the questions.
4. Be aware that you may have to redraw all or part of your diagram several times (typically, a few times for each set) as different conditional information is given for specific questions.
5. If a framework is not given, see if the information can be grouped by similarities or differences.
6. As you read each statement, look for concrete information that you can enter into your chart or that you can simply display. (For example, "Tom sits in seat 4," or "Cheryl coaches swimming.")

Drawing and Placing Information

1. Locate off to the side any information that you cannot place directly into your chart. (Whatever you can't put in, goes out; for example, "Jill will not sit next to Helen," or "A biology book must be next to a science book.")
2. Some very important statements may not fit into your chart. Remember to put a star or an asterisk by these big, general, and important statements.
3. If some statements are not immediately placeable in your chart (and they are not the big, general statements), you may have to return to them for later placing, after you have placed other statements. Remember to mark such statements with an arrow or some other symbol so you don't forget to return to them.
4. As you place information, use question marks (?) to mark information that is variable or could be placed in a number of different places in the diagram.
5. Underline and abbreviate or write out column headings and labels. Don't use single letters as they may be confused with the actual items (If you use "m" for males, it could be confused with an "m" for Manuel, one of the males).

6. If, as is true in many cases, no standard type of chart will apply to the problem, be aware that you can merely pull out information in a simple display or through simple notes. Remember to flow with the information given, looking for relationships between items.

Reasoning from the Conditions

1. No formal logic is required.
2. Apply evidence in both directions. For instance, if a statement tells you that a condition must be true, consider whether this means that certain other conditions must not be true. (For example: "All blue cars are fast" tells you that a slow car is *not* blue.)
3. Notice what information is used, and what is left to use. (For example, "Bob, Carl, Don, Ed, and Fred are riding the school bus home. Don, Ed, and Fred are sitting in seats one, two, and three, respectively." You should realize that Bob and Carl are left to be placed.)
4. Watch for actions and the subsequent reactions in initial conditions or from information given in the questions. (For example, "Dale, Ralph, and Art cannot be on the same team. Dale is on Team A." Your action is that Dale is on Team A; your immediate reaction is that Ralph and Art cannot be on Team A.)
5. Watch the number of items, places, and people (males to females, adults to children, etc.) you are working with. Sometimes these numbers are the basis for correct answers, and they can even tip off how to construct a diagram.
6. If the diagram you construct shows positions or specific dates or other limits, watch for items that will force you off the end or out of the limits. (For example, "There are five houses in a row on the north side of the street numbered 1, 2, 3, 4, 5 consecutively. There is one yellow house that is between two blue houses." Therefore, the yellow house cannot be in place 1 or 5, because there would be no room for a blue house. It would be forced off the end or out of bounds.)

When You Start Answering the Questions, Focus On:

Reading the Questions

1. Read the questions actively, marking the important words. You should first always circle what you are looking for (Which of the following must be true? All of the following are possible except . . .).
2. Notice and underline any *actions* given to you in a question (If <u>Bob is selected</u> for the team, who else must be selected?). Watch for any subsequent *reactions* (If Bob is selected, Tom can't be selected).
3. Keep in mind that any information given to you in a specific question (usually starting with the words "If . . . ," "Assume . . . ," "Suppose . . . ," "Given the fact that . . . ," and so on) can be used only for that question and not for any other questions.

4. Don't take any information from one question to another question. That is, if you get an answer on one question, don't use that information (answer) in any other questions.

Working with the Answer Choices

1. Using the elimination strategy mentioned in the introduction can be invaluable here. Watch for rule breakers, that is, statements that contradict initial conditions. If the conditions state "X cannot sit next to Y" then any answer choice with X sitting next to Y can be eliminated (unless of course, the initial condition was changed in the question for that particular question).

2. Watch for certain types of wrong answers known as *distracters*. Since *"could be"* and *"must be"* are often confused, a *"could be true"* answer choice is a great distracter (*attractive distracter*) for a question that asks what *must be true*.

Understand the distinction between *must be* and *could be*:

Must Be No exceptions All the time Always	***Could Be*** May be, but doesn't necessarily have to be

3. If a question looks like it's going to be difficult or time-consuming, you may wish to **scan the answer choices.** When you scan, **look for winners, losers, workers, and question marks:**

Winners—right answers that jump out at you or are easy to spot (circle the answer in your question booklet, mark it on your answer sheet, and move on)

Losers—answers that you can eliminate instantly or very easily (cross out the answer choice and move on)

Workers—answer choices that can be fairly easily worked out to determine if they are right or wrong (go on and work this one)

Question Marks—answer choices that you either can't work or don't know what to do with (put a question mark ? and move on)

AND A FINAL REMINDER: KEEP THE DRAWING SIMPLE; DON'T COMPLICATE YOUR THINKING.

The following sections provide some detailed examples of typical problem types and charts. These samples are intended to give you insight into the methods of charting that are possible. REMEMBER: Different students may prefer different types of charts. Use what is effective and efficient for you!

The Approach

Analyzing Types of Charts

The Connection Chart

One of the many types of charts is the connection chart. In constructing this chart, you should follow these steps:

1. Group or align items into general categories (remember you group items by similarities and differences).
2. Draw connections according to relationships between specific items. Your markings should indicate whether items always go together (x—y), never go together (x⤫y), are conditional (if x goes then y goes; x → y), and so on.

After you've drawn your chart, remember to take information forward and backward (what can and can't happen) and to watch for actions and subsequent reactions.

EXAMPLE

Sales manager Phil Forrester is trying to put together a sales team to cover the Los Angeles area. His team will consist of four members—two experienced and two new salesmen.

Sam, Fred, Harry, and Kim are the experienced salesmen.
John, Tim, and Dom are new.
Sam and Fred do not work together.
Tim and Sam refuse to work together.
Harry and Dom cannot work together.

Analysis—The setup

When drawing a connection chart, always prefer fewer connections to many connections. In this case, drawing connections between the workers who can work together will result in a complicated system of intersecting lines. Connecting those who *do not* or *cannot* work together results in a simple, clear chart:

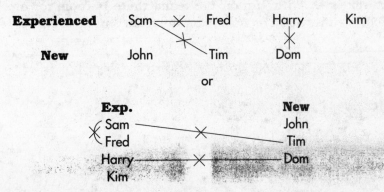

Each chart encourages you to use information in both directions, recognizing that, because connected workers *cannot* work together, unconnected workers *can* work together.

Notice that the conditions gave initial information about those who cannot work together, helping you to formulate the most efficient method of connecting the diagram. If the conditions had stated that some salesmen always work together and some never work together, you would have used a different type of marking to denote each type of connection. Also notice that the labels or headings should be written out or abbreviated *and* underlined.

Question 1

If Sam is made part of the team, the following must be the other members:

(A) John, Tim, Dom
(B) John, Dom, Kim
(C) Tim, Harry, Kim
(D) Dom, John, Fred
(E) John, Dom, Harry

Analysis
The correct answer is B. The team must consist of two experienced and two new salesmen. Sam is experienced, so the rest of the team must include one experienced and two new salesmen. (C) should be eliminated both because it contains two experienced salesmen and because Sam does not work with Tim; also eliminate (A) because it includes Tim. Eliminate (D) because Sam does not work with Fred, and eliminate (E) because Dom does not work with Harry.

Question 2

If Sam is not chosen as part of the sales team and Tim is, then which one of the following must be true?

(A) Dom and Harry are on the team.
(B) Kim and John are on the team.
(C) Harry and Fred are on the team.
(D) John or Dom is not on the team.
(E) Fred or Kim is not on the team.

Analysis
The correct answer is D. With Tim on the team, there is room for one other new salesman. Therefore, *either* John *or* Dom is on the team, but not both.

Question 3

Which one of the following must be true?

(A) Fred and Sam always work together.
(B) Kim and Dom never work together.
(C) Kim and Fred always work together.
(D) If John works, then Kim doesn't work.
(E) If Sam works, then Dom works.

Analysis

The correct answer is E. The key word in this question is *must*, which excludes possible but not necessary combinations. (A) is false, as the chart reveals. (B) is false because they *could* work together if Harry does not work. (C) is false because Kim and Fred do not have to work together. You could have the team of Kim, Sam, John, and Dom. This also eliminates (D). (E) must be true since Sam and Tim never work together; Sam must always work with Dom and John.

Question 4

If Dom is chosen as part of the sales team but John is not, then the other three members must be

(A) Fred, Tim, and Harry
(B) Fred, Tim, and Kim
(C) Harry, John, and Tim
(D) Tim, Dom, and Kim
(E) Sam, Fred, and Harry

Analysis

The correct answer is B. If Dom is chosen as part of the team and John is not, then Tim must be the other inexperienced member. So, if Dom and Tim both are chosen, then Sam and Harry are not chosen. The team now consists of Dom, Tim, Fred, and Kim.

Question 5

Which one of the following must be true?

(A) If Harry works, then John works.
(B) If Kim works, then John works.
(C) If John works, then Dom works.
(D) If Dom works, then John works.
(E) If John works, then Kim works.

Analysis

The correct answer is A. Since Harry will not work with Dom, then John must be one of the other inexperienced members in the group when Harry works. The other combinations (Kim and John, John and Dom) do not always work together.

EXAMPLE

A landscape designer wishes to use roses of different colors in a large planter. Seven colors of roses are available for selection: lavender, orange, pink, red, tan, white, and yellow. Only certain color combinations will be used based on the following conditions:

If lavender is used, then so is tan.
If red is used, then yellow is not used.
If orange, tan, or both are used, then so is red.
If pink is not used, then neither is lavender.
If white is not used, then yellow is used.

Analysis—The setup

From the information given, a simple connection chart could be constructed as follows:

```
Used            Not
L ➤ T
        R ──────➤ Y
   O/T ➤ R
                P ➤ L
        Y ◄───── W
```

Notice that the group headings are underlined and that the arrows are pointing in one direction. "If–then" statements should be represented by arrows pointing from the "if" to the "then."

Using this chart or display should make answering the questions much easier.

Question 1

If lavender is used, what is the least number of colors that can be used?

(A) 2
(B) 3
(C) 4
(D) 5
(E) 6

Analysis

The correct answer is D. If L is used, then so is T. If T is used, then so is R. If R is used, then Y is not. If Y is not used, then W is used. Since L is used, so must P. Therefore, Y cannot be used and O doesn't have to be used. Five is the correct answer. The following summarizes the results.

```
Used            Not
 L               Y
 T               O?
 R
 W
 P
```

Question 2

If tan is not used, which one of the following must be true?

(A) Pink is not used.
(B) Either lavender or red is used.
(C) Orange and red are the only two colors used.
(D) Either white or yellow or both are used.
(E) Both red and yellow are used.

Analysis

The correct answer is D. If T is not used, then neither is L. Since L is not used, P may or may not be used; therefore, answer (A) is incorrect. Since R may or may not be used, answer (B) is incorrect. Since R does not have to be used, answers (C) and (E) are incorrect. It is not possible for both W and Y not to be used; therefore, answer (D) is correct.

	Used	**Not**
		T
		L
	P?	
	R?	
Either	Y	W
or	W	Y
or	W, Y	

Question 3

Which one of the following sets of colors CANNOT be a complete set of colors used?

(A) orange, pink, red, and white
(B) yellow only
(C) lavender, red, tan, and white
(D) red and white
(E) pink, red, tan, and white

Analysis

The correct answer is C. Only answer choice (C) fails to meet the conditions. If P were not used, then L would not be used. Since L is used, so must P. All the other choices are possible.

Question 4

If exactly two colors are used, which of the following CANNOT be those two colors?

(A) red and white
(B) pink and white
(C) white and yellow
(D) orange and red
(E) pink and yellow

Analysis

The correct answer is D. If R is used, then Y is not used. If Y is not used, then W must be used. Therefore, if R is used, then so must W, and choice (D) is only O and R.

Question 5

If white is not used, then which one of the following must be true?

(A) Tan must be used.
(B) Pink must be used.
(C) Pink cannot be used.
(D) Yellow must be used.
(E) Yellow cannot be used.

Analysis

The correct answer is D. If W is not used, then Y must be used. T can't be used because then R would have to be used and then Y couldn't be used (eliminate A). Eliminate choices (B) and (C) since either *could* be true. Choice (E) cannot be true since Y must be used.

The Connection Chart with Placements

EXAMPLE

Seven students—John, Kim, Len, Molly, Neil, Owen, and Pam—will be assigned to three study stations—reading, writing, and math. Students are assigned to the stations under the following conditions:

Each student must be assigned to exactly one station.
Each station must have at least one student, but cannot have more than three students.
Kim and Len are always assigned to the same station.
Len and Molly are never assigned to the same station.
Pam is assigned to the reading station.
If John is assigned to math, then Kim is assigned to reading.
Neil is never assigned to writing.
Owen is never assigned to math.

Analysis—The setup

Your first step should be to set up the placement categories—reading, writing, and math. Be sure to underline the categories.

<u>Reading</u>   <u>Writing</u>   <u>Math</u>

From the condition "Each station must have at least one student, but cannot have more than three students," you could add the following:

	Reading	Writing	Math
?	_____	_____	_____
?	_____	_____	_____

Next, you could put information off to the side from the conditions "Kim and Len are always assigned to the same station" and "Len and Molly are never assigned to the same station."

	Reading	Writing	Math	
	_____	_____	_____	KL
?	_____	_____	_____	
?	_____	_____	_____	L̶M̶

The statement "Pam is assigned to the reading station" gives you a quick placement as follows:

	Reading	Writing	Math	
	P	_____	_____	KL
?	_____	_____	_____	
?	_____	_____	_____	L̶M̶

The conditional statement "If John is assigned to math, then Kim is assigned to reading" should be marked as follows:

K ⟵⎯⎯⎯⎯⎯⎯⎯⎯ J

	Reading	Writing	Math	
	P	_____	_____	KL
?	_____	_____	_____	
?	_____	_____	_____	L̶M̶

Notice that the arrow is pointing from J to K.

Finally, "Neil is never assigned to writing" and "Owen is never assigned to math" can be marked as follows:

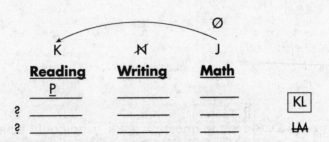

K   N̶   J   (Ø above J)

	Reading	Writing	Math	
	P	_____	_____	KL
?	_____	_____	_____	
?	_____	_____	_____	L̶M̶

Question 1

Which one of the following is a complete and accurate list of the students who could be assigned to reading?

(A) JKL
(B) LMO
(C) KLMN
(D) JKLMOP
(E) JKLMNOP

Analysis

The correct answer is E. Since Pam is assigned to reading, you could eliminate any answer that does not include P. Choices (A), (B), and (C) should be eliminated. Now take a careful look at the difference between (D) and (E). The difference is that choice (E) contains N, and since there is no reason that N could not be assigned to reading, (E) is the correct answer.

Question 2

Which one of the following is an acceptable assignment of students to stations?

(A) Reading: PKLN; Writing: MO; Math: J
(B) Reading: KLN; Writing: PO; Math: JM
(C) Reading: PJN; Writing: MO; Math: KL
(D) Reading: PMO; Writing: JN; Math: KL
(E) Reading: PN; Writing: MO; Math: JKL

Analysis

The correct answer is C. Since the question asks you for "an acceptable assignment," you should look for unacceptable assignments (rule breakers) and eliminate them. (A) can be eliminated because there can't be four students in reading. (B) can be eliminated because P is in writing and must be in reading. (D) can be eliminated because N cannot be in writing. (E) can be eliminated since "If John is assigned to math, then Kim is assigned to reading," so J and K cannot both be in math.

Question 3

Which one of the following is a pair of students who could be assigned to math?

(A) OM
(B) JL
(C) JK
(D) JN
(E) LM

Analysis

The correct answer is D. Since the question asks "who could be assigned to math," you should again look for those who couldn't (rule breakers). (A) can be eliminated because O cannot be in math. (B) can be eliminated because if J is in math, K must be in reading, so L must then be in reading. And because if J is in math, K must be in reading, so (C) can be eliminated. (E) can be eliminated because L and M cannot be assigned to the same station.

Question 4

If John is assigned to math, then which one of the following must be true?

(A) Molly is assigned to reading.
(B) Neil is assigned to writing.
(C) Molly and Owen are assigned to writing.
(D) Neil is assigned to Math and Owen is assigned to writing.
(E) Neil is assigned to Math and Len is assigned to writing.

Analysis
The correct answer is D. Once John is assigned to math, Kim and Len are assigned to reading and the display will look like this:

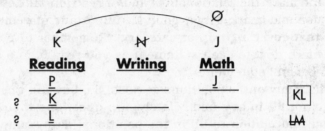

Therefore Neil must be in math and Owen must be in writing. Notice that (C) could be true, but doesn't necessarily have to be true.

Question 5

If Neil is assigned to reading, then which of the following could be true?

(A) John is assigned to math.
(B) Kim is assigned to reading.
(C) Molly is assigned to the same station as Kim.
(D) John is assigned to reading.
(E) Len is assigned to writing and Molly is assigned to reading.

Analysis
The correct answer is D. Once again, you should probably be looking for what can't be true and eliminate. If you place Neil in reading, the display would look like this:

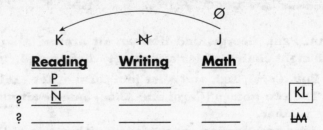

Now, since there are two students in reading, neither K nor L can be in reading and therefore J can't be in math. You can eliminate (A) and (B). You can eliminate (C); because K and L must be together, and M cannot be with L, so M could never be with K. If L is assigned to writing, then K is assigned to writing. If M is assigned to reading, then O must be assigned to writing (O can't in math and reading already has three), and then J is assigned to math. But if J is assigned to math, K must be in reading; therefore, eliminate (E).

The Position Chart

Another type of diagram is the position chart. The position chart is very common on the LSAT and appears in a variety of forms. In constructing this type of chart, you should follow these steps:

1. Look for a frame or framework (often given in the first condition or in a statement preceding the conditions).
2. Look for concrete information (that is, specific information to fill in the positions or information that shows restrictions or connections). Have techniques and symbols for showing restrictions (B cannot be next to A—B̶A) and connections (C is adjacent to D—CD) before you take the test.
3. List the items, people, or letters that will be used to fill in the positions, and mark the relationships and/or restrictions between them.
4. Watch for and mark large, general, important statements (statements that cover a group or category). Remember to place a small check mark next to each statement as you read it, and an asterisk next to general statements.
5. Fill in as many of the positions as possible, but don't be concerned if you can't fill in any immediately; the questions themselves may give you information to fill in the positions. (For example, if X sits in position 4, then which of the following sits in position 6?)
6. Watch for situations that push you out of bounds (for example, if Bill sits between Alice and Jan, then Bill cannot sit on either end— that would push Alice or Jan out of bounds).
7. Also watch for situations that lock you into certain positions. For example, consider this situation: There are seven seats in a row numbered 1 to 7 consecutively, and there are four boys and three girls to fill the seats. A statement like "no boys sit in adjacent seats" would lock you into certain positions, because you would immediately know that the boys must be in positions 1, 3, 5, and 7.
8. If you can't fill in any positions from the initial conditions, read some of the questions to get a feel for how much you should know and have filled in.

Keep in mind, whatever won't go in the chart immediately, goes out to the side for possible placement later (whatever won't go in, goes out).

EXAMPLE

John, Paul, George, and Herman sit around a square table with eight chairs, which are equally distributed.

Bob, Carol, Ted, and Alice join them at the table.

The two women (Carol and Alice) cannot sit next to each other.

John and Herman are seated on either side of George and are next to him.

Ted is seated next to Herman.

Carol is seated next to John, but not directly across from George.

John is directly across from Alice.

Analysis—The setup

Note that the statement preceding the six conditions immediately suggests that you draw a square table with two spaces on each side. The first piece of concrete information is condition 3, which tells you to seat John, George, and Herman in that order. Next, seat Ted next to Herman (#4), seat Carol next to John (#5), and seat Alice across from John (#6). Note that Carol and Alice are not sitting next to each other (#2), and that Paul and Bob are in *variable* positions on either side of Alice. The resulting chart is as follows:

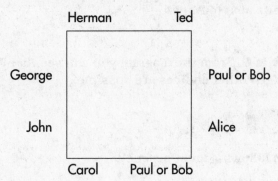

Question 1

Which men could switch positions without contradicting the seating arrangement?

(A) George and Herman
(B) John and George
(C) Paul and Ted
(D) Bob and Paul
(E) Bob and George

Analysis

The correct answer is D. As the chart points out, only Bob and Paul are in variable positions and, thus, interchangeable.

Question 2

Which of the following must be FALSE?

(A) George is not next to Ted.
(B) Alice is not next to Carol.
(C) Herman is next to Carol.
(D) George is across from Paul.
(E) Bob is not next to Paul.

Analysis

The correct answer is C. Working from the answer choices and inspecting the chart, you see that (C) *must* be false in any case, and that (D) *may* be false, depending upon where Paul is seated.

Question 3

Which of the following could be true?

(A) Herman sits next to Carol.
(B) Herman sits next to John.
(C) Ted sits next to Paul.
(D) John sits next to Paul.
(E) George sits next to Alice.

Analysis

The correct answer is C. From the diagram you can see that Paul could be in the seat next to Ted. None of the other choices are possible.

Question 4

Which of the following must be true?

(A) Ted sits next to Paul.
(B) Alice sits next to Paul.
(C) George sits next to Carol.
(D) Ted sits next to Bob.
(E) Bob sits next to John.

Analysis

The correct answer is B. Since the two seats next to Alice are taken by Paul and Bob, then Alice must sit next to Paul.

Question 5

If Arnold were now to take Ted's seat, then Arnold

(A) must now be next to Bob
(B) must be next to Alice
(C) must be across from Bob
(D) is either next to or across from Paul
(E) is either next to or across from George

Analysis

The correct answer is D. If Arnold takes Ted's seat, then either he is seated next to Paul, or else Paul is seated across from him.

EXAMPLE

A graphic artist is designing a modern type style for the alphabet. This type style is based on artistic design and relative sizes of the letters. At this point, the relative sizes among the letters that the artist has designed are as follows:

A is taller than B but shorter than C.
B is shorter than D but taller than E.
F is shorter than A but taller than B.
G is taller than D but shorter than F.
H is shorter than B.

Analysis—The setup

From the information given, a simple chart may be constructed using the following steps:

The first statement reads, "A is taller than B but shorter than C." Using a position chart where the top is the tallest and the bottom is the shortest, you have:

C

A

B

The first part of the second statement reads, "B is shorter than D. . . ." Notice that D can be *anywhere* taller than B, so a "range" for D has to be drawn:

Adding the second part of the second statement gives "B is shorter than D but taller than E." Since B is taller than E, E will be placed under B:

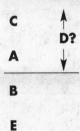

The third statement reads, "F is shorter than A but taller than B." Therefore F must fit between A and B:

According to the fourth statement, "G is taller than D but shorter than F." Therefore G is above D, but since it's below F, both G and D must fit between F and B:

C

A

F

G

D

B

E

The fifth statement reads, "H is shorter than B," so H must have a possible range anywhere under B:

C

A

F

G

D

B

E   H?

Note that H is in a variable position.

Question 1

Which one of the following could be FALSE, but is not necessarily false?

(A) E is shorter than D.
(B) C is taller than E.
(C) D is taller than F.
(D) H is taller than E.
(E) E is shorter than A.

Analysis
The correct answer is D. H may be taller than E, or it may be shorter than E. This is the only part of the chart that isn't definitely resolved.

Question 2

Which of the following could be true?

(A) D is taller than most of the others.
(B) A is the tallest.
(C) H is the shortest.
(D) D is not shorter than G.
(E) H is taller than F.

Analysis
The correct answer is C. H may be the shortest, because it could possibly be shorter than E.

Question 3

Which one of the following must be true?

(A) F is taller than D.
(B) H is the shortest of all.
(C) H is taller than D.
(D) E is the shortest of all.
(E) E is taller than H.

Analysis
The correct answer is A. Inspection of the chart reveals that F is taller than D. It also reveals that H cannot be taller than D and that H or E *could* be the shortest of all, since H is in a relatively variable position.

Question 4

If Q is added to the group and Q is taller than B but shorter than G, then Q must be

(A) taller than F
(B) shorter than D
(C) between D and F
(D) taller than only three of the others
(E) shorter than at least three of the others

Analysis

The correct answer is E. If Q is added to the group, it may be either taller or shorter than D. Therefore, only (E) is true.

Question 5

If Q and Z are both added to the group, and both are taller than H, then

(A) H is the shortest of all
(B) E is the shortest of all
(C) C is the tallest of all
(D) either Q or Z is the tallest of all
(E) either H or E is the shortest of all

Analysis

The correct answer is E. If Q and Z are added, and both are taller than H, we know little more except that H or E must still be the smallest. Q or Z could possibly be the tallest, but not necessarily so. Only (E) *must* be true.

EXAMPLE

In a parking lot, seven company automobiles are lined up in a row in seven adjacent parking spots.

> **There are two vans, which are both adjacent to the same sports car.**
> **There is one station wagon.**
> **There are two limousines, which are never parked adjacent to each other.**
> **One of the sports cars is always on one end.**

Analysis—The setup

From this information, you could have made the following display:

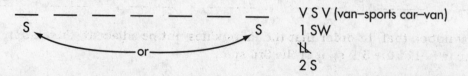

```
___  ___  ___  ___  ___  ___  ___    V S V (van–sports car–van)
 S                              S     1 SW
        ←————— or —————→              2 L
                                      2 S
```

Question 1

If the station wagon is on one end, one of the sports cars must be in the

(A) 2nd spot
(B) 3rd spot
(C) 4th spot
(D) 5th spot
(E) 7th spot

Analysis

The correct answer is C. In this question, two charts are possible:

S						SW

and

SW						S

Now notice that for *both* of the vans to be adjacent to the same sports car, there must be another sports car, and they must always be in the order V S V. Thus, the only way to place V S V in either of the above diagrams so that two limousines are never adjacent is to place V, S, and V in spots 3, 4, and 5, as follows:

S		V	S	V		SW

or

SW		V	S	V		S

Thus, the limousines will not be adjacent if one of the sports cars is in the 4th spot.

Question 2

If one of the vans is on one end, then the station wagon must be

(A) only in the 4th spot
(B) either in the 2nd or the 6th spot
(C) only in the 3rd spot
(D) either in the 3rd or the 5th spot
(E) only in the 6th spot

Analysis

The correct answer is D. Again there are two possible diagrams for this question:

V	S	V				S

and

S				V	S	V

Now notice that, in order that the limousines not be adjacent, the station wagon must be in either the 5th spot or the 3rd spot.

Question 3

If a limousine is in the 7th spot, then the station wagon could be in

(A) the 2nd spot
(B) the 3rd spot
(C) the 6th spot
(D) either the 2nd or 6th spot
(E) either the 2nd, 3rd, or 6th spot

Analysis

The correct answer is E. If a limousine is in the 7th spot, then a sports car, to be on an end, must be in the 1st spot:

S						L

Notice that the station wagon could now be in the 6th spot:

		V	S	V	L	
S	L	V	S	V	SW	L

or else in either the 2nd or the 3rd spot:

	L	SW				
S	SW	L	V	S	V	L

So the station wagon could be in either the 2nd, the 3rd, or the 6th spot.

Question 4

If one of the sports cars is in the 2nd spot, then the station wagon

(A) could be in the 5th spot
(B) could be in the 6th spot
(C) must be in the 5th spot
(D) must be in the 6th spot
(E) must be in the 3rd spot

Analysis

The correct answer is C. If one of the sports cars is in the 2nd spot, the other sports car must be in the 7th spot:

V	S	V				S

Thus, in order for the limousines not to be adjacent, the station wagon must be in the 5th spot.

Question 5

If both sports cars are adjacent to a van, the station wagon must be in

(A) the 2nd spot
(B) the 4th spot
(C) the 6th spot
(D) either the 2nd or 4th spot
(E) either the 2nd or 6th spot

Analysis

The correct answer is E. Two diagrams are necessary for this problem. If both sports cars are adjacent to a van, your diagrams will be:

S	V	S	V			

and

			V	S	V	S

Thus, in order for the limousines not to be adjacent, the station wagon must be in either the 2nd spot or the 6th spot.

Question 6

If an eighth car (a limousine) is added, and another parking spot is also added, then in order not to violate any of the original statements EXCEPT the number of limousines

(A) a limousine must be parked in the 2nd spot
(B) the station wagon must be parked in the 2nd spot
(C) the station wagon must be parked in the 6th spot
(D) a limousine must be parked on one end
(E) a limousine cannot be parked on either end

Analysis

The correct answer is D. If another limousine is added along with an eighth parking spot, all the original statements can be obeyed ONLY if a limousine is parked on one end. For example:

S	L	V	S	V	L	SW	L

Position Chart with the Diagram Provided

On occasion, the position chart or diagram will be provided. That is, instead of, or along with, a description of the set up, an actual diagram is given. Use the following steps if a chart or diagram is given:

1. Either redraw the chart or diagram or mark the diagram dark enough so you can understand your notes but also so you can erase without losing information.
2. Follow the same procedures you would use in filling in or completing the position chart.

Nine guests—A, B, C, D, E, F, G, H, I—attend a formal dinner party. Ten chairs are arranged around the rectangular dining room table as follows:

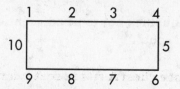

Seat 1 is directly across from seat 9.
Seat 2 is directly across from seat 8.
Seat 3 is directly across from seat 7.
Seat 4 is directly across from seat 6.
Seats 5 and 10 are at the ends of the table and are directly across from each other.
A, B, C, and D are females.
E, F, G, H, and I are males.
A and E are a married couple.
B and F are a married couple.
C and G are engaged to each other.
Each married couple always sits next to his or her spouse on one side of the table.
Members of the same sex never sit in adjacent seats.
Guests in end seats 5 and 10 are considered adjacent to seats on each side of them.
If G is in seat 10, then C is not in seat 5.
I is never in seat 6.
A is always in seat 1.

Analysis—The setup

From the initial conditions, the diagram and markings would look like this:

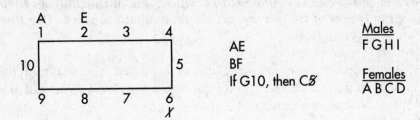

Question 1

Which one of the following could sit in seat 10?

(A) A
(B) C
(C) D
(D) F
(E) H

Analysis

The correct answer is E. Since guest A sits in seat 1, a male must sit in seat 10 if it is not empty. This eliminates (A), (B), and (C) since guests A, C, and D are females (A is in seat 1 anyway). Since guests B and F are a married couple, they must sit next to each other on a side. This eliminates (D). Guest H is a male and could sit in seat 10.

Question 2

Which one of the following is a complete and accurate list of guests who could sit in seat 3?

(A) A, B, C, D, E, F, G
(B) B, C, D, E, F
(C) B, C, D, E
(D) B, C, D
(E) B, C

Analysis

The correct answer is D. Since guest E is in seat 2, only a female could sit in seat 3. Since guest A is in seat 1, the remaining females are guests B, C, and D.

Question 3

If seat 9 is empty and G sits in seat 10, which one of the following could sit in seat 5?

(A) B
(B) D
(C) C
(D) H
(E) I

Analysis

The correct answer is B. From the information given in the question and the initial conditions, the diagram should look like this:

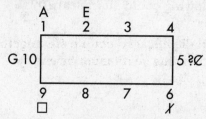

It can now be determined that seat 3 is a female, seat 4 is a male, and seat 5 is a female. You may have added to your diagram so it would now look like this:

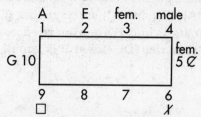

Seat 5 cannot be guest B, since guest B cannot be on the end. Guest H and I are males so (D) and (E) are eliminated. Since guest G is in seat 10, then guest C cannot be in seat 5 (from initial conditions), so only guest D is left.

Question 4

If C sits in seat 5, and F sits in seat 4, which one of the following could be the arrangement of seats from 1 to 10 respectively?

	1,	2,	3,	4,	5,	6,	7,	8,	9,	10
(A)	A,	B,	E,	F,	C,	G,	__,	I,	D,	H
(B)	A,	E,	B,	G,	C,	F,	D,	H,	__,	I
(C)	A,	E,	B,	F,	C,	I,	D,	__,	G,	H
(D)	A,	E,	B,	F,	C,	H,	D,	I,	__,	G
(E)	A,	E,	B,	F,	C,	G,	D,	H,	__,	I

Analysis

The correct answer is E. From the information given, the diagram should look like this:

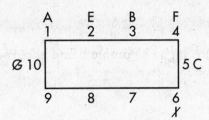

You could eliminate (A) because guest B cannot be in seat 2. Since guest F is in seat 4, guest B is in seat 3. This eliminates (B). (C) can be eliminated since male guests G and H cannot be seated next to each other. Since guest C is in seat 5, guest G cannot be in seat 10, so (D) is eliminated. (E) is a possible arrangement.

Question 5

If D sits in seat 5, and the engaged couple sits together in seats 7 and 8, which one of the following seats must be empty?

(A) 3
(B) 4
(C) 6
(D) 9
(E) 10

Analysis
The correct answer is D. From the information given, your chart should now look like this:

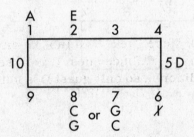

You should also be able to fill in seats 3 and 4 and determine that seats 6 and 10, if not empty, must be males. Your diagram should now have this information:

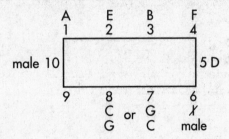

Since only male guests H and I are not seated, guest H must be in seat 6 and guest I in seat 10. This leaves seat 9 empty. In any other arrangement, two males are next to each other. (This also forces C into 7 and G into 8.)

Question 6

Which one of the following is a complete and accurate list of guests who could sit in seat 5?

(A) C
(B) D
(C) C, D
(D) B, C, D
(E) C, D, G

Analysis

The correct answer is C. First eliminate (D) since guest B must be on a side. If guest G is in seat 5, then the diagram would look like this:

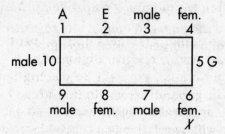

This requires two males to be next to each other, so seat 5 must be a female, either guest C or D.

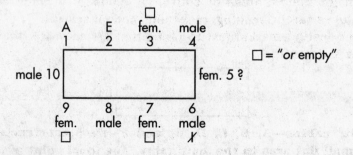

Question 7

If a female sits directly across from A, which one of the following must be true?

(A) Seat 3 is empty.
(B) Seat 4 is empty.
(C) Seat 6 is a female.
(D) Seat 7 is a female.
(E) Seat 8 is a male.

Analysis

The correct answer is E. If a female sits across from guest A, your diagram would now have the following information:

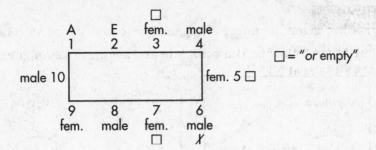

Since seats 3, 5, or 7 could be empty, only (E), a male is in seat 8, must be true.

The Map

Another type of display is the map. This is really a takeoff of the position diagram with some more possibilities. When completing a map display, keep the following in mind:

1. Maps can include actual distances (miles, yards, etc.) from one place to another, or simply relative alignments.
2. While constructing a map, you will be placing houses, cities, objects, or people in general areas, limited areas, or zones—north, south, east, west, northeast, southwest, and so on.
3. Placements often will be relative to a central location or other placements.
4. Sometimes the houses, cities, objects, or people will be placed directly north (due north), directly southeast, and so on.
5. Watch for limited areas or zones, as opposed to exact locations. This takes careful reading, reasoning, and placement.
6. Place question marks next to items that are movable (that is, not stuck in one spot).

EXAMPLE

Six cabins—A, B, C, D, E, and F—were constructed on a small flat area in the mountains. The focal point of the area was a statue that was constructed years before the cabins were constructed.

Cabin A is directly north of the statue.
Cabin C is directly west of the statue.
Cabin D is south of Cabin C.
Cabin E is west of Cabin A.
The statue is directly southeast of Cabin B and directly northwest of Cabin F.

Analysis—The setup

From the information given, a simple chart may be constructed as follows (possible ranges are denoted with arrows):

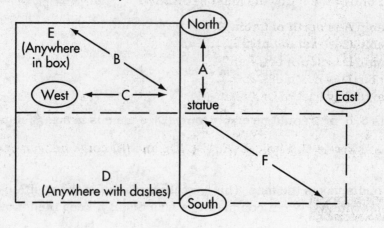

Or an even simpler map (if you can remember the zones) is possible:

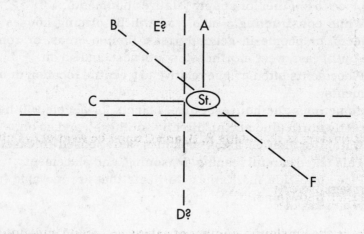

Question 1

Which one of the following must be true?

(A) Cabin B is east of Cabin C.
(B) Cabin B is west of Cabin C.
(C) Cabin F is west of Cabin E.
(D) Cabin D is south of Cabin B.
(E) Cabin D is east of Cabin A.

Analysis

The correct answer is D. Statements (A), (B), and (E) *could* be true, but do not necessarily have to be true. (C) is false. Only (D) must be true.

Question 2

Which one of the following must be FALSE?

(A) Cabin A is north of Cabin E.
(B) Cabin C is east of Cabin E.
(C) Cabin B is south of Cabin F.
(D) Cabin D is north of Cabin F.
(E) Cabin D is east of Cabin E.

Analysis
The correct answer is C. Choices (A), (B), (D), and (E) *could* be true, but (C) *must* be false.

Question 3

How many cabins must be west of Cabin A?

(A) 0
(B) 1
(C) 2
(D) 3
(E) 4

Analysis
The correct answer is D. Cabins E, B, and C must be west of A. Cabin D does not have to be west of Cabin A.

Question 4

What is the maximum number of cabins you could encounter traveling directly east from Cabin C?

(A) 0
(B) 1
(C) 2
(D) 3
(E) 4

Analysis
The correct answer is B. Traveling directly east from Cabin C, you could encounter Cabin E.

Question 5

If another cabin, Cabin G, is constructed directly north of Cabin F, then all of the following must be true EXCEPT

(A) Cabin A is west of Cabin G
(B) Cabin G is east of Cabin C
(C) Cabin D is south of Cabin G
(D) Cabin G is east of Cabin A
(E) Cabin B is west of Cabin G

Analysis

The correct answer is C. Adding Cabin G to the chart results in:

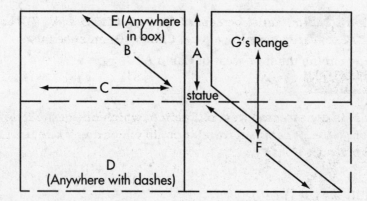

Statements (A), (B), (D), and (E) must be true. Statement (C) could be true, but does not necessarily have to be true.

Question 6

If Cabins H and J are constructed so that H is directly east of J, and H is directly north of A, then which one of the following must be true?

(A) Cabin H is north of Cabin B.
(B) Cabin C is west of Cabin J.
(C) Cabin H is south of Cabin D.
(D) Cabin E is south of Cabin H.
(E) Cabin F is east of Cabin J.

Analysis

The correct answer is E. Adding Cabins H and J to the chart results in:

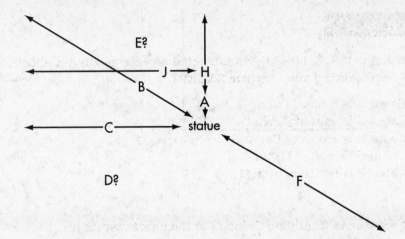

From the chart, Cabin F must be east of Cabin J. Choices (A), (B), and (D) could be true, but do not necessarily have to be true. Choice (C) must be false.

Question 7

If Cabin M is constructed west of Cabin A, which one of the following is a possible order of cabins a traveler could encounter while traveling directly northwest from F?

(A) BEDM
(B) DMBE
(C) MDEBC
(D) DMCBE
(E) MDABE

Analysis
The correct answer is B. Adding Cabin M to the chart results in:

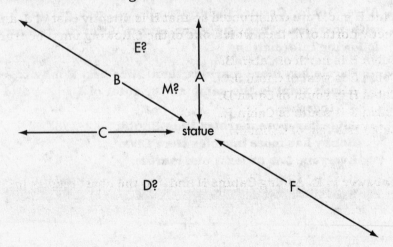

From the chart, you could possibly encounter DMBE while traveling northwest from F.

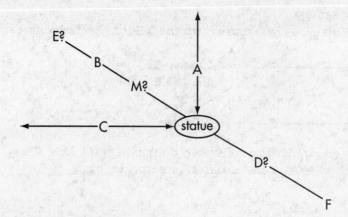

The Numerical Display or Numerical Position Diagram

This type of display or diagram deals with numerical relationships—lengths, heights, scores, and so on. When working with numerical information, keep the following in mind:

1. You may first need to simply list the relationships before making a display. This may help you see the complete picture.
2. When converting the information into a positional display, be sure to mark or signify what the directions mean (top-most, bottom-least, tallest, shortest, etc.).
3. Place question marks next to variables that can be moved or are not locked into a certain position.

EXAMPLE

Alice, Bobby, Carole, Dwight, and Elva were playing a game with marbles. When the game ended, Alice wrote down the following information:

Carole has more marbles than Alice and Bobby together.
Alice's total is the same as the total of Dwight and Elva together.
Alice has more marbles than Bobby.
Bobby has more marbles than Elva.
Everyone has at least one marble.

Analysis—The setup

From the information given, you can set up the following relationships:

$$C > A + B$$
$$A = D + E$$
$$A > B$$
$$B > E$$

Then you can construct the following diagram (Note: This chart is more easily realized by starting with the last condition and working up.):

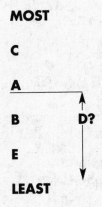

MOST

C

A

B   **D?**

E

LEAST

Question 1

Who ended the game with the most marbles?

(A) Alice
(B) Bobby
(C) Carole
(D) Dwight
(E) Elva

Analysis

The correct answer is C. Using the relationships you can see that Carole has more marbles than Alice and Bobby together. Because Alice has more marbles than Dwight, Elva, or Bobby each have alone, Carole must have most of all.

Question 2

If Dwight has more marbles than Bobby, who ended the game with the least marbles?

(A) Alice
(B) Bobby
(C) Carole
(D) Dwight
(E) Elva

Analysis

The correct answer is E. If Dwight has more marbles than Bobby, then Elva must have the least number of marbles. The arrangement would be as follows:

MOST

C

A
<u> </u>

D
<u> </u>

B

E

LEAST

Question 3

Which one of the following is a possible order of children going from most marbles to least?

(A) Alice, Bobby, Carole, Dwight, Elva
(B) Carole, Alice, Bobby, Elva, Dwight
(C) Carole, Bobby, Alice, Dwight, Elva
(D) Dwight, Carole, Alice, Bobby, Elva
(E) Carole, Alice, Elva, Bobby, Dwight

Analysis

The correct answer is B. From the original chart, we can see that Carole must have most of all, followed by Alice. Because Bobby has more marbles than Elva, only answer (B) can be a possible correct order.

Question 4

Which of the following must be true?

(A) Elva has more marbles than Dwight.
(B) Dwight has fewer marbles than Bobby.
(C) Alice has more marbles than Elva.
(D) Dwight and Bobby have the same number of marbles.
(E) Elva and Dwight have the same number of marbles.

Analysis

The correct answer is C. Only (C) *must* be true. In (A) and (E) Elva *could* have more marbles than Dwight, but not necessarily. She could have less *or the same*. Notice the possible range of placement for Dwight on the original chart. Again, in (B) and (D) Dwight's placement is uncertain: Dwight could have fewer, *the same,* or more marbles than Bobby.

Question 5

If Elva has 3 marbles and everyone has a different number of marbles, which of the following could NOT be the number of marbles that Alice could have?

(A) 5
(B) 6
(C) 7
(D) 8
(E) 9

Analysis

The correct answer is B. Using the relationships you can see that if Elva has 3 marbles, then Dwight can have any number *but* 3. Because Alice's total equals Dwight's and Elva's total together, Alice cannot have 3 + 3, or 6.

EXAMPLE

Five students, A, E, I, O, and U, were comparing the scores each received on a test and a quiz. The following was discovered:

A's quiz score was 80.
A's test score equals U's quiz score.
U's test score equals A's quiz score.
A's quiz score is 15 less than U's quiz score.
O's test score is 20 more than his quiz score and is 20 more than I's test score.
O's test score is 40 more than E's quiz score.
I's quiz score is 10 less than E's quiz score.

Analysis—The setup

You could have set up the following relationships from the information given

$$Aq = 80$$
$$At = Uq$$
$$Ut = Aq$$
$$Aq = Uq - 15$$
$$Ot = Oq + 20$$
$$Ot = It + 20$$
$$Ot = Eq + 40$$
$$Iq = Eq - 10$$

and you could have discovered that Ut = 80 (since Aq = Ut), Uq = 95 (since Aq = Uq − 15), At = 95 (since At = Uq), and Oq = It (since Ot = Oq + 20 and Ot = It + 20).

You might have used the following diagram to help visualize the solutions to these problems:

```
Quiz                    A         U
------------------------80--------95------------------------------------
Test                    U         A

Quiz          I <- - - - 10 - - - ->E<- - - - 20 - - - ->O
--------------------------------------------------------------------------
Test                                    I<- - - - 20 - - - ->O
```

Question 1

If E's quiz score is 60, what is O's quiz score?

(A) 80
(B) 70
(C) 60
(D) 50
(E) 40

Analysis

The correct answer is A. From the preceding information we can see that O's quiz score is 20 greater than E's quiz score. Thus, 80 is the correct answer.

Question 2

Which one of the following must be true?

(A) I's quiz score equals O's test score.
(B) E's quiz score equals U's quiz score.
(C) A's quiz score equals U's test score.
(D) E's quiz score equals O's quiz score.
(E) I's quiz score equals I's test score.

Analysis

The correct answer is C. From the diagram, A's quiz score equals U's test score. We do not have a relationship between E's quiz scores and A's or U's scores.

Question 3

What is U's test score?

(A) 55
(B) 65
(C) 80
(D) 95
(E) 100

Analysis

The correct answer is C. Because U's test score equals A's quiz score, and that is 80, the answer must be C.

Question 4

If I's test score is 45, what is O's test score?

(A) 25
(B) 35
(C) 45
(D) 55
(E) 65

Analysis

The correct answer is E. Because O's test score is 20 greater than I's test score, and I's test score is 45, O's test score must be 65.

Question 5

If E's quiz score is 50, which one of the following must be true?

(A) I's test score is 70.
(B) O's test score is 100.
(C) I's quiz score is 30.
(D) O's quiz score is 60.
(E) O's test score is 70.

Analysis

The correct answer is A. From the diagram, I's test score is 70. Using the relationships gives Ot = 50 + 40 = 90, Ot = It + 20; therefore It = 70.

Question 6

If O's quiz score is the same as U's quiz score, which one of the following must be true?

(A) I's test score is 90.
(B) O's test score is 110.
(C) I's quiz score is 70.
(D) E's quiz score is 75.
(E) O's quiz score is 80.

Analysis

The correct answer is D. This problem relates the two groups of scores together. Because A's quiz score is 80, U's quiz score is 95. Therefore, O's quiz score is 95. Thus, I's test score is 95. E's quiz score is 20 less than O's quiz score, thus it is 75, making (D) true.

The Information Chart

The information chart is helpful for spotting information and making deductions quickly. When putting together an information chart, you should follow these steps:

1. Carefully decide on the type of framework, categories, or labels. You may need to read all of the statements or conditions before deciding how to arrange the information.
2. If you have selected a good way of showing the information—proper labels, categories, and so on—the information should fit in fairly easily and be easy to understand and interpret.
3. Be sure to note variable positions or possibilities in your information chart (for example, Bob can work on Mondays or Tuesdays).

EXAMPLE

In order to open a new furniture store the following week, Mr. Worble hired a painter, a carpet layer, an electrician, and a carpenter. In scheduling the workmen, he had to consider the following conditions:

The painter is available only on Tuesday morning, Wednesday afternoon, and all day Friday.

The carpet layer is available only on Monday, Wednesday, and Friday mornings.

The electrician is available only on Tuesday morning and Friday afternoon.

The carpenter is available only on Monday morning, Tuesday all day, and Wednesday afternoon.

Unless otherwise stated, each workman must work alone in the store.

Unless otherwise stated, each workman is able to complete his own job in half a day.

Analysis—The setup

An information chart is suggested whenever you are trying to determine the points at which two sets of facts coincide. In this case, we chart the daily schedule of each worker, simply following the explicit information given.

	M	*T*	*W*	*T*	*F*
Painter		Morning	Afternoon		All day
Carpet layer	Morning		Morning		Morning
Electrician		Morning			Afternoon
Carpenter	Morning	All day	Afternoon		

Although we have written out "morning," "afternoon," and "all day," you may wish to abbreviate such terms.

Question 1

If the carpenter and the electrician must work on the same day to coordinate their efforts, but cannot work at the same time, who of the following will NOT be able to start work until Wednesday, at the earliest?

(A) painter
(B) carpet layer
(C) electrician
(D) carpenter
(E) carpet layer and electrician

Analysis

The correct answer is A. The carpet layer may work on Monday, and the carpenter and the electrician *must* work Tuesday (the only day they are available together). In this case, the painter (A) may not begin until Wednesday.

Question 2

If the painter needs the whole day on Friday to complete his job, the

(A) carpenter must work on Thursday
(B) electrician and carpet layer must work on the same day
(C) total job cannot be completed in one week
(D) electrician must work on Tuesday
(E) carpet layer and carpenter must work on the same day

Analysis

The correct answer is D. The electrician *must* work Tuesday, because his only other working day, Friday, interferes with the painter's work.

Question 3

Mr. Worble is expecting a supply of furniture on Thursday morning. Which one of the following must be true?

(A) The carpenter will be the only one finished before the merchandise arrives.
(B) Before the merchandise arrives, the painter will be finished, but the electrician will have to work Wednesday night.
(C) The carpet layer, the carpenter, and the electrician will be the only ones finished before the merchandise arrives.
(D) The carpet layer will have to work on the Tuesday before the merchandise arrives.
(E) All of the workers could have their jobs completed before the merchandise arrives.

Analysis

The correct answer is E. One possible plan is this: The carpet layer works Monday morning, the electrician works Tuesday morning, the carpenter works Tuesday afternoon, and the painter works Wednesday afternoon.

Question 4

If the store must be closed Monday and Tuesday and no worker may enter on those days, then, for all the work to be completed by the end of the week,

(A) the carpet layer must work Friday morning
(B) the painter must work Friday morning
(C) the painter must work Wednesday afternoon
(D) the painter must work Friday afternoon
(E) the carpet layer must work Friday afternoon

Analysis

The correct answer is B. If the store must be closed on Monday and Tuesday, then the carpenter must work Wednesday afternoon, and the electrician must work Friday afternoon, as these workers have no other available days to work. Since the painter cannot work Wednesday afternoon (the carpenter is already working then), he must work Friday morning. This leaves the carpet layer Wednesday morning to complete his work.

Question 5

If the store must be painted before any of the other work may begin, then, for all the work to be completed, all the following are true EXCEPT

(A) the carpenter may work Tuesday or Wednesday afternoon
(B) the electrician must work Friday afternoon
(C) the carpet layer must work Wednesday or Friday morning
(D) the electrician and the carpet layer may work the same day
(E) the painter and the electrician may work the same day

Analysis

The correct answer is E. If the store must be painted first, then the painter could do his work Tuesday morning. All of the choices then are true, except (E). The painter and electrician may not work the same day, because if it's Tuesday, then they both would work in the morning, which is not allowed. The only other day they could both work is Friday, but that wouldn't allow all the work to be completed if the painter first works Friday morning.

The Elimination Grid

This type of chart will assist you in eliminating many possibilities, thus narrowing your answer choices and simplifying the reasoning process. To set up an elimination grid you should:

1. Decide on the column and row headings.
2. Mark X's in squares or situations that are not possible.
3. Place check marks or fill in squares or situations that are possible.
4. Fill in any items that you can deduce or "eliminate" with the grid (for example, if Ann receives an A, she cannot receive a B, C, or D).

EXAMPLE

Two boys (Tom and Sal) and two girls (Lisa and Molly) each receive a different one of four different passing grades (A,B,C,D) on an exam.

(1) Both boys receive lower grades than Lisa.
(2) Sal did not get a B.
(3) Tom got a B.
(4) Molly did not get an A.

Analysis—The setup

Although a chart is not necessary to answer question 1, you could have constructed the following using the information given in the statements:

First, since both boys received lower grades than Lisa, we know that Lisa could not have gotten the C or D, and that neither of the boys could have gotten the A. Thus, your chart will look like this:

	A	B	C	D
Tom	X			
Sal	X			
Lisa			X	X
Molly				

From statements 2 and 3, we can fill in that Tom received the B (and thus the others didn't):

	A	B	C	D
Tom	X	✓	X	X
Sal	X	X		
Lisa		X	X	X
Molly		X		

Statement 4 allows us to indicate on our chart that Molly didn't get an A. Thus, we can see from our chart that Lisa *must* have gotten the A:

	A	B	C	D
Tom	X	✓	X	X
Sal	X	X		
Lisa		X	X	X
Molly	X	X		

Notice that we could have deduced that even without statement 4, as there was no other grade Lisa could possibly receive.

Now we know that Lisa received the A, and Tom received the B. But we cannot deduce Sal's or Molly's grade. Be aware that, on many problems like this, you will have to proceed to the questions with an incomplete chart.

Question 1

Which statement(s) may be deduced from only one of the other statements?

(A) statement 1
(B) statement 2
(C) statement 3
(D) statement 4
(E) statements 1 and 3

Analysis
The correct answer is B. Statement 2 may be deduced from statement 3. If Tom got the B, it must be true that Sal did not get the B.

Question 2

If Molly received the lowest grade, then Sal must have received

(A) the A
(B) the B
(C) the C
(D) the D
(E) either the A or the B

Analysis
The correct answer is C. Using the chart, if Molly received the lowest grade (D), then Sal must have gotten the C. Note that by elimination on the grid, the only possibilities for Sal and Molly were Cs and Ds.

Question 3

Which one of the following is a complete and accurate list of the grades that Sal could have received?

(A) A
(B) A, C
(C) B, D
(D) C, D
(E) B, C, D

Analysis
The correct answer is D. From our chart we can easily see that Sal could have received either the C or the D.

Question 4

Which one of the following is a complete and accurate list of the grades that Molly could NOT have received?

(A) A
(B) B
(C) B, C
(D) C, D
(E) A, B

Analysis
The correct answer is E. From our chart we can easily see that Molly could not have received either the A or the B. We could also have determined this from statements 3 and 4.

Question 5

If Sal received the D, then Molly received

(A) the A
(B) the B
(C) the C
(D) the D
(E) either the A or the D

Analysis
The correct answer is C. From our chart we can easily see that, if Sal received the D, then Molly must have received the C.

Question 6

If the grades that Sal and Lisa received were reversed, then which one of the original statements would no longer be true?

(A) statement 1
(B) statement 2
(C) statement 3
(D) statement 4
(E) statements 2 and 3

Analysis
The correct answer is A. If Sal and Lisa reversed their grades, then

Sal would get the A.
Tom would get the B.
Lisa received either the C or the D.
Molly received either the C or the D.

Therefore, only statement 1 ("Both boys receive lower grades than Lisa") would no longer be true.

Pulling Out Information

In some instances, no chart or diagram appears to fit the situation. If this is the case, then:

1. Simply pull out or note whatever information seems important to you.
2. Mark any relationships between the items you have pulled out.
3. Go on to the questions.

EXAMPLE

Tongo is a sport similar to racquetball, except in each game three players oppose each other. Sandy, Arnie, and Betsy are the only entrants in a tongo tournament. Sandy is a left-handed tongo player, while Arnie and Betsy are right-handed tongo players. The players must compete in the tournament according to the following rules:

The winner of each game receives 5 points; the second place finisher gets 3 points; and the third place finisher gets 1 point.

There are no tie games.

The one player with the most game points at the end of the tournament is the grand winner.

If, at the end of the tournament, two or more players have the same total number of points, there will be a playoff.

Analysis—The setup

You probably found that this set of conditions was not conducive to constructing any standard chart. As soon as this was evident, you should have simply pulled out information as follows:

L—Sandy	1st—5 pts.
R—Arnie	2nd—3 pts.
R—Betsy	3rd—1 pt.

Question 1

Which one of the following must be true?

(A) Betsy plays only right-handed opponents.
(B) Arnie never plays a right-handed opponent.
(C) Arnie plays just right-handed opponents.
(D) Sandy never plays right-handed opponents.
(E) Sandy always plays right-handed opponents.

Analysis

The correct answer is E. Since Sandy is the only left-handed player, then she must play only right-handed opponents.

Question 2

If, after three games, both right-handed players have each scored 9 points, which one of the following could be true?

(A) One of the right-handed players finished first twice.
(B) At least one of the right-handed players finished second three times.
(C) Both right-handed players each finished first, second, and third.
(D) The left-handed player finished first twice.
(E) The left-handed player was ahead after three games.

Analysis
The correct answer is C. Only (C) may be true. (A) is blatantly false, since two first-place wins would result in 10 points. (B) is incorrect because, if one player finished second in all three games, then there is no way a second player could score exactly 9 points in three games. (D) and (E) are incorrect since there must be 27 points scored during the three games with each player scoring 9 points.

Question 3

Which one of the following must be true?

(A) A player with no first-place game points cannot win the tournament.
(B) A player with only second-place game points can win the tournament.
(C) A player with no first-place game points can win the tournament.
(D) A player with no third-place game points must win the tournament.
(E) A player with no second-place game points cannot come in second.

Analysis
The correct answer is A. Only (A) is true. With no first-place game points, the most a player could score per game is 3 points. The best that that player could hope for would be that the other two players would split first place and third place on all the games. But even then, the other two players would average 3 points per game. At best a play-off would be necessary, and the player without a first-place finish would thus lose the tournament. (D) and (E) are false by example.

Question 4

If, after three games, Arnie has 11 points, Betsy has 9 points, and Sandy has 7 points, which one of the following must be false?

(A) After four games, there is a three-way tie.
(B) After four games, Betsy is alone in first place.
(C) After four games, Betsy is alone in third place.
(D) After four games, Sandy is alone in first place.
(E) After four games, Sandy is alone in third place.

Analysis
The correct answer is D. The only statement that could not be true is (D). Since the most Sandy could score after four games would be 12 points, Betsy and/or Arnie will at least tie her for first place.

Question 5

If, just before the last game, it is discovered that the left-handed player has finished first in every even-numbered game, then

(A) Sandy must win the tournament
(B) Sandy cannot win the tournament
(C) Arnie may win the tournament
(D) Betsy can't win the tournament
(E) Betsy must win the tournament

Analysis

The correct answer is C. Even though Sandy may have scored 5 points in every even-numbered game, she may not necessarily win the tournament. For instance, if, say, Arnie scores 5 points in every odd-numbered game, and if the tournament consists of an odd number of games, then Arnie will win the tournament. Sandy *can* win the tournament, but not necessarily *must* win the tournament. Betsy, also, could possibly win the tournament, if she scores first-place wins in every odd-numbered game.

Pulling Out Information with Display Given

EXAMPLE

A puzzle in a local newspaper gave a series of numerals in the following four four-letter sequences:

A B C D
D E H G
F B A K
H C F J

The rules for answering questions about the puzzle are as follows:

Each row represents a sequence, and some sequences could be the same.

Any letter that occurs in more than one sequence represents the same numeral in each of those sequences.

The numerals 6, 7, 8, and 9 are each represented once in each of the four sequences—no other numerals are represented.

The first letter of any sequence can represent only 6 or 7.

The last letter of any sequence cannot be 6.

Analysis—The setup

Since the display is already given, you should simply pull out information from the conditions and mark in or make notes as follows:

```
6/7    6̶
A B C D      6, 7, 8, 9
D E H G
F B A K
H C F J
```

You may have deduced some additional information from the conditions given. If you haven't, read a few questions to get a sense of what you need to know.

Question 1

What numeral is represented by A?

(A) 6
(B) 7
(C) 8
(D) 9
(E) 6 or 7

Analysis

The correct answer is A. This particular question is asking you something that you should have been able to deduce from the initial conditions. So, in this case, you can actually put your answer into the display. Otherwise, you cannot take information from one question and use it in another question.

Since A is in column 1, it must represent 6 or 7. Since D is in column 1, it must represent 6 or 7, but because D is in column 4, it cannot be 6. So D is 7. Since A and D are in row 1, and D is 7, A must represent 6.

Your display should now look like this:

```
6/7      6̶
A⁶ B  C  D⁷      6, 7, 8, 9
D⁷ E  H  G
F  B  A⁶ K
H  C  F  J
```

Notice that if A is 6 in row 1, then it is also 6 in row 3. Since D is 7 in row 1, it is 7 in row 2. Notice that you could have also figured out the value for F at this point.

Question 2

What numeral is represented by D?

(A) 6
(B) 7
(C) 8
(D) 9
(E) 6 or 7

Analysis

The correct answer is B. Since D is in column 1, it must represent 6 or 7, but because D is in column 4, it cannot be 6. So D must represent 7. You already knew this from finding A in the previous problem.

Question 3

Which of the following is a possible order of the numerals for the last sequence?

(A) 6 7 8 9
(B) 8 6 7 9
(C) 7 9 6 8
(D) 7 8 6 9
(E) 6 8 7 9

Analysis

The correct answer is E. From the display, since A is 6 (in row 3), F must represent 7. In the last row, if F is 7, H must be 6. The only sequences possible for HCFJ are 6, 8, 7, 9 or 6, 9, 7, 8.

Question 4

Which one of the following CANNOT be true?

(A) H represents 6.
(B) F represents 7.
(C) C represents 8.
(D) B represents 7.
(E) G represents 9.

Analysis

The correct answer is D. In row 1, since A is 6 and D is 7, B cannot be 7.

Question 5

If the additional rule is given that K represents 9, which one of the following must be true?

(A) G represents 8.
(B) E represents 8.
(C) B represents 8.
(D) J represents 9.
(E) F represents 9.

Analysis

The correct answer is C. Notice in row 3, if K represents 9, A must be 6 and F must be 7. Then B represents 8.

Venn Diagrams/Grouping Arrows

Another type of charting (also mentioned later in Chapter 4, Logical Reasoning) is the Venn Diagrams/Grouping Arrows. This type of diagram can be useful when information is given that shows relationships between sets or groups of sets. Keep in mind that:

1. Venn diagrams should be used only in very simple situations involving small numbers of items.
2. Grouping arrows seem to be more effective and simpler to work with, especially in complex situations.

Some very basic Venn diagrams and grouping arrows look like this:

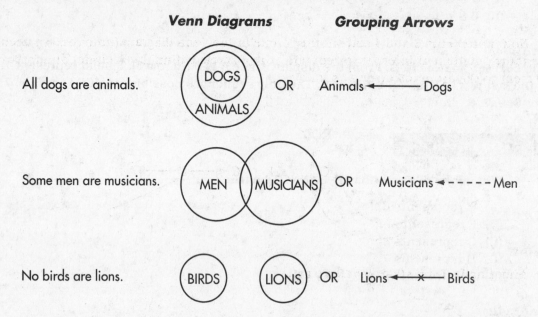

In diagramming more than two groups, you may find it helpful to draw the most general or largest category before drawing any of the others.

EXAMPLE

A pharmacist has labeled certain pills—A, B, C, D, and E—by the categories they fall into. Some of the categories overlap as follows:

(1) All As are Bs.
(2) All Bs are Cs.
(3) Some, but not all, Ds are As.
(4) All Ds are Bs.
(5) No Es are Cs.

Analysis—The setup

From statement 1 we may draw a Venn diagram or grouping arrows as follows:

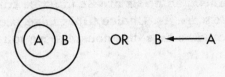

From statement 2 our diagrams or grouping arrows grow to look like this:

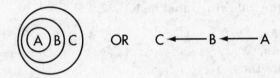

Now statements 3 and 4 add another circle in the Venn diagram (note that we need the fourth statement in order to "contain" the D circle within the B circle) or another element to the grouping arrows as follows:

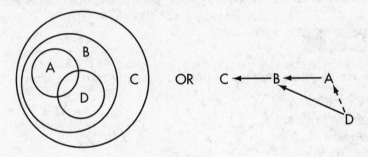

And, finally, from statement 5 we get:

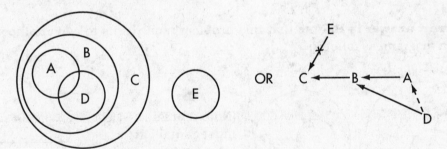

Now it will be relatively simple to answer the questions simply by referring to our final Venn Diagram or grouping arrows.

Question 1

Which one of the following must be true?

(A) All Cs are As.
(B) Some Es are Bs.
(C) All As are Ds.
(D) No Bs are Es.
(E) Some Es are As.

Analysis

The correct answer is D. From the grouping arrows or Venn Diagram, you can see that Bs and Es do not connect, so no Bs are Es must be true. Notice that (A) is false, all As are Cs, but not all Cs are As. Choice (B) is false because the Es are separate from the Bs. Choice (C) could be true, but doesn't have to be true. Choice (E) is false since no Bs are Es, no Es are Bs.

Question 2

Which one of the following must be FALSE?

(A) All Ds are As.
(B) No As are Es.
(C) Some As are Ds.
(D) Some Cs are Ds.
(E) No Bs are Es.

Analysis

The correct answer is A. Statement (3) says "Some, but not all, Ds are As."

Question 3

If all Es are Fs, then which one of the following must be true?

(A) All Fs are Es.
(B) Some Fs are Es.
(C) All As are Fs.
(D) Some Bs are Fs.
(E) No Fs are Cs.

Analysis

The correct answer is B. Note that this problem requires us to add another circle to our Venn diagram, as follows:

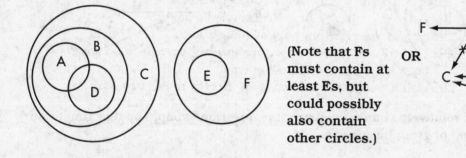

(Note that Fs must contain at least Es, but could possibly also contain other circles.)

Question 4

If some Gs are As, then which one of the following must be true?

(A) Some Gs are Ds.
(B) All Ds are Gs.
(C) All Bs are Gs.
(D) Some Es are Gs.
(E) Some Gs are Cs.

Analysis

The correct answer is E. This problem, too, requires us to add to our original Venn diagram. If some Gs are As, our Venn diagram must *at least* contain some Gs in the A circle (x notes location of some Gs):

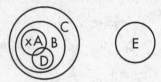

but it *could* also look like this:

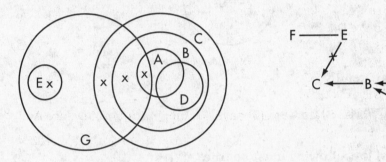

Another Venn-Type Diagram

EXAMPLE

Five school playground aides—Alice, Bert, Carrie, Diego, and Emma—are each given one circular area to supervise. Because some of the areas are used more often than others, the areas overlap as follows:

> Alice's area overlaps part of Bert's area.
> Bert's area overlaps part of Emma's area.
> Emma's area overlaps part of Alice's area.
> Part of Alice's and Bert's overlapping area is also overlapped by part of Emma's area.
> Carrie's area overlaps part of Bert's area, but no one else's area.
> Diego's area overlaps part of Emma's area, but no one else's area.

The playground aides must follow these rules:

> An aide can only treat a student who is injured in the aide's area.
> No more than two aides can ever treat an injured student.
> An injured student cannot be taken out of the aide's area.

Analysis—The setup

From the information given, you should have made a display similar to this:

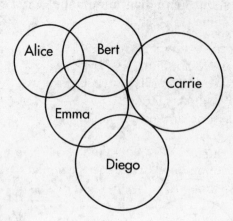

Check the overlaps carefully.

Question 1

Which one of the following must be true?

(A) Alice and Carrie could treat an injured student together.
(B) Bert and Diego could treat an injured student together.
(C) Emma could treat an injured student with Carrie.
(D) Alice and Bert could treat an injured student together.
(E) Diego and Alice could treat an injured student together.

Analysis

The correct answer is D. Since Alice and Bert's areas overlap, they could treat an injured student together. You could have eliminated each of the other choices because they don't overlap.

Question 2

If a student is injured in Emma's area, which one of the following is a complete and accurate list of the aids who could possibly treat the student?

(A) Emma
(B) Alice, Bert
(C) Alice, Bert, Emma
(D) Bert, Diego, Emma
(E) Alice, Bert, Diego, Emma

Analysis

The correct answer is E. Since Emma's area is overlapped by Alice, Bert, and Diego's areas, they could also treat the student if the student happened to be in the overlap.

Question 3

If a student is injured in Bert's area, which one of the following CANNOT be true?

(A) Bert must treat the student by himself.
(B) Alice could treat the student.
(C) Alice and Emma could treat the student together.
(D) Diego cannot treat the student.
(E) Carrie could treat the student.

Analysis
The correct answer is A. Since Bert's area is overlapped by other areas, he wouldn't have to treat the student by himself.

Question 4

If a student is injured in Bert's area, how many different possible combinations of one or two aides could treat the student?

(A) 3
(B) 4
(C) 5
(D) 7
(E) 8

Analysis
The correct answer is E. The possibilities are: (1) Bert; (2) Alice; (3) Emma; (4) Carrie; (5) Bert and Alice; (6) Bert and Emma; (7) Bert and Carrie; (8) Alice and Emma.

Question 5

If another school playground aide, Frank, is hired and assigned to supervise part of the areas supervised by Bert, Carrie, Diego, and Emma, then which one of the following must be true?

(A) Frank supervises all of Diego's area.
(B) Most of Emma's area is supervised by Frank.
(C) Part of Alice's area could be supervised by Frank.
(D) None of Alice's area is supervised by Frank.
(E) More of Bert's area is supervised by Frank than any other aide's area.

Analysis
The correct answer is C. Part of Alice's area could be supervised by Frank because the display could look like this:

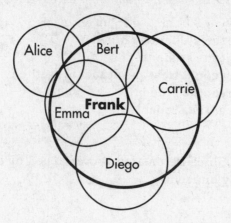

In Conclusion

You have just worked through some of the basic types of charts that you may encounter on the LSAT. Be aware that there are *many other possible charts and modifications of the charts presented.* In the following practice tests, as you work through some of the other possible charts, carefully review the explanations of each to assist you in understanding these other types.

Remember that the exact type of chart you make is not of critical importance. What is important is that you can get the necessary information from your chart, and that it is simple to understand. Do not spend a great deal of time trying to make an elaborate chart; a simple one will usually serve the purpose.

An Alternative General Approach

Some students, regardless of how much they review, analyze, and practice, cannot seem to finish the Analytical Reasoning section. They simply cannot work fast enough or make displays or rough diagrams quickly enough to see relationships and maintain a high level of correct answers. If you find that you consistently have a problem getting to or into the fourth set, you may wish to try this alternative approach: Focus your time on only three of the four sets. That is, try to set up and do well on the three sets and the questions that follow, and simply guess at the questions to the remaining set. You can skip one of the four sets and still receive a good score. The idea is to significantly raise your percentage of correct answers on the questions you *are* attempting. Remember, this is an alternative approach that you may wish to try if you are having a real problem getting to all four sets and maintaining a good level of correct answers. In using this method, you may wish to decide which set of questions you are going to skip after you have read the conditions and realize that the set is going to be problematic and difficult to complete.

Extra Practice: Analytical Reasoning

<u>Directions:</u> In this section you will be given a group of questions based on a specific set of conditions. Drawing a simple diagram may be helpful in answering some of the questions. You are to choose the best answer and mark the corresponding space on your answer sheet.

Use the answer sheet found on page 145.

<u>Questions 1–4</u>

There are four books standing next to each other on a shelf. The books are in order from left to right. The colors of the books are red, yellow, blue, and orange, but the placement of these books has not been determined. The following is known about the placement of the books:

The red book is between the yellow and blue books.

The blue book is between the orange and red books.

The orange book is not fourth.

1. If the orange book could be fourth, then which one of the following can be deduced?

   (A) The red book is fourth.
   (B) The blue book is not third.
   (C) The red book is next to the orange book.
   (D) The blue book is next to the yellow book.
   (E) The yellow book is not second.

2. If a white book is added to the shelf, and the fourth book is not necessarily an orange book, then which one of the following is a possible order of the books?

   (A) yellow, red, orange, blue, white
   (B) white, yellow, blue, red, orange
   (C) yellow, red, blue, white, orange
   (D) orange, blue, red, yellow, white
   (E) blue, red, yellow, orange, white

3. Which one of the following pairs are next to each other on the shelf?

   (A) yellow and blue
   (B) blue and orange
   (C) yellow and orange
   (D) red and orange
   (E) No books are next to each other on the shelf.

4. If a green book were placed just to the left of the blue book, what position would it be in (counting from the left)?

   (A) first
   (B) second
   (C) third
   (D) fourth
   (E) fifth

<u>Questions 5–8</u>

Doctors at Ventana Hospital have been researching an outbreak of three rare diseases, which they have labeled J, K, and L. In tracking the diseases and some of the people possibly infected, they have come up with the following information:

Disease J is always communicable; its symptoms are red splotches, which appear the day after infection.

Disease K is only communicable the day after infection; its symptoms are blue lips or red splotches, which appear the day of infection.

Disease L only infects concurrently with Disease J; its symptoms—swollen ears, which appear the day after infection—are negated by Disease K.

Peter had lunch with Paul on Tuesday.

Paul had dinner with Mary on Wednesday.

Symptoms appear for only one day.

The diseases J, K, and L are the only diseases involved in the outbreak and are the only ones being researched.

5. If Peter broke out in red splotches on Tuesday, which one of the following must be true?

   (A) Peter was infected with Disease K.
   (B) Peter was infected with Disease J.
   (C) Peter was infected with Disease L.
   (D) Peter could have given Disease K to Paul on Tuesday.
   (E) Peter didn't give Paul Disease K on Tuesday.

6. Which one of the following is a complete and accurate list of possible pairs of symptoms from the diseases?

   (A) blue lips and swollen ears
   (B) blue lips and swollen ears; red splotches and swollen ears
   (C) swollen ears and red splotches
   (D) blue lips and red splotches
   (E) swollen ears and red splotches; blue lips and red splotches

7. If Paul had red splotches on Tuesday, then he could NOT have given

   (A) Peter Disease J
   (B) Peter Disease K
   (C) Mary Disease J
   (D) Mary Disease K
   (E) Mary Disease L

8. If on Monday Peter was infected only with Disease K, then which of the following is a complete and accurate list of Mary's possible symptoms on Wednesday because of Peter's passing on Disease K?

   (A) swollen ears
   (B) blue lips
   (C) red splotches
   (D) swollen ears and blue lips
   (E) blue lips and red splotches

Questions 9–17

A head counselor is choosing people to go on a hiking trip. The head counselor must choose from among 3 adult counselors (A, B, C) and 9 campers (boys D, E, F, G, H, and girls J, K, L, M).
   At least two adult counselors must go on the hike.
   Camper D will not go without friends E and F.
   Campers J and L will not hike together.
   Camper M will not hike with counselor C.
   There can never be more boy campers than girl campers.

9. If camper D is chosen for the hike

   (A) camper L must be chosen
   (B) camper J cannot be chosen
   (C) camper L cannot be chosen
   (D) camper G cannot be chosen
   (E) camper H must be chosen

10. If camper K is NOT chosen for the hike

    (A) camper G cannot be chosen
    (B) camper H cannot be chosen
    (C) camper E cannot be chosen
    (D) camper D cannot be chosen
    (E) camper L cannot be chosen

11. If camper D is chosen for the hike, which one of the following CANNOT be true?

    (A) Camper H goes on the hike.
    (B) Camper K goes on the hike.
    (C) Counselor A goes on the hike.
    (D) Counselor B goes on the hike.
    (E) Camper M goes on the hike.

12. An acceptable combination of campers and counselors is

    (A) ABCDEFJKM
    (B) ABDEFJLM
    (C) ABGHJKM
    (D) ACDEFJK
    (E) ACEFGKLM

13. If counselor A is NOT chosen for the hike, then

    (A) camper D must be chosen
    (B) camper D cannot be chosen
    (C) camper J must be chosen
    (D) camper L cannot be chosen
    (E) camper F cannot be chosen

14. If counselor A is NOT chosen for the hike, then which one of the following must be true?

    (A) If camper E is chosen, camper K must be chosen.
    (B) If camper F is chosen, camper K must be chosen.
    (C) Camper J cannot be chosen.
    (D) Camper D cannot be chosen.
    (E) If camper L is chosen, camper F must be chosen.

15. If camper D is chosen for the hike, which one of the following could represent the other hikers?

    (A) ACEFJKM
    (B) ABGHKML
    (C) ABEFJKM
    (D) ABFGJKL
    (E) ACEFGKLM

16. What is the largest number of hikers that can go on the hike?

    (A) 5
    (B) 6
    (C) 7
    (D) 8
    (E) 9

17. Which one of the following must be true?

    (A) Campers K and M never hike together.
    (B) Campers E and G never hike together.
    (C) Campers D and G never hike together.
    (D) Campers J and M never hike together.
    (E) Campers D and M never hike together.

Questions 18–23

At 4:00 P.M. Howard, Iris, Jessie, Kelly, Lance, and Murray start playing video-games A, B, C, D, E, and F, respectively. They will play video games for one hour. At 4:15; 4:30, and 4:45, these players will switch video games using a different set of rules at each of the three designated switch times. The rules that are used are as follows:

   Rule 1: The player of video game A switches games with the player of video game B. The player of video game C switches games with the player of video game D. The player of video game E switches games with the player of video game F.

   Rule 2: The player of video game A switches games with the player of video game C. The player of video game B switches games with the player of video game D. The player of video game E switches games with the player of video game F.

   Rule 3: The player of video game A switches games with the player of video game F. The player of video game B switches games with the player of video game E.

   Rule 4: Howard switches video games with Lance, and Kelly switches video games with Murray.

18. If at 4:35, Howard is playing video game D, which one of the following must be true at 4:35?

    (A) Lance is playing video game F.
    (B) Jessie is playing the same game he started with at 4:00.
    (C) Iris is playing video game C.
    (D) Kelly is playing the same game she started with at 4:00.
    (E) Murray is playing video game B.

19. If at 4:20, Jessie is still playing the same game he started with at 4:00, which one of the following CANNOT be true at 4:20?

    (A) Kelly is playing video game D.
    (B) Murray is playing the video game that Howard was playing at 4:10.
    (C) Lance is playing the video game that Iris was playing at 4:05.
    (D) Iris is playing video game F.
    (E) Howard is playing video game E.

20. If at some time during the hour, Jessie is playing video game F, which one of the following could have been true 15 minutes earlier?

    (A) Howard was playing video game C.
    (B) Iris was playing video game E.
    (C) Kelly was playing video game A.
    (D) Lance was playing video game B.
    (E) Murray was playing video game D.

21. Which one of the following is a list of the times that Murray could be playing video game B?

    (A) 4:15–4:30 only
    (B) 4:30–4:45 only
    (C) 4:45–5:00 only
    (D) 4:15–4:30 and 4:45–5:00
    (E) 4:30–4:45 and 4:45–5:00

22. Which one of the following is a list of video games that Howard could be playing at 4:50?

    (A) A and B
    (B) A and C
    (C) B and D
    (D) C and D
    (E) D and E

23. If Jessie plays the same video game from 4:00 to 4:45, which one of the following must be true at 4:50?

    (A) Howard is playing video game A.
    (B) Iris is playing video game F.
    (C) Kelly is playing video game B.
    (D) Lance is playing video game D.
    (E) Murray is playing video game C.

Questions 24–27

The Alto family's children—Do, Rey, Mi, Fa, and So—are planning to sing at the annual holiday festival. All singers at the holiday festival are dressed in animal costumes, so it is impossible to distinguish who are the boys and who are the girls. The following is known about the Alto family's children:

Do is Rey's brother.
Rey is Mi's sister.
Mi is Fa's brother.
So is Rey's sister.

24. Which one of the following must be true?

    (A) Do is a boy.
    (B) Fa is a girl.
    (C) Rey is a boy.
    (D) Mi is a girl.
    (E) So is a boy.

25. Which one of the following could be FALSE?

    (A) Fa is Rey's brother.
    (B) Do is Mi's brother.
    (C) So is Fa's sister.
    (D) Rey is Fa's sister.
    (E) Mi is Rey's brother.

26. Which one of the following could be true?

    (A) Do is So's sister.
    (B) Mi is not Do's brother.
    (C) Rey is Mi's brother.
    (D) Fa is Rey's brother.
    (E) So is Do's brother.

27. If Fa is a girl, from the information given which one of the following must be true?

    (A) There are more brothers than sisters.
    (B) Fa is So's sister.
    (C) Do is older than Fa.
    (D) Mi is younger than So.
    (E) Rey is Fa's brother.

Questions 28–35

Four men, A, B, C, and D, and three women, E, F, and G, are auditioning for a new TV pilot. The director is deciding the order in which they should audition. Since many of the actors have other auditions to attend at different locations, the director must observe the following restrictions:

A must audition first or last.
D and E must audition consecutively, but not necessarily in that order.
Neither F nor G can audition last.
E cannot audition until B has auditioned.

28. Which one of the following must be true?

    (A) F cannot audition first.
    (B) D cannot audition first.
    (C) B cannot audition first or second.
    (D) A must audition before D auditions.
    (E) G must audition second.

29. If A auditions first, which one of the following CANNOT be true?

    (A) G auditions second.
    (B) F auditions before B auditions.
    (C) D auditions second.
    (D) B auditions fifth.
    (E) G auditions before B auditions.

30. If F and G audition first and second respectively, then which one of the following must be FALSE?

    (A) C auditions fourth.
    (B) B auditions fourth.
    (C) E auditions sixth.
    (D) D auditions fifth.
    (E) B auditions fifth.

31. Assume that B auditions first, and that F and G audition second and third respectively. Which one of the following must be FALSE?

    (A) E auditions sixth.
    (B) C auditions fifth.
    (C) D auditions fourth.
    (D) C auditions sixth.
    (E) E auditions fifth.

32. Suppose that D auditions ahead of E. If A auditions first and B auditions fifth, who must audition sixth?

    (A) D
    (B) E
    (C) F
    (D) G
    (E) C

33. Which one of the following is a possible order of auditions?

    (A) A, E, B, D, F, G, C
    (B) A, B, D, E, C, F, G
    (C) C, B, G, F, E, A, D
    (D) B, F, G, D, E, C, A
    (E) F, B, E, G, D, A, C

34. If the director decides NOT to audition two men consecutively, and if C auditions first, which one of the following must be true?

    (A) F auditions second.
    (B) G auditions second.
    (C) E auditions fifth.
    (D) D auditions fourth.
    (E) B auditions third.

35. Assume that all the women must audition consecutively. If F auditions third and G does NOT audition second, then which one of the following must be true?

    (A) A auditions first.
    (B) B auditions second.
    (C) C auditions seventh.
    (D) G auditions fifth.
    (E) D auditions sixth.

Questions 36–41

Eight weight lifters, Aaron, Bryan, Clifford, David, Ellen, Jason, Logan, and Prescott, have joined a local gym. No two of these lifters lift the same weight. The following statements describe the relative strength of the lifters:
  Ellen lifts more than Aaron.
  Bryan lifts less than Logan but more than Prescott.
  David lifts more than Logan.
  Jason lifts less than Aaron but more than Clifford.
  Logan lifts more than Jason.

36. Which one of the following statements must be true?

    (A) David lifts more than Jason.
    (B) Jason lifts more than Prescott.
    (C) Ellen lifts more than Bryan.
    (D) Clifford lifts more than Ellen.
    (E) Bryan lifts more than David.

37. If Prescott lifts more than Aaron, then which one of the following must be true?

    (A) Logan lifts more than Aaron.
    (B) Aaron lifts more than Bryan.
    (C) Ellen lifts more than Bryan.
    (D) David lifts more than Ellen.
    (E) Clifford lifts more than Logan.

38. If Aaron lifts more than David, what is the maximum number that can lift more than Logan?

    (A) 0
    (B) 1
    (C) 2
    (D) 3
    (E) 4

39. If 5 people lift less than Logan, then which one of the following must be true?

    (A) Bryan lifts more than Aaron.
    (B) Prescott lifts more than Aaron.
    (C) Clifford lifts more than Prescott.
    (D) Jason lifts more than David.
    (E) David lifts more than Aaron.

40. If Bryan lifts more than Aaron and Jason lifts more than Prescott, then who can lift more than Ellen?

    (A) Prescott, Bryan, Logan.
    (B) David, Prescott, Clifford.
    (C) Logan, Bryan, Prescott.
    (D) David, Logan, Jason.
    (E) Logan, David, Bryan.

41. If Prescott lifts more than Jason, then which one of the following must be false?

    (A) Bryan lifts more than Aaron.
    (B) Prescott lifts more than Ellen.
    (C) Ellen lifts more than David.
    (D) Aaron lifts more than Logan.
    (E) Bryan lifts more than David.

<u>Questions 42–47</u>

There are nine cans of soft drinks lined up on a shelf. The cans are numbered from 1 to 9, from left to right.

The first and fourth are different brands of cola.

The sixth and eighth are different brands of root beer.

The second, fifth, sixth, seventh, and ninth are the only caffeine-free soft drinks.

The second, third, fifth, seventh, and ninth cans contain unflavored beverages.

42. How many of the cans contain unflavored beverages that contain caffeine?

    (A) 0
    (B) 1
    (C) 2
    (D) 3
    (E) 4

43. In which one of the following places is a beverage that contains caffeine?

    (A) second
    (B) fourth
    (C) fifth
    (D) sixth
    (E) ninth

44. Which place contains a caffeine-free beverage that is not unflavored?

    (A) first
    (B) third
    (C) fourth
    (D) sixth
    (E) seventh

45. If the two root beers were replaced with two cans of orange flavored beverage containing caffeine, how many cans would contain either cola or caffeine but not both?

    (A) 0
    (B) 1
    (C) 2
    (D) 3
    (E) 4

46. If someone randomly chose two cans of caffeine-free beverage, which places could they be?

    (A) second and third
    (B) fourth and fifth
    (C) third and seventh
    (D) sixth and ninth
    (E) eighth and ninth

47. How many cans of flavored beverage are next to at least one can of caffeine-free beverage?

    (A) 0
    (B) 1
    (C) 2
    (D) 3
    (E) 4

<u>Questions 48–51</u>

Eight people—A, B, C, D, E, F, G, H—are to be seated at a square table, two people on each side.

B must sit directly across from H.

A must sit between and next to F and G.

C cannot sit next to F.

48. Which one of the following must be true?

    (A) C sits next to either B or H.
    (B) H must sit next to G.
    (C) F sits next to D or E.
    (D) A sits directly across from B.
    (E) F sits directly across from C or D.

49. If B does not sit next to G, then which one of the following is NOT possible?

    (A) If C sits next to B, then D could sit directly across from F.
    (B) If C sits next to D, then E could sit directly across from G.
    (C) C could sit next to G.
    (D) If C sits next to H, then B could sit between D and E.
    (E) If C sits next to B, then A could sit next to H.

50. If C sits directly across from F, who could NOT sit next to H?

    (A) C
    (B) D
    (C) E
    (D) G
    (E) A

51. How many different people could be seated directly across from A?

    (A) 1
    (B) 2
    (C) 3
    (D) 4
    (E) 5

Questions 52–57

A scientist starts experimenting with four chemicals—Alpha, Beta, Theta, and Zeta. These chemicals combine in the following ways:

Alpha combines with Beta, giving Zeta.
Theta combines with Zeta, giving Beta.
Zeta combines with Beta, giving Alpha.
Beta combines with Theta, giving Omega, which is the only odorless chemical.
Theta is formed only when Alpha and Zeta combine.
Alpha combines with Theta, giving Zeta.
The order of the combinations makes no difference in their outcome.

52. An odorless chemical may be formed from a combination of

    (A) Theta and Beta
    (B) Alpha and Beta
    (C) Beta and Zeta
    (D) Theta and Zeta
    (E) Alpha and Theta

53. Beta may be involved in the combination if the outcome is

    (A) Alpha or Theta
    (B) Alpha, Omega, or Zeta
    (C) Beta
    (D) Beta, Theta, or Zeta
    (E) Alpha, Beta, or Theta

54. If an odorless chemical combines with Zeta, the outcome is

    (A) Alpha
    (B) Beta
    (C) Theta
    (D) Zeta
    (E) unknown

55. Which one of the following must be true?

    (A) Zeta and Theta combine to give Beta.
    (B) Beta and Zeta combine to give Omega.
    (C) Alpha and Beta combine to give Theta.
    (D) Theta and Alpha combine to give Beta.
    (E) Alpha and Zeta combine to give Omega.

56. If the outcome of Alpha and Beta combine with the outcome of Alpha and Zeta, the result is

    (A) Alpha
    (B) Beta
    (C) Omega
    (D) Theta
    (E) Zeta

57. If Omega combines with Theta, the outcome is Zeta or Theta. Then the outcome of a combination of Omega and Theta is similar to the outcome of

    (A) Alpha with any other
    (B) Beta with any other
    (C) Theta with any other
    (D) Zeta with any other
    (E) Beta with Zeta

Questions 58–64

During a trip to a museum, Jilian and Mark each attend three historical lectures (D, E, and F) and three scientific lectures (R, S, and T). They do not attend the same lecture at the same time, although they both attend all six one-hour lectures. The lecture schedule must conform to the following conditions:

Mark must attend each scientific lecture prior to Jilian attending that same lecture.
Jilian must attend each historical lecture prior to Mark attending that same lecture.
Mark cannot attend two historical lectures consecutively.
Jilian must attend lecture T third.

58. Which one of the following could be true?

    (A) Mark attends R fourth.
    (B) Mark attends D fifth.
    (C) Mark attends E first.
    (D) Jilian attends T fifth.
    (E) Jilian attends F fourth.

59. If Jilian attends E second and Mark attends D second, which one of the following must be true?

    (A) Mark attends E fourth.
    (B) Jilian attends F fourth.
    (C) Mark attends S fifth.
    (D) Mark attends F fourth.
    (E) Jilian attends R sixth.

60. Which one of the following is an acceptable lecture schedule ordered from 1st to 6th?

    (A) Jilian: D, E, T, R, S, F
        Mark: T, D, R, E, F, S
    (B) Jilian: D, E, T, F, R, S
        Mark: R, T, E, S, D, F
    (C) Jilian: E, S, D, T, F, R
        Mark: S, E, T, D, R, F
    (D) Jilian: D, E, T, R, F, S
        Mark: T, D, R, F, S, E
    (E) Jilian: D, E, T, F, R, S
        Mark: T, D, R, E, S, F

61. Which one of the following is a complete and accurate list of when Jilian must attend a historical lecture?

    (A) first, second
    (B) second, third
    (C) first, second, fifth
    (D) first, third, fourth
    (E) first, fourth, fifth

62. If Mark attends lecture F fourth and Jilian attends lecture D first, which one of the following CANNOT be true?

    (A) Mark attends lecture R before lecture F.
    (B) Jilian attends lecture E after lecture R.
    (C) Lecture R is the fifth lecture attended by Jilian.
    (D) Lecture E is the second lecture attended by Mark.
    (E) Lecture D is the second lecture attended by Mark.

63. Which one of the following must be true?

    (A) Mark must attend lecture S fifth.
    (B) Jilian cannot attend lectures D and E consecutively.
    (C) Mark must attend lecture T first.
    (D) Jilian must attend lecture R before Mark attends lecture F.
    (E) Mark attends lecture S sixth.

64. If Mark attends lecture R third, then Jilian must attend which lecture sixth?

    (A) D
    (B) E
    (C) F
    (D) R
    (E) S

Questions 65–70

Kevin Kissalot, famous hairdresser to the stars, has scheduled eight one-hour appointments, one for each of his best customers: Arnie, Betah, Coco, Dodi, Elvis, Fetina, Greg, and Hector. Scheduling of appointments must conform to the following conditions:

> Elvis is scheduled immediately before Dodi.
> Fetina's appointment must be scheduled before Arnie's but after Greg's.
> Fetina's appointment must be scheduled either 3rd or 7th.
> Betah is scheduled 2nd only if Coco is scheduled 3rd or Arnie is scheduled 8th.

65. Which one of the following is an acceptable appointment schedule?

    (A) B C G F E D A H
    (B) E D B G C H F A
    (C) H B C G E A F D
    (D) H B F C G E D A
    (E) G B F C E D A H

66. It would NOT be possible for Arnie to be scheduled

    (A) 3rd
    (B) 4th
    (C) 5th
    (D) 6th
    (E) 7th

67. If Arnie is scheduled 6th and Hector is scheduled after Dodi, which one of the following could be true?

    (A) Greg is scheduled 5th.
    (B) Hector is scheduled 2nd.
    (C) Betah is scheduled 7th.
    (D) Dodi is scheduled 2nd.
    (E) Coco is scheduled 4th.

68. If Hector is scheduled 8th and Coco is scheduled 7th, which one of the following must be true?

   (A) Betah is scheduled 1st.
   (B) Dodi is scheduled 5th.
   (C) Greg is scheduled 1st.
   (D) Elvis is scheduled 6th.
   (E) Arnie is scheduled 6th.

69. If Betah is scheduled 2nd and Arnie is scheduled immediately after Coco, Hector could be scheduled

   (A) 1st
   (B) 3rd
   (C) 4th
   (D) 5th
   (E) 7th

70. Which one of the following is NOT an acceptable schedule of appointments from 1st to 8th?

   (A) G C F E D A B H
   (B) H G F A B C E D
   (C) B H C G E D F A
   (D) G B F H A E D C
   (E) H B C E D G F A

Questions 71–77

On the sixth floor of an office building there are eight offices in a row, numbered from 1 to 8. Five custodians are employed to clean these eight offices. They are Alisa, Bart, Clyde, Drew, and Ethel. The maximum number of offices that can be cleaned by one custodian is two. Each office is cleaned by only one custodian. The following conditions govern the cleaning assignments:

   Bart and Clyde are the only two custodians assigned to clean only one office each.
   Alisa does not clean the office at either end of the row of offices.
   One of the offices cleaned by Ethel is adjacent to both of the offices cleaned by Alisa.
   The lower numbered office cleaned by Ethel is numbered higher than the office cleaned by Bart.
   Office 7 has been assigned to Ethel.

71. If Drew cleans office 2, which one of the following CANNOT be true?

   (A) Bart cleans office 1.
   (B) Clyde cleans office 3.
   (C) Alisa cleans office 6.
   (D) Ethel cleans office 4.
   (E) Drew cleans office 4.

72. Which one of the following is true about the cleaning assignment for office 4?

   (A) The office is not cleaned by Alisa or Clyde.
   (B) The office is not cleaned by Clyde or Ethel.
   (C) The office is not cleaned by Bart or Drew.
   (D) The office is not cleaned by Alisa or Drew.
   (E) The office is not cleaned by Drew or Ethel.

73. Which one of the following represents a complete and accurate list of the offices that could be cleaned by Drew?

   (A) 1, 2, 3, 5, 6
   (B) 1, 2, 3, 5, 6, 8
   (C) 1, 2, 4, 8
   (D) 1, 2, 4, 6, 8
   (E) 2, 3, 4, 5, 6, 8

74. If Drew cleans office 8 and Drew and Alisa clean consecutive offices, then how many different cleaning assignments are possible?

   (A) one
   (B) two
   (C) three
   (D) four
   (E) five

75. Consecutive offices could be cleaned by which one of the following custodians?

   (A) Alisa
   (B) Bart
   (C) Clyde
   (D) Drew
   (E) Ethel

76. Which one of the following represents a complete and accurate list of custodians who could clean office 6?

   (A) Alisa, Clyde, Drew
   (B) Bart, Clyde, Ethel
   (C) Alisa, Bart, Clyde, Ethel
   (D) Clyde, Drew, Ethel
   (E) Alisa, Clyde, Drew, Ethel

77. If both end offices are cleaned by Drew, and Alisa and Clyde clean consecutive offices, which one of the following must be true?

    (A) Alisa cleans office 6.
    (B) Bart and Clyde clean consecutive offices.
    (C) Clyde cleans an even-numbered office.
    (D) Both of Alisa's offices are numbered lower than Clyde's.
    (E) Bart cleans office 2.

Questions 78–84

The Raxmeyers have seven daughters, each born two years apart. Their ages are 7, 9, 11, 13, 15, 17, and 19. Their names are Hilda, Ida, Joy, Kim, Loren, Marsha, and Nicole. The following conditions must be met:
  Joy is older than Marsha.
  Hilda is older than Loren but younger than Ida.
  Either Ida or Loren is 13 years old.
  Nicole is younger than Joy.
  The difference in ages between Marsha and Nicole is at least three years.

78. Which one of the following must be true?

    (A) Hilda is the oldest.
    (B) Kim is older than Joy.
    (C) Hilda is younger than Joy.
    (D) Ida is older than Loren.
    (E) Marsha is older than Loren.

79. If Loren is 4 years younger than Ida, then which one of the following could be true?

    (A) Marsha is 9 years old.
    (B) Hilda is 17 years old.
    (C) Joy is 15 years old.
    (D) Hilda is 9 years old.
    (E) Joy is 19 years old.

80. Which one of the following could be the order of the ages of the seven daughters from youngest to oldest?

    (A) L, H, K, I, M, N, J
    (B) M, H, N, L, J, I, K
    (C) N, K, M, L, H, I, J
    (D) M, L, N, H, I, J, K
    (E) L, M, H, I, J, N, K

81. If Ida is older than Joy, then how many different possible orders are there for the ages of the seven daughters?

    (A) three
    (B) four
    (C) five
    (D) six
    (E) seven

82. Which one of the following could be true?

    (A) Kim is two years older than Hilda.
    (B) Joy is two years younger than Marsha.
    (C) Loren is two years younger than Kim.
    (D) Joy is two years older than Hilda.
    (E) Hilda is two years older than Kim.

83. All of the following could be true EXCEPT:

    (A) If Loren is 13 years old, then Marsha is 7 years old.
    (B) If Hilda is 15 years old, then Nicole is 7 years old.
    (C) If Ida is 13 years old, then Kim is 7 years old.
    (D) If Ida is 17 years old, then Kim is 9 years old.
    (E) If Hilda is 11 years old, then Marsha is 7 years old.

84. If Kim is older than Joy, then Ida must be

    (A) 9 years old
    (B) 11 years old
    (C) 13 years old
    (D) 15 years old
    (E) 17 years old

Questions 85–90

Seven friends—Paul, Ron, Sam, Tom, Victor, Willard, and Zack—are having dinner together. Each orders one of two possible starters, soup or salad, but not both. The following conditions must be satisfied:

If Tom orders salad, then Willard orders soup.

If Tom orders soup, then Ron orders salad.

If Zack orders soup, then Paul orders salad.

If Paul orders salad, then Willard orders salad.

If Victor orders salad, then Willard orders soup.

If Sam orders soup, then Tom orders soup.

If Zack orders soup, then Victor orders salad.

If Victor orders salad, then Ron orders soup.

85. If Paul and Willard make different choices for their starters, then which one of the following must be true?

    (A) Sam orders soup.
    (B) Paul orders salad.
    (C) Victor orders soup.
    (D) Tom orders salad.
    (E) Zack orders soup.

86. If Victor orders salad, then which one of the following must be true?

    (A) Willard orders salad.
    (B) Sam orders soup.
    (C) Zack orders soup.
    (D) Paul orders salad.
    (E) Tom orders salad.

87. If Paul and Tom have the same starter, each of the following could be true EXCEPT:

    (A) Zack and Victor order different starters.
    (B) Victor and Willard order different starters.
    (C) Tom and Victor order different starters.
    (D) Willard and Sam order different starters.
    (E) Sam and Ron order different starters.

88. Which of the following pairs of friends together must order at least one soup?

    (A) Sam and Tom
    (B) Paul and Victor
    (C) Tom and Zack
    (D) Sam and Ron
    (E) Paul and Willard

89. If Ron orders soup, then which of the following must be true?

    (A) Tom orders soup.
    (B) Victor orders salad.
    (C) Zack orders soup.
    (D) Paul orders soup.
    (E) Willard orders salad.

90. What is the maximum number of friends who could order soup?

    (A) two
    (B) three
    (C) four
    (D) five
    (E) six

Answers and Explanations

Answers 1–4

By following statements 1–3, you could have made these two possible orders:

Y R B O or O B R Y

but statement 4 eliminates the first order, Y R B O.

1. **E** From statements 2 and 3, the red and blue books are between other books; thus, they cannot be first or fourth. Therefore, they are second and third. This leaves first and fourth positions for the orange and yellow books.

2. **D** Orange, blue, red, yellow, white is a possible order. Notice that each of the other orders could have been eliminated because each broke an initial statement:
   (A) Orange and blue are switched.
   (B) Blue and red are switched.
   (C) White must be on an end since the other four must be next to each other.
   (E) Blue cannot be on an end.

3. **B** This follows the order discovered from the initial conditions, YRBO.

4. **B** Because the blue book was in the second position, it will move to the third position, and the green book will take the second.

Answers 5–8

The following simple chart may be helpful in answering the questions:

Disease	When Communicable	Symptom
J	Always	Red splotches appear DAY AFTER INF.
K	Day after infection	Blue lips OR red splotches appear DAY OF INF.
L	Only with J	Swollen ears appear DAY AFTER INF. NEGATED BY DISEASE K

Tuesday	Wednesday
Peter and Paul	Paul and Mary

5. **E** Either (A) or (B) may be true, but neither necessarily *must* be true. (C) could be true if Disease L is concurrent with Disease J, but it doesn't necessarily have to be true. Choice (D) is false since Disease K wouldn't be communicable until the day after, Wednesday. Thus (E) *is* true: Peter did not give Paul Disease K, because Disease K isn't communicable until a day later, on Wednesday.

6. **E** A complete and accurate list of pairs is swollen ears and red splotches and blue lips and red splotches. Blue lips and swollen ears are not possible together: Disease L's symptoms are negated by Disease K. Swollen ears and red splotches will both appear the day after infection with Diseases J and L. Blue lips and red splotches will appear together if a person is infected with Disease K a day after infection by Disease J.

7. **B** If Paul had red splotches on Tuesday, then he either was infected with Disease J on Monday or was infected with Disease K on Tuesday. Therefore:
   Paul could have given Peter Disease J because J is always communicable.
   Paul could *not* have given Peter Disease K on Tuesday, because Disease K isn't communicable until the day after (Wednesday).
   Paul could have given Mary Disease J because Disease J is always communicable.
   Paul could have given Mary Disease K because Disease K is communicable a day after infection (Wednesday).

8. **E** If Peter was infected with Disease K on Monday, then:
   Peter could have infected Paul with Disease K on Tuesday (one day later); Paul in turn could have infected Mary on Wednesday. Thus, Mary could have blue lips.
   Mary's ears could not have been swollen because simply passing on Disease K would not manifest such a symptom.
   Peter could have given Paul Disease K on Tuesday; Paul in turn could have given it to Mary on Wednesday. Red splotches are

also a symptom of Disease K, which Mary could have shown on Wednesday.

Answers 9–17

Drawing the simple diagram, below, will help answer the questions.

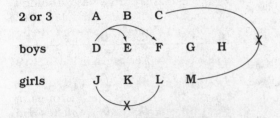

9. **D** If camper D is chosen, then campers E and F are also chosen. Thus three boys have been picked to go on the hike. Note that three girls, at most, can go on the hike. Since boys cannot outnumber girls, no other boys can be chosen.

10. **D** If camper K is not chosen, the maximum number of girls chosen can be two. Therefore, since boys cannot outnumber girls, D cannot be chosen, since selecting D means also selecting two more boys, E and F.

11. **A** If camper D is chosen, then boys E and F are also chosen. Since the maximum number of girls chosen can be three, no other boys may be chosen, since boys may not outnumber girls.

12. **C** Choices (A) and (E) include both C and M, which is not permitted. Choice (B) includes J and L, who will not hike together. In choice (D), boys outnumber girls, which is not permitted. Only choice (C) is an acceptable combination of campers and counselors.

13. **B** If counselor A is not chosen for the hike, then counselors B and C are chosen as there must be at least two counselors on the hike. Since counselor C is chosen, camper M (a girl) cannot be chosen. Therefore, the maximum number of girls on the hike can be two. Since boys cannot outnumber girls, D cannot be chosen, since selecting D would mean also selecting E and F, a total of three boys.

14. **D** If counselor A is not chosen, then counselors B and C will be chosen as there must be at least two counselors on the hike. If counselor C is chosen, camper M cannot be chosen, leaving the maximum number of girls possible on the hike at two. Therefore, since boys may not outnumber girls, D cannot be chosen, as choosing D would mean also selecting E and F, thus outnumbering the girls.

15. **C** Choices (A) and (E) included both C and M, which is not permitted. Choices (B) and (D) do not include camper E, who must accompany camper D. Only choice (C) includes acceptable companions for a hike with camper D.

16. **D** The largest number of hikers that can go on the hike is eight, as follows: three boys, three girls, and counselors A and B. (Example: A, B, D, E, F, J, K, M)

17. **C** The maximum number of girls possible for the hike is three. Therefore, since choosing camper D means also choosing campers E and F, no other boys (for instance, G) can be chosen, as boys would then outnumber girls.

Answers 18–23

From the information given, you could have made a simple chart showing how each rule works:

Rule 1 A B C D E F

Rule 2 A B C D E F

Rule 3 A B C D E F

Rule 4 H L K M

18. **C** The only way Howard can be playing video game D after two switches is if rule 1 then rule 2, or rule 2 then rule 1, is applied. The following is a diagram showing who is playing each video game after two switches. The order of rules 1 and 2 does not make any difference.

Choices (A) and (E) are incorrect since Lance and Murray are playing the same video games they were playing at 4:00. Choices (B) and (D) are wrong because Jessie and Kelly are playing different games from those they were playing at 4:00.

	A	**B**	**C**	**D**	**E**	**F**
	H	I	J	K	L	M
Rule 1	I	H	K	J	M	L
Rule 2	K	J	I	H	L	M

	A	**B**	**C**	**D**	**E**	**F**
	H	I	J	K	L	M
Rule 2	J	K	H	I	M	L
Rule 1	K	J	I	H	L	M

19. D If Jessie does not switch video games at 4:15, then either rule 3 or rule 4 must be applied at 4:15.

Choice (A) is incorrect since using rule 3, Kelly is playing video game D.

Choice (B) is incorrect since using rule 3, Murray is playing video game A.

Choice (C) is incorrect since using rule 3, Lance is playing video game B.

Choice (E) is incorrect since using rule 4, Howard is playing video game E.

	A	**B**	**C**	**D**	**E**	**F**
	H	I	J	K	L	M
Rule 3	M	L	J	K	I	H

	A	**B**	**C**	**D**	**E**	**F**
	H	I	J	K	L	M
Rule 4	L	I	J	M	H	K

20. A The only way Jessie can play video game F is if rule 2 is applied at 4:15 and rule 3 is applied at 4:30. Thus, 15 minutes earlier would be after rule 2 was applied.

Choice (B) is incorrect since Iris is playing video game D.

Choice (C) is incorrect since Kelly is playing video game B.

Choice (D) is incorrect since Lance is playing video game F.

Choice (E) is incorrect since Murray is playing video game E.

	A	**B**	**C**	**D**	**E**	**F**
	H	I	J	K	L	M
Rule 2	J	K	H	I	M	L
Rule 3	L	M	H	I	K	J

21. E The switch for Murray from video game F to video game B cannot be made in one switch. Thus, 4:20 is not possible. This eliminates choices (A) and (D). Since it is possible for Murray to be playing video game B after two switches or three switches, choices (B) and (C) are incorrect and choice (E) is correct.

	A	**B**	**C**	**D**	**E**	**F**
	H	I	J	K	L	M
Rule 1	I	H	K	J	M	L
Rule 3	L	M	K	J	H	I

	A	**B**	**C**	**D**	**E**	**F**
	H	I	J	K	L	M
Rule 2	J	K	H	I	M	L
Rule 3	L	M	H	I	K	J

	A	**B**	**C**	**D**	**E**	**F**
	H	I	J	K	L	M
Rule 3	M	L	J	K	I	H
Rule 1	L	M	K	J	H	I

	A	**B**	**C**	**D**	**E**	**F**
	H	I	J	K	L	M
Rule 3	M	L	J	K	I	H
Rule 4	K	H	J	M	I	L
Rule 2	J	M	K	H	L	I

22. E After three of the four rules are applied, it is not possible for Howard to be playing either video game B or video game C. Thus, any choice including video game B or C is incorrect.

After applying rules (in any order)	Howard will be playing the following video game
Rules 1, 2, and 3	D or F
Rules 1, 2, and 4	E
Rules 1, 3, and 4	A
Rules 2, 3, and 4	A or D

23. B In order for Jessie to play the same video game from 4:00 to 4:45, rules 3 and 4 must be used and 4:15 and 4:30. The order of rules 3 and 4 does not make a difference since both yield the same result.

	A	**B**	**C**	**D**	**E**	**F**
	H	I	J	K	L	M
Rule 3	M	L	J	K	I	H
Rule 4	K	H	J	M	I	L

	A	**B**	**C**	**D**	**E**	**F**
	H	I	J	K	L	M
Rule 4	L	I	J	M	H	K
Rule 3	K	H	J	M	I	L

	A	**B**	**C**	**D**	**E**	**F**
	K	H	J	M	I	L
Rule 1	H	K	M	J	L	I

	A	**B**	**C**	**D**	**E**	**F**
	K	H	J	M	I	L
Rule 2	J	M	K	H	L	I

If rule 1 or rule 2 is applied to the result of rules 3 and 4, Lance must play video game E and Iris must play video game F. Thus, choice (B) is the only one that must be true. Choices (A), (C), and (E) may be true, and choice (D) is false.

Answers 24–27

Constructing the following chart would be helpful in answering the questions:

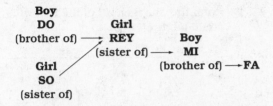

24. **A** Only statement (A) must be true. Because Do is Rey's brother, then Do is a boy. Because Rey is Mi's sister, then Rey is a girl. We do not know if Fa is a boy or a girl.

25. **A** Only statement (A) could be false, because we don't know if Fa is a boy or a girl.

26. **D** We do not know if Fa is a boy or a girl. Thus, (D) could be true. The others are false.

27. **B** We are not given any information about their ages. If Fa is a girl, then we have three sisters and two brothers.

Answers 28–35

From the information given, you could have constructed a diagram similar to this:

```
                                    ⌒
                              D–E
                          F   B ? E
                          G
A?                        A?
 1   2   3   4   5   6   7
```

Notice the information listed off to the side of the diagram.

28. **B** D cannot audition first since D and E have to audition consecutively, and B must audition before E.

29. **C** If A auditions first, then D cannot audition second because B must audition before E, and therefore also before D.

30. **E** If F and G audition first and second respectively, then A must audition last and the diagram for this question would look like this:

```
F   G                       A
1   2   3   4   5   6   7
```

Therefore, A must audition last and B cannot audition fifth (no room for D and E to follow B). C could possibly audition fourth.

31. **B** If B auditions first, and F and G audition second and third respectively, then A must audition last and the diagram for this question would look like this:

```
B   F   G                   A
1   2   3   4   5   6   7
```

Therefore, E auditions sixth could be true. C auditions fifth must be false because D and E must be next to each other. If C was fifth, he would split D and E. D auditions fourth could be true.

32. **A** If D auditions ahead of E, and if A auditions first and B fifth, then the diagram for this question would look like this:

```
A               B   D   E
1   2   3   4   5   6   7
```

Since B auditions fifth, then D must be sixth and E seventh.

33. **D** This question is most easily answered by eliminating the orders that are not possible. Choice (A) can be eliminated because E is ahead of B and not next to D. Choice (B) can be eliminated because G cannot audition last. Choices (C) and (A) can be eliminated because A is not first or last.

34. **E** From the new information given, men cannot audition consecutively; the diagram for this question would now look like this:

```
C       B       D       A
1   2   3   4   5   6   7
```

Therefore, B must audition third.

35. **E** If F auditions third and all the women must audition consecutively, then G must audition next to F, since E must be next to D. The diagram for this question would now look like this:

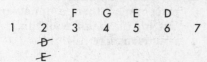

```
        F   G   E   D
1   2   3   4   5   6   7
   -D-
   -E-
```

Therefore, D must audition sixth.

Answers 36–41

The following diagram may prove helpful:

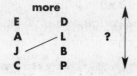

```
            more
        E   D        ↑
        A   L    ?
        J   B        ↓
        C   P
```

36. **A** Because David lifts more than Logan and Logan lifts more than Jason, David lifts more than Jason. Prescott and Bryan lift less than Logan, but we cannot say anything about their relationship to Jason. It is possible for Prescott to lift more than Ellen.

37. **A** Logan lifts more than Prescott. If Prescott lifts more than Aaron, so must Logan.

```
            D
            L
        E   B
            P
        A
        J
        C
```

38. **D** If Aaron lifts more than David, then Aaron, Ellen, and David each lift more than Logan.

```
        E
        A
            D
            L
        J
        C   B
            P
```

39. **E** If 5 people lift less than Logan, they must be Bryan, Prescott, Clifford, Jason, and Aaron. Thus, David and Ellen lift more than Logan, therefore, David lifts more than Aaron. Answer (C) may be true, but doesn't have to be.

```
            D
        E   L
        A   B
        J   P
        C
```

40. **E** Given these additional facts, we can redraw the diagram as follows:

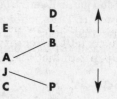

```
            D
        E   L        ↑
            B
        A
        J
        C       P    ↓
```

Thus, Logan, David, and Bryan can each lift more than Ellen.

41. **E** From the diagram, all of the following could be true:

```
        E   D        ↑
            L
        A   B    ?
            P
        J
        C
```

Answers 42–47

This diagram shows these relationships:

```
      CF          CF  CF  CF      CF
1   2   3   4   5   6   7   8   9
Cola        Cola    RB      RB
```

42. **B** Can 3 is the only one.

43. **B** Of the cans listed, only the fourth place (can 4) contains caffeine.

44. **D** The sixth place (can 6) is the can that meets the requirements.

45. **D** For this question, you should use the following diagram:

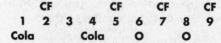

```
      CF          CF      CF      CF
1   2   3   4   5   6   7   8   9
Cola        Cola    O       O
```

After the replacement, the cans that meet the conditions are 3, 6, and 8.

46. **D** The five caffeine-free cans are 2, 5, 6, 7, and 9. Therefore choice (D), the sixth and ninth places, is the only valid one.

47. **E** All four flavored beverages are next to caffeine-free beverages.

Answers 48–51

From the information given, it would be helpful to construct a diagram to answer the questions.

NOTE: When more than one letter appears at a seat, those letters represent all the possible occupants of that seat.

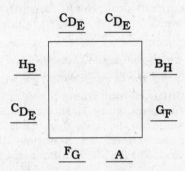

48. **A** From the diagram, C must sit next to B or H; therefore (A) is true. Taking a second look at the diagram, we can see that H doesn't have to sit next to G, and F doesn't have to sit next to D or E. Therefore, (B) and (C) are not necessarily true. Also, (D) is false since H sits directly across from B. Statement (E) is false since F could sit across from E.

49. **E** If B does not sit next to G, then we should adjust the diagram as follows:

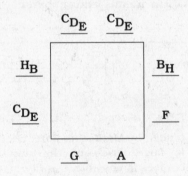

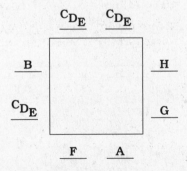

From these diagrams, we see that all statements are possible except (E). Since A sits between G and F, A cannot sit next to H under any circumstances.

50. **E** If C sits across from F, then H could sit next to any of these four (C, D, E, G) depending on the positions of B and H. A cannot sit next to H since A sits between G and F.

51. **C** B and H can't, since they must sit opposite each other. F and G can't, since they must sit next to A. That leaves only C, D, and E.

Answers 52–57

From the information given, you could make the following displays:

$$A + B = Z$$
$$T + Z = B$$
$$Z + B = A$$
$$B + T = O \quad \text{(O is odorless)}$$
$$A + Z = T$$
$$A + T = Z$$

OR

	A	B	T	Z
A	?	Z	Z	T
B	Z	?	O	A
T	Z	O	?	B
Z	T	A	B	?

(O is odorless)

52. **A** This answer may be derived directly from the statement: Beta combines with Theta, giving Omega. Omega is the only odorless chemical.

53. **B** From our chart or statements we can see that, if Beta is involved, then the outcome may be Alpha, Omega, or Zeta.

54. **E** We have no information about the results if the odorless chemical, Omega, combines with anything.

55. **A** From the chart or statements we can see that Zeta and Theta combine to give Beta.

56. **B** The outcome of Alpha and Beta is Zeta. The outcome of Alpha and Zeta is Theta. Thus, if the two outcomes (Zeta and Theta) combine, the result will then be Beta.

57. **A** Alpha with any other (with the exception of Omega, which we do not know) produces either Zeta or Theta, which is similar to the outcome of Omega with Theta.

58. **E** From the initial conditions, the following chart can be drawn:

	1	2	3	4	5	6
Jilian	D,E,F		T			R,S
Mark		D,E,F		D,E,F		D,E,F

Not (D), since Jilian attends T third. Not (A), (B), or (C), since Mark must attend historical lectures second, fourth, and sixth so that no two historical lectures are attended consecutively.

59. **A** Filling in Mark's possible schedule gives:

	1	2	3	4	5	6
Jilian	D,E,F		T			R,S
Mark	T	D,E,F	R,S	D,E,F	R,S	D,E,F

If Jilian attends E second and Mark attends D second, we get:

	1	2	3	4	5	6
Jilian	D	E	T	F,R,S	F,R,S	R,S
Mark	T	D	R,S	E	R,S	F

Notice that Mark must attend F sixth, after it is attended by Jilian.

E must therefore be attended fourth by Mark. Now choices can be eliminated. Not (B) since Jilian could attend F fourth or fifth. Not (C), since Mark could attend S third or fifth. Not (D), since Mark attends F sixth. Not (E), since Jilian could attend R fourth, fifth, or sixth.

60. **E** Referring to the initial chart and conditions, the unacceptable choices can be eliminated.

Not (A), since Mark must attend S before Jilian and Jilian must attend F before Mark. Also, Mark attends two historical lectures in a row. Not (B) since Mark attends two historical lectures in a row. Not (C), since Jilian attends T fourth. Not (D), since Mark attends F before Jilian.

61. **A** Using the initial chart and the conditions will give the following:

Jilian cannot attend a scientific lecture first, since Mark must attend all scientific lectures first. Thus, Jilian must attend an historical lecture first. Not (D) since Jilian must attend T third. Not (C) or (E), since both Jilian and Mark can attend a scientific lecture fifth: Jilian—D, E, T, F, R, S and Mark—T, D, R, E, S, F.

62. **D** Using and filling in the initial conditions chart will give the insight needed for this question.

	1	2	3	4	5	6
Jilian	D,E,F		T			R,S
Mark		D,E,F		D,E,F		D,E,F

If Mark attends lecture F fourth and Jilian attends lecture D first:

	1	2	3	4	5	6
Jilian	D	F	T	E,R,S	E,R,S	R,S
Mark	T	D	R,S	F	R,S	E

Lecture E is the sixth lecture attended by Mark; therefore, choice (D) is false. Each of the other four choices is possible.

63. **C** Not (A), (B), or (D) as the following counter example illustrates:

Jilian: D, E, T, S, F, R and
Mark: T, D, S, E, R, F.

Not (E), since Mark must attend an historical lecture sixth. The answer must be (C), since Mark must attend scientific lectures first, third and fifth, and must attend T before Jilian. Thus, first is the only possibility for T.

64. **E** Using the initial conditions chart, the following information can be included:

	1	2	3	4	5	6
Jilian	D,E,F		T			R,S
Mark	T	D,E,F	R	D,E,F	S	D,E,F

Mark attends lecture T first since he must attend it before Jilian. If he attends lecture R third, he must attend lecture S fifth. Since he must attend S before Jilian, Jilian must attend S sixth.

From the initial conditions, a simple display could have been drawn.

F?   F?   ED
1 2 3 4 5 6 7 8 G-F-A
B? C?   or   A?

65. **B** Using the simple display and the initial conditions makes eliminating the wrong answers much easier to do.

Not (A), since F is 4th and must be either 3rd or 7th. Not (C), since D does not immediately follow E. Also GFA is not in the correct order. Not (D), since GFA not in the correct order. Not (E), since C is not 3rd and A is not 8th, but B is 2nd.

66. **A** Using the initial conditions: Since Fetina's appointment must be before Arnie's and Fetina must be either 3rd or 7th, it is not possible for Arnie to be scheduled 3rd.

67. **C** Using the simple display and the initial conditions: Since Arnie is 6th, Fetina must be 3rd. Since Greg's appointment is before Fetina's, it must be either 1st or 2nd. Since Hector's appointment is after Dodi's, it must be either 7th or 8th. Therefore, the answer is not (A), since Greg must be 1st or 2nd. Not (B), since Hector is either 7th or 8th. Not (D), since Dodi is 5th. Not (E), since Coco must be either 7th or 8th.

1	2	3	4	5	6	7	8
B,C,G	B,C,G	F	E	D	A	B,C,H	B,C,H

68. **A** Using the simple display and the initial conditions: If Coco is 7th, then Fetina must be 3rd. Since Greg must be scheduled before Fetina, the only appointments open for Elvis and Dodi are 4th, 5th, and 6th, with Arnie taking the remaining slot. This leaves 1st and 2nd available for Betah. Betah cannot be 2nd, since Coco is not 3rd and Arnie is not 8th. Thus, Betah must be 1st. The display would look like this:

1	2	3	4	5	6	7	8
B	G	F	A,E	D,E	A,D	C	H

69. C Using the simple display and the initial conditions: Since Arnie is scheduled after Coco, Arnie must be 8th and Coco must be 7th and Fetina 3rd. Since Betah is 2nd, Greg must be 1st. Since Dodi must immediately follow Elvis, Elvis is 4th and Dodi is 5th, or Elvis is 5th and Dodi is 6th. Therefore, Hector must be either 4th or 6th. The display would look like this:

1	2	3	4	5	6	7	8
G	B	F	E,H	E,D	D,H	C	A

70. D Using the initial conditions and simple display: Answer choice (D) is not valid, since if Betah is 2nd, we must have either Coco 3rd or Arnie 8th.

Answers 71–77

From the information given, you could have constructed the following display:

```
A̶                          E   A̶   1B   2A
1  2  3  4  5  6  7  8       1C   2D
                                  2E
            B̶?  [AEA]
```

71. E Office 4 can be cleaned only by A or E. Therefore, answer choice (E) is incorrect. The other choices are possible as follows.

	1	2	3	4	5	6	7	8
(A)	B	A	E	A	D	D	E	C
(B) & (C)	B	D	C	A	E	A	E	D
(D)	B	D	A	E	A	C	E	D

72. C Office 4 can be cleaned only by A or E. Therefore, choice (C) is the only correct one.

73. B Office 4 can be cleaned only by A or E. Therefore, choices (C), (D), and (E) are incorrect. Choice (A) is incorrect because D can clean office 8, so this choice is accurate but not complete. Choice (B) is correct.

74. D There are four possible arrangements as follows. Thus, choice (D) is correct.

1	2	3	4	5	6	7	8
B	A	E	A	D	C	E	D
B	D	A	E	A	C	E	D
B	C	A	E	A	D	E	D
B	C	D	A	E	A	E	D

75. D Choices (B) and (C) are incorrect since they each clean only one office. Choice (A) is incorrect since the conditions state that A's offices are separated by one of E's offices. Answer (E) is incorrect since one of E's offices is between A's offices. Only choice (D) is possible as follows.

1	2	3	4	5	6	7	8
B	A	E	A	D	D	E	C

76. A Bart cannot clean office 6 since his office must be numbered lower than E's lowest. Also, Ethel cannot clean office 6 since E must be between A's and E is already cleaning office 7.

77. E There are two possible arrangements of rooms, as follows.

1	2	3	4	5	6	7	8
D	B	A	E	A	C	E	D
D	B	C	A	E	A	E	D

Choice (A) is incorrect since A may clean office 6. Choice (B) is incorrect since B and C may clean consecutive offices. Choice (C) is incorrect since C may or may not clean an even-numbered office. Choice (D) is incorrect since this may or may not be true. The only one that *must* be true is choice (E), Bart cleans office 2.

Answers 78–84

The six conditions could give the following display:

```
            L/I                    M̶N̶ or N̶M̶
7  9  11  13  15  17  19            N—J
                                    M—J
                                    L—H—I
```

You may have been able to deduce additional information.

78. D Choice (A) is incorrect since H is between L and I. Choice (B) is incorrect since Kim could be younger than Joy, as follows:

7	9	11	13	15	17	19
N	K	M	L	H	J	I

Choice (C) is incorrect since Hilda could be older than Joy, as follows:

7	9	11	13	15	17	19
N	K	M	L	J	H	I

Choice (E) is incorrect because Marsha could be younger than Loren, as illustrated above. Choice (D) is correct, since Hilda is older than Loren but younger than Ida.

79. E The correct answer is (E). Because there are only two possible basic setups, this could be true as follows:

7	9	11	13	15	17	19
M?	K	N?	L	H	I	J
M?	L	H	I	N?	K	J

Choice (A) is incorrect since if M were 9, it would be consecutive with N. Choice (B) is incorrect since if H was 17, L would be 15, which violates a condition. Choice (C) is incorrect since if J were 15, there would not be enough slots to the left of J for five daughters. Choice (D) is incorrect since if H were 9, I would be 11, which violates a condition.

80. C Choice (A) is incorrect since M and N are consecutive. Choice (B) is incorrect since H is not between L and I. Choice (D) is incorrect since I or L must be 13. Choice (E) is incorrect since N is older than J. Only choice (C) meets all the conditions.

81. B The correct choice is four. These four possibilities are shown below. If I is 19, L is 13, so H must be 15 or 17. Remember, M and N can't be next to each other.

7	9	11	13	15	17	19
N	K	M	L	H	J	I
M	K	N	L	H	J	I
N	K	M	L	J	H	I
M	K	N	L	J	H	I

82. D Choices (A) and (E) are incorrect. If Kim were two years older than Hilda, or Hilda were two years older than Kim, the following arrangements would result. In either case, M and N would be consecutive.

7	9	11	13	15	17	19
M	N	J	L	H?	K?	I
L	H?	K?	I	M	N	J

Choice (B) is incorrect since Joy is older than Marsha. Choice (C) is incorrect since M and N would be consecutive as follows:

7	9	11	13	15	17	19
M	N	J	L	K	H	I
L	K	H	I	M	N	J

Choice (D) is the correct choice as follows:

7	9	11	13	15	17	19
M	K	N	L	H	J	I

83. C Choice (C) is correct since if I is 13 and K is 7, you end up with M and N consecutive, as follows:

7	9	11	13	15	17	19
K	L	H	I	M	N	J

The other four choices are all possible, as follows:

	7	9	11	13	15	17	19
(A) & (D)	M	K	N	L	H	I	J
(B)	N	K	M	L	H	I	J
(E)	M	L	H	I	N	K	J

84. C Choice (C) is correct because, from the conditions, I must always be either 13, 17 or 19. If I was 17 or 19, M and N would be 7 and 9, and therefore consecutive. Thus, I must be 13. If I is 13, we could get the following:

7	9	11	13	15	17	19
M	L	H	I	N	J	K

Answers 85–90

The following display can be constructed from the conditions:

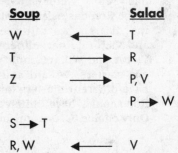

85. C If Paul orders salad, so must Willard. Therefore, Paul must order soup (eliminate B) and Willard orders salad. Since Willard orders salad, Tom must order soup (eliminate D). Thus, Ron must order salad. Zack must order salad. He cannot order soup. If Zack ordered soup, then Paul must order salad and Paul can't order the same as Willard (eliminate E). The correct choice is (C). Victor must order soup, since, if he ordered salad, that would force Ron and Willard to order soup (and Willard can't order the same as Paul). Sam can order either soup or salad (eliminate A).

Soup	Salad
P	W
T	R
V	Z
	← S →

86. **E** If Victor orders salad, then the following ordering arrangement results:

Soup	Salad
R	V
W	T
P	Z
	S

If Victor orders salad, then both Ron and Willard order soup. Since Ron orders soup, Tom must order salad. We know that Zack must order salad; otherwise, Paul, Victor, and Willard would have to order salad. Since Tom orders salad, so must Sam, Since Willard orders soup, so must Paul. From this diagram, it is clear that choice (E) is the correct choice.

87. **C** If Paul and Tom have the same starter, it must be soup. It cannot be salad because if Paul has salad, so must Willard, and if Tom has salad, Willard must have soup. This is a contradiction. Thus, Paul and Tom have soup. Ron has salad since Tom has soup. Victor must have soup since Ron has salad. From the following diagram we can see that Zack and Victor do have different starters, Victor and Willard could have different starters, Willard and Sam could have different starters, and Sam and Ron could have different starters. Only choice (C) is not true.

Soup	Salad
P	Z
T	R
V	

←— W —→
←— S —→

88. **B** The correct answer choice is (B). If Victor orders salad, then Willard orders soup. If Paul orders salad, then Willard orders salad. Willard cannot order both soup and salad. Each of the other choices is possible, as seen in the following two possible arrangements:

Soup	Salad	Soup	Salad
	Z	T	R
W	T	V	W
P	V		S
R	S		P
			Z

89. **D** If Ron orders soup, then Tom must order salad. If Tom orders salad, then Willard must order soup. Paul must order soup since Willard ordered soup. Sam must order salad since Tom ordered salad. Only Victor has a choice. Choice (A) is incorrect since Tom orders salad. Choice (B) is incorrect since Victor may or may not order salad. Choice (C) is incorrect since Zack must order salad. Choice (E) is incorrect since Willard orders soup.

Soup	Salad
R	T
W	Z
P	S

←— V —→

90. **D** The following arrangement results in a maximum of five friends ordering soup:

Soup	Salad
T	R
V	Z
P	
W	
S	

Answer Sheet
Extra Practice:
Analytical Reasoning

1. Ⓐ Ⓑ Ⓒ Ⓓ Ⓔ	19. Ⓐ Ⓑ Ⓒ Ⓓ Ⓔ	37. Ⓐ Ⓑ Ⓒ Ⓓ Ⓔ	55. Ⓐ Ⓑ Ⓒ Ⓓ Ⓔ	73. Ⓐ Ⓑ Ⓒ Ⓓ Ⓔ
2. Ⓐ Ⓑ Ⓒ Ⓓ Ⓔ	20. Ⓐ Ⓑ Ⓒ Ⓓ Ⓔ	38. Ⓐ Ⓑ Ⓒ Ⓓ Ⓔ	56. Ⓐ Ⓑ Ⓒ Ⓓ Ⓔ	74. Ⓐ Ⓑ Ⓒ Ⓓ Ⓔ
3. Ⓐ Ⓑ Ⓒ Ⓓ Ⓔ	21. Ⓐ Ⓑ Ⓒ Ⓓ Ⓔ	39. Ⓐ Ⓑ Ⓒ Ⓓ Ⓔ	57. Ⓐ Ⓑ Ⓒ Ⓓ Ⓔ	75. Ⓐ Ⓑ Ⓒ Ⓓ Ⓔ
4. Ⓐ Ⓑ Ⓒ Ⓓ Ⓔ	22. Ⓐ Ⓑ Ⓒ Ⓓ Ⓔ	40. Ⓐ Ⓑ Ⓒ Ⓓ Ⓔ	58. Ⓐ Ⓑ Ⓒ Ⓓ Ⓔ	76. Ⓐ Ⓑ Ⓒ Ⓓ Ⓔ
5. Ⓐ Ⓑ Ⓒ Ⓓ Ⓔ	23. Ⓐ Ⓑ Ⓒ Ⓓ Ⓔ	41. Ⓐ Ⓑ Ⓒ Ⓓ Ⓔ	59. Ⓐ Ⓑ Ⓒ Ⓓ Ⓔ	77. Ⓐ Ⓑ Ⓒ Ⓓ Ⓔ
6. Ⓐ Ⓑ Ⓒ Ⓓ Ⓔ	24. Ⓐ Ⓑ Ⓒ Ⓓ Ⓔ	42. Ⓐ Ⓑ Ⓒ Ⓓ Ⓔ	60. Ⓐ Ⓑ Ⓒ Ⓓ Ⓔ	78. Ⓐ Ⓑ Ⓒ Ⓓ Ⓔ
7. Ⓐ Ⓑ Ⓒ Ⓓ Ⓔ	25. Ⓐ Ⓑ Ⓒ Ⓓ Ⓔ	43. Ⓐ Ⓑ Ⓒ Ⓓ Ⓔ	61. Ⓐ Ⓑ Ⓒ Ⓓ Ⓔ	79. Ⓐ Ⓑ Ⓒ Ⓓ Ⓔ
8. Ⓐ Ⓑ Ⓒ Ⓓ Ⓔ	26. Ⓐ Ⓑ Ⓒ Ⓓ Ⓔ	44. Ⓐ Ⓑ Ⓒ Ⓓ Ⓔ	62. Ⓐ Ⓑ Ⓒ Ⓓ Ⓔ	80. Ⓐ Ⓑ Ⓒ Ⓓ Ⓔ
9. Ⓐ Ⓑ Ⓒ Ⓓ Ⓔ	27. Ⓐ Ⓑ Ⓒ Ⓓ Ⓔ	45. Ⓐ Ⓑ Ⓒ Ⓓ Ⓔ	63. Ⓐ Ⓑ Ⓒ Ⓓ Ⓔ	81. Ⓐ Ⓑ Ⓒ Ⓓ Ⓔ
10. Ⓐ Ⓑ Ⓒ Ⓓ Ⓔ	28. Ⓐ Ⓑ Ⓒ Ⓓ Ⓔ	46. Ⓐ Ⓑ Ⓒ Ⓓ Ⓔ	64. Ⓐ Ⓑ Ⓒ Ⓓ Ⓔ	82. Ⓐ Ⓑ Ⓒ Ⓓ Ⓔ
11. Ⓐ Ⓑ Ⓒ Ⓓ Ⓔ	29. Ⓐ Ⓑ Ⓒ Ⓓ Ⓔ	47. Ⓐ Ⓑ Ⓒ Ⓓ Ⓔ	65. Ⓐ Ⓑ Ⓒ Ⓓ Ⓔ	83. Ⓐ Ⓑ Ⓒ Ⓓ Ⓔ
12. Ⓐ Ⓑ Ⓒ Ⓓ Ⓔ	30. Ⓐ Ⓑ Ⓒ Ⓓ Ⓔ	48. Ⓐ Ⓑ Ⓒ Ⓓ Ⓔ	66. Ⓐ Ⓑ Ⓒ Ⓓ Ⓔ	84. Ⓐ Ⓑ Ⓒ Ⓓ Ⓔ
13. Ⓐ Ⓑ Ⓒ Ⓓ Ⓔ	31. Ⓐ Ⓑ Ⓒ Ⓓ Ⓔ	49. Ⓐ Ⓑ Ⓒ Ⓓ Ⓔ	67. Ⓐ Ⓑ Ⓒ Ⓓ Ⓔ	85. Ⓐ Ⓑ Ⓒ Ⓓ Ⓔ
14. Ⓐ Ⓑ Ⓒ Ⓓ Ⓔ	32. Ⓐ Ⓑ Ⓒ Ⓓ Ⓔ	50. Ⓐ Ⓑ Ⓒ Ⓓ Ⓔ	68. Ⓐ Ⓑ Ⓒ Ⓓ Ⓔ	86. Ⓐ Ⓑ Ⓒ Ⓓ Ⓔ
15. Ⓐ Ⓑ Ⓒ Ⓓ Ⓔ	33. Ⓐ Ⓑ Ⓒ Ⓓ Ⓔ	51. Ⓐ Ⓑ Ⓒ Ⓓ Ⓔ	69. Ⓐ Ⓑ Ⓒ Ⓓ Ⓔ	87. Ⓐ Ⓑ Ⓒ Ⓓ Ⓔ
16. Ⓐ Ⓑ Ⓒ Ⓓ Ⓔ	34. Ⓐ Ⓑ Ⓒ Ⓓ Ⓔ	52. Ⓐ Ⓑ Ⓒ Ⓓ Ⓔ	70. Ⓐ Ⓑ Ⓒ Ⓓ Ⓔ	88. Ⓐ Ⓑ Ⓒ Ⓓ Ⓔ
17. Ⓐ Ⓑ Ⓒ Ⓓ Ⓔ	35. Ⓐ Ⓑ Ⓒ Ⓓ Ⓔ	53. Ⓐ Ⓑ Ⓒ Ⓓ Ⓔ	71. Ⓐ Ⓑ Ⓒ Ⓓ Ⓔ	89. Ⓐ Ⓑ Ⓒ Ⓓ Ⓔ
18. Ⓐ Ⓑ Ⓒ Ⓓ Ⓔ	36. Ⓐ Ⓑ Ⓒ Ⓓ Ⓔ	54. Ⓐ Ⓑ Ⓒ Ⓓ Ⓔ	72. Ⓐ Ⓑ Ⓒ Ⓓ Ⓔ	90. Ⓐ Ⓑ Ⓒ Ⓓ Ⓔ

To remove, cut along dotted rule.

Chapter 4
LOGICAL REASONING

Introduction to Question Type

The LSAT will contain *two* Logical Reasoning sections that will count toward your score. The unscored experimental section could also be Logical Reasoning. Each Logical Reasoning section is 35 minutes in length and contains from 24 to 26 questions. *Since approximately half of your exam consists of Logical Reasoning questions, you should spend additional time reviewing, understanding, and practicing this question type.*

Logical Reasoning questions, which require you to apply your reading and reasoning skills, measure your aptitude for understanding, analyzing, utilizing, and criticizing various short passages and types of arguments. Your ability to reason logically and critically is tested by questions that require you to do the following:

- Recognize a point.
- Follow a chain of reasoning.
- Draw conclusions.
- Infer missing material.
- Apply principles from an argument.
- Identify methods.
- Evaluate arguments.
- Differentiate between fact and opinion.
- Analyze evidence.
- Assess claims critically.

Logical reasoning questions may take many forms. In analyzing these forms, consider their basic component parts:

1. **A *passage, argument* or *discussion***
   followed by
2. **A *question* based upon the preceding text**
   followed by
3. **The five *answer choices* (A, B, C, D, and E)**

The following discussion offers some tips for each of these parts.

The Approach

The Basic Components

1. The Passage, Argument, or Discussion

For the passage, read *actively;* that is, as you read you should mark the important parts with circles, exclamation points, etc., directly on the page of your question booklet. Reading actively helps you stay involved in the passage, it keeps you an active participant in the testing process, and it helps you note and highlight the important points mentioned, should you need to refer to the passage.

As you read you should also note the major issue being discussed, along with the few supporting points, if any.

2. The Question

For the question, it may be helpful to *preread actively;* that is, to read the question first, *before* reading the passage. That way you have an idea of what to look for as you read the passage. This is an effective technique only if the question is short. If the question is as long as (or longer than) the passage, this technique may not be helpful. Use your judgment.

As you read the question, note the key words and *circle* them, in the same manner as you mark the passage. Also note the *reference* of the question. Is it positive or negative? Is it asking what would strengthen the author's argument or what would weaken the author's argument? Is it asking what the author would agree or disagree with? Is it asking what the author believes, or what his critics would believe? Finally, be aware that questions often refer to *unstated* ideas: assumptions (a supposition or a truth taken for granted); implications/inferences (what would logically follow from a previous statement); and conclusions (the necessary consequence or result of the ideas in the passage). Assumptions and implications/inferences are usually not directly mentioned in the passage. Conclusions may or may not be mentioned. You must arrive at all three through logical thinking.

3. The Choices

For the choices, note that you must select the *best* of the five alternatives. Therefore, there may not be a perfect choice. There may also be two good choices. You are to pick the best of the five. Therefore, the elimination strategy (p. 11) is an effective way to approach the answer choices. Eliminate choices that are irrelevant (have nothing to do with the particular topic or issue), off-topic, or not addressed by the passage. Note that often a choice will be incorrect simply because one word in that choice is off-topic. Learn to look for and mark these off-topic key words.

Finally, be very careful as you read the passage, question, and choices, to watch for words that have very special meanings. The following words, for instance, are frequently used:

except   some   all   none   only   one

few   no   could   must   each

These types of words will often be the key to finding the best answer. Therefore, make sure to underline or circle them in your reading.

Analyzing Question Categories

The following sections give detailed examples of the most common types of Logical Reasoning questions, complete with important techniques and strategies. You should not try to memorize the different categories presented here, but rather use them as an aid in identifying strategies needed and in practicing techniques.

Author's Main Point or Main Idea

A very common Logical Reasoning question type will ask you to identify or understand the main point or main idea of the passage. This is also a common question type in the Reading Comprehension section.

As you read the short passage, focus on what the author is trying to say—the major issue. Each paragraph usually contains only one main idea, often stated in the first sentence.

Let's analyze the following passage:

EXAMPLE 1

> *Legal Analyst:* As the legal profession becomes more specialized and complex, clerical assistance must become more specialized as well. One legal secretary might be an expert in bankruptcy law, another an expert in criminal justice.

Which one of the following is the main point of the passage?

(A) A legal secretary may understand subjects other than law.

(B) A legal secretary should have special training in a particular branch of law.

(C) A legal secretary must be an expert in several types of law.

(D) Attorneys will hire only secretaries without legal experience so they can be trained on the job.

(E) Attorneys will still need legal secretaries with a very general background.

Analysis

The first sentence of the passage, a general statement about increasing specialization in the legal profession, states the main idea. It is followed by a more specific statement, which gives you additional information.

To help you focus on the main point, you may wish to use the following technique when practicing this question type. As you finish reading each paragraph, try to mentally summarize the paragraph in a few words. For example, after reading the sample above, you might summarize it by saying to yourself, "Legal secretaries should specialize in different types of law."

Next, note whether the paragraph states a particular attitude toward the subject. Typically the author will either approve or disapprove of the main point, or remain neutral. In the Example 1 passage, the author takes no position pro or con, but delivers the additional information in a matter-of-fact way.

The correct answer is (B). In this case, the main point is that legal secretaries must become more specialized, and the correct answer emphasizes "special training." Notice also that the correct answer here refers as well to the second sentence, which contains additional information about particular branches of law.

(A) is irrelevant. Although particular types of law are mentioned, subjects other than law are not. Note that this statement may certainly be true for some legal secretaries, but receives no support from the paragraph. (C) contradicts information in the passage; the passage discusses legal secretaries who specialize in one type of law, not several. (D) and (E) are not addressed in the passage. The passage does not discuss attorneys' hiring requirements or the need for legal secretaries with a very general background.

Remember, when asked for a main point, be sure to differentiate the main point from secondary or minor points.

EXAMPLE 2

The belief that positive thinking is the key to success can lead to laziness. It encourages some people to engage in slipshod work, in the hope that an optimistic mental attitude will take the place of hard, careful, dedicated work.

Which one of the following is the main idea of this passage?

(A) Laziness is always the result of positive thinking.
(B) Laziness is practiced by successful people.
(C) Laziness is only permissible after one has completed a hard day's work.
(D) Laziness may result from a reliance on positive thinking.
(E) Laziness may result from an assortment of mental attitudes.

Analysis

The correct answer is (D), which restates the opening statement that "positive thinking . . . can lead to laziness." However, the paragraph does not say that laziness is always the result; therefore (A) is incorrect. (B) is unreasonable and is contradicted by the paragraph. (C) is irrelevant; the paragraph does not discuss when laziness is permissible. (E) brings in an assortment of mental attitudes that are not addressed.

EXAMPLE 3

Few people understand poetry, and few prefer to read it. Although English professors speak in glowing terms about the greatness of Pope's *Rape of the Lock* and Tennyson's *Ulysses,* it seems that only other professors share their enthusiasm. To appreciate the greatness of difficult poetry, readers must exercise great patience and concentration, and must tolerate the unusual, compressed language of rhythm and rhyme; with so many urgent issues demanding our attention almost every hour of the day, choosing to figure out a poem seems an unlikely possibility.

In the passage above, the writer makes which one of the following arguments?

(A) English professors pay lip service to great poetry, but, in fact, rarely read it for pleasure.

(B) Even English professors may not really understand difficult poetry.

(C) Few laypeople will spend the time necessary to read difficult poetry.

(D) Simple poetry may continue to be popular, but only English teachers now read difficult poetry.

(E) To read difficult poetry requires patience, concentration, and tolerance.

Analysis

The correct answer is (C). The passage does not suggest that the English professors' enthusiasm is insincere (A) nor that they may fail to understand difficult poems (B). It argues that only English professors have the skills, time, and interest in poetry to deal with its difficulties, that laypeople are now unlikely to do so (C). The passage does not allude to simple poetry. (E) is tempting at first, but the argument of the passage is that understanding or appreciating poetry requires these skills, not simply reading it, so (C) is the best of the five choices.

Author Information or Author's Purpose

Another common Logical Reasoning question refers to a reading passage or paragraph and asks you to understand some things about the author. You may be asked to interpret what the author is trying to accomplish by this statement, or to predict the action and feeling of the author on similar or unrelated subject matter (tell whether the author would agree or disagree with some idea).

To answer this type of question, first look for the values and attitudes of the author. (Ask yourself, "Where is the author coming from?") Second, watch for word connotation: the author's choice of words can be very important. Third, decide the author's purpose and point of view, but don't OVERREAD. Keep within the context of the passage. Sometimes it will be advantageous to skim some of the questions (not the answer choices) before reading the short passage, so that you will know what to expect.

Remember while reading to mark the passage and look for *who, what, when, where, why,* and *how.* (See the section on "Active Reading" that begins on page 36.)

EXAMPLE 1

Recent studies show that the general public is unaware of most new legislation and doesn't understand 99% of the remaining legislation. This is mainly because of the public's inattention and lack of interest.

The author of this argument would most likely be

(A) in favor in new legislation
(B) against new legislation
(C) advocating public participation in legislation
(D) advocating the simplifying of the language of new legislation
(E) advocating more interesting legislation

Analysis

The correct answer is (C). The statement does not imply that an increase or decrease in legislation would change the public awareness; therefore (A) and (B) are incorrect. (C) follows in the tenor of the argument because the author's purpose appears to be centered around involvement. He points out that the general public is unaware because of inattention and lack of interest. (D) would be possible, *but* the author is not focusing his criticism on the complex wording of legislation and does not mention it as a reason for unawareness. Remember (1) *whom* the author is talking about—the general public, (2) *what* he mentions—their unawareness of most new legislation, and (3) *why* they are unaware—because of inattention and lack of interest. The author is not advocating more interesting legislation (E).

EXAMPLE 2

Writing Teacher: There are advantages and disadvantages to clear, simple writing. Sentences that are easy to understand are processed more quickly and efficiently by readers; those who can express themselves in simple terms are rarely misunderstood. However, prose that is crystal clear often lacks both complexity and imagination. Whether one chooses a style that is simple and clear or complex and unusual often depends upon the tolerance of one's readers.

The purpose of the writing teacher who makes this statement to a class is probably to

(A) encourage students to write more simply
(B) encourage students to imitate in their own pure style the points the teacher is making about pure style
(C) encourage students to be more imaginative in their writing

(D) remind students of the importance of the audience to a piece of writing

(E) urge students to combine simplicity and complexity, clarity and imagination in all their writing

Analysis

The correct answer is (D). The passage points out the disadvantages and advantages of both simple and complex prose and concludes with the reminder that the readers will determine which is appropriate. The passage does not favor one style over another as in (A) and (C), nor does it say that all writing should be both simple and complex (E). It argues for a style suitable to the audience.

Form of Argumentation

In this type of question, you are asked to decide what type of argument, logic, or reasoning the author is using (example, exaggeration, deduction, induction, etc.).

To answer this type of question, carefully follow the author's line of reasoning while focusing on his or her intent or purpose. Notice how the author starts and finishes the argument. Consider what the author has concluded or proved, or what point has been made or argued. Watch "if" and "how" specific points or examples are used in relation to more general statements.

EXAMPLE 1

Once again, refer to the argument used earlier concerning legislation.

Recent studies show that the general public is unaware of most new legislation and doesn't understand 99% of the remaining legislation. This is mainly because of the public's inattention and lack of interest.

To make the point, the author of this statement

(A) gives a general statement followed by supporting facts

(B) argues by pointing out the effects and then the cause

(C) uses specific examples to disprove an argument

(D) infers an outcome and then attempts to support that outcome

(E) assumes the conclusion is true and uses circular reasoning to state the premise

Analysis

The correct answer is (B). The author starts by making specific points about the general public. It is "unaware of most new legislation and doesn't understand 99% of the remaining legislation." This is followed by a statement of the cause: "This is mainly because of the public's inattention and lack of interest."

EXAMPLE 2

Editorial: In the twelfth century, people used the abacus (a simple device made of beads strung on wire) to perform complex calculations. Today we use electronic calculators, and the abacus has become obsolete. In fifty or one hundred years, the calculator will be as quaint and outmoded as the abacus. Every invention of man, every breakthrough of science will, if we wait long enough, be out of date and used no longer.

Which one of the following is a questionable technique used in the argument in this passage?

(A) It ignores the fact that the abacus is still in use in Asia.

(B) It generalizes from a single instance of obsolescence.

(C) It makes a prediction without specifying exactly when the prediction will come true.

(D) It mistakes a minor premise for a major premise and so deduces erroneously.

(E) It considers only scientific advances, but some inventions are not related to science.

Analysis

The correct answer is (B). The question calls for a questionable technique. The error here is the hasty generalization, based on a single instance of obsolescence. (A), (C), and (E) may be true but they do not point to a technique of argument. (D) is irrelevant and not true of this argument, which is not a syllogism.

Strengthening or Weakening the Author's Statement or Conclusion

This question type is very common on the LSAT. Here you are given a short reading passage or paragraph followed by the question "Which of the following would strengthen the author's statement the most?" or "Which of the following would most weaken the author's statement?" (Both of these questions may be asked. There are many possible varieties of this question type: "least likely to weaken," "strongest criticism of," and so on).

You may find it helpful to preread, or read the question before reading the short paragraph. Focus on the major point of the statement and "how" or "if" it is supported. Be aware of the strength of the statement or argument. Is it a harsh criticism of a certain system? Is it a mildly persuasive paragraph? What point is the author trying to make in supporting this cause?

Remember to always read actively, marking key words or phrases.

EXAMPLE 1

Psychiatrists and laypeople agree that the best sort of adjustment is founded upon an acceptance of reality, rather than an escape from it.

Which one of the following would probably most weaken the author's point?

(A) Psychiatrists and laypeople do not often agree.
(B) Reality is difficult to define.
(C) Escaping reality has worked for many.
(D) Accepting reality is often traumatic.
(E) Psychiatrists' definition of reality and laypeople's definition of reality are different.

Analysis

The correct answer is (C). If escaping reality has worked for many, then it becomes more difficult to defend the acceptance of reality theory. (A) would probably strengthen the point being made. (B) could strengthen or weaken the point. (D) and (E) are irrelevant.

EXAMPLE 2

The likelihood of America's exhausting her natural resources is growing less. All kinds of waste are being reworked and new uses are constantly being found for almost everything. We are getting more use out of our goods and are making many new by-products out of what was formerly thrown away. It is, therefore, unnecessary to continue to ban logging in national parks, nature reserves, or areas inhabited by endangered species of animals.

Which one of the following most seriously undermines the conclusion of this argument?

(A) The increasing amount of recycled material made available each year is equal to one-tenth of the increasing amount of natural material consumed annually.
(B) Recent studies have shown that the number of endangered animals throughout the world fluctuates sharply and is chiefly determined by changes in weather conditions.
(C) The logging industry contributes huge sums of money to the political campaigns in states where it has a financial interest.
(D) The techniques that make recycling possible are constantly improved so that more is reclaimed for lower costs each year.
(E) Political contributions by the recycling industry are now greater than those of the logging or animal protection interests.

Analysis

The correct answer is (A). First, remember to circle the words undermines and conclusion to help you focus on what you're looking for. Now let's look at the choices. (D) would support rather than undermine the conclusion. (B), (C), and (E) neither support nor weaken the argument, though with more information (C) and (E) might be relevant. If the recycled materials are equal to only one-tenth of the natural materials lost each year, the argument is seriously injured.

EXAMPLE 3

Some scientists have proposed that, over two hundred million years ago, one giant land mass—rather than various continents and islands—covered one-third of the earth. Long before there was any human life, and over vast periods of time, islands and continents drifted apart. Australia was the first to separate, while South America and Africa were late in splitting apart. Some islands, of course, were formed by volcanoes and were never part of the great land mass.

All the following would support the author's claim EXCEPT

(A) Many of the plants of the South American rain forests are markedly similar to those of the African rain forest.

(B) Australia has more animals that are not found on any other continent than have several of the much larger continents.

(C) Volcanic islands like Hawaii have ecosystems very different from those of continental lands with the same average temperature.

(D) The plants of similar conditions in South America have less in common with those of Australia than with those of Asia, Africa, or Europe.

(E) The primitive languages of Australia are unlike those of Africa, which resemble those of South America.

Analysis

The correct answer is (E). If Australia was the first continent to separate, it would follow that its flora and fauna would develop in isolation over a longer period of time. Similarly, we may expect the plants and animals of South America and Africa that separated later to be more alike. (A), (B), and (D) support these ideas. That the separately developed islands are different is also in accord with the passage. However, the languages of all the continents would have developed in isolation, since man did not evolve until after the break-up of the land mass, and it is surprising that African and South American languages are similar. Human likeness or difference are irrelevant to the claims of the passage.

EXAMPLE 4

Columnist: In America, a baseball game should be described as a series of solo performances: at any given moment, attention is focused on one player and one play. On the other hand, soccer involves all of the team most of the time: each player interacts with others constantly, so that no single individual seems responsible for success or failure. It is because spectators prefer concentrating on individual personalities that baseball remains a much more popular spectator sport than soccer.

Which one of the following, if true, can best be used to undermine the conclusion of this argument?

(A) Soccer is more popular with spectators in France than baseball.

(B) Among the ten most televised sports in America, by far the most watched is football, and the least watched are tennis and bowling.

(C) Many people watch only the baseball teams of the city in which they live and for whom they root.

(D) Compared to football and basketball, baseball games are much cheaper to attend.

(E) In some sections of the United States, soccer leagues for children under fifteen are more popular than Little League baseball.

Analysis

The correct answer is (B). The weakness of this argument is not its claim that baseball is more popular than soccer with spectators in America. This is true from the passage. The weakness is its claim that the reason for baseball's greater popularity is that it is an individual performance rather than a team sport. (B) cites a team sport that is more watched than baseball and two solo performance sports that are not very popular. (A) makes a good point, but the passage is concerned with spectators "in America." Even if (C) is true, it may be that these people watch the teams to see individual performances. (D) is true, but not as powerful a criticism as (B). (E) does not necessarily deal with spectators; popularity could refer to the number of participants.

Author Assumptions, Presuppositions, Underlying Principles

This is another very common question type in the Logical Reasoning section. Here you are again given a short reading passage or paragraph followed by questions asking about the author's possible assumptions, presuppositions, or underlying principles.

To answer this question type, you may wish to first read the question actively. Make a careful note of what part of the paragraph the question refers to. Is the question asking about the conclusion of the passage? (Which of the following assumptions must be made for the author to reasonably arrive at the stated conclusion?) Or about the opening statement? Or about the complete paragraph? (The complete paragraph may be only one or two sentences.)

Keep in mind that assumptions and presuppositions are things taken for granted, or supposed as facts. In the same sense, an underlying principle is the basis for the original statement. It is necessary for the conclusion to be logical. There may be a number of assumptions possible, but in most cases you are looking for the major assumption, not a minor one. In some cases the major assumption will be evident; you will know what the author is assuming before you even get to the answer choices. In other cases, the assumptions are more subtle, and the answer choices will be helpful by stating them for you.

EXAMPLE 1

Use the statement in Example 1 on page 155:

Psychiatrists and laypeople agree that the best sort of adjustment is founded upon acceptance of reality, rather than an escape from it.

The author of this statement assumes that

(A) there is only one sort of adjustment
(B) escaping reality is possible
(C) psychiatrists and laypeople disagree on most things
(D) psychiatrists never escape reality
(E) laypeople need many sorts of adjustments

Analysis

The correct answer is (B). In stating "rather than an escape from it [reality]," the author is assuming that escaping reality is possible.

EXAMPLE 2

It has been said that a weed is a flower whose virtue has not yet been discovered. As if to prove this point, a homeowner who was tired of constantly maintaining a pretty lawn and shrubbery decided to let weeds run wild in his yard. The result, so far, has been an array of lively shapes and colors. If everyone in the neighborhood would follow this leader, we could save time, effort, money, and water, and soon have one of the most unusual neighborhoods in the city.

Which one of the following is a basic assumption on which this argument depends?

(A) The neighborhood values convenience more than maintaining an attractive environment.

(B) All the other yards will look like the first homeowner's if the weeds are allowed to run wild.

(C) Allowing the weeds to take over will save money spent on maintaining a lawn.

(D) Other neighborhoods in the city will not follow the example of this neighborhood.

(E) The loss of jobs or revenue to gardeners and garden supply businesses is not so important as the time and money that will be saved.

Analysis

The correct answer is (A). Although all five of the propositions here may well be true, it is (A) that is the basic assumption of the argument. No one who highly values an attractive lawn and yard will want to let weeds take over, so for the argument to have any validity, its speaker must assume that an audience willing to allow the gain in convenience outweighs the loss in appearance of the neighborhood.

EXAMPLE 3

Four of the candidates for reelection in this state had been named among those who had more than 100 overdrafts on the House Bank. Two were Democrats, one was a Republican and one an Independent. One other Republican incumbent candidate had bounced over 50 checks. All of the Democrats favored increased federal spending on education and increased government regulation of firearms, while the Republicans opposed these measures. Of the five incumbents, only the Independent candidate was reelected.

Which one of the following is the most likely principle upon which the majority of voters cast their votes in the elections?

(A) The voters opposed any candidate who had more than 49 overdrafts on the House Bank.

(B) The voters opposed any candidates who favored increased federal spending.

(C) The voters opposed reelection of any members of the two major parties who bounced 50 or more checks.

(D) The voters opposed any candidate who favored increased firearms control.

(E) The voters opposed any candidate who opposed firearms legislation.

Analysis

The correct answer is (C). Since the Independent also bounced more than 100 checks, that cannot be the reason for the defeat of the other four candidates. Since we do not know how the Independent candidate stands on spending for education or on firearms regulation, the only factor to explain his victory is his not belonging to one of the two major parties.

EXAMPLE 4

Time and again studies have shown that 85% of the young adults sent to special juvenile prison farms lead productive lives when they are released. On the other hand, 85% of young adults of the same age who are sent to prisons for adults later return to prisons. The bad influence of the older inmates is permanent. We must expand the number of special juvenile prison farms so that all young adults convicted of crimes can be sent to a penal institution that will not maim them for life.

Which one of the following principles most helps to justify this argument?

(A) It is more expensive to house adult prisoners in prisons than to house young adults on prison farms.

(B) Young adults exposed to bad role models will imitate these models.

(C) Some young adults who are sent to prison farms later become criminals who are sent to prisons for adults.

(D) Some of the young adults who are sent to prisons for adults become productive members of society and never return to prison.

(E) Young adults who have been sent to prison farms on two occasions are more likely to return to prison than young adults who have been sent to prison farms only once.

Analysis

The correct answer is (B). This principle is the basis of the argument to prevent young adults from being exposed to adult felons. If the hope of penologists is to reintegrate young adults into society, these young adults must be kept away from bad models they are likely to imitate. (C) and (D) may be true, but they do not justify the argument. (A) is a practical matter, not a principle to justify the case. (E) would not justify the argument, and might, in fact, be used against it.

EXAMPLE 5

Drunken drivers in our state kill or maim people every day. I understand that only one out of 500 drunken drivers on the highway is flagged down by the police. Also, 50% of these arrests are made on four holiday weekends when the policing of highways is greatly increased. With these odds, I can afford to drink heavily and drive, as long as I am careful not to do so on holiday weekends.

Which one of the following is a necessary premise for the speaker's conclusion in the paragraph above?

(A) The odds against being arrested from drunken driving are greater on weekends than on weekdays.

(B) Fear of arrest is a good reason not to drink and drive.

(C) All that drunken drivers need to fear is being arrested.

(D) The chances of being arrested for drunken driving are greatest on four holiday weekends.

(E) The penalties for drunken driving are often incommensurate with the dangers to the public.

Analysis

The correct answer is (C). The speaker of this passage notes that drunk driving can kill and maim, but his concern is solely with the chances of his being arrested. His conclusion is based on the assumption that no other consequence of drunk driving need trouble him. (A), (B), (D), and (E) are not untrue, but they are not the underlying principle in the speaker's conclusion.

Inferences and Implications

In this very common question type you are asked to "read between the lines." Inferences and implications are not expressed in words in the passage, but may be fairly understood from the passage. If you draw or infer something from a passage, it is called an <u>inference</u>. From the author's point of view, if he or she imparts or implies something, it is called an <u>implication</u>. For the purposes of your exam, you should not be concerned with the differences in the terms, but in understanding what unstated information is in the passage. As you read the passage, focus on the main idea, what the author is suggesting but not actually saying, and what information you can be drawing.

As you approach the choices in inference and implication questions, look for the most direct answer that is not explicitly stated. That is the one that most directly ties back into the passage. Remember that your inference is NOT directly stated in the passage, but is implied by the passage.

EXAMPLE 1

Since 1890, the federal government and the individual states have passed a number of laws against corrupt political practices. But today many feel that political corruption is a regular occurrence, and deeply distrust their public leaders.

Each of the following can be reasonably inferred from the passage EXCEPT

(A) Corrupt political practices have been going on for many years.

(B) The laws against corrupt political practices have not been effective.

   (C) The federal government and the individual states are against corrupt political practices.

   (D) Many public leaders may be distrusted even though they are not corrupt.

   (E) Leaders in private industry are also involved in corrupt political practices.

Analysis

The correct answer is (E). Since the passage does not address leaders in private industry, you could not reasonably make an inference regarding their practices. Though (A), (B), (C), and (D) are not stated, all of them are reasonable inferences from the passage.

EXAMPLE 2

Teacher: **The ability to recognize grammar and usage errors in the writing of others is not the same as the ability to see such errors in one's own writing.**

The author of this statement implies that

   (A) a writer may not be aware of his own errors

   (B) grammar and usage errors are difficult to correct

   (C) grammar and usage errors are very common

   (D) one often has many abilities

   (E) recognizing grammar and usage errors and writing correctly use two different abilities

Analysis

The correct answer is (A). The author's statement points out that recognizing errors in others' work involves a different ability than recognizing errors in one's own work. Since these abilities are different, writers may not possess both abilities and therefore may not be aware of their own errors. (B) is irrelevant because its focus is "difficulty to correct," which is not addressed. (C) and (D) are incorrect because they are too general, addressing items that are not specific to the statement. (E), which is a common mistake, simply restates information in the statement.

EXAMPLE 3

A poll of journalists who were involved in the Senate campaign revealed that 80% believed Senator Smith's campaign was damaged by press reports about his record during his last six years in office. His opponent, the recently narrowly elected Senator Jones, believes he was benefited by press coverage of his campaign. Journalists believe the election was covered without bias, and the Senator was defeated because of his record, not, as he insists, because of unfair press coverage. Ninety percent of the voters who supported Senator Smith believe the press was unfair in this election, while 85% of the voters who supported Senator Jones thought the coverage free of any bias.

Which one of the following can be inferred from this passage?

(A) The press coverage of the Senate election was free from bias.

(B) Senator Smith lost the election because the press reported his record accurately.

(C) The public's view of the objectivity of the press is likely to be influenced by the election results.

(D) The election was close because of different perceptions of the bias of the press.

(E) Journalists are probably the best judges of bias in political campaign reportage.

Analysis

The correct answer is (C). We cannot be sure whether or not the reporting of the press was biased since the election was close and the pros and cons are nearly equal. The press cannot be counted on to be objective, so (A), (B), and (E) are not reasonable inferences. The large percentage of each candidate's supporters, whose views of the press coincide with the success or defeat of their candidates, strongly support the inference of (C). Whether or not (D) is true, we cannot tell.

Deductions

You may be asked to deduce information from a passage. Deductions are arrived at or attained from general premises—drawing information to a specific piece of information—from general laws to specific cases. In a deduction, if the general premises are true, then the deduction is necessarily true.

To answer this question type you may wish to first actively read the question. Focus on the general premises to see where they lead. As you continue reading, try to follow the logic as it narrows the possibilities of what must be true.

EXAMPLE 1

Years ago, a nationwide poll concluded that there are more televisions than there are bathtubs in American homes. No doubt that fact remains today, especially in light of the growing popularity of home computers. Now, in addition to owning televisions for entertainment, more and more families are purchasing TV monitors for use with a personal computer. We can safely guess that there are still many more people staring at a picture tube than singing in the shower.

Which one of the following statements can be deduced from this passage?

(A) Personal computers probably cost less than installing a shower or a bathtub.

(B) People can wash themselves without a tub or shower, but they cannot watch television unless they own a television set.

(C) TV monitors will work with personal computers in place of regular computer monitors.

(D) As many computers are sold today as television sets a few years ago.

(E) More television monitors are now used with personal computers than are used to watch commercial television broadcasts.

Analysis

The correct answer is (C). Though (A) and (B) may well be true, they are not deductions that we can make from the information in the passage. But (C) can be deduced since, "more and more families are purchasing TV monitors for use with a personal computer." TV monitors must work with these computers. Otherwise, people would not buy them for that purpose. (D) and (E) may or may not be true, but they are not deductions from the passage, simply additional information.

EXAMPLE 2

Antifreeze lowers the melting point of any liquid to which it is added so that the liquid will not freeze in cold weather. It is commonly used to maintain the cooling system in automobile radiators. Of course, the weather may become so cold that even antifreeze is not effective, but such a severe climatic condition rarely occurs in well-traveled places.

Which one of the following can be deduced from the passage?

(A) Well-traveled places have means of transportation other than automobiles.

(B) Antifreeze does not lower the melting point of certain liquids in extreme conditions.

(C) Severe climatic conditions rarely occur.

(D) It is not often that many travelers who use antifreeze have their cooling systems freeze.

(E) Antifreeze raises the melting point of some liquids.

Analysis

The correct answer is (D). Since severe climatic conditions rarely occur in well-traveled places, it is necessarily true that "It is not often that many travelers who use antifreeze have their cooling systems freeze." (A) mentions other means of transportation, which is not addressed in the passage. (B) refers to "certain" liquids, which again are not addressed. You cannot deduce that "severe climatic conditions rarely occur" (C), because the passage alludes to only well-traveled places. (E) discusses raising the melting point, which is irrelevant to the passage.

EXAMPLE 3

> Sociologists have noted that children today are less "childish" than ever; when they are still very young, perhaps only six or seven years old, children are already mimicking adult fashions and leading relatively independent lives. Dressed in designer jeans, an elementary school child is likely to spend much of every day fending for herself, taking charge of her own life while waiting for her working parents to arrive home. Children become less dependent on adults for their day-to-day decisions.

> From the passage above, since children are less dependent on adults for their day-to-day decisions, it must be true that

> (A) children need more supervision
> (B) children are growing up faster
> (C) children should be completely independent
> (D) parents should not leave children home alone
> (E) parents need to spend more "quality time" with their children

Analysis

The correct answer is (B). Since children today are "less childish than ever," and since they are "less dependent on adults for their day-to-day decisions," they must be "growing up" faster. Although (A), (D), and (E) are probably true, they are not necessarily true and therefore cannot be deduced from the passage.

Parallel Reasoning or Similarity of Logic

In this type you will be given a statement or statements and asked to select the statements that most nearly parallel the originals or use similar logic. First, you should decide whether the original statement is valid. (But don't take too much time on this first step because some of the others may tip you off to the correct choice.) If the statement is valid, your choice must be a valid statement. If the statement is invalid, your choice must be an invalid one. Your choice must preserve the same relationship or comparison.

Second, the direction of connections is important—general to specific (deduction), specific to general (induction), quality to thing, thing to quality, and so on.

Third, the tone of the argument should be the same. If the original has a negative slant, has a positive slant, or changes from negative to positive, then so must your choice.

Fourth, the order of each element is important. Remember: Corresponding elements must be in the same order as the original.

It may be helpful to substitute letters for complex terms or phrases, to simplify confusing situations and help you avoid getting lost in the wording. Direction and order are usually more easily followed by letter substitution.

Remember: Don't correct or alter the original; just reproduce the reasoning.

EXAMPLE 1

Alex said, "All lemons I have tasted are sour; therefore all lemons are sour."

Which one of the following most closely parallels the logic of the above statement?

(A) I have eaten pickles four times and I got sick each time; therefore, if I eat another pickle, I will get sick.
(B) My income has increased each year for the past four years; therefore, it will increase again next year.
(C) I sped to work every day last week and I did not get a ticket; therefore, they do not give tickets for speeding around here any more.
(D) All flormids are green. This moncle is red; therefore, it is not a flormid.
(E) Every teacher I had in school was mean; therefore, all teachers are mean.

Analysis

The correct answer is (E). First, the logic of the original is faulty; therefore, the correct choice must also be faulty, eliminating (D). Next, notice the direction of connections: generalization from a *few* experiences → generalization about *all* similar experiences. (A) and (B) each project the result of a few past experiences to only ONE similar experience. (C) starts from a few experiences, but finishes with a result that implies a change in a specific area. You could assume that "they" used to give tickets here.

EXAMPLE 2

Some serious novelists prefer scientific studies to literary studies. All science fiction writers are more interested in science than in literature. Therefore, some serious novelists are science fiction writers.

Which one of the following is most closely parallel to the flawed reasoning in the argument above?

(A) All trees have leaves. Some cactuses have leaves. Therefore, all trees are cactuses.

(B) All orchestras include violins and all chamber groups include violins. Therefore, some chamber groups are orchestras.

(C) Some animals sleep through the winter and some animals sleep through the summer. Therefore, all animals sleep through either the summer or the winter.

(D) All hotels have restaurants. Some shopping malls have restaurants. Therefore, some shopping malls are hotels.

(E) Some sweaters in this store are made of cotton. All shirts in this store are made of cotton. Therefore, all the wearing apparel in this store is made of cotton.

Analysis

The correct answer is (D). The stem asserts that all science fiction writers prefer science to literature and so do some serious novelists. It then concludes that some serious novelists must be science fiction writers. The "some serious novelists" who prefer science do not have to be science fiction writers, though they share a preference with them. The stem would have to say only science fiction writers prefer science to make this conclusion certain. The two terms used in the stem are "all" and "some," so we can exclude (B) and (C), which use "all" and "all" and "some" and "some." (D), though it gives the "some" term first and the "all" term second, is parallel to the passage.

EXAMPLE 3
(with a slight twist)

Why do you want to stop smoking?

Which one of the following most closely parallels the reasoning of this question?

(A) Why do you want to go to Italy?
(B) When will you decide on the offer?
(C) Will you ever play cards again?
(D) When do you want to learn to play tennis?
(E) Which desk do you like better?

Analysis

The correct answer is (C). This response is the only one that implies that the *action has already taken place*, as in the original question. To stop smoking, one must have been smoking *before*. To stop playing cards, one must have been playing cards *before*. (A) appears to be the closest, but this is only true regarding sentence structure, not reasoning. (B) and (D) are asking about future plans without implying anything about past actions. (D) does imply past lack of action. (E) merely asks for a comparison.

Argument Exchange

In this question type, two or more speakers are exchanging arguments or merely discussing a situation. You will then be asked to choose the statement that most strengthens or weakens either argument. Or you may be asked to find the inconsistency or flaw in an argument, or to identify the form of argument. In some instances you will be asked to interpret what one speaker might have thought the other meant by his response.

To answer these questions, you should first evaluate the strength and completeness of the statements. Are they general or specific? Do they use absolutes? Are they consistent?

Second, evaluate the relationship between responses. What kind of response did the first statement elicit from the second speaker?

Third, evaluate the intentions of the author in making his remarks. What was his purpose?

EXAMPLE 1

Tom: It is impossible to hit off the Yankee pitcher Turley.

Jim: You're just saying that because he struck you out three times yesterday.

Which one of the following would strengthen Tom's argument most?

(A) Tom is a good hitter.
(B) Turley pitched a no-hitter yesterday.
(C) Tom has not struck out three times in a game all season.
(D) Tom has not struck out all season.
(E) Turley has not given up a hit to Jim or Tom all season.

Analysis

The correct answer is (B). Tom's is a general statement about Turley's relationship to all hitters. All choices except (B) mention only Tom or Jim, not hitters in general.

EXAMPLE 2

Sid: The recent popularity of hot-air ballooning and bungee-jumping are instances of the latest quest for new types of adventure in the modern world.

Phil: That's ridiculous! Certainly these brightly colored floating globes of air are not modern inventions; rather, they recall the spectacle of county fairs and carnivals from the turn of the century.

Sid: Well, bungee-jumping wasn't around at the turn of the century.

Phil's best counter to Sid's last statement would be

(A) But bungee-jumping is used in fairs and carnivals.
(B) No, bungee-jumping is merely a newer version of a Polynesian ritual hundreds of years old.
(C) You do know that bungee-jumping is more dangerous than hot-air ballooning.
(D) Yes, but hot-air ballooning is more popular than bungee-jumping.
(E) No, but lots of other inventions are adventurous.

Analysis

The correct answer is (B). Sid's point is that these modern adventures are with modern inventions. His last statement is trying to say that bungee-jumping is modern. Phil's best counter would be to point out that bungee-jumping is not new.

EXAMPLE 3

Al: **To be a good parent, one must be patient.**
Bill: **That's not so. It takes much more than patience to be a good parent.**

Bill has understood Al's statement to mean that

(A) if a person is a good parent, he or she will be patient
(B) if a person is patient, he or she will make a good parent
(C) some patient people make good parents
(D) some good parents are patient
(E) a person cannot be a good parent unless he or she is patient

Analysis

The correct answer is (B). This is a problem in grasping an understanding of necessary and sufficient conditions. Al states that if one is a good parent then one is patient. Patience is necessary to be a good parent. However, Bill's response shows that he (Bill) has inferred that Al considers patience to be sufficient to be a good parent, not just a necessary condition. (B) reflects Bill's mistaken inference. (A) is incorrect because it accurately describes Al's statement. (C) and (D) are incorrect because Al's statement concerns "any" or "all" persons and not "some." (E) is incorrect because it is equivalent to (A) and thus accurately describes Al's statement.

Syllogistic Reasoning

Syllogistic reasoning is a slightly more formal type of reasoning. It deals with an argument that has two premises and a conclusion. This type of question gives you short propositions (premises) and asks you to draw conclusions, valid or invalid. You may be expected to evaluate assumptions—information that is or is not assumed.

First, if possible, simplify the propositions to assist your understanding. Second, draw diagrams (Venn diagrams; see p. 116 in Chapter 3), if possible. Third, replace phrases or words with letters to help yourself follow the logic.

EXAMPLE 1

All couples who have children are happy.
All couples either have children or are happy.

Assuming the above to be true, which one of the following CANNOT be true?

(A) All couples are happy.
(B) Some couples who are happy have children.
(C) Some couples who have children are not happy.
(D) Some couples have happy children.
(E) Children of happy couples are happy.

Analysis

The correct answer is (C). If all couples who have children are happy, and if all couples who don't have children are happy, then all couples are happy. Simplifying the two statements to "all couples are happy" makes this question much more direct and easier to handle. Thus (C) is false, since it contradicts the first statement; we have no information about children.

EXAMPLE 2

All As are Bs.
Some Cs are As.

Which one of the following is warranted based upon the above?

(A) All Bs are As.
(B) Some Cs are Bs.
(C) All Bs are Cs
(D) No Bs are As.
(E) All Cs are Bs.

Analysis

The correct choice is (B). Here is a diagram of the original information:

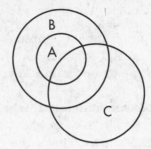

With this diagram, the following is evident:

(A) "All Bs are As" is false.
(B) "Some Cs are Bs" is true.
(C) "All Bs are Cs" is false.
(D) "No Bs are As" is false. If all As are Bs, then some Bs must be As.
(E) "All Cs are Bs" is false.

EXAMPLE 3

In this question, the second premise shows up in the actual question.

If the Dodgers do not finally win a championship for their fans this season, the team's manager will definitely not return to guide the club next year.

It follows logically from the statement above that, if the Dodgers win a championship this season, then next year the team's manager

(A) will definitely not return
(B) will probably not return
(C) will probably return
(D) will definitely return
(E) may or may not return

Analysis

The correct answer is (E). The passage states that if the Dodgers do not win the championship [condition A], then the manager will not return [condition B]. Thus we have if A then B. The question then asks, what follows if they *do* win the championship [a negation of condition A]? If A implies B, the negation of A [if the Dodgers do win the championship] does *not* imply the negation of B [the manager will return]. Hence, condition A or not A (win or lose) may be the case; the manager may or may not return. (C) is possible, but he may also not return. All we know for sure is that if he loses, he positively won't return.

Conclusions

Here you will be given a list of conditionals, statements, or a short paragraph, and asked to follow the logic to reach a valid conclusion.

In this type, you will first want to underline key terms to eliminate looking at excess wording.

Second, mark the direction of each statement. Where does it start and end? What connection is it making?

Third, look for the "kicker" statement. That's the one that starts the chain reaction; it gives you the information to work with other statements.

If there is no "kicker" statement, carefully check how the information given in one statement is relative to the information given in the next statement. This relationship may be enough to help you understand the reasoning.

In checking the validity of a conclusion, you should be looking for a key statement that leads you as directly as possible to that conclusion. Sometimes, if the choices don't start with the word "therefore," you may wish to insert the word "therefore" before the answer choices to help you see which one follows logically.

EXAMPLE 1

Senator Jones will vote for the Pork bill if he is reelected. If the Pork bill passes, then Senator Jones was not reelected. Senator Jones was reelected.

Which one of the following can be concluded from these statements?

(A) Senator Jones assisted in the passage of the Pork bill.
(B) The passage of the Pork bill carried Senator Jones to victory.
(C) Senator Jones voted against the Pork bill, but it passed anyway.
(D) The Pork bill didn't pass, even though Senator Jones voted for it.
(E) The Pork bill was defeated by a large majority.

Analysis

The correct answer is (D). Notice that the "kicker" statement that started the chain reaction is "Senator Jones was reelected." From this, we know that he voted for the Pork bill. But the Pork bill could not have passed; otherwise, he could not have been reelected.

EXAMPLE 2

Meteorology may qualify as a science, but there is a great deal of guesswork involved as well. Even with increased knowledge about wind currents and weather patterns, and the most sophisticated equipment, forecasters' predictions are often wrong. Even the movement of a phenomenon as prominent as a hurricane cannot be determined very far in advance.

Which one of the following is the best conclusion to the passage?

- (A) Therefore, we should be especially skeptical of weather predictions for the distant future.
- (B) Therefore, we cannot control the weather, but we can predict it.
- (C) Therefore, even though we cannot accurately predict the weather now, it will be possible in the near future.
- (D) Therefore, since we cannot predict the weather, our aim should be to control it.
- (E) Therefore, meteorology is a worthless science.

Analysis

The correct answer is (A). The passage points out that, although we can to some extent predict the weather, we are often wrong. This leads us to the conclusion that we cannot predict far in advance. (A) is the best answer. (B) and (D) do not follow since the passage does not mention controlling the weather. (C) does not follow since the passage does not address our gaining additional knowledge or more sophisticated equipment to help us in the future. The passage does not condemn meteorology, so (E) can be eliminated.

Logical Flaws

This common question type gives you a passage, statement, or argument, and asks you to find, understand, analyze, or name the type of flaw in the reasoning.

As you watch for logical flaws, notice that some are very evident, especially if the passage or argument seems nonsensical. Others are very subtle, and need a second look. If you don't spot the flaw immediately upon reading the passage, let the choices help. Remember, the choices are showing you some possibilities.

Also, reading the question first will stop you from trying to make complete sense from a nonsensical passage, or trying to follow the logic or reasoning when, by design of the question, it does not follow. You see that the question itself warned you that there was a flaw in the reasoning.

EXAMPLE 1

The new American revolution is an electronic one. Advances in sophisticated circuitry have yielded more gadgets than anyone could have imagined only a few years ago: calculators as small as a wristwatch and automobile dashboards full of digital readouts are two of the many products that have enhanced the quality of life. But we may become so dependent on solid-state circuits to do our thinking that we may forget how to do it ourselves. Certain birds living on islands where there were no predators have, in time, lost their ability to fly. We may just as easily lose the ability to perform even the simplest mathematical calculation without the aid of an electronic gadget.

Which one of the following best describes the flaw in the reasoning in this passage?

    (A) It assumes that a temporal sequence implies a causal relation.

    (B) It generalizes from one instance to every other instance of the same type.

    (C) It draws an analogy between two very different situations.

    (D) It wrongly assumes that no new and better electronic devices will be invented.

    (E) It assumes that what happens in America also happens in the rest of the world.

Analysis

The correct answer is (C). The flaw in the reasoning here is the comparison of two wholly unlike situations. The analogy compares men and birds and compares an event in the evolutionary history of certain birds that happened under unique circumstances over vast periods of time to what is supposed to be similar situations in the modern world, but which has in fact no real similarity.

EXAMPLE 2

With the continued water shortage in our area, the Water Department has had to restrict the use of water during daylight hours and to increase the cost of water to consumers. An average water bill has risen twenty-four dollars a year for three years in a row. Three years from now, our water costs will be astronomical.

A major flaw in the reasoning is that it

    (A) relies upon figures that are imprecise to support a conclusion

    (B) fails to indicate exactly how high expenses will be in three years

    (C) assumes the conditions of the past three years will continue

    (D) overlooks the possibility that conservation methods may improve in the next five years

    (E) ignores the likelihood of the high cost driving down the water usage

Analysis

The correct answer is (C). To follow the author's line of reasoning, the author must assume that "the conditions of the past three years will continue." This assumption is flawed since the conditions could change. The conclusion is therefore based on a faulty assumption.

EXAMPLE 3

In 1982 and 1983, when the limit on class size in grades 7, 8, and 9 was 25, our junior high school students had an average reading score of 79 and an average math score of 75 in the state tests administered at the end of grade 9. But, in 1984 and 1985, when the limit on class size was raised to 28, our junior high school students had average scores of 75 in the state reading tests and 75 in the state math tests. The increase in class size limitations has brought about the decline in state test scores.

Which one of the following is a major flaw in the reasoning in this passage?

(A) The author believes that test scores are accurate.
(B) The author fails to realize that some students' math test scores have not declined, though the average has.
(C) The author regards scores in math tests more important than scores in reading.
(D) The author assumes class size has caused the variation in test scores.
(E) The author does not know whether or not class size actually increased.

Analysis

The correct answer is (D). Since the class size limitations were increased and only the reading scores decreased, the author came to the conclusion that class size limitations caused the decline. But the math scores did not decrease, which would lead one to believe other factors are involved in the scores' decline. Also, because there were different class size limitations does not mean the sizes of the classes were different. The author's reasoning is flawed by his assumption that class size caused the variation. (E) is a fact, but is not the flaw in the author's reasoning.

Situation Analysis

This new question type requires you to select the situation, from the ones given, that most appropriately illustrates a principle expressed by the analysis of the situation in the passage.

To answer this question type, you should focus on the analysis and how it applies to the situation. After reading the situation, you may wish to read the analysis twice before proceeding to the question and the choices.

EXAMPLE 1

Situation: In order to discourage the use of tobacco products, the state imposes a 50-cent tax on each package of cigarettes. It employs the revenues generated by the cigarette tax to fund television advertisements whose purpose is to deteteenagers from smoking.

Analysis: The objective of both is to reduce smoking, and the success of the first may help to achieve the objective of the second.

The analysis provided for the situation above would be most appropriate in which one of the following situations?

(A) In order to reduce the number of cars on the five major highways into the city, the transportation board sets aside one lane in each direction for the exclusive use of cars carrying two or more passengers. To keep these lanes moving at higher speeds, taxis and buses are not allowed to use them.

(B) In order to stem the rising crime rate, the city council approves a budget that spends $600 million to increase the size of the police force. To avoid a tax increase, the money for the additional officer is provided by reducing the funding of gang prevention and neighborhood watch programs.

(C) In an effort to get rid of the rodents that have been feeding on the grain stored in his barn, Mr. McDonald buys five cats to live in the barn. To keep the cats warm and inside the barn, he carefully repairs all of the holes in the doors and walls where the wood has weathered.

(D) In order to reduce its liability insurance rates, the Ace Car Rental Agency no longer allows drivers under the age of twenty-one or over the age of seventy-five to drive its trucks and cars. To make up for the lost revenues, it offers lower rates on weekend rentals.

(E) To reduce the air pollution caused by automobile emissions, the city establishes bicycle lanes on many of the roads from the suburbs to the downtown working areas. To provide space for the bicycle lanes without the expense of widening the roads, the number of car lanes is reduced by one in all of the highways with multiple lanes.

Analysis

The correct answer is (C). As the increased taxes and the television advertising both contribute to the reduction of smoking, so the use of cats to prey on the grain-eating rodents, and the repairs to the barn that will keep the cats in and keep rodents out will both contribute to the preservation of the grain.

In (A), the restriction may or may not reduce the number of cars on the highways. By denying buses and taxis the use of the faster lanes, the city may actually increase the number of cars on the highways. There is no certainty that either of the two steps will work, and the success of the one will not contribute to the success of the other.

In (B), the reduction of funds that support gang- prevention and neighborhood watch programs will probably result in an increase in crime, rather then encourage its reduction.

Though it is possible that the reduction of weekend rental rates (D) may make up for lost revenues, the two objectives are not closely related, and success in the one will no contribute to success in the other.

In (E), if the automobiles must spend more time on the road because of increased congestion that results from the loss of a driving lane, air pollution will not be reduced.

EXAMPLE 2

Situation: In order to increase its advertising revenues, radio station WJBW changes its format from all news to the rap and salsa music that is popular with the younger listeners that advertisers prefer. To accommodate the revised format, the station reduces the time for commercial messages from 16 to 12 minutes each hour.
Analysis: The success of the first objective is undermined by meeting the requirements of the second.

The analysis provided for the situation above would be most appropriate in which one of the following situations?

(A) In order to improve profitability, Fox Produce Company raises only a popular yellow tomato that sells at a higher price than the red. It uses the profits from sales to expand the greenhouses in which it develops seedlings of the yellow tomato.

(B) The aquarium raises its fees in order to finance the construction of a wing to exhibit tropical jellyfish. In order to educate the public, its new Web site is devoted to information about jellyfish of the world's oceans.

(C) In order to increase her disposable income, Mrs. Scudder gives used clothing, books, and furniture to the church thrift shop for which she receives both federal and state income tax deductions. She uses the money she saves on her taxes to buy tax-free bond mutual funds.

(D) In order to increase its profits, a cable television company raises its fees to customers and adds an additional channel of nature programs. To make room for the new station, the company eliminates a popular classic movie channel, as well as a Spanish language station, and a successful all-news channel.

(E) In order to increase the value of their stock holdings, members of the Key Investment Club contribute at least $500 dollars each month to buy additional shares in the stock portfolio of the club. In order to diversify its holdings, the club invests only in stocks that it does not already own.

Analysis

The correct answer is (D). Though not an ideal answer, this is clearly the best of the five choices. In the original situation, the number of advertising minutes is reduced, and so the advertising revenues are likely to decline. In (D), though the station will increase revenues by raising its fees, the reduction in the number of channels and the elimination of two popular ones will probably lead to customer defections, and the plan to increase profits will be undermined.

In (A), the use of the profits to increase the availability of seedlings will contribute to, rather than injure, the success of the first objective.

In (B), there is no reason to believe that information on the Internet will have an effect one way or the other on the aquarium's ability to finance new construction.

In (C), both the tax deductions and the mutual funds will contribute to the disposable income that is sought.

In (E), it is impossible to say how the choice of stocks that are not already in the portfolio will affect the value of the holdings. It is possible, but not certain, that previously owned stocks would be better investments, so we cannot be sure how the second factor will affect the first.

Passage Completion

This question type requires you to choose a phrase or sentence that best completes the passage.

It is initially important that you preserve the meaning of the passage, completing or maintaining the same thought. Unity (same subject) and coherence (order of thoughts) should be carefully noted. Second, it is important that the words you choose fit stylistically, use the same vocabulary, and are from the same context. Many times you will be able to eliminate some choices that "just don't sound good."

EXAMPLE 1

English, with its insatiable and omnivorous appetite for imported food, has eaten until it has become linguistically unbuttoned. And the glutton has cloaked his paunch with the pride of the gourmet. We would not imply that a large vocabulary is bad, but rather that it is self-destructive if uncontrolled by _____.

Which one of the following is the best completion according to the context of this passage?

(A) a smattering of slang
(B) a fine sense of distinction

    (C) the removal of all but Anglo-Saxon derivatives

    (D) a professor who knows the limits of good usage

    (E) an unbuttoned tongue

Analysis

The correct answer is (B). The passage describes the English language itself; therefore, references to individuals, (D) and (E), are inappropriate. They do not maintain the same general level of thought. Since the author does not condemn a large and distinguished vocabulary, (A) and (C), which do, are both poor choices. (B) preserves the meaning of the passage and fits stylistically.

EXAMPLE 2

In a reversal of past trends, last year more lawyers left courtroom practice to go into the teaching of law than vice versa. Since courtroom practice on average yields a much higher annual income, this shift discredits the theory that _____.

Which one of the following best completes the last sentence in the passage above?

    (A) incomes in the teaching of law will at some future time match those of courtroom practice

    (B) the change in profession by those lawyers who are likely to increase their incomes can be predicted in advance

    (C) more lawyers have remained in the teaching of law in the past few years than previously was the case

    (D) lawyers under 40 years of age are more likely to change professions for financial rather than other reasons

    (E) lawyers are likely to move into those professions in which the income is highest

Analysis

The correct answer is (E). The passage argues a connection between lawyers, profession changes, and income. Any answer choice that does not address those items cannot be a logical conclusion. (E) addresses the three key items and offers a conclusion that is logically consistent with the apparent change from higher to lower paying professions. (A) is irrelevant because the passage does not address the "future." (B) is irrelevant because the passage does not address "prediction." (C) is irrelevant because the passage does not address "remained" in a profession, only changing. (D) is irrelevant because the passage does not address the "age" of lawyers.

Word Reference

Here a word, or group of words, is taken out of context, and you are asked either what the word or words mean or what they refer to. In this type of question, first consider the passage as a whole, then carefully examine the key word or words surrounding the selected ones.

EXAMPLE

> English, with its insatiable and omnivorous appetite for imported food, has eaten until it has become linguistically unbuttoned. And the glutton has cloaked his paunch with the pride of the gourmet. We would not imply that a large vocabulary is bad, but rather that it is self-destructive if uncontrolled by a fine sense of distinction.

As used here, the word "glutton" refers to

(A) an English language with a lack of Anglo-Saxon derivation
(B) one who never stops talking about foreign food
(C) an English language bursting with pride
(D) one who is bilingual
(E) an English language bursting with derivatives from foreign languages

Analysis
The correct answer is (E). The passage, as a whole, is commenting on the English language, and (E) is the only choice that equates "glutton" with the subject of the passage.

In Conclusion

As you have seen, Logical Reasoning includes a potpourri of problem types all requiring common sense and reasonableness in the answers. You should take care in underlining what is being asked so that you do not (for example) accidentally look for the valid conclusion when the invalid one is asked for. Because of the nature of the Logical Reasoning problems, it is very easy to get tangled in a problem and lose your original thought, spending too much time on the question. If you feel that you have become trapped or stuck, take a guess and come back later if you have time. Remember that you must work within the context of the question, so do not bring in outside experiences or otherwise complicate a problem. The Logical Reasoning question is looking not for training in formal logic, but just for common sense and reasonableness.

Remember: Logical Reasoning accounts for 50% of your LSAT score.

Review of Some General Strategies for Logical Reasoning

THE PASSAGE
Read *actively*, circling key words.
Note major issue and supporting points.

THE QUESTION
Preread (before reading the passage) *actively*.
Note its reference.
Watch out for *unstated* ideas:
assumptions, implications/inferences, and sometimes conclusions.

ANSWER CHOICES
Sometimes there may not be a *perfect* answer; thus choose the *best* of the five choices.
Use the elimination strategy.
Note that "wrong" words in a choice make that choice incorrect.
Watch for those off-topic key words.

Extra Practice: Logical Reasoning

Directions: In this section you will be given brief statements or passages and be required to evaluate the reasoning involved. In some instances, more than one choice will appear to be a possible answer. You are to choose the *best* answer. Use common sense and reasonableness in making your selection; then mark the correct answer.

Use the answer sheet found on page 213.

Use the answer sheet found on page 213.

Questions 1–3

Robots have the ability to exhibit programmed behavior. Their performance can range from the simplest activity to the most complex group of activities. They not only can build other robots, but also can rebuild themselves. Physically they can resemble humans, yet mentally they cannot. Even the most highly advanced robot does not have the capacity to be creative, have emotions, or think independently.

1. From the passage above, which one of the following must be true?

   (A) Robots could eventually take over the world.
   (B) The most complex group of activities involves being creative.
   (C) A robot should last forever.
   (D) Emotions, creativity, and independent thought can be written as programs.
   (E) Building other robots involves independent thinking.

2. The author of this passage would agree that

   (A) robots would eventually be impossible to control
   (B) in the near future, robots will be able to think independently
   (C) robots have reached their peak of development
   (D) there are dangers in robots that think for themselves
   (E) there are some tasks that are better done by robots than by humans

3. The author's assertions would be weakened by pointing out that

   (A) humans exhibit programmed behavior for the first few years of life
   (B) robots' behavior is not always predictable
   (C) building other robots requires independent training
   (D) internal feeling is not always exhibited
   (E) the most complex group of activities necessitates independent thinking

4. The management of Trans-Caribbean Airways has announced that the airline's bonus mileage program will be discontinued on July 1. A survey conducted on weekdays in February on the Miami to Port-of-Spain route asked passengers to rate in order of importance: low fares, on-time performance, prompt baggage handling, quality in-flight refreshments, and bonus mileage. More than 95 percent of the respondents put low fares and on-time performance either first or second, whereas less than 1 percent placed the bonus mileage program above fourth. Since bonus mileage is not important to Trans-Caribbean passengers, management has decided to eliminate it.

The decision of the management is based on all the following assumptions EXCEPT

(A) that because the bonus mileage program was not the passengers' first or second concern, it is not important to them

(B) that the passengers on the Miami to Port-of-Spain route reflect the opinion of other passengers of the Trans-Caribbean Airways

(C) that the passengers flying in February are representative of the airline's passengers throughout the year

(D) that other airlines will not attract Trans-Caribbean customers by offering attractive mileage bonus plans

(E) that the number of passengers who failed to complete the survey is statistically insignificant

5. *Botanist:* No plant in the botanical gardens blossoms twice in the same month. All of the plants in the botanical gardens that blossom in January are grown from either bulbs or tubers. None of the plants that blossom in January will flower again later in the year.

If the statements above are true, which one of the following must also be true?

(A) No plant in the botanical garden grown from a bulb will blossom in October.

(B) No plants in the botanical garden blossom twice in the year if they blossom first in January.

(C) None of the plants in the botanical gardens that blossom in June are grown from tubers.

(D) All of the plants in the botanical gardens grown from bulbs or tubers that did not blossom in January will flower later in the year.

(E) All plants in the botanical gardens grown from bulbs or tubers flower in January.

6. The simplest conceivable situation in which one human being may communicate with another is one in which structurally complementary communicants have been conditioned to associate the same words with the same things.

The sentence that would best complete this thought is:

(A) Therefore, dictionaries are of little value to foreigners.

(B) Therefore, man cannot communicate effectively with animals.

(C) Therefore, communication is a matter of relation.

(D) Therefore, communication is simplest following a common experience.

(E) Therefore, communication is dependent on complementary structures.

7. In a nationwide survey, four out of five dentists questioned recommended sugarless gum for their patients who chew gum.

   Which one of the following would most weaken the above endorsement for sugarless gum?

   (A) Only five dentists were questioned.
   (B) The dentists were not paid for their endorsements.
   (C) Only one of the dentists questioned chewed sugarless gum.
   (D) Patients do not do what their dentists tell them to do.
   (E) Sugarless gum costs much more than regular gum.

8. In Tom and Angie's class, everyone likes drawing or painting or both, but Angie does not like painting.

   Which one of the following statements cannot be true?

   (A) Angie likes drawing.
   (B) Tom likes drawing and painting.
   (C) Everyone in the class who does not like drawing likes painting.
   (D) No one in the class likes painting.
   (E) Tom dislikes drawing and painting.

9. *Mark:* The big test is tomorrow and I didn't study. I suppose I'll just have to cheat. I know it is wrong, but I have to get a good grade on the test.
   Amy: I don't think that's a good idea. Just go to the teacher, tell the truth, and maybe you can get a postponement.

   Amy attacks Mark's argument by

   (A) attacking his reasoning
   (B) applying personal pressure
   (C) implying that good triumphs over evil
   (D) presenting another alternative
   (E) suggesting a positive approach

Questions 10–11

The microwave oven has become a standard appliance in many kitchens, mainly because it offers a fast way of cooking food. Yet, some homeowners believe that the ovens are still not completely safe. Microwaves, therefore, should not be standard appliances until they are more carefully researched and tested.

10. Which one of the following, if true, would most weaken the conclusion of the passage above?

    (A) Homeowners often purchase items despite knowing they may be unsafe.
    (B) Those homeowners in doubt about microwave safety ought not to purchase microwaves.
    (C) Research and testing of home appliances seldom reveal safety hazards.
    (D) Microwaves are not as dangerous as steam irons, which are used in almost every home.
    (E) Homeowners often purchase items that they do not need.

11. Which one of the following, if true, would most strengthen the conclusion of the passage above?

    (A) Homeowners often doubt the advertised safety of all new appliances.
    (B) Speed of food preparation is not the only concern of today's homeowner.
    (C) Modern homeowners have more free time than ever before.
    (D) Food preparation has become almost a science, with more complicated and involved recipes.
    (E) Many microwave ovens have been found to leak radioactive elements.

12. Cats that eat Vitagatto Cat Food each day will have sleek coats and excellent night vision. Since Jane feeds her cats only white tuna or poached chicken breasts, they cannot have excellent night vision. Therefore they should be kept indoors at night to prevent injuries.

Which one of the following contains a reasoning error most similar to that in the argument above?

(A) Older houses in Canary Park sell for about $100,000, if the kitchen and bathrooms have been modernized. Arthur has put new fixtures in the bathrooms of his Canary Park house, but has not changed the kitchen. Therefore, the house will sell for less than $100,000 dollars.

(B) Plants that have never been exposed to fungicides are especially susceptible to mildew. Since Jarmilla never uses any chemicals in her garden, her plants are liable to be subject to mildew in wet or cloudy weather.

(C) Restaurants in Arlmont that buy their baked goods from Vonder's Bakery do brisk business at breakfast. Since Tamale Tom's restaurant does all its own baking, it will not have many breakfast customers, and should not open until lunchtime.

(D) Students who take the law exam preparation class offered by the English department receive scores above the national average. Sally has taken a more expensive and more time-consuming course from a private tutor. She will therefore receive a very high score and be accepted at Yale.

(E) Police in Allentown solve most of the robberies that take place in daylight hours, but more than half of the robberies that take place after 6 P.M. are unsolved. Since the Borden Furniture Company was robbed at midnight, the thieves will probably not be caught.

13. According to a count of the men and women listed in the Glenarm Telephone Directory, there are 10,000 more men than women in this city of only 100,000. But according to the last census report, the population of Glenarm is 55 percent female. All of the following can be used to explain this discrepancy EXCEPT

(A) not all phone users list their names in the directory

(B) married couples are more likely to use the husband's than the wife's name in the directory

(C) the census report has been faulted for undercounting the minority population of large cities

(D) the phone book count may be misled by initials or names that are not gender specific

(E) there are many more females under 14 than males

14. Given that this rock is white in color, it must be quartz.

The foregoing conclusion can be properly drawn if it is true that

(A) only quartz rocks are white in color

(B) quartz rocks are generally white in color

(C) other white rocks have proved to be quartz

(D) few other types of rocks are white in color

(E) all quartz rocks are white in color

Questions 15–16

"Even the smallest restaurant in Paris serves better breads than the best restaurants in New York," the visiting chef said. He was complaining about the quality of the bread available in America. "I was trained in France," he added, "so I understand bread-making. But in America, there are hardly any good bakers. You can tell just by looking at the roll baskets. In every restaurant I have visited in New York, the roll baskets are still full on every table at the end of the meal."

15. The chef's conclusions depends on all of the following assumptions EXCEPT

    (A) if the bread is good, all of it will be consumed
    (B) the quality of a restaurant can be determined by the quality of its breads
    (C) all good bakers are professionals
    (D) the norm for good bread-making is France
    (E) restaurants do not replenish roll baskets

16. All of the following are errors in the reasoning of the speaker in the passage above EXCEPT

    (A) the argument takes as fact what is unproven personal opinion
    (B) the argument assumes that New York restaurants represent American baking
    (C) the speaker claims complete knowledge of a large number of small restaurants in Paris
    (D) the speaker claims that he knows how to bake bread
    (E) the examples the speaker cites of good and bad bread makers are vague and unspecific

Questions 17–18

Some American auto factories are beginning to resemble their Japanese counterparts. In many Japanese factories, the workers enjoy the same status and privileges as their bosses. Everyone works in harmony, and there is much less of the tension and anger that results when one group dominates another.

17. With which one of the following would the author of the above passage most likely agree?

    (A) American work environments ought to emulate Japanese auto factories.
    (B) Japanese automobiles are better built than American automobiles.
    (C) Tension in the workplace enhances worker productivity.
    (D) Japanese culture differs so much from American culture that it precludes any overlap of styles.
    (E) Striving for managerial status induces worker productivity.

18. The argument gives logically relevant support for which one of the following conclusions?

    (A) Some American auto factories are experiencing changes in their work environments.
    (B) American auto workers envy their Japanese counterparts.
    (C) There is no tension or anger in Japanese factories.
    (D) Decrease in tension leads to higher productivity.
    (E) There is no tension or anger in American factories that follow Japanese models.

19. When we approach land, we usually sight birds. The lookout has just sighted birds.

    Which one of the following represents the most logical conclusion based upon the foregoing statements?

    (A) The conjecture that we are approaching land is strengthened.
    (B) Land is closer than it was before the sighting of the birds.
    (C) We are approaching land.
    (D) We may or may not be approaching land.
    (E) We may not be approaching land.

20. The presence of the gas Nexon is a necessary condition, but not a sufficient condition, for the existence of life on the planet Plex.

    On the basis of the foregoing, which of the following would also be true?

    (A) If life exists on Plex, then only the gas Nexon is present.
    (B) If life exists on Plex, then the gas Nexon may or may not be present.
    (C) If life exists on Plex, then the gas Nexon is present.
    (D) If no life exists on Plex, Nexon cannot be present.
    (E) If no life exists on Plex, Nexon is the only gas present.

21. The absence of the liquid Flennel is a sufficient condition for the cessation of life on the planet Fluke, but it is not a necessary condition.

    On the basis of the foregoing, which of the following would also be true?

    (A) If life on Fluke ceased to exist, there would have to have been an absence of the liquid Flennel.
    (B) If all liquid Flennel were removed from Fluke, life there would surely perish.
    (C) If all liquid Flennel were removed from Fluke, life there might or might not cease.
    (D) If all liquid Flennel were removed from Fluke, the cessation of life would depend upon other conditions.
    (E) Life on Fluke cannot cease so long as Flennel is present.

22. The gas rates in Edina are low only for the first 30 therms used each month; the next 30 cost twice as much, and all gas over 60 therms costs four times as much as the first 30. The city has very cold winters and warm summers. To heat an average-size two-bedroom home in the winter by gas is prohibitively expensive, but not as costly as electric heating. Consequently

    All of the following are logical conclusions to this passage EXCEPT

    (A) most homeowners use oil heating
    (B) many homes are kept at temperatures below 70 degrees in the winter
    (C) the consumption of gas is lower in the winter than in the summer
    (D) electric cooling is more common than electric heating
    (E) many homes have wood burning stoves and fireplaces

23. If the poodle was reared at Prince Charming Kennels, then it is a purebred.

    The foregoing statement can be deduced logically from which one of the following statements?

    (A) Every purebred poodle is reared at Prince Charming Kennels or at another AKC approved kennel.
    (B) The poodle in question was bred at either Prince Charming Kennels or at another AKC approved kennel.
    (C) The poodle in question either is a purebred or looks remarkably like a purebred.
    (D) The majority of poodles reared at Prince Charming Kennels are purebred.
    (E) There are no dogs reared at Prince Charming Kennels that are not purebred.

24. There is no reason to eliminate the possibility of an oil field existing beneath the Great Salt Lake. Therefore, we must undertake the exploration of the Salt Lake's bottom.

    The foregoing argument assumes which one of the following?

    (A) Exploration of the Salt Lake's bottom has not been previously proposed.
    (B) An oil field located beneath the lake would be easy to identify.
    (C) The Great Salt Lake is the only large inland body of water beneath which an oil field may lie.
    (D) The quest for oil is a sufficient motive to undertake exploration of the Salt Lake's bottom.
    (E) An oil field exists beneath the Great Salt Lake.

Questions 25–26

My course of study had led me to believe that all mental and moral feelings and qualities, whether of a good or of a bad kind, were the results of association; that we love one thing, and hate another, take pleasure in one sort of action or contemplation, and pain in another sort, through the clinging of pleasurable or painful ideas to those things, from the effect of education or of experience. As a corollary from this, I was convinced, that the object of education should be to form the strongest possible associations of the salutary class; associations of pleasure with all things beneficial to the great whole. It now seemed to me, on retrospect, that my teachers had occupied themselves but superficially with the means of forming and keeping up these salutary associations. They seemed to have trusted altogether to the old familiar instruments, praise and blame, reward and punishment. I did not doubt that by these means, begun early, and applied unremittingly, intense associations of pain and pleasure, especially of pain, might be created, and might produce desires and aversions capable of lasting undiminished to the end of life. But there must always be something artificial and casual in associations thus produced.

25. By "salutary" the author means

    (A) "the strongest possible associations"
    (B) ideas that "salute" one's mind
    (C) capable of giving pain
    (D) promoting some good purpose
    (E) those earning a middle-class income or better

26. All of the following questions are answered in the passage EXCEPT

    (A) Is there any sort of thinking that is not associational?
    (B) Is schooling the only cause of our lifelong "desires and aversions"?
    (C) What else besides education causes these associations?
    (D) What do teachers praise and what do they blame?
    (E) How long would the desires and aversions last?

27. The San Diego Chargers practice expertly for long hours every day and keep a written log of their errors.

    The above statement is an example of which one of the following assumptions?

    (A) Practice makes perfect.
    (B) To err is human.
    (C) People make mistakes; that's why they put erasers on pencils.
    (D) Practice is what you know, and it will help to make clear what now you do not know.
    (E) Writing is a mode of learning.

28. Pine trees may be taller than any other tree. Pines are never shorter than the shortest palms, and some palms may exceed the height of some pines. Peppertrees are always taller than palm trees. Peach trees are shorter than peppertrees but not shorter than all palms.

    Given the foregoing, which one of the following would be true?

    (A) Peach trees may be shorter than pine trees.
    (B) Peppertrees may be shorter than some peach trees.
    (C) Every pine is taller than every palm.
    (D) A particular palm could not be taller than a particular pine.
    (E) Now and then a peach tree may be taller than a pepper.

29. Most popular paperback novels are of low intellectual quality; therefore *Splendor Behind the Billboard,* an unpopular paperback novel, is probably of high intellectual quality.

The foregoing argument is most like which one of the following?

(A) Most locusts inhabit arid places; therefore, locusts are probably found in all deserts.
(B) Most acts of criminal violence have declined in number during the past few years; therefore, law enforcement during this period has improved.
(C) Most people who stop drinking gain weight; therefore, if Carl does not cease drinking, he will probably not gain weight.
(D) Most nations run by autocratic governments do not permit a free press; therefore the country of Endorff, which is run by an autocratic government, probably does not have a free press.
(E) Most new motor homes are equipped with air conditioning; therefore, Jim's new motor home may not be equipped with air conditioning.

Questions 30–31

Jane states, "All mammals have hair. This creature possesses no hair. Therefore, it is not a mammal."

30. Which one of the following most closely parallels the logic of Jane's statement?

(A) All reptiles have scales. This creature possesses scales. Therefore, it is a reptile.
(B) All physics tests are difficult. This is not a physics test. Therefore, it is not difficult.
(C) All American cars are poorly constructed. Every car sold by Fred was poorly constructed. Therefore, Fred sells only American cars.
(D) All mammals do not have hair. This creature possesses hair. Therefore, it may be a mammal.
(E) All lubricants smell. This liquid does not have an odor. Therefore, it is not a lubricant.

31. Which one of the following, if true, would most weaken Jane's argument?

(A) Animals other than mammals have hair.
(B) Some mammals do not have hair.
(C) Mammals have more hair than nonmammals.
(D) One could remove the hair from a mammal.
(E) Reptiles may have hair.

Questions 32–33

A recent study of Hodgkin's disease in young adults has examined a large number of sets of twins, half of them identical and half nonidentical. Identical twins have the same genetic makeup, but like any other siblings nonidentical twins share only about 50 percent of their genetic material. In the study of twins with Hodgkin's disease, the researchers found that the chances of the second of a set of identical twins also developing the disease was 100 times higher than in the case of the sibling of a nonidentical twin, or of any other average individual. The number of cases where both identical twins were affected was, however, not a very large proportion of the identical twin pairs.

32. Based on the information in this passage, we can infer all of the following EXCEPT

(A) genetic inheritance is one factor in determining the susceptibility to Hodgkin's disease
(B) if one twin of a set of nonidentical twins develops Hodgkin's disease, the chances of the second twin developing Hodgkin's disease are no greater than that of a person who is not a twin
(C) Hodgkin's disease is more likely to appear first in a twin who is one of a pair of identical twins than one of a pair of nonidentical twins
(D) genetics alone is not sufficient to cause Hodgkin's disease
(E) the chances of the second of a pair of identical twins whose twin has developed Hodgkin's disease also developing the disease are not very high

33. For which reason of the following are studies of identical twins likely to be valuable to medical research?

    (A) Identical twins are usually raised in the same environments.
    (B) Researchers using identical twins can discern differences more easily.
    (C) Identical twins may differ psychologically, but not physically.
    (D) Identical twins may reveal information related to genetics.
    (E) It is easier to arrange medical examinations at the same hospital for identical twins than for unrelated persons.

34. The frog population in the lake each year is determined by the number of two avian predators: egrets and blue herons. The weather has little effect on the egret population, but the number of herons varies according to the rainfall in the area. Therefore, a greatly changing frog population in the lake three years in a row will probably occur when the annual rainfall fluctuates widely for three years.

    Of the following arguments, which one most closely resembles this paragraph in the pattern of its reasoning?

    (A) The annual profit or loss of Acme Desk Company depends chiefly on the number of new office buildings in the city and on the stability of the mortgage rates. In a year when mortgage rates fluctuate, the building rate is also likely to fluctuate.
    (B) The parking lot at the university is filled to capacity on nights when the business school holds classes at the same hours as the extension college. If there are classes at the business school and no classes at the extension college, or classes at the extension college and no classes at the business school, the parking lots are three-quarters full.
    (C) The restaurant can sell a beef and cheese pizza for a one dollar profit if the price of cheese remains at less than two dollars per pound and the price of beef at less than one dollar per pound. For the last six months, cheese has sold at $1.95 per pound. Since the pizzas have failed to earn a profit of one dollar in this period, the price of beef must have risen to above one dollar per pound.
    (D) Farmers in the valley can legally purchase federal water at a reduced rate only if they raise cotton or if their farms are no larger than 960 acres. Several of the farmers who continue to purchase federal water at the reduced rate are raising only alfalfa. Therefore, their farms must be larger than 960 acres.
    (E) A cake will not collapse in the oven if the eggs have been brought to room temperature before mixing or if the sugar syrup is at a temperature above 140 degrees. The cake must have collapsed because the eggs were too cold or the sugar was not hot enough.

35. *Editorial:* Scientific studies have shown that second-hand tobacco smoke in the workplace greatly increases the number of workers who take more than fifteen days of sick-leave and the number of workers who suffer serious respiratory ailments. It has also been shown that the number of workers who die of lung cancer is twice as high in workplaces that permit smoking than in workplaces that do not. Therefore, the state must pass laws that require all companies to forbid smoking in the workplace.

    Which one of the following is the underlying principle in this argument?

    (A) Every individual has a responsibility for the well-being of every other individual with whom he or she comes into daily contact.
    (B) Employers who do not take care of the health of their workers risk increasing losses from absenteeism each year.
    (C) States must be permitted to outlaw any dangerous substances or implements.
    (D) States must be responsible for the safety of the workplace of all businesses in their jurisdiction.
    (E) Workers must be permitted to make their own decisions about their workplace.

36. For the post-election festivities, no athlete was invited to the White House unless he or she was more than 35 years old. No one older than 35 was both an athlete and invited to the White House.

    Which one of the following conclusions can be logically drawn from the statements above?

    (A) No one but athletes were invited to the White House.
    (B) No athlete was invited to the White House.
    (C) Only persons older than 35 were invited to the White House.
    (D) No one over 35 was invited to the White House.
    (E) Some athletes over 35 were invited to the White House.

37. At the Brightman Diet Center, 20 men and women who wished to lose ten pounds undertook a program that included an hour of exercise and a limit of 200 calories for breakfast and lunch each day. A second group of 20 men and women, similar in age and weight to the first group, exercised for only half an hour and ate up to 500 calories for breakfast and lunch each day. Surprisingly, at the end of three weeks, all 20 who had exercised less and consumed more calories at breakfast and lunch had lost more weight than members of the other group.

    Which one of the following best explains these unexpected results?

    (A) Some of those who lost more weight exercised longer than the half hour.
    (B) Forty people is too small a sample to produce any meaningful statistics.
    (C) The exercise of some of the members of those who lost more weight was more vigorous than that of members of the other group.
    (D) Those in the group that ate 500 calories for breakfast and lunch chose foods lower in fat and cholesterol than those in the other group.
    (E) The group that had eaten more and exercised less during the day ate fewer calories at dinner than those in the other group.

38. Of the 8,000 American victims of isochemic optic neuropathy, most are over 60. The condition occurs suddenly and normally in only one eye. Its cause is unknown, though doctors agree that an interruption of the blood flow to the optic nerve is a major factor. Untreated, most people recover full vision in six months. The most common treatment, an operation called optic nerve decompression surgery, has proven to be less effective than no treatment at all. Fewer regain their sight after the operation, and those who do require nine months to do so.

The conclusions of this paragraph would be most useful in support of an argument for

(A) increasing federal supervision of surgical procedures
(B) reducing the cost of surgical procedures
(C) reducing the number of surgical procedures
(D) expanding federal oversight of cosmetic surgery
(E) funding a study of isochemic optic neuropathy in men and women under 40

39. No one who is a member of the tennis team will smoke cigarettes. No first-rate athlete smokes cigarettes. Therefore, only first-rate athletes will become members of the tennis team.

The reasoning here is in error since the conclusion does not allow for the possibility of

(A) a nonsmoker on the tennis team who is a second-rate athlete
(B) a first-rate athlete who doesn't play tennis
(C) an ex-smoker who is a first-rate athlete
(D) a nonsmoker who is not a first-rate athlete
(E) a smoker who is a first-rate tennis player

40. The sale of clothing featuring characters from children's television programs such as Barney or the Power Rangers has increased enormously in the last five years. The number of children who watch television must also have increased greatly in the same period.

Which one of the following would fail to support this conclusion and at the same time explain the rise in clothing sales?

(A) The relaxation of trade barriers has substantially reduced the cost of Asian-made clothes in the last five years.
(B) Five years ago, the most popular children's television program, Sesame Street, was seen on educational television stations.
(C) In many areas, the three most popular children's television programs are carried on both cable and network television stations.
(D) There are now several stations, such as the Disney Channel or Nickelodeon, which intend most or all of their programs for a young or very young audience.
(E) Television programs directed at children have been increasingly attacked in the last five years for excessive violence.

41. Alfred Thomason, one of the ten brokers in the mortgage department of Kean and Landers, will certainly write more than $5 million in mortgages this year. Last year the department's sales totaled more than $50 million and this year's totals will be just as high.

Which one of the following contains the same kind of reasoning error as this passage?

(A) Jacobson expects the dahlias he exhibits in this year's flower show will win a prize. His dahlias failed to win in last year's exhibition, but he believes that the cause was a jealous judge who is not on this year's panel.

(B) The debate squad is expected to win the state tournament in May. They have won all nine of their debates this year, including a large tournament in Memphis competing against most of the teams highly regarded in the state competition.

(C) The Vasquez family plans to drive from Boston to Scottsdale in four days. Last winter the drive took six days, but they were delayed by bad weather in New England, Pennsylvania, and New Mexico.

(D) South Texas State's Edward Meany will represent his college in a two-day tournament for top golfers from 30 different colleges in the state. Since the team from South Texas State easily won the state intercollegiate golf championship, Meany should have no trouble winning this tournament.

(E) Seeded first in the NCAA championships in Atlanta, Laura Lomax should breeze through the tournament. She already has won the two tournaments she has entered, and has a 38-match winning streak.

42. Although it is subject to the variations of currencies and interest rates, the Asian influx is now a major factor in the Australian real estate market. Although many Australians are nervous about the waves of Asian immigration, their economy welcomes the purchase of Australian properties by investors from Asia who have no residential rights. Foreigners are permitted to purchase up to half of the units of a condominium, provided they do so before the condo is first occupied. They can also purchase real estate in areas designated as "integrated tourism resorts," though few exist at present. The average purchase price paid by foreign investors is 80 percent more than the average paid by Australian residents. The United States is still the largest foreign investor, and Singapore recently has replaced Britain in second place.

From which one of the following can we infer that Australian regulations of foreign investments in real estate are not determined by a policy designed to exclude Asians?

(A) Asians make purchases chiefly of the more expensive dwelling units.

(B) Asians pay higher average purchase prices than Australians.

(C) The largest foreign investor is the United States.

(D) Traditional ties to Great Britain are no longer important to many Australians.

(E) Asians can purchase property in "integrated tourism resorts."

43. Thirty-eight percent of people in America drink unfluoridated water and, as a result, have 25 percent more cavities. Early opponents of fluoridation, like the John Birch Society, claimed it was a demonic communist scheme to poison America. More recent opponents invoke the fear of cancer, though years of scientific studies have continued to declare fluoridation safe. Almost every dental and medical organization has endorsed the process, but cities as large as Los Angeles are still without it, though its yearly cost is about 50 cents per person.

The claim that fluoridation is a communist plot is cited here because

(A) it gives historic breadth to the argument

(B) it exemplifies the eccentricity of the opposition

(C) it is what the argument is attempting to refute

(D) it supports the assumption that fluoridation is dangerous

(E) it supports the conclusion of the argument

44. The sickle-cell trait is usually regarded as a characteristic of black Africans. As a single gene, it confers a resistance to malaria, but if the gene is inherited from two parents, it may lead to a dangerous form of anemia. That trait, however, is not a unique characteristic of black Africans but appears wherever malaria has been common. The gene occurs as often in areas of Greece and of southern Asia as it does in central Africa. A genetic grouping by how well they digest milk would separate Arabs and northern Europeans from southern Europeans, native Americans, and some Africans. Most Europeans, black Africans, and east Asians have a gene that determines how they inherit fingerprint patterns, but Mongolians and the Australian aborigines do not. We have the notion that race is important because the surface is what we see. We now have the means to look beneath the skin.

This paragraph is probably part of a longer article that seeks to show

(A) the importance of genetic inheritance in the incidence of disease

(B) the difficulty of finding a scientific definition of race

(C) the decline of parasitic diseases like malaria in the wake of the discovery of their causes

(D) that most of the genes in a member of one race are likely to be unique to that race

(E) the genetic determination of the higher incidence of certain diseases in different racial groups

Auto accident victims in this state can sue for both their medical costs and for "pain and suffering" awards. Because the "pain and suffering" awards can be very large, often when the medical expenses are high, victims have an incentive to inflate their medical needs and medical costs in order to receive a higher total payment. For the victims of automobile accidents of equivalent seriousness, medical costs in this state are 30 percent higher than in all four of the neighboring states that have no-fault insurance programs and do make "pain and suffering" awards. Motorists in this state pay more than $300 more for the same insurance coverage of motorists in the four adjoining states. A no-fault insurance system eliminating the lawsuits for "pain and suffering" and fairly compensating victims for medical costs would save the insured drivers of the state medical costs of nearly $1 billion.

45. This argument depends on all of the following assumptions EXCEPT

    (A) juries assume a higher medical cost signifies greater pain and suffering

    (B) accident victims may falsify the extent of their injuries

    (C) doctors and lawyers have no incentives to keep costs low

    (D) accident victims should not be rewarded for "pain and suffering"

    (E) the medical costs of automobile accidents exceed their legal costs

46. Which one of the following, if true, would weaken the persuasiveness of this argument?

    (A) The per-vehicle accident rate in this state is 4 percent higher than in the four neighboring states.

    (B) The average motorist in this state drives fewer miles than the average motorist in two of the four neighboring states.

    (C) There are more state patrolmen per driver in this state than in any other in the region.

    (D) Medical costs in the four neighboring states are 20 percent lower than in this state.

    (E) Though the sales tax rate is lower, the income tax is higher in this state than in any other in the region.

---

47. In order for Agri-Cola Corporation to show a profit this year, it must again sell $10 million worth of soft drinks in the United States and an equal amount overseas. Though sales in this country will certainly be equal to last year's, market unrest in Asia and South America will limit this year's overseas sales to at least $2 million less than last year's. It is therefore impossible that the company can show a profit this year.

The conclusion of this paragraph is correct if which one of the following is assumed?

    (A) Last year's overseas sales were more than $10 million.

    (B) This year's expenses on overseas sales can be reduced so that profits will increase.

    (C) This year's sales of domestic soft drinks may surpass last year's.

    (D) The margin of profit on this year's sales will not be higher than last year's.

    (E) Both this year and last, sales in the overseas markets are more profitable than sales in the domestic market.

<u>Questions 48–49</u>

Ecologist: It is true that the solution of the problem of global warming will require important changes in the way we use fossil fuels over the long term and that the free market must play an important role in making these changes possible. But these facts should not make us forget how crucial near-term limits on the emissions of "greenhouse gases" are to motivate these changes. When the issue was the limitation of ozone-reducing substances, it was short-term emissions limits that quickly brought the needed technologies to the marketplace. These technologies were not available until the international community had adopted specific limits on ozone-depleting substances.

48. By which one of the following means does the author of this passage make his case?

    (A) making a careful distinction between two key terms
    (B) questioning the accuracy of the evidence given to support the opposition's case
    (C) using an appropriate analogy
    (D) using the literal meaning of a word that could be construed as metaphoric
    (E) using premises that are contradictory

49. The author's case would be weakened if it could be shown that

    (A) the immediate economic consequences of reducing the emission of greenhouse gases will be catastrophic in both the industrialized world and developing countries
    (B) there has been virtually no research to develop a technology to deal with global warming
    (C) the long-term limits on greenhouse gas emissions may not be adopted for at least 25 years
    (D) many multinational corporations are reluctant to abide by any international agreements to limit the use of oil and oil-based products
    (E) many scientists are skeptical about the effect of fossil fuel use on global warming

50. *Robert:* Cattle are turning up dead all over the place with their eyes removed with surgical precision. Strange lights have been seen in the sky on the night before the bodies were discovered, and no human culprits have ever been found. It must be extraterrestrial invaders.

    June: Maybe it's some weird cult. Or a college student prank. I don't know all the facts of the story, and I have no certain explanation myself, but I am sure that it's not likely to be aliens who want to collect eyes from cattle.

    June responds to Robert's explanation by

    (A) demonstrating that his conclusion is inconsistent with the evidence that is advanced in its support
    (B) questioning the accuracy of the evidence on which his argument depends
    (C) providing evidence that contradicts his conclusion
    (D) refusing to deal with the logic of his argument
    (E) offering counter-explanations equally supported by the evidence

51. *Professor:* Did you study for this exam?
    Student: Yes. And I spent at least two hours on the endocrine system alone.
    Professor: And you reviewed the circulatory system?
    Student: I read that chapter three times.
    Professor: You aren't being honest here. If you'd studied, you wouldn't have confused such basic facts as the functions of the left and right ventricles.

    The professor's reasoning is flawed for each of the following reasons EXCEPT

    (A) it does not consider the possibility that lack of concentration can cause poor retention
    (B) it assumes the study regimen mentioned by the student would be effective
    (C) it assumes that basic facts are easy to remember
    (D) it connects repeated reading with retention
    (E) it ignores the possibility that the student may have been ill or tired during the exam, causing poor performance

52. People who dream in color are creative. Conrad is a creative person. Therefore, Conrad must dream in color.

The pattern of reasoning in the argument above is flawed most similarly to which of the following arguments?

(A) Ants leave scent trails for other ants to follow to food. Food scent trails are common among social insects. Therefore, all social insects leave scent trails.

(B) Redwood is extremely weather resistant. Cedar is less resistant but less expensive. Therefore, cedar is the choice of most builders.

(C) Plumbers and electricians often belong to unions. Sally wants to become an electrician. Therefore, Sally will probably join a union.

(D) Oak trees provide acorns as food for wildlife. Wildlife has many food sources. Therefore, oak trees are not necessary as a wildlife food source.

(E) Corn is not a good plant to grow in containers. Maize is not a good plant to grow in containers. Therefore, maize is corn.

Questions 53–54

Park visitor advisory: Chigger activity in the park is high. According to a popular misconception, chiggers burrow under one's skin, but they don't. They bite and hold on, exuding an enzyme that liquefies the skin so they can sip it up. The longer they stay attached and exude the enzyme, the more severe a person's reaction is likely to be. Chiggers, so small they can't be seen on the body without magnification, perch on the tops of weeds and other plants, particularly tall plants, and jump onto a person or animal coming close to them. They then often migrate to areas such as the ankles, waist, underarms, and groin because they are relatively weak and need something such as socks or a waistband to push against in order to bite into the skin. Preventive measures include spraying with an insect repellant and showering immediately upon returning from outside to dislodge the insects. If showering is not possible, a brisk rubdown with a rough towel is somewhat effective. Prophylactic measures after bites include application of an anti-itch medication and complete avoidance of scratching the bite, which causes more severe itching and may cause infection. The effects of chigger bites may last up to two weeks or more.
Parks and Recreation Supervisor

53. Which of the following assumptions is most likely being made by the Parks and Recreation Supervisor?

(A) Visitors to the park will invariably be bitten by chiggers but with varying levels of discomfort.

(B) Prophylactic measures are generally only marginally effective.

(C) Visitors to the park would like to avoid being bitten by chiggers.

(D) Showering will remove all chiggers on the body.

(E) Tight clothing will lessen the severity of chigger bites.

54. According to the information supplied by the supervisor, which of the following people would be LEAST likely to be affected by chigger bites?

   (A) Before going into the woods, Sheila sprays herself with insect repellant and then showers.
   (B) Consuela picks blackberries in the woods and towels herself off when she reaches her cabin.
   (C) George stays on the woodland paths, except for a strenuous climb up a rock face. He showers when he returns to his room.
   (D) Dimitri makes sure to spray insect repellant at waist, ankles, and wrists before taking his dirt bike up Thunder Mountain through the brush.
   (E) During her walk through the forest, Connie briskly towels herself off and applies insect repellent.

---

55. There are now almost three million undocumented immigrants living in the United States. They are taking jobs that legal citizens should have and using services that cost federal tax dollars to which they don't contribute. Consequently, these undocumented immigrants must be identified and deported immediately.

   Which of the following, if true, would most call into question the speaker's conclusion?

   (A) There are actually 3.2 million undocumented immigrants living in the United States.
   (B) Undocumented immigrants do pay taxes in the form of local sales taxes on their purchases.
   (C) Undocumented immigrants come primarily from Central and South America, important areas for the production of raw materials crucial to the United States.
   (D) The jobs taken by undocumented immigrants are largely those low-paid positions U.S. workers refuse to take.
   (E) New laws would need to be passed in order to grant amnesty to undocumented immigrants.

56. The Woodward family, in reviewing their electricity cost for the month of August, discovered the following facts: The electric company's average charge per kilowatt hour throughout their area was the same as it was in July. The Woodwards' total kilowatt usage in August was higher than it was in July, but their total expenditure for August's electricity was less than their expenditure in July.

   Of the following, which fact, if true, would most likely explain the difference between the July and August electricity charges?

   (A) The Woodwards had to repair their air conditioner during July.
   (B) The Woodwards' August electricity usage was more often at off-peak, lower-rate times than it was in July.
   (C) The electric company began buying electricity from a different, lower-cost source in August.
   (D) During August, the Woodwards lowered the temperature setting on their hot water heater and hung their clothes outside to dry rather than using the electric dryer.
   (E) In July, the Woodwards were away on vacation for two weeks.

57. *Pete:* Although it's a mistake to equate the life of a spotted owl and the life of a human, I agree with the ecoterrorists' concerns for the planet. It's undeniable that burning down buildings can stop overbuilding in natural environments, and embedding spikes in trees to harm loggers and their equipment can slow down clear-cutting operations.
   Anne: Then you think the ends can justify the means.

   Anne's response indicates she has most likely misunderstood Pete to believe which of the following?

   (A) Spotted owls are not as important as other endangered species.
   (B) Spikes in trees unacceptably endanger human life and arson unnecessarily endangers human possessions.
   (C) Environmentalists share the concerns of ecoterrorists in that they realize drastic measures must be taken to save the planet.
   (D) Human life must take precedence over the lives of other animals.
   (E) The need to stem the danger to the planet makes spiking trees acceptable.

58. In the United States, pharmaceutical plant research is hailed by most scientists as holding promise for important medical breakthroughs. Ninety percent of doctors actively promote the research. But the majority of people do not know enough about the process to make an informed decision on the necessity of protecting the rain forests in which most of the promising plants are discovered. Fewer than two out of a hundred can speak knowledgeably about the basics of the subject. Politicians in rain forest countries tend to denounce the research, stressing the economic needs of their citizens over the nebulous promise of new medicines.

If the information given above is true, which of the following must also be true?

(A) No politician in a rain forest country is among those who can speak knowledgeably about pharmaceutical plant research.
(B) Ten percent of doctors do not actively promote pharmaceutical plant research.
(C) Ninety-eight percent of people oppose pharmaceutical plant research.
(D) Most doctors are well informed about pharmaceutical plant research.
(E) Some doctors oppose pharmaceutical plant research.

59. Although the regulation that airline pilots be provided nine hours of rest in a twenty-four-hour period seems reasonable and prudent, serious safety concerns remain due to pilot fatigue. The nine hours of rest may be on paper only because schedule delays often mean the pilot is in the airport hours before a flight, and the time traveling to and checking into a hotel is counted as part of the rest time.

The argumentative technique used in the argument above is most accurately described by which of the following?

(A) setting up a hypothesis and then giving examples to both support and refute it
(B) citing specific information that calls a conclusion into question
(C) contrasting the details of two opposing points of view
(D) presenting an analogy between assumed and actual facts
(E) comparing the general attitude of the public with the more informed attitude of a regulatory body

60. The penny coin ought to be discontinued. People no longer want pennies taking space in pockets and purses, and the coins no longer serve any viable function in today's economy. There is no longer anything that can be purchased with a penny.

Of the following, which statement, if true, most strongly calls into question the above argument?

(A) The citizenry would not approve rounding up the sales tax to the nearest nickel, which would be necessary if the penny were eliminated.
(B) Pennies can be easily exchanged for other coins or bills.
(C) The elimination of the penny coin would immediately make coin collectors' penny mint sets more valuable.
(D) Penny candy has historically been widely available.
(E) Pennies cost the U.S. Mint more to make than they are worth.

61. *Janice:* Continued building on coastal shorelines is nothing but a recipe for disaster. The threat of hurricane destruction of homes and businesses is ever present, and erosion caused by construction activities is extremely destructive to the natural coastal environment. Both state and federal government should take more decisive steps to stop U.S. coastal development.
Wayne: People have a right to their property, the use of it, and any benefit they may derive from its ownership. Such rights should never be abridged by government without a compelling reason.

Which of the following best summarizes the point under discussion by Janice and Wayne?

(A) whether hurricane destruction and erosion constitute a compelling reason to ban coastal development

(B) the need for a ban on coastal development due to damage to property and the environment versus the property rights of individuals

(C) the possibility of a government buyout of existing private coastal property versus the grandfathering in of rights for existing property owners

(D) the need for a ban on coastal development based on the compelling reasons of loss of shore bird habitat and beach areas due to erosion

(E) whether the benefits derived from coastal property ownership offset the damage caused to the environment

62. State auto emission testing is less effective against air pollution than generally thought. Not all states require such testing before license renewal, and those that do may be more or less stringent in their checking procedures, allowing local garages, whose priorities may be earning the fee, not controlling emissions, to do the testing. It is clear that approximately 12 percent of vehicles, those that are older or malfunctioning, produce over 50 percent of emission pollution.

Of the following, which is most strongly supported by the information above?

(A) Consistent auto emission checking by all states would result in less emission pollution.

(B) Half of auto emission pollution is caused by 50 percent of older and malfunctioning vehicles.

(C) The general thought concerning the effectiveness of emission testing is irrelevant to a constructive handling of the problem.

(D) If checking stations themselves were regulated, making sure they efficiently enforced appropriate auto emission standards, the problem would be eliminated.

(E) A stringent federal program to identify and repair or delicense vehicles with unacceptable emission levels would most likely lower emission pollution.

63. The venomous brown recluse spider, as its name indicates, is not regularly seen because of its reclusive habits. Outdoors it may be discovered under stones and rocks, but it is more likely to inhabit indoor areas, particularly dark closet or drawer corners or any quiet and unused cranny. It is, however, also often seen in bathtubs.

Which one of the following, if true, LEAST explains the fact that brown recluse spiders are found in bathtubs?

(A) Although the brown recluse spider inhabits many indoor areas, it is most easily spotted in contrast to the often light-colored field of the bathroom fixtures.

(B) The insects upon which the brown recluse spider preys are likely to inhabit the moist areas of a bathroom.

(C) Since the brown recluse spider prefers to inhabit indoor areas, it can bite humans when they step into the tub, sometimes causing ulcerative sores that are slow to heal.

(D) The brown recluse spider is unable to negotiate the slick surface of bathroom fixtures.

(E) Since these spiders prefer to inhabit indoor areas, they are statistically likely to sometimes appear in bathtubs.

64. A research study on corporate behavior concludes that without the threat of government intervention, only a third as many recalls of dangerous products would occur as there are at present. Based on interoffice memos concerning products eventually recalled, the research finds that prior to recalling a product, company employees cite the possibility of government sanctions in two-thirds of the correspondence.

Based on the information above, the reasoning upon which the conclusion of the research study is based is likely to be flawed for all of the following reasons EXCEPT

(A) the study makes the assumption that companies should recall dangerous products on their own, without the impetus of government intervention or sanctions

(B) interoffice memos may be sent and received by low-level employees who have little or no input into the decision-making process of a company

(C) of all the recalled products studied, those that are dangerous may constitute only a small percentage of the whole

(D) citing the possibility of government sanctions does not necessarily make such sanctions a consideration in making the decision whether to recall or not

(E) the mention of the possibility of government sanctions in two-thirds of the correspondence does not necessarily equate to a reduction of two-thirds of recalled products

65. *Political analyst:* Contributions to political campaigns carry with them not only the possibility but the near certainty of conflicts of interest for politicians elected to office. When a politician votes on issues that will have an impact on the business interests of wealthy, generous constituents, it is highly likely that the politician's vote will be influenced. But needed as it is, pending campaign contribution reform legislation is in for a rocky road because the very politicians who benefit from campaign donations would have to vote to discontinue them.

Upon which of the following assumptions does the political analyst's argument most depend?

(A) Public and private good are inevitably at odds with one another when conflicts of interest arise in the political arena.

(B) Campaign contribution reform will be voted down by politicians in power because it is antithetical to their interests.

(C) Politicians, because they rely on contributions to their campaigns in order to be elected, would be ineffective champions for any sort of reform legislation while they are in office.

(D) Campaign contributors will make their points of view on legislation known to the politicians to whom they contributed.

(E) Those who receive campaign contributions are likely to adopt points of view reflecting those of the majority of their contributors.

66. Advertising and conducting closeout sales of summer merchandise should be banned until September. It's still hot in August, and people are still going on vacations, so they need the merchandise available to them.

Of the following principles, which one, if valid, most provides justification for the reasoning above.

(A) If closeout sales are advertised, they always take place.

(B) If closeout sales take place, they have not only been advertised, they are also successful.

(C) When one merchant has closeout of summer merchandise, all other merchants have closeout sales of summer merchandise.

(D) After a closeout sale of summer merchandise, no summer merchandise remains for sale until the following year.

(E) Advertising of closeout sales is regulated by law, and merchants may not falsely depict what is for sale, its price, and how long the sale will continue.

67. Sales of SUVs (sports utility vehicles), which use twice the gas that compact cars do for the same mileage, have not decreased even in periods of high gas prices. Automobile manufacturers have continued to produce these vehicles at an escalating rate and without any new fuel-efficient features. So the lowering of gas consumption is not a concern among purchasers and owners of these vehicles.

Which one of the following, if true, most weakens the argument above?

(A) In periods of high gas prices, owners of SUVs drive them twenty-five percent fewer miles than they do when gas prices fall.

(B) Fuel-efficient features were incorporated in the design of SUVs when they were first produced.

(C) SUV owners support the fact that manufacturers have designed many fuel-efficient features to use in these vehicles as soon as government regulations mandate them.

(D) The sales of SUVs in Europe have sharply declined compared to sales in the United States.

(E) SUV owners generally purchase the same lower octane fuel as do drivers of compact cars.

68. The dry heat of the southwestern United States has long been touted as an excellent environment for alleviating respiratory problems such as asthma and emphysema. But with the growing air pollution problems in southwestern cities, retirees with such conditions should not plan for the Southwest as their retirement home.

Which of the following is an assumption that the speaker above must make in order to appropriately draw his or her conclusion?

(A) Air pollution problems in the Southwest are as bad as or worse than those problems in other urban areas of the country.

(B) Retirees plan for housing and move to new areas when they stop working.

(C) The effect of air pollution on respiratory ailments offsets the benefit of dry heat for these ailments.

(D) Although respiratory problems have many causes, air pollution is certainly one of them.

(E) Air pollution problems in the Southwest reduce the dryness of the heat, causing it to be ineffective in alleviating respiratory problems.

69. Thirty minutes of exercise several times a week and, for those who are overweight, a reduction in weight of as little as 7 percent, can be effective in preventing or delaying the onset of adult type II diabetes. Therefore, if you are sedentary and obese, your chances of having this disease are higher than if you are thinner and active.

If the statements above are true, which one of the following must also be true?

(A) If you reduce your weight by 7 percent, your chances of remaining free of type II diabetes are enhanced.

(B) If you are not overweight, if you exercise, and if you don't have type II diabetes, your weight and exercise may be playing a role in your freedom from the disease.

(C) Thirty minutes of exercise several times a week and a reduction of weight by 7 percent will likely lengthen your life span.

(D) If you have type II diabetes, the addition of exercise and the careful attention to diet will make it more likely that your disease can be eliminated.

(E) If you do not have type II diabetes, you have controlled your weight and engaged in some exercise.

70. *Defense lawyer:* The releasing of computer viruses is a form of vandalism. That the vandalism is electronic does not change the fact that, like spray painting a wall or knocking down a mailbox, it is the destruction of property. So punishment for releasing computer viruses should be no harsher than for other types of vandalism.

Of the following, which most accurately describes the defense lawyer's argument?

(A) It draws a conclusion based on semantic differences in disparate points of view.

(B) It uses a metaphor to point out substantive variations in definition.

(C) It moves from a specific identification to general description.

(D) It proposes that seemingly unrelated events are members of the same larger category.

(E) It defines a principle and then posits an exception to that principle.

Answers and Explanations

1. **C** The passage states that robots not only can build other robots but also can rebuild themselves; therefore, they should last forever. (B) is probably true, but (C) must be true. According to the passage, (A) and (E) are not implied, and (D) is probably not true.

2. **E** There are tasks that robots can do better than humans. Any task in which not being able to think independently or not having emotions would be advantageous might be better done by robots. Tasks that require exposure to dangerous chemicals or radioactivity are also suitable for robots.

3. **E** The author states that the robot can do the most complex group of activities, but "does not have the capacity to . . . think independently." If the most complex group of activities necessitates independent thinking, then the author's assertions are in *direct* contradiction. (C) would be a good choice if it mentioned independent thinking, not training, as training is not mentioned in the passage.

4. **D** All of the four other answers are clearly assumptions that can be inferred from the details of the paragraph. Choice (D) may or may not be true, but unlike the other choices, there is nothing in the paragraph that supports it, since there is no reference to the policies of other airlines.

5. **B** Since none of the January blossoming plants will flower again later in the year, no plants that first blossom in January will flower twice in the year. (A), (C), and (E) may be untrue, because we are not told that all the bulbs and tubers in the garden blossom in January; we are told only that all the plants that blossom in January are from bulbs or tubers. (D) need not be true since some bulbs may not flower every year.

6. **D** (A) and (B) are irrelevant, and (C) and (E) are not as effective as (D) because they are just restatements of the thought, rather than a clarification.

7. **A** The phrase "four out of five" implies 80% of a large sample (nationwide). If only five dentists were in the sample, the reliability would certainly be in question. (B) would strengthen the endorsement, while (D) and (E) are irrelevant. (C) could weaken it, but not nearly as much.

8. **E** (A) must be true by the first statement because everybody in the class likes drawing or painting or both, so if Angie does not like painting, she must like drawing. This same logic holds for (C). "Everyone in the class who does not like drawing," must like painting. And (D), it is possible that no one in the class likes painting. But (E) cannot be true if everyone likes drawing or painting or both.

9. **D** (A) is incorrect since there is no attack on Mark's reasoning. (B) is incorrect because personal pressure is not implied. (C) is incorrect since it is hearsay. (E) is incorrect, since who is to say what a "positive" approach is? (E) could have been the correct choice if (D) were not a possibility.

10. **C** The conclusion of the passage is that, because of safety concerns, more research and testing ought to be done before microwaves become standard household appliances. If, however, research and testing are ineffective means of discerning safety problems, then research and testing would be irrelevant. This criticism seriously weakens the conclusion.

11. **E** If many microwave ovens have been found to leak radioactive elements, then the conclusion—that microwaves should not be standard appliances until they are more carefully researched and tested—is further strengthened because more safety concerns needed to be addressed.

12. **C** The pattern of reasoning here is since X follows from Y, if Y is absent, there will be no X. In choice (C), buying from the bakery (Y) results in good breakfast business (X). But the restaurant that does not buy from the bakery (Y is absent) will have poor breakfast business (X). In the original, the first step is an action (eating Vitagatto), whereas in choice (B) it is inaction that has a consequence.

13. **C** Choices (A), (B), (D), and (E) are all reasonable ways of explaining the discrepancies. If the census report did undercount, we would still need to know if it undercounted one gender more than the other.

14. **A** The conclusion can be properly drawn only if the condition, *"being white,"* is sufficient to rule out all but quartz. (A) allows the conclusion, *"must* be quartz," to be reached.

15. **B** Though this chef probably believes that the restaurants of Paris are superior, the passage passes judgment only on the breads, not on the restaurants of New York. It does assume that good bread will be eaten, that lacking French training there are hardly any good bakers in America, and that if the bread is good the roll basket will be empty. But it may have been refilled three times.

16. **D** The chef's claim to know how to bake bread is, no doubt, just, but the four other answers point to weaknesses to be seen in the passage. The speaker asserts American incompetence on the basis of flimsy evidence, and the assumption that American food can be judged on the basis of some New York restaurants generalizes about the small restaurants in Paris and is not specific about restaurants in New York or Paris.

17. **A** The tone of the passage is positive: workers "enjoy" the same status; "harmony"; less "tension and anger." One can therefore conclude that the author approves of the work environment of the Japanese auto factory for the workers' well-being, and any resemblance of American factories to those of the Japanese ought to be encouraged. Note that there is no indication at all regarding the quality of the goods produced (B).

18. **A** Only (A) is logically supported by the passage. There is no direct support regarding worker envy for (B). There may be less tension and anger in Japanese auto factories; however, to conclude that there is no tension or anger is not logically sound. Nothing in the passage describes the relation of tension to productivity (D).

19. **A** The key word in the statements given is "usually." "Usually" suggests a frequent or regular phenomenon. It implies that an event may be normally expected and allows one to draw a conclusion *stronger than* those contained in (D) and (E). "Usually" does not mean "with certainty." Therefore, the categorical conclusions of (B) and (C) are not appropriate.

20. **C** (A) is not true, since Nexon is not a sufficient condition for life; that is, Nexon alone is not enough. (B) is not true because Nexon must be present if there is life (necessary condition). (C) is true; Nexon must be present (it is a necessary condition). (C) does not suggest the absence of things other than Nexon and, therefore, does not contradict the original statement. (D) is untrue since Nexon alone is not a sufficient condition.

21. **B** (A) need not be true, because the absence of Flennel is not a necessary condition; that is, there can be other conditions that result in the end of life. (C) is not true, because the absence of Flennel is sufficient to end life (one cannot say life may "not cease"). (B) is true, given the absence of Flennel is sufficient to end life. Both (D) and (E) are untrue. Absence of Flennel is sufficient cause (D) but there might be other causes as well (E).

22. **C** Choices (A), (B), (D), and (E) are all logical conclusions. Since electric heat is very expensive and the winters are very cold but the summers are merely warm, choice (D) makes sense. But even with high costs, we expect gas consumption to be higher in the very cold winters.

23. **E** The statement presented can be logically made only if being reared at Prince Charming Kennels assures that a poodle is purebred. (E) provides such assurance. (A) does not state that only purebreds are reared and, therefore, does not assure that any given poodle from the kennels is pure.

24. **D** (A) may be eliminated because the argument does not rule out a possible previous proposal. (B) may be eliminated as no suggestion of easy identification or the necessity of easy identification is presupposed. (C) may be eliminated because the argument is independent of any comparison between the Great Salt Lake and any other body of water. (E) can be eliminated because the argument presents the weaker claim of the *possibility* of oil. (D) allows, if true, the *possibility* of oil to be sufficient cause for exploration.

25. **D** The context suggests that salutary associations are positive ones, and the phrase *associations of pleasure* immediately following the first mention of *salutary* certifies (D) as the best choice.

26. **D** (A) is answered in the first sentence, as are (B) and (C). In the first sentence we are told that all thinking is associational, and in the second, that both education and experience promote accusations. Nowhere, however, does the author mention just what teachers blame and praise.

27. **D** Only this choice addresses both parts of the statement, which implies that expert practice helps identify errors. (B) and (C) stress error only; (A) stresses practice only; and (E) stresses writing only.

28. **A** Refer to the following diagram:

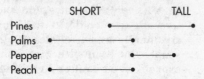

On the basis of the foregoing diagram, (B), (C), (D), and (E) are false.

29. **C** The structure of the given argument may be simplified:
Most are popular and low.
Splendor is not popular and high (not low).

(C) parallels this structure:
Most who stop do gain.
Carl does not stop and will not gain.

30. **E** The statement given can be simplified:
All have hair (mammal).
This does not have hair.
It is not (mammal).

Only (E) can be reduced to this same form:
All have smell (lubricants).
This does not have smell.
It is not (lubricant).

31. **B** (A) has no bearing because the argument is concerned only with mammals. (C) is not relevant; the argument does not address the amount of hair. (E) is likewise outside the argument's subject. (D) is a possible answer because the claim is that the absence of hair indicates a nonmammal. However, (B) is a better choice. (D) is a possibility—"One *could* remove." (B) points out that, without any other intervention, there *are* creatures with no hair that are also mammals.

32. **C** If the chances of a person with the same genetic makeup as someone who has developed the disease are 100 times higher than someone with different genes, genetic material must play some role. But if the proportion of people who do develop the disease is very small, genetics cannot be the only cause. The study supports (B) and (E), but gives no information on whether the disease is more likely to affect one identical twin than one nonidentical twin.

33. **D** Because they share the same genetic makeup, identical twins are especially useful in medical studies of the role of genes.

34. **C** The pattern of reasoning here is that X is caused by changes in either Y or Z. If Y is unchanged, and X happens, it must have been caused by Z. In (C), X is the rise in pizza costs, the steady Y is the cost of cheese, and the causative Z is the price of beef.

35. **D** Since the argument concerns state laws to be passed, the best choices must be those that refer to the responsibility of the state, (C) and (D). Of the two, (D) is clearly the more specific and directly relevant to the situation described in the paragraph.

36. **B** The first proposition states that if an athlete and invited, then over 35. The second proposition states that if over 35, then not both an athlete and invited. The propositions contradict each other. Therefore, no person can be both an athlete and invited.

37. **E** The most plausible answer here is that the group that lost more weight ate less at dinner. Presumably, members of the other group were much hungrier because they had exercised so much more and had less to eat at lunch, and so they ate more at dinner. (A) and (C) will not work if applied only to "some" of the group.

38. **C** If this surgical procedure does more harm than good, it would be wise not to perform it at all. This would reduce by one the number of needless surgical procedures.

39. **A** The passage insists that the tennis team will be composed only of first-rate athletes and nonsmokers. But there is no reason given to prevent a nonsmoker who is not a first-rate athlete from being on the team. Presumably he or she made up for lack of great natural ability with more practice.

40. **A** If the prices have gone down, the clothing sales might well increase, and television watching would be irrelevant. Options (B), (C), (D), and (E) have no information to explain the rise in sales apart from television.

41. **D** The error in the reasoning is the assumption that what was true of a group (the mortgage sales department) can predict something specific about a single member of that group (Thomason's presumed sales). The correct parallel is in (D), where the individual's performance (Meany's winning the golf championship) is based on the accomplishment of a group (the South Texas State golf team).

42. **C** If the largest foreign investor is the United States and the third largest is Britain, it appears that the rules are not intended to exclude Asians, since the same rules apply even more extensively to Europeans and Americans.

43. **B** The author, whose position is clearly in favor of fluoridation, refers to the "demonic scheme" to suggest the irrationality of the opposition. Choice (C) is careless. The argument is not trying to refute the notion of a communist plot.

44. **B** Only the first example (sickle-cell) is related to disease. The second concerns the response to lactose, and the third to fingerprints. What all three have in common is that they

cannot be predicted by race, and the passage is part of a consideration of the difficulty of providing a scientific definition of race.

45. **E** Options (A), (B), (C), and (D) assumptions are in the passage, but there is nothing here to support the idea that either medical or legal costs are greater.

46. **D** If all medical costs in the other states are much lower, the fact that the medical costs of automobile accident victims are also lower would be explained, and the argument that "pain and suffering" awards lead to higher medical costs would be weakened.

47. **D** Most of the paragraph is concerned with the sales figures. Only in the last sentence does the subject of profit arise, and we are never told exactly how sales relate to profit. To assume that there can be no profit with this decline in sales, we must also assume that the profit margin will not be higher.

48. **C** The author makes his point by using an analogy. That is, he argues that the passage of limits on ozone-depleting gases resulted in the rapid development of affordable technologies to deal with the problem, and suggests that unless short-term limits on greenhouse gases are enacted, there will be no urgency to develop the necessary technologies.

49. **B** If there has been no research to develop a technology to deal with global warming, the enactment of short-term limits would not bring the needed technologies to the marketplace. Choice (A) deals with "immediate economic consequences" but the issue is short- and long-term limits, not immediate ones.

50. **E** The suggestions of a cult or college prank are alternate explanations that are supported by the evidence as well as the alien invader notion. Though the evidence is questionable, the response here does not quarrel with its accuracy.

51. **C** The professor accuses the student of being less than honest about the study time mentioned and so is assuming that the two hours spent on the review of the endocrine system and the rereading of the chapter on the circulatory system three times

would have been effective (A), which is not necessarily the case. Consequently, the professor is saying, the student must be less than honest about the study time. But the student's study time and methods may not have been effective through poor concentration (B), lack of attention perhaps during the rereading (D), or physical problems during the exam itself (E) and may not be dishonest at all. The passage assumes only that the "basic facts" could have been learned in the study time that the student had specified; there is no evidence to suggest, however, that the professor considers the learning of basic facts to be easy.

52. **E** The argument is in this form: A (people who dream in color) are B (creative). C (Conrad) is B (creative). Therefore, C (Conrad) is A (one who dreams in color). The final statement logically doesn't follow because the first statement doesn't say *only* people who dream in color are creative. The only answer that follows this pattern is (E). A (corn) is B (not good in containers). C (maize) is B (not good in containers). Therefore, C (maize) is A (corn). This question is made more difficult by the fact that in reality maize actually is corn. But that doesn't change the flawed reasoning. Any other plant could have been substituted for maize in the pattern of this argument, producing a statement such as "tomatoes are corn." No other answer exhibits this flawed pattern of logic. Answer (C) is incorrect because Sally is not now an electrician, and there's nothing that suggests she will be, only that she wants to be.

53. **C** The only assumption made by the Parks and Recreation Supervisor is that visitors to the park would like to avoid being bitten. If the supervisor didn't make such an assumption, there would be no reason to write the advisory in the first place.

54. **C** Although George doesn't do all that he could to avoid bites, what he does is the most likely to be effective. By staying on the paths, he avoids the weeds and other plants that are likely to harbor chiggers. And climbing the rock face is unlikely to put him in harm's way from the insects because a rock face would not tend to have heavy plant growth. By showering when he returns, he's likely to dislodge any stray chiggers that might have gotten on his body. Sheila (A) showers after applying repellant, rendering it ineffective. Consuela (B), by venturing into a blackberry patch will probably have picked up chiggers, and toweling alone may not rid her of them. Dimitri (D) sprays only a few areas of his body and is going through heavy brush, where insects are likely to be. Connie (E) may be applying countermeasures too late into her walk.

55. **D** The fact that the immigrants are taking jobs that U.S. citizens won't take calls into question the speaker's statement that the immigrants are taking jobs away from legal citizens. It doesn't approach the speaker's contention that the immigrants use federal tax dollars for services, but it calls the conclusion into question more than does any other choice given. (B) is not correct because it mentions local taxes, not the federal taxes the speaker cites.

56. **B** Only this fact could explain the seeming inconsistency presented. The Woodwards used *more* kilowatt hours in August than in July, but they were charged *less* for those hours. The information given makes it clear that the electric company didn't lower their *average* rate. It remained the same as July's, so the company's buying cheaper electricity (C) isn't relevant. Neither is the fact that the Woodwards tried to conserve electricity in August. Since they used more hours in August than in July, they obviously weren't successful in that endeavor.

57. **E** Pete clearly says that he agrees with the *concerns* of the ecoterrorists. But he also suggests that the life of the spotted owl and the life of a human shouldn't be equated; in other words, methods used to save the planet should *not* endanger people (he doesn't comment on whether harming human possessions is unacceptable). The fact that Pete recognizes the effectiveness of the ecoterrorists' methods doesn't mean that he agrees with them. But Anne mistakenly believes that Pete agrees with the *methods* of the ecoterrorists, not only their *concerns*.

58. **B** If ninety percent of doctors actively promote pharmaceutical plant research, then it can be assumed that ten percent do not. But it doesn't follow that those who don't actively promote the research are opposed to it (E). It also can't be known from the facts given that all politicians in rain forest countries are ignorant about the subject (A) or that ninety-eight percent of people oppose the research (C) (they simply aren't knowledgeable about it). And even though ninety percent of doctors actively promote the research, it doesn't necessarily follow that they are well informed about it (D).

59. **B** The argument uses specific information (schedule delays, travel and check-in time) to call into question the conclusion that the allowance of nine hours of rest in a twenty-four hour period is reasonable and prudent. By this argumentative technique, the speaker suggests that pilots may not be getting the nine hours of rest they are thought to get. Although the argument does deal with a possible discrepancy between assumed and actual facts, it doesn't use an analogy (D).

60. **A** If the citizenry would not approve the rounding up of sales tax to the next nickel, then local government would have a real dilemma. They would lose money if the amount were rounded down, and they would be unable to collect their present sales tax if pennies were eliminated and consequently would lose needed funds. Of the answers given, this problem would most strongly call the elimination of the penny coin into question. The other answer choices either support (mildly or strongly) the argument (choices B and E) or are irrelevant (choices C and D).

61. **B** Janice promotes a ban on coastal development. Wayne, however, raises the question of property rights of individuals in this matter. All the other choices go too far, given the discussion presented. The conversation might go on to discuss whether Janice's points constitute a compelling reason for the ban (A), but it doesn't do so as presented. A government buyout or grandfathering in of rights (C) might be options discussed as the conversation progresses, but

they aren't here. The specific damage of lost shore bird habitat and beach areas aren't discussed (D), only erosion damage in general. And, although you might surmise that Wayne may contend that property rights offset the damage (E), he doesn't actually make that point.

62. **E** The passage states that not all states have emission testing. A first step in controlling the emission problem, then, would be to have testing on a national (federal) level. The fact that the testing program would be "stringent," that is, rigorous and exacting, indicates that it may be more effective than existing state programs. In addition, the choice suggests that these measures would "probably" be effective, not absolutely. Choice (A) isn't the best answer because there is no indication of the level of effectiveness of the state programs. Checking can be consistently bad as well as good, in which case the problem would not be reduced. The general view of emission testing is not irrelevant (C), although it may be incorrect, as public opinion can be important in the passing of laws and the functioning of government. Choice (D) overstates the effect when it says the problem would definitely be "eliminated."

63. **C** For choice (C) to explain why the spiders are found in bathtubs, it would have to be assumed that they intentionally lie there awaiting a chance to bite humans, which is illogical considering that, first, the spiders prefer isolated, dark, unused areas and, second, that they would somehow consider humans prey, which is not likely considering their size. All other choices give possible reasons for the phenomenon, although (E) does so fairly weakly. Choice (D) does explain the presence of the spiders, as they may fall into the tub and be unable to climb back out.

64. **A** According to the information, the study makes no ethical judgment on what the companies should or should not do; it simply reports, based on this research, on what is done. But given these facts, the other choices all indicate a likely flaw in the study's reasoning. The actual decision makers may not agree with the memo writers (B); the study seems to confuse dangerous recalled products

with all recalled products (C); the awareness of possible sanctions doesn't automatically make them factors in the decision (D); and the assumption that mention of sanctions in two-thirds of the correspondence equates to a two-thirds reduction of dangerous products (or even of all recalled products) is illogical (E).

65. **D** If contributors don't somehow make their points of view known to the politicians, it would be difficult for those points of view to be influential at voting time. Although the discussion does seem to suggest that public and private good may sometimes be in conflict, it doesn't assume that it would be "inevitably" so (A). Nor does the analyst imply that campaign contribution reform will necessarily be "voted down" (B), only that it will face challenges (a "rocky road"). Choice (C) mentions reform legislation in general, which isn't under discussion here. There is an assumption by the analyst that politicians may adopt the view of "wealthy, generous contributors," but choice (E) mentions the "majority" of contributors. The wealthy and generous donors may not be in the majority. Their number, as opposed to, say, donors of small sums, isn't mentioned.

66. **D** Although there are several logical problems with the reasoning in the passage, and no choice fully justifies its reasoning, choice (D) at least in part justifies it. If people actually still need summer merchandise in August, and if no summer merchandise remains after a sale, then an argument might be made that no such closeout sales should be allowed until September. No other choice indicates that no summer merchandise remains for consumers to buy in August.

67. **A** Only this choice definitely suggests that the SUV owners are concerned about the lowering of gas consumption at least to some extent and at least during periods of high gas prices, and weakens the argument that they are unconcerned. The fact that fuel-efficient features were originally incorporated in these vehicles is irrelevant, as the SUVs are now high gas users. Choice (C) is also irrelevant; these owners may simply

not want their vehicles banned and so support features that will still allow them to drive them. Because the conclusion about SUV owners' unconcern is not restricted to only U.S. drivers, choice (D) may seem to be a good answer, because it indicates a drop in sales in Europe. But the choice doesn't say why the drop in sales has occurred. Perhaps it's just a cultural change in preference. The purchase of lower octane fuel (E) doesn't necessarily have to do with the concern about amount of gas consumption, only with the cost of that consumption, and nothing indicates that these vehicles would need higher octane fuel in any case.

68. **C** If dry heat alleviates respiratory problems, and this speaker now recommends against the Southwest as a retirement destination for retirees with respiratory problems because of the air pollution, the speaker must make the assumption that the pollution substantially offsets the benefits of dry heat. Choice (D) is incorrect because air pollution is not listed as a *cause* of respiratory problems such as asthma or emphysema (although it perhaps could be), and such an assumption is not necessary to the argument, which addresses itself to those who already *have* respiratory difficulties. Choices (A), (B), and (E) are not assumptions that the speaker must make. Choice (A) deals with comparing pollution problems with those in other areas. Choice (B) deals with retirees' plans, and Choice (E) deals with the reduction of dryness of the heat.

69. **B** Choice (B) is the only choice that must be true if the statements are true. Note that the choice says that weight and exercise "may" be playing a role, which is true given the fact that we know they are effective in preventing or delaying the onset of the disease. The choice would not necessarily be true if it said they "are" definitely playing a role because other factors may be involved in the disease (say, genetic factors or simply your age). Choice E is incorrect for this same reason. Choice (A) is not necessarily true because it discusses weight alone, and the original statements speak only of the combi-

nation of exercise and weight reduction. Choice (C) is incorrect because you may die from other causes and life span would not be affected. Choice (D) introduces the elimination of the disease, which isn't discussed in the original statements, only the onset of the disease.

70. **D** The lawyer's argument proposes that seemingly unrelated events—the releasing of computer viruses, the spray painting of a wall, and the knocking over of a mailbox—are part of a larger category, vandalism. The argument doesn't deal with "disparate points of view" (A), a metaphor (B), a general description (C), or an exception to a principle (E). The argument goes on to draw a conclusion based on the fact that the events are part of one larger category, but even though choice (D) may not be a complete description of the lawyer's argument, it remains the best of the choices given.

Answer Sheet
Extra Practice:
Logical Reasoning

1. Ⓐ Ⓑ Ⓒ Ⓓ Ⓔ
2. Ⓐ Ⓑ Ⓒ Ⓓ Ⓔ
3. Ⓐ Ⓑ Ⓒ Ⓓ Ⓔ
4. Ⓐ Ⓑ Ⓒ Ⓓ Ⓔ
5. Ⓐ Ⓑ Ⓒ Ⓓ Ⓔ
6. Ⓐ Ⓑ Ⓒ Ⓓ Ⓔ
7. Ⓐ Ⓑ Ⓒ Ⓓ Ⓔ
8. Ⓐ Ⓑ Ⓒ Ⓓ Ⓔ
9. Ⓐ Ⓑ Ⓒ Ⓓ Ⓔ
10. Ⓐ Ⓑ Ⓒ Ⓓ Ⓔ
11. Ⓐ Ⓑ Ⓒ Ⓓ Ⓔ
12. Ⓐ Ⓑ Ⓒ Ⓓ Ⓔ
13. Ⓐ Ⓑ Ⓒ Ⓓ Ⓔ
14. Ⓐ Ⓑ Ⓒ Ⓓ Ⓔ
15. Ⓐ Ⓑ Ⓒ Ⓓ Ⓔ
16. Ⓐ Ⓑ Ⓒ Ⓓ Ⓔ
17. Ⓐ Ⓑ Ⓒ Ⓓ Ⓔ
18. Ⓐ Ⓑ Ⓒ Ⓓ Ⓔ

19. Ⓐ Ⓑ Ⓒ Ⓓ Ⓔ
20. Ⓐ Ⓑ Ⓒ Ⓓ Ⓔ
21. Ⓐ Ⓑ Ⓒ Ⓓ Ⓔ
22. Ⓐ Ⓑ Ⓒ Ⓓ Ⓔ
23. Ⓐ Ⓑ Ⓒ Ⓓ Ⓔ
24. Ⓐ Ⓑ Ⓒ Ⓓ Ⓔ
25. Ⓐ Ⓑ Ⓒ Ⓓ Ⓔ
26. Ⓐ Ⓑ Ⓒ Ⓓ Ⓔ
27. Ⓐ Ⓑ Ⓒ Ⓓ Ⓔ
28. Ⓐ Ⓑ Ⓒ Ⓓ Ⓔ
29. Ⓐ Ⓑ Ⓒ Ⓓ Ⓔ
30. Ⓐ Ⓑ Ⓒ Ⓓ Ⓔ
31. Ⓐ Ⓑ Ⓒ Ⓓ Ⓔ
32. Ⓐ Ⓑ Ⓒ Ⓓ Ⓔ
33. Ⓐ Ⓑ Ⓒ Ⓓ Ⓔ
34. Ⓐ Ⓑ Ⓒ Ⓓ Ⓔ
35. Ⓐ Ⓑ Ⓒ Ⓓ Ⓔ
36. Ⓐ Ⓑ Ⓒ Ⓓ Ⓔ

37. Ⓐ Ⓑ Ⓒ Ⓓ Ⓔ
38. Ⓐ Ⓑ Ⓒ Ⓓ Ⓔ
39. Ⓐ Ⓑ Ⓒ Ⓓ Ⓔ
40. Ⓐ Ⓑ Ⓒ Ⓓ Ⓔ
41. Ⓐ Ⓑ Ⓒ Ⓓ Ⓔ
42. Ⓐ Ⓑ Ⓒ Ⓓ Ⓔ
43. Ⓐ Ⓑ Ⓒ Ⓓ Ⓔ
44. Ⓐ Ⓑ Ⓒ Ⓓ Ⓔ
45. Ⓐ Ⓑ Ⓒ Ⓓ Ⓔ
46. Ⓐ Ⓑ Ⓒ Ⓓ Ⓔ
47. Ⓐ Ⓑ Ⓒ Ⓓ Ⓔ
48. Ⓐ Ⓑ Ⓒ Ⓓ Ⓔ
49. Ⓐ Ⓑ Ⓒ Ⓓ Ⓔ
50. Ⓐ Ⓑ Ⓒ Ⓓ Ⓔ
51. Ⓐ Ⓑ Ⓒ Ⓓ Ⓔ
52. Ⓐ Ⓑ Ⓒ Ⓓ Ⓔ
53. Ⓐ Ⓑ Ⓒ Ⓓ Ⓔ

54. Ⓐ Ⓑ Ⓒ Ⓓ Ⓔ
55. Ⓐ Ⓑ Ⓒ Ⓓ Ⓔ
56. Ⓐ Ⓑ Ⓒ Ⓓ Ⓔ
57. Ⓐ Ⓑ Ⓒ Ⓓ Ⓔ
58. Ⓐ Ⓑ Ⓒ Ⓓ Ⓔ
59. Ⓐ Ⓑ Ⓒ Ⓓ Ⓔ
60. Ⓐ Ⓑ Ⓒ Ⓓ Ⓔ
61. Ⓐ Ⓑ Ⓒ Ⓓ Ⓔ
62. Ⓐ Ⓑ Ⓒ Ⓓ Ⓔ
63. Ⓐ Ⓑ Ⓒ Ⓓ Ⓔ
64. Ⓐ Ⓑ Ⓒ Ⓓ Ⓔ
65. Ⓐ Ⓑ Ⓒ Ⓓ Ⓔ
66. Ⓐ Ⓑ Ⓒ Ⓓ Ⓔ
67. Ⓐ Ⓑ Ⓒ Ⓓ Ⓔ
68. Ⓐ Ⓑ Ⓒ Ⓓ Ⓔ
69. Ⓐ Ⓑ Ⓒ Ⓓ Ⓔ
70. Ⓐ Ⓑ Ⓒ Ⓓ Ⓔ

Chapter 5
WRITING SAMPLE

Introduction

The LSAT will include a 30-minute writing sample. You will be asked to respond to a general essay topic that requires no specialized knowledge, but does require you to write an argument for selecting one of two candidates or items based on given criteria. You should express yourself clearly and effectively.

The essay will *not* be scored, but will be forwarded to the law schools to which you apply. Different law schools have adopted different approaches to evaluating and weighing the quality of the essay.

You will write the essay in a "Writing Sample booklet," a paper folder with general directions on the outside, and the essay topic plus space for your response on the inside. A sheet of scratch paper is provided for organizing and/or outlining your ideas. A pen is also provided for the essay. The essay booklet restricts the length of your response to about *30 lines, each line about seven inches long.* Anything you write outside this restricted space will not be evaluated. Therefore, for practice purposes, restrict yourself to the same space that you will be given on the LSAT to become more comfortable with writing under these restricted conditions.

Following are general directions for the writing sample, a careful analysis of this essay requirement, and a series of steps you may want to follow as you compose your essay. Next, you will examine two completed essays, each written from a different perspective. The chapter concludes with a review of general tips for the writing sample and nine suggested topics for writing your own essays.

General Directions

You have 30 minutes to write an essay in response to a given topic. Take a few minutes to plan your work before you begin writing. DO NOT WRITE ON A TOPIC OF YOUR OWN CHOICE. ESSAYS THAT DO NOT ADDRESS THE GIVEN TOPIC ARE UNACCEPTABLE.

The quality of your writing is more important than the length of your response and content. There is no "right" or "wrong" answer to the question. Pay attention to organization, appropriate diction, and correct usage. You will not be expected to display any specialized knowledge in your response, nor will you be expected to write a "perfect" essay; law schools understand that you are writing under a time constraint and pressured circumstances.

Only the lined area in your booklet will be reproduced for the law schools, so do not write outside this space. *Do not* skip lines or use wide margins. These precautions, along with careful planning and legible handwriting that is not unduly large, will keep you within the allowed space.

The Approach

Analyzing the Writing Sample Topic

You will be asked to write an argument for hiring, promoting, selecting, etc., one of two candidates or items based on two or more criteria and two brief sketches of the candidates or items.

Some recent topics have included writing arguments in support of:

- Purchasing one of two films for a public television station
- Selecting one of two designs submitted for a commemorative sculpture
- Selecting one of two retirement communities for a retiree
- Selecting one of two ways of investing money inherited from an uncle
- Deciding which one of two schools to enter for an undergraduate business degree
- Selecting one of two proposals for an introductory course in computer training
- Selecting one of two athletes for a team

In each case the initial introductory statement was followed by two criteria, and then the background of each candidate, or a description of each film, or a description of each school, or a description of each option.

Let's take a closer look. A recent topic gave us its two criteria for hiring a mathematics teacher: (1) the high school's increased concern with computers and (2) its wish to develop the mathematics program at the school to incorporate work-study projects in the business community. The first candidate had a solid educational background, high school teaching and minor administrative experience, good references, and recent training in computers. The second candidate had a slightly different but equally good educational background and no high school teaching experience, but had worked as a teaching assistant in college and a tutor in community programs, as well as having solid credentials in computers and experience as an employee in financial work for a retail store and a bank.

What should be apparent is that it does _NOT_ matter which candidate you choose. The principles and qualifications will be written in such a way that you can write in favor of _EITHER_ candidate. Make your choice, and stick to it. Don't worry about the other candidate. What your readers will be looking for are clarity, consistency, relevance, and correctness of grammar and usage. Since you have only one-half hour to read the topic and to plan and write your essay, you will not be expected to produce a long or a subtle essay. But you must write on the topic clearly and correctly.

The questions will make clear the sort of audience you are writing for, and you can be sure that this audience is literate and informed about the issues in your paper. In the math teacher topic, for example, the assumed audience is whoever is to hire the math teacher. You do not need to tell this audience what she already knows, but you do want to make her focus upon the issues that support your case. Let us assume you are making the case for the experienced teacher with some computer training. Your essay should stress the obvious qualifications—his teaching experience and computer training. Where you have no direct evidence of expertise, you can invent, so long as you do so plausibly and work from details that are given in the question. You could, for example, argue that, although there are two criteria, the computer issue is really the more important since the students will not be able to find good work-study projects in the community until they have a greater knowledge of computers.

Assume you have chosen the second candidate. Your essay should focus upon her strengths (for example, her experience in business will help her in setting up a business-related program for the students). Where her qualifications are weaker (her lack of high school teaching experience), your essay can emphasize the other kind of teaching experience she has had. Do not be afraid to introduce details to support your argument that are your own ideas. Just be sure that, when you do present additional information, it is consistent with and arises plausibly from the information on the test.

So far, the writing topics have used two slightly different forms. The first (the math teachers) used two sentences, one for each of two equally weighted criteria, and then described the two equally qualified candidates. Another sample topic type also uses two sentences to describe the principles, but the first contains the two criteria, and the second sentence elaborates on one of them. For example, the two principles might be (1) lifeguards are promoted on the basis of years of service and community activities; and (2) community activities include lifesaving clinics, talks to school children, waterfront safety seminars, and high school swimming-team coaching. The biographies would then describe two candidates whose years of service differ slightly, and each of whom has some strength in the areas listed under (2). Since you are not told which of the two criteria is the more important, or which of the various sorts of community service is most important, you can decide for yourself how to weigh these factors, as long as you do so plausibly. You cannot contradict the question—for example, by saying length of service is not important—but you can argue that, although your candidate's length of service is slightly less than that of her competition, her overwhelming superiority in community service is more important.

Here is a suggested plan for approaching any writing sample of this sort.

The Phases of Writing

Phase 1—Prewriting

1. Read the two statements of policy or criteria at least twice, *actively*. (Circle or mark the essential points of the topic.) Are they equally weighted? If not, clarify the difference.
2. Read the biographies or descriptions at least twice, *actively*. Test them carefully against the policy or criteria statements.
3. Choose your candidate or item. Again set the qualifications or qualities beside those of the statements. Decide exactly what your choice's greatest strengths are. What are the limitations? Think about how these limitations can be invalidated or turned into strengths.
4. Outline your essay. It should be two or three paragraphs long. If you are selecting a candidate, paragraph 1 might focus on his or her obvious strengths that meet the given criteria. Paragraph 2, or paragraphs 2 and 3, might deal with how the candidate also shows promise of fulfilling the other requirements.

Phase 2—Writing

1. Do *not* waste time with a fancy opening paragraph on an irrelevant topic like the importance of math teachers or lifeguards in this complex modern world.
2. Start with a direction. Your first sentence should serve a purpose.
3. Support your argument with examples or other specifics.
4. Do *not* write a closing paragraph that simply repeats what you have already said.
5. Write legibly. Write clearly. Write naturally. Do *not* use big words for their own sake. Do not try to be cute or ironic or funny.
6. Remember that the assumed purpose of this paper is to convince a reader to prefer one candidate or item to another. Your real purpose, of course, is to show a law school that you can follow instructions and write an essay that is well organized, adheres to the point, and is grammatically correct.

Phase 3—Reading

1. Allow sufficient time to proofread your essay. At this point, add any information that is vital, and delete any information that seems confusing or out of place.
2. Don't make extensive changes that will make your writing less readable.
3. Check each sentence for mechanical errors (spelling, punctuation, grammar). Some common types of errors are these:

    *   using pronouns with no clear antecedents;
    *   lack of agreement between subject and verb;
    *   using the wrong verb tense;
    *   faulty parallelism in a series of items;
    *   misplaced or dangling modifiers;
    *   adjective-adverb confusion;
    *   misuse of comparative terms or comparisons.

Two Completed Writing Samples

Following are two handwritten "model" essays, written on LSAT Writing Sample booklet-type pages. These samples are based on the topic given in the Diagnostic Mini-Exam on page 30. Notice that each of the two sample essays is written from a different perspective.

Sample Topic

Read the following descriptions of Bergquist and Kretchmer, applicants for the job of Assistant Director on a major motion picture. *Then, in the space provided, write an argument for hiring either Bergquist or Kretchmer.* The following criteria are relevant to your decision:

- In addition to working closely with and advising the Director on creative decisions, the Assistant Director must work with all types of individuals—from stars to Teamster truck drivers—and elicit the best from every cast and crew member for the good of the motion picture.
- The Assistant Director is responsible for all the planning and organization—including paperwork, travel itinerary, meals, etc.—of the entire film project. He/she lays the groundwork for a successful "shoot."

BERGQUIST began her career in films as an Administrative Assistant to the president of a major film studio. As such, she often accompanied her employer in his wining and dining of stars, or to the set when problems arose. She double-checked contracts, shooting schedules, cast and crew checks, and kept a close eye on the budget of several multimillion-dollar films. When her boss was subsequently fired due to a poor season of films, Bergquist was able to secure a position as Assistant Editor at the studio, helping several highly respected film editors "cut" feature films. It was here that she learned about the creative end of the business, and soon after became the chief editor of an hour-long studio documentary, which won several awards. After two years, Bergquist was accepted into the Assistant Directors Training Program, and is presently a candidate for Assistant Director of this new $15,000,000 motion picture.

KRETCHMER was a principal/teacher for 12 years before embarking on a film career. She taught math at the New York School for the Creative Arts, and also worked with parents in the community, the board of education, and local government representatives in securing financing for the $20,000,000 school building. As Chairperson of the New Building Committee, she worked closely with architects, townspeople, contractors, and even children to understand their needs for the building. Today the building stands as a model for such schools everywhere. Eight years ago Kretchmer came to Hollywood and, through persistence and charm, secured a studio position and worked her way up to Chief Auditor, where she oversaw budgets on several multimillion-dollar films. She enrolled in the Assistant Directors Training Program, which she recently completed, and is now a candidate for the position of Assistant Director of this new film.

What sets Bergquist apart from Kretchmer is her understanding of, and experience in, the creative elements of filmmaking.

An Assistant Director (AD) advises the Director in key creative decisions: how to best structure and order the shooting schedule, how to begin and end scenes, and how best to shoot a scene or sequence. While the ultimate decision rests with the Director, the AD's input is vital. Like a caddy advising a golfer of the distance and terrain of the course, the AD's knowledge of the creative elements of filmmaking enhances her abilities in these tasks. Since a film's success often hinges on these creative decisions, the AD's contributions can be critical.

As an editor, Bergquist learned how a film is cut together and how the pieces must fit coherently. She cut her own films and won numerous awards, thus reflecting her understanding of good creative choices. This special knowledge of film (which Kretchmer lacks)—how shots must match, how moods and sequences build upon each other—is essential to the final success of any film.

Another Approach

Read the following descriptions of Bergquist and Kretchmer, applicants for the job of Assistant Director on a major motion picture. *Then, in the space provided, write an argument for hiring either Bergquist or Kretchmer.* The following criteria are relevant to your decision:
- In addition to working closely with and advising the Director on creative decisions, the Assistant Director must work with all types of individuals—from stars to Teamster truck drivers—and elicit the best from every cast and crew member for the good of the motion picture.
- The Assistant Director is responsible for all the planning and organization—including paperwork, travel itinerary, meals, etc.—of the entire film project. He/she lays the groundwork for a successful "shoot."

BERGQUIST began her career in films as an Administrative Assistant to the president of a major film studio. As such, she often accompanied her employer in his wining and dining of stars, or to the set when problems arose. She double-checked contracts, shooting schedules, cast and crew checks, and kept a close eye on the budget of several multimillion-dollar films. When her boss was subsequently fired due to a poor season of films, Bergquist was able to secure a position as Assistant Editor at the studio, helping several highly respected film editors "cut" feature films. It was here that she learned about the creative end of the business, and soon after became the chief editor of an hour-long studio documentary, which won several awards. After two years, Bergquist was accepted into the Assistant Directors Training Program, and is presently a candidate for Assistant Director of this new $15,000,000 motion picture.

KRETCHMER was a principal/teacher for 12 years before embarking on a film career. She taught math at the New York School for the Creative Arts, and also worked with parents in the community, the board of education, and local government representatives in securing financing for the $20,000,000 school building. As Chairperson of the New Building Committee, she worked closely with architects, townspeople, contractors, and even children to understand their needs for the building. Today the building stands as a model for such schools everywhere. Eight years ago Kretchmer came to Hollywood and, through persistence and charm, secured a studio position and worked her way up to Chief Auditor, where she oversaw budgets on several multimillion-dollar films. She enrolled in the Assistant Directors Training Program, which she recently completed, and is now a candidate for the position of Assistant Director of this new film.

Kretchmer has what Bergquist seriously lacks: the experience and ability to work well with all kinds of people—a crucial skill in the collaborative art/business of filmmaking.

Any film's lengthy end-credits attest to the huge number of people contributing talent—technicians, laborers, performing artists and others. As the director's right-hand person, the Assistant Director (AD) must help orchestrate that effort. She must "read" the personalities of different individuals and know how to appeal to each ego to garner the best from each.

As chairperson of a building committee, Kretchmer worked successfully with dozens of different personalities in pursuit of a common goal, not unlike a film project. In working with diverse personalities (parents, administrators, children, teachers, architects and builders, each with different goals) Kretchmer had to have a keen understanding of people and be able to know their strengths and limitations. This is precisely her most important task as a motion picture AD.

Working on the set with hundreds of different personalities requires a specially skilled individual: Kretchmer is that person.

Review of General Tips

1. Read the topic question at least twice, *actively:* circle or mark the essential points of the question. Note the main question or parts to be discussed, the audience you are addressing, and the persona or position from which you are writing.
2. Remember to *prewrite,* or plan before you write. Spend at least five minutes organizing your thoughts by jotting notes, outlining, brainstorming, clustering, etc.
3. As you write, keep the flow of your writing going. Don't stop your train of thought to worry about the spelling of a word. You can fix little things later.
4. Leave a few minutes to reread and edit your paper after you finish writing. A careful rereading will often catch careless mistakes and errors in punctuation, spelling, etc., that you didn't have time to worry about as you wrote.
5. Remember that a good essay will be

   - on topic,
   - well organized,
   - well developed with examples,
   - grammatically sound with few errors,
   - interesting to read, with a variety of sentence types,
   - clear, neat, and easy to read.

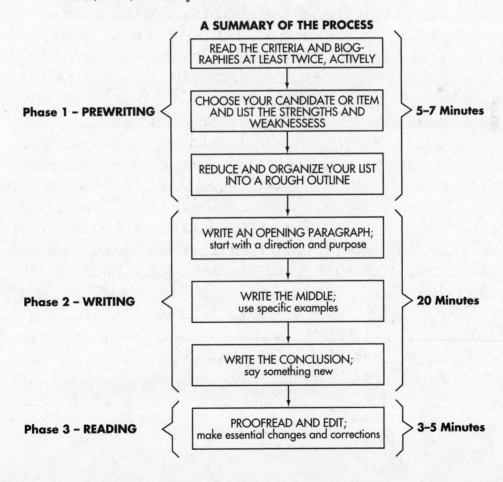

A SUMMARY OF THE PROCESS

Phase 1 – PREWRITING

- READ THE CRITERIA AND BIOGRAPHIES AT LEAST TWICE, ACTIVELY
- CHOOSE YOUR CANDIDATE OR ITEM AND LIST THE STRENGTHS AND WEAKNESSESS
- REDUCE AND ORGANIZE YOUR LIST INTO A ROUGH OUTLINE

5–7 Minutes

Phase 2 – WRITING

- WRITE AN OPENING PARAGRAPH; start with a direction and purpose
- WRITE THE MIDDLE; use specific examples
- WRITE THE CONCLUSION; say something new

20 Minutes

Phase 3 – READING

- PROOFREAD AND EDIT; make essential changes and corrections

3–5 Minutes

Practice: Writing Sample

After reviewing the completed essays, try some practice on your own. We have provided sample questions and booklet-type pages.

Try following the steps we have suggested, varying them slightly, if necessary, to suit your personal style. Have an honest critic read and respond to each practice essay you complete.

Writing Sample Topic 1

Read the following description of Arbit and Blatas, candidates for your party's nomination to the city council. *Then, in the space provided, write an argument for nominating either Arbit or Blatas.* Use the information in this description and assume that two general policies guide your party's decision on nomination:

- Nominations are based upon a combination of the probable success in the election and party service.
- Party service includes seniority, committee work, and fund-raising.

Arbit, a Rumanian-American, has lived in the district and worked for the party for fifteen years. He is chairman of two key party committees and a member of two others. His fund-raising picnic, begun ten years ago, now raises at least $10,000 every year. Arbit is 47, a trial lawyer, with no prior experience in elective office. Twenty percent of the district is Rumanian-American, almost all of whom support the party in every election.

Blatas, of Hungarian background, moved to the district seven years ago. She has worked for the party for seven years as a member of several party committees, and as Arbit's assistant in arranging the fund-raising picnic. A graduate of law school, she is 35, and was recently promoted to director of the city's real estate research office. She narrowly lost an election for city assessor two years ago. Thirty-five percent of the voters in the district are Hungarian-American.

Writing Sample Topic 2

Read the following descriptions of Arnot and Brecht, applicants for the position of head chef at *Chez Moi,* a highly successful New York restaurant. *Then, in the space provided, write an argument for hiring either Arnot or Brecht.* The following criteria are relevant to your decision:

- The chef at *Chez Moi* must be able to socialize freely and to discuss each day's menu with the patrons.
- *Chez Moi's* reputation depends upon the remarkable range and originality of its seafood and its desserts.

Chef Arnot was born in Normandy and trained in Paris. For fifteen years he has been the head chef at major international restaurants in Paris and Marseilles. While in Paris, he won a competition among the city's pastry chefs four times. In Marseilles, his specialty was Mediterranean seafood. He is among the most respected chefs in the world, known equally for his inventive recipes for fish and his short temper. His English is competent, but slow and heavily accented. He has, for the first time, agreed to accept a position outside of France.

Chef Brecht was born in Berlin and trained in Paris, London, and Rome. For the last five years, she has been the head chef in one of Chicago's most successful restaurants. Through her books and her television cooking programs, she has become the most widely known and most popular chef in America. She is especially renowned for her recipes for ice creams and sherbets. She has agreed to apply for the position at *Chez Moi* because of the restaurant's reputation and because it is located in New York, a center of the publishing and television industries.

Writing Sample Topic 3

Read the following descriptions of Selig and Druck, two applicants for the position of receptionist for the medical offices of four physicians (general practitioners). *Then, in the space provided, write an argument for hiring either Selig or Druck.* The following criteria are relevant to your decision:

- The receptionist must answer the phone, schedule appointments for each of the physicians, and relay messages from the physicians to their patients when necessary.
- The receptionist must screen patients over the phone, in order to decide whether to schedule an immediate appointment.

Selig has worked as a registered nurse for ten years and in the emergency room at City Hospital for the last eighteen months. Before this, she was the head nurse in a small suburban hospital staffed by twelve physicians and twenty nurses and aides. She recently decided to leave her position as an emergency room nurse and seek a job with more regular hours and duties. Since high school, Selig has spent two evenings each week counseling the distraught people who phone the free, state-supported "crisis hot line" for help. She has prevented a number of suicides by encouraging the caller to reveal his location and wait for help.

Druck recently moved into the area, leaving his position as office manager for a busy medical corporation in another state. He has long been involved in medical work, having completed two years of medical school before deciding that he was most interested in the business and personnel decisions associated with enhanced patient care. After a series of jobs manning the front office for various private practices, Druck accepted the managerial position only to discover that it kept him more out of touch with the patients themselves than he would like. Druck is a regular subscriber to the major medical journals.

Writing Sample Topic 4

The *Times-Herald,* a large metropolitan newspaper, is about to add a new strip to its comic page. The editorial board must decide between two features that do not now appear in any of the city's other newspapers. *In the space provided, write an argument to be presented to the editorial board in support of one of the two following comic strips.* Two considerations should guide your decision:

- The newspaper wishes to improve its reputation for serious journalism.
- The newspaper wishes to increase its circulation.

Described by *Time* magazine as "America's most beloved comic strip," *Tom Jordan, M.D.* is a serial that depicts the life of a handsome young doctor at a large New York hospital. It appears in more newspapers in the United States than any other comic. Its stories combine medical information, romance, and moral uplift. Each story takes thirty-two weeks to complete. An especially popular recent episode dealt with Tom Jordan's saving the life of an orphaned leukemia victim; others in the recent past have dealt with drug addiction among the very rich, kidney transplants, and anorexia. *Tom Jordan, M.D.* is the work of a group of four cartoonists.

Bart Pollard's comic, *D.C.,* was the first strip cartoon to win a Pulitzer Prize. Its satiric treatment of Democrats and Republicans, of clergymen, doctors, lawyers, and athletes, has at one time or another given such offense that a number of newspapers that had contracted to run the feature have refused to print it. In Washington, Pollard's *D.C.* is called the "comic strip that everyone hates, but everyone reads." A cabinet officer who closely resembled a character pilloried in the comic has recently filed a libel suit against Pollard. Readership of the strip is especially high on college campuses.

Writing Sample Topic 5

The Animal Protection Society must decide on a speaker to address its annual fund-raising dinner. *In the space provided, write an argument in support of one of the two following choices.* Two considerations guide your decision:

- The society must immediately raise as much money as possible to support an emergency airlift to save an endangered species of crane.
- The society wishes to increase the number of life members, subscribers who can be counted on to give money every year.

Jan Gilbert is a comedienne and the star of a popular television talk show. On her program, she frequently invites keepers from the San Diego Zoo, who bring with them lion cubs, talking mynah birds, lemurs, and other small animals that appeal to large audiences. A dog lover, she often appears in public and on television with her miniature poodle, which travels with her wherever she goes. She is an active fund-raiser for conservative political causes. Because of her love of animals, she has agreed to waive half of her usual personal appearance fee of $12,000.

Katrina Nelson is a distinguished zoologist. She is an adjunct research professor at Cambridge University and has spent fourteen years in Africa observing the behavior of packs of Cape hunting dogs, jackals, and hyenas. A film she made on the scavengers and predators of Africa has been shown on educational television stations. She is the author of five books, including one on the animals of Africa that have become extinct in this century. She is an experienced and skillful public speaker. Her lecture fee is $500.

Writing Sample Topic 6

Read the following descriptions of two 1-hour television series, *Love 'Em and Leave 'Em* and *Down and Out*, that are competing for a spot in the network lineup. *Then, in the space provided, write an argument for deciding which of the two the network should choose.* The following criteria are relevant to your decision:

- The only available time slot for the chosen series is 10 P.M. on a weeknight.
- Network executives prefer a series that can deal with controversial issues while providing action and adventure.

Love 'Em and Leave 'Em deals with a metropolitan newspaper columnist who writes a daily "advice to the lovelorn" column and often gets involved in the private lives and problems of those who write her letters. Her father is a criminal attorney, and her sister is a police lieutenant. The columnist holds a degree in psychology and provides free counseling a few hours a week at a halfway house for rehabilitated drug addicts. She is always arguing with the managing editor of the newspaper, who wants a column that is entertaining but not controversial.

Down and Out portrays the week-to-week lives of a minor league baseball team. Two members of the team work as private detectives during the off season and are always alert to "shady" situations. The owner of the team is a former U.S. senator who always preferred baseball to politics but still acts as a presidential advisor at times. The team players are an ethnic and racial mix; some are as young as eighteen and some in their early thirties; the private life and personal background of each individual player remain to be developed. The team manager, a former All-Star, has two sons on the team.

Writing Sample Topic 7

The Sundown Realty Company has purchased a large parcel of land for development in Date City. The company must decide between two building plans. *In the space provided, write an argument in support of one of the two plans.* Base your decision on the following considerations:

- The design of the development must be approved by an environmental commission that is likely to be unsympathetic to radical changes in the landscape.
- The construction must be completed, and at least half of the units sold, within eighteen months. All of the units must be sold within two years.

Plan One calls for the building of fifty free-standing one-story units distributed along the fairways of a newly constructed nine-hole golf course. Three of the nine holes will have small water hazards. Buyer studies of the area have shown clearly that the highest demand for new homes is for those on golf courses. The fifty houses will be well within the density limit set by the environmental committee, and none of the houses would be visible from outside the development. The units will be built of local wood and stone. Each will cost $200,000.

Plan Two calls for five multi-storied buildings, each containing twenty units built around an activities building, tennis courts, and pool. The five buildings will be placed far apart in natural wooded areas on the property. Only the top stories will be visible above the trees, and only a few trees on the property will have to be removed for the construction. The units will sell for $100,000 or $150,000 each, and will be constructed from aged brick.

Writing Sample Topic 8

Southwest Pacific University is facing a severe budget crisis and must make up for a shortfall of $1,000,000 in the next fiscal year. *In the space provided, write an argument for Plan A or Plan B.* Keep in mind that the Board of Trustees has determined that the savings must be made under the following conditions:

- Direct and indirect costs to the students should be avoided as much as possible.
- The quality of academic instruction at the school must in no way be compromised.

Plan A would discontinue several campus services that are now running at a loss, including all the food services on campus that are now subsidized by the university. Any student activities such as band, debate, drama, and men's and women's athletics, which are now financially dependent on the university, must become self-supporting, and student admission fees will be charged for all activities that are not operating at a profit. A fund-raising drive among parents and alumni is the first priority of the administration.

Plan B would freeze all faculty and staff salaries, and cancel all paid sabbatical leaves for two years. Throughout the university, a 10% reduction in non-academic staff will take place at once. Tuition fees will remain unchanged, but student users' fees will be assessed for laboratory equipment, printing costs, and computer time. Obtaining state and federal grants is the first priority of the administration.

Writing Sample Topic 9

The Black Hills County Art Museum, a small, well-run institution, must decide how to spend a large state grant. The money was given with the understanding that the museum would accomplish two objectives. *In the space provided, write an argument in favor of Plan A or Plan B.* Keep these objectives in mind:

- The museum will open an area for the display of Native American artifacts.
- The museum will substantially increase its revenues from memberships, contributions, and sales.

Plan A: The museum will use all of the money to construct a display space large and secure enough to attract several of the major popular traveling art exhibits each year. At present, the display space at the museum is too small to be used to present the art exhibits that attract attention in the national media. With the large university population in the area, there is a local audience for such shows, and with the new galleries, the museum could become the most important exhibition space in a six-state area. A leading modern architect has expressed interest in designing the new gallery at a greatly reduced fee. By selling some of the museum's permanent collection, space could be made available for Native American art exhibits.

Plan B: The museum will use the money to construct a new, small gallery for the display of Native American art, and to construct classrooms, a sculpture garden, a museum shop, and a restaurant. The museum has never sponsored a program of art education for either its adult supporters or local schoolchildren, but the many college teachers, along with the museum staff, would provide a fine core of instructors. The museum has never had a shop or a restaurant, though many of its wealthiest supporters have encouraged these additions. The sculpture garden would also serve as an ideal place to display the large Native American carvings that are too tall to be shown inside the buildings.

Writing Sample Topic 10

The Chief Operating Officer of the Springfield Municipal Zoo must decide between two projects to be funded by a recently received large unrestricted grant. Write an essay in which you argue for one of the two projects based on the following considerations:

- The zoo wishes to improve its reputation as a conservation center.
- The zoo wishes to increase attendance and contributions from the public.

Project One is the building of facilities to house and display the endangered Arabian oryx. Springfield is one of a handful of American cities in whose climate the oryx might breed. The new buildings would include a library and conference center. The grant would also provide for the purchase of the animals and the hiring of specialized veterinarians to care for them.

Project Two is the renovation of four large cat exhibits. At present, the zoo's small holdings of a lion, cheetah, jaguar, and tiger are displayed in small areas that are often overcrowded with patrons. If the new exhibits are built, the zoo will be able to increase the size of its collection of large cats, currently among the most popular animals with the public.

Writing Sample Topic 11

The Overseers of the Augsburg Opera Festival must choose a designer-director for a new production of a four-part Wagner opera. Write an essay in which you argue for one of the two candidates with the following in mind:
- The festival hopes to attract worldwide attention while keeping within a limited budget.
- The festival wishes to continue to please its most generous benefactors, whose tastes are rigidly conservative.

Dieter Hoffman is Germany's leading set and lighting designer. He has no experience as an opera director but has staged highly successful productions of Shakespeare and modern dance. He is especially celebrated for his highly imaginative use of lighting. His short-tempered directing style has been widely reported.

Alain du Bois is a prominent French film and stage director, experienced in opera but known especially for his blockbuster films of epic adventure. His most recent film went far over budget, but returned a huge profit and won a number of international awards. He is especially celebrated for his handling of large crowd scenes and the precise realism of his settings.

Writing Sample Topic 12

A major west-coast newspaper wishes to hire a political cartoonist to comment on state and national issues. There are two candidates. Write an essay in support of one of the two, bearing the following facts in mind:

- The paper wishes to enliven the nonpartisan stance of its editorial page.
- The paper is anxious not to alienate its largely conservative readers.

Conrad Hodge is a successful Seattle political cartoonist whose work is topical, timely, and conventional. He is well-informed about local and national politics, and has contacts with sources of political information not available to most reporters.

Ralph Kane is a prize-winning cartoonist with the Washington Post. His work is provocative, and occasionally ribald. He usually takes a liberal view of social issues and a conservative one on economic topics. Raised and educated in California, he is knowledgeable about politics on the west coast.

Writing Sample Topic 12

Writing Sample Topic 13

Artful Cinema, Inc., must decide on a location in which to shoot a new dramatic film about life in a nineteenth century New England fishing village. Write an essay in favor of one of the two proposed locations, keeping in mind the following:

- Artful Cinema wishes to keep production costs as low as possible.
- Artful Cinema wishes to make the film as authentic as possible.

Lewis, Novia Scotia, is a small coastal town with countryside and seascapes ideal for the film. Its waterfront was entirely rebuilt after World War II. The sets for the waterfront scenes in the picture would have to be built by Canadian workmen. The town has adequate accommodations at a reasonable cost, and the fees for filming in Canada are much lower that those in the United States.

Yarmouth, Maine, is a small fishing port constructed chiefly in the mid-nineteenth century. It is the town in the novel on which the film is based. Because Yarmouth is small and isolated, the cast and crew would have to commute from some distance away. The state has said that it is willing to discuss the reduction of the very high fees it normally charges for filming in Maine.

Writing Sample Topic 14

The aldermen of the town of Waverley must decide between two proposed construction projects: a large new housing development that would include luxury homes and low-cost housing to be built on parkland now owned by the city, and a large mall containing both commercial and residential spaces. Write an essay in which you argue for one of the two projects based on the following considerations:

- The town hopes to qualify for federal grants that support the construction of low-cost housing.
- The town wishes to increase its tax base to be able to support future school construction and maintenance.

Arrow Corporation has proposed the construction of a large gated residential community of luxury homes in exchange for the ownership of lands that are now part of the city's largest public park. At the same time, they would also construct low-cost housing on adjacent land. Because of the desirable location, the new homes are expected to sell rapidly at high prices.

Beta, Inc. has proposed the development of a large area near downtown that is currently in decline. The project would include a large retail mall with stores, cinemas, restaurants, and a number of small, modestly priced residential condominiums. Several department stores have already expressed interest in opening branches in this location.

Writing Sample Topic 15

Mindgrowth Corporation, a producer of television programs for use in high schools and on educational television channels, must decide between two candidates for a position with the company. Write an essay in which you argue for one of the candidates based on the following considerations:

- Mindgrowth wishes to increase its catalog of programs dealing with world geography and U.S. history.
- Mindgrowth wishes to expand the use of computer-generated graphics in its productions.

David is a former high-school teacher with advanced degrees in computer science and history. For the past three years, he has been employed as a writer and project director for a small documentary film company. His film on the ecology of Tahiti was nominated for an award at the Sundance Film Festival.

Marie has a doctorate in computer sciences from M.I.T. and is currently a highly paid executive at a large manufacturer of computer graphic software. A lifelong reader with a strong interest in history, she is eager to work in a more creative environment, and to do so is willing to work at a much lower salary than she now earns.

PART THREE

PRACTICE

Mastering Problem Types
and Time Pressures

Chapter 6

MODEL TEST ONE

This chapter contains full-length Model Test One. It is geared to the format of the LSAT, and it is complete with answers and explanations. It is equivalent to the LSAT in question structure, number of questions, level of difficulty, and time allotments. (The questions used are not taken directly from the LSAT, as those questions are copyrighted and may not be reproduced.)

Model Test One should be taken under strict test conditions. The test ends with a 30-minute Writing Sample, which is not scored.

Section	Description	Number of Questions	Time Allowed
I.	Reading Comprehension	28	35 minutes
II.	Analytical Reasoning	24	35 minutes
III.	Logical Reasoning	26	35 minutes
IV.	Analytical Reasoning	24	35 minutes
V.	Logical Reasoning	25	35 minutes
	Writing Sample		30 minutes
TOTALS:		127	3 hours 25 minutes

Now please turn to the next page, remove your answer sheet, and begin Model Test One.

Answer Sheet—Model Test One

Section 1	Section 2	Section 3	Section 4	Section 5
1. Ⓐ Ⓑ Ⓒ Ⓓ Ⓔ	1. Ⓐ Ⓑ Ⓒ Ⓓ Ⓔ	1. Ⓐ Ⓑ Ⓒ Ⓓ Ⓔ	1. Ⓐ Ⓑ Ⓒ Ⓓ Ⓔ	1. Ⓐ Ⓑ Ⓒ Ⓓ Ⓔ
2. Ⓐ Ⓑ Ⓒ Ⓓ Ⓔ	2. Ⓐ Ⓑ Ⓒ Ⓓ Ⓔ	2. Ⓐ Ⓑ Ⓒ Ⓓ Ⓔ	2. Ⓐ Ⓑ Ⓒ Ⓓ Ⓔ	2. Ⓐ Ⓑ Ⓒ Ⓓ Ⓔ
3. Ⓐ Ⓑ Ⓒ Ⓓ Ⓔ	3. Ⓐ Ⓑ Ⓒ Ⓓ Ⓔ	3. Ⓐ Ⓑ Ⓒ Ⓓ Ⓔ	3. Ⓐ Ⓑ Ⓒ Ⓓ Ⓔ	3. Ⓐ Ⓑ Ⓒ Ⓓ Ⓔ
4. Ⓐ Ⓑ Ⓒ Ⓓ Ⓔ	4. Ⓐ Ⓑ Ⓒ Ⓓ Ⓔ	4. Ⓐ Ⓑ Ⓒ Ⓓ Ⓔ	4. Ⓐ Ⓑ Ⓒ Ⓓ Ⓔ	4. Ⓐ Ⓑ Ⓒ Ⓓ Ⓔ
5. Ⓐ Ⓑ Ⓒ Ⓓ Ⓔ	5. Ⓐ Ⓑ Ⓒ Ⓓ Ⓔ	5. Ⓐ Ⓑ Ⓒ Ⓓ Ⓔ	5. Ⓐ Ⓑ Ⓒ Ⓓ Ⓔ	5. Ⓐ Ⓑ Ⓒ Ⓓ Ⓔ
6. Ⓐ Ⓑ Ⓒ Ⓓ Ⓔ	6. Ⓐ Ⓑ Ⓒ Ⓓ Ⓔ	6. Ⓐ Ⓑ Ⓒ Ⓓ Ⓔ	6. Ⓐ Ⓑ Ⓒ Ⓓ Ⓔ	6. Ⓐ Ⓑ Ⓒ Ⓓ Ⓔ
7. Ⓐ Ⓑ Ⓒ Ⓓ Ⓔ	7. Ⓐ Ⓑ Ⓒ Ⓓ Ⓔ	7. Ⓐ Ⓑ Ⓒ Ⓓ Ⓔ	7. Ⓐ Ⓑ Ⓒ Ⓓ Ⓔ	7. Ⓐ Ⓑ Ⓒ Ⓓ Ⓔ
8. Ⓐ Ⓑ Ⓒ Ⓓ Ⓔ	8. Ⓐ Ⓑ Ⓒ Ⓓ Ⓔ	8. Ⓐ Ⓑ Ⓒ Ⓓ Ⓔ	8. Ⓐ Ⓑ Ⓒ Ⓓ Ⓔ	8. Ⓐ Ⓑ Ⓒ Ⓓ Ⓔ
9. Ⓐ Ⓑ Ⓒ Ⓓ Ⓔ	9. Ⓐ Ⓑ Ⓒ Ⓓ Ⓔ	9. Ⓐ Ⓑ Ⓒ Ⓓ Ⓔ	9. Ⓐ Ⓑ Ⓒ Ⓓ Ⓔ	9. Ⓐ Ⓑ Ⓒ Ⓓ Ⓔ
10. Ⓐ Ⓑ Ⓒ Ⓓ Ⓔ	10. Ⓐ Ⓑ Ⓒ Ⓓ Ⓔ	10. Ⓐ Ⓑ Ⓒ Ⓓ Ⓔ	10. Ⓐ Ⓑ Ⓒ Ⓓ Ⓔ	10. Ⓐ Ⓑ Ⓒ Ⓓ Ⓔ
11. Ⓐ Ⓑ Ⓒ Ⓓ Ⓔ	11. Ⓐ Ⓑ Ⓒ Ⓓ Ⓔ	11. Ⓐ Ⓑ Ⓒ Ⓓ Ⓔ	11. Ⓐ Ⓑ Ⓒ Ⓓ Ⓔ	11. Ⓐ Ⓑ Ⓒ Ⓓ Ⓔ
12. Ⓐ Ⓑ Ⓒ Ⓓ Ⓔ	12. Ⓐ Ⓑ Ⓒ Ⓓ Ⓔ	12. Ⓐ Ⓑ Ⓒ Ⓓ Ⓔ	12. Ⓐ Ⓑ Ⓒ Ⓓ Ⓔ	12. Ⓐ Ⓑ Ⓒ Ⓓ Ⓔ
13. Ⓐ Ⓑ Ⓒ Ⓓ Ⓔ	13. Ⓐ Ⓑ Ⓒ Ⓓ Ⓔ	13. Ⓐ Ⓑ Ⓒ Ⓓ Ⓔ	13. Ⓐ Ⓑ Ⓒ Ⓓ Ⓔ	13. Ⓐ Ⓑ Ⓒ Ⓓ Ⓔ
14. Ⓐ Ⓑ Ⓒ Ⓓ Ⓔ	14. Ⓐ Ⓑ Ⓒ Ⓓ Ⓔ	14. Ⓐ Ⓑ Ⓒ Ⓓ Ⓔ	14. Ⓐ Ⓑ Ⓒ Ⓓ Ⓔ	14. Ⓐ Ⓑ Ⓒ Ⓓ Ⓔ
15. Ⓐ Ⓑ Ⓒ Ⓓ Ⓔ	15. Ⓐ Ⓑ Ⓒ Ⓓ Ⓔ	15. Ⓐ Ⓑ Ⓒ Ⓓ Ⓔ	15. Ⓐ Ⓑ Ⓒ Ⓓ Ⓔ	15. Ⓐ Ⓑ Ⓒ Ⓓ Ⓔ
16. Ⓐ Ⓑ Ⓒ Ⓓ Ⓔ	16. Ⓐ Ⓑ Ⓒ Ⓓ Ⓔ	16. Ⓐ Ⓑ Ⓒ Ⓓ Ⓔ	16. Ⓐ Ⓑ Ⓒ Ⓓ Ⓔ	16. Ⓐ Ⓑ Ⓒ Ⓓ Ⓔ
17. Ⓐ Ⓑ Ⓒ Ⓓ Ⓔ	17. Ⓐ Ⓑ Ⓒ Ⓓ Ⓔ	17. Ⓐ Ⓑ Ⓒ Ⓓ Ⓔ	17. Ⓐ Ⓑ Ⓒ Ⓓ Ⓔ	17. Ⓐ Ⓑ Ⓒ Ⓓ Ⓔ
18. Ⓐ Ⓑ Ⓒ Ⓓ Ⓔ	18. Ⓐ Ⓑ Ⓒ Ⓓ Ⓔ	18. Ⓐ Ⓑ Ⓒ Ⓓ Ⓔ	18. Ⓐ Ⓑ Ⓒ Ⓓ Ⓔ	18. Ⓐ Ⓑ Ⓒ Ⓓ Ⓔ
19. Ⓐ Ⓑ Ⓒ Ⓓ Ⓔ	19. Ⓐ Ⓑ Ⓒ Ⓓ Ⓔ	19. Ⓐ Ⓑ Ⓒ Ⓓ Ⓔ	19. Ⓐ Ⓑ Ⓒ Ⓓ Ⓔ	19. Ⓐ Ⓑ Ⓒ Ⓓ Ⓔ
20. Ⓐ Ⓑ Ⓒ Ⓓ Ⓔ	20. Ⓐ Ⓑ Ⓒ Ⓓ Ⓔ	20. Ⓐ Ⓑ Ⓒ Ⓓ Ⓔ	20. Ⓐ Ⓑ Ⓒ Ⓓ Ⓔ	20. Ⓐ Ⓑ Ⓒ Ⓓ Ⓔ
21. Ⓐ Ⓑ Ⓒ Ⓓ Ⓔ	21. Ⓐ Ⓑ Ⓒ Ⓓ Ⓔ	21. Ⓐ Ⓑ Ⓒ Ⓓ Ⓔ	21. Ⓐ Ⓑ Ⓒ Ⓓ Ⓔ	21. Ⓐ Ⓑ Ⓒ Ⓓ Ⓔ
22. Ⓐ Ⓑ Ⓒ Ⓓ Ⓔ	22. Ⓐ Ⓑ Ⓒ Ⓓ Ⓔ	22. Ⓐ Ⓑ Ⓒ Ⓓ Ⓔ	22. Ⓐ Ⓑ Ⓒ Ⓓ Ⓔ	22. Ⓐ Ⓑ Ⓒ Ⓓ Ⓔ
23. Ⓐ Ⓑ Ⓒ Ⓓ Ⓔ	23. Ⓐ Ⓑ Ⓒ Ⓓ Ⓔ	23. Ⓐ Ⓑ Ⓒ Ⓓ Ⓔ	23. Ⓐ Ⓑ Ⓒ Ⓓ Ⓔ	23. Ⓐ Ⓑ Ⓒ Ⓓ Ⓔ
24. Ⓐ Ⓑ Ⓒ Ⓓ Ⓔ	24. Ⓐ Ⓑ Ⓒ Ⓓ Ⓔ	24. Ⓐ Ⓑ Ⓒ Ⓓ Ⓔ	24. Ⓐ Ⓑ Ⓒ Ⓓ Ⓔ	24. Ⓐ Ⓑ Ⓒ Ⓓ Ⓔ
25. Ⓐ Ⓑ Ⓒ Ⓓ Ⓔ	25. Ⓐ Ⓑ Ⓒ Ⓓ Ⓔ	25. Ⓐ Ⓑ Ⓒ Ⓓ Ⓔ	25. Ⓐ Ⓑ Ⓒ Ⓓ Ⓔ	25. Ⓐ Ⓑ Ⓒ Ⓓ Ⓔ
26. Ⓐ Ⓑ Ⓒ Ⓓ Ⓔ	26. Ⓐ Ⓑ Ⓒ Ⓓ Ⓔ	26. Ⓐ Ⓑ Ⓒ Ⓓ Ⓔ	26. Ⓐ Ⓑ Ⓒ Ⓓ Ⓔ	26. Ⓐ Ⓑ Ⓒ Ⓓ Ⓔ
27. Ⓐ Ⓑ Ⓒ Ⓓ Ⓔ	27. Ⓐ Ⓑ Ⓒ Ⓓ Ⓔ	27. Ⓐ Ⓑ Ⓒ Ⓓ Ⓔ	27. Ⓐ Ⓑ Ⓒ Ⓓ Ⓔ	27. Ⓐ Ⓑ Ⓒ Ⓓ Ⓔ
28. Ⓐ Ⓑ Ⓒ Ⓓ Ⓔ	28. Ⓐ Ⓑ Ⓒ Ⓓ Ⓔ	28. Ⓐ Ⓑ Ⓒ Ⓓ Ⓔ	28. Ⓐ Ⓑ Ⓒ Ⓓ Ⓔ	28. Ⓐ Ⓑ Ⓒ Ⓓ Ⓔ
29. Ⓐ Ⓑ Ⓒ Ⓓ Ⓔ	29. Ⓐ Ⓑ Ⓒ Ⓓ Ⓔ	29. Ⓐ Ⓑ Ⓒ Ⓓ Ⓔ	29. Ⓐ Ⓑ Ⓒ Ⓓ Ⓔ	29. Ⓐ Ⓑ Ⓒ Ⓓ Ⓔ
30. Ⓐ Ⓑ Ⓒ Ⓓ Ⓔ	30. Ⓐ Ⓑ Ⓒ Ⓓ Ⓔ	30. Ⓐ Ⓑ Ⓒ Ⓓ Ⓔ	30. Ⓐ Ⓑ Ⓒ Ⓓ Ⓔ	30. Ⓐ Ⓑ Ⓒ Ⓓ Ⓔ

To remove, cut along dotted rule.

SECTION I
TIME — 35 MINUTES
28 QUESTIONS

<u>Directions:</u> Read the passages and answer the questions following each passage by blackening the appropriate space on the answer sheet. You may refer back to the passages when answering the questions. Answer all questions on the basis of what is stated or implied.

Although statutory law (a law enacted by the legislature) expressly forbids strikes by government workers, the
(line) constitutional validity of these laws as
(5) well as their interpretative applications have been under attack in various cases, the most publicized case being that of the federal government air traffic controllers.
(10)   The First Amendment to the United States Constitution guarantees the right of free speech. The constitutional issue to be resolved therefore is whether strikes are a form of "symbolic speech"
(15) or "symbolic conduct" that should be accorded the same degree of First Amendment protection as verbal communications. In a case that involved private rather than public employees, a
(20) Texas Court held that picketing as an incident to a labor dispute is a proper exercise of freedom of speech. The court went on to say that only a "clear and present danger of substantive evil will
(25) justify an abridgement of the right to picket." Later, the New Jersey state court concluded that even though picketing is protected by freedom of speech, this does not mean that
(30) statutes prohibiting strikes are constitutionally invalid. This case involved a constitutional interpretation of the New Jersey statute. The court stated that the justification of this
(35) statute is based on the ground of "clear and present danger" that would result to the state if the performance of functions of a public utility was ceased or impaired by a strike. Those in favor of
(40) no-strike clauses seem to concede that strikes are a form of symbolic speech that should be accorded the same degree of First Amendment protection as verbal speech. Their justification for
(45) upholding these clauses is the "clear and present danger" doctrine. They tend

to believe that strikes by government employees automatically present a "clear and present danger of substantive
(50) evil." However, according to the U.S. Supreme Court, legislatures cannot be relied upon to make a determination of what constitutes a "clear and present danger." In effect this is what happened
(55) when President Reagan ordered the firing of the air traffic controllers, based on the antistrike clause pronounced by Congress. The Supreme Court held that courts themselves must determine
(60) what constitutes a clear and present danger. The Supreme Court went on to say that mere public inconvenience or annoyance is not enough to constitute a clear and present danger. Thus, the
(65) public inconvenience and annoyance created by the curtailment of air traffic as a result of the controllers' strike may not be sufficient to constitute such a danger. The argument that a clear and
(70) present danger resulted from the emergency staffing of control towers by military and supervisory personnel is invalidated by the fact that the airlines have run safely since the strike.
(75)   This is not to suggest that every employee should automatically have the right to strike. However, constitutional consideration of due process and freedom of speech should bar denying
(80) government workers, as a class, the right to strike. A close look should be taken at what actually constitutes a "clear and present danger of substantive evil." It is an evasion for courts to allow
(85) legislatures to prejudge all government services to be different for "strike" purposes than those provided by the private sector. The court itself should look at such factors as the nature of
(90) the service in determining whether particular no-strike clauses are constitutionally valid. The nature of the

GO ON TO THE NEXT PAGE ➤

provider of the service (i.e., government v. private) is not a compelling (95) justification for upholding no-strike clauses.

1. According to the passage, strikes by government workers are

   (A) constitutionally invalid
   (B) forbidden by statutory law
   (C) permissible when there is no danger of substantial evil
   (D) permissible when there is no public inconvenience or annoyance
   (E) permissible when there is no danger to national security and safety

2. If government workers as a class are denied the right to strike, it can be argued that they have been denied all of the following EXCEPT

   (A) due process
   (B) freedom of speech
   (C) the clear and present danger doctrine
   (D) redress from abnormally dangerous working conditions
   (E) an abridgment of the right to picket

3. According to the passage, the "clear and present danger" justification of forbidding a strike has been misapplied for all of the following reasons EXCEPT

   (A) the dangers were determined by the executive branch
   (B) the dangers are often merely inconveniences
   (C) the dangers were determined by the courts
   (D) strikes by government workers do not automatically present dangers
   (E) the inconvenience caused by the air traffic controllers may not have been a danger

4. The fact that there was no rise in the number of airline accidents in the first six months after the firing and replacement of the striking air traffic controllers undermines the

   (A) government's argument that a strike would present a danger to the public
   (B) argument that the no-strike clause violates first amendment rights
   (C) argument that a strike is a form of symbolic speech
   (D) air traffic controllers' argument that they left their jobs because of dangerous working conditions
   (E) argument that no-strike clauses discourage more highly qualified individuals from applying for positions

5. The author of the passage objects to the current situation in which

   (A) all employees equally have the right to strike
   (B) the government regards national security more important than an individual's freedom
   (C) the Supreme Court avoids taking a position in its dealing with regret-to-strike cases
   (D) an unfair burden of proof is placed upon workers who leave jobs they believe to have unsafe working conditions
   (E) a false distinction is made between workers doing similar jobs for the government and private employees

6. Which one of the following might the author cite to exemplify another of the harmful effects of the no-strike rule?

   (A) It deters the highly skilled from taking government jobs.
   (B) It can be used as a precedent in the private sector.
   (C) It places too much power in the hands of the judicial branch of the government.
   (D) It encourages the courts to determine whether or not particular no-strike clauses are valid.
   (E) It protects some workers from abnormally dangerous working conditions.

GO ON TO THE NEXT PAGE ➤

1   1   1   1   1

Virginia Woolf's development as a
novelist was deeply influenced by her
struggle to reconcile feminism and art.
line Long before the aesthetic creed of
(5) Bloomsbury came into being she had
learned from her father that a work of
literature is no better than the morality
which it is intended to express—a
lesson she never forgot. Virginia Woolf
(10) was a passionate moralist, though she
directed all her fervor into one narrow
channel. The impulse to write *Three
Guineas* possessed her for years,
"violently . . . persistently, pressingly,
(15) compulsorily," until she carried it into
action. This moral fervor was not
contained within the limits of her tracts,
nor could it have been. Feminism is
implicit in her novels. The novels are
(20) not, of course, didactic in the narrow
sense of pleading for specific reforms,
but they illustrate the dangers of
one-sidedness and celebrate the
androgynous mind.
(25) Virginia Woolf's main emphasis in her
feminist writings, as in the novels, was
on self-reform, and on art as a means to
that end. Novels and tracts alike grew
out of a preoccupation with her own
(30) spiritual dilemma. Fiction was the
medium within which Virginia Woolf
controlled and directed this intense self-
absorption. When she deserted art for
propaganda, as in *Three Guineas,* her
(35) self-absorption got the upper hand.
Thus, paradoxically, she was truer to
her feminist ideas as a novelist than as
a pamphleteer. Her social conscience
and her aesthetic vision were mutually
(40) dependent. She could express her
feminism only by means of her art; but
her art owed its character to her
feminism.
The contrast between Virginia Woolf's
(45) failure in *Three Guineas* and her
triumph in *The Years* confirms this
impression. In the first, confining
herself to political and social
controversy, she lost her grasp of reality
(50) and ended up talking to herself. In the
second, striving, as she said, "to give
the whole of the present society . . .
facts as well as the vision," she
transcended purely personal
(55) preoccupations and created a lasting
work of art. Virginia Woolf's direct

attack on social evil is too shrill and
self-indulgent to succeed, even as
propaganda. On the other hand, her
(60) symbolic representation of the
Wasteland—pollution, faithlessness,
remorse—has a lucid objectivity that
forces the reader to see through her
eyes. The tract, with all its talk of
(65) reform, is one-sided. The novel is whole.
In Virginia Woolf's case, the myth of
the artist as more or less helpless agent
of his own creative drive seems to have
a foundation in fact. She needed the
(70) discipline of art, because it permitted
her to express her intense moral
indignation, while at the same time
controlling the disintegrating effects of
that indignation upon her personality.
(75) Art produced feelings of release and
harmony, such as she associated with
the androgynous mind. When she
avoided that discipline, as in *Three
Guineas,* her writing tended to become
(80) morbid. In relation to the radiance of
Virginia Woolf's artistic successes,
therefore, *Three Guineas* represents a
kind of negative definition. Through it
we can glance into the heart of her
(85) darkness.

7. According to the passage, Woolf's father
influenced her

(A) choice of writing as a career
(B) belief in the importance of self-
reform
(C) belief that literature should have a
moral base
(D) desire to write tracts and pamphlets
(E) views on the equality of men and
women

GO ON TO THE NEXT PAGE ➤

1   1   1   1   1

8. We can infer from the passage that the "spiritual dilemma" mentioned in line 30 refers to a

   (A) need to transcend one-sidedness and encompass both the masculine and feminine
   (B) desire to retire from the world rather than participate actively in society
   (C) need to choose between artistic endeavors and social work
   (D) desire to pursue a writing career and a desire to raise a family
   (E) need to transcend lucid objectivity and express passion in her work

9. According to the passage, which one of the following best characterizes Woolf's feminism?

   (A) a faith in feminine creativity and intuition
   (B) an integration of the masculine and the feminine
   (C) an indignation toward social institutions
   (D) an emphasis on social equality
   (E) a morbid preoccupation with self

10. The function of the third paragraph of the passage is to provide a

   (A) concrete example of the points made in paragraph 2
   (B) view contrasting with the one presented in paragraph 1
   (C) transition between paragraphs 2 and 4
   (D) subtopic to the main topic of paragraph 1
   (E) exegesis of the works introduced in paragraph 1

11. Which one of the following oppositions does the author principally address in the passage?

   (A) Woolf's aesthetic creed and the aesthetic creed of the Bloomsbury group
   (B) Woolf's novels of social reform and Woolf's novels of individual soul-searching
   (C) masculinity and femininity
   (D) social injustice and self-reform
   (E) Woolf's propaganda and Woolf's art

12. From the passage we can infer that the author

   (A) questions the validity of the Bloomsbury aesthetic creed
   (B) approves of symbolism only when used for social reform
   (C) finds Woolf's fiction more successful than her nonfiction
   (D) believes Woolf's social concerns are trivial
   (E) dislikes literature written in the cause of social reform

13. Which one of the following would be the best title for this passage?

   (A) *Three Guineas* and *The Years:* A Study
   (B) Virginia Woolf's Success
   (C) Virginia Woolf: Problems with Nonfiction
   (D) Virginia Woolf: Reconciling Feminism and Art
   (E) Masculine vs. Feminine: A Study of Virginia Woolf

GO ON TO THE NEXT PAGE ➤

Much as they may deplore the fact, historians have no monopoly on the past and no franchise as its privileged
line interpreters to the public. It may have
(5) been different once, but there can no longer be any doubt about the relegation of the historian to a back seat. Far surpassing works of history, as measured by the size of their public and
(10) the influence they exert, are the novel, works for the stage, the screen, and television. It is mainly from these sources that millions who never open a history book derive such conceptions,
(15) interpretations, convictions, or fantasies as they have about the past. Whatever gives shape to popular conceptions of the past is of concern to historians, and this surely includes
(20) fiction.

Broadly speaking, two types of fiction deal with the past—historical fiction and fictional history. The more common of the two is historical fiction, which
(25) places fictional characters and events in a more or less authentic historical background. Examples range from *War and Peace* to *Gone With the Wind*. Since all but a few novelists must place their
(30) fictional characters in some period, nearly all fiction can be thought of as in some degree historical. But the term is applied as a rule only to novels in which historical events figure prominently.
(35) Fictional history, on the other hand, portrays and focuses attention upon real historical figures and events, but with the license of the novelist to imagine and invent. It has yet to
(40) produce anything approaching Tolstoy's masterpiece. Some fictional history makes use of invented characters and events, and historical fiction at times mixes up fictional and nonfictional
(45) characters. As a result the two genres overlap sometimes, but not often enough to make the distinction unimportant.

Of the two, it is fictional history that
(50) is the greater source of mischief, for it is here that fabrication and fact, fiction and nonfiction, are most likely to be mixed and confused. Of course, historians themselves sometimes mix
(55) fact with fancy, but it is a rare one who does it consciously or deliberately, and

he knows very well that if discovered he stands convicted of betraying his calling. The writer of fictional history,
(60) on the other hand, does this as a matter of course and with no compunction whatever. The production and consumption of fictional history appear to be growing of late. Part of the
(65) explanation of this is probably the fragmentation of history by professionals, their retreat into specializations, their abandonment of the narrative style, and with it the
(70) traditional patronage of lay readers. Fictional history has expanded to fill the gap thus created but has at the same time gone further to create a much larger readership than history books
(75) ever had.

14. We can infer from the passage that the author is probably

   (A) a historian
   (B) a historical novelist
   (C) a literary critic
   (D) a social commentator
   (E) a literary historian

15. According to the passage, which one of the following is likely to have contributed to the increasing popularity of fictional history?

   (A) a change in the demographics of lay readers of history
   (B) an increase in the audience for movies and television
   (C) a decline in historians' use of a storytelling style
   (D) an increase in historians' mixing fact and fancy
   (E) a decline in the writing ability of professional historians

GO ON TO THE NEXT PAGE ➤

16. The author's attitude toward fictional history can best be summarized in which one of the following statements?

    (A) Masterpieces such as *War and Peace* and *Gone With the Wind* could not be created in the fictional history genre.
    (B) Fictional history is responsible for leading the reading public away from traditional historical works.
    (C) Fictional history provides a useful service by filling the gap for readers not interested in traditional history.
    (D) Writers of fictional history should not mix historical figures with fictional characters.
    (E) Fictional history can mislead readers about actual historical events.

17. Of the following, which one would the author consider most likely to cause a reader to confuse fact and fiction?

    (A) a book about the Watergate scandal with fictionalized dialogue between President Nixon and his attorney general, John Mitchell
    (B) a book about a fictional platoon in Vietnam during the last days of the war
    (C) a fictional account of the adventures of a group of servants in the White House under Eisenhower, Kennedy, Johnson, and Nixon
    (D) an account of the assassination of President Kennedy as viewed by a Texas adolescent on the parade route
    (E) a book based on newspaper accounts about the reaction to the Cuban missile crisis in the United States, the U.S.S.R., and Western Europe

18. The function of the second paragraph of the passage is to

    (A) reinforce the argument about fictionalized history presented in the first paragraph
    (B) define and contrast fictional history and historical fiction
    (C) emphasize the superiority of historical fiction to fictional history
    (D) provide context for the analysis in the third paragraph
    (E) clarify the difference between history and fiction

19. According to the passage, the author would agree with all of the following statements EXCEPT

    (A) historical fiction and fictional history are of concern to the professional historian
    (B) the works of today's professional historians tend to be more specialized than historical works of the past
    (C) professional historians understand that they should not mix fact and fiction in their works
    (D) a historical event presented as a TV miniseries is likely to be accepted as true by many people
    (E) fictional history has succeeded because of a failure of the academic history curriculum

20. The author's attitude about the issue of fiction and history is presented most clearly in

    (A) paragraph 1, lines 1–7
    (B) paragraph 1, lines 17–20
    (C) paragraph 2, lines 35–41
    (D) paragraph 3, lines 49–53
    (E) paragraph 3, lines 62–64

21. The tone of this passage could best be described as

    (A) hostile and didactic
    (B) moderate and concerned
    (C) pedantic and detached
    (D) ironic and condescending
    (E) philosophical and enlightened

GO ON TO THE NEXT PAGE ➤

Faith healing, or spirit healing, by
definition, is the physical healing of the
body of an individual by means of that
line individual's religious faith and the
(5) consequent intervention by deities in
the healing process, spiritual
intervention of other sorts in the course
of a disease, or the efficacious effect on
the physical body by force of will, either
(10) the will of the affected person or that of
another person who has such power or
who can channel such power from
elsewhere. While looked upon by "hard"
science as worthy of no attention other
(15) than the heaping upon it of denigration
and a dismissive shake of the head, faith
healing has enjoyed a long and
continuous history of practice and
acceptance among the peoples of the
(20) world. And debunking and calumny
notwithstanding, it remains in many
people a deep-seated belief in modern
society, and elements of the practice
find their way even into "standard"
(25) medical therapies.

Faith healing advocates point to
historical practices, reputed to have
been successful in treating a myriad of
illnesses, to bolster their cases. Native
(30) American "medicine," for example, in
which the medicine man, or shaman,
functioned as a combination of priest,
physician, and magician, relied, at least
in part, on the shaman's ability to create
(35) belief by the sick individual in either
cure or curse, and is said to have been
highly effective in producing either
recovery or descent into greater illness
and death, whichever was desired by the
(40) shaman. While certain herbs or other
substances as well as such devices as
drums, rattles, and totems were used in
treatment, it was the shaman's force of
will and its effect on the strength of the
(45) belief system of the treated person that
was paramount. Voodoo practices share
some of the points of view found in
ancient Native American healing, using
dolls, fetishes, charms, and cabalistic
(50) totems in causing belief in the sufferer,
as do the practices of certain
fundamentalist religions—for example,
in the ritual of the "laying on of hands,"
in which a deity's intervention is
(55) channeled through a minister and in
which a sufferer believes himself or

herself to be cured and so apparently is
cured.

Modern proponents of forms of faith
(60) healing most often now promote a
combination of spirituality, which does
not necessarily involve religion, and
science as the most effective team in
the process of combating disease. One
(65) point of view suggests that modern
society has lost its connection with its
community and its strong belief in the
religion and tradition of that
community. Because of that weakened
(70) belief system, the real-world therapeutic
effects of healing rituals have been lost,
and only the strengthening of belief will
reclaim the beneficial results produced
historically by faith healing, whether
(75) that belief is in the force of an
individual's own will or in outside
healing forces. Holistic medicine, in
which the emphasis is on treating the
"whole" individual, not only the
(80) person's disease, shares at least in part
some of these modern faith healers'
points of view in that it does not
discount the importance of the mindset
of the ill person, nor does it discount
(85) the truism of "healthy mind, healthy
body" or the effect on the physical body
of the will to live. And while faith
healing undoubtedly is often practiced
by those most of society is convinced
(90) are charlatans, self-promoting and self-
defined psychics, and those motivated
simply by greed, some of its tenets are
finding their way into the mainstream of
medical practice, just as certain
(95) medicinal herbs used by ancient
healers, "medicines" once ridiculed,
have now been found to have curative
powers previously unknown and
unappreciated.

GO ON TO THE NEXT PAGE ➤

22. The main point of the passage is most
accurately expressed by which one of
the following?

(A) If modern society has lost its faith
in the force of will to heal disease,
then it can reclaim that faith by
studying the effects faith healers
have had throughout history and in
various cultures.

(B) Holistic medicine has its roots in
the practices of shamans, voodoo
priests, and other religious figures
and not in the practices of psychics
and other charlatans.

(C) Practices of using totems, herbs,
charms, and other devices are
central to the effect faith healing
has on the ill person and are
effective even in modern medical
practices when the desired result is
to strengthen the individual's belief
system.

(D) Faith healing is a long-accepted
ritual that some have thought to be
beneficial in combating disease, and
although it may or may not have
been effective, some of the beliefs of
faith healing advocates have been
incorporated into modern medical
practice.

(E) Modern medical practitioners have
been remiss in dismissing the
claims of faith healing because
scientists have been surprised by
the effectiveness of some of the
ancient medicines used by healers.

23. Each of the following is indicated by the
passage EXCEPT

(A) some faith healing is practiced by
charlatans

(B) the rituals of voodoo practitioners
share some elements of Native
American medicine

(C) the term "holistic" is a modern term

(D) faith healing can be based strictly
on religious belief

(E) faith healing may have been
historically paired with drug
treatment

24. The primary purpose of the concluding
paragraph is to

(A) combine historical and modern
perspectives on the effectiveness of
faith healing

(B) discuss spirituality and faith as a
basis for the efficacy of faith healing

(C) differentiate historical attitudes of
faith healers from the attitudes of
modern medical practitioners

(D) provide a synthesis of scientific
objections to spirit healing

(E) discuss elements of faith healing in
modern medicine and suggest some
reasons for the inclusion of those
elements

25. The author would be most likely to agree
with which one of the following?

(A) There is no proof that faith healing
has ever been effective;
consequently, the inclusion of
elements of faith healing in modern
medicine is without rational
foundation.

(B) Open-minded behavior on the part of
scientists may lead to some
important discoveries in medicine;
simply because something has not
been rigorously tested may not
mean it isn't effective.

(C) The "laying on of hands" is a
delusion in the ill person produced
by the force of the minister's will.

(D) "Healthy mind, healthy body" is a
truism believed by ancient
practitioners of faith healing as well
as modern ones.

(E) The belief in a deity's intervention
in the healing process is as much
an indication of rational thought
processes as is the belief in
"healthy mind, healthy body."

26. The passage suggests that which one of the following is true about practitioners of holistic medicine?

(A) Practitioners of holistic medicine are well aware of the lost opportunities in treatment because effective, natural medicines have gone unrecognized.

(B) Because holistic medicine involves treating the whole person rather than simply the person's disease, it necessarily involves trained psychological intervention in the healing processes.

(C) Practitioners of holistic medicine are likely to refer some cases to faith healers when hard science fails to effect a cure.

(D) Holistic medicine practitioners, in treating the whole person rather than simply the person's disease, are likely to investigate the mindset of the individual in the context of that mindset's effect on the course of a disease, even though the individual in question may disagree with the connection between the will to live and the outcome of treatment.

(E) Holistic medicine and the practices of ancient faith healers have little in common because the point of modern medical science, of whatever kind, is to use all available methods to competently treat patients.

27. According to the passage, modern practitioners of faith healing would be likely to engage in all of the following activities EXCEPT

(A) relying on surgery and radiation alone to cure an individual of cancer

(B) the laying on of hands in order to effect an immediate and startling cure without recourse to more traditional medical treatment

(C) creating an atmosphere in which a patient feels free to discuss an illness at length, even to the point of admitting despair and suicidal thoughts

(D) calling upon deities to intervene in the healing process and channeling the power of the deities to effect healing

(E) referring patients to licensed medical doctors for long-term care

28. The author's primary purpose in the passage is to

(A) compare and contrast the methods of faith healers in the past and the methods of faith healers today

(B) explain some of the practices of faith healers both now and in the past and suggest the part of faith healers in modern medicine

(C) promote the acceptance of faith healers as viable alternatives to "standard" medical therapies

(D) identify those practices of faith healers that are unacceptable in modern society and those that are slowly gaining acceptance, even among promoters of "hard" science

(E) present medical alternatives for the reader who is searching for methods of treating his or her illness or that of another

STOP

IF YOU FINISH BEFORE TIME IS UP, CHECK YOUR WORK ON THIS SECTION OF THE TEST ONLY.
DO NOT GO ON TO THE NEXT SECTION OF THE TEST UNTIL TIME IS UP FOR THIS SECTION.

2　　**2**　　**2**　　**2**　　**2**

SECTION II
TIME — 35 MINUTES
24 QUESTIONS

Directions: In this section you will be given groups of questions based on different sets of conditions. Drawing a simple diagram may be helpful in answering some of the questions. You are to choose the best answer and mark the corresponding space on your answer sheet.

Questions 1–6

The Bell Canyon Condominium is a four-story building with a single penthouse apartment on the fourth floor. There are two apartments on each of the three other floors. The apartments are owned by A, B, C, D, E, F, and G.

  A's apartment is on one of the floors higher than B's.
  C's apartment is on one of the floors lower than D's.
  C's apartment is on one of the floors lower than E's.
  F and G's apartments are on the same floor.

1. Which one of the following could be the owner of the penthouse?

  (A) B
  (B) C
  (C) E
  (D) F
  (E) G

2. If F's apartment is on the second floor, which one of the following must be true?

  (A) C's apartment is on the first floor.
  (B) D's apartment is on the third floor.
  (C) A's apartment is on the fourth floor.
  (D) G's apartment is on the first floor.
  (E) B's apartment is on the third floor.

3. If D owns the penthouse apartment, on which floor or floors could G's apartment be located?

  (A) the first floor only
  (B) the second floor only
  (C) the third floor only
  (D) the second or the third floor
  (E) the first, second, or third floor

4. If D's and E's apartments are on the same floor, which one of the following must be true?

  (A) D and E are on the third floor.
  (B) D and E are on the second floor.
  (C) A is on the fourth floor.
  (D) B and C are on the first floor.
  (E) F and G are on the second floor.

5. If C's apartment is on the first floor, and A is the owner of the penthouse, which one of the following must be true?

  (A) G's apartment is on the third floor.
  (B) D's apartment is on the second floor.
  (C) E's apartment is on the second floor.
  (D) B's apartment is on the first floor.
  (E) F's apartment is on the second floor.

6. Which one of the following is possible?

  (A) A and C are on the same floor.
  (B) A and E are on the same floor.
  (C) A is on the first floor.
  (D) D is on the first floor.
  (E) C is on the fourth floor.

2   **2**

Questions 7–12

A new bank has decided to stay open only on weekends—all day Saturday and Sunday—and no other days. The bank has hired two managers (U and V), four tellers (W, X, Y, and Z), and two operations officers (S and T), for a total of exactly eight full-time employees. No part-time employees are hired. Each employee works a complete day when working.

  A manager must be on duty each day.
  The managers cannot work on the same day.
  At least two tellers must be working on the same day.
  W and X will not work on the same day.
  S and Z will only work on Saturday.
  No employee can work on consecutive days, but each employee must work on Saturday or Sunday.

7. Which one of the following could be false?

   (A) If U works on Saturday, then V works on Sunday.
   (B) If X works on Saturday, then W works on Sunday.
   (C) T can work either day.
   (D) If W works on Saturday and Y works on Sunday, then X works on Sunday.
   (E) If U works on Sunday, then X works on Saturday.

8. Which one of the following is an acceptable group of employees that could work on Saturday?

   (A) ZWYST
   (B) UVWYZS
   (C) VWXZT
   (D) UZST
   (E) VWZS

9. What is the greatest number of employees that can work on Saturday?

   (A) 2
   (B) 3
   (C) 4
   (D) 5
   (E) 6

10. If W works on Sunday, then which one of the following must be true?

   (A) X works on Saturday.
   (B) Y works on Saturday.
   (C) T works on Sunday.
   (D) Z works on Sunday.
   (E) U works on Saturday.

11. Which one of the following must be true?

   (A) T always works the same day as Y.
   (B) S never works the same day as U.
   (C) Z never works the same day as X.
   (D) If W works on Sunday, then Y always works on Saturday.
   (E) Only two tellers work on Saturday.

12. Which one of the following is a complete and accurate list of the employees who have the possibility of working on Sunday?

   (A) UWYZ
   (B) UWYS
   (C) UVWXT
   (D) UVWXYT
   (E) UVWXYTS

GO ON TO THE NEXT PAGE ➤

Questions 13–19

Three division office managers, Fred, Al, and Cynthia, draw office assistants each day from the clerical and typing pools available to them. The clerical pool consists of Lyndia, Jim, Dennis, and Sylvia. The typing pool consists of Edra, Gene, and Helen. The office assistants are selected according to the following conditions:

Fred always needs at least one typist, but never more than two assistants.

Al always needs at least two assistants, but never more than three.

Sylvia or Gene and one other assistant always work for Cynthia.

Gene and Lyndia always work together.

Dennis and Edra will not work together.

No more than two typists work for the same manager, but all three typists must work each day.

13. If Gene works for Fred and all of the assistants work, then which one of the following must be FALSE?

(A) Jim works for Cynthia.
(B) Sylvia works for Cynthia.
(C) Lyndia works for Fred.
(D) Dennis works for Al.
(E) Edra works for Al.

14. If Sylvia doesn't work for Cynthia, then which one of the following must be true?

(A) Edra works for Fred.
(B) Gene works for Al.
(C) Lyndia works for Cynthia.
(D) Dennis works for Al.
(E) Helen works for Cynthia.

15. Assume that Lyndia and Jim work for Al. Which one of the following must be true?

(A) Gene works for Al.
(B) Edra works for Cynthia.
(C) Helen works for Fred.
(D) Edra works for Fred.
(E) Helen works for Cynthia.

16. Assume that Sylvia and Jim work for Al. If all of the assistants work, then which one of the following must be true?

(A) Edra works for Al.
(B) Gene works for Fred.
(C) Lyndia works for Al.
(D) Helen works for Fred.
(E) Dennis works for Fred.

17. Which one of the following must be FALSE?

(A) Helen and Edra never work for Cynthia on the same day.
(B) Edra can work for Cynthia.
(C) Dennis and Gene never work for Fred on the same day.
(D) Jim and Sylvia never work for Fred on the same day.
(E) Lyndia and Sylvia can work for Al on the same day.

18. If Jim works for Cynthia and all of the assistants work, then

(A) Dennis works for Al.
(B) Edra works for Al.
(C) Helen works for Al.
(D) Lyndia works for Al.
(E) Sylvia works for Fred.

19. Assume that Al needs only two assistants and Fred needs only one assistant. If Helen works for Fred, then which one of the following must be true?

(A) Jim works for Al.
(B) Sylvia doesn't work.
(C) Dennis doesn't work.
(D) Edra works for Al.
(E) Edra works for Cynthia.

2 ● 2 ● 2 ● 2 2

Questions 20–24

Four teams (Red, Blue, Green, and Yellow) participate in the Junior Olympics, in which there are five events. In each event participants place either 1st, 2nd, 3rd, or 4th. First place is awarded a gold medal, 2nd place is awarded a silver medal, and 3rd place is awarded a bronze medal. There are no ties and each team enters one contestant in each event. All contestants finish each event.

The results of the Junior Olympics are:
    No team wins gold medals in two consecutive events.
    No team fails to win a medal within two consecutive events.
    The Blue team wins only two medals, neither of them gold.
    The Red team only wins three gold medals, and no other medals.

20. If the green team wins only one gold medal, then which one of the following must be true?

    (A) The yellow team wins two gold medals.
    (B) The red team wins only two bronze medals.
    (C) The yellow team wins only one gold medal.
    (D) The yellow team wins only silver medals.
    (E) The green team wins only bronze medals.

21. Which one of the following must be true?

    (A) The yellow team wins only bronze and gold medals.
    (B) The yellow team wins five medals.
    (C) The green team cannot win a silver medal.
    (D) The yellow team cannot win a bronze medal.
    (E) The green team wins exactly three medals.

22. If the yellow team wins five silver medals, then the green team must win

    (A) more silver than gold
    (B) more gold than bronze
    (C) two gold, two bronze, one silver
    (D) two gold, three bronze
    (E) six medals

23. All of the following must be true EXCEPT

    (A) the green team wins five medals
    (B) the yellow team wins five medals
    (C) if the green team wins one gold medal, the yellow team wins one gold medal
    (D) if the green team wins only one silver medal, the yellow team wins only one silver medal
    (E) if the yellow team wins only silver medals, the green team cannot win a silver medal

24. If a fifth team, Orange, enters all events and wins only three consecutive silver medals, which one of the following must be true?

    (A) If green wins a gold in the 2nd event, it also wins a bronze in the 3rd event.
    (B) If green wins a gold in the 2nd event, it also wins a silver in the 4th event.
    (C) If yellow wins a gold in the 2nd event, green wins a bronze in the 3rd event.
    (D) If yellow wins a gold in the 2nd event, blue wins a silver in the 3rd event.
    (E) If red wins a gold in the 1st event, orange wins a silver in the last event.

STOP

IF YOU FINISH BEFORE TIME IS UP, CHECK YOUR WORK ON THIS SECTION OF THE TEST ONLY.
DO NOT GO ON TO THE NEXT SECTION OF THE TEST UNTIL TIME IS UP FOR THIS SECTION.

3   **3**   **3**   **3**   **3**

SECTION III
TIME — 35 MINUTES
26 QUESTIONS

<u>Directions:</u> In this section you will be given brief statements or passages and will be required to evaluate the reasoning involved. In some instances, more than one choice will appear to be a possible answer. You are to choose the *best* answer. Use common sense and reasonableness in making your selection; then mark the proper space on the answer sheet.

1. Though the benefits of the hot tub and the Jacuzzis have been well publicized by their manufacturers, there are also some less widely known dangers. Young children, of course, cannot be left unattended near a hot tub, and even adults have fallen asleep and drowned. Warm water can cause the blood vessels to dilate and the resulting drop in blood pressure can make people liable to fainting, especially when they stand up quickly to get out. Improperly maintained water can promote the growth of bacteria that can cause folliculitis.

   The main point of this passage is that

   (A) the benefits of the hot tub and the Jacuzzi have been overrated
   (B) the dangers of the hot tub and Jacuzzi outweigh their potential publicized benefits
   (C) users of hot tubs and Jacuzzis should be aware of the dangers connected with their use
   (D) the hot tub and Jacuzzi are dangerous only when improperly maintained
   (E) the hot tub is potentially beneficial in the treatment of high blood pressure

2. *Chariots of Fire* may have caught some professional critics off guard in 1982 as the Motion Picture Academy's choice for an Oscar as the year's best film, but it won wide audience approval as superb entertainment.

   Refreshingly, *Chariots of Fire* features an exciting story, enchanting English and Scottish scenery, a beautiful musical score, and appropriate costumes.

   All of these attractions are added to a theme that extols traditional religious values—without a shred of offensive sex, violence, or profanity.

   Too good to be true? See *Chariots of Fire* and judge for yourself.

   Those who condemn the motion picture industry for producing so many objectionable films can do their part by patronizing wholesome ones, thereby encouraging future Academy Award judges to recognize and reward decency.

   Which one of the following is a basic assumption underlying the final sentence of the passage?

   (A) Academy judges are not decent people.
   (B) The popularity of a film influences academy judges.
   (C) Future academy judges will be better than past ones.
   (D) There are those who condemn the motion picture industry.
   (E) *Chariots of Fire* is a patronizing film.

GO ON TO THE NEXT PAGE ➤

3   **3**   **3**   **3**   **3**

3. *Andy:* All teachers are mean.
   Bob: That is not true. I know some doctors who are mean too.

   Bob's answer demonstrates that he thought Andy to mean that

   (A) all teachers are mean
   (B) some teachers are mean
   (C) doctors are meaner than teachers
   (D) teachers are meaner than doctors
   (E) only teachers are mean

4. Theodore Roosevelt was a great hunter. He was the mighty Nimrod of his generation. He had the physical aptitude and adventurous spirit of the true frontiersman. "There is delight," he said, "in the hardy life of the open; in long rides, rifle in hand; in the thrill of the fight with dangerous game." But he was more than a marksman and tracker of beasts, for he brought to his sport the intellectual curiosity and patient observation of the natural scientist.

   Which one of the following would most weaken the author's concluding contention?

   (A) Theodore Roosevelt never studied natural science.
   (B) Actually, Theodore Roosevelt's sharpshooting prowess was highly exaggerated.
   (C) Theodore Roosevelt always used native guides when tracking game.
   (D) Theodore Roosevelt was known to leave safaris if their first few days were unproductive.
   (E) Theodore Roosevelt's powers of observation were significantly hampered by his nearsightedness.

5. The following is an excerpt from a letter sent to a law school applicant:

   "Thank you for considering our school to further your education. Your application for admission was received well before the deadline and was processed with your admission test score and undergraduate grade report.

   "We regret to inform you that you cannot be admitted for the fall semester. We have had to refuse admission to many outstanding candidates because of the recent cut in state funding of our program.

   "Thank you for your interest in our school and we wish you success in your future endeavors."

   Which one of the following can be deduced from the above letter?

   (A) The recipient of the letter did not have a sufficiently high grade point average to warrant admission to this graduate program.
   (B) The recipient of the letter was being seriously considered for a place in the evening class.
   (C) The law school sending the letter could not fill all the places in its entering class due to a funding problem.
   (D) Criteria other than test scores and grade reports were used in determining the size of the entering class.
   (E) The school sending the letter is suffering severe financial difficulties.

GO ON TO THE NEXT PAGE ➤

3   **3**   **3**   **3**   **3**

<u>Questions 6–7</u>

At birth we have no self-image. We cannot distinguish anything from the confusion of light and sound around us. From this beginning of no-dimension, we gradually begin to differentiate our body from our environment and develop a sense of identity, with the realization that we are a separate and independent human being. We then begin to develop a conscience, the sense of right and wrong. Further, we develop social consciousness, where we become aware that we live with other people. Finally, we develop a sense of values, which is our overall estimation of our worth in the world.

6. Which one of the following would be the best completion of this passage?

   (A) The sum total of all these developments we call the self-image or the self-concept.

   (B) This estimation of worth is only relative to our value system.

   (C) Therefore, our social consciousness is dependent on our sense of values.

   (D) Therefore, our conscience keeps our sense of values in perspective.

   (E) The sum total of living with other people and developing a sense of values makes us a total person.

7. The author of this passage would most likely agree with which one of the following?

   (A) Children have no self-dimension.

   (B) Having a conscience necessitates the ability to differentiate between right and wrong.

   (C) Social consciousness is our most important awareness.

   (D) Heredity is predominant over environment in development.

   (E) The ability to distinguish the difference between moral issues depends on the overall dimension of self-development.

8. *Editorial:* A previously undisclosed transcript has revealed that Richard Nixon's secret White House slush fund that was used to silence the Watergate burglars came from illegally donated campaign money. After Nixon resigned, his successor, Gerald Ford, pardoned him. The same Gerald Ford has joined Presidents Carter and Bush in urging campaign funding reforms. Recent hearings have shown all too clearly that both parties have been guilty of highly questionable fund-raising practices. Unless the laws are changed, the shoddy practices of the last thirty years will undoubtedly continue.

Which one of the following most accurately states the main point of the argument?

   (A) It is hypocritical of Gerald Ford to urge campaign reform after his pardon of Richard Nixon.

   (B) Both the Democrats and the Republicans have been guilty of unethical campaign fund-raising practices.

   (C) The laws governing campaign fund-raising must be reformed.

   (D) Reform of campaign fund-raising has been supported by former presidents of both parties.

   (E) We cannot expect that those who benefit from a problem will wish to take steps to solve it.

GO ON TO THE NEXT PAGE ➤

3   **3**   **3**   **3**   **3**

Questions 9–10

In a report released last week, a government-funded institute concluded that there is "overwhelming" evidence that violence on television leads to criminal behavior by children and teenagers.

The report based on an extensive review of several hundred research studies conducted during the 1970s, is an update of a 1972 Surgeon General's report that came to similar conclusions.

9. Which one of the following is the most convincing statement in support of the argument in the first paragraph above?

(A) A 50-state survey of the viewing habits of prison inmates concluded that every inmate watches at least 2 hours of violent programming each day.

(B) A 50-state survey of the viewing habits of convicted adolescents shows that each of them had watched at least 2 hours of violent programming daily since the age of 5.

(C) One juvenile committed a murder that closely resembled a crime portrayed on a network series.

(D) The 1972 Surgeon General's report was not nearly as extensive as this more recent study.

(E) Ghetto residents who are burglarized most often report the theft of a television set.

10. The argument above is most weakened by its vague use of the word

(A) violence
(B) government
(C) extensive
(D) update
(E) overwhelming

Questions 11–12

Violence against racial and religious minority groups increased sharply throughout the county last year, despite a slight decline in statewide figures. Compiling incidents from police departments and private watchdog groups, the County Human Relations Committee reported almost 500 hate crimes in the year, up from only 200 last year. It was the first increase since the committee began to report a yearly figure six years ago. The lower statewide figures are probably in error due to underreporting in other counties; underreporting is the major problem that state surveyors face each year.

11. All of the following, if true, would support the conclusion or the explanation of the discrepancy in the state and county figures EXCEPT

(A) the number of hate crimes and those resulting in fatalities has increased in neighboring states

(B) anti-immigration sentiment was fanned this year by an anti-immigration ballot referendum

(C) funding for police departments throughout the state has decreased

(D) many law-abiding members of minority groups are fearful or distrustful of the police

(E) all of the counties in the state have active private watchdog groups that carefully monitor hate crimes

12. The author of this passage makes his case by

(A) establishing the likelihood of an event by ruling out several other possibilities

(B) combining several pieces of apparently unrelated evidence to build support for a conclusion

(C) contrasting a single certain case with several others with less evidence in their support

(D) assuming that what is only probable is certain

(E) using a general rule to explain a specific case

GO ON TO THE NEXT PAGE ➤

13. The study of village communities has become one of the fundamental methods of discussing the ancient history of institutions. It would be out of the question here to range over the whole field of human society in search for communal arrangements of rural life. It will be sufficient to confine the present inquiry to the varieties presented by nations of Aryan race, not because greater importance is to be attached to these nations than to other branches of humankind, although this view might also be reasonably urged, but principally because the Aryan race in its history has gone through all sorts of experiences, and the data gathered from its historical life can be tolerably well ascertained. Should the road be sufficiently cleared in this particular direction, it will not be difficult to connect the results with similar researches in other racial surroundings.

Which one of the following, if true, most weakens the author's conclusion?

(A) Information about the Aryan race is no more conclusive than information about any other ethnic group.
(B) The experiences and lifestyle of Aryans are uniquely different from those of other cultures.
(C) The Aryan race is no more important than any other race.
(D) The historical life of the Aryans dates back only 12 centuries.
(E) Aryans lived predominantly in villages, while today 90 percent of the world population live predominantly in or around major cities.

14. Although any reasonable modern citizen of the world must abhor war and condemn senseless killing, we must also agree that honor is more valuable than life. Life, after all, is transient, but honor is _____.

Which one of the following most logically completes the passage above?

(A) sensible
(B) real
(C) eternal
(D) of present value
(E) priceless

Questions 15–16

Bill said, "All dogs bark. This animal does not bark. Therefore it is not a dog."

15. Which one of the following most closely parallels the logic of this statement?

(A) All rocks are hard. This lump is hard. Therefore, it may be a rock.
(B) All foreign language tests are difficult. This is not a foreign language test. Therefore, it is not difficult.
(C) All Blunder automobiles are poorly built. Every auto sold by Joe was poorly built. Therefore, Joe sells Blunder automobiles.
(D) Rocks beat scissors, scissors beat paper, and paper beats rocks. Therefore, it is best to choose paper.
(E) All paint smells. This liquid does not smell. Therefore, it is not paint.

16. Which one of the following would weaken Bill's argument the most?

(A) Animals other than dogs bark.
(B) Some dogs cannot bark.
(C) Dogs bark more than cockatiels.
(D) You can train a dog not to bark.
(E) You can train birds to bark.

17. In the last three years the number of arrests for burglary and robbery in Sandy Beach has declined by more than 30 percent. At the same time, the city has reduced the size of its police force by 25 percent.

Which one of the following helps to resolve an apparent discrepancy in the information above?

(A) Neighborhood Watch programs have always been active in Sandy Beach.
(B) The number of reported burglaries and robberies in Sandy Beach has increased in the last three years.
(C) Compared to other cities in the state, Sandy Beach has one of the lowest crime rates.
(D) By using motorcycles rather than foot patrols, the police are able to cover larger areas of the city using fewer officers.
(E) Many of the residents of Sandy Beach have installed expensive security systems in their homes.

GO ON TO THE NEXT PAGE ➤

3   **3**   **3**   **3**   **3**

Questions 18–19

California and Nevada officials have questioned the impartiality of the board of scientists from the National Academy of Science who assess the safety of proposed nuclear dumping sites. They claim that the panels are heavily weighted in favor of the nuclear power companies that have been lobbying for the creation of nuclear dump sites in the deserts of the Southwest. At least ten members of the panels are or have been employees of the Department of Energy, but none is associated with any environmental organization. Environmentalists fear that long-lived nuclear wastes may leach into the groundwater and ultimately into the waters of the Colorado River. They also point out that 90 percent of the budget of the National Academy's Radioactive Waste Management Board is provided by the Department of Energy. The inventory of radioactive waste has been growing larger and larger in temporary storage places, but so far there has been virtually no agreement about a permanent dump site.

18. The officials who question the impartiality of the Management Board assume that the Department of Energy

    (A) supports the activities of the nuclear power industry
    (B) supports the activities of environmental groups
    (C) wishes to delay the selection of permanent nuclear waste dumping sites for as long as possible
    (D) is indifferent to the growing mass of nuclear wastes in temporary storage sites
    (E) has declined to take a stand for or against the use of nuclear power

19. The Nuclear Waste Management Board could best allay doubt of its impartiality if it were to

    (A) publish the results of its studies of the feasibility of locating nuclear waste dumps in the deserts of the Southwest
    (B) add one or two environmentalists to the panels that assess locations for nuclear dump sites
    (C) make public the sources of all its funding
    (D) recommend desert sites at a greater distance from the Colorado River
    (E) base decisions on feasibility studies by scientists with no connection to the National Academy

20. The law of parsimony urges a strict economy upon us; it requires that we can never make a guess with two or three assumptions in it if we can make sense with one.

    Which one of the following is the main point of the author's statement?

    (A) Complications arise from economy.
    (B) Simplify terminology whenever possible.
    (C) Don't complicate a simple issue.
    (D) Assumptions are necessarily simple in nature.
    (E) Excess assumptions never clarify the situation.

GO ON TO THE NEXT PAGE ➤

21. You can use a bottle opener to open the new beer bottles. You do not need to use a bottle opener to open the new beer bottles.

Which one of the following most closely parallels the logic of these statements?

(A) You must turn on the switch to light the lamp. If you turn on the switch, the lamp may not light.
(B) A cornered rattlesnake will strike, so do not corner a rattlesnake.
(C) If you do not study you will fail the test. If you do study, you may fail the test.
(D) Every candidate I voted for in the election lost his race. I must learn to vote better.
(E) I can move the sofa with my brother's help. If my brother is not available, I'll get a neighbor to help me.

22. To be admitted to Bigshot University, you must have a 3.5 grade-point average (GPA) and a score of 800 on the admissions test, a 3.0 GPA and a score of 1000 on the admissions test, or a 2.5 GPA and a score of 1200 on the admissions test. A sliding scale exists for other scores and GPAs.

Which one of the following is inconsistent with the above?

(A) The higher the GPA, the lower the admissions test score needed for admission.
(B) Joe was admitted with a 2.7 GPA and a score of 1100 on the admissions test.
(C) No student with a score of less than 800 on the admissions test and a 3.4 GPA will be admitted.
(D) More applicants had a GPA of 3.5 than had a GPA of 2.5.
(E) Some students with a score of less than 1200 on the admissions test and a GPA of less than 2.5 were admitted.

23. The Census Bureau's family portrait of America may remind us of the problems we face as a nation, but it also gives us reason to take heart in our ability to solve them in an enlightened way. The 1980 census was the first in history to show that the majority of the population in every state has completed high school. And the percentage of our people with at least 4 years of college rose from 11 percent in 1970 to 16.3 percent in 1980. That's progress—where it really counts.

Which one of the following assumptions underlies the author's conclusion in the above passage?

(A) Greater numbers of high school and college degrees coincide with other firsts in the 1980 census.
(B) Greater numbers of high school and college degrees coincide with greater numbers of well-educated people.
(C) Greater numbers of high school and college degrees coincide with a great commitment to social progress.
(D) Greater numbers of high school and college degrees coincide with a better chance to avoid national catastrophe.
(E) Greater numbers of high school and college degrees coincide with the 1980 census.

24. *Advertisement:* Add No-NOCK to your car and watch its performance soar. No-NOCK will give it more get-up-and-go and keep it running longer. Ask for No-NOCK when you want better mileage!

According to the advertisement above, No-NOCK claims to do everything EXCEPT

(A) improve your car's performance
(B) increase your car's life
(C) improve your car's miles per gallon
(D) cause fewer breakdowns
(E) stop the engine from knocking

GO ON TO THE NEXT PAGE ➤

3   **3**   **3**   **3**   **3**

25. So many arrogant and ill-tempered young men have dominated the tennis courts of late that we had begun to fear those characteristics were prerequisites for championship tennis.

Tennis used to be a gentleman's game. What is sad is not just that the game has changed. With so much importance placed on success, it may be that something has gone out of the American character—such things as gentleness and graciousness.

Which one of the following statements, if true, would most weaken the above argument?

(A) The American character is a result of American goals.
(B) Tennis has only recently become a professional sport.
(C) Some ill-tempered tennis players are unsuccessful.
(D) The "gentlemen" of early tennis often dueled to the death off the court.
(E) Some even-tempered tennis players are successful.

26. *Dolores:* To preserve the peace, we must be prepared to go to war with any nation at any time, using either conventional or nuclear weapons.
Fran: Which shall it be, conventional weapons or nuclear weapons?

Fran mistakenly concludes that the "either . . . or" phrase in Dolores's statement indicates

(A) fear
(B) indecision
(C) a choice
(D) a question
(E) a refusal

STOP

IF YOU FINISH BEFORE TIME IS UP, CHECK YOUR WORK ON THIS SECTION OF THE TEST ONLY.
DO NOT GO ON TO THE NEXT SECTION OF THE TEST UNTIL TIME IS UP FOR THIS SECTION.

4   **4**   **4**   **4**   **4**

SECTION IV
Time — 35 minutes
24 Questions

Directions: In this section you will be given groups of questions based on different sets of conditions. Drawing a simple diagram may be helpful in answering some of the questions. You are to choose the best answer and mark the corresponding space on your answer sheet.

Questions 1–6

A group of tourists is planning to visit a cluster of islands—U, V, W, X, Y, and Z, connected by bridges. The tourists must stay on each island visited for exactly three days and three nights. Each bridge takes one hour to cross, may be crossed in either direction, and can be crossed only in the morning to give the tourists a full day on the island.

    The islands are connected by bridges only as indicated below:

U is connected to W, X, and Y
V is connected to Y and Z
X is connected to Z and W
Y is connected to X and Z

1. If the group visits island W first, eight days later it could NOT be at which one of the following islands?

    (A) U
    (B) V
    (C) X
    (D) Y
    (E) Z

2. If the group stays on island X for three nights, it CANNOT spend the next three days and nights on island

    (A) U
    (B) V
    (C) W
    (D) Y
    (E) Z

3. Which one of the following is a possible order of islands visited in 12 days and nights?

    (A) UWYZ
    (B) UVYZ
    (C) UYVX
    (D) UXZV
    (E) UWYX

4. If the group visits island W first and can visit an island more than once, but does not use a bridge more than once, what is the greatest number of visits it can make?

    (A) 5
    (B) 6
    (C) 7
    (D) 8
    (E) 9

5. Assume the group visits island X first, and does not use a bridge more than once. Assume also that the group does stay at island Y twice. What is the greatest number of different islands the group can visit?

    (A) 3
    (B) 4
    (C) 5
    (D) 6
    (E) 7

6. Assume another island, T, is added to the tour. Assume also that T is connected only to U. Which one of the following statements must be true?

    (A) On the eighth day of a tour, starting its visit at island T, the group could be on island V.
    (B) On the fifth day of a tour, starting its visit at island T, the group could be on island X.
    (C) On the seventh day of a tour, starting its visit at island T, the group could be on island U.
    (D) On the eighth day of a tour, starting its visit at island V, the group could be on island T.
    (E) On the tenth day of a tour, starting its visit at island Z, the tour group could be on island T.

GO ON TO THE NEXT PAGE ➤

4   4   4   4   4

Questions 7–13

Teams A and B play a series of 9 games. To win the series, a team must win the most games, but must also win a minimum of 3 games.

There are no ties in the first 3 games.
Team A wins more of the last 3 games than team B.
Team B wins more of the last 5 games than team A.
The last game is a tie.
Games 1 and 3 are won by the same team.

7. Which one of the following must be true?

   (A) One team must win 5 games to win the series.
   (B) There are no ties.
   (C) One team wins at least 2 of the first 3 games.
   (D) The same team wins the last 5 games.
   (E) The last three games are won by one team.

8. Considering all of the conditions mentioned above, game 6

   (A) could be won by team A
   (B) could be won by team B
   (C) could be a tie
   (D) must be won by team A
   (E) must be won by team B

9. If game 7 is won by team A, then

   (A) game 8 is a tie
   (B) game 2 is a tie
   (C) game 4 is won by team A
   (D) game 5 is a tie
   (E) game 6 is won by team A

10. Which one of the following must be true?

    (A) There is only 1 tie in the last 5 games.
    (B) Team A wins 2 of the first 3 games.
    (C) Team B can win 3 of the last 5 games.
    (D) Game 4 is a tie.
    (E) Team A can win only 1 of the last 5 games.

11. If team A wins game 1 and game 4, then which one of the following must be FALSE?

    (A) Team A wins game 3.
    (B) Team A wins game 2.
    (C) Team B wins game 2.
    (D) Team A wins the series.
    (E) Team B wins the series.

12. Assume that game 4 is won by the winner of game 5. If game 2 is not won by the winner of game 3, then which one of the following must be true?

    (A) Team A wins game 7.
    (B) Team B is the winner of the series.
    (C) Team A wins game 2.
    (D) Team B wins game 1.
    (E) Team A wins game 3.

13. Which one of the following must be true?

    (A) For team A to win the series, team A must win exactly two of the first four games.
    (B) For team B to win the series, team B must win exactly one of the first four games.
    (C) For team A to win the series, team A must win only three of the first seven games.
    (D) For team B to win the series, team B must win at least three of the first four games.
    (E) For team A to win the series, team A must win two consecutive games.

GO ON TO THE NEXT PAGE ➤

Questions 14–18

Eight busts of American Presidents are to be arranged on two shelves, left to right. Each shelf accommodates exactly four busts. One shelf is directly above the other shelf. The busts are of John Adams, George Washington, Abraham Lincoln, Thomas Jefferson, James Monroe, John Kennedy, Theodore Roosevelt and Franklin Delano Roosevelt.

The Roosevelt busts may not be directly one above the other.

The bust of Kennedy must be adjacent to the bust of a Roosevelt.

The bust of Jefferson must be directly above the bust of John Adams.

The busts of Monroe, Adams, Kennedy and Franklin Delano Roosevelt must be on the bottom shelf.

The bust of Monroe must be third from the left.

14. If the bust of Theodore Roosevelt is second from the left on one shelf, which one of the following must be true?

    (A) The bust of Adams must be first on a shelf.
    (B) The bust of Adams must be third on a shelf.
    (C) The bust of Kennedy must be first on a shelf.
    (D) The bust of Kennedy must be second on a shelf.
    (E) The bust of Kennedy must be third on a shelf.

15. Which one of the following must be true about the bust of Monroe?

    (A) It is next to the bust of Adams.
    (B) It is next to the bust of Kennedy.
    (C) It is next to the bust of Franklin Delano Roosevelt.
    (D) It is directly under the bust of Lincoln.
    (E) It is directly under the bust of Theodore Roosevelt.

16. If the bust of Washington is first, directly above Kennedy's, all of the following must be true EXCEPT

    (A) the bust of Jefferson is fourth
    (B) the bust of Theodore Roosevelt is third
    (C) the bust of Franklin Delano Roosevelt is second
    (D) the bust of Lincoln is third
    (E) the bust of Adams is fourth

17. Which one of the following is not a possible order for the busts on either shelf?

    (A) Washington, Lincoln, Theodore Roosevelt, Jefferson
    (B) Franklin Delano Roosevelt, Kennedy, Monroe, Adams
    (C) Theodore Roosevelt, Lincoln, Washington, Jefferson
    (D) Lincoln, Theodore Roosevelt, Washington, Jefferson
    (E) Kennedy, Adams, Monroe, Franklin Delano Roosevelt

18. If the bust of Lincoln is next to the bust of Jefferson, all of the following are true EXCEPT

    (A) if the bust of Kennedy is first, the bust of Theodore Roosevelt is also first
    (B) if the bust of Washington is first, the bust of Franklin Delano Roosevelt is also first
    (C) if the bust of Washington is second, the bust of Kennedy is also second
    (D) if the bust of Kennedy is second, the bust of Theodore Roosevelt is also second
    (E) if the bust of Washington is second, the bust of Franklin Delano Roosevelt is also second

GO ON TO THE NEXT PAGE ➤

4   4   4   4   4

<u>Questions 19–24</u>

Six houses are numbered from 1 to 6 in order from left to right. Each house is to be painted a different color. Each house is to be painted by a different painter. Each painter paints using only colors he or she likes. No two painters use the same color.

    The first house is painted by a painter who likes only orange, white, and yellow.

    The second house is painted by a painter who likes only blue, green, and yellow.

    The third and fourth houses are painted by painters who each like only red and yellow.

    The fifth house is painted by a painter who likes only blue, green, red, and yellow.

    The sixth house is painted by a painter who likes only red, orange, violet, and white.

19. Which one of the following could be true?

    (A) The first house is painted yellow.
    (B) The second house is painted red.
    (C) The fifth house is painted red.
    (D) The fifth house is painted yellow.
    (E) The sixth house is painted orange.

20. What is the maximum number of possible color combinations for the six houses if orange is not used?

    (A) four
    (B) five
    (C) six
    (D) seven
    (E) eight

21. Which one of the following would provide sufficient information to determine the color of each of the six houses?

    (A) The houses that are painted blue, white, and yellow.
    (B) The houses that are painted blue, red, violet, and yellow.
    (C) The houses that are painted green, orange, red, and white.
    (D) The houses that are painted blue, green, red, and yellow.
    (E) The houses that are painted blue, green, orange, and white.

22. If the primary colors are red, blue, and yellow, and the secondary colors are green, orange, and violet, which one of the following could be true?

    (A) The second and fifth houses are painted primary colors.
    (B) The third and sixth houses are painted primary colors.
    (C) The second and fifth houses are painted secondary colors.
    (D) The first and fourth houses are painted secondary colors.
    (E) The second and sixth houses are painted secondary colors.

23. If the violet house is next to the green house and the blue house is next to the yellow house, then which one of the following must be true?

    (A) The first house is white.
    (B) The first house is orange.
    (C) The third house is red.
    (D) The fourth house is red.
    (E) The fifth house is blue.

24. Suppose that the painter of the third house also likes the color pink. If all the other conditions remain the same, then each of the following could be true EXCEPT

    (A) the fourth house is yellow and the sixth house is red
    (B) the second house is green and the sixth house is white
    (C) the second house is yellow and the third house is red
    (D) the first house is yellow and the fifth house is blue
    (E) the first house is white and the second house is yellow

STOP

IF YOU FINISH BEFORE TIME IS UP, CHECK YOUR WORK ON THIS SECTION OF THE TEST ONLY.
DO NOT GO ON TO THE NEXT SECTION OF THE TEST UNTIL TIME IS UP FOR THIS SECTION.

5   **5**

SECTION V
TIME — 35 MINUTES
25 QUESTIONS

<u>Directions:</u> In this section you will be given brief statements or passages and will be required to evaluate the reasoning involved. In some instances, more than one choice will appear to be a possible answer. You are to choose the best answer. Use common sense and reasonableness in making your selection; then mark the proper space on the answer sheet.

1. Chrysanthemums that have not been fertilized in July will normally not blossom in October. In October, the chrysanthemums did not blossom.

   With the premises given above, which one of the following would logically complete an argument?

   (A) Therefore, the chrysanthemums were not fertilized in July.
   (B) Therefore, the chrysanthemums may not have been fertilized in July.
   (C) Therefore, the chrysanthemums may blossom later in the fall.
   (D) Therefore, the chrysanthemums will blossom in the fall.
   (E) Therefore, the chrysanthemums will not blossom later in the fall.

2. When asked about the danger to public health from the spraying of pesticides by helicopters throughout the county, the County Supervisor replied, "The real danger to the public is the possibility of an infestation of harmful fruit-flies, which this spraying will prevent. Such an infestation would drive up the cost of fruits and vegetables by 15 percent."

   Which one of the following is the most serious weakness in the Supervisor's reply to the question?

   (A) He depends upon the ambiguity in the word "danger."
   (B) His response contains a self-contradiction.
   (C) He fails to support his argument concretely.
   (D) He fails to answer the question that has been asked.
   (E) His chief concern is the economic consequences of spraying.

3. So far this year researchers have reported the following:

   Heavy coffee consumption can increase the risk of heart attacks.
   Drinking a cup of coffee in the morning increases feelings of well-being and alertness.
   Boiled coffee increases blood cholesterol levels.
   Coffee may protect against cancer of the colon.

   If all these statements are true, which one of the following conclusions can be drawn from this information?

   (A) Reducing coffee consumption will make people healthier.
   (B) Reducing coffee consumption will make people feel better.
   (C) People at risk for heart attack should limit their coffee drinking.
   (D) Percolated coffee will not affect cholesterol levels.
   (E) People at risk for cancer should reduce their coffee consumption.

GO ON TO THE NEXT PAGE ➤

5   **5**

4. *Governor:* Compared with children in other states, infants born in California weigh more, survive the first years in greater numbers, and live longer. The hysteria about the danger of pesticides in California has attracted attention simply because a few Hollywood stars have appeared on television talk shows. Pesticides are the responsibility of the California Department of Food and Agriculture, and we can be sure its members are doing their job.

The governor's argument would be weakened if all of the following were shown to be true EXCEPT

(A) rates of melanoma and some forms of leukemia in California are above national norms
(B) the three highest positions at the California Department of Food and Agriculture are held by farm owners
(C) synthetic pesticide residues in food cause more cancer than do "natural pesticides" that the plants themselves produce
(D) more Californians suffer the consequences of air pollution than do the citizens in any other state
(E) children of farm workers are three times more likely to suffer childhood cancers than children of urban parents

5. Should we allow the Fire Department to continue to underpay its women officers by using policies of promotion that favor men?

The question above most closely resembles which one of the following in terms of its logical features?

(A) Should the excessive tax on cigarettes, liquor, and luxury goods be unfairly increased again this year?
(B) Should corrupt politicians be subject to the same sentencing laws as blue-collar felons?
(C) Should the police chief be chosen by examination score regardless of gender or seniority?
(D) Should the religious right be allowed to determine the censorship laws for all of society?
(E) Are liberal political values an appropriate basis for all of the social values in this state?

6. If airline fares have risen, then either the cost of fuel has risen or there are no fare wars among competing companies. If there are no fare wars among competing companies, the number of airline passengers is larger than it was last year.

According to the passage above, if there has been a rise in airline fares this month, which one of the following CANNOT be true?

(A) There are no fare wars among competing airlines.
(B) The cost of fuel has risen, and the number of passengers is the same as last year.
(C) The cost of fuel has risen, there are no fare wars, and the number of passengers is larger than it was last year.
(D) There are no fare wars, and the number of passengers is larger than it was last year.
(E) The cost of fuel has risen, there are no fare wars, and the number of passengers is smaller than it was last year.

GO ON TO THE NEXT PAGE ➤

7. Only 75 years ago, the best fishing in the world was the Grand Banks of the North Atlantic. But now overfishing and man's pollution have decimated the area. There will be no fishing industry in the Americas in a very few years. The waters off Newfoundland now yield less than half the catch of five years ago, and less than one quarter of the total of ten years ago. The cod has almost disappeared. The number of fishermen in Newfoundland and New England has declined, and their yearly earnings are now at an all-time low. Yet radar has made fishing methods more efficient than ever.

Which one of the following identifies most clearly a faulty assumption in the reasoning of this passage?

(A) Ten years is too short a time period to use to draw conclusions about the natural world.
(B) The argument assumes that the waters off Newfoundland are representative of all the American oceans.
(C) The pollution of the sea may have been caused by natural as well as by human forces.
(D) The argument does not allow for the possibility that the catch may increase in size in the next five years.
(E) The argument fails to consider that the decline in the catch may be due to factors other than pollution.

8. A cigarette advertisement in a magazine asks, "What do gremlins, the Loch Ness monster, and a filter cigarette claiming 'great taste' have in common?" The answer is "You've heard of all of them, but don't really believe they exist." The advertisement contains no pictures, and no additional text except the words Gold Star Cigarettes and the Surgeon General's warning in a box in the lower corner.

Which one of the following conclusions can be drawn from the information given above?

(A) Cigarette advertising depends upon visual appeal to create images for specific brands.
(B) All cigarette advertising depends on praising a specific brand.
(C) Gold Star Cigarettes are non-filters.
(D) The writers of this advertisement do not believe in advertising.
(E) The writers of this advertisement do not believe the Surgeon General's warning is true.

GO ON TO THE NEXT PAGE ➤

5   **5**

9. The traffic on the Imperial Highway has always been slowed by the dangerous curves in the road. It was built when cars were much smaller and less powerful, and very few drivers traveled between Imperial City and Fremont. All this has changed. The cost of widening and straightening the road would now be many times greater than building the proposed new toll road on the borders of the Imperial Wetlands reserve. Environmentalists fear the construction noise and waste will harm the wildlife in the reserve, and have urged that the toll road not be constructed.

Which one of the following, if true, would most strengthen the case of the environmentalists?

(A) None of the animals living in the Imperial Wetlands is on the list of endangered species.

(B) The traffic congestion on the Imperial Highway increases each year.

(C) The cost of building the new road will be amortized in ten years by the tolls collected.

(D) There are several less direct routes the toll road could take between Fremont and Imperial City.

(E) The environmentalists threaten to bring a lawsuit in federal court to halt construction of the road.

10. Despite the very large increase in the federal tax on luxury items, the value of the stock of Harry Evans, Inc., seller of the world's most expensive jewelry, continues to rise. Six months after the introduction of the tax, Evans's stock is at an all-time high. Moreover, sales in the United States continue to increase. In other countries, where Evans does 30 percent of its business, there have been no rises in excise taxes and the company will open new stores in Tokyo, Monte Carlo, and Singapore. According to a company spokesperson, _____.

Which one of the following most logically completes this paragraph?

(A) American customers who can afford to shop at Evans are not likely to be deterred by a rise in luxury taxes

(B) American customers are expected to spend far less at Evans because of the tax rise

(C) American sales are not significant enough to affect the overall profits of the firm

(D) the company will probably be forced to close most of its stores in America

(E) state taxes are more likely to influence jewelry sales than federal taxes

GO ON TO THE NEXT PAGE ➤

5   **5**

11. *Speaker:* A recent study of cigarette smokers has shown that, of cancer patients who are heavy smokers of unfiltered cigarettes, 40 percent will die of the disease. For cancer patients who are light smokers of filter cigarettes, the percentage is 25 percent.

Which one of the following conclusions can be drawn from the information above?

(A) There are more heavy smokers of unfiltered cigarettes than light smokers of filter cigarettes.

(B) More heavy smokers of unfiltered cigarettes die of cancer than light smokers of filter cigarettes.

(C) A heavy smoker of unfiltered cigarettes who has cancer is more likely to die than a light smoker of unfiltered cigarettes.

(D) A heavy smoker of unfiltered cigarettes who has cancer may be more likely to die than a light smoker of unfiltered cigarettes.

(E) A heavy smoker of unfiltered cigarettes who has cancer is more likely to die than a light smoker of filtered cigarettes who has cancer.

Questions 12–13

Archeologists have come to the support of Arctic anthropologists. A small minority of anthropologists assert that Stone-Age tribes of the Arctic domesticated wolves and trained them to haul sleds. Excavations have recently found evidence to support this claim. Archeologists have found wolf bones near the site of a Stone-Age village. They have also found walrus bones that might have been used on primitive sleds. The small minority of anthropologists believe that their theories have been proved.

12. Which one of the following is true of the evidence cited in the paragraph above?

(A) It is not relevant to the anthropologists' conclusions.

(B) It conclusively contradicts the anthropologists' conclusions.

(C) It neither supports nor refutes the anthropologists' conclusions positively.

(D) It supports the anthropologists' conclusions authoritatively.

(E) It conclusively supports only a part of the anthropologists' conclusions.

13. Which one of the following, if true, would best support the theory of the anthropologists?

(A) Wolves are known to have fed upon the garbage of villages in northern Europe.

(B) Wolves as a species are easily domesticated and trained.

(C) Almost all Stone-Age Arctic tools were made of walrus bone.

(D) Stone-Age villages were located on the migration routes of the caribou herds upon which wolves preyed.

(E) The earliest sled part found in the Arctic was made one thousand years after the Stone Age.

GO ON TO THE NEXT PAGE ➤

5   **5**

Questions 14–15

The following criticism of a self-portrait by Vincent van Gogh appeared in a magazine in 1917:

"Here we have a work of art which is so self-evidently a degenerate work by a degenerate artist that we need not say anything about the inept creation. It is safe to say that if we were to meet in our dreams such a villainous looking jailbird with such a deformed Neanderthal skull, degenerate ears, hobo beard and insane glare, it would certainly give us a nightmare."

14. The author of this passage makes his point by using

   (A) invective
   (B) analogy
   (C) citation of authority
   (D) paradox
   (E) example

15. In relation to the first sentence of the quotation, the second sentence is

   (A) an example of an effect following a cause
   (B) a specific derived from a general principle
   (C) a logical conclusion
   (D) a contradiction
   (E) a personal experience in support of a generalization

16. A company called Popcorn Packaging is promoting the use of popcorn as a cushioning material in packing. Unlike the commonly used Styrofoam beads or chips, popcorn can be recycled as a food for birds or squirrels and can serve as a garden mulch. Used out of doors, popcorn disappears almost overnight, while the Styrofoam beads may be in the environment for centuries. Even before we became ecology conscious, popcorn was used in packing in the 1940s. Since it now costs less to produce than Styrofoam, there is every reason to return to wide-scale use of packaging by popcorn.

Which one of the following, if true, would most seriously weaken the author's argument?

   (A) A package using popcorn as a cushioning material will weigh less than a package using Styrofoam beads.
   (B) Popcorn may attract rodents and insects.
   (C) A large number of squirrels can damage a garden by consuming flowering bulbs.
   (D) Less than 1 percent of the material now used for package cushioning is recycled.
   (E) Styrofoam replaced popcorn in the early 1950s because it was cheaper to produce.

17. This produce stand sells fruits and vegetables. All fruits are delicious, and all vegetables are rich in vitamins. Every food that is vitamin-rich is delicious, so everything sold at this stand is delicious.

Which one of the following assumptions is necessary to make the conclusion in the argument above logically correct?

   (A) The stand sells many fruits and vegetables.
   (B) This produce stand sells only fruits and vegetables.
   (C) Something cannot be both vitamin-rich and delicious.
   (D) Some stands sell fruits that are not delicious.
   (E) Some vegetables are delicious.

GO ON TO THE NEXT PAGE ➤

5   **5**

18. Voter turnout in primary elections has declined steadily from 1982 to 1990. In 1990, more than 80 percent of the Americans eligible to vote failed to do so. Only 11.9 percent of the Democrats and 7.7 percent of the Republicans went to the polls. The largest number of voters turned out for elections in the District of Columbia (28 percent) and in Massachusetts, where the 32 percent total was the highest since 1962. In each of the twenty-four other states holding elections, the number of voters was smaller than it had been in 1986 and 1982.

Based on the information in this passage, which one of the following must be true?

(A) The turnout in the District of Columbia was affected by favorable weather conditions.
(B) Fewer than 20 percent of the eligible major-party voters voted in the 24 states other than Massachusetts.
(C) The voter turnout in Massachusetts is always higher than the turnouts in other states.
(D) The voter turnout decline is a signal of a nationwide voter rebellion.
(E) More voters cast their votes in general elections than in primary elections.

19. Each year the number of schools that no longer allow smoking on school property grows larger. Four states, New Jersey, Kansas, Utah, and New Hampshire, now require tobacco-free schools. The Tobacco Institute has fought against regulations restricting smoking everywhere from airlines to restaurants on the grounds that they trample on the rights of smokers, but is conspicuously absent from school board lobbyists. Tobacco industry spokesmen have denounced the rules treating teachers like children, but have said they will not go on record to defend policies that affect children.

Which one of the following, if true, best accounts for the Tobacco Institute's behavior?

(A) The tobacco industry is presently fighting the charge that it attempts to recruit new smokers among minors.
(B) The tobacco industry can depend on continued high profits from overseas operations, where restrictions do not exist.
(C) Most tobacco companies are highly diversified corporations whose profits no longer depend wholly on tobacco products.
(D) The tobacco industry believes the rights of children to be equal to the rights of adults.
(E) The tobacco industry agrees with the schools that have rules against tobacco.

5   **5**

A number of lawsuits have been brought against popular singing groups charging that suicidal themes in their songs have led to teenage suicides. So far, the courts have found that the lyrics are protected by the First Amendment. But what if this should change, and a court decides that suicidal themes in popular songs are dangerous? In fact, the songs that have been charged so far are antisuicide; they present sardonically the self-destructive behavior of drinking, drugs, and escape by death. They describe a pitiful state of mind, but they do not endorse it.

Blaming suicide on the arts is nothing new. In the late eighteenth century, Goethe's popular novel *Werther* was said to be the cause of a rash of suicides in imitation of the novel's hero. If we begin to hold suicide in books or music responsible for suicides in real life, the operas of Verdi and Puccini will have to go, and *Romeo and Juliet* and *Julius Caesar* will disappear from high school reading lists.

20. The author of this passage argues by

    (A) providing examples to support two opposing positions
    (B) using an observation to undermine a theoretical principle
    (C) disputing an interpretation of evidence cited by those with an opposing view
    (D) predicting personal experience from a general principle
    (E) accusing the opposing side of using inaccurate statistical information

21. Which one of the following is an assumption necessary to the author's argument?

    (A) A lyric presenting suicide in a favorable light should not have First Amendment protection.
    (B) Literature or music cannot directly influence human behavior.
    (C) Many record albums already carry labels warning purchasers of their dangerous contents.
    (D) The audience, not the performer, is responsible for the audience's actions.
    (E) Freedom of speech is the most threatened of our personal freedoms.

---

22. Haven't you at some time had a favorite song or book or film that was not well known but later became popular? And didn't you feel somehow betrayed and resentful when what you had thought was unique became commonplace? On a larger scale, the same thing happens to novelists or film makers who have enjoyed critical esteem without popular success. Let them become public sensations, and the critics who praised their work will attack them virulently.

This paragraph most likely introduces an article on a film maker who has made a

    (A) series of commercially successful films
    (B) series of commercially unsuccessful films
    (C) single film, a commercial success
    (D) single film, a commercial failure
    (E) critical success and a commercial success

GO ON TO THE NEXT PAGE ➤

5   **5**

23. Studies of the effects of drinking four or more cups of coffee per day have shown that coffee consumption increases work efficiency by improving the ability to process information. People who drink two cups of coffee in the morning are more alert and feel better than those who do not. But there are other factors to be considered.

Which one of the following sentences would provide the most logical continuation of this paragraph?

(A) Contrary to popular belief, drinking coffee cannot erase the effect of alcohol.
(B) Some studies suggest that coffee drinking will protect against cancer of the colon.
(C) Combined with the stress of heavy exercise, coffee drinking may be the cause of higher blood pressure.
(D) Drinking two or more cups of coffee per day increases the risk of heart attacks in men.
(E) Many people cannot distinguish between the taste of decaffeinated and that of regular coffee.

24. All of the members of the chorus will sing in the performance of the oratorio *Messiah.* Some of these are highly trained professionals, some are gifted amateurs, and some are singers of mediocre ability.

If the statements above are true, which one of the following must also be true?

(A) *Messiah* will be performed by highly trained professionals, gifted amateurs, and some singers of mediocre ability.
(B) Some of the members of the chorus are not highly trained professionals, gifted amateurs, or singers of mediocre ability.
(C) *Messiah* will be performed by some highly trained professionals, but not all of them are in the chorus.
(D) Not all of those in the chorus who are gifted amateurs will perform in the oratorio.
(E) All of those who will perform *Messiah* are members of the chorus.

25. *Politician:* The passage of laws that limit elected officials to one or two terms in office is an admission that voters are civic fools, unable to tell good lawmakers from bad ones. To ban all the politicians when the real intention is to get rid of the corrupt ones is to burn the house down to get rid of the vermin.

The author of this passage makes his point chiefly by

(A) defining a key term
(B) exposing a self-contradiction
(C) drawing an analogy
(D) questioning the evidence of his opponents
(E) citing an example

STOP

END OF MULTIPLE-CHOICE EXAMINATION. IF YOU FINISH BEFORE TIME IS UP, CHECK YOUR WORK ON THIS SECTION ONLY. DO NOT GO BACK TO ANY OTHER SECTION OF THE EXAMINATION.

Writing Sample

Directions: You have 30 minutes to write an essay in response to a given topic. Take a few minutes to plan your work before you begin writing. DO NOT WRITE ON A TOPIC OF YOUR OWN CHOICE. ESSAYS THAT DO NOT ADDRESS THE GIVEN TOPIC ARE UNACCEPTABLE.

The quality of your writing is more important than the length of your response or the content. Pay attention to organization, appropriate diction, and correct usage. You will not be expected to display any specialized knowledge in your response, nor will you be expected to write a "perfect" essay; law schools understand that you are writing under a time constraint, and will allow for the minor lapses in writing ability that might occur under this circumstance.

Only the lined area in your booklet will be reproduced for the law schools, so do not write outside this space. *Do not* skip lines or use wide margins. These precautions, along with careful planning and legible handwriting that is not unduly large, will keep you within the allowed space.

Sample Topic

Read the following descriptions of Jackson and Brown. *Then, in the space provided, write an argument for deciding which of the two should be assigned the responsibility of hiring teachers for the Hapsville School System.* The following criteria are relevant to your decision:

- The taxpayers want educators who can instill in students the desire to learn and an excitement for knowledge, something that has been lacking in their schools.
- A majority of students' parents believe that their children should be equipped, upon graduation, to earn a living, and thus favor a more trade-oriented (rather than academic) approach to schooling.

JACKSON was appointed as Superintendent of Schools by the Hapsville School Board, which was elected by the community's taxpayers. As a 30-year resident of Hapsville (population 45,000), Jackson is unique in that he holds not only a doctorate in administration, but also a master's degree in education. He taught in the Hapsville schools for 16 years until he served on the state Commission on Education. He has always favored a progressive approach to education, although it may not always have been popular with the town's population. Through the years he has brought many fine teachers to the faculty, because of his willingness to encourage new classroom techniques.

BROWN is a 52-year resident of Hapsville, having been born in the same house in which he now lives. He was elected to the School Board 13 years ago, and continues to win nearly unanimous reelection every two years. As the foremost developer in the Four Counties area, Mr. Brown has had the opportunity to build hundreds of new homes in the six housing developments he's planned and actualized, and, in the interim, has employed hundreds of Hapsville residents as carpenters, electricians, plumbers, architects, landscapers, groundskeepers, etc. As such, he is held in high esteem by most of the town, not only for his providing livelihoods for many, but also for his fair and realistic outlook on life. Mr. Brown feels strongly that the key to life is having a marketable skill.

Answer Key

Section I: Reading Comprehension

1. **B**	6. **A**	11. **E**	16. **E**	21. **B**	26. **D**
2. **C**	7. **C**	12. **C**	17. **A**	22. **D**	27. **A**
3. **A**	8. **A**	13. **D**	18. **B**	23. **A**	28. **B**
4. **A**	9. **B**	14. **A**	19. **E**	24. **E**	
5. **E**	10. **A**	15. **C**	20. **D**	25. **B**	

Section II: Analytical Reasoning

1. **C**	5. **D**	9. **D**	13. **A**	17. **E**	21. **B**
2. **A**	6. **B**	10. **A**	14. **C**	18. **D**	22. **D**
3. **E**	7. **E**	11. **E**	15. **A**	19. **C**	23. **D**
4. **C**	8. **E**	12. **D**	16. **D**	20. **C**	24. **C**

Section III: Logical Reasoning

1. **C**	6. **A**	11. **E**	16. **B**	21. **E**	26. **B**
2. **B**	7. **B**	12. **C**	17. **B**	22. **E**	
3. **E**	8. **C**	13. **B**	18. **A**	23. **B**	
4. **D**	9. **B**	14. **C**	19. **E**	24. **E**	
5. **D**	10. **E**	15. **E**	20. **C**	25. **D**	

Section IV: Analytical Reasoning

1. **B**	5. **D**	9. **A**	13. **E**	17. **E**	21. **C**
2. **B**	6. **E**	10. **E**	14. **D**	18. **C**	22. **E**
3. **D**	7. **C**	11. **E**	15. **A**	19. **E**	23. **D**
4. **E**	8. **E**	12. **B**	16. **D**	20. **A**	24. **C**

Section V: Logical Reasoning

1. **B**	6. **E**	11. **E**	16. **B**	21. **D**
2. **D**	7. **B**	12. **C**	17. **B**	22. **E**
3. **C**	8. **C**	13. **B**	18. **B**	23. **D**
4. **D**	9. **D**	14. **A**	19. **A**	24. **A**
5. **A**	10. **A**	15. **D**	20. **C**	25. **C**

Model Test Analysis

Doing model exams and understanding the explanations afterwards are of course important in acquainting you with typical LSAT question types and successful approaches to the questions. However, another benefit of carefully analyzing these model tests is to understand the kinds of errors you are making and thus work to minimize them. For instance, if a very high percentage of your incorrect answers is due to "careless error" or "misread problem" then perhaps you are working much too fast and should slow your pace accordingly. If your incorrect answers are due primarily to "lack of knowledge," then a careful rereading and reworking of the appropriate question-type chapter may be in order. Or if you find that you aren't completing a large number of questions because of lack of time, you may need to either increase your speed or learn to use the "one-check, two-check" technique more effectively.

This kind of analysis of the model tests will enable you to identify your particular weaknesses and thus remedy them.

Model Test One Analysis

Section	Total Number of Questions	Number Correct	Number Incorrect	Number Unanswered*
I. Reading Comprehension	28			
II. Analytical Reasoning	24			
III. Logical Reasoning	26			
IV. Analytical Reasoning	24			
V. Logical Reasoning	25			
TOTALS:	127			

*At this stage in your preparation, you should not be leaving any blank answer spaces. At least fill in a guess, as there is no penalty for a wrong answer.

Reasons for Incorrect Answers

You may wish to evaluate the explanations before completing this chart.

Section	Total Number Incorrect	Lack of Knowledge	Misread Problem	Careless Error	Unanswered or Wrong Guess
I. Reading Comprehension					
II. Analytical Reasoning					
III. Logical Reasoning					
IV. Analytical Reasoning					
V. Logical Reasoning					
TOTALS:					

Explanation of Answers

Section I

Passage 1

1. **B** The first sentence of the passage makes it clear that government workers are forbidden to strike by statutory law.

2. **C** If strikes are a form of symbolic speech, the denial of the right to strike is arguably a denial of free speech. It also can be argued that it denies due process, the right to picket, and the right to avoid abnormally dangerous working conditions.

3. **A** The courts, not the legislative or the executive branches, must determine the "clear and present danger," according to the Supreme Court decision described in the second paragraph.

4. **A** Because the firing of the controllers had the same effect as a strike, it appears that there was no danger to the public.

5. **E** The author points out that workers in government who do that same job as workers in private industry cannot strike. The passage argues that the nature of the service should determine the right to strike, not the employer.

6. **A** It is possible that the "highly qualified" may seek employment outside of government, because of the no-strike clause. Choices (B), (C), (D), (E) are not plausible weaknesses of the no-strike rule.

Passage 2

7. **C** See lines 4–9. Her father also may have influenced her in the ways suggested in (A), (B), (D), and (E), but these answers are not suggested by the passage itself.

8. **A** We can infer from lines 19–24 that this was Woolf's dilemma, particularly because in lines 25–28 we learn that the emphasis in her feminism was self-reform. E is incorrect; "lucid objectivity" is cited as a strength of her novel *The Years*, not something that needed to be overcome. C is not supported by the passage because there is nothing to suggest that Virginia Woolf wished to pursue "social work." Similarly, (B) and (D) are not supported by any information in the passage.

9. **B** In the passage, the integration of masculine and feminine (the androgynous mind) and the danger of one-sidedness (lines 18–24) describe Woolf's feminism. Although C and D might also characterize her feminism, the passage emphasizes a need for wholeness. A is not supported by the passage. E might be suggested in lines 30–35 and lines 77–80 but it is *not* presented as a characterization of her feminism.

10. **A** Paragraph two is concerned with the superiority of Woolf's novels to her tracts in dealing with her feminist concerns. Paragraph three contrasts a tract and a novel to illustrate this point. Paragraph three doesn't present a contrast to or a subtopic of paragraph one (B, D), nor does it act as a transition (C). (In fact, the passage could move smoothly from paragraph two to paragraph four even if paragraph three were missing. What would be missing would be a concrete example—i.e., answer A.) Paragraph two does not present an exegesis (E).

11. **E** This opposition is at the heart of the passage—see paragraphs two, three, and four. Different types of novels are *not* contrasted (B), nor is Woolf's aesthetic creed contrasted to the aesthetic creed of the Bloomsbury group (A). (A contrast is suggested in lines 4–9, but it is minor, and not explained or developed.) C is incorrect; the passage explicitly addresses Woolf's *avoidance* of such a contrast and her belief in the androgynous mind. D is unclear and inaccurate.

12. **C**   See paragraph four. Although the author does say that Woolf's primary emphasis was on self-reform, he does not suggest that her social concerns were trivial (D). Nothing in the passage suggests that the author is criticizing the Bloomsbury aesthetic creed (A). Similarly, although the author finds Woolf's novels more successful than her tracts, it is a giant leap to infer that he dislikes social reform literature in general (E). (B) is clearly incorrect.

13. **D**   The passage states this idea in the first line and then continues throughout to develop the subject of the importance of both feminism and art in Woolf's writing. See lines 37–43. (A) is too limited; these two works are used to illustrate the main point of the passage. (B) is broad and imprecise. (C) is also imprecise. (E) is incorrect; opposition of masculine and feminine is not part of the passage.

Passage 3

14. **A**   The author is obviously most concerned with the work of historians and the current state of written history, which is what prompts his discussion of fiction in relation to history. See lines 4–7, 17–20, 53–59, 64–70. Literature and literary concerns (answer C) are secondary.

15. **C**   See lines 68–69: "... their abandonment of the narrative style...." A decline in the writing *ability* of historians (E) is not implied. And although the author does mention the movies and television, he does not attribute the growth of fictional history to an increase in their audiences (B).

16. **E**   This attitude is clearly stated in lines 49–53. B may seem correct, but the author does not say that fictional history on its own has won the audience away from traditional history. On the contrary, he suggests that professional historians themselves may be partly responsible for the growth of fictional history (lines 64–68).

17. **A**   This book would most clearly fit the definition of fictional history given in lines 35–39. According to the author, it is fictional history that causes the greatest confusion (lines 49–53). (B) and (C) would be classified as historical fiction according to the author's definitions, and (D) and (E) as nonfiction.

18. **B**   The second paragraph is devoted to defining and contrasting the two terms. (D) might be considered a possible answer but is less clear and specific. The other answers are simply inaccurate.

19. **E**   Nothing in the passage suggests a judgment of history taught in the schools. The other statements are all supported in the passage: (A)—lines 17–20; (B)—lines 64–68; (C)—lines 53–59; (D)—lines 12–16.

20. **D**   Throughout the passage the author is most concerned with the growth of fictional history and its effects. None of the other answers present his *attitude* as clearly, though (C) does define fictional history.

21. **B**   The author is obviously concerned with the "mischief" that the mixture of history with fiction can cause. However, he presents his concern in a moderate fashion. He is not hostile, he does not preach, he is not pedantic, nor does he display irony. (E) suggests an elevated tone not present in the passage.

Passage 4

22. **D**   The author simply presents facts, both historical and modern, concerning faith healing and doesn't necessarily suggest that it is effective, only that some aspects of it now appear in modern medical practice. All of the other choices suggest opinions not given by the author or facts not in evidence in the passage.

23. **A** "Charlatans" are mentioned in the passage only in the context of what "most of modern society is convinced" of, but the author does not indicate that it is true or proven that faith healing is practiced by charlatans. Choice (C) is suggested by the passage; the term *holistic* is used in the discussion of modern medicine. Note that it would be incorrect if it said "*only* a modern term," which is not suggested.

24. **E** The final paragraph discusses the modern medical world and its inclusion of certain elements of faith healing. It doesn't deal with historical attitudes at all, choices (A) and (C), or with scientific objections (D). Although it mentions spirituality and faith (B), that choice is too narrow to best describe the purpose of the entire paragraph.

25. **B** In the last paragraph, the author says that "certain medicinal herbs used by ancient healers, 'medicines' once ridiculed, have now been found to have curative powers previously unknown and unappreciated." In mentioning that fact, it is likely that the author would appreciate open-minded behavior on the part of scientists and their not dismissing a drug or procedure simply because it has not yet been fully tested.

26. **D** Because holistic medicine practitioners attempt to treat the "whole" person, they are likely to investigate not only the physical condition of their patients but also the psychological condition. The fact that an individual being treated might disagree with the importance of the "will to live" would not logically be likely to keep practitioners from conducting that investigation in some manner in order to do their job as they feel appropriate. We have no information from the passage that holistic practitioners are necessarily aware of the lost opportunities in finding medicines (A); that trained psychological personnel would be involved (B), although one could assume they *might* be; or that patients would be referred to faith healers (C). Holistic practitioners and ancient faith healers *do* have something in common (E)—they are both concerned with the affect of the mind on the state of the body.

27. **A** Faith healers would be unlikely to rely solely on physical intervention in a disease. From the passage, it is clear that modern practitioners of faith healing "*most* often promote a combination of spirituality . . . and science," so they might well refer a patient for long-term physical care (E), but it is *not* clear that *all* of them involve science in their treatment, so it is likely that some would engage in the activities of (B) and (D). Given the information, it's likely that *all* such practitioners would engage in (C), creating a comfortable psychological atmosphere so as to understand the patient's state of mind in order to improve it.

28. **B** The author's tone is factual, presenting information for the reader about faith healing practices and the place in modern medicine that some of them might have. The author isn't promoting a particular point of view concerning faith healing, (C) and (D), or particularly addressing readers looking for medical alternatives (E). Although there is some comparison of past practices with modern ones, in that modern practices often accept hard science as well, choice (A), this choice is too narrow to be the best answer.

Section II

Answers 1-6

From the information given, you could have made the following diagram:

```
Higher   A   D   E        Pent. 4  ___
         ?   ?   ?  [FG]        3  ___  ___
Lower    B   C   C             2  ___  ___
                               1  ___  ___
```

1. **C** Since F and G are on the same floor, they can't be on 4. Since B and C are below A or D/E, they can't be on 4; therefore only A, D, or E can be on 4.

2. **A** If F's apartment is on 2, so is G's. For B and C to be below A, D, and E, B and C must be on 1 and A, D, and E on 3 and 4, but we don't know exactly where on 3/4.

3. **E** If D is on 4, G (and F) *can* be on 3, 2, or 1.

```
D       D       D
FG      AE      AE
AE      FG      BC
BC      BC      FG
```

4. **C** If D and E are on the same floor, A must be on 4. All the other answers are possible but *not* certain.

5. **D** If A is on 4 or C on 1, the arrangement must be either

```
A                A
FG      or       DE
DE               FG
BC               BC
```

6. **B** A and E can be on the same floor if D is on 4.

```
D                D
AE      or       AE
FG               BC
BC               FG
```

Answers 7-12

From the information given, you may have constructed a simple grouping display of information similar to this:

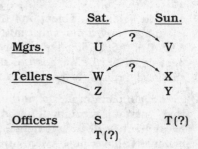

Another possible display might look like this:

```
              Sat.        Sun.
                     ?
Mgrs.          U --------- V
                     ?
Tellers ------ W --------- X
               Z           Y

Officers       S           T(?)
               T(?)
```

7. **E** From the original information, a manager must be on duty each day and the managers cannot work on the same day. Therefore (A) must be true. (E) does not have to be true, since U's schedule has no bearing on X's schedule. Since W and X will not work on the same day, (B) must also be true. There is no restriction placed on T.

8. **E** V, W, Z, S can work on Saturday without breaking any of the conditions given. Choice (A) is missing a manager. Choice (B) has two managers working on the same day. Choices (C) and (D) have W and X working on the same day.

9. **D** Five employees, U or V, X or W, Z, S, and T are the greatest number to work on Saturday.

10. **A** Since W and X will not work on the same day, (A) must be true. (B) is false since Y must work on Sunday. (C) could be true. Since W's schedule has no effect on Z and U, (D) and (E) may be true or false.

11. **E** Since no employee can work on consecutive days, and there are four tellers, then two must work on Saturday.

12. **D** U, V, W, X, Y, Z, and T have the possibility of working on Sunday; S and Z do not.

Answers 13–19

From the information given, you could have constructed the following simple diagram and display of information:

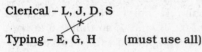

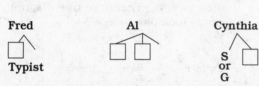

13. **A** From the diagram and information above, if Gene works for Fred, then Lyndia also works for Fred, and Sylvia must work for Cynthia. Since Dennis and Edra will not work together, one of them must work for Cynthia; therefore choice (A) must be false. Jim cannot work for Cynthia.

14. **C** Using the diagram, if Sylvia doesn't work for Cynthia, then Gene must work for Cynthia. If Gene works for Cynthia, then Lyndia must also work for Cynthia, since Gene and Lyndia always work together.

15. **A** If Lyndia and Jim work for Al, then Gene must also work for Al, and Sylvia must work for Cynthia. The diagram would look like this:

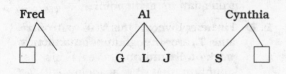

First, (A) is true since Gene and Lyndia always work together. Stop there. Go no further. Edra could work for Cynthia or Fred, and also Helen could work for Cynthia or Fred.

16. **D** If Sylvia and Jim work for Al, then Gene and Lyndia must work for Cynthia. Since Dennis and Edra cannot work together, one of them must work for Fred and the other for Al. The diagram would now look like this:

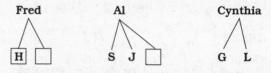

Therefore, only (D) is true.

17. **E** From the diagram, if Lyndia and Sylvia work for Al, then Gene also must work for Al. But either Sylvia or Gene must work for Cynthia. Therefore (E) must be false.

18. **D** From the diagram, if Jim works for Cynthia, then Sylvia must also work for Cynthia, since Gene and Lyndia must work together. Gene and Lyndia cannot work for Fred, because then Dennis and Edra (who cannot work together) would work for Al. Therefore, Lyndia must work for Al. The diagram would look like this:

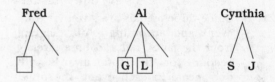

19. **C** If Al needs only two assistants and Fred needs only one, and if Helen works for Fred, then the diagram would look like this:

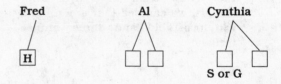

Since Gene and Lyndia must work together, they can work for either Al or Cynthia. Since Edra (typist) must work and Dennis and Edra cannot work together, then Dennis doesn't work. Otherwise, Dennis and Edra would work together. Statements A, B, D, and E *could* be true.

Answers 20–24

Drawing a diagram, below, will help answer the questions.

EVENTS

	1	2	3	4	5
RED	G	—	G	—	G
BLUE	—	B/S	—	B/S	—
GREEN					
YELLOW					

Since the red team wins only 3 gold medals, it must win gold medals in events 1, 3, and 5, since no team wins gold medals in consecutive events. Also, note that since blue wins only two medals (neither of them gold), it must have won medals in events 2 and 4, so that it didn't fail to win a medal within two consecutive events. Be aware then that green and yellow, therefore, must each have won medals in all five events.

20. **C** If the green team wins only one gold medal, there remains only one gold medal, which the yellow team must win.

21. **B** Since three medals are given for each event, and, according to our diagram from the facts, red and blue already account for their total awards with one medal in each event, the other two medals in each event must go to yellow and green. Thus, yellow and green will each be awarded five medals.

22. **D** By completing the chart such that the yellow team wins five silver medals, we can see that green must win two gold and three bronze medals.

	1	2	3	4	5
RED	G	—	G	—	G
BLUE	—	B/S	—	B/S	—
GREEN					
YELLOW	S	S	S	S	S

23. **D** We know choices (A) and (B) are both true: both the green and yellow teams each must win five medals. Therefore (E) is also true. Choice (C) is true because three of the gold medals are already won by the red team; since blue doesn't win gold, if green wins one gold, yellow wins the remaining gold medal. Choice (D) is not true: if the green team wins only one silver medal, the yellow team must win at least two silver medals.

24. **C** If a fifth team enters all events and wins only three consecutive silver medals, it must win the silver in events 2, 3, and 4, so that it does not fail to win a medal within two consecutive events. Therefore our diagram would look like this:

	1	2	3	4	5
RED	G	—	G	—	G
BLUE	—	B	—	B	—
GREEN					
YELLOW					
ORANGE	—	S	S	S	—

Therefore, if yellow wins a gold in the 2nd event, green must win a medal in the 3rd event (since no team fails to win a medal within two consecutive events). Thus, green must win a bronze in the 3rd event.

Section III

1. **C** The passage is more restrained in its criticism than (A) or (B), while (D) and (E) are only elements of the paragraph, not its main point.

2. **B** By urging moviegoers to patronize films *in order to* influence academy judges, the author reveals his assumption that the academy will be influenced by the number of people paying to see a movie.

3. **E** Bob's answer shows that he thinks that people other than teachers are mean. His thought was that Andy meant otherwise.

4. **D** The author's concluding contention is that Roosevelt was not only a good marksman, but also an intellectually curious and patient man. If Roosevelt was known to leave safaris which were not immediately productive, this fact would substantially weaken the author's contention about Roosevelt's "patient observation."

5. **D** The words "because of a recent cut in state funding of our program" indicate that another criterion was used in determining entering class size besides candidates' scores and grades, namely, the financial situation of the college. The words *seriously* in choice (B) and *severe* in choice (E) are not necessarily supported by the passage, and thus make those choices incorrect. Since grade point average is only one of several criteria for admission, we cannot deduce (A) with certainty.

6. **A** This sentence not only fits well stylistically but completes the thought of the passage by tying it into the opening statement.

7. **B** The author of this passage actually defines conscience as the ability to sense right and wrong.

8. **C** The main point of the paragraph is the need for campaign reform. Choice (D) supports the argument, while the other three choices are assumptions that might arise, but these are not the main point of the paragraph.

9. **B** This choice offers the most thorough and comprehensive evidence that the viewing of violent television precedes criminal behavior. (A) is not the best choice because it describes viewing habits that follow rather than precede criminal behavior.

10. **E** The use of "overwhelming" leaves the evidence unspecified, thus opening to challenge the extent and nature of the report's data.

11. **E** All of the first four statements can be used to explain the underreporting. In D, for example, if the size of police departments has declined, they would have less manpower available to gather and report information. E is a reason against underreporting rather than an explanation for it.

12. **C** The argument uses the case of the county to call the state figures into question. The underreported figures are "less evidence."

13. **B** If the experiences and lifestyle of the Aryan race are uniquely different from those of other cultures, it would seriously weaken the author's conclusion that studying the Aryan race will be helpful in understanding the experiences and life styles of other races. That its communal arrangements are *unique* would make comparison between the Aryan race and other cultures impossible.

14. **C** The author presents a *contrast* between life and honor: in particular, the final sentence suggests that life and honor have opposite qualities. Of the choices, the only opposite of *transient* is *eternal*.

15. **E** The logic of this statement goes from the general absolute ("all") to the specific ("this animal"), concluding with specific to specific. Symbolically, if P implies Q, then *not* Q implies *not* P. (E) goes from general absolute ("all") to specific ("this liquid"), concluding with specific to specific. Notice how and where the inverse ("not") is inserted. Using symbols, we have that, if P implies Q, then *not* Q implies *not* P.

16. **B** This is a close one. (B) and (D) both weaken the argument by pointing out that all dogs do not always bark, but (B) is absolute. (D) is tentative, since a dog trained not to bark might do so by accident.

17. **B** The apparent discrepancy in the paragraph is why should arrests decline when there are fewer policemen to arrest the criminals? One explanation is that though the number of arrests has declined, the number of crimes has risen, and because there are fewer police officers, more crimes are unsolved.

18. **A** The complaint about ex-employees of the Department of Energy on the board, and the financial tie of the National Academy Board to the Energy Department indicate the officials' belief that the Department of Energy supports the nuclear power industry against the views of environmentalists.

19. **E** Though adding one or two environmentalists might help, they would still be outnumbered by the ten panel members with ties to the Department of Energy. Of the five choices, E offers the best hope of impartiality.

20. **C** (A) contradicts the statement's urging of economy. (B) introduces an irrelevant word, "terminology." (D) and (E) are *absolute* statements about assumptions, but the statement itself is *relative*, urging us only to simplify our assumptions *if one such simplification is possible; in other words, "If an issue is simple, don't complicate it."*

21. **E** The question demonstrates a solution and the fact that an alternative exists.

22. **E** (A) is obviously true. (B) also satisfies the conditions. (C) is correct, since 3.5 was required with a score of 800. (D) is correct, since we do not know anything about numbers of applicants. (E) is inconsistent, since a score of 1200 is required with a GPA of 2.5. (E) specifies a score *less than* 1200. Therefore, a GPA greater than (*not less than*) 2.5 would be required for admittance.

23. **B** To speak in positive terms about the increase in school degrees, the author must assume that the degrees indicate what they are supposed to indicate, that is, well-educated individuals. (A) and (E) are empty statements; (C) and (D) are altogether unsubstantiated by either expressed or implied information.

24. **E** Although the brand name is No-NOCK, the advertisement makes no claim to stop the engine from knocking. All the other claims are contained in the advertisement.

25. **D** The choice repudiates the suggestion that gentleness and graciousness were once part of the American character. (B), another choice worth considering, is not best because it does not address the temperament of tennis players as directly as does (D).

26. **B** By asking Dolores to choose between conventional and nuclear weapons, Fran has concluded that Dolores's statement calls for a decision. (C), worth considering, is not best because Fran supposes that Dolores has *not* made a choice—hence her question.

Section IV
Answers 1–6

From the information given, you should have constructed a diagram similar to this:

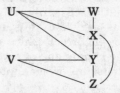

1. **B** From the diagram, if the group begins on island W, it could not reach island V in the eight days. Remember three days would have to be spent on W and three on X.

2. **B** From the diagram, if the group stays on island X for three nights, then the group cannot get to island V on the next visit.

3. **D** To answer this question, you must try each answer choice and eliminate the ones that do not connect. From the diagram, the only possible order listed would be U X Z V.

4. **E** From the diagram, if the group visits island W first, it could go to X to Y to Z, back to X, to U back to Y, to V and back to Z. A total of 9 visits. You could work from the choices, but remember to start from the highest number.

5. **D** From the diagram, the group could go from X to W to U to Y to V to Z to Y. This would be 6 different islands.

6. **E**   Adding island T to the diagram connected only to U could look like this:

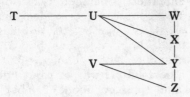

From this revised diagram, only (E) must be true. On the tenth day of a tour starting on Z, the tour group could be on island T. It would go from Z to Y to U to T or Z to X to U to T.

Answers 7–13

From the information given, you could have constructed the following diagram:

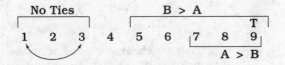

Notice the simple markings to show:

There are no ties in the first 3 games.

Team A wins more of the last 3 games than team B.

Team B wins more of the last 5 games than team A.

The last game is a tie.

Games 1 and 3 are won by the same team.

From this information you could deduce that team A wins either game 7 or 8, but not both, and team B cannot win any of the last 3 games. (If team A won both, team B could not win more of the last 5 games.) If team A wins game 7, then 8 is a tie, and if team A wins game 8, then 7 is a tie.

You could also deduce that team B must win games 5 and 6. Your diagram now looks like this:

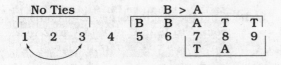

7. **C**   From the information given, since games 1 and 3 are won by the same team, then one team wins at least 2 of the first 3 games.

8. **E**   From the diagram, game 6 must be won by team B.

9. **A**   From the diagram, if game 7 is won by team A, then game 8 must be a tie.

10. **E**   From the diagram, you can see that (E) must be true.

11. **E**   If team A wins games 1 and 4, then it must also win game 3. This would give team A four wins total, and team B could only win three, therefore team B could not win the series. For this question, the diagram would now look like this:

A   A A B B   A   T
1   2 3 4 5 6   7 8   9

12. **B**   If game 4 is won by the winner of game 5, then team B wins game 4. If game 2 is not won by the winner of game 3, then team B wins either game 2 or 3. This gives team B at least four wins and team A only a possible three wins, therefore B is the winner of the series.

13. **E**   From the original diagram, team A must win either games 1, 2, and 3, or games 1, 3, and 4 to win the series. [This also eliminates choice (A).] If team B wins exactly one of the first four games [choice (B)], then team B cannot win the series as team A will win at least three games. If team A wins only three of the first seven games [choice (C)], then team A could still lose the series as team B could win games 2, 4, 5, and 6, with team A winning only games 1, 3, and 7. Team B could win the series by winning two of the first four games, eliminating choice (D).

Answers 14–18

Drawing a simple diagram, below, will help answer the questions.

```
                              TR
                               *
                                       J    FDR
M, A, K, FDR →  __ __ __ M  A       K – FDR or
                                         FDR – K
```

Note that, once Madison is placed in position 3 on the bottom, Adams must go in position 4 in order to leave spots for Kennedy to be adjacent to Franklin Delano Roosevelt.

14. **D** If Theodore Roosevelt is second from the left (on top), then Franklin Delano Roosevelt must be first on the bottom since one Roosevelt may not be above the other. Therefore, Kennedy must be second on the bottom.

15. **A** Adams must go to the far right on the bottom to allow Kennedy to be adjacent to Franklin Delano Roosevelt.

16. **D** If Washington and Kennedy are both first on their shelves, then Franklin Delano Roosevelt must be second on the lower shelf. Therefore, Theodore Roosevelt cannot be second on the top shelf and therefore must be third. Thus, statement D cannot be true.

17. **E** Since Adams must be on the right in the second row, only (E) is not possible.

18. **C** If Lincoln is next to Jefferson, that leaves Theodore Roosevelt and Washington for the first two positions on the top shelf. All of the choices are therefore true except (C) because that choice would place one Roosevelt above the other, which is not permitted.

Answers 19–24

The following display can be drawn from the information given:

```
1   2   3   4   5   6
O   B   R   R   B   R
W   G   Y   Y   G   O
Y   Y           R   V
                Y   W
```

19. **E** The only two color choices for houses 3 and 4 are R and Y. Therefore, houses 3 and 4 must be the two houses painted R and Y. Therefore, no other house is painted R or Y. Thus, choice (A) is incorrect. Choices (B), (C), and (D) are incorrect for the same reason.

20. **A** If orange is not used, the color choices reduce to the following possibilities:

```
1   2   3   4   5   6
W   B   R   R   B   W
    G   Y   Y   G   V
```

There is one way to paint houses 1 and 6. Since house 1 must be W, house 6 must be V. There are two ways to paint houses 2 and 5: BG or GB. There are two ways to paint houses 3 and 4: RY or YR. Therefore, there are $1 \times 2 \times 2$ ways, or 4 ways to paint the houses.

21. **C** Since houses 3 and 4 are the R and Y houses, the possible color combinations reduce to the following:

```
1   2   3   4   5   6
O   B   R   R   B   O
W   G   Y   Y   G   V
                    W
```

Choice (A) is incorrect since, if house 1 is painted W, we still do not know the color of house 6. Choice (B) is incorrect since, if house 6 is painted V, we still do not know the color of house 1. Choice (D) is incorrect since we do not know the colors of houses 1 or 6. Choice (E) is incorrect since we do not know the colors of houses 3 and 4. Choice (C) is correct since all colors are determined. If you know G you know B, if you know R you know Y, and if you know W you know O.

22. **E** Since houses 3 and 4 are the R and Y houses, the possible color combinations reduces to the following (p = primary, s = secondary):

```
1    2    3    4    5    6
Os   Bp   Rp   Rp   Bp   Os
W    Gs   Yp   Yp   Gs   Vs
                         W
```

Choice (A) is incorrect since it is not possible for both the second and sixth house to be Bp. Choice (B) is incorrect since the sixth house cannot be painted a primary color. Choice (C) is incorrect since it is not possible for both the second and fifth house to be Gs. Choice (D) is incorrect since the fourth house must be painted a primary color. Choice (E) is the only possible combination.

23. **D** Since houses 3 and 4 are the R and Y houses, the possible color combinations reduce to the following:

1	2	3	4	5	6
O	B	R	R	B	O
W	G	Y	Y	G	V
					W

If the V house is next to the G house, the possible combinations reduce to the following:

1	2	3	4	5	6
O	B	R	R	G	V
W		Y	Y		

If the B house is next to the Y house, the possible combinations reduce to the following:

1	2	3	4	5	6
O	B	Y	R	G	V
W					

Choices (A) and (B) are incorrect since the first house could be either O or W. Choice (C) is incorrect since the third house is not R. Choice (E) is incorrect since the fifth house is not B. Choice (D) is correct.

24. **C** If the painter of the third house also likes pink, then the possible color combinations are as follows:

1	2	3	4	5	6
O	B	R	R	B	R
W	G	Y	Y	G	O
Y	Y	P		R	V
					Y
					W

Choices (A), (B), (D), and (E) are possible as follows:

1	2	3	4	5	6	
O	B	P	Y	G	R	(A)
O	G	R	Y	B	W	(B)
Y	G	P	R	B	W	(D)
W	Y	P	R	G	V	(E)

Choice (C) is correct, since if the second house is yellow, the fourth house, not the third house, must be red.

Section V

1. **B** The correct answer must use both premises. The first qualifies the assertion with "normally," so (A) will not follow, but (B) (with the qualifier "may") will. (C) may or may not be true, but it is not a logical conclusion based on the two premises. (D) and (E), like (A), do not use both premises.

2. **D** The question asked concerns the danger to public health, but the reply does not deal with this issue at all. It changes the subject.

3. **C** Reducing coffee consumption in general will not guarantee a healthier population (A) if "heavy" consumers do not reduce their coffee intake. Reducing coffee consumption would make those who drink a morning cup of coffee feel less well (B). (C) is a logical conclusion since heavy consumption increases heart attack risk. There is no information in the passage to justify the assertion about percolated coffee (D). If coffee may protect against colon cancer, (E) is not true.

4. **D** The issue of the danger of pesticides is addressed by (A), (C), and (E), while (B) calls into question the objectivity of the Food and Agriculture Department. But (D) deals with a different issue: air pollution. And if air pollution is a cause of illness, pesticides may be less to blame.

5. **A** The question contains its own prior judgment (underpay, unfair promotion policies) on what it asks, regardless of a "yes" or "no" answer. Similarly, the adjective "excessive" and the adverb "unfairly" prejudge any answer in choice (A).

6. **E** Since fares have risen, the cost of fuel has risen or there are no fare wars. And if there are no fare wars, the number of passengers is larger. Only (E) cannot be true. (B) is possible if fuel costs have risen, and there are fare wars.

7. **B** Though the argument for a decline in fishing off Newfoundland is convincing, the generalization that the "fishing industry in the Americas" will disappear is here based only on information about the Atlantic waters off Canada. It is possible that other areas have not been so affected.

8. **C** The advertisement asserts filter cigarettes cannot have great taste. A reasonable inference is that Gold Star is not a filter cigarette. (A) is contradicted by this ad without visual appeal. (B) is contradicted by this ad, which does not specifically praise a brand. (D) is illogical given the existence of this ad. Nothing in the ad supports (E).

9. **D** Choices (A), (B), and (C) strengthen the case for building the toll road. The environmentalists may be able to make their case for one of the other possible routes that, if less direct, would not disturb the reserve. With the information we have, the value of (E) is indeterminable.

10. **A** There is nothing in the paragraph to support (E), and there are details that contradict (B), (C), and (D). That "sales in the United States continue to increase" supports (A).

11. **E** The passage does not give the information that would lead to the conclusion in (A), (B), or (C). (E) is a better answer than (D), the odds against the heavy smoker being 40 in 100 as opposed to 25 in 100 for the light smoker.

12. **C** The presence of wolf bones and walrus bones near a village is not evidence that wolves were trained to haul sleds; it does not disprove the theory, however.

13. **B** Choices (A), (C), (D), and (E) would undermine the theory. But if wolves were easily domesticated and trained, it would make the theory of their domestication by Stone-Age tribes more plausible.

14. **A** The author makes his point by invective, an abrasive verbal attack.

15. **D** The first sentence asserts the needlessness of commenting on the picture; the second nonetheless makes a detailed criticism.

16. **B** If popcorn attracts rodents and insects, warehouses where packages using popcorn are stored would have vermin problems.

17. **B** Only (B) is a necessary assumption. It must be assumed that no other items (for example dressings, recipes, spices, etc.) are sold at the stand in order to conclude definitively that everything sold there is delicious.

18. **B** Though (E) is probably true, it is not a conclusion based on the information in the passage. But the passage does assert that only 19.67 percent (11.9 plus 7.7) of the eligible voters in the Democratic and Republican parties went to the polls.

19. **A** Choices (B) and (C), although true, are not relevant, while (D) and (E) are probably untrue. That it is only in the schools that the tobacco spokesmen are silent supports the inference of (A).

20. **C** In both paragraphs, the author disputes the interpretations of his opponents.

21. **D** The author assumes that an audience is able to evaluate a work and determine its own course of action.

22. **E** The opening lines describe esteem without popularity, later followed by popular success.

23. **D** The "But" introducing the last sentence suggests that a contrast, a disadvantage of coffee, is to follow. Either (C) or (D) is possible, but since exercise has not been an issue, (D) is the better choice.

24. **A** Only choice (A) must be true. There may be other performers as well as the chorus members (the orchestra, for example) in the performance, so (E) is incorrect.

25. **C** The passage draws an analogy comparing corrupt politicians to vermin.

Chapter 7
MODEL TEST TWO

This chapter contains full-length Model Test Two. It is geared to the format of the LSAT, and it is complete with answers and explanations. It is equivalent to the LSAT in question structure, number of questions, level of difficulty, and time allotments. (The questions used are not taken directly from the LSAT, as those questions are copyrighted and may not be reproduced.)

Model Test Two should be taken under strict test conditions. The test ends with a 30-minute Writing Sample, which is not scored.

Section	Description	Number of Questions	Time Allowed
I.	Logical Reasoning	26	35 minutes
II.	Reading Comprehension	28	35 minutes
III.	Analytical Reasoning	24	35 minutes
IV.	Logical Reasoning	26	35 minutes
V.	Reading Comprehension	28	35 minutes
	Writing Sample		30 minutes
TOTALS:		132	3 hours 25 minutes

Now please turn to the next page, remove your answer sheet, and begin Model Test Two.

Answer Sheet—Model Test Two

Section 1	Section 2	Section 3	Section 4	Section 5
1. Ⓐ Ⓑ Ⓒ Ⓓ Ⓔ	1. Ⓐ Ⓑ Ⓒ Ⓓ Ⓔ	1. Ⓐ Ⓑ Ⓒ Ⓓ Ⓔ	1. Ⓐ Ⓑ Ⓒ Ⓓ Ⓔ	1. Ⓐ Ⓑ Ⓒ Ⓓ Ⓔ
2. Ⓐ Ⓑ Ⓒ Ⓓ Ⓔ	2. Ⓐ Ⓑ Ⓒ Ⓓ Ⓔ	2. Ⓐ Ⓑ Ⓒ Ⓓ Ⓔ	2. Ⓐ Ⓑ Ⓒ Ⓓ Ⓔ	2. Ⓐ Ⓑ Ⓒ Ⓓ Ⓔ
3. Ⓐ Ⓑ Ⓒ Ⓓ Ⓔ	3. Ⓐ Ⓑ Ⓒ Ⓓ Ⓔ	3. Ⓐ Ⓑ Ⓒ Ⓓ Ⓔ	3. Ⓐ Ⓑ Ⓒ Ⓓ Ⓔ	3. Ⓐ Ⓑ Ⓒ Ⓓ Ⓔ
4. Ⓐ Ⓑ Ⓒ Ⓓ Ⓔ	4. Ⓐ Ⓑ Ⓒ Ⓓ Ⓔ	4. Ⓐ Ⓑ Ⓒ Ⓓ Ⓔ	4. Ⓐ Ⓑ Ⓒ Ⓓ Ⓔ	4. Ⓐ Ⓑ Ⓒ Ⓓ Ⓔ
5. Ⓐ Ⓑ Ⓒ Ⓓ Ⓔ	5. Ⓐ Ⓑ Ⓒ Ⓓ Ⓔ	5. Ⓐ Ⓑ Ⓒ Ⓓ Ⓔ	5. Ⓐ Ⓑ Ⓒ Ⓓ Ⓔ	5. Ⓐ Ⓑ Ⓒ Ⓓ Ⓔ
6. Ⓐ Ⓑ Ⓒ Ⓓ Ⓔ	6. Ⓐ Ⓑ Ⓒ Ⓓ Ⓔ	6. Ⓐ Ⓑ Ⓒ Ⓓ Ⓔ	6. Ⓐ Ⓑ Ⓒ Ⓓ Ⓔ	6. Ⓐ Ⓑ Ⓒ Ⓓ Ⓔ
7. Ⓐ Ⓑ Ⓒ Ⓓ Ⓔ	7. Ⓐ Ⓑ Ⓒ Ⓓ Ⓔ	7. Ⓐ Ⓑ Ⓒ Ⓓ Ⓔ	7. Ⓐ Ⓑ Ⓒ Ⓓ Ⓔ	7. Ⓐ Ⓑ Ⓒ Ⓓ Ⓔ
8. Ⓐ Ⓑ Ⓒ Ⓓ Ⓔ	8. Ⓐ Ⓑ Ⓒ Ⓓ Ⓔ	8. Ⓐ Ⓑ Ⓒ Ⓓ Ⓔ	8. Ⓐ Ⓑ Ⓒ Ⓓ Ⓔ	8. Ⓐ Ⓑ Ⓒ Ⓓ Ⓔ
9. Ⓐ Ⓑ Ⓒ Ⓓ Ⓔ	9. Ⓐ Ⓑ Ⓒ Ⓓ Ⓔ	9. Ⓐ Ⓑ Ⓒ Ⓓ Ⓔ	9. Ⓐ Ⓑ Ⓒ Ⓓ Ⓔ	9. Ⓐ Ⓑ Ⓒ Ⓓ Ⓔ
10. Ⓐ Ⓑ Ⓒ Ⓓ Ⓔ	10. Ⓐ Ⓑ Ⓒ Ⓓ Ⓔ	10. Ⓐ Ⓑ Ⓒ Ⓓ Ⓔ	10. Ⓐ Ⓑ Ⓒ Ⓓ Ⓔ	10. Ⓐ Ⓑ Ⓒ Ⓓ Ⓔ
11. Ⓐ Ⓑ Ⓒ Ⓓ Ⓔ	11. Ⓐ Ⓑ Ⓒ Ⓓ Ⓔ	11. Ⓐ Ⓑ Ⓒ Ⓓ Ⓔ	11. Ⓐ Ⓑ Ⓒ Ⓓ Ⓔ	11. Ⓐ Ⓑ Ⓒ Ⓓ Ⓔ
12. Ⓐ Ⓑ Ⓒ Ⓓ Ⓔ	12. Ⓐ Ⓑ Ⓒ Ⓓ Ⓔ	12. Ⓐ Ⓑ Ⓒ Ⓓ Ⓔ	12. Ⓐ Ⓑ Ⓒ Ⓓ Ⓔ	12. Ⓐ Ⓑ Ⓒ Ⓓ Ⓔ
13. Ⓐ Ⓑ Ⓒ Ⓓ Ⓔ	13. Ⓐ Ⓑ Ⓒ Ⓓ Ⓔ	13. Ⓐ Ⓑ Ⓒ Ⓓ Ⓔ	13. Ⓐ Ⓑ Ⓒ Ⓓ Ⓔ	13. Ⓐ Ⓑ Ⓒ Ⓓ Ⓔ
14. Ⓐ Ⓑ Ⓒ Ⓓ Ⓔ	14. Ⓐ Ⓑ Ⓒ Ⓓ Ⓔ	14. Ⓐ Ⓑ Ⓒ Ⓓ Ⓔ	14. Ⓐ Ⓑ Ⓒ Ⓓ Ⓔ	14. Ⓐ Ⓑ Ⓒ Ⓓ Ⓔ
15. Ⓐ Ⓑ Ⓒ Ⓓ Ⓔ	15. Ⓐ Ⓑ Ⓒ Ⓓ Ⓔ	15. Ⓐ Ⓑ Ⓒ Ⓓ Ⓔ	15. Ⓐ Ⓑ Ⓒ Ⓓ Ⓔ	15. Ⓐ Ⓑ Ⓒ Ⓓ Ⓔ
16. Ⓐ Ⓑ Ⓒ Ⓓ Ⓔ	16. Ⓐ Ⓑ Ⓒ Ⓓ Ⓔ	16. Ⓐ Ⓑ Ⓒ Ⓓ Ⓔ	16. Ⓐ Ⓑ Ⓒ Ⓓ Ⓔ	16. Ⓐ Ⓑ Ⓒ Ⓓ Ⓔ
17. Ⓐ Ⓑ Ⓒ Ⓓ Ⓔ	17. Ⓐ Ⓑ Ⓒ Ⓓ Ⓔ	17. Ⓐ Ⓑ Ⓒ Ⓓ Ⓔ	17. Ⓐ Ⓑ Ⓒ Ⓓ Ⓔ	17. Ⓐ Ⓑ Ⓒ Ⓓ Ⓔ
18. Ⓐ Ⓑ Ⓒ Ⓓ Ⓔ	18. Ⓐ Ⓑ Ⓒ Ⓓ Ⓔ	18. Ⓐ Ⓑ Ⓒ Ⓓ Ⓔ	18. Ⓐ Ⓑ Ⓒ Ⓓ Ⓔ	18. Ⓐ Ⓑ Ⓒ Ⓓ Ⓔ
19. Ⓐ Ⓑ Ⓒ Ⓓ Ⓔ	19. Ⓐ Ⓑ Ⓒ Ⓓ Ⓔ	19. Ⓐ Ⓑ Ⓒ Ⓓ Ⓔ	19. Ⓐ Ⓑ Ⓒ Ⓓ Ⓔ	19. Ⓐ Ⓑ Ⓒ Ⓓ Ⓔ
20. Ⓐ Ⓑ Ⓒ Ⓓ Ⓔ	20. Ⓐ Ⓑ Ⓒ Ⓓ Ⓔ	20. Ⓐ Ⓑ Ⓒ Ⓓ Ⓔ	20. Ⓐ Ⓑ Ⓒ Ⓓ Ⓔ	20. Ⓐ Ⓑ Ⓒ Ⓓ Ⓔ
21. Ⓐ Ⓑ Ⓒ Ⓓ Ⓔ	21. Ⓐ Ⓑ Ⓒ Ⓓ Ⓔ	21. Ⓐ Ⓑ Ⓒ Ⓓ Ⓔ	21. Ⓐ Ⓑ Ⓒ Ⓓ Ⓔ	21. Ⓐ Ⓑ Ⓒ Ⓓ Ⓔ
22. Ⓐ Ⓑ Ⓒ Ⓓ Ⓔ	22. Ⓐ Ⓑ Ⓒ Ⓓ Ⓔ	22. Ⓐ Ⓑ Ⓒ Ⓓ Ⓔ	22. Ⓐ Ⓑ Ⓒ Ⓓ Ⓔ	22. Ⓐ Ⓑ Ⓒ Ⓓ Ⓔ
23. Ⓐ Ⓑ Ⓒ Ⓓ Ⓔ	23. Ⓐ Ⓑ Ⓒ Ⓓ Ⓔ	23. Ⓐ Ⓑ Ⓒ Ⓓ Ⓔ	23. Ⓐ Ⓑ Ⓒ Ⓓ Ⓔ	23. Ⓐ Ⓑ Ⓒ Ⓓ Ⓔ
24. Ⓐ Ⓑ Ⓒ Ⓓ Ⓔ	24. Ⓐ Ⓑ Ⓒ Ⓓ Ⓔ	24. Ⓐ Ⓑ Ⓒ Ⓓ Ⓔ	24. Ⓐ Ⓑ Ⓒ Ⓓ Ⓔ	24. Ⓐ Ⓑ Ⓒ Ⓓ Ⓔ
25. Ⓐ Ⓑ Ⓒ Ⓓ Ⓔ	25. Ⓐ Ⓑ Ⓒ Ⓓ Ⓔ	25. Ⓐ Ⓑ Ⓒ Ⓓ Ⓔ	25. Ⓐ Ⓑ Ⓒ Ⓓ Ⓔ	25. Ⓐ Ⓑ Ⓒ Ⓓ Ⓔ
26. Ⓐ Ⓑ Ⓒ Ⓓ Ⓔ	26. Ⓐ Ⓑ Ⓒ Ⓓ Ⓔ	26. Ⓐ Ⓑ Ⓒ Ⓓ Ⓔ	26. Ⓐ Ⓑ Ⓒ Ⓓ Ⓔ	26. Ⓐ Ⓑ Ⓒ Ⓓ Ⓔ
27. Ⓐ Ⓑ Ⓒ Ⓓ Ⓔ	27. Ⓐ Ⓑ Ⓒ Ⓓ Ⓔ	27. Ⓐ Ⓑ Ⓒ Ⓓ Ⓔ	27. Ⓐ Ⓑ Ⓒ Ⓓ Ⓔ	27. Ⓐ Ⓑ Ⓒ Ⓓ Ⓔ
28. Ⓐ Ⓑ Ⓒ Ⓓ Ⓔ	28. Ⓐ Ⓑ Ⓒ Ⓓ Ⓔ	28. Ⓐ Ⓑ Ⓒ Ⓓ Ⓔ	28. Ⓐ Ⓑ Ⓒ Ⓓ Ⓔ	28. Ⓐ Ⓑ Ⓒ Ⓓ Ⓔ
29. Ⓐ Ⓑ Ⓒ Ⓓ Ⓔ	29. Ⓐ Ⓑ Ⓒ Ⓓ Ⓔ	29. Ⓐ Ⓑ Ⓒ Ⓓ Ⓔ	29. Ⓐ Ⓑ Ⓒ Ⓓ Ⓔ	29. Ⓐ Ⓑ Ⓒ Ⓓ Ⓔ
30. Ⓐ Ⓑ Ⓒ Ⓓ Ⓔ	30. Ⓐ Ⓑ Ⓒ Ⓓ Ⓔ	30. Ⓐ Ⓑ Ⓒ Ⓓ Ⓔ	30. Ⓐ Ⓑ Ⓒ Ⓓ Ⓔ	30. Ⓐ Ⓑ Ⓒ Ⓓ Ⓔ

To remove, cut along dotted rule.

1   1   1   1   1

SECTION I
TIME — 35 MINUTES
26 QUESTIONS

<u>Directions:</u> In this section you will be given brief statements or passages and will be required to evaluate the reasoning involved. In some instances, more than one choice will appear to be a possible answer. You are to choose the *best* answer. Use common sense and reasonableness in making your selection; then mark the proper space on the answer sheet.

<u>Questions 1–2</u>

Professor: Probability is a curiously unstable concept. Semantically speaking, it is an assumption, a pure artifice, a concept that may or may not be true, but nevertheless facilitates a logical process. It is not a hypothesis because, by its very nature, it cannot be proved. Suppose we flip a coin that has a distinguishable head and tail. In our ignorance of the coming result we say that the coin has one chance in two of falling heads up, or that the probability of a head turning up is one-to-two. Here it must be understood that the one-to-two is not "true" but is merely a species of the genus probability.

1. The professor assumes that

   (A) nothing about our coin influences its fall in favor of either side or that all influences are counterbalanced by equal and opposite influences
   (B) probability can be dealt with without the use of logic
   (C) an assumption must be plausible
   (D) the probability of the coin's landing on an edge is counterbalanced by the probability of its not landing on an edge
   (E) probability can be precisely calculated

2. The last sentence implies that

   (A) probability is not absolute
   (B) one-to-two is merely a guess
   (C) one-to-two is a worthless ratio
   (D) truth is not important
   (E) genus is a category of species

3. Self-confidence is a big factor in success. The person who thinks he can, will master most of the things he attempts. The person who thinks he can't, may not try.

   The author of these statements would agree that

   (A) nothing is impossible
   (B) no task is too large
   (C) success relies on effort
   (D) self-confidence is of most importance
   (E) trying is half the battle

4. People who risk riding on roller coasters are more likely to take risks in other areas of their lives than those who avoid roller coasters. So roller coaster riders are more likely than others to be successful in situations in which taking risks can result in benefit to them.

   If the above comments are true, they most strongly support which of the following statements?

   (A) No roller coaster riders avoid taking risks in other areas of their lives, but some may take more risks than others.
   (B) Risk taking in life decisions is important not only because of the possible financial gain but because of the psychological benefits produced.
   (C) Some people who are not roller coaster riders may take more risks in other areas of their lives than do roller coaster riders.
   (D) Mountain climbing is riskier than riding on roller coasters, so people who climb mountains will be more successful in other areas of their lives than are roller coaster riders.
   (E) Risk taking in one type of activity indicates a likelihood of risk taking in other types of activities.

GO ON TO THE NEXT PAGE ➤

5. *Anthropologist:* For many years, anthropologists believed that the longevity of the men of the island of Zobu was the result of their active lives and their eating only fish from the lagoon and fruits and vegetables grown on the island. However, recent studies of the inhabitants of nearby Luku, where the way of life and diet are virtually identical with Zobu's, have revealed that the men there rarely survive beyond early middle age.

If the information in this paragraph is correct, it best supports which one of the following ?

(A) There are important differences in the lagoons of the two islands of which scientists are unaware.

(B) The inhabitants of Luku and Zobu probably have many ancestors in common.

(C) The longevity of the natives of Zobu is not due simply to their diet and way of life.

(D) Some, though not all, of the residents of Luku live as long as some of the residents of Zobu.

(E) Since longevity depends on so many different factors, it is useless to compare longevity in one area with that in another.

Questions 6–7

Because college-educated men and women as a group earn more than those without college educations, and because in Eastern Europe and Latin America, 105 women are enrolled in colleges for every 100 men, the total earnings of college women in these areas should be equal to, if not greater than, the earnings of college men. But college women in Eastern Europe and in Latin America earn only 65 percent of what college men in these countries earn.

6. Which one of the following, if true, is most useful in explaining this discrepancy?

(A) The earning power of both men and women rises sharply in accord with their level of education.

(B) In some countries of Western Europe, the earning power of college-educated women is higher than that of men in Eastern Europe and Latin America.

(C) In Eastern Europe, more men than women who enter college fail to complete their educations.

(D) The largest percentage of women in Eastern European and Latin American universities study to become teachers; the largest percentage of men study engineering.

(E) In Eastern Europe and Latin America, about 60 percent of the total workforce is college educated.

7. Which of the following is a faulty assumption based on the statistics of the passage?

(A) The passage assumes all of the college women enter the workforce.

(B) The passage assumes conditions in Eastern Europe and in Latin America are the same.

(C) The passage assumes that men and women should be paid equally.

(D) The passage assumes that college-educated women outnumber women who have not attended college in Eastern Europe and Latin America.

(E) The passage assumes that all college-educated workers will be paid more than workers who do not have college educations.

GO ON TO THE NEXT PAGE ➤

8. *Economist:* When consumers are in a buying mood, and the cost of money is low, a shrewd retailer with a popular product will reduce prices of items that are selling slowly and make up for any loss by raising prices on the product or products that are popular.

In which one of the following situations are these recommendations observed?

(A) At Easter, John's Markets offered one dozen eggs at half their usual price, hams and turkeys at a 40 percent discount, but because of heavy rains, raised the price of many green vegetables.

(B) This Christmas Arrow Clothiers is offering six-month interest free charge accounts to any customers who purchase $50 or more of merchandise from their stock of discontinued summer wear and the fashionable new op-art neck wear.

(C) Since interest rates have reached a yearly low, the price of tax-free bonds is near an all-time high. Discount Brokerage has launched a campaign to sell off all of its holding in precious metals mutual funds that are now at a their lowest price in years.

(D) Angus Jewelry is offering special savings for customers who make purchases in May. With graduations coming soon, they are offering engraved gold Swiss watches, as well as lower prices on heart-shaped jewelry items that were featured on Valentine's Day.

(E) Travel agents in Orlando are capitalizing on the lowered air-fares to lure tourists by offering special rates on hotel accommodations and discounted admission tickets to two of the large theme parks in the area.

9. While some cities impose tough, clear restrictions on demolitions of older buildings, our city has no protection for cultural landmarks. Designation as a landmark by the Cultural Heritage Commission can delay a demolition for only one year. This delay can be avoided easily by an owner's demonstrating an economic hardship. Developers who simply ignore designations and tear down buildings receive only small fines. Therefore, _____.

Which one of the following best completes the passage above?

(A) the number of buildings protected by Cultural Heritage Commission designation must be increased

(B) developers must be encouraged to help preserve our older buildings

(C) the designation as landmark must be changed to delay demolition for more than one year

(D) developers who ignore designations to protect buildings must be subject to higher fines

(E) if our older buildings are to be saved, we need clearer and more rigorously enforced laws

10. In ballet schools throughout the country, 95 percent of the students and teachers are female, and 5 percent are male, but professional dance companies need at least 45 percent male dancers.

Which one of the following, if true, would help to explain these statistics?

(A) The social acceptance of dancing as a profession is much higher for females than for males.

(B) Modern choreographers can create dances that can be performed by companies with more female than male dancers.

(C) There are fewer dances than songs in most films and stage musicals.

(D) Men who have classical ballet training develop the same muscles as are used in track events such as the hurdles and the high jump.

(E) Women's bodies are more likely to mature at an earlier age than men's.

GO ON TO THE NEXT PAGE ➤

1   1   1   1   1

<u>Questions 11–12</u>

Sixty percent of the American people, according to the latest polls, now believe that inflation is the nation's most important problem. This problem of inflation is closely related to rising prices. The inflation rate has been 10 percent or more most of this year. Undoubtedly, our gluttonous appetite for high-priced foreign oil has been a major factor. We have been shipping billions of dollars overseas, more than foreigners can spend or invest here. Dollars are selling cheaply and this has forced the value of the dollar down. Government programs now being inaugurated to slow this trend are at best weak, but deserve our support, as they appear to be the best our government can produce. Hopefully, they won't fail as they have in the past.

11. The author of this passage implies that

   (A) inflation cannot be stopped or slowed, because of a weak government
   (B) the fear of inflation is not only unwarranted, but also detrimental
   (C) 40 percent of non-Americans believe inflation is not the most important problem
   (D) foreign oil is the sole reason for the sudden increase in inflation
   (E) the present programs will probably not slow inflation

12. Which one of the following contradicts something in the preceding passage?

   (A) Foreign oil is actually underpriced.
   (B) The inflation rate has not risen for most of this year.
   (C) Overseas investors are few and far between.
   (D) Our government is trying a new approach to end inflation.
   (E) The weakness of the programs stems from lack of support.

13. Sales of new homes in Arizona fell almost 20 percent in the month of February, compared to last year. Analysts attribute the decline to several factors. Record rainfalls kept both builders and buyers indoors for most of the month. The rise in the interest rates have brought mortgage rates to a ten-month high. Both the sales of new homes and housing starts have reached new lows. With every indication that mortgage rates will remain high for the rest of the year, Arizona home-builders foresee a very grim year ahead.

Which one of the following would add support to the conclusion of this passage?

   (A) Last year's sales increased in the second half of the year, despite some increase in interest rates.
   (B) Last year's sales were accelerated by good weather in January and February.
   (C) Widespread advertising and incentives to attract buyers this February were ineffective.
   (D) Rain in Arizona usually ends late in February.
   (E) Home sales and building starts throughout the country are about the same this year as last year.

14. No one reads *Weight-Off* magazine unless he is fat. Everyone reads *Weight-Off* magazine unless he eats chocolate.

Which one of the following is inconsistent with the above?

   (A) No one is fat and only some people eat chocolate.
   (B) Some people are fat and no one eats chocolate.
   (C) Everyone is fat.
   (D) No one is fat and no one reads *Weight-Off.*
   (E) No one who is fat eats chocolate.

GO ON TO THE NEXT PAGE ➤

1   **1**   **1**   **1**   **1**

15. *Jerry:* Every meal my wife cooks is fantastic.
    Dave: I disagree. Most of my wife's meals are fantastic, too.

    Dave's response shows that he understood Jerry to mean that

    (A) Dave's wife does not cook fantastic meals
    (B) only Jerry's wife cooks fantastic meals
    (C) every one of Jerry's wife's meals is fantastic
    (D) not every one of Jerry's wife's meals is fantastic
    (E) no one cooks fantastic meals all the time

Questions 16–17

Commentators and politicians are given to enlisting the rest of America as allies, sprinkling such phrases as "Americans believe" or "Americans will simply not put up with" into their pronouncements on whatever issue currently claims their attentions. They cite polls showing 60 or 80 or 90 percent support for their views. There may (or may not) have been such polls, but even if the polls are real, their finer points will not be reported because they usually contradict the speaker's point. The alleged 80 percent support for a balanced budget amendment, for example, plummets to less than 30 percent if the pollster so much as mentions an entitlement program like social security. People do have opinions, but they are rarely so specific or so unequivocal as your news broadcaster or your senator would lead you to believe.

16. The argument of this passage would be less convincing if it could be shown that

    (A) In a recent poll, 80 percent of the Americans responding supported a balanced budget amendment.
    (B) Most polls used by television commentators are conducted by telephone calls lasting less than 35 seconds.
    (C) Far more Americans are indifferent to or badly informed about current affairs than are well informed.
    (D) The polls' predictions of who will be elected president have been correct about every presidential election since Truman defeated Dewey.
    (E) Many polls are based on samples that do not accurately represent the demographics of an area.

17. The argument of this passage proceeds by using all of the following EXCEPT

    (A) supporting a general point with a specific example
    (B) questioning the honesty of politicians and commentators
    (C) reinterpreting evidence presented as supporting a position being rejected
    (D) pointing out inherent inconsistencies in the claims of the politicians and commentators
    (E) exposing the limitations of arguments based on statistics

GO ON TO THE NEXT PAGE ➤

1   **1**   **1**   **1**   **1**

18. The most often heard complaint about flights on Scorpio Airlines is that there is insufficient room in the cabin of the plane to accommodate all of the passengers' carry-on baggage. The number of passengers who carry on all of their luggage rather than checking it at the ticket counter has increased so much that on more than half of the flights on Scorpio Airlines passengers have difficulty finding space for their bags in the cabin of the plane. The company is considering ways to alleviate this problem.

All of the following are plausible ways of dealing with the problem EXCEPT

(A) reducing the allowable size of carry-on luggage
(B) charging passengers who carry on more than one bag a fee
(C) increasing the fares of flights on lightly traveled routes
(D) reducing the seating capacity of the cabins to provide more space for luggage
(E) offering a price reduction to ticket buyers who check their bags

19. X: "We discover new knowledge by the syllogistic process when we say, for example, 'All men are mortal; Socrates is a man; therefore Socrates is mortal.'"

Y: "Yes, but the fact is that if all men are mortal we cannot tell whether Socrates is a man until we have determined his mortality—in other words, until we find him dead. Of course, it's a great convenience to assume that Socrates is a man because he looks like one, but that's just a deduction. If we examine its formulation—'Objects that resemble men in most respects are men; Socrates resembles men in most respects; therefore Socrates is a man'—it's obvious that if he is a man, he resembles men in *all* necessary respects. So it's obvious we're right back where we started."

X: "Yes, we must know all the characteristics of men, and that Socrates has all of them, before we can be sure."

Which one of the following best expresses X's concluding observation?

(A) In deductive thinking we are simply reminding ourselves of the implications of our generalizations.
(B) It is often too convenient to arrive at conclusions simply by deduction instead of induction.
(C) Socrates' mortality is not the issue; the issue is critical thinking.
(D) Socrates' characteristics do not necessarily define his mortality.
(E) The key to the syllogistic process is using theoretical, rather than practical, issues of logic.

GO ON TO THE NEXT PAGE ➤

20. It takes a good telescope to see the moons of Neptune. I can't see the moons of Neptune with my telescope. Therefore, I do not have a good telescope.

Which one of the following most closely parallels the logic of this statement?

(A) It takes two to tango. You are doing the tango. Therefore, you have a partner.

(B) If you have a surfboard, you can surf. You do not have a surfboard. Therefore, you cannot surf.

(C) You need gin and vermouth to make a martini. You do not have any gin. Therefore, you cannot make a martini.

(D) If you know the area of a circle, you can find its circumference. You cannot figure out the circumference. Therefore, you do not know the area.

(E) You can write a letter to your friend with a pencil. You do not have a pencil. Therefore, you cannot write the letter.

Questions 21–22

Over 90 percent of our waking life depends on habits which for the most part we are unconscious of, from brushing our teeth in the morning, to the time and manner in which we go to sleep at night. Habits are tools which serve the important function of relieving the conscious mind for more important activities. Habits are stored patterns of behavior which are found to serve the needs of the individual that has them and are formed from what once was conscious behavior which over years of repetition can become an automatic behavior pattern of the unconscious mind.

21. It can be inferred that the author bases his beliefs on

(A) the testimony of a controlled group of students

(B) biblical passages referring to the unconscious state

(C) an intense psychological research

(D) extensive psychological research

(E) recent findings of clinical psychologists

22. The last sentence implies that

(A) all repetitious patterns become unconscious behavior

(B) conscious behavior eventually becomes habit

(C) the unconscious mind causes repetitive behavior

(D) automatic behavior patterns of the conscious mind are not possible

(E) habits can be good or bad

GO ON TO THE NEXT PAGE ➤

Questions 23–24

It should be emphasized that only one person in a thousand who is bitten by a disease-carrying mosquito develops symptoms that require hospitalization, according to Dr. Reeves. But it is a potentially serious disease that requires close collaboration by citizens and local government to prevent it from reaching epidemic proportions.

Citizens should fill or drain puddles where mosquitoes breed. They should repair leaking swamp coolers and be sure swimming pools have a good circulating system. Make sure drain gutters aren't clogged and holding rainwater. Keep barrels and other water-storage containers tightly covered. Use good window screens.

23. Which one of the following statements, if true, would most strengthen the advice given in the second paragraph above?

 (A) Leaking swamp coolers are the primary cause of mosquito infestation.
 (B) It is possible to completely eliminate mosquitoes from a neighborhood.
 (C) No one can completely protect herself from being bitten by a mosquito.
 (D) Tightly covered water containers do not ensure the purity of the water in all cases.
 (E) Window screens seldom need to be replaced.

24. What additional information would strengthen the clarity of the second sentence above?

 (A) The names of some local governments that have fought against disease.
 (B) The name of the disease under discussion.
 (C) The names of those bitten by disease-carrying mosquitoes.
 (D) The full name of Dr. Reeves.
 (E) A description of the symptoms that a bitten person might develop.

25. That which is rare is always more valuable than that which is abundant. And so we are continually frustrated in our attempts to teach young people how to use time wisely; they have too much of it to appreciate its value.

Which one of the following statements, if true, would most weaken the argument above?

 (A) Appreciation is not the same as obedience.
 (B) "Abundant" is a term whose definition varies widely.
 (C) Currency that is based on rare metals is more valuable than currency that is not.
 (D) Many young people possess an intuitive knowledge of what time is, a knowledge they lose around middle age.
 (E) The leisure time of people aged 18–24 has decreased by 80 percent over the last 10 years.

26. Many theorists now believe that people cannot learn to write if they are constantly worrying about whether their prose is correct or not. When a would-be writer worries about correctness, his ability for fluency is frozen.

With which one of the following statements would the author of the above passage probably agree?

 (A) Writing theorists are probably wrong.
 (B) Writing prose is different from writing poetry.
 (C) Literacy is a function of relaxation.
 (D) Fear blocks action.
 (E) Most good writers are careless.

STOP

IF YOU FINISH BEFORE TIME IS UP, CHECK YOUR WORK ON THIS SECTION OF THE TEST ONLY.
DO NOT GO ON TO THE NEXT SECTION OF THE TEST UNTIL TIME IS UP FOR THIS SECTION.

2   **2**

Directions: Read the passages and answer the questions following each passage by blackening the appropriate space on the answer sheet. You may refer back to the passages when answering the questions. Answer all questions on the basis of what is stated or implied.

The Sixth Amendment's right to the "assistance of counsel" has been the subject of considerable litigation in
line twentieth-century American courts. The
(5) emphasis has traditionally centered on the degree to which a criminal defendant can demand the assistance of counsel in various courts and at different hierarchical stages of the
(10) criminal proceeding. Although past courts have alluded to the idea that a defendant has a converse right to proceed without counsel, the issue had not been squarely addressed by the
(15) United States Supreme Court until late in its 1974–75 term. At that time, the Court held that within the Sixth Amendment rests an implied right of self-representation.
(20) As early as 1964, Justice Hugo Black wrote that "the Sixth Amendment withholds from federal courts, in all criminal proceedings, the power and authority to deprive an accused of his
(25) life or liberty unless he has or waives the assistance of counsel." However, recognizing that the Sixth Amendment does not require representation by counsel, it is quite another thing to say
(30) that the defendant has a constitutional right to reject professional assistance and proceed on his own. Notwithstanding such a logical and legal fallacy, the Court has, by way of opinion, spoken of
(35) a Sixth Amendment "correlative right" to dispense with a lawyer's help. Many lower federal courts have seized upon this and supported their holdings on it, in whole or in part.
(40) The basic motivation behind this proffered right of self-representation is that "respect for individual autonomy requires that (the defendant) be allowed to go to jail under his own banner if he
(45) so desires" and that he should not be forced to accept counsel in whom he has no confidence. Courts have ruled

that neither due process nor progressive standards of criminal justice require
(50) that the defendant be represented at trial by counsel. The Supreme Court, in its 1975 decision, held that a defendant in a state criminal trial has a constitutional right to waive counsel
(55) and carry on his own case *in propria persona.* In raising this obscure privilege to a constitutional level, the Court stated that, so long as the defendant is made aware of the
(60) dangers and disadvantages of self-representation, his lack of technical legal knowledge will not deprive him of the right to defend himself personally.
The Court conceded that the long line
(65) of right to counsel cases have alluded to the idea that the assistance of counsel is a prerequisite to the realization of a fair trial. However, the Court noted that the presence of counsel is of minor
(70) significance when a stubborn, self-reliant defendant prohibits the lawyer from employing his knowledge and skills. This line of reasoning is concluded with the observation that
(75) "the defendant and not his lawyer or the state, will bear the personal consequences of a conviction." The logical extension of this premise brings the Court to its decision that,
(80) recognizing the traditional American respect for the individual, the defendant "must be free personally to decide whether in his particular case counsel is to his advantage."

GO ON TO THE NEXT PAGE ➤

1. According to the passage, the chief purpose of the Sixth Amendment is to

   (A) assure a defendant the assistance of counsel in capital cases
   (B) assure a defendant the assistance of counsel in civil cases
   (C) assure a defendant the assistance of counsel in criminal cases
   (D) allow a defendant to represent himself in a criminal trial
   (E) allow a defendant to represent himself in a civil trial

2. The "logical and legal fallacy" referred to in line 33 is probably

   (A) the ability to waive a right does not automatically give rise to a replacement of that right
   (B) the right to reject implies a correlative right to refuse to reject
   (C) the right to dispense with a lawyer's help
   (D) the right to legal assistance
   (E) the defendant who chooses to go to jail is free to do so

3. From the passage, the phrase "in propria persona" in lines 55–56 means

   (A) in his own person
   (B) by an appropriate person
   (C) in place of another person
   (D) improperly
   (E) by using a stand-in

4. In allowing a defendant to refuse counsel, the Supreme Court may have reasoned all of the following EXCEPT

   (A) a defendant who objected to a court-appointed attorney would prevent the lawyer from defending him effectively
   (B) the assistance of counsel is necessary to the realization of a fair trial
   (C) in the event of an unfavorable verdict, the defendant will suffer the consequences
   (D) American tradition recognizes the individual's freedom to make decisions that will affect him
   (E) it is possible that a defendant might defend himself more effectively than a court-appointed lawyer

5. A defendant who is acting as counsel in his own defense must be

   (A) given additional legal assistance
   (B) allowed to give up his own defense if he chooses to do so before the trial has concluded
   (C) warned of the disadvantages of self-representation
   (D) assisted by the judge in areas where the defendant's lack of knowledge of technical legal terms is deficient
   (E) tried before a jury

6. All of the following are objections that might be raised to self-representation EXCEPT

   (A) by accepting the right to self-representation, a defendant must waive his right to assistance of counsel
   (B) a defendant determined to convict himself can do so more easily
   (C) if the right to self-representation is not asserted before the trial begins, it is lost
   (D) self-representation has a tradition in American law that dates back to the colonial period
   (E) a self-representation defendant may be unruly or disruptive

African art could have been observed and collected by Europeans no earlier than the second half of the fifteenth
(line) century. Before that time Europe knew
(5) of Africa only through the writing of classical authors such as Pliny and Herodotus and the reports of a few Arabic travelers. Unfortunately, until the latter years of the nineteenth century
(10) Europe was little interested in the arts of Africa except as curiosities and souvenirs of exotic peoples. Indeed, with the growth of the slave trade, colonial exploitation, and Christian missionizing
(15) the arts were presented as evidence of the low state of heathen savagery of the African, justifying both exploitation and missionary zeal. Even with the early growth of the discipline of anthropology
(20) the assumption was that Africa was a continent of savages, low on the scale of evolutionary development, and that these savages, because they were "preliterate," could, by definition, have
(25) no history and no government worth notice.

In recent years the development of critical studies of oral traditions, of accounts by Islamic travelers of the
(30) great Sudanese kingdoms, of the descriptions of the coast by early European travelers, and—above all—of the concept of cultural relativism, has led to a far more realistic assessment of
(35) the African, his culture, history, and arts.

Cultural relativism is, in essence, the attitude whereby cultures other than one's own are viewed in *their* terms and
(40) on *their* merits. As an alternative to the prejudgment of missionaries and colonials it allows us to view the cultures and arts of the African without the necessity of judging his beliefs and
(45) actions against a Judeo-Christian moralistic base, or his art against a Greco-Renaissance yardstick.

Curiously, the "discovery" and enthusiasm for African art early in this
(50) century was not based on an objective, scientific assessment but rather resulted from an excess of romantic rebellion at the end of the last century against the Classical and Naturalist
(55) roots of western art. Unfortunately this uncritical adulation swept aside many

rational concerns to focus upon African sculpture as if it were the product of a romantic, rebellious, *fin de siècle*,
(60) European movement. Obviously, African art is neither anti-classical nor anti-naturalistic: to be either it would have had to have had its roots in Classicism or in Naturalism, both European in
(65) origin. Nor was the concept of rebellion a part of the heritage of art in sub-Saharan Africa; rather, as we shall see, it was an art conservative in impulse and stable in concept.

(70) We may admire these sculptures from a purely twentieth century esthetic, but if we so limit our admiration we will most certainly fail to understand them in the context of their appearance as
(75) documents of African thought and action.

In sharp contrast to the arts of the recent past in the Western world, by far the greatest part, in fact nearly all of the
(80) art of the history of the world, including traditional Africa, was positive in its orientation; that is, it conformed in style and meaning to the expectations— the norms—of its patrons and audience.
(85) Those norms were shared by nearly all members of the society; thus, the arts were conservative and conformist. However, it must be stressed that they were not merely passive reflections, for
(90) they contributed actively to the sense of well-being of the parent culture. Indeed, the perishable nature of wood—the dominant medium for sculpture— ensured that each generation reaffirmed
(95) its faith by re-creating its arts.

7. According to the passage, before the latter part of the nineteenth century, Europeans viewed African art as

(A) simple and direct
(B) odd but beautifully crafted
(C) savage and of little value
(D) ugly and of grotesque proportions
(E) warlike and lacking in beauty

GO ON TO THE NEXT PAGE ➤

8. According to the passage, which one of the following contributed to the initial dismissal of African art by Europeans?

(A) Europeans valued color and sophisticated techniques, both of which were absent in African arts.
(B) It was easier to justify exploitation of Africans if their art was dismissed as heathen.
(C) Europeans were made uncomfortable by the Africans' tendency to depict coarse acts and vulgar positions.
(D) It was important to reject African art because it was dangerous to a stable European society.
(E) It was believed that an influx of African art could seriously disrupt the market for European art.

9. According to the passage, all of the following contributed to a change in the European view of African art EXCEPT

(A) the writings of Pliny
(B) cultural relativism
(C) Islamic travel accounts
(D) descriptions by early European travelers
(E) studies of oral traditions

10. Which one of the following most accurately represents the concept of cultural relativism as defined in the passage?

(A) The words "good" and "bad" are irrelevant when judging between works of art.
(B) One cannot enjoy a work of art without a complete understanding of the culture from which it came.
(C) The best art will always be art that is positive in its orientation.
(D) If an artist goes outside his own tradition in creating a work of art, that work of art will be inferior.
(E) To determine the success of a work of art, it should be judged against the values of its own culture.

11. According to the passage, the early twentieth-century European view of African art was inadequate because it

(A) was based on a limited number of objects available to the Western world
(B) was a result of a romantic rebellion against traditions in Western art
(C) did not take into account the importance of oral traditions
(D) was dependent on classical rather than naturalistic standards
(E) was dictated by the judgments of Christian missionaries

12. Which one of the following best describes the author's point about the relationship between twentieth-century Western art and African art?

(A) African art and twentieth-century Western art both have their roots in a desire to escape tradition and rediscover man's primitive state.
(B) The techniques used in African sculpture are remarkably similar to the techniques used in twentieth-century Western sculpture.
(C) It isn't possible to enjoy African art if we judge it by twentieth-century European aesthetic standards.
(D) Compared to twentieth-century Western art, African art is conservative and conformist, in that it is in keeping with the expectations of its society.
(E) Because it was produced by artists unschooled in technique, African art does not display the sophistication and ingenuity of twentieth-century Western art.

GO ON TO THE NEXT PAGE ➤

2   **2**   **2**   **2**   **2**

13. According to the author, the use of wood in African art is especially significant because

    (A) it is a simpler, more available medium than marble
    (B) unlike the hardness of stone, its relative softness allows intricate carvings representing African beliefs
    (C) it represents a rebellion from the media used in Western sculpture and a return to African roots
    (D) it is unique to primitive cultures uncorrupted by the Western world.
    (E) its impermanence ensures that each generation creates new art reaffirming the beliefs of the culture

14. In this passage, one of the principal methods the author uses to develop his subject is

    (A) discussion and explanation of reactions to African art in the Western world
    (B) examination and analysis of several specific African works of art
    (C) criticism and refutation of Western traditions such as Classicism and Naturalism
    (D) description and explanation of African religious and social beliefs
    (E) discussion and analysis of the aesthetic principles at the foundation of African art

GO ON TO THE NEXT PAGE ➤

In the competitive model—the economy of many sellers each with a small share of the total market—the
line restraint on the private exercise of
(5) economic power was provided by other firms on the same side of the market. It was the eagerness of competitors to sell, not the complaints of buyers, that saved the latter from spoliation. It was
(10) assumed, no doubt accurately, that the nineteenth-century textile manufacturer who overcharged for his product would promptly lose his market to another manufacturer who did not. If all
(15) manufacturers found themselves in a position where they could exploit a strong demand, and mark up their prices accordingly, there would soon be an inflow of new competitors. The
(20) resulting increase in supply would bring prices and profits back to normal.

As with the seller who was tempted to use his economic power against the customer, so with the buyer who was
(25) tempted to use it against his labor or suppliers. The man who paid less than the prevailing wage would lose his labor force to those who paid the worker his full (marginal) contribution to the
(30) earnings of the firm. In all cases the incentive to socially desirable behavior was provided by the competitor. It was to the same side of the market—the restraint of sellers by other sellers and
(35) of buyers by other buyers, in other words to competition—that economists came to look for the self-regulatory mechanisms of the economy.

They also came to look to
(40) competition exclusively and in formal theory still do. The notion that there might be another regulatory mechanism in the economy had been almost completely excluded from economic
(45) thought. Thus, with the widespread disappearance of competition in its classical form and its replacement by the small group of firms if not in overt, at least in conventional or tacit,
(50) collusion, it was easy to suppose that since competition had disappeared, all effective restraint on private power had disappeared. Indeed, this conclusion was all but inevitable if no search was
(55) made for other restraints, and so

complete was the preoccupation with competition that none was made.

In fact, new restraints on private power did appear to replace
(60) competition. They were nurtured by the same process of concentration which impaired or destroyed competition. But they appeared not on the same side of the market but on the opposite side,
(65) not with competitors but with customers or suppliers. It will be convenient to have a name for this counterpart of competition and I shall call it countervailing power.
(70) To begin with a broad and somewhat too dogmatically stated proposition, private economic power is held in check by the countervailing power of those who are subject to it. The first begets
(75) the second. The long trend toward concentration of industrial enterprise in the hands of a relatively few firms has brought into existence not only strong sellers, as economists have supposed,
(80) but also strong buyers, a fact they have failed to see. The two develop together, not in precise step, but in such manner that there can be no doubt that the one is in response to the other.

15. Which one of the following would be the best title for this passage?

(A) Capitalism and the Competitive Model
(B) Competition and the Concept of "Countervailing Power"
(C) Problems in American Capitalism
(D) The Importance of Economic Regulatory Mechanisms
(E) The Failure of the Classic Competition Model

16. In the classic competition model, when competitive manufacturers marked up prices because of strong demand, a return to normal was provided by

(A) new manufacturers entering the market
(B) refusal to buy on the part of customers
(C) governmental intervention in the form of regulation
(D) repositioning of the labor force
(E) failure of weaker manufacturers

2   **2**   **2**   **2**   **2**

17. In the classic competition model, the incentive for manufacturers to behave in a socially desirable way toward workers was provided by

 (A) competition for the labor supply
 (B) competition for the customer
 (C) imbalance between supply and demand
 (D) self-regulation among competitors
 (E) humanistic economic theory

18. According to the author, which one of the following statements is true?

 (A) The classic model of competition was inadequate because it ignored the role of labor and rewarded individual greed.
 (B) The classic model of competition provided self-regulation prior to, but not after, the Industrial Revolution.
 (C) The classic model of competition was undermined by the "restraint of sellers by other sellers and of buyers by other buyers."
 (D) The classic model of competition was replaced by concentration of industrial enterprise and collusion among manufacturers.
 (E) The classic model of competition was destroyed by the growth of "countervailing power."

19. Examples of "countervailing power" in the regulation of the economic power of manufacturers could include all of the following EXCEPT

 (A) organized customer boycotts
 (B) cooperative buying organizations
 (C) large retail chains
 (D) retailers developing their own sources of supply
 (E) organizations that network manufacturers

20. According to the author, a weakness of economic thought has been

 (A) a preoccupation with competition
 (B) a failure to recognize the need for reasonable government regulation
 (C) a belief in the "trickle-down" theory
 (D) a failure to recognize concentration of industrial enterprise
 (E) a bias toward unregulated capitalism

21. Which one of the following best describes the structure of this passage?

 (A) The first three paragraphs describe the strengths of economic competition and the fourth and fifth paragraph describe its weaknesses.
 (B) The first paragraph presents the historical perspective on competition, the second and third present examples of its effect on the economy, and the fourth and fifth paragraphs set forth the idea of "countervailing power."
 (C) The first two paragraphs describe how competition is thought to work, the third paragraph provides a transition, and the fourth and fifth paragraphs describe "countervailing power."
 (D) The first three paragraphs describe the classic model of competition, while the fourth and fifth paragraphs describe "countervailing power."
 (E) The first three paragraphs present a view of competition in opposition to the author's, while the fourth and fifth paragraphs present the author's view.

GO ON TO THE NEXT PAGE ➤

Although genetics is all about inheritance, inheritance is certainly not all about genetics. Nearly all inherited
line characteristics more complicated than a
(5) single change in the DNA involve gene and environment acting together. It is impossible to sort them into convenient compartments. An attribute such as intelligence is often seen as a cake
(10) which can be sliced into so much "gene" and so much "environment." In fact, the two are so closely blended that trying to separate them is more like trying to unbake the cake. Failure to
(15) understand this simple biological fact leads to confusion and worse.

Not far from Herbert Spencer's (and his neighbor Karl Marx's) tomb, in Hampstead—a notably affluent part of
(20) London—is a large red-brick house. It was occupied by Sigmund Freud after he fled Austria to avoid racial policies which descended from the Galtonian ideal. On his desk is a collection of
(25) stone axes and ancient figurines. Freud's interest in these lay in his belief that behavior is controlled by biological history.

Everyone, he thought, recapitulates
(30) during childhood the phases which humans experienced during evolution. Freud saw unhappiness as a sort of living fossil, the emergence of ancient behavior which was inappropriate today.
(35) Like Galton he viewed the human condition as formed by inheritance. The libido and ego are, he wrote, "at bottom heritages, abbreviated recapitulations of the development which all mankind has
(40) passed through from its primeval days." Freud hoped that once he had uncovered the inherited fault which underlies mental illness, he might be able to cure it.
(45) Today's Freudians have moved away from their master's Galtonizing of behavior. They feel that nurture is more important. Analysis looks for childhood events rather than race-memories. In so
(50) doing it is in as much danger as was Freud of trying to unbake the cake of human nature. Any attempt to do so is likely to prove futile.

The Siamese cat shows how futile the
(55) task may be. Siamese have black fur on the tips of the ears, the tail and the feet, but are white or light brown elsewhere. The cats carry the "Himalayan" mutation, which is also found in rabbits
(60) and guinea pigs (but not, unfortunately, in humans). Breeding experiments show that a single gene inherited according to Mendel's laws is involved. At first sight, then, the Siamese cat fur is set in its
(65) nature: if coat color is controlled by just one gene then surely there is no room for nurture to play a part.

However, the Himalayan mutation is odd. The damaged gene cannot produce
(70) pigment at normal body temperature but works perfectly if it is kept cool. This is why the colder parts of the cat's body, its ears, nose, and tail (and, for a male, its testicles) are darker than the rest. An
(75) unusually dark cat can be produced by keeping a typical Siamese in the cold and a light one by bringing it up in a warm room. Inside every Siamese is a black cat struggling to get out. It is
(80) meaningless to ask whether its pattern is due to gene or environment. It is due to both. What the Siamese cat—and every living creature—inherits is an ability to respond to the environment in
(85) which it is placed.

22. The function of paragraph one in the passage is to

(A) define the terms used in the passage
(B) present arguments against a prevailing viewpoint
(C) state the central thesis of the passage
(D) introduce a metaphor used to unite the passage
(E) provide scientific background for the passage

2   **2**   **2**   **2**   **2**

23. The author uses the example of Freud in paragraph two primarily to

   (A) provide a prominent example of the belief that behavior is controlled by biology

   (B) present historical context for the nature vs. nurture argument

   (C) show Freud's limitations as a scientist and indicate the danger of his approach to therapy

   (D) explain how Freud's concepts of ego and libido are related to genetic inheritance

   (E) emphasize the close connection between psychology and genetic research

24. The sentence "Inside every Siamese is a black cat struggling to get out" (lines 78–79) refers to the fact that

   (A) given the recessive nature of the Himalayan mutation, the black color on a Siamese cat will appear only in particular areas

   (B) if the dominant coat-color genes of a Siamese cat can fully suppress the Himalayan-mutated recessive genes, the cat's coat will be light brown

   (C) although genetically intended to be light brown, a Siamese cat will show black areas because of the Himalayan mutation and warm temperatures

   (D) because of the way the Himalayan mutation operates, the coat color of a Siamese will be dark if the cat is kept in the cold

   (E) without the Himalayan mutation combining with cold temperatures, the coat of a Siamese cat will be entirely black

25. Which one of the following summarizes the best example of irony in the passage?

   (A) People who believe nature and nurture are inseparable are basically trying to unbake the cake of human nature.

   (B) Freud fled Austria because of racial policies based on Galtonian theories that Freud himself believed.

   (C) After leaving Austria, Freud came to London, where he was able to live in an expensive neighborhood.

   (D) Studying how a gene works in a Siamese cat can explain how genes work in human beings.

   (E) Modern Freudians have moved far away from Freud's beliefs concerning the causes of people's problems.

26. Which one of the following statements supports the author's thesis in the passage?

   (A) Children of criminals, even when removed from the home environment, will in all likelihood exhibit criminal behavior.

   (B) Given a genetic history of lung cancer, a person who smokes will be in greater danger of contracting the disease than one who doesn't.

   (C) Although it poses some dangers, genetic engineering will lead in the future to a world free from disease and anti-social behavior.

   (D) Social programs for improving living conditions in the inner city are ultimately futile because of the genetic heritage of most people who live there.

   (E) Although intelligence seems to be determined largely by environment, creative talent in fields such as art, music, and literature is clearly genetic.

GO ON TO THE NEXT PAGE ➤

2 **2** **2** **2** **2**

27. All of the following statements are supported by information in the passage EXCEPT

(A) Freud saw the development of child to adult as parallel to the development of primitive man to modern man

(B) although Freud viewed inappropriate behavior as a result of biological history, he did believe therapy might cure it

(C) modern Freudians have shifted their views of behavior from Freud's views and by doing so avoided the danger of oversimplification

(D) in Freud's explanation of human behavior, his definitions of both the libido and the ego depend on his acceptance of Galtonian theory

(E) according to Freud, a person's dysfunctional adult behavior would be an inappropriate manifestation of behavior inherited from ancient man

28. Which one of the following best describes the structure of the passage?

(A) Paragraph one states the author's thesis, paragraphs two and three present ideas opposing the thesis, paragraphs four and five provide a concrete example that supports the thesis.

(B) Paragraph one asks a rhetorical question, paragraphs two and three provide commonly held incorrect answers, paragraphs four and five state the correct answer through use of an example.

(C) Paragraph one states the author's thesis, paragraph two presents an opposing argument, paragraph three is a transition, paragraph four provides an example supporting the thesis, paragraph five restates the thesis.

(D) Paragraph one presents historical background for a commonly held belief, paragraphs two and three develop the belief, paragraph four presents a different view, paragraph five states the author's opinion.

(E) Paragraph one presents one side of a well-known controversy, paragraphs two and three present the other side, paragraphs four and five reconcile the opposing viewpoints.

STOP

IF YOU FINISH BEFORE TIME IS UP, CHECK YOUR WORK ON THIS SECTION OF THE TEST ONLY.
DO NOT GO ON TO THE NEXT SECTION OF THE TEST UNTIL TIME IS UP FOR THIS SECTION.

3 **3** **3** **3** **3**

SECTION III
TIME — 35 MINUTES
24 QUESTIONS

Directions: In this section you will be given groups of questions based on different sets of conditions. Drawing a simple diagram may be helpful in answering some of the questions. You are to choose the best answer and mark the corresponding space on your answer sheet.

Questions 1–6

There are five flagpoles lined up next to each other in a straight row in front of a school. Each flagpole flies one flag (red, white, or blue) and one pennant (green, white, or blue). The following are conditions that affect the placement of flags and pennants on the poles:

On a given flagpole, the pennant, and the flag cannot be the same color.
Two adjacent flagpoles cannot fly the same color flags.
Two adjacent flagpoles cannot fly the same color pennants.
No more than two of any color flag or pennant may fly at one time.

1. If the 2nd and 5th pennants are blue, the 2nd and 5th flags are red, and the 3rd flag is white, then which one of the following must be true?

   (A) Two of the flags are white.
   (B) Two of the pennants are white.
   (C) The 4th pennant is green.
   (D) If the 1st pennant is green, then the 1st flag is blue.
   (E) If the 1st flag is white, then the 1st pennant is green.

2. If the 1st flag is red and the 2nd pennant is blue, then which one of the following is NOT necessarily true?

   (A) The 2nd flag is white.
   (B) If the 5th flag is red, then the 3rd flag is blue.
   (C) If the 4th pennant is green, then the 1st pennant is white.
   (D) If the 1st and 5th flags are the same color, then the 3rd flag is blue.
   (E) If the 4th pennant is green and the 5th pennant is white, then the 1st and 3rd pennants are different colors.

3. If the 1st and 3rd flags are white and the 2nd and 4th pennants are blue, then which one of the following is FALSE?

   (A) The 4th flag is red.
   (B) The 1st pennant is green.
   (C) The 3rd pennant is not red.
   (D) The 5th pennant is green.
   (E) There is one blue flag.

4. If the 1st and 4th flags are blue and the 3rd pennant is white, then which one of the following must be true?

   (A) If the 1st pennant is green, then the 5th pennant is white.
   (B) If the 5th pennant is white, then the 1st pennant is green.
   (C) The 2nd flag is red.
   (D) The 5th flag is red.
   (E) The 1st pennant is green.

5. If the 2nd flag is red and the 3rd flag is white, and the 4th pennant is blue, then which one of the following must be true?

   (A) If the 5th flag is white, then two of the pennants are blue.
   (B) If the 1st flag is white, then the 2nd flag is white.
   (C) If the 1st pennant is blue, then the 5th pennant is green.
   (D) If the 1st pennant is green, then the 5th flag is not blue.
   (E) If the 1st and 5th flags are the same color, then the 1st and 5th pennants are not the same color.

GO ON TO THE NEXT PAGE ➤

3   **3**   **3**   **3**   **3**

6. If the 1st flag and the 2nd pennant are the same color, the 2nd flag and the 3rd pennant are the same color, the 3rd flag and the 4th pennant are the same color, and the 4th flag and the 5th pennant are the same color, then which one of the following must be true?

(A) The 1st pennant is white.
(B) The 2nd flag is not white.
(C) The 5th flag is red.
(D) The 3rd pennant is blue.
(E) The 4th flag is white.

Questions 7–13

In the Norfolk Library returned book section there are ten books standing next to each other on a shelf. There are two math books, two science books, three English books, and three poetry books. The books are arranged as follows:
   There is a math book on one end and an English book on the other end.
   The two math books are never next to each other.
   The two science books are always next to each other.
   The three English books are always next to each other.

7. If the 8th book is a math book, then which one of the following must be true?

(A) The 5th book is a science book.
(B) The 7th book is an English book.
(C) The 6th book is not a poetry book.
(D) The 4th book is next to an English book.
(E) The 9th book is a science book.

8. If the 9th book is an English book and the 5th and 6th books are poetry books, then which one of the following must be true?

(A) There is a math book next to a poetry book.
(B) The 2nd book is a science book.
(C) The 3 poetry books are all next to one another.
(D) The 7th book is a math book.
(E) The 4th book is not a poetry book.

9. If the 1st book is a math book and the 7th book is a science book, then which one of the following could be FALSE?

(A) Both math books are next to poetry books.
(B) All three poetry books are next to each other.
(C) The 2nd book is a poetry book.
(D) The 10th book is an English book.
(E) The 6th book is a science book.

10. If the 4th book is a math book and the 5th book is a science book, then which one of the following must be true?

(A) An English book is next to a science book.
(B) If the 7th book is a poetry book, then the 3rd book is an English book.
(C) If the 8th book is an English book, then the 2nd book is a poetry book.
(D) If the 10th book is a math book, then a poetry book is next to an English book.
(E) The three poetry books are next to each other.

11. If no two poetry books are next to each other, then which one of the following must be true?

(A) A science book is next to a math book.
(B) The 7th book is a poetry book.
(C) The 8th book is an English book.
(D) An English book is next to a science book.
(E) A poetry book is next to an English book.

12. If a science book is next to an English book, but not next to a poetry book, then which one of the following must be true?

(A) The 7th book is a poetry book.
(B) The 3rd book is an English book or a math book.
(C) The 5th or the 6th book is a math book.
(D) The 3 poetry books are not next to each other.
(E) The 7th or the 10th book is a math book.

GO ON TO THE NEXT PAGE ➤

3   **3**   **3**   **3**   **3**

13. If the 7th and 8th books are poetry books, how many different arrangements are there for the 10 books?

   (A) 1
   (B) 2
   (C) 3
   (D) 4
   (E) 5

Questions 14–19

Freshman at State College must enroll in at least 3 classes chosen from Greek, Latin, Sex Lab, Marriage/Family Relations, American History, and Roman History. In addition to enrolling in at least one language (Greek or Latin), freshman class choices are governed by the following rules:
   Enrollment in the Sex Lab requires concurrent enrollment in Marriage/Family Relations.
   Enrollment in Marriage/Family Relations does not require concurrent enrollment in the Sex Lab.
   Freshmen may not enroll in American History and Latin at the same time.
   Anyone enrolled in Roman History must also be enrolled in Greek.

14. What is the maximum number of courses that a freshman can take?

   (A) 3
   (B) 4
   (C) 5
   (D) 6
   (E) 7

15. If a freshman wishes to enroll in American History and the Sex Lab, then which one of the following is true?

   (A) She must enroll in at least four classes.
   (B) She cannot enroll in Marriage/Family Relations.
   (C) She may enroll in Latin.
   (D) She cannot enroll in Roman History.
   (E) She must enroll in Roman History.

16. If a freshman does not enroll in Greek, what is the maximum number of classes he can take?

   (A) 1
   (B) 2
   (C) 3
   (D) 4
   (E) 5

17. If a freshman enrolls in Latin, which one of the following classes must be taken in addition to Latin?

   (A) Marriage/Family Relations or Sex Lab
   (B) Greek or American History
   (C) Roman History or Greek
   (D) Roman History or Sex Lab
   (E) Greek or Marriage/Family Relations

18. If a freshman does not wish to take American History or Greek, what is the maximum number of classes he can take?

   (A) 1
   (B) 3
   (C) 4
   (D) 5
   (E) 6

19. If a freshman enrolls in Latin, which one of the following must be true?

   (A) He enrolls in only three classes.
   (B) He enrolls in Sex Lab.
   (C) He may choose from four classes.
   (D) He enrolls in Marriage/Family Relations.
   (E) He cannot enroll in Marriage/Family Relations.

GO ON TO THE NEXT PAGE ➤

3   **3**   **3**   **3**   **3**

Questions 20–24

Seven track and field coaches, A, B, C, D, E, F, and G, are each assigned to coach exactly one of four activities—sprints, distance, jumpers, and throwers. Coaching assignments are made subject to the following conditions:
- Each sport is coached by one or two of the seven coaches.
- B coaches jumpers.
- Neither E nor F is a distance coach.
- If C coaches sprints, F and G coach throwers.
- If D coaches distance or throwers, A and G do not coach either distance or throwers.

20. If C and E coach sprints, which one of the following must be true?

   (A) Distance has two coaches.
   (B) G coaches jumping.
   (C) A coaches jumping or throwing.
   (D) D coaches jumping.
   (E) Jumping has one coach.

21. If G coaches jumping and A coaches distance, which one of the following must be true?

   (A) D coaches sprints.
   (B) F coaches throwing.
   (C) E coaches sprints.
   (D) C coaches distance.
   (E) F coaches sprints.

22. If D coaches throwing, which one of the following CANNOT be true?

   (A) G coaches sprints.
   (B) A coaches jumping.
   (C) E coaches sprints.
   (D) F coaches throwing.
   (E) C coaches jumping.

23. If G is the only throwing coach, which one of the following could be true?

   (A) D coaches distance.
   (B) If F coaches sprints, D coaches sprints.
   (C) A coaches jumping.
   (D) If F coaches jumping, D coaches jumping.
   (E) C and D coach the same sport.

24. If A does not coach sprints and D coaches distance, which one of the following CANNOT be true?

   (A) C coaches distance.
   (B) E coaches throwing.
   (C) G coaches jumping.
   (D) F coaches sprints.
   (E) E coaches sprints.

STOP

IF YOU FINISH BEFORE TIME IS UP, CHECK YOUR WORK ON THIS SECTION OF THE TEST ONLY.
DO NOT GO ON TO THE NEXT SECTION OF THE TEST UNTIL TIME IS UP FOR THIS SECTION.

4   4   4   4   4

SECTION IV
TIME — 35 MINUTES
26 QUESTIONS

<u>Directions:</u> In this section you will be given brief statements or passages and will be required to evaluate the reasoning involved. In some instances, more than one choice will appear to be a possible answer. You are to choose the *best* answer. Use common sense and reasonableness in making your selection; then mark the proper space on the answer sheet.

<u>Questions 1–2</u>

The spate of bills in the legislature dealing with utility regulation shows that our lawmakers recognize a good political issue when they see one. Among the least worthy is a proposal to establish a new "Consumers Utility Board" to fight proposed increases in gas and electric rates.

    It is hardly a novel idea that consumers need representation when rates are set for utilities which operate as monopolies in their communities. That's exactly why we have a state Public Utilities Commission.

    Supporters of the proposed consumer board point out that utility companies have the benefit of lawyers and accountants on their payrolls to argue the case for rate increases before the PUC. That's true. Well, the PUC has the benefit of a $40 million annual budget and a staff of 900—all paid at taxpayer expense—to find fault with these rate proposals if there is fault to be found.

1. Which one of the following is the best example to offer in support of this argument against a Consumers Utility Board?

    (A) the percentage of taxpayer dollars supporting the PUC
    (B) the number of lawyers working for the Consumers Utility Board
    (C) the number of concerned consumers
    (D) a PUC readjustment of rates downward
    (E) the voting record of lawmakers supporting the board

2. Which one of the following would most seriously weaken the above argument?

    (A) Private firms are taking an increasing share of the energy business.
    (B) Water rates are also increasing.
    (C) The PUC budget will be cut slightly, along with other state agencies.
    (D) Half of the PUC lawyers and accountants are also retained by utilities.
    (E) More tax money goes to education than to the PUC.

3. Most of those who enjoy music play a musical instrument; therefore, if Maria enjoys music, she probably plays a musical instrument.

Which one of the following most closely parallels the reasoning in the statement above?

    (A) The majority of those who voted for Smith in the last election oppose abortion; therefore, if the residents of University City all voted for Smith, they probably oppose abortion.
    (B) If you appreciate portrait painting you are probably a painter yourself; therefore, your own experience is probably the cause of your appreciation.
    (C) Most of those who join the army are male; therefore, if Jones did not join the army, Jones is probably female.
    (D) Over 50 percent of the high school students polled admitted hating homework; therefore, a majority of high school students do not like homework.
    (E) If most workers drive to work, and Sam drives to work, then Sam must be a worker.

GO ON TO THE NEXT PAGE ➤

4. *Mayor:* There must be no official or unofficial meeting of two or more members of the City Council that is not open to the public or a matter of public record. Though certain subjects can only be discussed in private, the danger of elected officials pursuing a private agenda, rather than what most benefits the public, is a serious concern in an age when politicians are too often willing to promote their private interests behind closed doors.

On which one of the following grounds is this argument especially subject to criticism?

(A) It treats popular opinion as if it were conclusive evidence.
(B) It misleadingly generalizes from the actions of a few to the actions of an entire group.
(C) It concedes the point that effectively undermines its argument.
(D) It uses an ambiguous term without making clear which meaning of the term applies here.
(E) It reaches a conclusion based on limited evidence chosen only because that evidence supports the argument.

5. "Good personnel relations of an organization depend upon mutual confidence, trust, and goodwill. The basis of confidence is understanding. Most troubles start with people who do not understand each other. When the organization's intentions or motives are misunderstood, or when reasons for actions, practices, or policies are misconstrued, complete cooperation from individuals is not forthcoming. If management expects full cooperation from employees, it has a responsibility of sharing with them the information which is the foundation of proper understanding, confidence, and trust. Personnel management has long since outgrown the days when it was the vogue to 'treat them rough and tell them nothing.' Up-to-date personnel management provides all possible information about the activities, aims, and purposes of the organization. It seems altogether creditable that a desire should exist among employees for such information which the best-intentioned executive might think would not interest them and which the worst-intentioned would think was none of their business."

The above paragraph implies that one of the causes of the difficulty that an organization might have with its personnel relations is that its employees

(A) have not expressed interest in the activities, aims, and purposes of the organization
(B) do not believe in the good faith of the organization
(C) have not been able to give full cooperation to the organization
(D) do not recommend improvements in the practices and policies of the organization
(E) can afford little time to establish good relations with their organization

4   4   4   4   4

6. Of all psychiatric disorders, depression is the most common; yet, research on its causes and cures is still far from complete. As a matter of fact, very few facilities offer assistance to those suffering from this disorder.

The author would probably agree that

(A) depression needs further study
(B) further research will make possible further assistance to those suffering from depression
(C) most facilities are staffed by psychiatrists whose specialty is not depression
(D) those suffering from depression need to know its causes and cures
(E) depression and ignorance go hand in hand

7. *Editorial:* The politicians who wish to see the schools run like businesses will have some trouble establishing a standard of accountability. In the business world, profits provide a clear standard, measurable in numbers. But in public education, standards are culturally derived, and differ very widely among age, ethnic, and political groups. We can evaluate a school's record keeping or its facilities, but there is no way to use the standards of quality control that are used to judge the profitability of a business and apply them to the academic performance of students throughout a public school system.

To which one of the following is the writer of this passage objecting?

(A) the assumption that a school and a business are analogous
(B) the belief that profitability is a universal standard
(C) the assumption that schools, like businesses, can show a financial profit
(D) the belief that school vouchers are undemocratic
(E) the assumption that record keeping and facilities are adequate gauges of business success

8. *Ivan:* What the Church says is true because the Church is an authority.
Mike: What grounds do you have for holding that the Church is a genuine authority?
Ivan: The authority of the Church is implied in the Bible.
Mike: And why do you hold that the Bible is true?
Ivan: Because the Church holds that it is true.

Which one of the following is the best description of the reasoning involved in the argument presented in the foregoing dialogue?

(A) deductive
(B) inductive
(C) vague
(D) pointed
(E) circular

9. *Mary:* All Italians are great lovers.
Kathy: That is not so. I have met some Spaniards who were magnificent lovers.

Kathy's reply to Mary indicates that she has misunderstood Mary's remark to mean that

(A) every great lover is an Italian
(B) Italians are best at the art of love
(C) Spaniards are inferior to Italians
(D) Italians are more likely to be great lovers than are Spaniards
(E) there is a relationship between nationality and love

GO ON TO THE NEXT PAGE ➤

4   **4**   **4**   **4**   **4**

<u>Questions 10–11</u>

Mr. Dimple: Mrs. Wilson's qualifications are ideal for the position. She is intelligent, forceful, determined, and trustworthy. I suggest we hire her immediately.

10. Which one of the following, if true, would most weaken Mr. Dimple's statement?

   (A) Mrs. Wilson is not interested in being hired.
   (B) There are two other applicants whose qualifications are identical to Mrs. Wilson's.
   (C) Mrs. Wilson is currently working for a rival company.
   (D) Mr. Dimple is not speaking directly to the hiring committee.
   (E) Mrs. Wilson is older than many of the other applicants.

11. Which one of the following, if true, offers the strongest support of Mr. Dimple's statement?

   (A) All the members of the hiring committee have agreed that intelligence, trustworthiness, determination, and forcefulness are important qualifications for the job.
   (B) Mr. Dimple holds exclusive responsibility for hiring new employees.
   (C) Mr. Dimple has known Mrs. Wilson longer than he has known any of the other applicants.
   (D) Mrs. Wilson is a member of Mr. Dimple's family.
   (E) Mrs. Dimple is intelligent, forceful, determined, and trustworthy.

12. All of the candidates for the spring track team must have participated in fall cross-country and winter track. Some runners, however, find cross-country tedious, and refuse to run in the fall. Thus, some winter track runners who would like to be members of the spring track teams are not permitted to try out.

In which one of the following is the reasoning most like that of this passage?

   (A) Mice become aggressive if confined in close quarters for an extended period of time, or if they are deprived of protein-rich foods. Therefore, highly aggressive mice have been closely confined and denied high-protein foods.
   (B) Roses grown in full sun are less susceptible to mildew than roses grown in partial shade. Roses grown in partial shade are also more susceptible to black spot. Thus, roses should be grown in full sun.
   (C) To qualify for the June primary, a candidate for office must reside in the district for six months and gather 500 signatures of district residents who support the candidate. Thus, a longtime district resident would not qualify for the June primary if she gathered only 300 signatures.
   (D) A convenience store sells three chocolate bars for a dollar, and a large soft drink for 50 cents. A competitor sells four chocolate bars for a dollar, and a medium-size soft drink for 50 cents. Therefore, neither of the two stores offers more for the same price.
   (E) The City Council has passed an ordinance that allows cyclists to use the city bike paths only if they are over 12 years old and are wearing bicycle helmets. Thus, parents with children under 12 will be unable to cycle with their families on the city bike paths unless they wear helmets.

GO ON TO THE NEXT PAGE ➤

4　　**4**　　**4**　　**4**　　**4**

13. When a dental hygienist cleans your teeth, you may not see much evidence that she is supervised by a dentist. Hygienists often work pretty much on their own, even though they are employed by dentists. Then why can't hygienists practice independently, perhaps saving patients a lot of money in the process? The patients would not have to pay the steep profit that many dentists make on the hygienists' labors.

Which one of the following statements weakens the argument above?

(A) Some patients might get their teeth cleaned more often if it costs less.
(B) Some dentists do not employ dental hygienists.
(C) Hygienists must be certified by state examinations.
(D) A dentist should be on hand to inspect a hygienist's work to make sure the patient has no problems that the hygienist is unable to detect.
(E) In some states, there are more female hygienists than male.

14. There are those of us who, determined to be happy, are discouraged repeatedly by social and economic forces that cause us nothing but trouble. And there are those of us who are blessed with health and wealth and still grumble and complain about almost everything.

To which one of the following points can the author be leading?

(A) Happiness is both a state of mind and a state of affairs.
(B) Both personal and public conditions can make happiness difficult to attain.
(C) Happiness may be influenced by economic forces and by health considerations.
(D) No one can be truly happy.
(E) Exterior forces and personal views determine happiness.

15. "Keep true, never be ashamed of doing right; decide on what you think is right and stick to it."—*George Eliot*

If one were to follow Eliot's advice, one

(A) would never change one's mind
(B) would do what is right
(C) might never know what is right
(D) would never be tempted to do wrong
(E) would not discriminate between right and wrong

16. To paraphrase Oliver Wendell Holmes, taxes keep us civilized. Just look around you, at well-paved superhighways, air-conditioned schools, and modernized prisons, and you cannot help but agree with Holmes.

Which one of the following is the strongest criticism of the statement above?

(A) The author never actually met Holmes.
(B) The author does not acknowledge those of us who do not live near highways, schools, and prisons.
(C) The author does not assure us that he has been in a modernized prison.
(D) The author does not offer a biographical sketch of Holmes.
(E) The author does not define "civilized."

4   4   4   4   4

Questions 17–18

Information that is published is part of the public record. But information that a reporter collects, and sources that he contacts, must be protected in order for our free press to function free of fear.

17. The above argument is most severely weakened by which one of the following statements?

    (A) Public information is usually reliable.
    (B) Undocumented evidence may be used to convict an innocent person.
    (C) Members of the press act ethically in most cases.
    (D) The sources that a reporter contacts are usually willing to divulge their identity.
    (E) Our press has never been altogether free.

18. Which one of the following statements is consistent with the argument above?

    (A) Privileged information has long been an important and necessary aspect of investigative reporting.
    (B) Not all the information a reporter collects becomes part of the public record.
    (C) Tape-recorded information is not always reliable.
    (D) The victim of a crime must be protected at all costs.
    (E) The perpetrator of a crime must be protected at all costs.

Questions 19–21

A federal court ruling that San Diego County can't sue the government for the cost of medical care of illegal aliens is based upon a legal technicality that ducks the larger moral question. But the U.S. Supreme Court's refusal to review this decision has closed the last avenue of legal appeal.

The medical expenses of indigent citizens or legally resident aliens are covered by state and federal assistance programs. The question of who is to pay when an undocumented alien falls ill remains unresolved, however, leaving California counties to bear this unfair and growing burden.

19. The author implies that

    (A) the U.S. Supreme Court has refused to review the federal court ruling
    (B) the burden of medical expenses for aliens is growing
    (C) the larger moral question involves no legal technicalities
    (D) San Diego should find another avenue of appeal
    (E) the federal government is dodging the moral issue

20. Which one of the following arguments, if true, would most seriously weaken the argument above?

    (A) There are many cases of undocumented aliens being denied medical aid at state hospitals.
    (B) A private philanthropic organization has funded medical aid programs that have so far provided adequate assistance to illegal aliens nationwide.
    (C) Illegal aliens do not wish federal or state aid, because those accepting aid risk detection of their illegal status and deportation.
    (D) Undocumented aliens stay in California only a short time before moving east.
    (E) Judges on the Supreme Court have pledged privately to assist illegal aliens with a favorable ruling once immigration laws are strengthened.

GO ON TO THE NEXT PAGE ➤

4   4   4   4   4

21. Which one of the following changes in the above passage could strengthen the author's argument?

    (A) adding interviews with illegal aliens
    (B) a description of the stages that led to a rejection by the Supreme Court
    (C) a clarification with numbers of the rate at which the burden of medical expenses is growing
    (D) the naming of those state and federal assistance programs that aid indigent citizens
    (E) the naming of those California counties that do not participate in medical aid to illegal aliens

---

22. *Historian:* History is strewn with the wreckage of experiments in communal living, often organized around farms and inspired by religious or philosophical ideals. To the more noble failures can now be added Mao Tse-tung's notorious Chinese communes. The current rulers of China, still undoing the mistakes of the late Chairman, are quietly allowing their agricultural communes to _____.

    Which one of the following is the most logical completion of the passage above?

    (A) evolve
    (B) increase
    (C) recycle
    (D) disintegrate
    (E) organize

23. *Sal:* Herb is my financial planner.
    Keith: I'm sure he's good; he's my cousin.

    Which one of the following facts is Keith ignoring in his response?

    (A) Financial planning is a professional, not a personal, matter.
    (B) Sal is probably flattering Keith.
    (C) Professional competence is not necessarily a family trait.
    (D) "Good" is a term with many meanings.
    (E) Sal's financial planner is no one's cousin.

24. Many very effective prescription drugs are available to patients on a "one time only" basis. Suspicious of drug abuse, physicians will not renew a prescription for a medicine that has worked effectively for a patient. This practice denies a patient her right to health.

    Which one of the following is a basic assumption made by the author?

    (A) A new type of medicine is likely to be more expensive.
    (B) Physicians are not concerned with a patient's health.
    (C) Most of the patients who need prescription renewals are female.
    (D) Most physicians prescribe inadequate amounts of medicine.
    (E) Patients are liable to suffer the same ailment repeatedly.

Questions 25–26

Forty years ago, hardly anybody thought about going to court to sue somebody. A person could bump a pedestrian with his Chrysler Airflow and the victim would say something like, "No harm done," and walk away. Ipso facto. No filing of codicils, taking of depositions or polling the jury. Attorneys need not apply.

25. Which one of the following sentences most logically continues the above passage?

    (A) The Chrysler Airflow is no longer the harmless machine it used to be.
    (B) Fortunately, this is still the case.
    (C) Unfortunately, times have changed.
    (D) New legislation affecting the necessity for codicils is a sign of the times.
    (E) But now, as we know, law schools are full of eager young people.

GO ON TO THE NEXT PAGE ➤

4   **4**   **4**   **4**   **4**

26. Which one of the following details, if true, would most strengthen the above statement?

   (A) There were fewer courthouses then than now.

   (B) The marked increase in pedestrian accidents is a relatively recent occurrence.

   (C) Most citizens of 40 years ago were not familiar with their legal rights.

   (D) The number of lawsuits filed during World War II was extremely low.

   (E) Most young attorneys were in the armed forces 40 years ago.

STOP

IF YOU FINISH BEFORE TIME IS UP, CHECK YOUR WORK ON THIS SECTION OF THE TEST ONLY.
DO NOT GO ON TO THE NEXT SECTION OF THE TEST UNTIL TIME IS UP FOR THIS SECTION.

5 **5** **5** **5** **5**

SECTION V
TIME — 35 MINUTES
28 QUESTIONS

Directions: Read the passages and answer the questions following each passage by blackening the appropriate space on the answer sheet. You may refer back to the passages when answering the questions. Answer all questions on the basis of what is stated or implied.

In the negotiation of tax treaties, developing nations, as a group, share two objectives somewhat at odds with those of developed-nation treaty
(5) partners. One such goal, attracting foreign investment, is in the broader context of foreign policy objectives. In the narrower realm of tax policy a common developing-country objective is
(10) to maximize the public capture of revenues from foreign investment activities.

Unfortunately for potential Third World treaty partners, this latter goal
(15) can conflict directly with the desires of both First World governments and individual investors. The preference of First World authorities for restricted source-based taxation is due to
(20) considerations of administrative feasibility. Such restrictions, though formally reciprocal, only produce equitable revenue effects when investment flows between treaty
(25) partners are relatively equal. However, when investment flows primarily in one direction, as it generally does from industrial to developing countries, the seemingly reciprocal source-based
(30) restrictions produce revenue sacrifices primarily by the state receiving most of the foreign investment and producing most of the income—namely, the developing country partner. The benefit
(35) is captured either by the taxpayer in the form of reduced excess credits, or by the treasury of the residence (First World) state as the taxpayer's domestically creditable foreign tax
(40) liabilities decrease. The potential public revenue gain to the residence state further bolsters the industrial nations' preference for restrictions on source-based taxation—at the direct expense of
(45) the treaty partner's revenue goals.

The facilitation of foreign investment by tax treaties, whereas potentially serving the tax-policy goal of maximizing public revenue, also (or
(50) even instead) may serve broader economic objectives of developing countries. Foreign investments may be seen as essential sources of technical and managerial knowledge, capital, jobs,
(55) and foreign exchange. As such, the significance of foreign investments as an immediate source of public revenue could pale next to their longer-term "ripple effect" on development. In the
(60) negotiation of tax treaties, then, a developing country might be expected to ignore revenue goals and accept substantial limitations on source-based taxation, at least insofar as such
(65) limitations could be expected to encourage investment.

Frequently, however, Third World nations take a considerably more aggressive approach, seeking treaty
(70) terms that, in effect, provide subsidies to private investors at the expense of First World treaty partners. The United States traditionally has followed a strict policy of "capital export neutrality,"
(75) providing no tax incentives for investment in the Third World through either the Internal Revenue Code or tax treaty provisions.

1. Normally, a developing country will negotiate a tax treaty for the purpose of

(A) attracting foreign workers
(B) decreasing tax revenues
(C) attracting international investment and reducing tax revenues
(D) attracting foreign investment and increasing tax revenues
(E) decreasing dependence on special interest local investors

GO ON TO THE NEXT PAGE ➤

2. We can infer that a reciprocal source-based taxation treaty between a First World and a developing nation will produce

   (A) greater revenues for the First World nation
   (B) greater revenues for the developing nation
   (C) equal revenues for each country
   (D) no revenues for either country
   (E) losses to the economy of the First World nation

3. In negotiated treaties with developing countries, a First World country is likely to prefer

   (A) unrestricted source-based taxation
   (B) reciprocal restricted source-based taxation
   (C) nonreciprocal source-based taxation
   (D) equal investment flow between the partners
   (E) limited investment flow between the partners

4. In a treaty with a developing country that generates an excess of foreign tax credits, all of the following are likely EXCEPT

   (A) the treaty will require some reduction of at-source taxation
   (B) the treaty will discourage private investors
   (C) the treaty will not produce what is perceived as the optimal revenue-producing balance
   (D) the treaty will require some expansion of at-source taxation
   (E) the excess of tax credits will be larger if the source country reserves more taxing jurisdiction

5. According to the passage, all of the following are potential advantages of foreign investment to developing countries EXCEPT

   (A) increased managerial expertise
   (B) increased capital
   (C) increased availability of new materials
   (D) increased foreign exchange
   (E) increased employment

6. A developing country that did not insist upon immediate higher public revenues might be expected to

   (A) deter foreign investment
   (B) increase foreign investment
   (C) avoid the "ripple effect"
   (D) decrease employment
   (E) decrease the availability of raw materials

GO ON TO THE NEXT PAGE ➤

5   ⬥**5**⬥   ⬥**5**⬥   ⬥**5**⬥   **5**

How buildings are depicted indicates how they are perceived. To the serious travelers of the eighteenth century, like
line James Stuart and Nicholas Revett who
(5) took it upon themselves to record the legendary remains of Greece for the first time since antiquity, there are two modes of perception: the topical and the archaeological. To introduce each
(10) monument, they resorted to the picturesque tableau. They show the Parthenon at the time of their visit in 1751, when Athens was a sleepy provincial town within the Ottoman
(15) Empire and the Akropolis served as the headquarters for the Turkish governor. The temple stands in a random cluster of modest houses; in it we can see a Turk on horseback and, through the
(20) colonnade, the vaulted forms of the small Byzantine church that rose within the body of the temple during the Middle Ages. This is what the Parthenon looks like today, the authors are saying; and
(25) this depiction carries at once the quaint appeal of an exotic land and that sense of the vanity of things which comes over us at the sight of the sad dilapidation of one-time splendors.
(30)   But when they turn from romance to archaeology, the task of showing the Parthenon not as it is now but as it was then, Stuart and Revett restrict themselves to the measured drawing.
(35) They re-create, in immaculate engravings of sharp clear lines, the original design of the temple in suitably reduced scale and with a careful tally of dimensions. We are confronted again
(40) with the traditional abstractions of the architect's trade. Indeed, those architects who, in subsequent decades, wished to imitate the Parthenon as a venerable form of rich associational
(45) value could do so readily from these precise plates of Stuart and Revett, without once having seen Athens for themselves. In nineteenth century Philadelphia, for example, the
(50) disembodied facade of the Parthenon is reconstructed as the Second Bank of the United States in an urban milieu that is completely alien to the setting of the prototype.
(55)   Against the engravings of Stuart and Revett, we might pit two pencil sketches

of the Akropolis made by Le Corbusier during his apprenticeship travels in the early years of this century. The close-up
(60) view is neither picturesque nor archaeological. It does not show us the ubiquitous tourists scrambling over the site, for example, nor any other transient feature of local relevance. Nor
(65) is the sketch a reproducible paradigm of the essential design of the Parthenon. Instead, we see the temple the way Le Corbusier experienced it, climbing toward it up the steep west slope of this
(70) natural citadel, and catching sight of it at a dynamic angle through the inner colonnade of the Propylaia, the ceremonial gate of the Akropolis. The long view shows the building in relation
(75) to the larger shapes of nature that complement its form: the pedestal of the Akropolis spur that lifts it up like a piece of sculpture and the Attic mountain chain on the horizon which
(80) echoes its mass. And when Le Corbusier draws on this experience later in his own work, it is the memory of the building as a foil to nature that guides his vision.

7. From paragraph one, which one of the following best describes Stuart and Revett's pictures of the remains of ancient Greece?

(A) They show the grandeur of the Akropolis and depict the surrounding mountain ranges.
(B) They emphasize the original design and dimensions of the building.
(C) They show the antiquities as they appeared at the time of the pictures, not as they appeared in ancient Greece.
(D) Human figures and modest houses dominate the scenes that are shown in the pictures, whereas the natural surroundings are missing entirely.
(E) They are designed to contrast classical Grecian architecture with Byzantine architecture from the Middle Ages.

GO ON TO THE NEXT PAGE ➤

8. Which one of the following best summarizes the author's point about Stuart and Revett's first set of pictures (paragraph one)?

   (A) Although the pictures are from 1751, they capture the way the Greek monuments looked to the average Greek citizen at the time they were constructed.

   (B) By mixing grand monuments such as the Akropolis with modest houses, Stuart and Revett are making an ironic comment about architecture.

   (C) Stuart and Revett's intention was to give as exact a picture as possible of the dimensions, scale, and grandeur of the original Greek antiquities.

   (D) The pictures have a quaint appeal but they also convey a sense of the vanity of human efforts by showing the effects of time on the Greek antiquities.

   (E) The pictures capture not just the beauty and grandeur of the Greek antiquities but also suggest the positive spirit possessed by the people who created them.

9. In paragraph two, Stuart and Revett's engravings that depict the Parthenon are best described as

   (A) exact and measured
   (B) romantic and abstract
   (C) topical and picturesque
   (D) exotic and quaint
   (E) uninteresting and pedantic

10. In paragraph two, the author mentions the Second Bank of the United States (lines 51–52) in order to

    (A) show how Stuart and Revett's archaeological plates were exact enough to allow the Parthenon to be copied without an architect ever seeing the original building

    (B) emphasize that classical architecture was so timeless that a building such as the Parthenon could be copied in an entirely alien environment and still retain its beauty

    (C) indict Stuart and Revett for allowing inferior copies of Greek antiquities to be made, thereby detracting from the splendor of the original structures

    (D) show the difference in the way that architecture was depicted in nineteenth-century America from the way it was depicted in eighteenth-century England as illustrated in Stuart and Revett's plates

    (E) contrast the inferiority of imitative nineteenth-century architecture with the greatness of classical Greek architecture

11. According to the author, Le Corbusier's sketches of the Akropolis primarily show its

    (A) beauty and importance as a monument
    (B) relationship to its natural surroundings
    (C) importance as a citadel in Athens
    (D) connection to the common man in ancient Greece
    (E) role as a model for other monuments

GO ON TO THE NEXT PAGE ➤

5   **5**

12. Which one of the following can be inferred from information in the passage?

   (A) Classical Greek architecture, although often imitated, has never been surpassed.
   (B) The engraving process is the most effective way to create accurate architectural drawings.
   (C) The same building, depending on how it is depicted, may elicit various responses from a viewer.
   (D) Romantic depictions of structures are generally superior to strictly archaeological drawings.
   (E) Stuart and Revett were superior to Le Corbusier in depicting architecture in various ways.

13. Which one of the following does the author primarily use to make his point about architectural depiction?

   (A) anecdote and allusion
   (B) irony and understatement
   (C) metaphor and personification
   (D) logical argument and persuasion
   (E) description and contrast

GO ON TO THE NEXT PAGE ➤

5   5   5   5   5

War and change—political and economic foremost, but social and cultural not far behind—have been
(line) linked in America from the beginning.
(5) War was the necessary factor in the birth of the new American republic, as it has been in the birth of every political state known to us in history. War, chiefly the Civil War, in U.S. history has
(10) been a vital force in the rise of industrial capitalism, in the change of America from a predominantly agrarian and pastoral country to one chiefly manufacturing in nature. War, in
(15) focusing the mind of a country, stimulates inventions, discoveries, and fresh adaptations. Despite its manifest illth*, war, by the simple fact of the intellectual and social changes it
(20) instigates, yields results which are tonics to advancement.

By all odds, the most important war in U.S. history, the war that released the greatest number and diversity of
(25) changes in American life, was the Great War, the war that began in Europe in August 1914 and engulfed the United States in April 1917. Great changes in America were immediate.
(30) In large measure these changes reflected a release from the sense of isolation, insularity, and exceptionalism that had suffused so much of the American mind during the nineteenth
(35) century. The early Puritans had seen their new land as a "city upon a hill" with the eyes of the world on it. It was not proper for the New World to go to the Old for its edification; what was
(40) proper was for the Old World, grown feeble and hidebound, to come to America for inspiration. A great deal of that state of mind entered into what Tocqueville called the "American
(45) Religion," a religion compounded of Puritanism and ecstatic nationalism.

What we think of today as modernity—in manners and morals as well as ideas and mechanical things—
(50) came into full-blown existence in Europe in the final part of the nineteenth century, its centers such

cities as London, Paris, and Vienna. In contrast America was a "closed" society,
(55) one steeped in conventionality and also in a struggle for identity. This was how many Europeans saw America and it was emphatically how certain somewhat more sophisticated Americans saw
(60) themselves. The grand tour was a veritable obligation of better-off, ambitious, and educated Americans— the tour being, of course, of Europe.

Possibly the passage of American
(65) values, ideas, and styles from "closed" to "open," from the isolated to the cosmopolitan society, would have taken place, albeit more slowly, had there been no transatlantic war of 1914–1918.
(70) We can't be sure. What we do know is that the war, and America's entrance into it, gave dynamic impact to the processes of secularization, individualization, and other kinds of
(75) social-psychological change which so drastically changed this country from the America of the turn of the century to the America of the 1920s.

14. In the passage the author makes all of the following points about war EXCEPT

(A) war increases the pace of changes that might occur anyway
(B) war stimulates new inventions and discoveries
(C) war causes social and intellectual changes
(D) war in a capitalistic society is inevitable
(E) war sometimes stimulates a closed society toward greater openness

*illth = ill effects (word coined by the author earlier in the full selection)

GO ON TO THE NEXT PAGE ➤

5   **5**   **5**   **5**   **5**

15. If true, which of the following best illustrates the author's point about the effects of war on American society?

   (A) During World War II, the Germans developed a variety of lethal nerve gas to use in the field.
   (B) The development of radioactive isotopes used in treating cancer grew out of research to build the atomic bomb used in World War II.
   (C) The American influenza epidemic of 1919 in all likelihood was a result of the return of infected soldiers from the battlefields of World War I.
   (D) After the Civil War and the abolition of slavery in the South, racial intolerance across America grew in bitterness.
   (E) A significant drain on America's material resources was a result of relaxed immigration policies occurring after World War II.

16. According to the author, World War I was the most important war in U.S. history because it

   (A) ended the notion of a war to end all wars
   (B) resulted in a weakened Germany that in turn led to Hitler's appeal
   (C) changed America from a dominantly agrarian country to a manufacturing country
   (D) led to more changes and a wider diversity of changes than any other American war
   (E) made Americans more aware of advances made in European centers such as London, Paris, and Vienna

17. The main purpose of paragraph three is to

   (A) characterize the American mind in the nineteenth century
   (B) define Tocqueville's concept of American religion
   (C) indicate the main cause of America's entrance into World War I
   (D) contrast Civil War America with World War I America
   (E) indicate the areas of America's strength at the start of World War I

18. According to the author, which one of the following contributed to America's insularity before World War I?

   (A) The inability of all but the most wealthy, educated Americans to travel abroad
   (B) The nationalistic view that the New World (America) shouldn't turn to the Old World (Europe) for ideas
   (C) The emphasis on agrarian pursuits as opposed to belief in industry and technology
   (D) The puritanical idea that traveling widely in the world exposed one to sin and corruption
   (E) The superiority of the New World (America) to a feeble, decadent Old World (Europe)

19. Which one of the following best describes the main subject of this passage?

   (A) a comparison of wars in America
   (B) the benefits of war to society
   (C) the importance of World War I to changes in America
   (D) the contrast between the New World (America) and the Old World (Europe)
   (E) secularization and individualization in American society

20. The relationship of paragraph one to the rest of the passage is best described by which one of the following?

   (A) It presents a popular view that is proved inadequate by the rest of the passage.
   (B) It introduces a philosophical question that is then answered in the rest of the passage.
   (C) It outlines the contents of each of the other four paragraphs in the passage.
   (D) It sets up the first of four examples developed in the rest of the passage.
   (E) It presents a general idea that introduces the specific topic developed in the rest of the passage.

GO ON TO THE NEXT PAGE ➤

21. According to information in the passage, all of the following inferences can be made EXCEPT

(A) well-to-do nineteenth-century American parents would be more likely to send their son to Europe than to California

(B) European "ecstatic nationalism" would be greater after World War I than before it

(C) religious influence in the daily workings of American society would be less evident in 1920 than 1900

(D) a census in America 20 years after the Civil War would indicate more manufacturing operations than before the war

(E) in the nineteenth century, avant garde movements in art and literature would be more likely to originate in Europe than in the U.S.

GO ON TO THE NEXT PAGE ➤

The theory of natural selection cites the fact that every organism produces more gametes and/or organisms than
line can possibly survive. If every gamete
(5) produced by a given species united in fertilization and developed into offspring, the world would become so overcrowded in a short period of time that there would be no room for
(10) successive generations. This does not happen. There is a balance that is maintained in the reproduction of all species and therefore natural populations remain fairly stable, unless
(15) upset by a change in conditions. In the struggle for existence, some organisms die and the more hardy survive.

The differences that exist between organisms of the same species, making
(20) one more fit to survive than another, can be explained in terms of variations. Variations exist in every species and in every trait in members of a species. Therefore some organisms can compete
(25) more successfully than others for the available food or space in which to grow, or they can elude their enemies better. These variations are said to add survival value to an organism. Survival value
(30) traits are passed on to the offspring by those individuals that live long enough to reproduce. As time goes on, these special adaptations for survival are perpetuated and new species evolve
(35) from a common ancestral species. The environment is the selecting agent in natural selection because it determines which variations are satisfactory for survival and which are not.
(40) The major weakness in Darwin's theory of natural selection is that he did not explain the source, or genetic basis, for variations. He did not distinguish between variations that are hereditary
(45) and those that are nonhereditary, making the assumption that all variations that have survival value are passed on to the progeny. Like Jean Baptiste Lamarck, Darwin believed in
(50) the inheritance of even acquired characteristics.

Hugo De Vries (1845–1935), a Dutch botanist, explained variations in terms of mutations. His study of 50,000 plants
(55) belonging to the evening primrose species enabled him to identify changes in the plants that were passed on from parent to offspring. In 1901 De Vries offered his mutation theory to explain
(60) organic evolution. Today, we know that mutations are changes in genes that can come about spontaneously or can be induced by some mutagenic agent. Spontaneous mutation rates are very
(65) low, and mutations alone do not affect major changes in the frequencies of alleles, which are alternative forms of genes that occupy a given place on a chromosone.
(70) An important cause of variation within species is genetic recombination that results from sexual reproduction. The genes of two individuals are sorted out and recombined into a new
(75) combination, producing new traits—and thus variation.

Gene flow is also responsible for the development of variations. It is the movement of new genes into a
(80) population. Gene flow often acts against the effects of natural selection. Genetic drift is a change in a gene pool that takes place in a population as a result of chance. If a mutation occurs in a gene of
(85) one person, and that person does not reproduce, the gene is lost to the population. Sometimes a small population breaks off from a larger one. Within that population is a mutant gene,
(90) and because the mating within the small population is very close, the frequencies of the mutant gene will increase. In the Amish population, for example, where there is little or no outbreeding, an
(95) increase in the homozygosity of the genes in the gene pool is evinced in the high frequencies of genetic dwarfism and polydactyly (six fingers). The isolated smaller population has a
(100) different gene frequency than the larger population from which it came. This is known as the "founder principle." Genetic drift and the random mutations that increase or decrease as the result
(105) of genetic drift are known as non-Darwinian evolution.

Another cause of variation is speciation, or the forming of new species from a species already in
(110) existence. This can happen when a population becomes geographically divided and part of the original species

GO ON TO THE NEXT PAGE ➤

continues life in a new habitat. The separated populations cannot
(115) interbreed. Over evolutionary time, different environments present different selective pressures, and the change in gene pools will eventually produce new species.

22. The passage supports which one of the following statements?

(A) Spontaneous mutations cause the most significant evolutionary changes.
(B) Darwin's theory of evolution depends on rejecting the idea that acquired characteristics can be inherited.
(C) Variations among individual members of a species occur only when new genes move into an established population of that species.
(D) It is possible for a survival value trait to be eliminated from a species.
(E) New species are generally the result of genetic recombination.

23. Which one of the following, if true, would support the idea that acquired characteristics can be inherited?

(A) A spontaneous mutation causes some members of a rodent population to develop webbed feet. This segment of the population becomes isolated and is unable to breed with the original group. An exceptionally high frequency of webbed feet occurs in the successive generations of the isolated segment.
(B) A gene from a virus is experimentally transmitted to a fruit fly, making it vulnerable to carbon dioxide poison. This vulnerability is then passed on to the fruit fly's offspring.
(C) Antelopes raised in captivity are released into the wild. They run significantly more slowly than the wild antelope. After a year, the released antelopes' speed equals that of the wild antelopes.
(D) A population of long-haired dogs is shaved and bred with a population of hairless dogs. Their offspring include more hairless than long-haired pups.
(E) Fourteen different species of finches live on the Galapagos Islands. It is determined that all descended from a single species of finch found on mainland Peru.

24. The passage provides explanations for each of the following EXCEPT

(A) genetic drift
(B) the founder principle
(C) survival value
(D) speciation
(E) homozygosity

5 **5** **5** **5**

25. Random mutations are known as non-Darwinian evolution because they

    (A) are not necessarily related to the survival value of an organism
    (B) are more infrequent than spontaneous mutations
    (C) tend to refute Darwin's theories about the formation of species
    (D) occur only in small populations that have been isolated
    (E) were first described by Hugo De Vries, not Charles Darwin

26. The founder principle

    (A) accounts for genetic dwarfism
    (B) supports the importance of "weeding out" non-adaptive organisms
    (C) explains the concept of homozygosity
    (D) relates to gene frequencies in isolated populations
    (E) refutes Darwin's theory of natural selection

27. Based on the passage, which one of the following can be inferred about Charles Darwin?

    (A) Darwin did not believe the theory of genetic inheritance.
    (B) Darwin did not believe that genetic theories were relevant to evolution.
    (C) Darwin's work was more concerned with the survival value of traits than with the mechanics of how they were inherited.
    (D) Darwin's theories did not include a recognition that variation within members of a species was crucial to evolution.
    (E) Darwin was more interested in traits that were acquired and passed on than he was in genetically inherited traits.

28. In the passage, the author's primary concern is to

    (A) address briefly the history of evolutionary theory
    (B) provide a brief overview of the concept of variation
    (C) expose the weakness inherent in Darwin's evolutionary theory
    (D) differentiate between genetic and evolutionary theories
    (E) describe one of the ways in which nonadaptive traits can be inherited

STOP

END OF MULTIPLE-CHOICE EXAMINATION. IF YOU FINISH BEFORE TIME IS UP, CHECK YOUR WORK ON THIS SECTION ONLY. DO NOT GO BACK TO ANY OTHER SECTION OF THE EXAMINATION.

Writing Sample

Directions: You have 30 minutes to write an essay in response to a given topic. Take a few minutes to plan your work before you begin writing. DO NOT WRITE ON A TOPIC OF YOUR OWN CHOICE. ESSAYS THAT DO NOT ADDRESS THE GIVEN TOPIC ARE UNACCEPTABLE.

The quality of your writing is more important than the length of your response or the content. Pay attention to organization, appropriate diction, and correct usage. You will not be expected to display any specialized knowledge in your response, nor will you be expected to write a "perfect" essay; law schools understand that you are writing under a time constraint, and will allow for the minor lapses in writing ability that might occur under this circumstance.

Only the lined area in your booklet will be reproduced for the law schools, so do not write outside this space. *Do not* skip lines or use wide margins. These precautions, along with careful planning and legible handwriting that is not unduly large, will keep you within the allowed space.

Sample Topic

Read the following descriptions of Thomas and Peters, candidates for the position of head coach of the Ventura Vultures professional football team. *Then, in the space provided, write an argument for appointing either Thomas or Peters.* Use the information in this description and assume that the two general policies below equally guide the Vultures' decision on the appointment:

- The head coach should possess the ability to work with players and coaching staff toward achieving a championship season.
- The head coach should successfully manage the behind-the-scenes activities of recruiting, analyzing scouting reports, and handling the media and fans in order to enhance the public relations and image of the team.

THOMAS has been General Manager of the Vultures for the past ten years. A physical education major with a master's in psychology, he knows the player personnel as well as anyone, including the coaching staff. His on-target assessment of player skills and weaknesses has been instrumental in building a more balanced team over the past decade through his skillful trading and recruitment of college athletes. As the chief managing officer, he has also enhanced the team's image by his careful press relationship and understated approach when negotiations with star players reached an impasse. He rarely alienates players, coaches, press, or fans with his even-handed (though sometimes unemotional) attitude, and the Vultures' owners feel fortunate that they were able to entice him away from his high school coaching position, which he left 10 years ago. He has never played either pro or college ball.

PETERS is presently a wide receiver and defensive end for the Vultures. A one-time star, Peters has played both offense and defense for the Vultures since their inception in the league 14 years ago, a remarkable feat equaled by few in the game. He was elected captain of the team the past five years because of his charisma, although he occasionally angers management and fellow players with his strong comments about his philosophy of the game. His only experience in the front office was leading a player charity benefit for the Vultures, which raised more than $2,000,000 for abused Ventura County children. Although a high school dropout, Peters is a self-made man who firmly believes the key to life is having a strong educational background, even though he sometimes feels uncomfortable around college-educated athletes. The Vulture owners believe Peters may provide the emotional charge the team needs at its helm to win its first championship.

Answer Key

Section I: Logical Reasoning

1. **A**	6. **D**	11. **E**	16. **D**	21. **D**	26. **D**
2. **A**	7. **A**	12. **D**	17. **D**	22. **B**	
3. **D**	8. **B**	13. **C**	18. **C**	23. **B**	
4. **E**	9. **E**	14. **A**	19. **A**	24. **B**	
5. **C**	10. **A**	15. **B**	20. **D**	25. **E**	

Section II: Reading Comprehension

1. **C**	6. **D**	11. **B**	16. **A**	21. **C**	26. **B**
2. **A**	7. **C**	12. **D**	17. **A**	22. **C**	27. **C**
3. **A**	8. **B**	13. **E**	18. **D**	23. **A**	28. **A**
4. **B**	9. **A**	14. **A**	19. **E**	24. **D**	
5. **C**	10. **E**	15. **B**	20. **A**	25. **B**	

Section III: Analytical Reasoning

1. **E**	5. **A**	9. **B**	13. **B**	17. **E**	21. **A**
2. **C**	6. **C**	10. **C**	14. **C**	18. **B**	22. **E**
3. **D**	7. **D**	11. **E**	15. **A**	19. **C**	23. **B**
4. **B**	8. **A**	12. **C**	16. **C**	20. **D**	24. **C**

Section IV: Logical Reasoning

1. **D**	6. **B**	11. **A**	16. **E**	21. **C**	26. **D**
2. **D**	7. **A**	12. **C**	17. **B**	22. **D**	
3. **A**	8. **E**	13. **D**	18. **A**	23. **C**	
4. **C**	9. **A**	14. **D**	19. **E**	24. **E**	
5. **B**	10. **B**	15. **B**	20. **B**	25. **C**	

Section V: Reading Comprehension

1. **D**	6. **B**	11. **B**	16. **D**	21. **B**	26. **D**
2. **A**	7. **C**	12. **C**	17. **A**	22. **D**	27. **C**
3. **B**	8. **D**	13. **E**	18. **B**	23. **B**	28. **B**
4. **D**	9. **A**	14. **D**	19. **C**	24. **E**	
5. **C**	10. **A**	15. **B**	20. **E**	25. **A**	

Model Test Analysis

Doing model exams and understanding the explanations afterwards are of course important in acquainting you with typical LSAT question types and successful approaches to the questions. However, another benefit of carefully analyzing these model tests is to understand the kinds of errors you are making and thus work to minimize them. For instance, if a very high percentage of your incorrect answers is due to "careless error" or "misread problem," then perhaps you are working much too fast and should slow your pace accordingly. If your incorrect answers are due primarily to "lack of knowledge," then a careful rereading and reworking of the appropriate question-type chapter may be in order. Or if you find that you aren't completing a large number of questions because of lack of time, you may need to either increase your speed or learn to use the "one-check, two-check" technique more effectively.

This kind of analysis of the model tests will enable you to identify your particular weaknesses and thus remedy them.

Model Test Two Analysis

Section	Total Number of Questions	Number Correct	Number Incorrect	Number Unanswered*
I. Logical Reasoning	26			
II. Reading Comprehension	28			
III. Analytical Reasoning	24			
IV. Logical Reasoning	26			
V. Reading Comprehension	28			
TOTALS:	132			

*At this stage in your preparation, you should not be leaving any blank answer spaces. At least fill in a guess, as there is no penalty for a wrong answer.

Reasons for Incorrect Answers

You may wish to evaluate the explanations before completing this chart.

Section	Total Number Incorrect	Lack of Knowledge	Misread Problem	Careless Error	Unanswered or Wrong Guess
I. Logical Reasoning					
II. Reading Comprehension					
III. Analytical Reasoning					
IV. Logical Reasoning					
V. Reading Comprehension					
TOTALS:					

Explanation of Answers

Section I

1. **A** The author must assume that "nothing about our coin influences its fall in favor of either side or that all influences are counterbalanced by equal and opposite influences"; otherwise "our ignorance of the coming result" is untrue. Also, he mentions that the chances are one out of two that the coin will fall heads up; this could not be correct if the coin had been weighted or tampered with.

2. **A** (A) is implied by the author's statement that one-to-two is not "true." (B), (C), (D), and (E) are not implied and would not follow from the passage.

3. **D** The author is actually pointing out that self-confidence is of most importance. (C) and (E) focus on behavior, while the author is focusing on mental attitude.

4. **E** Only choice (E) is supported by these comments. The comments suggest that riding on roller coasters is taking a risk and that this risk translates to a proclivity to taking other risks in life. The passage doesn't suggest, however, that *no* roller coaster riders avoid taking risks elsewhere (A), nor does it have any bearing on the importance of taking risks (B). Choice (C) is a difficult one to eliminate because the passage certainly doesn't rule out this possibility (the passage says "than other," not "than *all* others")—but it doesn't directly support it, either. The comments have nothing to do with varying levels or types of risk taking (D).

5. **C** If the diet and way of life of the men of the two islands are alike, but the life expectancies are very different, the cause of the difference is probably something other than diet and the way of life. Some of the other answers are reasonable inferences, but they do not follow so clearly from the paragraph as (C).

6. **D** None of the other four choices offer information that explains the discrepancy. If the women in college are preparing for a profession that pays less (teaching) than the profession the men will enter (engineering), the discrepancy is explained.

7. **A** To conclude that the women should earn as much or more than the men, the passage must assume that all of the men and all of the women, or at least an equal number, enter the workforce. It also assumes that all of them, or at least an equal number, graduate from college, though the passage says only "are enrolled."

8. **B** The six-month interest-free charge is the money at a low cost; the stock of discontinued summer wear is the slow selling product, and the fashionable new neck wear is the popular product. None of the other choices covers all three conditions.

9. **E** Though all of the choices are plausible, (E) deals with all three of the problems mentioned in the paragraph. Each of the other choices deals only with one.

10. **A** The statistics present the very small percentage of male dance students. Of the five statements, (A) does throw light on the figures. If dancing is not a socially accepted career for men, it is not surprising that there are few students. The other four statements have no real relevance to the statistics.

11. **E** The author states that the present programs are at best weak and hopefully won't fail as they have in the past.

12. **D** The statement that "Hopefully, they won't fail as they have in the past" tells us that our government is *not* trying a new approach to end inflation. (A) is close, but the passage states that foreign oil is "high-priced," not "overpriced." "High-priced" tells us the relative cost, not the actual comparative value.

13. **C** The conclusion is the prediction of a grim year for home-builders. Choices (A), (B), (D), and (E) do not point to continued bad sales, but (C), revealing that sales fell even with advertising and incentives, supports the prediction of a bad year ahead.

14. **A** Three possibilities exist:
(a) You read *Weight-Off* magazine, are fat, and do not eat chocolate.
(b) You are fat, eat chocolate, but do not read *Weight-Off* magazine.
(c) You eat chocolate, are not fat, and do not read *Weight-Off* magazine.

Thus,
(A) is inconsistent by (a) and (b). (B) is not inconsistent if (b) and (c) are void of people. (C) is not inconsistent if (c) is void of people. (D) and (E) are not inconsistent by (c) and (a).

15. **B** Dave felt that Jerry implied that no one except Jerry's wife cooks fantastic meals.

16. **D** Only (D) offers an instance of success in the polls. (A) simply repeats a point of the passage without including the qualification that comes later. Choices (B), (C), and (E) would support rather than undermine the viewpoint of the passage.

17. **D** The passage does not point inherent inconsistencies. It does support a point with a specific example (the two figures on the balanced budget poll), question the honesty of politicians (the phrase "or may not"), reinterprets the 80 percent support figure, and shows how statistics can be used to mislead.

18. **C** Decreasing the fares on lightly traveled routes might attract some passengers away from the overcrowded more popular flights, but increasing the fares would not help to solve the luggage problem. The four other suggestions are plausible ways of dealing with the lack of space.

19. **A** X's new realization is expressed in his final sentence: "We must know all the characteristics of men, and that Socrates has all of them, before we can be sure." The "characteristics of men" are what is implied by the generalization "man," in "Socrates is a man." Therefore, deductive thinking is simply reminding ourselves of the particular specifics implied by generalizations.

20. **D** Symbolically, A is necessary to have B (a good telescope to see moons of Neptune). You do not have B (can't see moons with my telescope). Therefore, you cannot have A (a good telescope). (D) is the only choice that follows this line of reasoning. Symbolically, A is necessary to have B (knowing area of circle to find circumference). You do not have B (can't figure out circumference). Therefore, you cannot have A (area of circle).

21. **D** Extensive psychological research would most likely give the information that the author discusses. (E) limits the research to clinical psychologists and to recent findings.

22. **B** "Conscious behavior eventually becomes habit" is indirectly stated in the last sentence. (A) is a close answer, but that absolute word "all" is inconsistent with the words "can become" in the last sentence. This does not imply that they *must* become unconscious behavior.

23. **B** The given advice would be strengthened by the assurance that such measures are effective. Each of the other choices either weakens the advice, or addresses only a portion of the paragraph.

24. **B** The disease under discussion is termed "it," and thus its identity is unclear. The other choices either are not applicable to the second sentence or refer to terms that require no further definition.

25. **E** (E) weakens the argument that young people have abundant time. The other choices are only tangentially relevant to the argument.

26. **D** The passage says that worrying about writing unfortunately keeps one from writing at all; (D) summarizes this viewpoint. (B) and (C) are irrelevant notions; (A) contradicts the author's implied support for writing theorists; and (E) is an unreasonable, unsupported conclusion.

Section II

Passage 1

1. **C** The chief purpose of the Sixth Amendment was to assure the assistance of counsel in criminal cases. The guarantee to the right to self-representation was not the chief purpose of the amendment though the amendment has been used to support it.

2. **A** The phrase refers to the end of the second paragraph. The author regards the waiving of the right to counsel as a choice, which should not be seen as a guarantee of the right of self-representation.

3. **A** The phrase *"in propria persona"* means "in his own person," "by himself," or "by herself."

4. **B** If the Court had believed a fair trial was impossible without the assistance of counsel, it would not have allowed self-representation.

5. **C** The passage emphasizes the importance of warning a defendant of the risks of self-representation.

6. **D** Though true, the tradition of self-representation is not a valid objection to the practice. In fact, it might be cited as an argument in favor of self-representing defendants.

Passage 2

7. **C** The passage states that African arts were curiosities, and were presented as evidence of the "low state of heathen savagery of the African." The implication of lines 18–26 is that the arts, like the government and history, were not worth notice. (D) and (E) are incorrect; nothing is implied concerning the proportions or the subjects of African art. (A) and (C) both suggest a positive reaction to the art; this reaction is not supported by the passage.

8. **B** See lines 12–18. (C), whether true or not, is not supported by the passage. (D) is incorrect; Africa wasn't a threat to European society. In fact, Africans were exploited or made objects of missionary zeal. (A) and (E) are clearly irrelevant or incorrect.

9. **A** The writings of Pliny are cited as one of the early sources of knowledge about Africa—not one of the factors contributing to a change in the European view. See lines 27–36 for support of (B), (C), (D), and (E).

10. **E** Lines 37–40 make it clear that cultural relativism refers to viewing a culture in its own terms and on its own merits rather than judging it by the standards of one's own culture. (E) most clearly defines this point of view in relation to art. (A) is incorrect; the passage does not suggest that value judgments about works of art cannot be made, as long as the works are judged against the values of their own culture. (B) and (C) are irrelevant to the idea of cultural relativism. (D) is also irrelevant, and its judgment is not supported by any statements in the passage.

11. **B** See lines 48–55. The author states that when the attitude towards African art did change, it changed as a result of an "excess of romantic rebellion" against Classicism and Naturalism, not as a result of an objective assessment. No point is made in the passage about the availability of African art (A). (C) is unclear, and (D) is clearly inaccurate. The judgments of missionaries (E) were irrelevant to the twentieth-century European assessment of African art.

12. **D** See lines 77–87. One of the author's main points is that African art was very much in tune with its audience, unlike modern European art, which represented a rebellion against European traditions. (A) is the opposite of the point the author makes about African art. (B) and (E) are irrelevant and not supported by information in the passage. (C) is incorrect because although the author says we cannot have full understanding of African art if we judge it by twentieth-century Western aesthetic standards, we can still "admire" the works in a limited way. See lines 70–76.

13. **E** See lines 91–95. The author states that the works of art, while conservative and conformist, were not "passive reflections" of the culture; the perishable nature of wood ensured that every generation reaffirmed its faith. No comparison between wood and stone is made (with the exception of the implied comparison of impermanence and permanence). Therefore, (A) and (B) are incorrect. Also, no point is made about Western art or the Western world (C), (D).

14. **A** Throughout the passage the author talks about European or Western reactions to African art, from the earliest knowledge of Africa in Europe until the twentieth-century reassessment of African art. No specific works are analyzed (B), nor is any information included about African religious and social beliefs (D) or African aesthetic principles (E).

Passage 3

15. **B** (B) is the best choice because the passage first describes the classic model of competition and then introduces what the author refers to as the concept of "countervailing power." Although the ideas in (D) and (E) are both present in the passage, these titles are too restrictive. (A) is incomplete, and (C) is clearly wrong, in that the passage doesn't specifically address "American capitalism."

16. **A** (A) is directly from the passage (lines 18–21). Although (B) and (C) might occur, these are not part of the classic competition model described by the author. (E) would certainly not provide a return to normal prices; although it might offer a change in *supply*, it would not alter *demand*. Answer (D) is simply unclear.

17. **A** (A) is the best choice. See lines 26–32. (D) and (E) are clearly wrong. (C) is unclear. The second-best answer is (B), since the behavior of manufacturers is ultimately related to competition for the customer. However, (A) is the more specific answer provided by the passage.

18. **D** (D) is the best choice. See lines 45–53. (A) is incorrect because the classic model of competition does *not* ignore the role of labor (lines 26–30). Also, although the author might agree that greed undermined the classic model, this is not an issue addressed in the passage. (B) is incorrect because the author does not relate change in self-regulation of competition to any particular event, nor does he place it in a specific time frame. (C) is clearly the opposite of the point made in the passage. The restraint of "sellers by other sellers and buyers by other buyers" is part of the classic model of competition. (E) is incorrect because, according to the author, "countervailing power" did not destroy competition but grew as a result of a change in the classic model, i.e., the reduction of the number of competitors and resulting concentration of power among a small group of firms.

19. **E** Organizations that network manufacturers would not provide a customer- or supplier-generated restraint on them, which is the way the author defines "countervailing power." All of the other choices are possible wielders of "countervailing power."

20. **A** In lines 32–45 and lines 53–57, the author makes it clear that economists have almost exclusively focused on the classic model of competition in considering restraints on manufacturers. (B) is incorrect because the author does not discuss government regulation or the lack of it as part of economic theory. Similarly, (C) is incorrect; the "trickle-down" theory (i.e., that what is good for those at the top will ultimately benefit those at the bottom) is also not mentioned in the passage. (D) is contradicted in the passage; according to the author, economists did recognize the trend toward concentration (lines 45–53, 75–81). Finally, although the author might agree with (E), the passage suggests that economists have been preoccupied with the classic model of competition (including its built-in restraints) rather than biased toward "unregulated" capitalism. The preoccupation with the classic models led them to ignore other types of restraint in the economy.

21. **C** The passage sets up the classic model of competition in paragraphs one and two. Paragraph three is a shift in the discussion to the idea that there might be a restraining mechanism exclusive of the competitive model that economists haven't recognized. Paragraphs four and five describe this restraining mechanism. The second-best answer is (D); however, paragraph three does provide a transition, which makes (C) the better choice.

Passage 4

22. **C** The second and third sentences of paragraph one state the thesis of the passage, which the rest of the paragraph explains further. (D) is incorrect because although the cake metaphor is introduced, it is referenced only once later in the passage. No terms are defined in paragraph one (A) nor are arguments presented (B).

23. **A** See lines 26–31. Although Freud does provide historical context (B), the author's primary purpose in including him is to explain by using a prominent example the argument that genetic inheritance is responsible for behavior.

24. **D** In the example of the Siamese cat, the author states that the cat's coat-color gene (the Himalayan mutation) dictates dark fur, but pigment is produced only if the temperature is cold. See lines 68–78. The example is used to show the inseparable contributions of "nature" and "nurture." (A) and (B) are both incorrect because nothing in the passage addresses the concept of dominant or recessive genes. (C) and (E) are simply inaccurate statements.

25. **B** See lines 20–24 and 35–36. There is irony (a disparity) in the fact that Freud would subscribe to theories that led to his flight from Austria. The author uses the irony to underline the point he makes in lines 14–16 of paragraph one. (E) is incorrect because although there may be irony in modern Freudians moving so far away from Freud's beliefs, the author does not make this point ironically.

26. **B** This statement most clearly supports the author's point that what is inherited is an ability to respond to the environment. Trying to separate the effects of inheritance and environment is not productive. Like the Himalayan mutation and its connection to temperature in Siamese cats, if there were a lung-cancer-causing gene in humans, its manifestation might depend on environment (smoking or not smoking). (A), (C), (D), and (E) all suppose being able to separate the effects of genes and environment, which the author argues isn't possible in most cases.

27. **C** The passage does not support this statement. See lines 49–52. The author indicates that today's Freudians separate nature and nurture and therefore oversimplify human behavior. The other statements are supported: (A)—lines 29–31; (B)—lines 41–44; (D)—lines 35–40; (E)—lines 32–34.

28. **A** After the statement of the thesis that traits and behaviors cannot be separated into those that are genetically caused and those that are environmentally caused, the author illustrates the "nature" argument using Freud and the "nurture" argument using modern Freudians. In the final two paragraphs he presents the example of the Himalayan mutation in Siamese cats to support his initial thesis. (B) is incorrect because paragraph one does not pose a rhetorical question; (C) is incorrect because paragraph three is not a transition.

Section III
Answers 1–6

UPPER-case letters denote colors given in the problem, and lower-case letters denote deduced colors.

1. **E**

	1	2	3	4	5	
	b/w	R	W	b	R	(flag)
	w/g	B	g	w	B	(pennant)

The 3rd pennant cannot be blue or white, so therefore it is green. The 4th flag cannot be white or red, so it must be blue. The 4th pennant cannot be green or blue, so it must be white. The 1st flag cannot be red, so it is either blue or white. The 1st pennant cannot be blue, so it must be green or white.

2. **C**

1	2	3	4	5	
R	w	r/b			(flag)
g/w	B	g/w			(pennant)

(A) is clearly true. If the 5th flag is red, then the 3rd flag cannot be, since the 1st flag is red and we can have only two of any one color. Thus, (B) is true. If the 4th pennant is green, then the 3rd pennant must be white. But that does not determine the color of the 1st pennant. Thus, (C) is not necessarily true. (D) is the same as (A) and is also true. If the 4th pennant is green, this implies that the 3rd pennant must be white. If the 5th pennant is white, then the 1st pennant cannot be. Therefore (E) is true.

3. **D**

1	2	3	4	5	
W	r	W	r	b	(flag)
g	B	g	B	w	(pennant)

The facts in this problem determine the complete configuration of flags and pennants. (D) is the one statement that is false.

4. **B**

1	2	3	4	5	
B	w	r	B		(flag)
		W	g		(pennant)

Statement (B) is true since the 1st pennant cannot be blue or white. Statement A is false since the 5th pennant could be blue or white. Statement (C) is false since it is white. Statements (D) and (E) are false since they could be white.

5. **A**

1	2	3	4	5	
	R	W	r		(flag)
		g	B		(pennant)

If the 5th flag is white, then the 5th pennant must be green. Thus the 1st and 2nd pennants cannot be green and cannot be the same color, so one of them is blue. Therefore, (A) is true. All the other statements are false.

6. **C**

1	2	3	4	5	
W	B	W	B	r	(flag)
g	W	B	W	B	(pennant)

1	2	3	4	5	
B	W	B	W	r	(flag)
g	B	W	B	W	(pennant)

Since blue and white are the two common colors between flags and pennants, the above are the only two arrangements possible. In both cases, the 5th flag is red and the 1st pennant is green.

Answers 7–13

7. **D**

1	2	3	4	5	6	7	8	9	10
E	E	E					M		M

If the 8th book is a math book, then the three English books must be in positions 1, 2, and 3, since they cannot be in positions 8, 9, and 10. Thus, the other math book is in position 10. The 4th book must be next to the English book in position 3.

8. **A**

1	2	3	4	5	6	7	8	9	10
M			P	P			E	E	E

If the 9th book is an English book, then so are the 8th and 10th books. Thus there is a math book in position 1. The science books must be in positions 2 and 3 *or* 3 and 4. This leaves only positions 4 and 7 for the other math book. Thus (A) is always true. (C) could be true, but does not have to be true. The 3rd poetry book could be in position 2.

9. **B**

1	2	3	4	5	6	7	8	9	10
M					S	S	E	E	E

If the 1st book is a math book, then the 8th, 9th, and 10th books must be the English books. If the 7th book is a science book, so must be the 6th book. This means that the other math book must be either the 3rd, the 4th, or the 5th book. The remainder of the books are poetry books, including the 2nd book.

10. **C**

1	2	3	4	5	6	7	8	9	10
M	P	P	P	M	S	S	P	E	E	E

or

E	E	E	M	S	S	P	P	P	M

If the 4th book is a math book and the 5th book is a science book, then the 6th book is also a science book. This leaves two possible arrangements for the remaining books, as shown above. Statement (C) is the only correct one.

11. **E**

1	2	3	4	5	6	7	8	9	10
E	E	P						P	M

or

M	P					P	E	E	E

The poetry books must be in positions 4 and 9 *or* 2 and 7, depending on whether the math book is in position 1 or 10. See diagrams above. For example, let us assume that the math book is the 10th book. In order for no two poetry books to be next to each other, the 4th and 9th books must be poetry books, with the 3rd poetry book in either position 6 or 7, depending on the positions of the science books. The same argument holds if the 1st book is a math book.

12. **C**

1	2	3	4	5	6	7	8	9	10
E	E	E	S	S	M	P	P	P	M

and

M	P	P	P	M	S	S	E	E	E

These are the two possible arrangements. We see that (A) is false, (B) could be false, (D) is false, and (E) could be false. Only (C) is always true.

13. **B**

1	2	3	4	5	6	7	8	9	10
E	E	E	M	S	S	P	P	P	M

and

E	E	E	S	S	M	P	P	P	M

These are the only two possible combinations; thus, (B) is the correct answer.

Answers 14–19

A simple chart, as follows, will help to answer the questions:

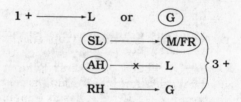

14. **C** From the chart we can see that a freshman can take everything except Latin (if he takes American History) or take everything except American History (if he takes Latin).

15. **A** In order to enroll in American History and the Sex Lab, a freshman must take Marriage/Family Relations plus Greek. Therefore, only (A) is true.

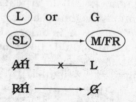

16. **C** If a freshman does not enroll in Greek, he can take only Latin, Sex Lab, and Marriage/Family Relations.

17. **E** If a freshman enrolls in Latin, his course load could consist of Latin, Greek, and Roman History; or it could consist of Latin, Sex Lab, and Marriage/Family Relations; or it could consist of Latin, Greek, and Marriage/Family Relations.

18. **B** If a freshman does not take Greek or American History, he must take Latin, and cannot take Roman History (because Roman History requires taking Greek). Therefore, the other two courses left for him to take are Sex Lab and Marriage/Family Relations.

19. **C** If a freshman enrolls in Latin, he may choose from any of the classes except American History. Thus, he may choose from Greek, Sex Lab, Marriage/Family Relations, and Roman History—a total of four.

Answers 20–24

From the information given, you could have constructed the following display:

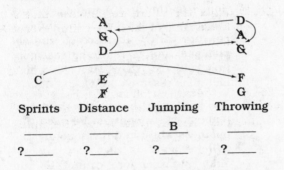

Sprints	Distance	Jumping	Throwing
		B	
?____	?____	?____	?____

20. **D** If C and E are both sprint coaches, then from the original conditions F and G coach throwers. Since G coaches throwers, D cannot coach distance, so D must coach jumping.

Sprints	Distance	Jumping	Throwing
C		B	F
? E	?____	? D	? G

21. **A** If G coaches jumping and A coaches distance we have:

Sprints	Distance	Jumping	Throwing
	A	B	
?____	?____	? G	?____

If D coaches distance or throwing, A must coach sprints or jumping. Since A coaches distance, D cannot coach distance or throwing. This means D must coach sprints. The other choices are possible, but not necessarily true.

Sprints	Distance	Jumping	Throwing
D	A	B	
?____	?____	? G	?____

22. **E** If D coaches throwing, A and G cannot coach distance or throwing. This leaves only C to be the distance coach. So C CANNOT coach jumping.

Sprints	Distance	Jumping	Throwing
	E̶		
	F̶		
	C	B	D
?____	?____	?____	?____
	A̶		A̶
	G̶		G̶

23. **B** If G is the only throwing coach, we have the following:

Sprints	Distance	Jumping	Throwing
	E̶		
	F̶		
		B	G
?____	?____	?____	? X

If D coaches distance or throwers, G must coach sprints or jumping. Since G coaches throwing, D does not coach distance or throwers. Thus, A and C must coach distance giving the following arrangement:

Sprints	Distance	Jumping	Throwing
	E̶		
	F̶		
	A	B	G
?____	? C	?____	? X
	D̶		D̶

Choice (A) is incorrect since D doesn't coach distance.
Choice (C) is incorrect since A coaches distance.
Choice (D) is incorrect since, if F coaches jumping, D and E must coach sprints.
Choice (E) is incorrect since C and D coach different sports.

24. **C** If D coaches distance, A and G do not coach distance or throwing.

		E	
		F̶	
Sprints	Distance	Jumping	Throwing
A̶	D	B	___
?___	?___	?___	?___
		A̶	A̶
		G̶	G̶

Since A does not coach sprints, then A must coach jumping. So A and B coach jumping; therefore, G CANNOT coach jumping.

		E	
		F̶	
Sprints	Distance	Jumping	Throwing
A̶	D	B	___
?___	?___	? A	?___
		A̶	A̶
		G̶	G̶

Section IV

1. **D** This choice provides the most direct evidence of the effectiveness of the PUC consumer action. Each of the other choices is only tangentially related to the argument.

2. **D** This choice most seriously weakens the author's contention that the PUC acts in the public interest. (C) is a weaker choice, especially because "slightly" softens the statement.

3. **A** This choice parallels both the reasoning and the structure of the original. The original reasoning may be summarized as follows: most $X \rightarrow Y$; therefore $X \rightarrow Y$ (probably).

4. **C** By conceding that certain subjects can *only* be discussed in private, the argument self-destructs. Several of the other Choices are tempting, but none is as much to the point as Choice (C).

5. **B** Since good personnel relations of an organization, according to the passage, rely upon "mutual confidence, trust and goodwill," one of the causes of personnel difficulties would most certainly be the employees' not believing in the good faith of the organization.

6. **B** In the second sentence, the author implies that the lack of facilities is related to the lack of research mentioned in the first sentence. In any case, the passage reveals the author's concern with both research and assistance, and therefore agrees more fully with (B) than with (A), which mentions research only.

7. **A** The "*But*" that begins the third sentence marks a contrast between the business world and the schools. The writer's point is that they are not alike and therefore cannot be run using the same standards of judgment.

8. **E** The correct answer is "circular." The argument that what the Church says is true is ultimately based upon this same assertion.

9. **A** Kathy believes Mary to have meant that *only Italians* are great lovers. Therefore, Kathy takes issue with this and points out in her reply that there are non-Italians who are great lovers. (A), if replaced for Mary's statement, would make Kathy's reply a reasonable one.

10. **B** Only (B) addresses Dimple's assumption that Mrs. Wilson is the *only* applicant whose qualifications are ideal. Other choices are irrelevant to the *argument*, although some may be relevant to the implied situation.

11. **A** Only (A) addresses the substance of Dimple's argument.

12. **C** The passage offers a pattern in which failure to meet one of two specific requirements results in a failure to qualify for something. In (C), the fall and winter track seasons become the residence requirement and the collecting of signatures. Failure to complete both leads to disqualification (for the spring team, for the June primary).

13. **D** The author of the argument avoids the issue of *quality*. The statement that stresses the incompleteness of the pro-hygienist position weakens it. (B) and (E) are irrelevant.

14. **D** The passage describes two types of obstacles to happiness: exterior forces and personal attitude. Both these factors are mentioned in (A), (B), (C), and (E). (D) requires the assumption that the two categories discussed by the author are the only categories.

15. **B** (A) may be eliminated because changing one's mind need not involve issues of right and wrong (in the moral sense that Eliot implies). (C) and (E) may be eliminated because they refute the underlying assumption of Eliot's words, that one can tell what is right. The passage does not address the issue of temptation (D).

16. **E** Without an implied or explicit definition of "civilized," the relevance of the examples is vague, at best. (A) and (D) are irrelevant considerations, and (B) and (C), although possibly relevant, do not address the most apparent weakness of the passage.

17. **B** (A) and (C) strengthen the argument. Although (D) and (E) partially weaken certain aspects of the argument, only (B) introduces a situation which suggests that freedom of the press may have harmful consequences.

18. **A** (B) and (C) are irrelevant to the argument. (D) and (E) contradict the implied assertion that a free press must be protected at all costs. Only (A) offers a statement both favorable to the concept of a free press and directly relevant to the subject discussed: the use of privileged information.

19. **E** By stating that "a legal technicality . . . ducks the . . . moral question," the author is implying that the federal government which benefits from the technicality is associated with dodging the issue. (A) and (B) restate explicit information; (C) is implausible; and (D) contradicts information in the passage.

20. **B** Private medical aid would render the author's argument unnecessary. (C), a choice worth considering, is not the best one because the author's focus is less on the aliens' needs than on the monetary burden borne by the counties.

21. **C** By documenting the rate at which the medical expense burden grows, the author could strengthen the argument that the situation he describes is indeed a burden.

22. **D** The passage talks about communes as failures. Therefore, the most logical completion must be a negative term consistent with failure. The only negative choice is (D).

23. **C** By linking Herb's ability with his "cousinhood," Herb is assuming that the latter determines the former; therefore, he is ignoring (C). (B) is irrelevant. (A) is too vague to be the best answer. (D) is inapplicable, because Keith uses "good" in a context that makes its meaning clear. Finally, (E) refers to contradictory information.

24. **E** In order to argue for the value of renewable prescriptions, the author must first assume that more medicine may be necessary, or, in other words, that the patient may suffer a relapse. Without the possibility of relapse, a call for more medicine that has already effected a cure ("worked effectively") is illogical.

25. **C** The passage consistently implies a difference between the past and the present, and (C) makes this contrast explicit. (B) contradicts the implication of the passage, while (A) and (D) narrow the focus unnecessarily, and (E) is irrelevant.

26. **D** This fact would strengthen the merely impressionistic evidence that lawsuits were less prevalent 40 years ago. It is the only choice dealing directly with the implied subject of the passage—lawsuits.

Section V

Passage 1

1. **D** According to the first paragraph, a developing country hopes to attract foreign investment and increase its revenues from taxation ("maximize the public capture of revenues").

2. **A** Unless the investment flow is equal in each direction, the First World nation from which the greater revenue is likely to come is more likely to benefit.

3. **B** According to the second paragraph, reciprocal source-based taxation produces revenue sacrifices by the state receiving most of the foreign investment, that is, the developing country.

4. **D** Excess foreign tax credits are a disincentive to private investors. If the at-source taxation is reduced, there will be fewer excess foreign credits.

5. **C** The passage makes no reference to the availability of raw materials. The four other options are cited.

6. **B** A country that reduced its revenue expectations would be expected to increase foreign investment.

Passage 2

7. **C** See lines 9–15. The point of the paragraph is to show how Stuart and Revett depicted the way the antiquities looked at the time of their visit in 1751. (A) is incorrect; not only is grandeur not shown but it is also undermined by the modest houses, Turkish influences, and sleepy atmosphere, (B) is also incorrect; these drawings are described in paragraph two. (D) is incorrect because the description does not say that the human figures and houses "dominate" the scenes. (E) is incorrect; although the Byzantine church is briefly mentioned, the paragraph does not contrast its architecture to the Grecian architecture.

8. **D** See lines 23–29. The author describes Stuart and Revett's topical drawings as being picturesque and conveying a sense of "the vanity of things." (A) is incorrect; the point is clearly made that the drawings do not show the monuments as they originally looked. (B) is also incorrect; although the contrast is shown, there is no implication that Stuart and Revett are making an ironic comment. (C) is true for the depictions described in the second paragraph, not the first. (E) is not supported by any information in the passage.

9. **A** See lines 30–39. The engravings are described by the author as archaeological; they re-create the original design and provide a "careful tally of dimensions." (C) and (D) describe the drawings discussed in paragraph one. The term "romantic," used in answer (B), also describes the drawings discussed in paragraph one. (E) is not supported by the passage; "traditional abstractions of the architect's trade" do not necessarily equal "uninteresting and pedantic" drawings.

10. **A** See lines 41–54. (B) and (E) are incorrect; no judgment is made as to the success of the Philadelphia building. (C) is also incorrect because no criticism of Stuart and Revett is suggested. (D) is inaccurate because the Philadelphia building is not a "depiction," as are the Stuart and Revett plates.

11. **B** The focus of the Le Corbusier sketches, according to the author, is on the way they show the Akropolis in relation to its natural surroundings. See lines 73–84. (A), (C), (D), and (E) are not supported by information in the passage.

12. **C** This inference is suggested by the point of the entire passage—that buildings are depicted according to how they are perceived. If they are depicted in various ways, it is implied that a viewer will have different responses, depending on the depiction. None of the other answers is supported by information in the passage. Nothing implies that classical architecture is superior to all other architecture (A) or that engraving is a superior process for depicting architecture (B). Also, there is not sufficient information to rank Stuart and Revett as superior to Le Corbusier (E) or to see romantic depiction as superior to archaeological drawings (D). In fact, the passage indicates that there are different ways to depict architecture, not that one way is superior to another.

13. **E** The author describes the three methods of depiction (topical, archaeological, in relation to nature) and contrasts them. The passage does not employ anecdote or allusion (A), irony or understatement (B), personification (C), or logical argument and persuasion (D).

Passage 3

14. **D** The author says that war and change have been inevitably linked in America, and that war has been a vital force in the rise of capitalism, but he does *not* say that war is inevitable. All of the other answers are supported by the passage: (A)—lines 64–78; (B)—lines 13–16; (C)—lines 16–20; (E)—lines 64–69.

15. **B** See lines 13–16. Radioactive isotopes used in treating cancer are an example of a positive advance caused by preparations for war. On the other hand, lethal nerve gases (A), in addition to being a German and not an American development, did not lead to positive peacetime uses. (C), (D), and (E), while possibly effects of wars that have changed America, did not "yield results which are tonics to advancement."

16. **D** See lines 21–28. (C) is incorrect; the author states that this is a result of the Civil War. (E) is a statement supported by the passage, but is not the primary reason for World War I's importance. (A) and (B) are not supported by information in the passage.

17. **A** In this paragraph the author paints a picture of, and indicates some of the reasons for, the "isolation, insularity, and exceptionalism" of America before World War I. The paragraph does define "American Religion" (B), but this is too limited an answer to describe the paragraph's main point. (C) and (E) are not covered in this paragraph. There is no contrast drawn between Civil War America and World War I America (D).

18. **B** See lines 36–45. (A) is incorrect; the grand tour is cited as an example that sophisticated Americans saw a trip to Europe as necessary to overcome insularity and complete an education. No social comment is made about its availability only to the rich. (D) is also incorrect; Puritanism is cited in paragraph four, but not in the context indicated in this answer, i.e., the sin and corruption of the world. (E) might seem correct at first, but the passage does not state that America was in fact superior to Europe; it comments on the *view* that Americans had of their country. (C) is irrelevant; this point is not made in relation to America's insularity.

19. **C** After the first paragraph introduces the idea of war as a force of change, the passage is devoted to the importance of World War I in changing American society. (B) is incorrect; paragraph one concerns some of the benefits of war, but this is not the main topic of the passage; it is an underlying idea. (A) is also incorrect; the passage mentions the Civil War briefly but is mostly concerned with World War I. (D) and (E) are points touched on in the passage, but neither is the main subject.

20. **E** War as a force for change (the topic of paragraph one) is a general idea that introduces the passage's main subject of World War I. It is not a "popular view" that is refuted in the passage (A), nor does the passage ask a question (B). The first paragraph doesn't outline the contents of the passage (C), nor does it set up the first of four examples (D).

21. **B** "Ecstatic nationalism" is part of what Tocqueville called "American Religion." It would not increase in Europe after World War I. (A) can be inferred because Europe was seen as a necessity in a young man's education. (California would have been considered the Wild West.) The inference in (C) is supported by lines 70–78; (D), by lines 8–13, (E), by lines 46–56.

Passage 4

22. **D** In lines 81–87, the passage describes genetic drift, a change in the gene pool that occurs by chance. If an organism with a survival trait gene doesn't reproduce, the gene is lost. (A) is incorrect; the passage does not indicate which mutations are most "significant." (B) is contrary to fact; see lines 48–51. (C) is contradicted by several examples in the passage of the ways variations occur, and genetic recombination (E) is not cited as the cause of the formation of new species.

23. **B** The vulnerability to carbon dioxide was a trait from a gene that was transmitted to the fruit fly by an outside agent; it is therefore an acquired characteristic. That the fruit fly's offspring exhibit the same vulnerability supports the theory that acquired characteristics can be inherited. In (A), the webbed feet are not an acquired characteristic but a result of mutation and were perpetuated by inbreeding. (C) has no relevance to the question of inheritance, and in (D), the shaving of the dogs has nothing to do with the number of hairless offspring; genetic inheritance (dominant and recessive genes) account for that. (E) does not address the issue of how characteristics were transmitted.

24. **E** (A), (B), (C), and (D) are all explained (however briefly) in the passage. Although (E) is mentioned in line 95, it is not defined or explained.

25. **A** By definition, random mutations occur by chance and are therefore not necessarily related to any survival trait. Darwin's theory states that natural selection accounts for the perpetuation of traits. (B) is incorrect; although spontaneous mutations are said to be infrequent, the frequency of random mutations is not addressed. That random mutations occur doesn't refute or replace Darwin's evolutionary concept; it is simply another possibility for explaining the inheritance of certain traits (C). Both (D) and (E) are factually incorrect.

26. **D** The founder principle (lines 101–102) is that a smaller, isolated population has a gene frequency different from the larger population from which it came. (A) is incorrect because although the passage states that more genetic dwarfism occurs in the Amish population as a result of the founder principle, it does not state that the founder principle explains all genetic dwarfism. The principle doesn't refute the theory of natural selection (E) nor does it explain homozygosity (C), although the term is related. (B) is incorrect; nothing intrinsic in the principle supports the importance of "weeding out" non-adaptative organisms.

27. **C** Darwin was more concerned with why certain traits were passed on (survival of the fittest) than with the mechanics of inheritance. (A) and (B) are incorrect; the passage doesn't imply that Darwin had any opinion about genetics. (In fact, the concept of the gene was developed after Darwin's work.) (D) is incorrect because Darwin recognized that variation among members of a species was central to the idea of natural selection. Although the passage states that he believed acquired characteristics could be inherited, it does not imply that he felt acquired traits were more important than hereditary ones (E).

28. **B** Most of the passage deals briefly with how variation occurs, not with the history of a theory (A) or the differences between genetic and evolutionary theories (D). (C) may seem to be a good answer because the author mentions that Darwin's failure to address the source of variations is "a major weakness." "Expose," however, is too strong a word; the passage is focused not on Darwin's weakness but rather on brief explanations of variation. (E) is a minor, not the primary, concern of the passage.

Chapter 8

MODEL TEST THREE

This chapter contains full-length Model Test Three. It is geared to the format of the LSAT, and it is complete with answers and explanations. It is equivalent to the LSAT in question structure, number of questions, level of difficulty, and time allotments. (The questions used are not taken directly from the LSAT, as those questions are copyrighted and may not be reproduced.)

Model Test Three should be taken under strict test conditions. The test ends with a 30-minute Writing Sample, which is not scored.

Section	Description	Number of Questions	Time Allowed
I.	Reading Comprehension	28	35 minutes
II.	Analytical Reasoning	24	35 minutes
III.	Logical Reasoning	26	35 minutes
IV.	Reading Comprehension	28	35 minutes
V.	Logical Reasoning	25	35 minutes
	Writing Sample		30 minutes
TOTALS:		131	3 hours 25 minutes

Now please turn to the next page, remove your answer sheet, and begin Model Test Three.

Answer Sheet—Model Test Three

Section 1	Section 2	Section 3	Section 4	Section 5
1. Ⓐ Ⓑ Ⓒ Ⓓ Ⓔ	1. Ⓐ Ⓑ Ⓒ Ⓓ Ⓔ	1. Ⓐ Ⓑ Ⓒ Ⓓ Ⓔ	1. Ⓐ Ⓑ Ⓒ Ⓓ Ⓔ	1. Ⓐ Ⓑ Ⓒ Ⓓ Ⓔ
2. Ⓐ Ⓑ Ⓒ Ⓓ Ⓔ	2. Ⓐ Ⓑ Ⓒ Ⓓ Ⓔ	2. Ⓐ Ⓑ Ⓒ Ⓓ Ⓔ	2. Ⓐ Ⓑ Ⓒ Ⓓ Ⓔ	2. Ⓐ Ⓑ Ⓒ Ⓓ Ⓔ
3. Ⓐ Ⓑ Ⓒ Ⓓ Ⓔ	3. Ⓐ Ⓑ Ⓒ Ⓓ Ⓔ	3. Ⓐ Ⓑ Ⓒ Ⓓ Ⓔ	3. Ⓐ Ⓑ Ⓒ Ⓓ Ⓔ	3. Ⓐ Ⓑ Ⓒ Ⓓ Ⓔ
4. Ⓐ Ⓑ Ⓒ Ⓓ Ⓔ	4. Ⓐ Ⓑ Ⓒ Ⓓ Ⓔ	4. Ⓐ Ⓑ Ⓒ Ⓓ Ⓔ	4. Ⓐ Ⓑ Ⓒ Ⓓ Ⓔ	4. Ⓐ Ⓑ Ⓒ Ⓓ Ⓔ
5. Ⓐ Ⓑ Ⓒ Ⓓ Ⓔ	5. Ⓐ Ⓑ Ⓒ Ⓓ Ⓔ	5. Ⓐ Ⓑ Ⓒ Ⓓ Ⓔ	5. Ⓐ Ⓑ Ⓒ Ⓓ Ⓔ	5. Ⓐ Ⓑ Ⓒ Ⓓ Ⓔ
6. Ⓐ Ⓑ Ⓒ Ⓓ Ⓔ	6. Ⓐ Ⓑ Ⓒ Ⓓ Ⓔ	6. Ⓐ Ⓑ Ⓒ Ⓓ Ⓔ	6. Ⓐ Ⓑ Ⓒ Ⓓ Ⓔ	6. Ⓐ Ⓑ Ⓒ Ⓓ Ⓔ
7. Ⓐ Ⓑ Ⓒ Ⓓ Ⓔ	7. Ⓐ Ⓑ Ⓒ Ⓓ Ⓔ	7. Ⓐ Ⓑ Ⓒ Ⓓ Ⓔ	7. Ⓐ Ⓑ Ⓒ Ⓓ Ⓔ	7. Ⓐ Ⓑ Ⓒ Ⓓ Ⓔ
8. Ⓐ Ⓑ Ⓒ Ⓓ Ⓔ	8. Ⓐ Ⓑ Ⓒ Ⓓ Ⓔ	8. Ⓐ Ⓑ Ⓒ Ⓓ Ⓔ	8. Ⓐ Ⓑ Ⓒ Ⓓ Ⓔ	8. Ⓐ Ⓑ Ⓒ Ⓓ Ⓔ
9. Ⓐ Ⓑ Ⓒ Ⓓ Ⓔ	9. Ⓐ Ⓑ Ⓒ Ⓓ Ⓔ	9. Ⓐ Ⓑ Ⓒ Ⓓ Ⓔ	9. Ⓐ Ⓑ Ⓒ Ⓓ Ⓔ	9. Ⓐ Ⓑ Ⓒ Ⓓ Ⓔ
10. Ⓐ Ⓑ Ⓒ Ⓓ Ⓔ	10. Ⓐ Ⓑ Ⓒ Ⓓ Ⓔ	10. Ⓐ Ⓑ Ⓒ Ⓓ Ⓔ	10. Ⓐ Ⓑ Ⓒ Ⓓ Ⓔ	10. Ⓐ Ⓑ Ⓒ Ⓓ Ⓔ
11. Ⓐ Ⓑ Ⓒ Ⓓ Ⓔ	11. Ⓐ Ⓑ Ⓒ Ⓓ Ⓔ	11. Ⓐ Ⓑ Ⓒ Ⓓ Ⓔ	11. Ⓐ Ⓑ Ⓒ Ⓓ Ⓔ	11. Ⓐ Ⓑ Ⓒ Ⓓ Ⓔ
12. Ⓐ Ⓑ Ⓒ Ⓓ Ⓔ	12. Ⓐ Ⓑ Ⓒ Ⓓ Ⓔ	12. Ⓐ Ⓑ Ⓒ Ⓓ Ⓔ	12. Ⓐ Ⓑ Ⓒ Ⓓ Ⓔ	12. Ⓐ Ⓑ Ⓒ Ⓓ Ⓔ
13. Ⓐ Ⓑ Ⓒ Ⓓ Ⓔ	13. Ⓐ Ⓑ Ⓒ Ⓓ Ⓔ	13. Ⓐ Ⓑ Ⓒ Ⓓ Ⓔ	13. Ⓐ Ⓑ Ⓒ Ⓓ Ⓔ	13. Ⓐ Ⓑ Ⓒ Ⓓ Ⓔ
14. Ⓐ Ⓑ Ⓒ Ⓓ Ⓔ	14. Ⓐ Ⓑ Ⓒ Ⓓ Ⓔ	14. Ⓐ Ⓑ Ⓒ Ⓓ Ⓔ	14. Ⓐ Ⓑ Ⓒ Ⓓ Ⓔ	14. Ⓐ Ⓑ Ⓒ Ⓓ Ⓔ
15. Ⓐ Ⓑ Ⓒ Ⓓ Ⓔ	15. Ⓐ Ⓑ Ⓒ Ⓓ Ⓔ	15. Ⓐ Ⓑ Ⓒ Ⓓ Ⓔ	15. Ⓐ Ⓑ Ⓒ Ⓓ Ⓔ	15. Ⓐ Ⓑ Ⓒ Ⓓ Ⓔ
16. Ⓐ Ⓑ Ⓒ Ⓓ Ⓔ	16. Ⓐ Ⓑ Ⓒ Ⓓ Ⓔ	16. Ⓐ Ⓑ Ⓒ Ⓓ Ⓔ	16. Ⓐ Ⓑ Ⓒ Ⓓ Ⓔ	16. Ⓐ Ⓑ Ⓒ Ⓓ Ⓔ
17. Ⓐ Ⓑ Ⓒ Ⓓ Ⓔ	17. Ⓐ Ⓑ Ⓒ Ⓓ Ⓔ	17. Ⓐ Ⓑ Ⓒ Ⓓ Ⓔ	17. Ⓐ Ⓑ Ⓒ Ⓓ Ⓔ	17. Ⓐ Ⓑ Ⓒ Ⓓ Ⓔ
18. Ⓐ Ⓑ Ⓒ Ⓓ Ⓔ	18. Ⓐ Ⓑ Ⓒ Ⓓ Ⓔ	18. Ⓐ Ⓑ Ⓒ Ⓓ Ⓔ	18. Ⓐ Ⓑ Ⓒ Ⓓ Ⓔ	18. Ⓐ Ⓑ Ⓒ Ⓓ Ⓔ
19. Ⓐ Ⓑ Ⓒ Ⓓ Ⓔ	19. Ⓐ Ⓑ Ⓒ Ⓓ Ⓔ	19. Ⓐ Ⓑ Ⓒ Ⓓ Ⓔ	19. Ⓐ Ⓑ Ⓒ Ⓓ Ⓔ	19. Ⓐ Ⓑ Ⓒ Ⓓ Ⓔ
20. Ⓐ Ⓑ Ⓒ Ⓓ Ⓔ	20. Ⓐ Ⓑ Ⓒ Ⓓ Ⓔ	20. Ⓐ Ⓑ Ⓒ Ⓓ Ⓔ	20. Ⓐ Ⓑ Ⓒ Ⓓ Ⓔ	20. Ⓐ Ⓑ Ⓒ Ⓓ Ⓔ
21. Ⓐ Ⓑ Ⓒ Ⓓ Ⓔ	21. Ⓐ Ⓑ Ⓒ Ⓓ Ⓔ	21. Ⓐ Ⓑ Ⓒ Ⓓ Ⓔ	21. Ⓐ Ⓑ Ⓒ Ⓓ Ⓔ	21. Ⓐ Ⓑ Ⓒ Ⓓ Ⓔ
22. Ⓐ Ⓑ Ⓒ Ⓓ Ⓔ	22. Ⓐ Ⓑ Ⓒ Ⓓ Ⓔ	22. Ⓐ Ⓑ Ⓒ Ⓓ Ⓔ	22. Ⓐ Ⓑ Ⓒ Ⓓ Ⓔ	22. Ⓐ Ⓑ Ⓒ Ⓓ Ⓔ
23. Ⓐ Ⓑ Ⓒ Ⓓ Ⓔ	23. Ⓐ Ⓑ Ⓒ Ⓓ Ⓔ	23. Ⓐ Ⓑ Ⓒ Ⓓ Ⓔ	23. Ⓐ Ⓑ Ⓒ Ⓓ Ⓔ	23. Ⓐ Ⓑ Ⓒ Ⓓ Ⓔ
24. Ⓐ Ⓑ Ⓒ Ⓓ Ⓔ	24. Ⓐ Ⓑ Ⓒ Ⓓ Ⓔ	24. Ⓐ Ⓑ Ⓒ Ⓓ Ⓔ	24. Ⓐ Ⓑ Ⓒ Ⓓ Ⓔ	24. Ⓐ Ⓑ Ⓒ Ⓓ Ⓔ
25. Ⓐ Ⓑ Ⓒ Ⓓ Ⓔ	25. Ⓐ Ⓑ Ⓒ Ⓓ Ⓔ	25. Ⓐ Ⓑ Ⓒ Ⓓ Ⓔ	25. Ⓐ Ⓑ Ⓒ Ⓓ Ⓔ	25. Ⓐ Ⓑ Ⓒ Ⓓ Ⓔ
26. Ⓐ Ⓑ Ⓒ Ⓓ Ⓔ	26. Ⓐ Ⓑ Ⓒ Ⓓ Ⓔ	26. Ⓐ Ⓑ Ⓒ Ⓓ Ⓔ	26. Ⓐ Ⓑ Ⓒ Ⓓ Ⓔ	26. Ⓐ Ⓑ Ⓒ Ⓓ Ⓔ
27. Ⓐ Ⓑ Ⓒ Ⓓ Ⓔ	27. Ⓐ Ⓑ Ⓒ Ⓓ Ⓔ	27. Ⓐ Ⓑ Ⓒ Ⓓ Ⓔ	27. Ⓐ Ⓑ Ⓒ Ⓓ Ⓔ	27. Ⓐ Ⓑ Ⓒ Ⓓ Ⓔ
28. Ⓐ Ⓑ Ⓒ Ⓓ Ⓔ	28. Ⓐ Ⓑ Ⓒ Ⓓ Ⓔ	28. Ⓐ Ⓑ Ⓒ Ⓓ Ⓔ	28. Ⓐ Ⓑ Ⓒ Ⓓ Ⓔ	28. Ⓐ Ⓑ Ⓒ Ⓓ Ⓔ
29. Ⓐ Ⓑ Ⓒ Ⓓ Ⓔ	29. Ⓐ Ⓑ Ⓒ Ⓓ Ⓔ	29. Ⓐ Ⓑ Ⓒ Ⓓ Ⓔ	29. Ⓐ Ⓑ Ⓒ Ⓓ Ⓔ	29. Ⓐ Ⓑ Ⓒ Ⓓ Ⓔ
30. Ⓐ Ⓑ Ⓒ Ⓓ Ⓔ	30. Ⓐ Ⓑ Ⓒ Ⓓ Ⓔ	30. Ⓐ Ⓑ Ⓒ Ⓓ Ⓔ	30. Ⓐ Ⓑ Ⓒ Ⓓ Ⓔ	30. Ⓐ Ⓑ Ⓒ Ⓓ Ⓔ

SECTION I
TIME — 35 MINUTES
28 QUESTIONS

<u>Directions:</u> Read the passages and answer the questions following each passage by blackening the appropriate space on the answer sheet. You may refer back to the passages when answering the questions. Answer all questions on the basis of what is stated or implied.

The Constitution of the United States protects both property rights and freedom of speech. At times these rights
line conflict. Resolution then requires a
(5) determination as to the type of property involved. If the property is private and not open to the general public, the owner may absolutely deny the exercise of the right of free speech thereon. On
(10) the other hand, if public land is at issue, the First Amendment protections of expression are applicable. However, the exercise of free speech thereon is not absolute. Rather it is necessary to
(15) determine the appropriateness of the forum. This requires that consideration be given to a number of factors including: character and normal use of the property, the extent to which it is
(20) open to the public, and the number and types of persons who frequent it. If the forum is clearly public or clearly private, the resolution of the greater of rights is relatively straightforward.
(25) In the area of quasi-public property, balancing these rights has produced a dilemma. This is the situation when a private owner permits the general public to use his property. When persons seek
(30) to use the land for passing out handbills or picketing, how is a conflict between property rights and freedom of expression resolved?
The precept that a private property
(35) owner surrenders his rights in proportion to the extent to which he opens up his property to the public is not new. In 1675, Lord Chief Justice Hale wrote that when private property is
(40) "affected with a public interest, it ceases to be private." Throughout the development of Anglo-American law, the individual has never possessed absolute dominion over property. Land becomes
(45) clothed with a public interest when the owner devotes his property to a use in which the public has an interest. In

support of this position the chairman of the board of the Wilde Lake Shopping
(50) Center in Columbia, Maryland said:

The only real purpose and justification of any of these centers is to serve the people in the area—not the merchants, not the architects,
(55) not the developers. The success or failure of a regional shopping center will be measured by what it does for the people it seeks to serve.

These doctrines should be applied
(60) when accommodation must be made between a shopping center owner's private property rights and the public's right to free expression. It is hoped that when the Court is asked to balance
(65) these conflicting rights it will keep in mind what Justice Black said in 1945: "When we balance the Constitutional rights of owners of property against those of the people to enjoy (First
(70) Amendment) freedom(s) . . . we remain mindful of the fact that the latter occupy a preferred position."

1. In which one of the following cases would the owner of the property probably be most free to restrict the freedom of speech?

(A) an amusement park attended by five million people each year owned by a multinational company
(B) a small grocery store owned by a husband and wife
(C) an enclosed shopping mall owned by a single woman
(D) a fenced public garden and park owned by a small town
(E) an eight-unit residential apartment building owned by a large real estate company

GO ON TO THE NEXT PAGE ➤

2. A conflict between property rights and freedom of speech might arise in all of the following situations, EXCEPT

   (A) protesters carrying signs outside a cinema in an enclosed shopping mall
   (B) a disgruntled employee passing out leaflets in front of a hairdresser's salon
   (C) a religious order soliciting funds and converts in the swimming pool area of a condominium
   (D) a candidate for mayor handing out flyers in front of his opponent's headquarters
   (E) environmentalists carrying signs at the entrance to an oil refinery

3. According to the passage, an owner's freedom to deny freedom of speech on his property is determined by all of the following EXCEPT

   (A) whether or not the land is open to the public
   (B) the nature of and the usual use of the property
   (C) the type of person who frequents the land
   (D) the nature of character of the owner
   (E) how many people use the property

4. We can infer from the passage that the author believes that shopping malls in America

   (A) should be in the service of the people who frequent them
   (B) have a right to prohibit distribution of advertising handbills
   (C) have a right to prohibit the distribution of religious printed matter
   (D) have a right to control any distributed materials
   (E) should permit any charitable solicitations

5. According to the passage, the idea that a property owner's rights decline as the property is more used by the general public

   (A) is peculiar to recent Supreme Court decisions
   (B) is attested to by a three-hundred-year-old opinion
   (C) conflicts with the idea that property affected with a public interest ceases to be private
   (D) is in accord with the idea that ownership confers absolute dominion
   (E) is now universally accepted in Great Britain and in Canada

6. All other things being equal, the courts must favor

   (A) First Amendment rights over property rights
   (B) Fourth Amendment rights over property rights
   (C) property rights over First Amendment rights
   (D) property rights and First Amendment rights equally
   (E) property rights and Fourth Amendment rights equally

GO ON TO THE NEXT PAGE ➤

1   1   1   1   1

When completing *David Copperfield*, Dickens experienced a powerful aftereffect that left him confused about
line "whether to laugh or to cry . . . strangely
(5) divided . . . between sorrow and joy." He felt that he had been turned inside out, his inner life now visible, in partly disguised forms, in the shadowy world of ordinary daylight. The story he had
(10) written was so deeply personal that "no one can believe [it] in the reading, more than I have believed it in the writing." Having transformed his private memories and his emotional life into a
(15) public myth about himself, particularly his development from an abandoned child into a great popular artist surrounded by love and success, he felt the excitement both of exposure and
(20) catharsis. Exorcising the wounds of childhood and young adulthood, he also dramatized the unresolved problems of his personality and his marriage, anticipating the turmoil that was to
(25) come. Though energized by the process of writing, he was also exhausted by "heaps of Copperfieldian blots," by that "tremendous paroxysm of Copperfield." Towards the end, he felt "rigid with
(30) Copperfield . . . from head to foot." When he finally put down his pen in October 1850, he took up his "idea of wandering somewhere for a day or two." Almost inevitably, he went back "to
(35) Rochester . . . where I was a small boy."
    In *David Copperfield* he re-created in mythic terms his relationship with his mother, his father, his siblings, particularly Fanny, and with his wife and
(40) his wife's sisters. The novel was more precious to him than his own children because the favorite child was himself. Soon after beginning, he confessed that he had stuck to that fictional name
(45) through the exploration of alternative titles because he had, even at the earliest stage, recognized that he was writing a book about himself.
    His passion for names also expressed
(50) his need to pattern and control. After the birth of Katie in 1839, he assumed the right to name all his children (Catherine had "little or nothing to say" about that). The elaborate christening of
(55) Alfred D'Orsay Tennyson Dickens provides the representative example of the novelist imposing his literary constructs on other people's lives as well as his own. When it came to his
(60) family, he did not admit of any distinction. When it came to his novels, the distinction between self and other was subordinated to the dramatization of the many varieties of the single self.
(65) Changing Charles Dickens into David Copperfield had the force both of unconscious reversal and of minimal autobiographical distancing. At the heart of the novel was a partly mediated
(70) version of himself that represented his effort to claim that he had come through, that all was well with him as he approached the age of forty.

7. Which one of the following best expresses the main idea of the passage?

(A) The creation of *David Copperfield* was, for Dickens, a painful, wrenching experience.
(B) While writing *David Copperfield*, Dickens put his novel above everything else, including his children.
(C) In creating *David Copperfield*, Dickens transformed his memories and feelings into a public myth about himself.
(D) In addition to being autobiographical, *David Copperfield* is a prophetic novel.
(E) *David Copperfield*, in addition to being Dickens' most auto-biographical novel, is also his greatest masterpiece.

GO ON TO THE NEXT PAGE ➤

1   **1**   **1**   **1**   **1**

8. The author's primary intention in this passage is to

   (A) provide a psychological study of Dickens' motivations for writing *David Copperfield* and suggest a basis for evaluating the novel
   (B) create a picture of Dickens as a writer burdened by childhood memories and contrast this with his public image
   (C) show the connection between Dickens as a self-centered husband and father and as a literary genius
   (D) present Dickens' reactions to writing *David Copperfield* and comment on the novel's relationship to his life and personality
   (E) describe Dickens as he finished *David Copperfield* and show how that novel became a turning point in his career

9. The purpose of the last sentence of paragraph one (lines 34–35) is to

   (A) show Dickens' complete exhaustion after finishing *David Copperfield*
   (B) emphasize the connection between Dickens' writing of *David Copperfield* and his own childhood memories
   (C) indicate Dickens' emotional response to writing *David Copperfield* and his inability to separate reality from fiction
   (D) inform the reader of Dickens' actual origins as opposed to the fictional origins created in *David Copperfield*
   (E) show that in finishing *David Copperfield* Dickens had finally exorcised the traumas of his childhood

10. Which one of the following can be inferred about Charles Dickens' life from information presented in the passage?

    (A) His marriage would end badly.
    (B) His most successful works were heavily autobiographical.
    (C) He was a distant, uncaring father.
    (D) His relationship with his sister Fanny had been significant to him.
    (E) Because of the problems in his childhood, he was a man driven by the need for public success.

11. According to the passage, the title of *David Copperfield* is most significant because it

    (A) demonstrates Dickens' view of the protagonist as a version of himself
    (B) with the unconscious reversal of initials, shows Dickens' inability to come to terms with his life
    (C) demonstrates Dickens' need to pattern and control his experience
    (D) is a prime example of Dickens' passion for names
    (E) represents both Dickens seeing the protagonist as himself and playing a game with the reader

12. The primary effect of lines 50–54—"After the birth of Katie in 1839, he assumed the right to name all his children (Catherine had 'little to say' about that)"—is to

    (A) suggest that Catherine Dickens was an inadequate mother
    (B) indicate that Dickens' creativity with names extended to his family
    (C) show that Dickens tended to confuse art with life
    (D) suggest the relationship between Dickens and Catherine
    (E) indicate that Dickens put his work over his family life

13. Which one of the following best describes the author's tone in the passage?

    (A) cool and ironic
    (B) argumentative and sarcastic
    (C) detached and condescending
    (D) intimate and persuasive
    (E) objective and analytical

GO ON TO THE NEXT PAGE ➤

1   1   1   1   1

14. Which one of the following best describes the structure of the passage?

(A) Paragraph one focuses on Dickens' reactions to writing *David Copperfield,* while paragraph two includes more of the author's comments and ties in related points.

(B) Paragraph one recounts Dickens' problems in writing *David Copperfield,* while paragraph two describes his creative solutions and his reactions to the work.

(C) Paragraph one presents Dickens' opinions of *David Copperfield,* while paragraph two provides the author's critique and relates the book to Dickens' other works.

(D) Paragraph one describes Dickens' relationship to his novels, while paragraph two describes his relationship to his family.

(E) Paragraph one shows the effect of his childhood on Dickens, while paragraph two describes his later life and its effect on his novels.

GO ON TO THE NEXT PAGE ➤

American society in the eighteenth century operated according to the logic of a closed system. Whatever the scope
line of concern—a family, a community, a
(5) new nation, an empire—the guiding assumptions in each case established a framework of rules or principles, a container of truth that defined relationships and consequences inside
(10) its bounds. Sometimes the source of these principles lay in heavenly writ, sometimes in natural law, more often in some blend of the sacred and the secular. Always, however, they existed
(15) above and prior to human actions, and therefore they always stood ready as a measure of virtue in the present and a basis for prescriptions about the future. Rarely were these truths considered
(20) incomprehensible. Although ordinary citizens might require a learned elite to explain them, their meaning nevertheless fell within the ken of human reason. Hence, everyone was
(25) obligated to adapt their ways to these overarching rules, as they were commonly understood, and anyone could reasonably judge others, wherever they lived, by their degree of conformity
(30) to the same immutable principles.

Applying these principles was a delicate art that demanded quite different skills in a familiar, local setting than in a broad, impersonal one.
(35) The center of eighteenth-century society was the family in a community. Across an impressive American diversity, family and community interconnected in a great many forms, ranging from
(40) Mennonite settlements where the community almost swallowed its families to kinship systems in South Carolina and Virginia with a very loose attachment to a county seat or a region.
(45) Every variation, however, set family units to manage the particulars of everyday life in a manner that constrained each unit by the values all of them held in common. These
(50) controls, in turn, were reinforced by an assumption of the community's permanence. People expected to spend a lifetime with the same faces, the same family names, the same pattern of
(55) institutions, the same routines of work and pleasure, and as they judged these

intimate relations by their superstructure of truths, they drew upon an accretion of knowledge about
(60) individuals and families and customary ways to estimate, day by day, the state of their immediate society.

The farther their vision extended beyond the community however, the
(65) more people relied upon an explicit demonstration that the affairs concerning them in a wider environment were actually abiding by the correct principles. An obsession with the exact
(70) privileges of a colonial legislature and the precise extent of Britain's imperial power, the specifics of a state constitution and the absolute necessity of a federal one, all expressed this urge
(75) for a careful articulation as proof that the right relationship with external powers did indeed prevail. Unlike the calculations of a community's health, which gave significance to everybody's
(80) accumulated knowledge about their neighbors and their traditions, these broad applications of principle belonged almost exclusively to an elite. The more a wider world affected the life of a
(85) community, the more its members looked to an elite for mediation—to explain distant events, to negotiate with distant authorities. During times of crisis relationships inside a community
(90) that might otherwise have been quite fluid tended to solidify behind a very few leaders in order to meet an external danger.

GO ON TO THE NEXT PAGE ➤

15. According to the passage, which one of the following best describes the closed nature of eighteenth-century American society?

(A) People in the society were expected to stay in the positions they were born to rather than to strive to achieve higher rank.

(B) The society was run according to principles laid down in the Bible, and all citizens were expected to adhere to these.

(C) A respect for tradition led citizens to entrust the workings of the community to a knowledgeable elite and to follow a small group of strong leaders.

(D) The society operated on the assumption that set principles existed that could be used both to live by and to measure actions against.

(E) People in the society expected to remain in the same area and among the same people for their entire lives, which ensured they would know each other well.

16. In paragraph two of the passage, the author refers to Mennonite settlements and kinship systems (lines 36–44) in order to

(A) suggest that America in the eighteenth century was inhabited by a diverse population with different ideas

(B) provide examples of the variety of religious sects existing in eighteenth-century America

(C) illustrate that while eighteenth-century American families and communities interacted, they did so in different ways

(D) emphasize that religious principles were essential in eighteenth-century America to ensure the strength of the society

(E) show the superiority of eighteenth-century American communities based on religious ties to those based on kinship ties alone

17. According to information in the passage, which one of the following was an effect of a community's permanence?

(A) It allowed people to develop looser state governments that did not require written laws and principles.

(B) It allowed people to know their communities well enough to make confident judgments about them.

(C) It limited the growth of communities and therefore the dissemination of principles necessary to maintain a closed system.

(D) It prevented an influx of outsiders who would stand in opposition to the community's principles.

(E) It limited innovations in thought and action that might ultimately lead to changes in the community's principles.

18. The function of the second paragraph of the passage is to

(A) explain in detail the historical background of the closed system introduced in paragraph one

(B) describe the roles of family and community in maintaining the closed system defined in paragraph one

(C) illustrate the contrast between the strong influence of communities and the closed system described in paragraph one

(D) provide a transition between the closed system shown in paragraph one and the political activities described in paragraph three

(E) contrast communities built on religious ties with communities built on kinship ties

1   **1**   **1**   **1**   **1**

19. From information in the passage, which one of the following best explains the statement that a federal constitution was an "absolute necessity" (line 73)?

(A) People did not trust a strong centralized government because of their past experiences.

(B) People wanted explicit details set forth in matters that affected them but were outside their immediate community.

(C) People wanted to prevent the development of an elite governing body that would operate without any restrictions.

(D) People demanded strong safeguards in writing to prevent British imperial power from encroaching on them.

(E) People trusted written documents much more than they trusted unwritten principles, in spite of their respect for the principles.

20. Which one of the following best describes the relationship between the points made in paragraph three and the description of the society in paragraph one?

(A) Because the society operated in adherence to immutable general principles (paragraph one), people needed assurance that events beyond their usual scope of activities were also in accordance with these principles (paragraph three).

(B) Because people lived in a closed system that allowed little variation in belief (paragraph one), they mistrusted anyone outside who seemed to adhere to a different set of principles (paragraph three).

(C) Because the society was based heavily on religious principles and beliefs (paragraph one), people were unsure of themselves in dealing with secular concerns such as legislatures and constitutions (paragraph three).

(D) Because eighteenth-century American society was generally stable and operated on clear principles (paragraph one), people found it difficult to deal with change and tended to follow strong leaders in times of crisis (paragraph three).

(E) Because the society relied on families to pass on general principles and community ideals (paragraph one), people judged outside events and affairs according to the way their own family units operated (paragraph three).

GO ON TO THE NEXT PAGE ➤

1   1   1   1   1

21. From information in the passage, which one of the following can we infer would be the *least likely* advice to come from an average eighteenth-century American?

   (A) Trust the voice within you, and always question authority.
   (B) Gain wisdom by listening to those older and more experienced than you.
   (C) Hold your reputation dear, for you may be judged by your good name.
   (D) Be a pillar of strength in both community and family.
   (E) Be vigilant in pursuing truth, and turn to God for guidance.

22. Which one of the following best expresses the main idea of the passage?

   (A) Eighteenth-century American society was both a culmination of and a reaction to America's colonial status.
   (B) Eighteenth-century American society relied primarily on families and communities to ensure that rules and laws were obeyed.
   (C) The primary contrast in eighteenth-century American society was between self-enclosed communities and communities as part of a wider environment.
   (D) Eighteenth-century American society was based on a set of accepted rules that provided a framework for people's actions and judgments.
   (E) The set principles upon which eighteenth-century American society was built were applied both effectively and ineffectively, depending on the context.

GO ON TO THE NEXT PAGE ➤

Taxonomy, the science of classifying and ordering organisms, has an undeserved reputation as a harmless,
line and mindless, activity of listing,
(5) cataloguing, and describing—consider the common idea of a birdwatcher, up at 5:30 in the morning with binoculars, short pants, and "life list" of every bird he has seen. Even among scientists,
(10) taxonomy is often treated as "stamp collecting." It was not always so. During the eighteenth and early nineteenth centuries, taxonomy was in the forefront of the sciences. The greatest
(15) biologists of Europe were professional taxonomists—Linnaeus, Cuvier, Lamarck. Darwin's major activity during the twenty years separating his Malthusian insights from the
(20) publication of his evolutionary theory was a three-volume work on the taxonomy of barnacles. Thomas Jefferson took time out from the affairs of state to publish one of the great
(25) taxonomic errors in the history of paleontology—he described a giant sloth claw as a lion's three times the size of Africa's version. These heady days were marked by discovery as naturalists
(30) collected the fauna and flora of previously uncharted regions. They were also marked by the emergence of intellectual structure, as coherent classifications seemed to mirror the
(35) order of God's thought.

America played its part in this great epoch of natural history. We often forget that 150 years ago much of our continent was as unknown and
(40) potentially hazardous as any place on earth. During the eighteenth century, when most naturalists denied the possibility of extinction, explorers expected to find mammoths and other
(45) formidable fossil creatures alive in the American West. There are a number of passionate, single-minded iconoclasts who fought the hostility of the wilderness, and often of urban literary
(50) people, to disclose the rich fauna and flora of America. For the most part, they worked alone, with small support from patrons or government. The Lewis and Clark expedition is an exception—and
(55) its primary purpose was not natural history. We may now look upon tales of

frontier toughness and perseverance as the necessary mythology of a nation too young to have real legends. But there is
(60) often a residue of truth in such tales, and naturalists are among the genuine pioneers.

Alexander Wilson walked from New England to Charleston peddling
(65) subscriptions to his *American Ornithology*. Thomas Nuttall—oblivious to danger, a Parsifal under a lucky star, vanquishing every Klingsor in the woods, discovered some of the rarest,
(70) most beautiful, and most useful of American plants. J. J. Audubon drank his way across Europe selling his beautiful pictures of birds to lords and kings. John Lawson, captured by
(75) Tuscarora Indians, met the following fate according to an eyewitness: "They struck him full of fine small, splinters or torchwoods like hog's bristles and so set them gradually afire." David Douglas
(80) fell into a pit trap for wild cattle and was stomped to death by a bull.

23. According to the passage, taxonomy was considered to be an important science from about

(A) 1700 to 1800
(B) 1700 to 1830
(C) 1700 to 1950
(D) 1800 to 1930
(E) 1818 to 1918

24. As they are used in the first paragraph (line 30), "flora and fauna" refer to

(A) lands and waters
(B) botanists and zoologists
(C) plants and animals
(D) cataloging and describing
(E) mythology and folklore

GO ON TO THE NEXT PAGE ➤

25. We can infer from the passage that

    (A) taxonomy was favorably regarded in the sixteenth and seventeenth centuries
    (B) taxonomy was invented in the eighteenth century
    (C) the number of kinds of barnacles is very large
    (D) Lamarck and Linnaeus were amateur scientists
    (E) most of the world's plants have already been classified

26. The relation of the third paragraph to the rest of the passage may be best described as

    (A) a comic contrast to the seriousness of the first two paragraphs
    (B) specific examples of the pioneers mentioned in the second paragraph
    (C) examples of American taxonomists to set against the exclusively European names of the first paragraph
    (D) real taxonomists of the western United States as opposed to the legendary figures of the second paragraph
    (E) examples of the tall tales of the frontier days

27. In the third paragraph, Parsifal and Klingsor were probably a

    (A) hunter and his prey
    (B) German taxonomist and his subject of study
    (C) knight and his enemy
    (D) a colonizer and the colonized
    (E) a mythical animal and its master

28. This passage is best described as a(n)

    (A) description of the modern bias against taxonomy
    (B) comparison of nineteenth-century and twentieth-century scientists
    (C) account of famous American naturalists
    (D) history and defense of taxonomy
    (E) argument for the renewed study of the classification of organisms

STOP

IF YOU FINISH BEFORE TIME IS UP, CHECK YOUR WORK ON THIS SECTION OF THE TEST ONLY.
DO NOT GO ON TO THE NEXT SECTION OF THE TEST UNTIL TIME IS UP FOR THIS SECTION.

2 **2** **2** **2**

SECTION II
TIME — 35 MINUTES
24 QUESTIONS

<u>Directions:</u> In this section you will be given groups of questions based on different sets of conditions. Drawing a simple diagram may be helpful in answering some of the questions. You are to choose the best answer and mark the corresponding space on your answer sheet.

<u>Questions 1–6</u>

A radio station will play eight songs during its "Winners" hour. Each song will be played once. The eight songs represent the following types of music: Jazz, Rock, and Country, with at least two songs of each type. The following restrictions are placed on the order and type of songs:

 All the jazz songs are played consecutively.

 No two rock songs are played consecutively.

 No two country songs are played consecutively.

 A rock song must be played before a jazz song is played.

 There are more jazz songs than country songs.

1. If four jazz songs are played and the first and last songs are of the same type, which one of the following must be true?

 (A) A jazz song is played second.
 (B) A jazz song is played third.
 (C) A rock song is played seventh.
 (D) A rock song is played eighth.
 (E) A country song is played first.

2. If three rock songs are played and a country song is played sixth, which one of the following CANNOT be true?

 (A) A jazz song is played second.
 (B) A rock song is played fifth.
 (C) A rock song is played first.
 (D) A country song is played last.
 (E) A country song is played first.

3. If a jazz song is played third, and the first and last songs are of the same type, which one of the following CANNOT be true?

 (A) A jazz song is sixth.
 (B) A country song is sixth.
 (C) A country song is first.
 (D) A rock song is second.
 (E) A rock song is seventh.

4. If all the jazz songs are played last, how many different arrangements of song types are possible?

 (A) one
 (B) two
 (C) three
 (D) four
 (E) five

5. If a country song is played first and seventh, which one of the following must be true?

 (A) A country song is sixth.
 (B) A jazz song is sixth.
 (C) A country song is third.
 (D) A jazz song is second.
 (E) A jazz song is third.

6. If a single classical song is added to the play list (making nine songs in all) and it is to be played fourth and a country song is to be played fifth, which one of the following must be true?

 (A) A jazz song is sixth.
 (B) A jazz song is last.
 (C) A rock song is second.
 (D) A rock song is third.
 (E) A country song is last.

GO ON TO THE NEXT PAGE ➤

2   **2**   **2**   **2**   **2**

Questions 7–13

Seven students—George, Hal, Ken, Jon, Neil, Lynn, and Melanie—are playing a game involving play money. The only bills used are play dollar bills. No coins are used.

> Jon has more bills than Lynn, Melanie, and Neil combined.
>
> The total of Lynn's and Melanie's bills are equal to Neil's bills.
>
> Melanie has more bills than Ken and George combined.
>
> Hal has fewer bills than George.
>
> Ken and George have the same number of bills.

7. Which one of the following students has the most bills?

    (A) Ken
    (B) George
    (C) Jon
    (D) Lynn
    (E) Melanie

8. Which one of the following students has the fewest bills?

    (A) Melanie
    (B) Neil
    (C) George
    (D) Ken
    (E) Hal

9. Which one of the following must be true?

    (A) Melanie has fewer bills than Ken.
    (B) Neil has more bills than Lynn.
    (C) Lynn has fewer bills than Melanie.
    (D) Lynn has more bills than George.
    (E) George has more bills than Melanie.

10. Assume that Ken is given one bill from Hal. Assume also that Melanie has more bills than Ken, George, and Lynn combined. If none of the students has the same number of bills, which one of the following is a possible order from highest to lowest of students who have the most bills?

    (A) Jon, Melanie, Lynn, Neil, Ken, George, Hal

    (B) Jon, Neil, Melanie, Lynn, George, Ken, Hal
    (C) Neil, Jon, Melanie, George, Ken, Hal, Lynn
    (D) Jon, Neil, Ken, Melanie, George, Lynn, Hal
    (E) Jon, Neil, Melanie, Ken, George, Hal, Lynn

11. Assume that Lynn does not have the same number of bills as Ken. Which one of the following must be FALSE?

    (A) Lynn has the same number of bills as Hal.
    (B) Neil has twice as many bills as Melanie.
    (C) George has more bills than Hal and Lynn combined.
    (D) George does not have the same number of bills as Lynn.
    (E) Jon has fewer than twice the number of Lynn's and Melanie's bills combined.

12. If Lynn and Melanie have the same number of bills, then which one of the following must be FALSE?

    (A) Neil has more bills than Melanie.
    (B) Melanie has more bills than Ken, George, and Hal combined.
    (C) George has fewer bills than Hal and Ken combined.
    (D) Neil has fewer bills than Lynn, George, and Hal combined.
    (E) Jon has more bills than Lynn, Ken, George, and Hal combined.

13. Assume that Tom decides to join the game. Assume also that he is given bills from the bank. If his total number of bills are more than Ken's and fewer than Lynn's, which one of the following must be true?

    (A) Melanie has fewer bills than Tom.
    (B) Tom has fewer bills than George.
    (C) Lynn has fewer bills than Melanie.
    (D) Melanie and Lynn have the same number of bills.
    (E) Lynn has more bills than Hal.

GO ON TO THE NEXT PAGE ➤

2   **2**

<u>Questions 14–20</u>

At the snack bar at a party, Alli, Boris, Cisco, and Dan are eating cookies. There are five kinds of cookies to choose from— chocolate chip cookies, oatmeal cookies, sugar cookies, peanut butter cookies, and raisin cookies. Each of these four people eat at least two kinds of cookies. Their choices are governed by the following rules:

At most two of them eat oatmeal cookies.

At least two of them eat sugar cookies.

Alli does not eat any sugar cookies.

Boris and Cisco do not eat the same type of cookie.

Boris eats chocolate chip cookies.

Cisco eats sugar cookies.

No one eats both raisin cookies and sugar cookies.

If someone eats raisin cookies, they also eat peanut butter cookies.

14. Which one of the following must be true?

(A) Cisco eats chocolate chip cookies.
(B) Alli eats chocolate chip cookies.
(C) Boris does not eat peanut butter cookies.
(D) Dan does not eat raisin cookies.
(E) Alli does not eat peanut butter cookies.

15. If Boris eats exactly three kinds of cookies, which one of the following must be true?

(A) Cisco eats exactly three kinds of cookies.
(B) Dan eats only sugar cookies.
(C) If Alli eats oatmeal cookies, Dan eats oatmeal cookies.
(D) Boris eats oatmeal cookies.
(E) Cisco eats oatmeal cookies.

16. Which one of the following CANNOT be true?

(A) No one eats raisin cookies.
(B) Alli and Dan both eat oatmeal cookies.
(C) Alli and Dan both eat chocolate chip cookies.
(D) Boris and Cisco eat the same number of kinds of cookies.
(E) Dan does not eat raisin cookies.

17. Which pair of cookie types could each be eaten by at least three different people?

(A) chocolate chip and oatmeal
(B) oatmeal and peanut butter
(C) chocolate chip and peanut butter
(D) oatmeal and sugar
(E) sugar and raisin

18. Which pair of cookie types contains a cookie type eaten by exactly two different people?

(A) chocolate chip and oatmeal
(B) oatmeal and peanut butter
(C) chocolate chip and peanut butter
(D) oatmeal and raisin
(E) sugar and raisin

19. If Alli does not eat chocolate chip or raisin cookies, which one of the following could be true?

(A) Dan eats oatmeal cookies.
(B) More people eat chocolate chip cookies than sugar cookies.
(C) Only one person eats peanut butter cookies.
(D) Cisco does not eat peanut butter cookies.
(E) Boris eats sugar cookies.

20. Which cookie type could be eaten by none of the people?

(A) chocolate chip
(B) oatmeal
(C) sugar
(D) peanut butter
(E) raisin

GO ON TO THE NEXT PAGE ➤

2   **2**

Questions 21–24

The National Domino League is planning to expand by adding one more team. All of the players for the new team will be chosen from the existing teams. Each team must make three players eligible to be chosen for the new team.

(1) The players eligible to be chosen from Team 1 are A, B, and C.
(2) The players eligible to be chosen from Team 2 are D, E, and F.
(3) The players eligible to be chosen from Team 3 are G, H, and K.
(4) The new team must choose two players from each of the three teams.
(5) B refuses to play with D.
(6) If C is chosen, then K must be chosen.
(7) G and H refuse to play together.

21. If A is not chosen, then how many members of the new team are determined?

(A) 2
(B) 3
(C) 4
(D) 5
(E) 6

22. If D is chosen, then which one of the following groups of three players could NOT be chosen?

(A) A, G, K
(B) B, C, G
(C) C, E, K
(D) A, E, G
(E) E, H, K

23. Which one of the following is (are) true?

(A) C must be chosen.
(B) If A is chosen, then F must be chosen.
(C) If B is chosen, then E must be chosen.
(D) E must be chosen.
(E) If G is chosen, then K is not chosen.

24. In addition to facts (1), (2), (3), and (4), which of the facts lead(s) to the conclusion that K must be chosen?

(A) (5)
(B) (6)
(C) (7)
(D) (6) and (7)
(E) (5), (6), and (7)

STOP

IF YOU FINISH BEFORE TIME IS UP, CHECK YOUR WORK ON THIS SECTION OF THE TEST ONLY.
DO NOT GO ON TO THE NEXT SECTION OF THE TEST UNTIL TIME IS UP FOR THIS SECTION.

3   **3**   **3**   **3**   **3**

SECTION III
TIME — 35 MINUTES
26 QUESTIONS

<u>Directions</u>: In this section you will be given brief statements or passages and will be required to evaluate the reasoning involved. In some instances, more than one choice will appear to be a possible answer. You are to choose the *best* answer. Use common sense and reasonableness in making your selection; then mark the proper space on the answer sheet.

1. *Mr. Kent:* Recent studies show that reduction in the maximum speed limit from 65 mph to 55 mph substantially reduces the number of highway fatalities.

   The preceding statement would be most weakened by establishing that

   (A) most fatal car accidents occur at night
   (B) most accidents occurring at speeds between 45 and 55 mph are nonfatal
   (C) few fatal accidents involve only one vehicle
   (D) prior to this reduction, 97 percent of fatal accidents occurred below 45 mph
   (E) prior to the reduction, 97 percent of fatal accidents occurred between 55 and 65 mph

2. Board member Smith will vote for the busing of students if she is reelected to the board. If the busing of students is passed by the board, then Smith was not reelected to the board. Smith was reelected to the board.

   Given the foregoing information, which one of the following can be concluded?

   (A) Smith assisted in the passage of student busing.
   (B) The passage of busing carried Smith to a reelection victory.
   (C) Smith voted against busing; however, it still passed.
   (D) Busing was defeated despite Smith's vote in favor of it.
   (E) Student busing was voted down by a majority of the board.

3. Daniel Webster said, "Falsehoods not only disagree with truths, but usually quarrel among themselves."

   Which one of these would follow from Webster's statement?

   (A) Quarreling is endemic to American political life.
   (B) Truth and falsehood can be distinguished from one another.
   (C) Liars often quarrel with each other.
   (D) Those who know the truth are normally silent.
   (E) Truth and falsehood are emotional, rather than intellectual, phenomena.

GO ON TO THE NEXT PAGE ➤

3   **3**   **3**   **3**   **3**

4. A recording industry celebrity observed: "I am not a star because all my songs are hits; all my songs are hits because I am a star."

Which one of the following most nearly parallels this reasoning?

(A) A college professor noted: "I am the final word in the classroom not because my judgment is always correct, but my judgment in the classroom is always correct because I am the instructor."

(B) A nurse observed: "I am not competent in my duties because I am a nurse, but I am competent in my duties because of my training in nursing."

(C) A dance instructor noted: "I am not the instructor because I know all there is about dance; rather I am an instructor because of my ability to teach dancing."

(D) A recording industry celebrity observed: "I am not wealthy because I am a star; I am wealthy because so many people buy my recordings."

(E) A recording industry celebrity observed: "I am not a star because my every song is enjoyed; I am a star because people pay to watch me perform."

5. *Economist:* As a rule, the price of gasoline at the pump increases when the oil refineries in the United States are operating at below 75 percent of capacity. If the unrest in the Middle East continues, the shipment of oil to the United States will decline and refineries here will have to operate at 60 percent of capacity for at least six months.

If the statements above are correct, which one of the following is the most likely conclusion?

(A) Imports from oil producing areas other than the Middle East are likely to increase next year.

(B) A sudden resolution of tensions in the Middle East will have little or no effect on the price of gasoline.

(C) Oil prices decline only when refineries in the United States operate at more than 75 percent of their capacity.

(D) The rise or fall in gasoline prices is determined by supply and demand and not by political events.

(E) It is likely that prices of gasoline in the United States will increase in the next year.

GO ON TO THE NEXT PAGE ➤

3   **3**   **3**   **3**   **3**

6. If a speaker were highly credible, would an objectively irrelevant personal characteristic of the speaker influence the effectiveness of her communication? For example, if a Nobel prize-winning chemist were speaking on inorganic chemistry, would she induce a lesser change in the opinions of an audience if she were known to be a poor cook? Would the speaker's effectiveness be different if she were obese rather than trim, sloppy rather than neat, ugly rather than attractive?

   By failing to consider irrelevant aspects of communicator credibility, studies in communication science have unknowingly implied that audiences are composed of individuals who are responsive only to objectively relevant aspects of a speaker.

   Which one of the following represent(s) assumptions upon which the foregoing passage is based?

   (A) Audiences are composed of people who are responsive only to objectively relevant aspects of a communicator.
   (B) Objectively irrelevant personal characteristics have a bearing on a speaker's effectiveness.
   (C) Some characteristics of a communicator are of greater relevance than others.
   (D) A trim speaker is likely to be more persuasive than an obese one.
   (E) Irrelevant aspects of a communication have more effect on an audience than the content of a speech.

Questions 7–8

I read with interest the statements of eminent archaeologists that the presence of a crude snare in an early Neolithic grave indicates that man of this period subsisted by snaring small mammals. I find this assertion open to question. How do I know the companions of the deceased did not toss the snare into the grave with the corpse because it had proved to be totally useless?

7. The author employs which one of the following as a method of questioning the archaeologists' claims?

   (A) evidence that contradicts the conclusion drawn by the archaeologists
   (B) a doubtful tone about the motives of the archaeologists
   (C) a body of knowledge inconsistent with that employed by the archaeologists
   (D) an alternative to the conclusion drawn by the archaeologists
   (E) the suggestion that archaeological studies are of little use

8. Which one of the following best expresses the author's criticism of the archaeologists whose statements he questions?

   (A) They have not subjected their conclusions to scientific verification.
   (B) They have stressed one explanation and ignored others.
   (C) They have drawn a conclusion that does not fit the evidence upon which it was based.
   (D) They failed to employ proper scientific methods in arriving at their conclusion.
   (E) They have based their conclusion on behaviors exhibited by more modern humans.

GO ON TO THE NEXT PAGE ➤

9. Semanticists point out that words and phrases often acquire connotations tinged with emotions. Such significances are attached because of the context, the history of the usage of the expression, or the background of the person reading or listening. Thus, "the hills of home" may evoke a feeling of nostalgia or a pleasant sensation; but "Bolshevik" may arouse derision or disgust in the minds of many people.

   The term "progressive education" has gone through several stages in the connotative process. At one time progressive education was hailed as the harbinger of all that was wise and wholesome in classroom practice, such as the recognition of individual differences and the revolution against formalized dictatorial procedures. However, partly because of abuses on the fanatical fringe of the movement, many people began to associate progressive schools with frills, fads, and follies. What had been discovered and developed by Froebel in Germany, by Pestalozzi in Switzerland, by Montessori in Italy, and by men like Parker and Dewey in the United States was muddled in a melange of mockery and misunderstanding and submerged in satirical quips. As a result, many educators have recently avoided the expression and have chosen to call present educational practices "new" or "modern" rather than "progressive."

Which one of the following would most seriously weaken the author's argument?

(A) In a recent poll of American voters, 76 percent responded that they would certainly not vote for the Progressive Labor Party.
(B) Open classrooms have recently fallen out of the educational limelight.
(C) New techniques in teaching cognitive skills, called "progressive learning," have recently met with widespread approval in middle class public schools.
(D) Parker and Dewey were well respected by academicians and educational theorists.
(E) Every new advance in education is first denounced as a "fad."

10. *Bill:* Professor Smith has been late for class almost every morning.
    Dave: That can't be true; he was on time yesterday.

Dave apparently believes that Bill has said which one of the following?

(A) Professor Smith is seldom late.
(B) Professor Smith does not enjoy teaching.
(C) Professor Smith has been late every day without exception.
(D) Professor Smith was late yesterday.
(E) Professor Smith informs Bill of his whereabouts.

11. Sunbathers do not usually spend much time in the shade. Shade prevails during most of June in La Jolla. It is June 14.

Which one of the following conclusions would be logically defensible, based upon the foregoing premises?

(A) La Jolla is the site of frequent sunbathing.
(B) The sun is not shining today.
(C) There are sunbathers in La Jolla today.
(D) There may be sunbathers in La Jolla today.
(E) There are more sunbathers in La Jolla in July than in June.

12. *Political Theorist:* Although American politicians disagree about many things, none of them disagrees with Wendell Wilkie's assertion that "the Constitution does not provide for first- and second-class citizens."

Wilkie's statement implies that

(A) the Constitution provides for third- and fourth-class citizens
(B) first-class citizens don't need to be provided for
(C) there is no such thing as a second-class citizen
(D) the Constitution makes no class distinctions
(E) no citizens can be first and second class simultaneously

GO ON TO THE NEXT PAGE ➤

3　　**3**　　**3**　　**3**　　**3**

13. There are 500 students in the school. In the fall semester, 30 were in the glee club, 30 were members of the debating society, and 40 were on the staff of the school newspaper. In the spring semester, all three of these activities had twice as many participants. Thus, in the course of the school year, all but 200 of the 500 students in the school participated in these extracurricular activities.

All of the following can be used to question the conclusion of this passage EXCEPT

(A) some students participated in more than one activity in the fall semester
(B) some students participated in an activity in more than one semester
(C) some students participated in activities in only the fall semester
(D) some students never participated in activities
(E) some students participated in more than one activity in both semesters

14. Nothing can come of nothing; nothing can go back to nothing.

Which one of the following follows most logically from the above statement?

(A) Something can come out of something; something can go back to something.
(B) Something can come out of nothing; something can go back to nothing.
(C) Nothing can come out of something; nothing can go back to something.
(D) Something must come out of something; something must go back to something.
(E) Something must come out of something; nothing can go back to nothing.

15. The president has vowed in speeches across the country that there will be no increase in taxes and no reduction in defense; he has repeatedly challenged Congress to narrow the deficit through deeper spending cuts. Congressional critics have responded with labored comparisons between a bloated Pentagon and the nation's poor being lacerated by merciless budget cutters. In Democratic cloakrooms, laments about the "intolerable deficit" are code words for higher taxes.

Which one of the following additions to the passage would make clear the author's position on the budget issue?

(A) Everyone agrees that the president's budget deficit of around 100 billion is highly undesirable, to say the least.
(B) Everyone agrees that the president's budget deficit is both undesirable and unavoidable.
(C) Everyone agrees that this will be a summer of hot debate in Congress over the president's budget proposal.
(D) Everyone agrees that the partisan disagreement over the president's budget proposal will be won by those who create the most persuasive terminology.
(E) Everyone agrees that the president's budget proposal is a product of careful, honest, but sometimes misguided analysis.

GO ON TO THE NEXT PAGE ➤

3   **3**   **3**   **3**   **3**

16. *The average wage in this plant comes to exactly $7.87 per working day.* In this statement *average* has the strict mathematical sense. It is the quotient obtained by dividing the sum of all wages for a given period by the product of the number of workers and the number of days in the period.

    Which one of the following is the most logical implication of the passage above?

    (A) More workers in the plant earn $7.87 per day than those who do not earn $7.87 per day.
    (B) Any particular worker in the plant receives $7.87 per day.
    (C) There must be workers in the plant who earn far more than $7.87 per day.
    (D) If some workers in the plant earn more than $7.87 per day, there must be others in the plant who earn less than $7.87 per day.
    (E) There must be workers in the plant who earn exactly $7.87 per day.

17. *Magazine article:* Davy "Sugar" Jinkins is one of the finest boxers to have ever fought. Last week Davy announced his retirement from the ring, but not from the sport. Davy will continue in boxing as the trainer of "Boom Boom" Jones. With Jinkins handling him, we are sure that Boom Boom will become a title contender in no time.

    The foregoing article is based upon all of the following assumptions EXCEPT

    (A) boxers who have a good trainer can do well
    (B) those who were good boxers can be fine trainers
    (C) Jones is capable of being trained
    (D) title contenders should be well trained
    (E) Jinkins did well as a boxer

18. You can solve a problem. You cannot solve a dilemma, for it requires a choice between two disagreeable alternatives.

    All of the following exemplify a dilemma EXCEPT

    (A) Amleth must avenge his father's death by killing his assassins. He must also protect his mother who was one of the murderers.
    (B) the zoo has one vacant enclosure that is suitable for the exhibition of hyenas or lesser kudus. Hyenas prey upon kudus. The zoo will lose a federal grant if it fails to exhibit both kinds of animals.
    (C) Ames must relocate his business in Belmont or Arlington. Office rentals are much more expensive in Belmont; office locations in Arlington are inconvenient for customers.
    (D) to have enough meat to feed the four guests I must buy two pounds of beef. But one pound of beef costs two dollars and I have only three dollars.
    (E) I must park my car on Ash or Maple Street and go to the market. If I park on Ash Street, I will probably get a parking ticket; if I park on Maple Street, my radio will probably be stolen.

19. The stores are always crowded on holidays. The stores are not crowded; therefore, it must not be a holiday.

    Which one of the following most closely parallels the kind of reasoning used in the above sentences?

    (A) The stores are always crowded on Christmas. The stores are crowded; therefore, it must be Christmas.
    (B) Reptiles are present on a hot day in the desert. Reptiles are absent in this desert area; therefore, this cannot be a hot desert day.
    (C) There is a causal relationship between the occurrence of holidays and the number of people in stores.
    (D) The voting places are empty; therefore, it is not an election day.
    (E) The stores are always empty on Tuesdays. It is Tuesday; therefore, the stores will be empty.

GO ON TO THE NEXT PAGE ➤

3   **3**   **3**   **3**   **3**

Questions 20–21

For one to be assured of success in politics, one must have a sound experiential background, be a polished orator, and possess great wealth. Should an individual lack any one of these attributes, he most certainly will be considered a dark horse in any campaign for public office. Should an individual be without any two of these attributes, he cannot win an election. If Nelson Nerd is to win the presidency, he must greatly improve his ability as a public speaker. His extraordinary wealth is not enough.

20. The author of the above passage appears to believe that

    (A) Nerd is the wealthiest candidate
    (B) Nerd is a sufficiently experienced politician
    (C) being a good public speaker alone can win one a high public office
    (D) if Nerd's public speaking improves, he will win the presidency
    (E) Nerd is not a dark horse now

21. Which one of the following would most weaken the speaker's claims?

    (A) Nerd is not the wealthiest candidate running for president.
    (B) The incumbent president had little relevant experience before coming into office and has always been a poor public speaker.
    (C) Of the individuals elected to public office, 0.001 percent have lacked either oratory skill, experience, or money.
    (D) Nerd failed in his last bid for the presidency.
    (E) The incumbent president, who is running for reelection, is as wealthy as Nerd.

22. Tom is test driving a blue car. After driving for a short while he comes to the following conclusion: Since this car is blue, it must not accelerate quickly.

    The foregoing conclusion can be properly drawn if it is also known that

    (A) all red cars accelerate quickly
    (B) there are some slow blue cars
    (C) all blue cars may not accelerate slowly
    (D) all cars that accelerate quickly are red
    (E) all slow cars are red

Questions 23–24

As almost everyone is painfully aware, the federal government has butted into almost every sector of human existence in recent years. But this manic intrusiveness isn't always the government's fault. Sometimes there is a compulsion to enlist Uncle Sam as a superbusybody.

23. Which one of the following is one of the author's basic assumptions?

    (A) Most of his readers have suffered government intrusion.
    (B) All government intrusion is unwarranted.
    (C) Government intrusion is always government-initiated.
    (D) All memories of government intrusion are painful memories.
    (E) At no time has the federal government practiced nonintrusiveness.

24. Which one of the following most nearly restates the final sentence?

    (A) Most of the time government is responsible for government intrusion.
    (B) Sometimes government does more than intrude; it compels intrusion.
    (C) Sometimes Uncle Sam himself enlists in the ranks of the intruders.
    (D) Sometimes Uncle Sam is compulsive rather than merely symbolic.
    (E) Sometimes the government itself is not responsible for government intrusion.

GO ON TO THE NEXT PAGE ➤

3   **3**   **3**   **3**   **3**

25. Those who dictate what we can and cannot see on television are guilty of falsely equating knowledge with action. They would have us believe that to view violent behavior is to commit it.

On the basis of the content of the above passage, we may infer that the author would believe which one of the following?

(A) Knowing how to manufacture nuclear weapons leads to nuclear war.
(B) Those guilty of committing a crime were not necessarily influenced by an awareness that such crimes occurred.
(C) Media censorship is based upon logical justification.
(D) Know your enemy.
(E) The truth shall set you free.

26. In 1975, the U.S. Supreme Court ruled that the federal government has exclusive rights to any oil and gas resources on the Atlantic Outer Shelf beyond the three-mile limit.

Which one of the following must be true in order for this ruling to be logical?

(A) The U.S. Supreme Court has met recently.
(B) The Atlantic Outer Shelf may possibly contain oil and gas resources.
(C) No oil and gas resources exist within the three-mile limit.
(D) In 1977, the Court reversed this ruling.
(E) Oil and gas on the Atlantic Shelf has not been explored for in the past three years.

STOP

IF YOU FINISH BEFORE TIME IS UP, CHECK YOUR WORK ON THIS SECTION OF THE TEST ONLY.
DO NOT GO ON TO THE NEXT SECTION OF THE TEST UNTIL TIME IS UP FOR THIS SECTION.

SECTION IV
TIME — 35 MINUTES
28 QUESTIONS

Directions: Read the passages and answer the questions following each passage by blackening the appropriate space on the answer sheet. You may refer back to the passages when answering the questions. Answer all questions on the basis of what is stated or implied.

The Constitution gives the Congress power to make the laws that determine the election of senators and
line representatives. At first Congress
(5) exercised its power to supervise apportionment by simply specifying in the statutes how many representatives each state was to have. From 1842 until the 1920s, it went further and required
(10) that the districts be relatively compact (not scattered areas) and relatively equal in voting population.

Major shifts in population occurred in the twentieth century: large numbers
(15) of farmers could no longer maintain small farms and moved to the cities to find employment; rapidly growing industries, organized in factory systems, attracted rural workers; and
(20) many blacks who could no longer find work in southern agriculture moved to the North to get better jobs and get away from strict Jim Crow living conditions. The rural areas of the country became
(25) more sparsely populated while the city populations swelled.

As these changes were occurring, Congress took less interest in its reapportionment power, and after 1929
(30) did not reenact the requirements. In 1946, voters in Illinois asked the Supreme Court to remedy the serious malapportionment of their state congressional districts. Justice
(35) Frankfurter, writing for the Court, said the federal courts should stay out of "this political thicket." Reapportionment was a "political question" outside the jurisdiction of
(40) these courts. Following this holding, malapportionment grew more severe and widespread in the United States.

In the Warren Court era, voters again asked the Court to pass on issues
(45) concerning the size and shape of electoral districts, partly out of

desperation because no other branch of government offered relief, and partly out of hope that the Court would reexamine
(50) old decisions in this area as it had in others, looking at basic constitutional principles in the light of modern living conditions. Once again the Court had to work through the problem of separation
(55) of powers, which had stood in the way of court action concerning representation. In this area, too, the Court's rulings were greeted by some as shockingly radical departures from "the American
(60) way," while others saw them as a reversion to the democratic processes established by the Constitution, applied to an urbanized setting.

1. The primary purpose of the passage is to

(A) criticize public apathy concerning apportionment
(B) describe in general the history of political apportionment
(C) argue for the power of the Supreme Court
(D) describe the role of the Warren Court in political apportionment
(E) stress that reapportionment is essentially a congressional concern

2. The author implies which one of the following opinions about federal supervision of apportionment?

(A) Federal supervision is unnecessary.
(B) Federal supervision is necessary.
(C) Apportionment should be regulated by the Court.
(D) Apportionment should be regulated by Congress.
(E) Court rulings on apportionment violate "the American way."

GO ON TO THE NEXT PAGE ➤

3. In the third paragraph, "malapportionment" refers to the

(A) influx of farmers into the city
(B) Jim Crow phenomenon
(C) shift from rural to urban populations
(D) distribution of voters in Illinois
(E) unfair size and shape of congressional districts

4. We may infer that during the Warren Court era

(A) the most dissatisfied voters lived in cities
(B) the constituency was dissatisfied
(C) the separation of powers became important for the first time
(D) the public turned its attention away from issues of apportionment
(E) a ballot issue concerning electoral apportionment passed

5. The passage answers which one of the following questions?

(A) Does the Constitution delegate authority for supervising apportionment?
(B) Do population shifts intensify racism?
(C) Should the Constitution still be consulted, even though times have changed?
(D) Why did the Warren Court agree to undertake the issue of representation?
(E) How did the Warren Court rule on the separation of powers issue?

6. We may conclude that Justice Frankfurter was

(A) a member of the Warren Court
(B) not a member of the Warren Court
(C) opposed to reapportionment
(D) skeptical about the separation of powers
(E) too attached to outmoded interpretations of the Constitution

7. In the passage the author is primarily concerned with

(A) summarizing history
(B) provoking a controversy
(C) suggesting a new attitude
(D) reevaluating old decisions
(E) challenging constitutional principles

GO ON TO THE NEXT PAGE ➤

Primitive humans knew intuitively that there was a world of the spirit, and that intuitive knowledge progressed and
line expanded into the history of many
(5) religious movements. While the majority of humans probably have never given up their belief in a world of the spirit, the success of scientific materialism encouraged the claim to a universe that
(10) excluded everything but that which could be weighed, measured, or dissected. As children, not yet plagued by the knowledge of science, we all shared a common heritage of
(15) humankind in the belief in the world that we could not see. But in time, the harshness of rational day's spotlight changed our "childlike" beliefs into the pejorative "childish," and we ceased to
(20) believe or rather could no longer admit to ourselves that we did.

Not so with the young Irish poet, dramatist, and essayist William Butler Yeats. Somehow he escaped the
(25) "rationalistic" strictures to which most thoroughly civilized people succumb. Born into a nation whose people were steeped in the traditions of prehistory, in the lore of the faeries and the Druids,
(30) he remained free to believe. Much of his younger life, spent with his mother's people in Sligo, tended to enhance this belief. In his autobiography, he recalls instances of supernatural forces at work
(35) upon his imagination. He awoke screaming from a dream one night insisting that his grandfather had been in a shipwreck, which proved the next day to have been true. In his first close
(40) brush with death, when his brother Robert died, he said, "Next day at breakfast I heard people telling how my mother and the servant had heard the banshee crying the night before he
(45) died."

It was during this period that many of the symbols of Irish mythology took hold of his mind, symbols that were to recur throughout his poetic career,
(50) refined and enlarged, but in some measure the same. Such is the symbol of the tree, which perhaps had its genesis in the folktale of the Island of Innisfree and was repeated over and
(55) over throughout his poems. The study of magic and the occult became a

primary force in Yeats's life and such a part of him that to read his poetry we must at least have an understanding of
(60) its meaning to him and the depth to which it affected everything he wrote.

For the reader, rather than becoming lost in the intricacies of Yeats's occult practices, it may be more to the point to
(65) realize that all of the rituals involved are calling to a deep-seated capacity for reaction in all of us. Yeats sees the poet as a supernatural artist who enchants his own mind when he would enchant
(70) the minds of others. He is conjuring up the imagination, but the imagination far more enlarged that that which we normally conceive, and he does this by means of symbols. He says of them, "I
(75) cannot now think symbols less than the greatest of all powers whether they are used consciously by the masters of magic or half unconsciously by their successors the poet, the musician, and
(80) the artist. . . . Whatever the passions of man have gathered about, becomes a symbol in the great memory." It is this great mind, and great memory, to which Yeats is calling and which he insists can
(85) be evoked by symbols, whether from Celtic lore, the Upanishads, or the Noh plays, if they be appropriate. Yeats calls to us to remember what we have not forgotten, an elemental force, a reality
(90) outside that of materialistic science. His hidden things embrace all that humans have forgotten to open their minds to, not in past time or future time, but in that reality that knows no time.

GO ON TO THE NEXT PAGE ➤

4   4   4   4   4

8. The passage best supports which one of the following statements?

   (A) The great memory arises from the cultural history of individual nations.
   (B) To understand Yeat's writing, one is obliged to understand the specific occult and magic rituals he practiced in the context of the times.
   (C) One's acceptance of and belief in the lore of faeries and Druids is enhanced if one's environment is also accepting.
   (D) Imagination in writing is rationalistic, relying also on symbol and nonscientific reality.
   (E) Yeats's writing is rooted in mythology and consequently calls to the child in the adult and the adult in the child.

9. The organization of the passage is best described by which one of the following?

   (A) An author is introduced; the author's titles are discussed; generalities about humankind are drawn; suggestions are made concerning extrapolating an understanding of one kind of writing to aid in the understanding of other kinds of writing.
   (B) Symbols are defined; the use of symbols in a particular work is investigated; the great memory is connected to other authors' works; generalizations are made concerning the concept of time and the ideal.
   (C) Concepts about humanity are introduced; the same concepts are connected with an author's works and life; the author's attitude toward those concepts is explored.
   (D) Humanity's understanding of literary symbolism is defined; the author's understanding of such symbolism is discussed; symbolism in other works is investigated.
   (E) The history of mythological beliefs is outlined; the similarities of one mythology to other mythologies is considered; these mythologies are connected to the concept of the great memory.

10. Of the following statements, the passage best supports which one as compatible with Yeats's beliefs?

    (A) Although the rationalistic approach of science is essential in the modern world, it can be used only marginally in art, whereas mythology can be combined with it to produce a viable synthesis.
    (B) The symbolism of the tree is likely to evoke similar effects in readers from different areas of the world.
    (C) The Upanishads, Celtic lore, and the Noh plays were written in times when childlike beliefs were the norm among adults, not the exception as they are now.
    (D) The cry of the banshees is inevitably connected with the death of someone close to the person who hears them.
    (E) Magic and the occult have a place in materialistic science and could enhance people's understanding of and belief in that science.

11. Of the following titles, which one best describes the passage's content?

    (A) "Irish Mythology in the Writing of William Butler Yeats."
    (B) "Rationalism vs. Symbolic Reality"
    (C) "Childhood Belief and Adult Pragmatism: A Loss of Innocence"
    (D) "Mythology and the Occult in the Folktale of the Island of Innisfree"
    (E) "Yeat's Use of Mythology and Symbolism"

GO ON TO THE NEXT PAGE ➤

12. The author most likely mentions Celtic lore, the Upanishads, and the Noh plays for which one of the following reasons?

   (A) The three examples suggest that symbolism may be found in all cultures and that Yeats believed these symbols to be common to them.

   (B) Celtic lore is part of Yeats's literary base, while the Upanishads and the Noh plays come from other cultures, which would not use Celtic lore as part of their system of symbols.

   (C) Celtic lore is an example of a nonliterary tradition; the Upanishads illustrate religious writing; and the Noh plays combine both forms.

   (D) The three examples illustrate the "strictures to which most thoroughly civilized people succumb."

   (E) All three examples involve use of magic and the occult.

13. Of the following, according to the information in the passage, which statement is LEAST consistent with Yeats's life and beliefs?

   (A) Dreams involve symbols common to humankind.

   (B) Artists, poets, and musicians are aware of the power and magic of the symbols they use.

   (C) Childhood beliefs remain in the subconscious minds of adults.

   (D) Symbolism is based in emotion, not rational thought.

   (E) Civilized societies focus on the rational rather than the symbolic.

14. Which one of the following sentences would most logically begin a new paragraph following the third paragraph of the passage as given?

   (A) The innocuous ghosts and goblins of modern Halloween are much less threatening than those they are historically derived from.

   (B) Yeats became increasingly disillusioned with Irish politics.

   (C) Yeats died in 1939 in France, but he is buried in Ireland, in the land of his childhood, the land of the banshees and the faeries.

   (D) Yeats's interest in the occult survived into adulthood and affected even his choice of a marriage partner, Georgie Hyde-Lees, who was herself interested in automatic writing through what she called her "communicators."

   (E) If you are ten years old, you are alone, and it is night, you feel you are the only person in the world, and you believe in the world of the unseen.

GO ON TO THE NEXT PAGE ➤

4   4   4   4   4

The paganism of the Greeks and Romans, though a religion without salvation or afterlife, was not
line necessarily indifferent to man's moral
(5) behavior. What has misled some historians is that this religion, without theology or church, was, if I may put it this way, more an á la carte religion than a religion with a fixed menu. If an
(10) established church is a "one-party state," then paganism was "free enterprise." Each man was free to found his own temple and preach whatever god he liked, just as he might open a new
(15) inn or peddle a new product. And each man made himself the client of whichever god he chose, not necessarily his city's favorite deity: The choice was free.
(20)   Such freedom was possible because between what the pagans meant by "god" and what Jews, Christians, and Moslems mean, there is little in common but the name. For the three
(25) religions of the Book, God is infinitely greater than the world which he created. He exists solely as an actor in a cosmic drama in which the salvation of humankind is played out. The pagan
(30) gods, by contrast, live their lives and are not confined to a metaphysical role. They are part of this world, one of three races that populate the earth: animals, which are neither immortal nor gifted
(35) with reason; humans, who are mortal but reasonable; and gods, who are immortal and reasonable. So true is it that the divine race is an animal genus that every god is either male or female.
(40) From this it follows that the gods of all peoples are true gods. Other nations might worship gods unknown to the Greeks and Romans, or they might worship the same gods under different
(45) names. Jupiter was Jupiter the world over, just as a lion is a lion, but he happened to be called Zeus in Greek, Taranis in Gallic, and Yao in Hebrew. The names of the gods could be
(50) translated from one language to another, just like the names of planets and other material things. Belief in alien gods foundered only where it was the product of an absurd superstition, something
(55) that smacked of a fantastic bestiary. The Romans laughed at the gods with animal

bodies worshiped by the Egyptians. In the ancient world religious people were as tolerant of one another as are Hindu
(60) sects. To take a special interest in one god was not to deny the others.
    This fact was not without consequence for man's idea of his own place in the natural order. Imagine a
(65) circle, which represents the world according to the religions of the Book. Given man's importance in the cosmic drama, he occupies at least half the circle. What about God? He is so
(70) exalted, so awesome, that he remains far above the circle. To represent Him, draw an arrow, pointing upward from the center of the circle and mark it with the sign of infinity. Now consider the pagan
(75) world. Imagine a sort of staircase with three steps. On the lowest step stand the animals; on the next step, humans; and on the third step, the gods. In order to become a god, one did not need to
(80) rise very far. The gods stood just above humans, so that it often makes sense to translate the Latin and Greek words for "divine" as "superhuman."

15. Which one of the following best expresses the main idea of the passage?

(A) Under Greek and Roman paganism, people were not bound by a set theology or teachings from a sacred book.
(B) In Greek and Roman paganism, humans differed from animals in that they possessed reason.
(C) Greek and Roman paganism was not, as some historians have claimed, indifferent to man's morality.
(D) Central to Greek and Roman paganism was the belief that the gods were of this world, not above it.
(E) Greek and Roman paganism cannot accurately be called a "religion" because of its concept of the gods.

GO ON TO THE NEXT PAGE ➤

4   4   4   4   4

16. In the first paragraph, the effect of the metaphors "à la carte/fixed menu" and "free enterprise/one-party state" is to

 (A) suggest the immorality of the gods
 (B) indicate the origins of the gods
 (C) suggest the earthbound quality of the gods
 (D) suggest the selfishness and pettiness of the gods
 (E) indicate the economic role of the gods

17. The central contrast between an "à la carte" religion and a "fixed menu" religion is best expressed as

 (A) choice among many gods vs. obedience to one true god
 (B) belief in female gods vs. belief in male gods
 (C) choice among holy books vs. adherence to one holy book
 (D) belief in life on earth vs. belief in life in heaven
 (E) choice among varieties of worship vs. acceptance of one liturgy

18. To develop his points, the author uses all of the following methods EXCEPT

 (A) contrast
 (B) example
 (C) figurative language
 (D) irony
 (E) explanation

19. From information in the passage, we can infer which one of the following would be true under Greek and Roman paganism?

 (A) People would be happier and more fulfilled.
 (B) Religious wars would be less likely.
 (C) Family life would be less significant.
 (D) The arts would flourish.
 (E) People would behave immorally.

20. According to the author, why have some historians assumed that the Greeks and Romans were indifferent to man's moral behavior?

 (A) Their gods had no significant power.
 (B) They laughed at the religious practices of others.
 (C) Their religion did not include salvation.
 (D) Their gods were immoral role models.
 (E) They viewed gods and animals as the same.

21. The passage attributes the religious tolerance under paganism to the fact that

 (A) human reason was valued over faith
 (B) no one god was seen as the "true god"
 (C) religion was not at the center of human activity
 (D) the same gods were worshiped by different nations
 (E) gods were not taken seriously

22. The purpose of the third paragraph of the passage is to

 (A) summarize and evaluate the contrasts between paganism and religions of the Book
 (B) show the connection between the concepts of the "divine" and the "superhuman"
 (C) contrast the place of man in relation to God under paganism and under religions of the Book
 (D) explain the conflicts between the concept of monotheism and the concept of polytheism
 (E) simplify the points made in paragraphs one and two so that they will be more understandable to the reader

GO ON TO THE NEXT PAGE ➤

In contrast to the planets, the stars seem to be motionless, or fixed to their spots on the celestial sphere. But it only looks that way because they are so far away from us—distances that are measured in light-years. In reality the fixed stars also move in the sky, but they do so at such a slow pace that their motion (called "proper" motion) becomes visually apparent only over thousands of years and otherwise can be proven to exist only through precision measurements.

The fixed stars shine with their own light. They are suns like our Sun, that is, spheres of incandescent gases (called plasma by scientists). In the interior of these spheres, energy is produced through thermonuclear reactions. The number of suns in the universe is vast beyond guessing. The unaided eye can detect about 4,000 stars on a very clear night; a telescope reveals many millions in the region of the Milky Way alone.

The stars are so far removed from Earth that their distance is difficult to measure. Distances up to about 70 light-years can be established with relative accuracy by using a method similar to triangulation, which is used by surveyors. Greater stellar distances are determined indirectly. Because a star (like any other luminous body) appears fainter the farther away it is, scientists try to calculate a star's magnitude theoretically by applying methods based on physics. They then compare the results with the actual magnitude observed. However, this method is less accurate, and the distances given by different astronomers vary considerably, diverging sometimes as much as 100 percent, especially for very remote stars.

Many stars do not always exhibit the same brightness. Instead they change their magnitude in cycles anywhere from several hours to several years in length, but most commonly with so-called periods of up to 100 days. In many of these variable stars the magnitudinal fluctuations occur with considerable regularity, whereas in others they follow no clearly recognizable pattern. There are two reasons for the fluctuations in brightness. Either the physical characteristics of the star change—it may be growing larger or smaller or its surface temperature may rise and drop—or the star is concealed by another star that stands in our direct line of vision—as the Sun is hidden by the Moon in a solar eclipse—and blocks the light of the star behind it from our view for a certain period.

One of the most fascinating areas of research in modern astronomy is the study of the life history of stars. Stars are formed from huge interstellar gas clouds in whose interior gases and particles of matter gradually concentrate. A star is born when, at the core of this concentrated mass, energy is first produced through the conversion of hydrogen, the most prevalent element in space, into helium. The star then goes on to spend the main part of its life in a stable state, shining with a steady light.

But at some point all the hydrogen is used up and the star enters its next life stage. It tries to find alternate sources of energy by transforming the helium it has produced. But this is accomplished only with difficulty. The interior parts of the star contract while the outer ones expand. The star swells up in size and becomes a red giant. Eventually, when all sources of energy are exhausted, the star's life comes to an end. The star goes through a final, cataclysmic reaction and then either dies in a spectacular supernova explosion or simply ceases to emit light. The outer layers go hurling into space as gas nebulas, and what remains is either a star corpse whose glow gradually fades away—a white dwarf—or a neutron star. Conditions in such a neutron star are beyond anything imaginable: The mass of the entire Sun can be compressed into a ball 6 to 12 miles in diameter, and one cubic centimeter of matter weighs 10 million to 1 billion tons. The life span of a star depends largely on its initial mass. Heavy stars with more than five times the mass of our Sun live a relatively short time, about 100 to 200 million years, whereas stars like our Sun have a life span of 7 to 10 billion years.

GO ON TO THE NEXT PAGE ➤

23. Which one of the following is the most likely reason astronomers vary in their calculations of a distant star's magnitude?

   (A) Distance measurements of remote stars can be made only indirectly using theoretical methods.
   (B) Triangulation is a surveyor's, not an astronomer's, method and is therefore imprecise in measuring star distances.
   (C) Astronomers do not agree on the concept of light-years and therefore their calculations have different bases.
   (D) Some astronomers use sophisticated and precise measuring instruments, whereas others rely on theoretical methods.
   (E) Fluctuations in the brightness of remote stars cause magnitude measurements to be estimates at best.

24. Based on the passage, all of the following statements about stars are true EXCEPT

   (A) the accuracy of distance determinations for remote stars is open to question
   (B) no one knows the number of stars in the universe
   (C) stars are composed of both gases and particles of matter
   (D) heavy stars have a shorter life span than stars of smaller mass
   (E) a star's life span depends on the types of incandescent gases in its core

25. Which one of the following inferences can be made about the cycle of stars?

   (A) If a star uses up its hydrogen, it becomes a "white dwarf."
   (B) A neutron star remaining after a supernova explosion is highly concentrated.
   (C) Supernova explosions occur only when stars are created.
   (D) The brightest stars will most likely have the longest life.
   (E) The sun is able to transform hydrogen into helium, which means that its life span is longer than most stars.

26. Which one of the following best describes the organization of the passage?

   (A) The first paragraph introduces the subject of stars. Paragraphs 2, 3, 4, and 5 enumerate the difficulties inherent in studying the stars. Paragraph 6 draws a conclusion.
   (B) The first four paragraphs describe qualities of stars. Paragraphs 5 and 6 explain a star's cycle.
   (C) The first three paragraphs make general statements about stars. Paragraphs 4, 5, and 6 provide concrete examples.
   (D) The first paragraph includes a thesis statement about stars. Paragraphs 2 through 4 present arguments supporting the thesis. Paragraphs 5 and 6 develop a subtopic.
   (E) Each of the six paragraphs of the passage discusses a different aspect of star formation and destruction.

27. The author of the passage would agree with all of the following statements EXCEPT

   (A) a star's energy is produced by the conversion of helium to hydrogen
   (B) a star may change in brightness because it is blocked by another star
   (C) the surface temperature of a star can fluctuate
   (D) before a star dies, its outer parts expand
   (E) a neutron star may remain after the death of a star

28. Which one of the following best describes the purpose of the passage?

   (A) to summarize the life span of stars
   (B) to contrast stars and planets
   (C) to encourage the study of astronomy
   (D) to describe the difficulties inherent in the study of stars
   (E) to provide general information about stars

STOP

IF YOU FINISH BEFORE TIME IS UP, CHECK YOUR WORK ON THIS SECTION OF THE TEST ONLY.
DO NOT GO ON TO THE NEXT SECTION OF THE TEST UNTIL TIME IS UP FOR THIS SECTION.

5 **5** **5** **5** **5**

SECTION V
TIME — 35 MINUTES
25 QUESTIONS

Directions: In this section you will be given brief statements or passages and will be required to evaluate the reasoning involved. In some instances, more than one choice will appear to be a possible answer. You are to choose the *best* answer. Use common sense and reasonableness in making your selection; then mark the proper space on the answer sheet.

Questions 1–2

By passing more and more regulations allegedly to protect the environment, the state is driving the manufacturing industry away. And when the employers leave, the workers will follow. The number of new no-growth or environmental rules passed each year is increasing by leaps and bounds. Rich environmentalists who think they are sympathetic to workers have no real sympathy for the blue-collar employees who are injured by their activities. One major manufacturer has been fined for failing to establish a car-pool plan. Another is accused of polluting the air with industrial emissions, although everyone knows that two thirds of the pollutants come from cars and trucks. No wonder the large manufacturers are moving to states with fewer restrictive laws. And as the manufacturers go, unemployment and the number of workers leaving the state will rise more rapidly than ever before.

1. The author's argument that strict environmental laws will eventually lead to loss of workers in the state will be most weakened if it can be shown that

(A) so far, the number of manufacturers who have left the state is small
(B) the unemployment rate has climbed steadily in the last three years
(C) most workers who leave the state give as their reason for leaving the poor environmental quality
(D) several other manufacturing states have strict environmental laws
(E) rich environmentalists are more powerful in many other states

2. Which one of the following is NOT an argument of this passage?

(A) Environmentalists are responsible for depriving workers of their jobs.
(B) When workers leave a state, it is a sign that manufacturers will follow.
(C) A car-pool law should not be enforced, as cars and trucks are responsible for most air pollution.
(D) Large manufacturers prefer states with fewer restrictions.
(E) A rise in unemployment will lead to an increase in workers leaving the state.

GO ON TO THE NEXT PAGE ➤

3. *Dick:* There will be a disastrous rise in the temperatures on Earth unless we are able to reduce the carbon dioxide content of the atmosphere to the levels of the 1980s. The only way to do this is to reduce drastically our use of carboniferous fuels.

   Harry: The fear of too much carbon dioxide in the atmosphere is unwarranted. Throughout geological time, the oceans have absorbed carbon dioxide from the atmosphere and precipitated it as limestone. Since the ocean waters are alkaline and contain large amounts of calcium and magnesium, they can control any excessive carbon dioxide in the atmosphere.

   In replying to Dick, Harry does which one of the following?

   (A) questions Dick's assumption that reducing the use of carboniferous fuels will reduce the amount of carbon dioxide in the atmosphere
   (B) denies that the reduction of the use of carbon-producing fuel will reduce the likelihood of global warming
   (C) asserts that the reduction of carbon dioxide in the atmosphere is not the only way to avoid global warming
   (D) suggests that reducing the use of fuels that produce carbon dioxide is economically unfeasible
   (E) challenges Dick's belief that the increasing amounts of carbon dioxide in the atmosphere are dangerous

4. Unlike most graduates of American high schools, all graduates of high schools in Bermuda have completed four years of advanced mathematics.

   Which one of the following, if true, would best explain the situation described above?

   (A) Math anxiety is higher in the United States than in Bermuda.
   (B) There are far more high schools and high school students in the United States than in Bermuda.
   (C) More students in America take full-time jobs without completing high school.
   (D) Math programs in American high schools are frequently understaffed.
   (E) High schools in Bermuda require four years of advanced mathematics for graduation.

5. Psychological novels are superior to novels of adventure. Immature readers prefer novels of adventure to novels with less action and greater psychological depth. The immature reader, who prefers James Bond's exploits to the subtleties of Henry James, can be identified easily by his choice of inferior reading matter.

   A criticism of the logic of this argument would be likely to find fault with the author's

   (A) presupposing the conclusion he wishes to prove
   (B) failure to define "adventure" clearly
   (C) failure to cite possible exceptions to this rule
   (D) hasty generalization on the basis of a limited specific case
   (E) inaccurate definitions of key terms

5   **5**

6. *Literary critic:* A good mystery novel should have three strengths: an interesting location, complex and engaging characters, and a plot that is unpredictable but observes probability. If two of the three are especially good, the book may please many readers. In Kate Rudman's latest mystery story, the detective and the suspects are original and entertaining and the plot is full of surprises, but the book will probably disappoint most readers.

If the above is true, we can infer that

(A) it is too easy for a reader to solve the mystery before the detective can do so

(B) the setting is unrealized and the events of the book are hard to believe

(C) the solution depends on information that is unfairly concealed from the reader, and the setting is the same as that of Rudman's last novel

(D) the language of the book is unsuitable for children and, at the end, evil wins out over good

(E) most mystery readers are satisfied if a story has an interesting detective and a plot that is full of surprises

7. In professional athletics, the small number of record-setting performers in each thirty-year span is remarkably consistent. In hockey, for example, 5 percent of all the professional players were responsible for more than half of the new records, and 95 percent of the new records were set by only 8 percent of the players. Similar percentages were found in baseball, football, and basketball records, where the numbers of participants are much higher.

If the statements above are true, which one of the following conclusions may be most reasonably inferred?

(A) An increase in the number of athletic teams playing hockey, football, or baseball would significantly increase the number of record-setting performances.

(B) Reducing the number of athletic teams playing hockey, football, or baseball would not necessarily cause a decrease in the number of record-setting performances.

(C) Record-setting performances would increase if the number of amateur teams were increased.

(D) Many record-setting performances are not recorded by statisticians.

(E) As records become higher with the passage of time, fewer and fewer records will be broken.

GO ON TO THE NEXT PAGE ➤

8. By refusing to ban smoking in restaurants, the city council has put the financial well-being of restaurant owners above the health of the citizens of this city. No doubt the council would support the restaurateurs if they decided to use asbestos tablecloths and to barbecue using radioactivity. These devices would be no more risky.

The author of this paragraph makes her case by arguing

(A) from experience
(B) from example
(C) by authority
(D) from observation
(E) from analogy

9. The GOP's attempt to win the South has, however indirectly, played on the racial anxiety of white voters. It has produced a vocabulary of civility to conceal their opposition to school integration ("forced busing") and affirmative action ("quotas"). And, to the horror of regular Republicans, the party's candidate for senator in Louisiana is a neo-Nazi and Ku Klux Klan alumnus. The ease with which this candidate has merged his bigotry with a respectable conservative social agenda is frightening. There is, however, a ray of hope. The candidate is supported by about 30 percent of the voters.

The passage above is structured to lead to which one of the following conclusions?

(A) If the candidate disavows his views, he will lose his support; but if he does not disavow them, he cannot gain any new supporters.
(B) And that 30 percent has grown from only 15 percent three weeks ago.
(C) We cannot predict now whether that percentage will increase or decrease before the election.
(D) Two opponents also have about 30 percent of voters with another 10 percent undecided.
(E) There is still a possibility that Louisiana, with its unmatched history of corrupt, demagogic, and ineffectual state politics, will support his candidacy.

Questions 10–11

The gill-net is used to catch halibut and sea bass, but up to 72 percent of what it ensnares is not marketable and is thrown back dead. Gill-nets are often called "walls of death" because they entangle and painfully kill mammals such as dolphins, whales, and sea otters. To use the gill-net at sea is like strip mining or clear-cutting on land.

Powerful lobbyists representing the commercial fishing industry have prevented the legislature from passing a ban on the use of gill-nets within the three-mile limit. They claim that the banning of gill-nets will raise the price of fish. They also charge that the law would benefit rich sport fishermen who want the ocean for their yachts.

10. In the first paragraph, the case against gill-nets is made by using

(A) statistical analysis
(B) ambiguity and indirection
(C) biased definitions
(D) simile and metaphor
(E) understatement

11. Which one of the following, if true, would support the argument in favor of a ban on gill-nets within the three-mile limit?

(A) Less than one percent of the fish sold in this country is imported from abroad.
(B) Gill-net users catch all but two percent of their fish within the three-mile limit.
(C) The halibut population has fallen to a near extinction level.
(D) There is a serious overpopulation of the coastal sea otter.
(E) Coastal sea otters have nearly destroyed the abalone beds along the coast.

GO ON TO THE NEXT PAGE ➤

5   **5**

12. According to the Supreme Court, the First Amendment does not protect "obscene" speech. To the "obscene," the Court explained, speech must appeal to a "prurient" interest, describe conduct in a way "patently offensive to contemporary community standards," and lack serious literary, artistic or scientific value.

All of the following arguments can be used to question the validity of the Court's definition of "obscene" EXCEPT

(A) there is no certain way of knowing just what an "appeal" to "prurient interest" is
(B) the phrase "patently offensive" is impossible to define precisely
(C) no two communities are likely to have the same standards of decency
(D) most juries are incapable of determining what is "serious" artistic or literary value
(E) there is no writing that is without some "scientific value"

13. There are no edible fish in the streams of this county because there are no pesticide controls.

Which one of the following assumptions must be made before the conclusion above can be reached?

(A) Edible fish cannot be found in areas where there are no pesticide controls.
(B) If there are pesticide controls, there will be many edible fish.
(C) Without adequate pesticide controls, the fish population will rapidly decline.
(D) If there are pesticide controls, there will be some edible fish.
(E) With pesticide controls, the fish population will rapidly increase.

14. For eighteen years, a state has had three conservative congressmen, all representing the agricultural counties in the northern parts of the state. It also has three liberal congressmen from the large capital city in the south. One of the two senators is a liberal from the south, and the other is a conservative from the north.

Which one of the following can be inferred from this passage?

(A) Voters in the southern parts of the state will always vote liberal.
(B) Voters in the northern part of the state are likely to vote liberal in the next election.
(C) Voters in the state are influenced more by a candidate's political leanings than by where the candidate lives.
(D) The population of the three northern counties is about equal to the population of the capital city.
(E) The governor of the state is probably a liberal.

GO ON TO THE NEXT PAGE ➤

5   **5**

15. In the United States, people can get their medications. Those who say they can't are being vocal about it just to get another free ride. HMOs offer drug coverage at only a minimal copay; other private policies have many drug options; state programs offer discounted prescriptions for low income families; and drug companies make free medications available to those who cannot afford them.

    All of the following, if true, would weaken the argument above EXCEPT

    (A) drug companies change the types of medications they offer free from month to month
    (B) incomes may vary considerably from month to month and year to year
    (C) the definition of what is a "minimal" copay varies depending on the income of the individual paying it
    (D) private insureers set rates based on previous prescription usage of an individual
    (E) drug companies sell drugs in other countries for less than they do in the United States, so people are forced to order their medications by mail from those countries or go there to purchase them

16. *Political Analyst:* Over the last three decades, the President's party has lost an average of 22 House of Representatives seats and two Senate seats in the midterm elections. This year, with a popular Republican President in the White House, GOP strategists had hoped to pick up seats in the House and the Senate. But the polls show these expectations are unrealistic. This should be an election with results much like those of the recent past.

    According to information in this passage, the election should

    (A) produce large Republican gains in the House and the Senate
    (B) produce about 25 new House and Senate seats for the Democrats
    (C) result in virtually no change in the balance of Republican and Democratic members of the House
    (D) produce small Republican gains in the House and even smaller gains in the Senate
    (E) produce two new Republican seats in the Senate

17. Ten percent of the state lottery winners interviewed by researchers of the paranormal have reported that they had visions or other signs instructing them to select the winning numbers. On the basis of these results, the researchers claim to have proved the existence of paranormal gifts.

    Which one of the following pieces of additional information would be most relevant in assessing the logical validity of the researcher's claim?

    (A) the total sum of money these men and women win on the lottery
    (B) the percentage of lottery players who win money
    (C) the percentage of contestants interviewed who were not lottery winners
    (D) the percentage of lottery players who had visions or signs but did not win money
    (E) the amount of money the lottery winners spend each year on lottery tickets

GO ON TO THE NEXT PAGE ➤

5   **5**   **5**   **5**   **5**

18. By spraying with pesticides like malathion, we can eradicate dangerous pests like the fruit-fly. But malathion spraying also destroys the ladybug, the best natural predator of aphids. Areas that have been sprayed with malathion are now free of the fruit-fly, but infested with aphids. This is the price we must pay to protect our citrus crop.

    The argument above assumes all of the following EXCEPT

    (A) pesticide spraying is the only way to eradicate the fruit-fly
    (B) the aphid infestation is caused by the lack of ladybugs
    (C) a pesticide that would kill fruit-flies and spare ladybugs cannot be made
    (D) the use of pesticides has disadvantages
    (E) the aphid infestation could be prevented by introducing a natural predator other than the ladybug

19. The Superintendent of Education complains that the share of the total state budget for education has decreased in each of the last four years; he blames the fall-off on the steady rise in the cost of law enforcement. Organizations opposing increased spending on education point out that the amount of money the state has spent on education has increased by at least three million dollars in each of the last four years.

    Which one of the following, if true, best resolves the apparent contradiction in the passage above?

    (A) The total state budget has increased more rapidly than the expenditure for education.
    (B) Both the pro- and con-educational-spending spokesmen have failed to take inflation into account.
    (C) Law-enforcement costs have not risen as rapidly as the superintendent claims.
    (D) Some educational expenses are not included in the state budget, but are paid by local taxes.
    (E) School construction is paid for by funds from bonds, not by funds from the state budget.

20. How can I write any of the essays when there are so many essays to be written?

    In terms of its logical structure, the remark above most closely resembles which one of the following?

    (A) How can he buy a new car when he is already deeply in debt?
    (B) How can she increase her collection of books when it is already so large?
    (C) How can he iron any of his shirts when he has so many shirts that need ironing?
    (D) How can she visit London and Paris when she has not yet visited New York and Washington?
    (E) How can they raise horses when they already raise so many cows?

21. Great playwrights do not develop in countries where there is no freedom of opinion. Repressive countries are likely to produce great satiric writers.

    If both of these statements are true, which of the following is the most logical continuation?

    (A) Therefore, countries with no restrictions on expression will produce great satiric playwrights.
    (B) Therefore, great satirists in repressive countries will use forms other than the play.
    (C) Therefore, playwrights in repressive countries will not write satire.
    (D) Therefore, great satiric writers will not develop in countries where there is freedom of speech.
    (E) Therefore, no great satire is likely to be written in dramatic forms.

GO ON TO THE NEXT PAGE ➤

22. Contrary to the expectations of the Canadian government, a majority of the Mohawk population in Quebec is calling for native sovereignty. The Mohawk separatists cite a written agreement from colonial times in which Great Britain recognized the Mohawks' separateness from Canada. Unfortunately, the various Mohawk factions, each with its own agenda, have made it difficult to reach lasting agreements. What satisfies one group displeases another. The bleak outlook is for _____.

Which one of the following most logically concludes this paragraph?

(A) continued struggle within the tribe and between the tribe and the Canadian government

(B) some kind of compromise which recognizes the rights of both the Indians and the government of Canada

(C) some sort of agreement among the divided groups within the Mohawk tribe

(D) the establishment of a separate Mohawk state with its sovereignty recognized by the Canadian government

(E) a decline in Mohawk militarism and a series of fence-mending conferences

23. A new law will require labels giving consumers more nutritional information on all prepackaged foods manufactured in the United States. Food sold by restaurants or grocers with annual sales of less than $500,000 will be exempt. The required labels will reveal the number of servings, the serving size, the number of calories per serving, and the amount of fat, cholesterol, sodium, and dietary fiber.

The effectiveness of the new labels in improving overall U.S. nutrition could be seriously questioned if which one of the following were shown to be true?

(A) More than 80 percent of the food sold in this country is not prepackaged.

(B) More than 80 percent of the prepackaged food sold in this country is marketed by the eight major food corporations.

(C) The amount of money Americans spend on prepackaged foods for microwaving has more than tripled every year for the last five years, and the trend is expected to continue.

(D) An increasingly large number of consumers now read the nutritional information on food packages.

(E) Small retailers who manufacture packaged foods sell to only a tiny percentage of American food buyers.

5 ⬦**5**⬦ ⬦**5**⬦ ⬦**5**⬦ **5**

24. A year ago the presidential science advisor announced prematurely that the United States would reveal its plan for combating global warming at the World Climate Conference in Geneva, Switzerland. Five European countries have already announced plans to make reductions in carbon dioxide emissions, and five others have committed themselves to goals of stabilizing their emissions. But the United States is still unprepared to announce targets or a schedule for reducing carbon dioxide emissions.

Which one of the following sentences would provide the most logical continuation of this paragraph?

(A) The Geneva Conference will be the last international meeting before negotiations on a global-warming convention begin next year.

(B) The United States accounts for about 22 percent of the carbon dioxide pumped into the atmosphere, while the former Soviet Union accounts for 18 percent.

(C) By adopting renewable energy strategies that would permit stabilization of carbon dioxide emissions, the United States could save millions of dollars.

(D) The British Prime Minister and top environmental officials of many nations will attend the conference in Geneva.

(E) Anticipating a debate in which the Europeans will criticize the United States for failing to act, the administration is downplaying the importance of the conference.

25. There is increasing reason to believe that Americans are talking themselves into a recession. Consumers are becoming more and more pessimistic, and the index of consumer confidence has plunged to its lowest level in years. What bothers analysts is fear that consumer pessimism about the economy will lead to spending cuts and become a self-fulfilling prophecy, speeding the onset of a recession.

Widespread predictions in the media of a coming recession may be one reason for the pessimistic attitudes of consumers. They may be bracing for a recession by cutting back on spending plans for new cars, vacations, and restaurant meals—the very behavior pattern that analysts say will intensify the slump. Real estate values have been in decline for a year and a half, and the stock market has declined for four months in a row. When the economy is on the ropes, waning consumer confidence can deliver the knock-out punch.

The argument in the passage above would be weakened if it were shown that

(A) in the 1955 recession, the widespread concern over the President's health precipitated an economic downturn

(B) although consumer spending in the last fiscal quarter was the same as last year's, most of that strength stemmed from unusual government military spending

(C) the steady rise in car sales has continued, despite the phasing out of discount prices and low-interest car loans

(D) the predicted recession after the steep fall in stock prices two years ago did not lead to recession

(E) some consumers are more eager than ever to maintain the living standards they have enjoyed for the last two years

STOP

END OF MULTIPLE-CHOICE EXAMINATION. IF YOU FINISH BEFORE TIME IS UP, CHECK YOUR WORK ON THIS SECTION ONLY. DO NOT GO BACK TO ANY OTHER SECTION OF THE EXAMINATION.

Writing Sample

Directions: You have 30 minutes to write an essay in response to a given topic. Take a few minutes to plan your work before you begin writing. DO NOT WRITE ON A TOPIC OF YOUR OWN CHOICE. ESSAYS THAT DO NOT ADDRESS THE GIVEN TOPIC ARE UNACCEPTABLE.

The quality of your writing is more important than the length of your response or the content. Pay attention to organization, appropriate diction, and correct usage. You will not be expected to display any specialized knowledge in your response, nor will you be expected to write a "perfect" essay; law schools understand that you are writing under a time constraint, and will allow for the minor lapses in writing ability that might occur under this circumstance.

Only the lined area in your booklet will be reproduced for the law schools, so do not write outside this space. *Do not* skip lines or use wide margins. These precautions, along with careful planning and legible handwriting that is not unduly large, will keep you within the allowed space.

Sample Topic

The State Legislature has appropriated funds to build a new maximum security prison somewhere in Metropolis County. The prison is to house one hundred prisoners convicted of serious crimes and also the two hundred prisoners awaiting trial or being tried in Metropolis City. These prisoners are now held at the overcrowded and antiquated Metropolis City Jail. Two locations have been proposed.

As an aide to the state senator who represents Metropolis County, you have been asked to write an argument to be presented to the Legislature in support of one of the sites. Two considerations guide your decision:

- The state funds for building and maintaining the prison and for transporting the prisoners to the courts are limited.
- The senator is eager to increase his popular support in anticipation of the upcoming election.

The Metropolis City site is located ten minutes from the court buildings near the downtown district. This area of the city is densely populated and has a high, slowly declining, crime rate. Residents of the district strongly oppose the building of the prison in their neighborhood, especially since a number of prisoners have recently escaped from the old Metropolis City Jail. Art preservation groups also oppose the proposed location since it would require the destruction of two buildings with unique architectural features. The estimated cost for the land and the construction of the prison on the Metropolis City site is eight million dollars.

The Deer Valley site is located in the sparsely populated Metropolis County, seventy-five miles from the court buildings. Deer Valley is a small town in a depressed rural area. Many of the residents of Deer Valley favor the construction of the prison, since they believe it will bring new jobs to the area. The roads between Deer Valley and Metropolis are narrow, and in a winter when the rains or snows are heavy, they may be impassable. The cost of utilities in Deer Valley is about twice the cost of utilities in Metropolis City. The estimated building cost in Deer Valley is seven million dollars.

Answer Key

Section I: Reading Comprehension

1. **E**	6. **A**	11. **A**	16. **C**	21. **A**	26. **B**
2. **C**	7. **C**	12. **D**	17. **B**	22. **D**	27. **C**
3. **D**	8. **D**	13. **E**	18. **B**	23. **B**	28. **D**
4. **A**	9. **B**	14. **A**	19. **B**	24. **C**	
5. **B**	10. **D**	15. **D**	20. **A**	25. **C**	

Section II: Analytical Reasoning

1. **B**	5. **E**	9. **B**	13. **E**	17. **C**	21. **D**
2. **E**	6. **D**	10. **E**	14. **D**	18. **E**	22. **B**
3. **B**	7. **C**	11. **E**	15. **E**	19. **D**	23. **C**
4. **C**	8. **E**	12. **D**	16. **B**	20. **E**	24. **C**

Section III: Logical Reasoning

1. **D**	6. **C**	11. **D**	16. **D**	21. **B**	26. **B**
2. **D**	7. **D**	12. **D**	17. **E**	22. **D**	
3. **C**	8. **B**	13. **D**	18. **D**	23. **A**	
4. **A**	9. **C**	14. **D**	19. **B**	24. **E**	
5. **E**	10. **C**	15. **A**	20. **B**	25. **B**	

Section IV: Reading Comprehension

1. **B**	6. **B**	11. **E**	16. **C**	21. **B**	26. **B**
2. **B**	7. **A**	12. **A**	17. **A**	22. **C**	27. **A**
3. **E**	8. **C**	13. **B**	18. **D**	23. **A**	28. **E**
4. **E**	9. **C**	14. **D**	19. **B**	24. **E**	
5. **A**	10. **B**	15. **D**	20. **C**	25. **B**	

Section V: Logical Reasoning

1. **C**	6. **B**	11. **C**	16. **B**	21. **B**
2. **B**	7. **B**	12. **E**	17. **D**	22. **A**
3. **E**	8. **E**	13. **A**	18. **E**	23. **A**
4. **E**	9. **A**	14. **D**	19. **A**	24. **E**
5. **A**	10. **D**	15. **E**	20. **C**	25. **C**

Model Test Analysis

Doing model exams and understanding the explanations afterwards are of course important in acquainting you with typical LSAT question types and successful approaches to the questions. However, another benefit of carefully analyzing these model tests is to understand the kinds of errors you are making and thus work to minimize them. For instance, if a very high percentage of your incorrect answers is due to "careless error" or "misread problem," then perhaps you are working much too fast and should slow your pace accordingly. If your incorrect answers are due primarily to "lack of knowledge," then a careful rereading and reworking of the appropriate question-type chapter may be in order. Or if you find that you aren't completing a large number of questions because of lack of time, you may need to either increase your speed or learn to use the "one-check, two-check" technique more effectively.

This kind of analysis of the model tests will enable you to identify your particular weaknesses and thus remedy them.

Model Test Three Analysis

Section	Total Number of Questions	Number Correct	Number Incorrect	Number Unanswered*
I. Reading Comprehension	28			
II. Analytical Reasoning	24			
III. Logical Reasoning	26			
IV. Reading Comprehension	28			
V. Logical Reasoning	25			
TOTALS:	131			

*At this stage in your preparation, you should not be leaving any blank answer spaces. At least fill in a guess, as there is no penalty for a wrong answer.

Reasons for Incorrect Answers

You may wish to evaluate the explanations before completing this chart.

Section	Total Number Incorrect	Lack of Knowledge	Misread Problem	Careless Error	Unanswered or Wrong Guess
I. Reading Comprehension					
II. Analytical Reasoning					
III. Logical Reasoning					
IV. Reading Comprehension					
V. Logical Reasoning					
TOTALS:					

Explanation of Answers

Section I

Passage 1

1. **E** Each of the first four cases is public or quasi-public land. The last is private, not likely to be open to the general public and therefore the owner may deny free speech on the property.

2. **C** In this instance, the property is clearly private; in the other cases, it is not always clear whether the property is public or private.

3. **D** The nature or character of the owner of the property is not a factor mentioned by the passage. All of the four other options are alluded to in the opening paragraphs of the passage.

4. **A** The author approvingly quotes the words of a mall chairman in support of this position. Choice (E) may not be true if the charity seekers are offensive.

5. **B** The passage cites Lord Chief Justice Hale's remarks of 1675. (C) and (D) are false and the passage does not discuss current practice in Canada and Great Britain (E).

6. **A** The passage concludes with Justice Black's remarks on the "preferred position" of First Amendment freedoms.

Passage 2

7. **C** This is the best answer because the passage recounts both Dickens' realization that the novel, based on his memories, was deeply personal and also his recognition that he was creating a "mediated version" of himself. See lines 13–20, 65–73. (A) covers only paragraph one of the passage; (B) is a secondary point, not the main idea. The novel can hardly be called prophetic (C), although one line suggests it "anticipated" turmoil in his marriage. However, this is not a main idea. (E) is an opinion not presented or suggested in the passage.

8. **D** This answer is supported by the main points in both paragraphs one and two. The author does not present a "psychological study of motivations" (A) nor does he primarily contrast two aspects of Dickens (B), (C). (E) is inaccurate; the passage does not show that the novel became a turning point in his life.

9. **B** The line indicates that writing the book has called up his childhood memories and therefore "almost inevitably" led him back to the place where he was a small boy. The line does not indicate complete exhaustion (A) nor does it suggest that he was unable to separate reality and fiction (C). (D) is simply inaccurate. It is too far a leap to infer that because he returns to Rochester, he has overcome the trauma of his childhood (E), particularly because of the inclusion of the words "almost inevitably."

10. **D** This is the best of the answers because Fanny's significance is clearly suggested in lines 36–40. Although (A) might seem correct because future turmoil in his marriage is indicated (lines 22–25), an end to the marriage is not implied. (C) is incorrect because although it is suggested that he sometimes put his work and his own ego above his family, coolness and distance are not implied. (B) and (E) are not supported by information in the passage.

11. **A** Although (C) and (D) are accurate statements, they are not the *most significant* reasons for Dickens' choice of the name. Lines 65–73 suggest that (A) is the correct answer. (B) and (E) are not supported by information in the passage.

12. **D** This is the best answer because the parenthetical phrase concerning Catherine indicates her reaction to her husband's assumption of the right to name the children, which in turn suggests something about their relationship. Failing to insist on naming her children does not indicate that she is an inadequate mother (A). (B), (C), and (E) are simply not suggested in this line.

13. **E** The author is primarily objective and analytical in the passage. (A) is incorrect because although there is perhaps some irony (e.g., lines 40–42), it is minor. (B), (C), and (D) are simply incorrect; the author is neither argumentative, condescending, nor persuasive, for example.

14. **A** The first paragraph includes an account of Dickens' reactions to writing the novel, using many of his own quotations. The second paragraph relies on more commentary from the author, and also introduces related points, such as Dickens' choice of the novel's title and his interest in names. (E) is incorrect because paragraph one doesn't show the *effect* of Dickens' childhood on him, nor does the second paragraph connect his later life with his novels. Similarly, (B), (C), and (D) all include inadequate (or inaccurate) descriptions of the two paragraphs of the passage.

Passage 3

15. **D** This summarizes the main point of paragraph one. See lines 3–10, 24–30. (B) is incorrect because the principles were only sometimes laid down in "heavenly writ." (E) is a correct statement but not the best description of the society. (A) is not supported by the passage. (C) is inaccurate.

16. **C** The author gives two examples—a settlement where community was dominant and settlements where kinship was dominant—to illustrate that although community and family always operated together, they did so in different ways. The examples are not included to show a diverse population (A) nor is any point illustrated or judgment made of religious and nonreligious communities (B), (D), (E).

17. **B** See lines 49–62. Permanence allowed people to have a much better knowledge of others in their community, the routines, customs, and history. This in turn made it easier to measure the state of the community against a "superstructure of truth." (D) and (E), while possibly true, are not supported by the passage. (A) and (C) are simply inaccurate.

18. **B** Paragraph two focuses on the roles of both community and family and shows how they operated together to maintain the principles of the closed system of society. See lines 45–52. Paragraph two does not provide historical background (A) nor does it provide a contrast with paragraph one (C). It is not a transition (D) nor does it contrast types of communities (E).

19. **B** The point of paragraph three is that people required "careful articulation" and "explicit demonstration" in matters that were beyond their local community. A federal constitution would be an absolute necessity to them so that they could ensure it was in agreement with correct principles. (E) is incorrect because people did trust unwritten general principles on matters within their communities. (A), (C), and (D) are either irrelevant or unsupported by information in the passage.

20. **A** Paragraph one stresses the importance of general governing principles, and paragraph three is concerned with how people ensured adherence to those principles when events were beyond their immediate community. (B) is incorrect; there is no reference to mistrust of outsiders. (D) is also incorrect because there is no reference to people's reaction to change. (C) and (E) are simply inaccurate statements.

21. **A** The passage emphasizes the framework of rules and principles that defined the society. Questioning authority and trusting yourself above all would not be likely advice. (B), (C), (D), and (E) are all suggested by information given in the passage.

22. **D** This states the main idea presented in paragraph one, with its implications developed in paragraphs two and three. (B) is the second-best answer but emphasizes a secondary point rather than the main point. (E) is incorrect because the passage does not draw the contrast between effective and ineffective application of the principles. (C) suggests a minor point, and (A) is inaccurate.

Passage 4

23. **B** The first paragraph says that taxonomy was "in the forefront of the
sciences" in "the eighteenth and
early nineteenth centuries."

24. **C** The terms refer to plants and
animals.

25. **C** The passage gives us no information
to support (A), (B), or (E). (D) is untrue (they were among the "greatest
biologists of Europe"). That Darwin
spent many years and wrote three
volumes about the taxonomy of barnacles suggest that there are a large
number of kinds to describe.

26. **B** The third paragraph gives examples
of the "genuine pioneers" mentioned
at the end of the second paragraph.
The scientists of the first paragraph
are not "exclusively European,"
(Jefferson).

27. **C** Parsifal was a naive knight of German
legend and Klingsor was his enemy, a
magician with an enchanted garden.
The reference to Parsifal's bravery
and the use of the word "vanquished"
should suggest this answer.

28. **D** Though the passage does include (A),
(B), and (C), the best choice here is
(D), which describes all three para-
graphs in the passage.

Section II

Answers 1–6

From the information given you should pull
out information and list the two possibilities:

```
        1 2 3 4 5 6 7 8

JJJJ or JJJ
RR
CC
```

```
R ? J
```

Two Possibilities:
```
JJJJ            JJJ
R R    or     R R R
C C            C C
```

1. **B** If four jazz songs are played and the
first and last song are of the same
type, there are two possible arrangements. Remember, at least two of
each type of song are required. Start
by placing the first and last song; for
example, two rock songs. It is apparent that there is only one place for
the four jazz songs, since, other than
jazz, no two songs of the same type
can be consecutive.

```
R C J J J J C R
C R J J J J R C
```

In both arrangements a jazz song is
played third. For each of the other
answer choices, there are two types
of songs played.

2. **E** If three rock songs are played, the
remaining five songs must be made
up of two country songs and three
jazz songs, since there must be more
jazz songs than country songs. Since
a rock song must precede the first
jazz song, there is only one arrangement where a country song is played
sixth.

```
R J J J R C R C
```

3. **B** There are four possible arrangements
where a jazz song is played third and
the first and last songs of the same
type.

```
R J J J C R C R
R C J J J R C R
R C J J J J C R
C R J J J J R C
```

In none of the arrangements is the
sixth song a country song.

4. **C** There is only one arrangement containing three jazz songs where all
three jazz songs are last. There are
two arrangements containing four
jazz songs. The songs at the beginning of the play list must alternate.

```
R C R C R J J J
R C R C J J J J
C R C R J J J J
```

5. **E** If a country song is played first and
seventh, there is only one possible
arrangement using three jazz songs
and one arrangement using four jazz
songs. In both cases, a jazz song is
being played third.

C	R	J	J	J	R	C	R
C	R	J	J	J	J	C	R

6. **D** Since a country song was fifth, the first three songs must be rock-country-rock. This leaves only three arrangements for the remaining songs.

R	C	R	K	C	J	J	J	J
R	C	R	K	C	J	J	J	R
R	C	R	K	C	R	J	J	J

In all three arrangements, there is a rock song played third.

Answers 7–13

From the information given, you could have made the following relationships:

$$J > L + M + N$$
$$N = L + M$$
$$M > K + G$$
$$G > H$$
$$K = G$$

7. **C** From the diagram above, since Jon has more bills than Lynn, Melanie, and Neil combined and since Melanie has more bills than Ken and George combined, then Jon has the most bills.

8. **E** Since Hal has fewer bills than George, and George has fewer bills than Melanie, and Melanie has fewer bills than Neil, and Neil has fewer bills than Jon, then Hal has the fewest number of bills. At this point you may have deduced most of the order of students:

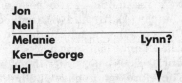

If you realized these relationships immediately from the initial conditions, you should have made this part of your first diagram.

9. **B** From the chart for the previous problem we see that only choice (B) must be true.

10. **E** Using this new information with the order chart, we have the following chart:

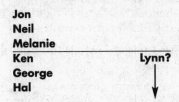

You may have approached this problem by eliminating the incorrect choices.

11. **E** Since Neil has the same number of bills as Lynn and Melanie combined, and Jon has more bills than Lynn, Melanie, and Neil combined, therefore Jon has more bills than twice the number of Lynn's and Melanie's bills. Choice (E) is false.

12. **D** If Lynn and Melanie have the same number of bills, then Lynn has more bills than Ken and George combined. Since George has more bills than Hal and since Neil has the same number of bills as Lynn and Melanie combined, then Neil has more bills than Lynn, George, and Hal combined.

13. **E** If Tom has more bills than Ken and fewer than Lynn, the order of students would now be as follows:

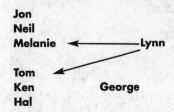

Therefore, Lynn having more bills than Hal is the only one that must be true.

Answers 14–20

From the information given, you may have set up the following display:

```
        ⌢×
       /   \
Alli  Boris Cisco Dan
____   C    S    ____    O —1 or 2
                         S —2 or more
____  ____  ____  ____
?→____ ____ ____ ____    C
                         O
                         S⌝
                        ⌐P⌟×
                         ⌐R⌟
```

Since Boris eats chocolate chip cookies, Cisco does not. Since Cisco eats sugar cookies, Boris does not. We are given that Alli does not eat sugar cookies and at least two people must eat sugar cookies, so Dan must eat sugar cookies. Anyone who eats sugar cookies does not eat raisin cookies, thus Dan does not eat raisin cookies. Your display should now look like this:

```
        ⌢×
       /   \
Alli  Boris Cisco Dan
____   C    S    S      O —1 or 2
       S̶    S̶    R̶      S —2 or more
            C̶
                         C
                         O
                         S⌝
                        ⌐P⌟×
                         ⌐R⌟
```

14. **D** From the display above you can see that Dan does not eat raisin cookies.

15. **E** If Boris eats exactly three kinds of cookies they must be chocolate chip, peanut butter, and raisin. Since Boris eats chocolate chip cookies but does not eat sugar cookies, he must eat two of the remaining three—peanut butter, raisin, oatmeal. But Cisco cannot eat raisin, so if Boris eats raisin, he must eat peanut butter. Since Cisco must eat at least two types, he must eat sugar cookies and oatmeal cookies. The display should look like this:

```
        ⌢×
       /   \
Alli  Boris Cisco Dan
____   C    S    S
       P    O
       R    R̶    R̶
```

16. **B** At most, two people eat oatmeal cookies, thus, if Alli and Dan eat oatmeal cookies, Boris and Cisco cannot. Thus, Boris must eat at least one more type of cookie. Either Boris eats peanut butter cookies, or raisin and peanut butter cookies. Either way, Boris eats peanut butter cookies. Thus, Cisco cannot eat peanut butter cookies. This is not a possible arrangement since Cisco must eat at least two types of cookies. The display would look like this:

```
        ⌢×
       /   \
Alli  Boris Cisco Dan
       C    S    S
O      S̶         O
       P    R̶    R̶
            C̶
            P̶
```

17. **C** The general conditions state that oatmeal cookies can only be eaten by a maximum of two people, thus, choices (A), (B), and (D) are incorrect. Choice (E) can be eliminated since Alli cannot eat sugar cookies and Boris does not eat them either. Therefore, by process of elimination, choice (C) must be correct.

18. **E** This problem follows directly from the given conditions. Sugar cookies is the only cookie type that must be eaten by exactly two different people.

19. **D** If Alli does not eat chocolate chip or raisin cookies (or sugar cookies), she must eat oatmeal and peanut butter cookies, since those are the only ones left.

Ṣ			
Alli	Boris	Cisco	Dan
O	C	S	S
O	R	Ṛ	Ṛ
Ç	P	Ç	
Ṛ			

It is possible for Boris to eat raisin and peanut butter cookies, which would preclude Cisco from eating peanut butter cookies.

Choice (A) is not possible. If Dan eats oatmeal cookies, Boris and Cisco cannot, since at most two people eat oatmeal cookies. In order for Cisco to eat two kinds of cookies, he must eat peanut butter cookies. If Cisco eats peanut butter cookies, Boris cannot. But this is not possible, since Boris needs to eat two types of cookies too, and he cannot eat raisin cookies without peanut butter cookies.

Choice (B) is incorrect, since two people eat sugar cookies and at most two can eat chocolate chip cookies.

Choice (C) is incorrect. If only Alli eats peanut butter cookies, Boris does not eat peanut butter or raisin cookies. Thus Boris would have to eat oatmeal cookies in order to eat two types. But Cisco would also have to eat oatmeal cookies in order to eat two types. Boris and Cisco cannot both eat oatmeal cookies. Choice (E) is incorrect because the initial conditions state that Cisco eats sugar cookies, so Boris could not.

20. **E** Raisin cookies cannot be eaten by Cisco and Dan, and they do not have to be eaten by Alli or Boris. We can also eliminate the other choices. From initial conditions, chocolate chip cookies are eaten by at least one person and sugar cookies are eaten by two people. This eliminates choices (A) and (C). If no one eats peanut butter cookies, no one can eat raisin cookies either. This would force Boris and Cisco to eat oatmeal cookies, but they can't eat the same cookie. This eliminates choice (D). If no one eats oatmeal cookies, Cisco must eat peanut butter cookies, since he must eat two kinds of cookies. Boris must eat raisin cookies in order to eat at least two kinds of cookies, but if he eats raisin cookies, he must eat peanut butter cookies as well. This is not possible, since Cisco is already eating peanut butter cookies. This eliminates choice (B).

Answers 21–24

From the information given, it would be helpful to construct the following chart to answer the questions:

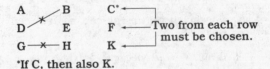

*If C, then also K.

21. **D** If A is not chosen, then B and C are chosen. Since C is chosen, K is chosen too. Since B is chosen, D is not chosen. Thus, E and F are chosen. So, if A is not chosen, B, C, E, F, and K must be chosen.

22. **B** If D is chosen, then B is not chosen. Therefore, (B) could NOT be chosen. Also, A and C must be chosen. If C is chosen, then so is K. E or F is chosen. G or H is chosen.

23. **C** If B is chosen, then D is not chosen. Thus, E and F are chosen. Notice that statement 6 is not two-directional.

24. **C** Since G and H do not play together, only one will be chosen. Thus, K must be chosen.

Section III

1. **D** If 97 percent of fatalities occurred *below* 45 mph, then a reduction in the maximum speed from 65 to 55 mph would have little impact, no more than a 3 percent reduction (if we assume that all other fatalities occurred between 55 and 65 mph). (A) and (C) are not relevant, (B) provides no conclusive data, and (E) *strengthens* the argument.

2. **D** The information states:
   1. If busing passes, then Smith was not reelected.
   2. Smith was reelected.
   Therefore, busing failed.
   3. If Smith is reelected she will vote for busing.
   4. Smith was reelected.
   Therefore, Smith voted for busing.

   (A) and (B) are wrong, because busing failed. (C) is wrong because Smith voted for busing. (E) is wrong because there are insufficient data to support it.

3. **C** Webster is stating that not only do lies disagree with truth, but they usually also disagree with other lies. Thus, it would follow that liars often quarrel with other liars.

4. **A** The given argument can be reduced to:

is not	S (star)	because	H (hit)
is	H	because	S

   (A) exhibits the structure closest to that of the given argument:

is not	F (final word)	because	C (correct)
is	C (correct)	because	F ("Instructor" is the final word.)

5. **E** The logic here is straightforward. If the refineries are operating at 60 percent, not 75 percent of their capacity, then oil prices will probably rise.

6. **C** The discussion points out that (A) is an implication (rather than an assumption) of the studies. (B) is also not an assumption but is a restatement of the discussion's central issue. In order to consider speaker characteristics as either relevant or irrelevant, the author must assume that such a distinction exists; that assumption is expressed by (C). The passage does not assume a trim speaker will be "more persuasive" (D) or that irrelevant aspects are more influential than content (E), though it does suggest that these are issues worth examining.

7. **D** The final sentence of the passage offers an alternative explanation of the phenomenon introduced in the first sentence.

8. **B** The author, by offering an alternative explanation, stresses the scientists' unwillingness to consider such alternatives. (A), a choice worth considering, should be eliminated because the alternative suggested by the author is no more verifiable than the assertion he criticizes.

9. **C** The author argues that the term "progressive" is avoided by educators because of abuses in the progressive education movement, and that therefore, recently new, educational practices have avoided being tagged with the name "progressive." If choice (C) were true—that "progressive learning" has recently met with approval in middle class public schools—it would contradict the author's statement about the connotation of the word "progressive" and seriously weaken his argument.

10. **C** The misunderstanding arises from Dave's assumption that Bill has said *every* morning, not *almost* every morning. (D), although worth considering, is not best because it does not address the scope of Bill's remark.

11. **D** Because the first two statements are not absolute, we may conclude sunbathing is unlikely but still possible. There is no information in the passage to support (A), (B), (C), or (E).

12. **D** (A) and (B) are, by commonsense standards, implausible. (C) might be a valid statement, but it is not implied by Wilkie's assertion, which makes no distinction between first- and second-class citizens, and so implies (D).

13. **D** Since the passage does not say that the 200 students in spring activities were all different and all different from the 100 in fall activities, the total number of students could be much lower than 300. A single student could participate in all three activities in both semesters. (C) could apply if there were more than one activity, but (D) is a correct assumption in any case.

14. **D** If *nothing* produces only nothing, then the production of something *must* require something. (A) makes the production of something from something a possibility; however, the original statement implies that the something/something relationship is imperative.

15. **A** Only (A) makes an unqualified negative assessment; each of the other choices is either a neutral statement or one that attempts to balance positive and negative terms.

16. **D** The term *average* in the passage implies that if some workers earned more than $7.87 per day, others must have earned less. In choice (C) the words *far more than* make that choice not necessarily true.

17. **E** The magazine is sure that Jones will be a contender soon, and all that is offered to support this is the fact that Jinkins will train him. Therefore, (A) and (B) are the assumptions motivating the passage. (E) is not an assumption, but rather a statement made explicitly in the article.

18. **D** All the other examples are dilemmas. Amleth must choose between failure to avenge or failure to protect his mother; the zoo must choose between the loss of the grant and the loss of a kudu. Ames must choose between higher rent and customer inconvenience. The driver must choose between a parking ticket and losing a radio. In (D), there is no choice between disagreeable alternatives. If you don't have enough money, you can't buy enough meat.

19. **B** The structure of question 19 may be simplified as follows:

C (crowded) <u>whenever</u> <u>H</u> (holiday)
Not C; <u>therefore</u>, <u>not H</u>

(B) is most nearly parallel to the relationships presented in the question:
R (reptiles) <u>whenever</u> <u>D</u> (hot desert day)

Not R (absent); <u>therefore</u>, not <u>D</u>.

20. **B** (A) is not a strong choice; the author indicates only that Nerd is *very* wealthy. The author does not compare Nerd's wealth to that of the other candidates. (C) contradicts the third sentence of the author's statement. Since the author tells us that Nerd has the necessary wealth and should acquire skill as a speaker, the author must believe that the third attribute (experience) is not an issue. In other words, the author believes that Nerd has satisfactory experience. The passage does not assert that an improvement in Nerd's public speaking will guarantee a win (D). Since Nerd has wealth and experience but inadequate speaking skills, he is a dark horse (E).

21. **B** (A) would not weaken the argument, since being wealthy, but not necessarily wealthiest, is all that is called for. (D) and (E) are consistent with the expressed or implied information in the argument. Although (C) is a possible answer choice, (B) is superior; it directly contradicts the author's assertions.

22. **D** The given statement tells us only that the car is blue. For us to be *assured* that it is slow we must know either that every blue car is slow *or* that no blue car accelerates quickly. (D) restricts quick acceleration to red cars.

23. **A** The argument obviously avoids absolute terms, relying instead on words such as "almost" and "sometimes." Therefore, it would seem consistent that a basic assumption would also avoid absolute terms; only (A) does so. In addition, (A) makes explicit the assumption underlying the first sentence of the passage.

24. **E** The second sentence diminishes the government's "fault" and the final sentence continues this idea; the only restatement that takes into account extragovernmental responsibility for intrusion is (E).

25. **B** The key phrase in the author's remarks is "*falsely* equating knowledge [viewing] with action [crime]." (A) is poor because it links knowledge with action. (C) is poor because the author indicates that those who dictate what we see (in other words, the censors) are guilty of drawing false (illogical) relationships. (D) and (E) are not relevant to the author's argument. (B) is consistent with the author's position that knowledge and action do not necessarily go hand in hand.

26. **B** A ruling on resources must at least presume the possibility that such resources exist; otherwise it is absurd. All other choices are irrelevant to the ruling.

Section IV
Passage 1

1. **B** Each of the other choices is too specific and/or not indicative of the *neutral* rather than argumentative *tone* of the passage.

2. **B** In the fourth paragraph, the author notes that after Congress had stopped enacting its reapportionment power, "serious malapportionment" problems ensued; the author thus implies that federal supervision is necessary. (C), (D), and (E) are issues on which the author does not imply an opinion.

3. **E** A clue to this answer occurs in paragraph 5, in which "malapportionment" is replaced by "the size and shape of electoral districts." Each of the other choices *may contribute* to malapportionment, but each is too specific to be the best choice.

4. **E** In the fifth paragraph we learn that the *voters* asked the Warren Court to rule on apportionment issues; therefore, we must assume that a ballot was taken that expressed the voters' opinions.

5. **A** Question 1 is answered in the first paragraph. The other questions, although they may be implied as *issues* in the passage, are not answered.

6. **B** Justice Frankfurter did not declare his opinion about reapportionment per se, but did declare that the Supreme Court should not address the issue; the Warren Court, on the other hand, did deliberate over the reapportionment issue. Therefore, we may conclude that Frankfurter was not a member of the Warren Court.

7. **A** The passage is a summary of events that occurred through the century, relative to apportionment. Each of the other choices has the author writing a passage calculated to persuade rather than to inform.

Passage 2

8. **C** The passage says, "Born into a nation whose people were steeped in the traditions of prehistory, in the lore of the faeries and the Druids, he remained free to believe." Choice (C) reiterates this idea, that the environment of the believer enhances the belief. The great memory (A), however, is not confined to a single environment, but rather exists for all humans. Choice (B) is incorrect because the passage suggests the opposite: The reader need not know the specific occult practices in order to understand Yeats's writing. Choice (D) is incorrect because, according to the passage, imagination, as Yeats understands it, is *not* rationalistic, and (E) is incorrect because although the writing may call to the child, it does not call to the adult, who has lost belief.

9. **C** Choice (C) directly follows the progression of the passage's paragraphs. The first paragraph discusses the primitive and childhood belief in "the world that we could not see," that is, certain concepts about humanity. The second and third paragraphs connect that belief with Yeats's belief and background. The final paragraph deals with Yeats's use of that belief in his writing, that is, his attitudes toward these concepts. None of the other choices follows the development of the passage.

10. **B** The passage states that Yeats conjures up the imagination by the use of symbols, which are in the "great memory." It's appropriate to think, then, that Yeats would agree that the symbol of the tree is also part of the "great memory" and that it would evoke similar responses in readers not only in a particular environment but throughout the world.

11. **E** Choice (E) is the most straightforward and complete title for the passage. The other choices describe only a portion of the passage.

12. **A** The passage says. "It is this great mind, and great memory, to which Yeats is calling and which he insists can be evoked by symbols, whether from Celtic lore, the Upanishads, or the Noh plays." The sentence illustrates the commonality of symbols, even in works from different cultures—Celtic lore (Ireland, Scotland, Wales), the Upanishads (Hindu religious writing), and Noh plays (Japan).

13. **B** If, as Yeats suggests, the successors of "the masters of magic," the "poet, the musician, and the artist," may use symbols "half unconsciously," then he would most likely not agree that they are "aware of the power and magic of the symbols they use."

14. **D** The second paragraph deals with the young Yeats living in Sligo. The third paragraph extends this time into the near future, a time in which Yeats became fascinated with symbols, and the final sentence says, "we must at least have an understanding of its [the occult's] meaning to him and the depth to which it affected everything he wrote." The final paragraph changes focus to comment on the reader and on Yeats's general attitudes toward symbolism. The only choice given that could logically fit between these two paragraphs is (D), which follows the discussion of Yeats's early interest in the occult with a paragraph that would probably go on to detail his involvement with the study of the occult in later life. All the other choices disrupt the flow and organization of the passage.

Passage 3

15. **D** The passage is concerned with the earthly nature of the pagan gods and the implications of that earthly nature. (A), (B), and (C) are correct statements but are subtopics or minor points.

16. **C** Both metaphors, which involve eating out in restaurants and conducting business, suggest the earthbound nature of the gods. (A) and (D) are incorrect because they address qualities not attributed to the gods in this passage.

17. **A** "A la carte" means that each menu item is chosen separately (cf. choice of gods), while "fixed menu" refers to an entire meal ordered as one item (cf. one true god). It is clear in paragraph one that the choice is among deities, not among holy books (C) or varieties of worship (E).

18. **D** There is no irony in the passage. For examples of *contrast*, see lines 24–31; for *example*, see lines 41–52; for *figurative language*, see lines 7–17; for *explanation*, see lines 62–78.

19. **B** See lines 57–65. According to the passage, tolerance was an aspect of paganism, making religious wars unlikely. (A), (C), and (D) are not implied in the passage, and (E) is contradicted.

20. **C** Lines 1–9 imply that "morality" is sometimes erroneously linked to salvation and an afterlife, and that historians have made this error with paganism because of the nature of the religion. (A) and (D) are not suggested by information in the passage, (B) is irrelevant, and (E) is inaccurate.

21. **B** See lines 40–41, 57–61. (D) is a correct statement but does not explain the basis of religious tolerance. (A), (C), and (E) are not supported anywhere in the passage.

22. **C** Paragraph three essentially creates a diagram in words to explain man's relationship to God in both paganism and the religions of the Book. (A) and (E) might be considered correct but both are imprecise; paragraph three doesn't actually summarize or evaluate, nor does it simplify all the points in paragraphs one and two.

Passage 4

23. **A** See lines 26–28 and lines 33–34. Astronomers use a method *similar* to triangulation, but only to measure distances up to about 70 light-years; also, nothing indicates that the method is imprecise (B). Conflicting beliefs of astronomers are not addressed in the passage (C) nor is the quality of their instrumentation (D). (E) is not supported in the passage.

24. **E** A star's life span depends largely on its initial mass, not the types of gases at its core. See lines 95–97. All the other statements are true. (A) is supported by paragraph 3, (B) by lines 20–23, (C) by paragraph 5, and (D) by paragraph 6.

25. **B** Support for this inference can be found in lines 100–105. (A) is incorrect because not all stars that lose their hydrogen become white dwarfs (see lines 95–99). (C) is contradicted by lines 94–95. (D) is not supported; initial mass is the only factor cited to account for a star's life span. Although the passage states that the Sun has a long life, it does not imply that the reason is its ability to transform hydrogen into helium but rather its size (E).

26. **B** Of the choices, (B) is the best. Although (D) recognizes the difference between the first four and the last two paragraphs, it says that the first paragraph includes a thesis statement. This passage does not develop a thesis. (A), (C), and (E) do not refer to the shift in focus in paragraphs 5 and 6.

27. **A** Hydrogen is converted to helium, not helium to hydrogen. See paragraph 5, (B) and (C) are supported in paragraph 4, and (D) and (E) in paragraph 6 (lines 86–87 and 99).

28. **E** Although the author might want to encourage the study of astronomy (C), the method used to present material is informational, not motivational. (A), (B), and (D) are all aspects of the passage but too limited to describe its purpose.

Section V

1. **C** The passage argues that environmental restrictions will lead to losses of jobs and hence workers, but if workers are already leaving because the environmental quality is poor, the argument is seriously weakened.

2. **B** The passage makes no comment on workers leaving before a manufacturer. It argues that the loss of manufacturers leads to a loss of workers (E).

3. **E** Harry does not need to deal with the connection between excessive carbon dioxide and global warming, because he does not believe there is too much carbon dioxide in the atmo-sphere. He argues that the oceans take care of the gas, so there is no danger.

4. **E** Though choices (A), (B), (C), and (D) might contribute to increased study of math in Bermuda, (E) leaves no doubt. High schools in Bermuda require four years of advanced math for graduation; high schools in the United States do not.

5. **A** Though all of the choices are plausible here, (A) is the best choice. The first sentence asserts the conclusion ("superior"), and the second asserts a consequence ("immature . . . prefer"). The last repeats what has already been insisted upon.

6. **B** The critic requires a good mystery to have "an interesting location," and "a plot that observes probability." If the book in question is disappointing, it may well have "an unrealized setting" and events that "are hard to believe."

7. **B** The passage suggests that records are set only by rare, superior performers, and an increase or decrease in the number of participants would not significantly change the number of record-setting performances.

8. **E** The passage makes its point by analogy, comparing the dangers of smoking to the dangers of asbestos and radioactivity.

9. **A** The passage is clearly hostile to the racist candidate, and has found a "ray of hope." The conclusion should logically predict his defeat. Choice (A) also draws a conclusion related to the part of the paragraph that refers to "regular Republicans."

10. **D** The argument uses both simile ("like strip mining or clear-cutting") and metaphor ("walls of death").

11. **C** If the halibut population is endangered, the banning of gill-nets would improve the fish's chance for survival. If (A) and (B) are true, the fisheries' argument about the price rise has more merit. If (D) and (E) are true, the reduction of the sea otter population would be more defensible.

12. **E** Choices (A), (B), (C), and (D) are reasonable objections, but the argument that *no* writing is without some scientific value is an overstatement.

13. **A** The assumption is that where there are no pesticide controls, no edible fish can be found, not the reverse as in (B), (D), and (E).

14. **D** The results of the elections and the fact that there are three congressmen from the north and three from the south suggest that the populations are nearly equal. Choice (A) would be a likely choice if "always" were changed to "usually." Choice (B) is unlikely, and the passage gives us no reason either to believe in or to disbelieve (C) and (E).

15. **E** The argument is that, one way or another, people can afford to buy their medications. Choice (E), in some measure, supports that argument or at the least is irrelevant to it. People who travel to buy their prescriptions or order them by mail *are*, it would seem, able to afford them somehow. All the other choices weaken the argument, with choices (B), (C), and (D) each suggesting reasons people could't afford the drugs and (A) indicating that the type of drug needed may not be available free from the drug companies.

16. **B** If the results are like those of the "recent past," the total should approximate "an average of 22 House" and "2 Senate seats."

17. **D** The conclusion could be more reasonably assessed if we knew how often the paranormal signs had been false. The issue is not how many contestants win money or how much money they win. The issue is the paranormal aid.

18. **E** The words "this is the price we must pay" (that is, we must suffer aphid infestation because the rutabagas have been destroyed) indicated that the author makes all of the assumptions of (A), (B), (C), and (D). The idea of (E) may be true, but it is not an assumption of the passage.

19. **A** The apparent contradiction disappears if the total state budget has increased enough so that the *expenditure* on education has been raised by three million each year while at the same time the *percentage* spent on education is a smaller part of the whole budget.

20. **C** In each case, the verb ("iron" . . . "need ironing"; "write" . . . "to be written") is repeated, while the adjective ("many") modifies the repeated noun.

21. **B** The first statement asserts that great playwrights will not develop in repressive countries. Therefore, the great satirists which repressive countries will produce (the second statement) will not write plays.

22. **A** The details of the paragraph and the phrase "bleak outlook" suggest that a settlement is not likely.

23. **A** If the new labels will appear on less than 20 percent of the food sold, they will not be very effective.

24. **E** As the United States is still unwilling to act, its downplaying the conference is a predictable response. Though several of the other choices are plausible, none follows so clearly from what the paragraph has already said.

25. **C** If there has been a steady rise in car sales, consumers cannot be "cutting back on spending plans for new cars," as the predictions assert.

Chapter 9

MODEL TEST FOUR

This chapter contains full-length Model Test Four. It is geared to the format of the LSAT, and it is complete with answers and explanations. It is equivalent to the LSAT in question structure, number of questions, level of difficulty and time allotments. (The questions used are not taken directly from the LSAT, as those questions are copyrighted and may not be reproduced.)

Model Test Four should be taken under strict test conditions. The test ends with a 30-minute Writing Sample, which is not scored.

Section	Description	Number of Questions	Time Allowed
I.	Analytical Reasoning	24	35 minutes
II.	Logical Reasoning	26	35 minutes
III.	Logical Reasoning	25	35 minutes
IV.	Reading Comprehension	27	35 minutes
V.	Analytical Reasoning	24	35 minutes
	Writing Sample		30 minutes
TOTALS:		126	3 hours 25 minutes

Now please turn to the next page, remove your answer sheet, and begin Model Test Four.

Answer Sheet—Model Test Four

Section 1	Section 2	Section 3	Section 4	Section 5
1. Ⓐ Ⓑ Ⓒ Ⓓ Ⓔ	1. Ⓐ Ⓑ Ⓒ Ⓓ Ⓔ	1. Ⓐ Ⓑ Ⓒ Ⓓ Ⓔ	1. Ⓐ Ⓑ Ⓒ Ⓓ Ⓔ	1. Ⓐ Ⓑ Ⓒ Ⓓ Ⓔ
2. Ⓐ Ⓑ Ⓒ Ⓓ Ⓔ	2. Ⓐ Ⓑ Ⓒ Ⓓ Ⓔ	2. Ⓐ Ⓑ Ⓒ Ⓓ Ⓔ	2. Ⓐ Ⓑ Ⓒ Ⓓ Ⓔ	2. Ⓐ Ⓑ Ⓒ Ⓓ Ⓔ
3. Ⓐ Ⓑ Ⓒ Ⓓ Ⓔ	3. Ⓐ Ⓑ Ⓒ Ⓓ Ⓔ	3. Ⓐ Ⓑ Ⓒ Ⓓ Ⓔ	3. Ⓐ Ⓑ Ⓒ Ⓓ Ⓔ	3. Ⓐ Ⓑ Ⓒ Ⓓ Ⓔ
4. Ⓐ Ⓑ Ⓒ Ⓓ Ⓔ	4. Ⓐ Ⓑ Ⓒ Ⓓ Ⓔ	4. Ⓐ Ⓑ Ⓒ Ⓓ Ⓔ	4. Ⓐ Ⓑ Ⓒ Ⓓ Ⓔ	4. Ⓐ Ⓑ Ⓒ Ⓓ Ⓔ
5. Ⓐ Ⓑ Ⓒ Ⓓ Ⓔ	5. Ⓐ Ⓑ Ⓒ Ⓓ Ⓔ	5. Ⓐ Ⓑ Ⓒ Ⓓ Ⓔ	5. Ⓐ Ⓑ Ⓒ Ⓓ Ⓔ	5. Ⓐ Ⓑ Ⓒ Ⓓ Ⓔ
6. Ⓐ Ⓑ Ⓒ Ⓓ Ⓔ	6. Ⓐ Ⓑ Ⓒ Ⓓ Ⓔ	6. Ⓐ Ⓑ Ⓒ Ⓓ Ⓔ	6. Ⓐ Ⓑ Ⓒ Ⓓ Ⓔ	6. Ⓐ Ⓑ Ⓒ Ⓓ Ⓔ
7. Ⓐ Ⓑ Ⓒ Ⓓ Ⓔ	7. Ⓐ Ⓑ Ⓒ Ⓓ Ⓔ	7. Ⓐ Ⓑ Ⓒ Ⓓ Ⓔ	7. Ⓐ Ⓑ Ⓒ Ⓓ Ⓔ	7. Ⓐ Ⓑ Ⓒ Ⓓ Ⓔ
8. Ⓐ Ⓑ Ⓒ Ⓓ Ⓔ	8. Ⓐ Ⓑ Ⓒ Ⓓ Ⓔ	8. Ⓐ Ⓑ Ⓒ Ⓓ Ⓔ	8. Ⓐ Ⓑ Ⓒ Ⓓ Ⓔ	8. Ⓐ Ⓑ Ⓒ Ⓓ Ⓔ
9. Ⓐ Ⓑ Ⓒ Ⓓ Ⓔ	9. Ⓐ Ⓑ Ⓒ Ⓓ Ⓔ	9. Ⓐ Ⓑ Ⓒ Ⓓ Ⓔ	9. Ⓐ Ⓑ Ⓒ Ⓓ Ⓔ	9. Ⓐ Ⓑ Ⓒ Ⓓ Ⓔ
10. Ⓐ Ⓑ Ⓒ Ⓓ Ⓔ	10. Ⓐ Ⓑ Ⓒ Ⓓ Ⓔ	10. Ⓐ Ⓑ Ⓒ Ⓓ Ⓔ	10. Ⓐ Ⓑ Ⓒ Ⓓ Ⓔ	10. Ⓐ Ⓑ Ⓒ Ⓓ Ⓔ
11. Ⓐ Ⓑ Ⓒ Ⓓ Ⓔ	11. Ⓐ Ⓑ Ⓒ Ⓓ Ⓔ	11. Ⓐ Ⓑ Ⓒ Ⓓ Ⓔ	11. Ⓐ Ⓑ Ⓒ Ⓓ Ⓔ	11. Ⓐ Ⓑ Ⓒ Ⓓ Ⓔ
12. Ⓐ Ⓑ Ⓒ Ⓓ Ⓔ	12. Ⓐ Ⓑ Ⓒ Ⓓ Ⓔ	12. Ⓐ Ⓑ Ⓒ Ⓓ Ⓔ	12. Ⓐ Ⓑ Ⓒ Ⓓ Ⓔ	12. Ⓐ Ⓑ Ⓒ Ⓓ Ⓔ
13. Ⓐ Ⓑ Ⓒ Ⓓ Ⓔ	13. Ⓐ Ⓑ Ⓒ Ⓓ Ⓔ	13. Ⓐ Ⓑ Ⓒ Ⓓ Ⓔ	13. Ⓐ Ⓑ Ⓒ Ⓓ Ⓔ	13. Ⓐ Ⓑ Ⓒ Ⓓ Ⓔ
14. Ⓐ Ⓑ Ⓒ Ⓓ Ⓔ	14. Ⓐ Ⓑ Ⓒ Ⓓ Ⓔ	14. Ⓐ Ⓑ Ⓒ Ⓓ Ⓔ	14. Ⓐ Ⓑ Ⓒ Ⓓ Ⓔ	14. Ⓐ Ⓑ Ⓒ Ⓓ Ⓔ
15. Ⓐ Ⓑ Ⓒ Ⓓ Ⓔ	15. Ⓐ Ⓑ Ⓒ Ⓓ Ⓔ	15. Ⓐ Ⓑ Ⓒ Ⓓ Ⓔ	15. Ⓐ Ⓑ Ⓒ Ⓓ Ⓔ	15. Ⓐ Ⓑ Ⓒ Ⓓ Ⓔ
16. Ⓐ Ⓑ Ⓒ Ⓓ Ⓔ	16. Ⓐ Ⓑ Ⓒ Ⓓ Ⓔ	16. Ⓐ Ⓑ Ⓒ Ⓓ Ⓔ	16. Ⓐ Ⓑ Ⓒ Ⓓ Ⓔ	16. Ⓐ Ⓑ Ⓒ Ⓓ Ⓔ
17. Ⓐ Ⓑ Ⓒ Ⓓ Ⓔ	17. Ⓐ Ⓑ Ⓒ Ⓓ Ⓔ	17. Ⓐ Ⓑ Ⓒ Ⓓ Ⓔ	17. Ⓐ Ⓑ Ⓒ Ⓓ Ⓔ	17. Ⓐ Ⓑ Ⓒ Ⓓ Ⓔ
18. Ⓐ Ⓑ Ⓒ Ⓓ Ⓔ	18. Ⓐ Ⓑ Ⓒ Ⓓ Ⓔ	18. Ⓐ Ⓑ Ⓒ Ⓓ Ⓔ	18. Ⓐ Ⓑ Ⓒ Ⓓ Ⓔ	18. Ⓐ Ⓑ Ⓒ Ⓓ Ⓔ
19. Ⓐ Ⓑ Ⓒ Ⓓ Ⓔ	19. Ⓐ Ⓑ Ⓒ Ⓓ Ⓔ	19. Ⓐ Ⓑ Ⓒ Ⓓ Ⓔ	19. Ⓐ Ⓑ Ⓒ Ⓓ Ⓔ	19. Ⓐ Ⓑ Ⓒ Ⓓ Ⓔ
20. Ⓐ Ⓑ Ⓒ Ⓓ Ⓔ	20. Ⓐ Ⓑ Ⓒ Ⓓ Ⓔ	20. Ⓐ Ⓑ Ⓒ Ⓓ Ⓔ	20. Ⓐ Ⓑ Ⓒ Ⓓ Ⓔ	20. Ⓐ Ⓑ Ⓒ Ⓓ Ⓔ
21. Ⓐ Ⓑ Ⓒ Ⓓ Ⓔ	21. Ⓐ Ⓑ Ⓒ Ⓓ Ⓔ	21. Ⓐ Ⓑ Ⓒ Ⓓ Ⓔ	21. Ⓐ Ⓑ Ⓒ Ⓓ Ⓔ	21. Ⓐ Ⓑ Ⓒ Ⓓ Ⓔ
22. Ⓐ Ⓑ Ⓒ Ⓓ Ⓔ	22. Ⓐ Ⓑ Ⓒ Ⓓ Ⓔ	22. Ⓐ Ⓑ Ⓒ Ⓓ Ⓔ	22. Ⓐ Ⓑ Ⓒ Ⓓ Ⓔ	22. Ⓐ Ⓑ Ⓒ Ⓓ Ⓔ
23. Ⓐ Ⓑ Ⓒ Ⓓ Ⓔ	23. Ⓐ Ⓑ Ⓒ Ⓓ Ⓔ	23. Ⓐ Ⓑ Ⓒ Ⓓ Ⓔ	23. Ⓐ Ⓑ Ⓒ Ⓓ Ⓔ	23. Ⓐ Ⓑ Ⓒ Ⓓ Ⓔ
24. Ⓐ Ⓑ Ⓒ Ⓓ Ⓔ	24. Ⓐ Ⓑ Ⓒ Ⓓ Ⓔ	24. Ⓐ Ⓑ Ⓒ Ⓓ Ⓔ	24. Ⓐ Ⓑ Ⓒ Ⓓ Ⓔ	24. Ⓐ Ⓑ Ⓒ Ⓓ Ⓔ
25. Ⓐ Ⓑ Ⓒ Ⓓ Ⓔ	25. Ⓐ Ⓑ Ⓒ Ⓓ Ⓔ	25. Ⓐ Ⓑ Ⓒ Ⓓ Ⓔ	25. Ⓐ Ⓑ Ⓒ Ⓓ Ⓔ	25. Ⓐ Ⓑ Ⓒ Ⓓ Ⓔ
26. Ⓐ Ⓑ Ⓒ Ⓓ Ⓔ	26. Ⓐ Ⓑ Ⓒ Ⓓ Ⓔ	26. Ⓐ Ⓑ Ⓒ Ⓓ Ⓔ	26. Ⓐ Ⓑ Ⓒ Ⓓ Ⓔ	26. Ⓐ Ⓑ Ⓒ Ⓓ Ⓔ
27. Ⓐ Ⓑ Ⓒ Ⓓ Ⓔ	27. Ⓐ Ⓑ Ⓒ Ⓓ Ⓔ	27. Ⓐ Ⓑ Ⓒ Ⓓ Ⓔ	27. Ⓐ Ⓑ Ⓒ Ⓓ Ⓔ	27. Ⓐ Ⓑ Ⓒ Ⓓ Ⓔ
28. Ⓐ Ⓑ Ⓒ Ⓓ Ⓔ	28. Ⓐ Ⓑ Ⓒ Ⓓ Ⓔ	28. Ⓐ Ⓑ Ⓒ Ⓓ Ⓔ	28. Ⓐ Ⓑ Ⓒ Ⓓ Ⓔ	28. Ⓐ Ⓑ Ⓒ Ⓓ Ⓔ
29. Ⓐ Ⓑ Ⓒ Ⓓ Ⓔ	29. Ⓐ Ⓑ Ⓒ Ⓓ Ⓔ	29. Ⓐ Ⓑ Ⓒ Ⓓ Ⓔ	29. Ⓐ Ⓑ Ⓒ Ⓓ Ⓔ	29. Ⓐ Ⓑ Ⓒ Ⓓ Ⓔ
30. Ⓐ Ⓑ Ⓒ Ⓓ Ⓔ	30. Ⓐ Ⓑ Ⓒ Ⓓ Ⓔ	30. Ⓐ Ⓑ Ⓒ Ⓓ Ⓔ	30. Ⓐ Ⓑ Ⓒ Ⓓ Ⓔ	30. Ⓐ Ⓑ Ⓒ Ⓓ Ⓔ

To remove, cut along dotted rule.

1   1   1   1   1

SECTION I
TIME — 35 MINUTES
24 QUESTIONS

Directions: In this section you will be given groups of questions based on different sets of conditions. Drawing a simple diagram may be helpful in answering some of the questions. You are to choose the best answer and mark the corresponding space on your answer sheet.

Questions 1–6

A committee is being selected from a pool of ten people. The men in the pool are A, B, G, and H. The women are C, D, E, F, I, and J. The Democrats are D, E, F, G, and H. The Republicans are A, B, C, I, and J.

The committee being formed must have six members. Not more than four members may come from the same political party.

At least two men must serve on the committee.

A will not serve on the same committee as H.

G will not serve on the same committee as D.

E will not serve on the same committee as J.

1. If four Democrats are selected, which one of the following must be true?

   (A) H may not be selected.
   (B) B must be selected.
   (C) A cannot be selected.
   (D) G must be selected.
   (E) D cannot be selected.

2. If B, G, H, and J are selected, which one of the following must be true?

   (A) E may be selected.
   (B) A must be selected.
   (C) C cannot be selected.
   (D) If F is selected, then C is selected.
   (E) If I is not selected then F must be selected.

3. If A and B cannot be selected, which one of the following is true?

   (A) J must be selected.
   (B) C must be selected.
   (C) G may not be selected.
   (D) E cannot be selected.
   (E) D must be selected.

4. If G and H cannot be selected and J must be selected, which one of the following CANNOT be selected?

   (A) I and C
   (B) I and D
   (C) I and F
   (D) C and D
   (E) D and F

5. If H is not selected and both J and D are selected, which one of the following must be selected?

   (A) B and C
   (B) I and D
   (C) I and F
   (D) C and D
   (E) A and F

6. If A, B, I, and J are selected, which one of the following must be true?

   (A) G must be selected.
   (B) C can be selected.
   (C) E can be selected.
   (D) F must be selected.
   (E) D cannot be selected.

GO ON TO THE NEXT PAGE ➤

Questions 7–12

The West Valley JCC is sponsoring a First Annual Talent Show. Five contestants—A, B, C, D, and E—are entered in the talent show. The contestants are ranked 1st through 5th and there are no ties. No ties means that no contestants are ranked in the same place at the same time.

Contestant A places ahead of contestant B.
Contestant C places 1st or last.
Contestant D places 1st or last.

7. If E finishes ahead of A, then which one of the following must be true?

   (A) B finishes ahead of D.
   (B) B finishes 4th.
   (C) E finishes 3rd.
   (D) C finishes ahead of A.
   (E) C finishes 5th.

8. If C finishes ahead of B, then which one of the following must be FALSE?

   (A) D is 5th.
   (B) E is 2nd.
   (C) B is 4th.
   (D) A finishes ahead of D.
   (E) A finishes 4th.

9. If B finishes ahead of E, then which one of the following must be true?

   (A) A is 2nd.
   (B) B is 4th.
   (C) E finishes ahead of D.
   (D) C is 1st.
   (E) D is not 1st.

10. If C and B finish in consecutive positions, then which one of the following must be true?

    (A) D finishes 1st.
    (B) E finishes ahead of A.
    (C) B finishes ahead of E.
    (D) C finishes 1st.
    (E) A finishes 2nd.

11. If a sixth contestant, F, places 4th, and B finishes behind F, then which one of the following must be FALSE?

    (A) A and E finish consecutively.
    (B) A must place ahead of D.
    (C) B is 5th.
    (D) B and E do not finish consecutively.
    (E) B finishes behind D.

12. If E finishes 2nd and F, a sixth contestant, finishes next to C, then which one of the following must be true?

    (A) F finishes ahead of B.
    (B) B finishes 4th.
    (C) A finishes ahead of D.
    (D) F finishes ahead of D.
    (E) C finishes 1st.

GO ON TO THE NEXT PAGE ➤

Questions 13–18

Along the coast of Zambatania there are four major cities, X, Y, Z, and Q. Each of these cities lies on a straight road that runs from east to west.
   City X is 30 miles from city Y.
   City Z is 40 miles from city Y.
   City Q is 2 miles from city Z.

13. Which one of the following could be true?

   (A) City Z is 30 miles from city X.
   (B) City Z is 40 miles from city X.
   (C) City Z is 10 miles from city X.
   (D) City Y is 50 miles from city Z.
   (E) City Q is 80 miles from city Z.

14. All of the following could be true EXCEPT

   (A) city Q is 38 miles from city Y
   (B) city Q is 42 miles from city Y
   (C) city Q is 68 miles from city X
   (D) city Q is 8 miles from city X
   (E) city Q is 38 miles from city X

15. If city Q is 12 miles from city X, then

   (A) city Z is 70 miles from city X
   (B) city Q is 38 miles from city Y
   (C) city Q is 8 miles from city Y
   (D) city Q is 18 miles from city Y
   (E) city Z is 10 miles from city X

16. Each of the following is a possible order of cities along the coast road EXCEPT

   (A) XYQZ
   (B) XYZQ
   (C) QZYX
   (D) XQZY
   (E) QZXY

17. If a traveler takes the coast road, beginning his trip at X and ending at Q, he must travel

   (A) through city Y
   (B) through both Y and Z
   (C) through Z
   (D) at least 10 miles
   (E) at least 8 miles

18. If a fifth city, M, is located on the same straight coast road, and M is 5 miles from city Y, all of the following could be true EXCEPT

   (A) M is 35 miles from city X
   (B) M is 35 miles from city Z
   (C) M is 45 miles from city Z
   (D) M is 49 miles from city Q
   (E) M is 47 miles from city Q

GO ON TO THE NEXT PAGE ➤

1   1   1   1   1

<u>Questions 19–24</u>

A professor is constructing 3 unique exams (A, B, and C) consisting of 3 questions each. There are 4 essay questions (1, 2, 3, and 4) and 5 short-answer questions (5, 6, 7, 8, and 9) to choose from. Each question is to be used once and only once based on the following conditions:

There must be at least one essay question on each exam.

Questions 5 and 7 must be on the same exam.

Questions 1 and 6 cannot be on the same exam.

Question 4 is not on exam A.

Question 6 is not on exam A.

Questions 4 and 9 cannot be on the same exam.

19. If question 3 is on exam B and question 2 is on exam C, which one of the following CANNOT be true?

   (A) Question 9 is on exam A.
   (B) There are 2 essay questions on exam A.
   (C) There are 2 essay questions on exam B.
   (D) Question 4 is on exam B.
   (E) There are 2 essay questions on exam C.

20. If questions 8 and 9 are on exam C, which one of the following must be true?

   (A) Question 1 is on exam A.
   (B) Question 5 is on exam B.
   (C) Question 6 is on exam C.
   (D) Question 4 is on exam B.
   (E) Question 2 is on exam C.

21. If question 7 is on exam B, which one of the following could be true?

   (A) Questions 1 and 9 are on exam C.
   (B) Questions 8 and 9 are on exam C.
   (C) Questions 1 and 8 are on exam B.
   (D) Questions 2 and 5 are on exam A.
   (E) Questions 2 and 3 are on exam A.

22. If question 9 is the only short-answer question on exam B, which one of the following must be true?

   (A) Question 7 is on exam C.
   (B) Question 3 is on exam A.
   (C) Question 8 is on exam C.
   (D) Question 1 is on exam B.
   (E) Question 2 is on exam A.

23. If questions 2 and 7 are on exam C, which one of the following must be true?

   (A) Question 9 is on exam A.
   (B) Question 1 is on exam B.
   (C) Question 3 is on exam A.
   (D) Question 8 is on exam B.
   (E) Question 6 is on exam C.

24. If questions 8 and 9 are on the same exam and question 2 is on exam A, which one of the following CANNOT be true?

   (A) Question 9 is on exam B.
   (B) Question 3 is on exam A.
   (C) Question 4 is on exam C.
   (D) Question 1 is on exam B.
   (E) Question 6 is on exam C.

STOP

IF YOU FINISH BEFORE TIME IS UP, CHECK YOUR WORK ON THIS SECTION OF THE TEST ONLY.
DO NOT GO ON TO THE NEXT SECTION OF THE TEST UNTIL TIME IS UP FOR THIS SECTION.

2   **2**

SECTION II
TIME — 35 MINUTES
26 QUESTIONS

Directions: In this section you will be given brief statements or passages and will be required to evaluate the reasoning involved. In some instances, more than one choice will appear to be a possible answer. You are to choose the *best* answer. Use common sense and reasonableness in making your selection; then mark the proper space on the answer sheet.

Questions 1–2

It has long been apparent that the nation's violent crime problem is disproportionately a juvenile crime problem. Those under age 18 constitute a fifth of the population, but account for nearly half of the arrests for the seven major crimes on which the FBI maintains national statistics. The statistical trend lines suggest the problem is growing; the number of juveniles arrested for murder and aggravated assault rose 82 percent and 91 percent respectively from 1967 to 1976. Yet, under the laws of most states, courts are obliged to treat these young hard-core hoodlums as if they were little worse than wayward delinquents.

1. The author of this passage would argue that

   (A) crime has increased because of juveniles
   (B) young hard-core hoodlums account for nearly 50 percent of the seven major crimes
   (C) our legal system is biased in favor of hardened criminals
   (D) arrests for aggravated assault are growing more rapidly than those for murder
   (E) a fifth of our population is comprised of wayward delinquents

2. The author of this passage assumes all of the following EXCEPT

   (A) statistical trend lines are accurate predictors
   (B) 1967 to 1976 were not abnormal years
   (C) the laws of most states are consistent involving juveniles
   (D) the laws governing juvenile criminals are lenient in most states
   (E) the nation's nonviolent crime problem does not involve juveniles

---

3. Any single adult female lion in a pride is capable of killing a warthog or a Thompson's gazelle unassisted. But to bring down an eland at least two, and probably three, lionesses must cooperate. Therefore, the capture of two warthogs and one eland will require at least four adult females.

All of the following are faulty assumptions in the passage EXCEPT

   (A) all eland kills require at least two lions
   (B) all elands are killed by two lions
   (C) no warthogs are killed by two lions
   (D) no lion kills twice
   (E) no lion kills three times

4. The average number of fatal cases of influenza in the winter months in the Boston area is likely to decline noticeably if 50 percent of the population over the age of fifty is inoculated in October or November. If the government program that supplies information about influenza and makes free shots widely available is discontinued to save money, the number of men and women over age fifty who have been inoculated before the flu season begins this year will sharply decrease.

If the statements are true, which one of the following is the conclusion most likely to follow from the statements above?

(A) Programs that contribute to the health of the community should not be dependent on public funding.
(B) The severity and frequency of influenza outbreaks in the winter months can vary widely from year to year.
(C) The number of influenza fatalities this winter will probably increase.
(D) The number of fatal cases of influenza will sharply increase this year.
(E) The number of fatal cases in men and women less than fifty years old is likely to remain unchanged.

5. *Transit Official:* In order to increase the number of riders and improve its financial position, the Central Transit Company has purchased new air-conditioned buses for its routes from the west side and the east side to the city center. The routes from the north side and the south side continue to use the older buses, which are not air-conditioned. In the six spring and summer months since the new buses were put into service, the ridership on the west side and east side routes has increased. Therefore, the purchase of the new buses was a wise expenditure.

Which one of the following, if true, most calls into question the conclusion of this passage?

(A) The ridership on the bus routes from the north and south has increased more than that on the east and west routes in the spring and summer.
(B) The increased ridership on the north and south routes normally falls off in the fall and winter.
(C) The price of fares on all the city bus routes was increased early in the spring, though the increase was a very small one.
(D) There are more buses on the north and south routes to the city center than on the east and west routes.
(E) If more commuters in the city take the buses to work than drive their own cars, the traffic congestion problem in the downtown area will be solved.

Questions 6–7

Nutritionist: Recent studies show that the height of the average American has increased 2 inches in the past 10 years, lending support to the view that modern foods stimulate growth.

6. The argument would be strengthened by pointing out that

(A) statistical studies were done on which foods were eaten
(B) modern foods are unhealthy
(C) all average heights are increasing
(D) comparisons have been studied in control groups
(E) there is no such thing as an average American

7. This argument would be weakened most by pointing out that

(A) statistics don't lie
(B) there are too many variables in this type of study
(C) the genetic background of the subjects was not investigated
(D) the sample group used was small
(E) some people's height decreased

2 **2** **2** **2** **2**

Questions 8–9

A glance at the five leading causes of death in 1900, 1910, and 1945, years representing in some measure the early and late practice of physicians still active, shows a significant trend. In 1900 these causes were (1) tuberculosis, (2) pneumonia, (3) enteritis, typhoid fever, and other acute intestinal diseases, (4) heart diseases, and (5) cerebral hemorrhage and thrombosis. Ten years later the only change was that heart disease had moved from fourth to first place, tuberculosis now being second, and pneumonia third. In 1945, however, the list had changed profoundly. Heart diseases were far out in front; cancer, which had come up from eighth place, was second; and cerebral hemorrhage and thrombosis, third. Fatal accidents, which had been well down the list, were now fourth, and nephritis was fifth. All of these are, of course, composites rather than single diseases, and it is significant that, except for accidents, they are characteristic of the advanced rather than the early or middle years of life.

8. Which one of the following is the most logical conclusion from the passage above?

(A) A cure for cancer will be found within the decade.
(B) Many of the medical problems of today are problems of the gerontologist (specialist in medical problems of old age).
(C) Older persons are more accident-prone than are younger persons.
(D) Tuberculosis has been all but eliminated.
(E) Heart disease has never been a real threat to the aged.

9. Which one of the following is not indicated by the passage?

(A) As one grows older he is more subject to disease.
(B) Pneumonia is no longer among the five most common causes of death.
(C) Compared to mortality rates for acute intestinal diseases, the mortality rate for cancer has increased.
(D) The incidence of heart disease has increased.
(E) Fatal accidents today claim more lives than ever.

GO ON TO THE NEXT PAGE ➤

2   **2**   **2**   **2**   **2**

10. A recent study of children between 2 and 4 years old has shown that in this period of their lives, they show no preference for cereals that have been sweetened either naturally or artificially. But almost all of the same group four years later preferred sweetened cereals. This change shows that the preference for sweetened foods is acquired rather than natural, and that without the example of others using sweeteners, whether in television advertisements or in the home, children would avoid the chief causes of obesity and cavities.

Which one of the following, if true, would provide the best support for this argument?

(A) A second study showed that children who had eaten sweetened food between the ages of 2 and 4 showed no greater preference for sweetened foods at the ages of 6 to 8 than children who had not eaten sweetened foods at the younger age.

(B) A second study showed that children between 4 and 6 who had been sequestered from advertising for sweeteners preferred sugar-free cereals when they were 6 to 8 years old.

(C) Studies of children 6 to 8 who ate sweetened foods show those who live in areas where the water is fluoridated had fewer cavities than children who ate unsweetened foods and lived in areas where the water was not fluoridated.

(D) Studies have shown that the influence of parents upon their children's behavior at early ages is measurably greater than the influence of peer groups or school teachers.

(E) Contrary to what advertisers claim, both adults and children have no difficulty in distinguishing between naturally and artificially sweetened foods or beverages.

Questions 11–12

Within the unconscious realm of the mind, of which we are normally unaware, lie our basic drives and the coordination and control of our bodily functions and chemistry. This dark area of the mind constitutes about 90 percent of our mind and is responsible for about 95 percent of our behavior. We are dimly aware of its existence through our dreams, spontaneous recall of forgotten memories, and slips of speech.

11. Which one of the following is implied in the passage?

(A) Ninety-five percent of our behavior is controlled by 90 percent of our mind.

(B) Five percent of our behavior is uncontrolled.

(C) Dreams, spontaneous recall, and slips of speech constitute about 90 percent of our behavior.

(D) The conscious mind controls our body chemistry.

(E) About 10 percent of our mind controls 5 percent of our behavior.

12. The author of this passage assumes that

(A) all humans have the same bodily functions and chemical balance

(B) it is difficult to define the unconscious realm of the mind

(C) behavior modification could not take place in the conscious realm of the mind

(D) our basic drives and the coordination and control of our bodily functions take place in the same half of the brain

(E) a small part of our mind controls a small part of our behavior

2 **2** **2** **2** **2**

13. All teachers like some of their students. No teacher likes all of his or her students.

If the statements are true, then all of the following must be true EXCEPT

(A) some teachers dislike some of their students
(B) all teachers dislike some of their students
(C) no teacher dislikes all of his or her students
(D) most teachers like most of their students
(E) no teacher likes all of his or her students

Questions 14–15

A landowner in Africa at the turn of the twentieth century had difficulty in finding out whether or not the workers he employed had carried out their assignments because the workers, eager to please their colonial boss, answered "Yes" to every question. One planter claimed that he could solve this problem. He planned to elicit the same information twice, by asking questions in such a way that the first time the right answer was "Yes" and the second time the right answer was "No." His solution was bound to fail. So is any attempt to find the truth with only self-report, that is, a single interested party's word, to depend on. Without some kind of second opinion or corroborating evidence, we can never know the truth. How can we trust what an involved person tells us, an interested party who may not even realize that he is deceiving himself?

14. The landowner's device for finding the truth could not possibly succeed because

(A) the workers answering "No" might not tell the truth
(B) the workers would not answer "No"
(C) it would be hard to phrase the question to which the "No" answer was correct
(D) the workers will give the answers that will most please the landowner
(E) workers who had carried out their assignments will tell the truth when they answer "Yes"

15. With which of the following generalizations would the author of this passage be most likely to agree?

(A) You cannot ask a question so that "Yes" or "No" is the correct answer.
(B) Self-reporting can always be verified by consulting a second source of information.
(C) If something is true for me, it does not matter whether or not it is true for others.
(D) Because of language and cultural differences, there can never be real communication between an African and a European.
(E) There are many things that we can never know at all, and many that we will never know exactly.

16. On-the-job training alone, of course, cannot solve the unemployment problem. The national economic recession is basically responsible for the recent surge in unemployment. The administration is pinning its chief hope for full employment on its program for revitalizing the economy.

Which one of the following topics would most logically precede the passage above?

(A) successful economic plans of the past
(B) government policies preceding the administration
(C) the motives of the administration
(D) causes of the recession
(E) opportunities for on-the-job training

GO ON TO THE NEXT PAGE ➤

17. On the one hand, "little white lies" are sinful; on the other hand, when we lie in order to save a friend from unnecessary pain, the "whiteness" of our lie becomes more apparent. Those who tell the whole truth all of the time are sure to leave misery in their wake.

The author makes which one of the following arguments?

(A) Lying is either sinful or virtuous.
(B) Truthtellers are sure to be miserable.
(C) Little white lies are the only justifiable lies.
(D) It is good to lie in order to avoid hurting someone.
(E) Pain is the result of truth.

18. *Advertisement:* Cleenup Soap will scour your pots and pans while it whitens your sink. You'll want Cleenup for all your clean-up chores, especially the hard jobs around the house.

The advertisement above implies that Cleenup Soap

(A) is better than the rest
(B) is the best soap for household clean-up chores
(C) can be used for many cleaning jobs
(D) is economically the best buy
(E) can be used only for jobs around the house

19. *Landlord:* When are you going to pay last month's rent?
Renter: First, I've already paid it. Second, I don't owe you anything. Third, not until you fix the heater.

The weakness in the renter's response is best expressed by which one of the following?

(A) He contradicts himself.
(B) He dislikes his landlord.
(C) He assumes the landlord has a poor memory.
(D) He repeats himself.
(E) He makes no sense.

20. If people would use cloth towels and napkins instead of paper, less paper would be manufactured. So we should replace paper napkins and towels with cloth, and the forests of the world will not be consumed so rapidly.

This argument depends on which one of the following assumptions?

(A) The pace at which the forests are being consumed should be reduced.
(B) Washing cloth towels and napkins will consume resources less valuable than forests.
(C) The cost of paper napkins and towels may be less than that of cloth.
(D) The economic advantages of using cloth napkins and towels outweigh those of using paper.
(E) People are rarely willing to give up a convenience for an advantage that is not immediately perceptible.

21. *State Legislator:* The law requiring motorcyclists to wear protective helmets should be enacted immediately. The individual's loss of freedom of choice is trivial when set beside the suffering and the costs to the state of head injuries that are the result of not wearing safety helmets.

Which one of the following, if true, weakens this argument?

(A) With the recent reductions in the speed limit, the number of motorcycle accidents has been sharply reduced.
(B) Cyclists complain that helmets obscure their vision when they are worn under normal driving conditions.
(C) Highway patrolmen report that most of the motorcyclists that they arrest for speeding are wearing helmets.
(D) The state's expense for the long-term care of people who suffer severe head injuries in highway accidents is less than $1 million monthly.
(E) The fees for the registration of motorcycles in this state have increased every year for the past five years.

GO ON TO THE NEXT PAGE ➤

2   **2**   **2**   **2**   **2**

22. You do not succeed unless you take a gamble. Gambling is foolish. Therefore, only fools succeed.

   Which one of the following would weaken the conclusion the most?

   (A) Most fools gamble.
   (B) Most fools do not succeed.
   (C) Some succeed without gambling.
   (D) Most successful gamblers are not foolish.
   (E) A fool and his money are soon parted.

23. Christopher Lasch is, in one sense, a modern-day Aesop. The ancient Greek philosopher once said, "Self-conceit may lead to self-destruction," and this warning is echoed by Lasch in his best-selling study, *The Culture of Narcissism*.

   Which of the following excerpts from the above passage is least relevant to a comparison between Lasch and Aesop?

   (A) "warning is echoed"
   (B) "ancient Greek philosopher"
   (C) "modern-day Aesop"
   (D) "best-selling"
   (E) "in one sense"

24. In the Soviet Union, it was a crime for anyone to offer religious instruction to a person under the age of 18. The overtly religious were systematically excluded from any higher education or position of professional responsibility. By definition, every person holding official power was an atheist. And religious activists, most especially those who shared Dr. Graham's evangelical spirit, were prime candidates for the torment of life in the Gulag Archipelago.

   Which of the following assumptions does the author of the above passage necessarily make about his readers?

   (A) They knew who Dr. Graham was.
   (B) They were enemies of the Soviet Union.
   (C) They were not religious activists.
   (D) They had been offered religious instruction.
   (E) They may have become evangelical themselves.

25. There is something sinister about progress. Just look at the folks who cling to the past, and whom do you find?—friendly, neighborly types who respect traditional religious and moral values and who fear a machine age that will replace the leisurely back-fence conversation with instantaneous "telephonatronics."

   With which of the following would the author be likely to agree?

   (A) Progress is our most important product.
   (B) We have nothing to fear except fear itself.
   (C) Lack of progress coincides with a migration from the cities.
   (D) The enemies of the future are always the very nicest people.
   (E) The best people own no machines.

26. Far too often today, concern about nuclear weapons is focused exclusively on the superpowers. The issue of nuclear proliferation is, at best, considered secondary. Yet more and more nations are moving to the threshold of the nuclear club. The search for ways to curb nuclear proliferation deserves as much attention as the quest for arms control between the United States and Russia.

   Which of the following statements, if true, would weaken the argument above?

   (A) Nuclear proliferation is given more attention than human rights.
   (B) All nations, including the United States and Russia, have promised not to abuse their nuclear technology.
   (C) An arms reduction by the United States and Russia will result in an overall arms reduction by other countries.
   (D) Two adversary middle-Eastern countries have aimed nuclear missiles at each other.
   (E) Arms control in general has never before received as much attention as it has in this decade.

STOP

IF YOU FINISH BEFORE TIME IS UP, CHECK YOUR WORK ON THIS SECTION OF THE TEST ONLY.
DO NOT GO ON TO THE NEXT SECTION OF THE TEST UNTIL TIME IS UP FOR THIS SECTION.

3   **3**   **3**   **3**   **3**

SECTION III
TIME — 35 MINUTES
25 QUESTIONS

<u>Directions:</u> In this section you will be given brief statements or passages and will be required to evaluate the reasoning involved. In some instances, more than one choice will appear to be a possible answer. You are to choose the *best* answer. Use common sense and reasonableness in making your selection; then mark the proper space on the answer sheet.

1. *Mayor:* If the stadium improvement bond measure on the November ballot is passed by the electorate, the city will be able to host a New Year's Day bowl game. This assures huge tourist revenues for the businesses of the city, and so the electorate will certainly approve the bond measure.

   Which one of the following assumptions, if true, will verify the argument that the measure will pass?

   (A) Any bond measure that does not bring revenues to the city will not be approved in November.
   (B) Any bond measure that would prevent the city's hosting a New Year's Day bowl game will not be approved this November.
   (C) No bond measure that does not bring large revenues to the businesses of city will be defeated in the November election.
   (D) No bond measure that brings large revenues to the city's businesses will be defeated in November.
   (E) Next year's tourist revenues will be twice as large as this year's.

2. Industrial nations have agreed to a global ban on dumping industrial waste at sea. About 80 percent of all ocean pollution is generated on land, with 10 percent coming from industrial wastes disposed of by ships at sea, and the rest thrown or discharged from routine operation of oceangoing vessels. The measure calls for phasing out all industrial waste dumping at sea by 2010. Spokesmen for the environmental group Greenpeace praised the resolution, but _____.

   Which one of the following is the most logical conclusion of the passage above?

   (A) expressed grave concern about the 10 percent of the wastes that are not accounted for
   (B) expressed grave concern about the pollution generated on land
   (C) expressed a hope that the 2010 date could be extended to the year 2015
   (D) expressed concern about the pollution generated by nonindustrial nations
   (E) expressed concern about the decline in the ocean mammal population

GO ON TO THE NEXT PAGE ➤

3 **3** **3** **3** **3**

3. The band always practices on Tuesday afternoons when the weather is good. The band is not practicing this afternoon.

Which one of the following can be logically deduced from the premises above?

(A) Therefore, the weather is not good.
(B) Therefore, today must be Wednesday.
(C) Therefore, the band will practice tomorrow if the weather is good.
(D) Therefore, if today's weather is bad, today must be Tuesday.
(E) Therefore, if the weather is good, today cannot be Tuesday.

4. *Critic:* With the end of the cold war, many Americans see an end to the nightmare fear of nuclear destruction. But for antinuclear activists the threat has merely changed its form. Hardly any nuclear weapons have been destroyed, and new and more dangerous weapons are still being developed. If the threat of an American-Soviet showdown has declined, the danger in other quarters has increased. Compared with the weapons we have now, the Hiroshima bomb was far more powerful.

The logic of the paragraph would be most improved by the elimination of which one of its five sentences?

(A) the first ("With the end . . .")
(B) the second ("But for antinuclear . . .")
(C) the third ("Hardly any nuclear . . .")
(D) the fourth ("If the threat . . .")
(E) the fifth ("Compared with the . . .")

Questions 5–6

The dire shortage of rental housing in the city is the result of our unfair, strict rent-control laws. As long as we have rent control, no new rental units will be built, because they offer no chance of profit to landlords. But if rent controls are eliminated, new apartments will eventually be built, and when there is no longer a shortage of rental units, rents will no longer go up.

5. All of the following are assumptions of the author of the passage EXCEPT

(A) the motive for building new housing is expectation of profit
(B) the only builders of new housing are private companies
(C) the reason no new rental housing is being built is rent control
(D) if rent controls are eliminated, apartment construction will be inhibited by other factors
(E) at the present level, rents are unfairly low

6. Which one of the following, if true, would support the argument of this passage?

(A) There is a shortage of low-cost housing.
(B) There is no shortage of high-cost rental housing.
(C) The population of the city declines steadily each year.
(D) A city nearby with no rent control has a shortage of low-cost rental housing.
(E) Fewer rental units were built this year in a city nearby with no rent control than were built here.

GO ON TO THE NEXT PAGE ➤

7. Unfortunately, the only things that get much attention today in the American public debate are extreme and dubious claims. In issue after issue, the discussions are dominated by extravagant statements, with no concern for the middle ground where truth is most likely to lie. The situation is bad enough in all fields, but it is even worse when it comes to environmental affairs. Every claim from one side predicts an unspeakable environmental disaster. Every claim from the opposite camp foretells economic suicide as the result of any regulatory control.

Which one of the following best describes a weakness of this passage?

(A) It fails to point to a specific area of concern.

(B) It is guilty of the same sort of overstatement it complains about.

(C) It justifies its conclusion on the basis of an alternate conclusion's being untrue.

(D) It assumes a cause and effect without showing that the cause came first.

(E) It fails to take into account the economic factors that propel media presentations of public debate.

8. For the sixth year in a row, the average score for males taking the mathematics section of a nationally administered examination for high school seniors was ten points higher than the average score for females. Both males and females had taken twenty or more full-year academic classes in high school, and the socioeconomic background of the test takers was virtually the same. This result shows clearly the bias of the test in favor of males.

The argument of this passage would be weakened if which one of the following were shown to be true?

(A) Regardless of gender, the higher a student's grades are in high school, the higher his or her scores on nationally administered examinations are likely to be.

(B) The highest scoring performers on the exam were students who had taken four or more years of mathematics courses.

(C) The highest scoring ethnic group on the examination was Asian-Americans.

(D) While 40 percent of the female test takers had studied computer programming, only 38 percent of the male test takers had.

(E) Females taking the test had completed an average of 1.3 fewer mathematics and natural science classes than males.

GO ON TO THE NEXT PAGE ➤

3　　　**3**　　　**3**　　　**3**　　　**3**

9. All vegetables for sale in this market are low in calories; therefore this market sells only low-calorie vegetables.

   Which one of the following is most like the argument above?

   (A) All the classes in this catalog offer three units of credit; therefore all three-unit courses are listed in this catalog.
   (B) All graduates of this high school have completed four science courses; therefore all graduates know chemistry, biology, and physics well.
   (C) All the machines in this factory are powered by electricity; therefore this factory uses only electrically powered machines.
   (D) All the players on this football team exercise for three hours daily; therefore all football players should exercise for three hours each day.
   (E) All the articles in this magazine were written by women; therefore the editors of this magazine must all be female.

10. If members of the City Council vote to impose a surtax on gasoline to raise money for the new railway system, they will certainly be voted out of office in the June election by the unified action of voters in the western precincts, who argue that the system will not be of use to them. The following year, when construction of the system is complete, the support of voters in the eastern precincts will be so great that only Council members who voted for the railway will certainly be elected at that time.

    To assure continued election to the City Council, a member would have to

    (A) vote against the gasoline surtax
    (B) find an alternate way of financing the railway
    (C) appeal to the voters in the eastern precincts in the June election
    (D) support the gasoline surtax, but oppose the construction of the railway
    (E) oppose both the gasoline tax and the construction of the railway

GO ON TO THE NEXT PAGE ➤

3   **3**   **3**   **3**   **3**

Questions 11–12

The new clean-air legislation is going to cost a great deal of money. Industry and consumers will share costs that are predicted to run to $10 billion a year by 2005, and $20 billion ten years later. Electric bills in the Midwest are likely to increase by 20 percent. Gasoline will cost 10 cents per gallon more to refine. Car costs will increase by more than $100 a car. And cleaner air will not show as a productivity gain for the economy. Small companies that cannot pass added costs on to their customers will be especially hard pressed.

For very good reasons, the American public has decided that clean air is worth the high price. The pollution control industry, of course, will get a big boost. So will makers of catalytic converters and ethanol products, as well as many specialized engineering firms. The implementation of the clean-air legislation may lead to the commercial development of wind- or solar-generated electricity, new power sources for trains, and nonpolluting cars. Good public policy may become good business.

11. The passage as a whole is structured to lead to which one of the following conclusions?

   (A) The costs of implementing the new clean-air legislation will be enormous.
   (B) The clean-air legislation will so improve public health that the large costs are a good investment.
   (C) The high cost of cleaning the air may be accompanied by the development of new business opportunities.
   (D) The implementation of the clean-air act will lead to large rises in the cost of electricity, gasoline, and automobiles.
   (E) Regardless of the cost, it is essential to put an end to air pollution.

12. Which one of the following best describes the organization of the argument of this passage?

   (A) The passage deals with specific details in the first paragraph and with general principles in the second.
   (B) The passage deals with economic issues in the first paragraph and social issues in the second.
   (C) The passage presents the liabilities of the legislation in the first paragraph and some possible benefits in the second.
   (D) The passage evaluates the legislation in the first paragraph in a way which the second paragraph contradicts.
   (E) The passage uses examples and analogies in the first paragraph, while the second paragraph uses only examples.

Questions 13–14

Assume that the following statements are true:
   (1) Left-handed people never live in apartments.
   (2) People who live in apartments are always suspicious.
   (3) People who don't live in apartments are always thin.

13. If David is left-handed, which one of the following cannot be true?

   (A) David does not live in an apartment.
   (B) David is not suspicious.
   (C) David is thin.
   (D) David is suspicious.
   (E) David is not thin.

14. If Jane is left-handed, all of the following could be true EXCEPT

   (A) Jane is not suspicious
   (B) Jane is suspicious
   (C) Jane is thin
   (D) Jane does not live in an apartment
   (E) Jane lives in an apartment

GO ON TO THE NEXT PAGE ➤

3   **3**   **3**   **3**   **3**

15. *Magazine Article:* Chemists studying the lithium level in water supplies of ten Texas cities have correlated those levels with the incidence of crime. They have found that communities with no lithium in the drinking water have consistently higher rates of suicides, homicides, violent crimes, and drug abuse than cities with naturally high levels of lithium in the drinking water. A second study of prison inmates has shown that violent offenders have lower levels of lithium in their bodies than do nonviolent offenders. Lithium is now used to treat manic depressive illness.

Which one of the following can be inferred from the article above?

(A) The suicide rate and level of violent crime could probably be reduced by increasing lithium levels in the water supply.

(B) No two different scientific studies can prove exactly the same thing.

(C) There is a need to repeat similar studies in other parts of the country.

(D) The crime rate of a city can be predicted by examining the lithium levels in its water supply.

(E) The suicide rate will probably be lower in cities with a high rate of drug abuse and violent crime.

16. The use of referendums or initiatives on the state ballot allows the electorate to make decisions about important issues such as the environment, taxes, education, and crime. It exposes the electorate to a deluge of communication that is cynical and manipulative. Negative techniques in initiative campaigns are often used by candidates in the election that follows.

The reasoning in the passage above is flawed because the passage

(A) does not give examples of issues that can be decided by initiative

(B) presents inconsistent judgments on initiatives

(C) deals only with state, not national, elections

(D) fails to discriminate between initiatives and referendums

(E) regards advertising in elections negatively

17. *Dave:* According to my doctor, by adding high-fiber foods to your diet, you can help your weight-loss program.
Jane: That's not true. My sister eats some high-fiber foods, and she is seriously overweight.

Dave can best counter Jane's assertion by pointing out that

(A) it has not yet been scientifically proved that adding high-fiber foods to the diet will cause weight loss

(B) Jane's sister may be avoiding high-fiber foods, although Jane doesn't know this

(C) Jane's sister is the exception that proves the rule

(D) other components of Jane's sister's diet may be the cause of her being overweight

(E) the metabolism of every human being is unique

GO ON TO THE NEXT PAGE ➤

3   **3**   **3**   **3**   **3**

18. *Editorial:* Let me say at once that I believe all the UFOs that people claim to have seen or visited are either figments of the imagination or explainable phenomena. I disagree with the UFO believers' charge that unbelievers are close minded and so self-centered that we cannot imagine a civilization more scientifically advanced than ours. Why do all the aliens turn out to look like oddly formed humans? Why do UFOs always appear in the sticks, rather than, say, in New York City or on the White House lawn? Why do these aliens never stick around long enough to be interviewed on television? Why don't they kidnap the president of MIT or Cal. Tech. instead of some tobacco farmer from rural Carolina?

The author of this passage makes his point chiefly by

(A) drawing an analogy
(B) disputing evidence cited by those with an opposing view
(C) using personal experience to derive a general principle
(D) basing a conclusion upon a specific case
(E) showing that the opposition's argument is based upon a contradiction

19. There are two basic clothing styles designed today for children. One is pseudo-Victorian, imitations of the clothes that Lewis Carroll's Alice might have worn. The other is a miniature version of the clothes the parents are now wearing. These may include cocktail dresses or fake mink coats, rock-star clothes, and leather anything, together with the new lines of children's perfumes and cosmetics. On the basis of this evidence, I infer two types of parents. One hopes to shield the child from contemporary reality. The other wants children to reflect what the parents have become, a mirror for themselves.

All of the following are true of the evidence the author of this passage cites EXCEPT

(A) it is based on observation
(B) it supports the author's conclusions
(C) it may not be the only evidence to support the author's conclusions
(D) it is used to support ideas that assume that children's clothes express adults' hopes
(E) it is irrelevant to the conclusions the author reaches

20. *Jane:* All New Yorkers are rude.
    Jack: No. I know many people from Pittsburgh who are very impolite.

Jack's answer reveals that he has interpreted Jane's statement to mean that

(A) rudeness can be restricted to a single city
(B) New Yorkers are worse than people who live in other cities
(C) only New Yorkers are rude
(D) New Yorkers are likely to be more rude than people from anywhere else
(E) degrees of rudeness can be measured

3 **3** **3** **3** **3**

Questions 21–22

A large National Science Foundation grant was recently awarded to Florida State University. The money will fund a center to study high-energy magnetism. Competing for the grant was MIT, which, according to the NSF review panels, had the better physicists. But the state of Florida pledged financial and political support that won it the award. Defenders of the award point out that, though the government would appear to get the best value by investing in the best institution, by diversifying the locations of its awards, the NSF has created new centers of research of world-class standing.

The real reason is a fundamental shift in the way we spend money on science. For years the primary reason scientists got money was for national security. But nowadays economic development is a primary cause. Consequently, politics is becoming more important than dispassionate peer reviews. The state with more than 25 percent of the members of the National Academy of Sciences gets just over 10 percent of the science funds, because its congressional delegation is splintered. The economic benefits are, at best, unpredictable. The benefits to science are even more doubtful.

21. Which one of the following, if true, would support the awarding of the grant to Florida?

(A) The NSF has already awarded a large number of grants to Florida State University.
(B) The NSF has already awarded a large number of grants in the South.
(C) The science review panels described the physics department at Florida State as adequate.
(D) The University of Texas, once a mediocre research institution, has with government support become a world-class center of scientific research.
(E) The physics department at MIT is universally regarded as the best in the country.

22. Which one of the following, if true, would weaken the argument of the second paragraph?

(A) The area around Los Alamos, a recipient of huge government funding, has not developed in the last 30 years.
(B) The development of the Silicon Valley in California is due chiefly to its climate and quality of life.
(C) Economic development of an area depends chiefly on an infrastructure of entrepreneurial faculty and venture capital.
(D) The proximity of the National Institutes of Health has made Montgomery, Maryland, a center of biotechnology entrepreneurialism.
(E) The unity of a congressional delegation profoundly influences its effectiveness in pork-barrel competition.

23. Every time I am beaten at golf, I become short-tempered, and I curse at anyone who makes me short-tempered.

Which one of the following can be logically concluded about the speaker of the passage above?

(A) He curses anyone who beats him at golf.
(B) Everyone whom he curses makes him short-tempered.
(C) People whom he beats at golf are not cursed at.
(D) Every time he curses he has been beaten at golf.
(E) He does not curse when he is not short-tempered.

GO ON TO THE NEXT PAGE ➤

3   **3**   **3**   **3**   **3**

Questions 24–25

Candidate: The mayor's attempt to ban smoking in the restaurants in the city was irresponsible. Everyone knows that smoking is unhealthy for the smoker and for the people near him. We know that traffic, smog, pesticides, and overeating are bad for us. Shall we ban all cars from the city? After all, it's not the nondriver's fault that so many others are addicted to the automobile.

Fortunately the City Council voted against the mayor's proposed smoking ban. The councilors realized that banning smoking in city restaurants would result in patrons' going to the suburbs. Though many councilors, like the mayor, are nonsmokers, they unselfishly voted to protect the livelihood of thousands of restaurant owners and workers.

24. The author makes his criticism of the mayor chiefly by

   (A) drawing an analogy
   (B) ridiculing his logic
   (C) questioning his assumptions
   (D) defining his areas of disagreement
   (E) exposing his contradictions

25. Which one of the following, if true, would tend to weaken the author's argument?

   (A) Studies of the danger of second-hand cigarette smoke are still inconclusive.
   (B) Cigarette manufacturers are large contributors to the campaign funds of the mayor.
   (C) Profits of restaurants with separate smoking and nonsmoking areas have increased.
   (D) Restaurants in cities that have banned smoking report no decline in their profits.
   (E) Some of the city council members are nonsmokers.

STOP

IF YOU FINISH BEFORE TIME IS UP, CHECK YOUR WORK ON THIS SECTION OF THE TEST ONLY.
DO NOT GO ON TO THE NEXT SECTION OF THE TEST UNTIL TIME IS UP FOR THIS SECTION.

4   **4**   **4**   **4**   **4**

SECTION IV
TIME — 35 MINUTES
28 QUESTIONS

<u>Directions:</u> Read the passages and answer the questions following each passage by blackening the appropriate space on the answer sheet. You may refer back to the passages when answering the questions. Answer all questions on the basis of what is stated or implied.

Moviemakers have always been interested in politicians, and vice-versa. As early as 1912, Raoul Walsh followed
line Pancho Villa around, filming his
(5) ambushes and executions. In Russia, Sergei Eisenstein made several films at Stalin's request, including *Alexander Nevski* in 1938 and *Ivan the Terrible* in 1945, both of which made the new
(10) regime appear to be the heir of a glorious revolutionary tradition. Hitler himself charged Leni Riefenstahl to film the Nazi rallies at Nuremberg in 1934. The result was *Triumph of the Will,*
(15) which took two years to make and included oceans of swastika flags, miles of military parades, stylized eagles, rolling drums, and an omnipresent Hitler whose profile stood out against
(20) the sky.

But the movies soon helped create a political style less stridently heroic and melodramatic than that inspired by the theater and opera. At the beginning, of
(25) course, early cinema techniques encouraged the leader to pantomime heavily with excessive gestures and expressions. The result was similar to expressionist theater. But it soon
(30) became clear the cinema offered possibilities unknown on the stage; for example, the close-up, which abolished the distance between the actor and the audience and made exaggerated
(35) gestures unnecessary. With the actor's image enlarged on the screen, even a trembling of the lips or batting the eyelids would be magnified. When the talkies appeared, the theatrical delivery
(40) of lines was no longer the rule. A conversational tone—even a whisper— was easily heard by the audience, making actors adopt a more natural style.
(45) Political leaders have adapted their style to this evolution of the dramatic arts. The hero leader necessarily has a style more suited to the theater or silent movies and is less able to use the new
(50) tone required by cinema and television, which is more sober, allusive, and elliptical. In this sense, de Gaulle was of the theater generation while Giscard d'Estaing belongs to the cinema and
(55) television generation that understands the need for a more nuanced "stage presence."

Another result of the cinema has been to make actors more influential as
(60) models to imitate, since they are so much more visible. From 1920 to 1932, stars were inaccessible, marmoreal, and inimitable. They were idols, surrounded by an aura of myth. In short, they were
(65) the cinema equivalent of the hero leader. During the 1930s and 1940s, the star became more human. He or she, though still shining brightly, was less exceptional, a bit more like the rest of
(70) us. The star became a model that could be imitated—like the charm leader.

And finally in the 1950s and after, stars became virtually the reflection of the spectator if not, indeed, his double.
(75) It became more difficult to imitate a star, since he or she was already like everyone else. This corresponded to the political Mr. Everyman.

GO ON TO THE NEXT PAGE ➤

4   **4**   **4**   **4**   **4**

1. Franklin Roosevelt's "Fireside Chats" (seemingly informal radio talks with his constituency) might have been mentioned in this passage as an example of the

    (A) same mode of propaganda practiced by the Germans and Russians
    (B) unpopularity of excessive theatricality during the 1930s and 1940s
    (C) use of a new medium for political communications
    (D) more natural style of presentation that developed in both movies and politics
    (E) mastery of nuance

2. Overall, the passage develops a comparison between

    (A) bandits and political leaders
    (B) actors and politicians
    (C) moviemakers and politicians
    (D) Nazis and Communists
    (E) de Gaulle and d'Estaing

3. The author's attitude toward the factualness of the two films mentioned that Eisenstein made for Stalin is

    (A) enthusiastic
    (B) satiric
    (C) angry
    (D) skeptical
    (E) ambiguous

4. The author might agree that the exaggerated gestures in Hitler's speeches were influenced by

    (A) the Führer's desire to outdo Russian propaganda
    (B) Leni Riefenstahl's direction
    (C) the style of movie heroes
    (D) the dramatic style of the theater and opera
    (E) Hitler's effort to stress profile features

5. Which one of the following is the most appropriate title for this passage?

    (A) Political Influences on the Movies
    (B) The Waning of Expressionist Theater
    (C) Propaganda as Entertainment
    (D) Four Countries and Theatricality
    (E) Government as Cinema

6. According to the passage, after 1932 both actors and politicians began to seem

    (A) less like mirror images of each other
    (B) less introverted
    (C) more popular
    (D) less unique
    (E) more involved in each other's profession

7. By developing an analogy between the movies and politics, the author assumes which one of the following?

    (A) Public life is an art form.
    (B) Movies about politics generate government policies.
    (C) Before the advent of the movies, politics lacked character.
    (D) Events in life can be imitations of art.
    (E) Movies have been the most important influence on politics in recent history.

GO ON TO THE NEXT PAGE ➤

4   4   4   4   4

Literary periods are slippery concepts. When dates are established and cultural developments are outlined, *line* predecessors and successors have a way (5) of making them dissolve. One discovers that the Romantic Period in English literature so comfortably introduced as extending from 1800 to 1830 has a long Pre-Romantic development and that it (10) really isn't over yet. The same thing is true of American literary history, perhaps more so. But if there is one date that seems to make a decisive cut in the continuity of twentieth-century (15) America, it is probably the stock market crash at the end of October 1929. By 1930 reassessment was forced on the American consciousness.

The Twenties have a character of (20) their own, an individualized and particularized decade for which there has come to be felt considerable nostalgia among the older generation. Clear memories can hardly regard these (25) years as the good old days (this was the era of prohibition and gangsters), but one of the blessings of the human condition is the tendency to forget unpleasantness and remember what one (30) chooses to remember. Perhaps even the Sixties will become a happy recollection in the twenty-first century.

Three major designations arose in the Twenties to define the Twenties as a (35) cultural phenomenon: the Jazz Age, the Lost Generation, and the Wasteland—all with significant literary associations. Of them all the Jazz Age, as represented best in F. Scott Fitzgerald's fiction, was (40) most clearly cut off by the stock market collapse and the ensuing depression. It is the period of the Twenties alone. But the Lost Generation (as proclaimed in the double epigraph from *Ecclesiastes* (45) and Gertrude Stein in the 1926 *The Sun Also Rises*—"You are all a lost generation."—Gertrude Stein in conversation) continued to be lost in the Thirties. The uprootedness and (50) disillusionment of the post-World War I fiction writers, many of whom had participated in that war and perhaps particularly of the Paris expatriate group including Hemingway, Elliot Paul, Henry (55) Miller, and others, pursued them into the depression and beyond. The third

term, the Wasteland, established by T. S. Eliot in his 1922 poem, had perhaps an even longer life; it has come to (60) represent an age extending from the Twenties to 1945 and may indeed suggest the central features of the landscape of this larger period. The Wasteland poets, including Ezra Pound, (65) Eliot himself, and possibly William Carlos Williams, Archibald MacLeish, and e. e. cummings, although many of them had written distinctive poetry even before 1920 and certainly before 1930, (70) continued to develop and sharpen both their verse and their ideas into the Thirties and Forties. The Wasteland runs into and disappears in the Age of Anxiety. Such American writers as (75) Gertrude Stein, Ezra Pound, T. S. Eliot, Williams, cummings, and Hemingway are included in the post-1930 Canon rather than in the pre-1930 one. They had all certainly made a mark in the (80) literary world before 1930, but they were ahead of their time and made a larger and deeper mark after that date.

It is in this fashion that American literature approaches the period which (85) begins in 1930, trailing clouds of several impulses—some would say glory—as it comes. Realism and naturalism are by this time established as dominant modes, but antirealistic frames of (90) reference like expressionism, surrealism, psychology, and religious idealogy are also operative.

8. The passage suggests that literary periods may be demarcated by

(A) a death of a major writer
(B) a publication of a uniquely original work
(C) an economic event outside of the literary sphere
(D) an election of a new president
(E) the accession of a new king or queen

GO ON TO THE NEXT PAGE ➤

4   **4**   **4**   **4**   **4**

9. In view of the author's skepticism in the first paragraph about the strict demarcation of literary and historical periods, he would probably agree with which of the following statements about the stock market crash?

   (A) Economics did not impinge upon the Romantic Age.
   (B) The stock market crash affected economic history but not literary history.
   (C) The crash was the focus of a series of events that both preceded it and followed it.
   (D) The crash was not a welcome phenomenon.
   (E) The crash motivated a wave of new poems and novels.

10. When the author says in the third paragraph, "It is the period of the Twenties alone," (line 42) he probably means that

   (A) the Jazz Age was a phenomenon of the Twenties only
   (B) he will discuss the 1920s only
   (C) "it" is a synonym for "period"
   (D) the stock market crash and the depression occurred in the 1920s
   (E) the 1920s alone constituted a cultural phenomenon

11. We may conclude that the author regards the 1960s as

   (A) a worse decade than the 1920s
   (B) a replica of the 1920s
   (C) a happy recollection
   (D) not the best of times
   (E) a political and artistic disaster

12. From the information given in the second and third paragraphs, we can infer that the "nostalgia" for the Twenties is partly due to the fact that

   (A) the writers of the Twenties were superior to the writers of the Thirties
   (B) compared to the Thirties, most of the Twenties were more prosperous economically
   (C) the novels of Hemingway and Fitzgerald are more optimistic than those of Gertrude Stein
   (D) Eliot's "The Wasteland" describes the life of the Twenties
   (E) the public is still sympathetic to the ideals of prohibition

13. According to the author, the literature of the 1930s was dominated by

   (A) romanticism
   (B) realism
   (C) impressionism
   (D) expressionism
   (E) surrealism

GO ON TO THE NEXT PAGE ➤

4   4   4   4   4

Just as the members of the Inter-American Tropical Tuna Commission have subscribed to annual quotas on the
line tuna harvest, they are agreed that
(5) cooperation is essential in limiting the porpoise kill. The common interest is preservation of the tuna industry. And since modern fishing methods exploit the cozy relationship between the
(10) yellowfin tuna and the porpoise, tuna fishing would become less profitable if the number of porpoises decreased. Tuna and porpoise are often found together at sea, and the fishermen have
(15) learned to cast their nets where they see the porpoises, using them to locate the tuna. The problem is that many porpoises die in the nets.

The commission deliberations
(20) acknowledged the environmental pressures that have led to strict regulation of U.S. tuna crews under federal law. Delegates also recognized that porpoise protection goals are
(25) relatively meaningless unless conservation procedures are adopted and followed on an international basis. Commission supervision of survey, observer, and research programs won
(30) general agreement at the eight-nation conference. The method and timetable for implementing the program, however, remain uncertain.

Thus the federal regulation that
(35) leaves U.S. crews at a disadvantage in the tuna-harvest competition remains a threat to the survival of the tuna fleet. Still, the commission meetings have focused on the workable solution. All
(40) vessels should be equipped with the best porpoise-saving gear devised; crews should be trained and motivated to save the porpoise; a system must be instituted to assure that rules are
(45) enforced. Above all, the response must be international. Porpoise conservation could well be another element in an envisioned treaty that remains unhappily elusive at the continuing
(50) Law-of-the-Sea Conference.

The tuna industry interest in saving porpoises is bothersome to many who also want to save the porpoise, but object to the industry motivation for
(55) doing so. For fishermen, saving the porpoise is valuable only because the porpoise leads them to tuna. For more compassionate souls, however, the porpoise is not just a tuna finder, but,
(60) more important, the sea creature that seems most human. Fredson Delacourte, national chairman of the "People for Animals" drive, says this: "It is especially sad that these sea
(65) creatures, in spite of their keen intelligence, cannot outwit the tuna fishermen who, anxious to meet their annual quota, ensnare and destroy porpoises as well. But it is even sadder
(70) that the tuna industry is so intent upon using the porpoise so greedily." Mr. Delacourte praises the fishing industry for its plans to save the porpoises, at the same time that he wishes their
(75) motives were more altruistic. He insists that any "law of the sea" should be essentially a moral law rather than an economic one.

14. The primary purpose of this passage is to

(A) resolve a controversy
(B) discuss the protection of porpoises
(C) praise the Law-of-the-Sea Conference
(D) implement a program for new fishing techniques
(E) create international cooperation

15. Fredson Delacourte and the tuna industry do NOT share which one of the following?

(A) a wish that international fishing crews cooperate
(B) information about the tuna/porpoise relationship
(C) a common interest in the porpoise/tuna relationship
(D) a common desire to protect porpoises
(E) a common motive for the preservation of porpoises

16. The author presents the information in this passage

(A) cynically
(B) angrily
(C) objectively
(D) humorously
(E) indifferently

GO ON TO THE NEXT PAGE ➤

4   4   4   4   4

17. The author implies that the government and industry representatives concerned with porpoise conservation may lack which one of the following?

    (A) knowledge
    (B) influence
    (C) greed
    (D) compassion
    (E) purpose

18. Fredson Delacourte would probably object to which one of the following?

    (A) a reduced tuna quota
    (B) the use of animal fur for coats
    (C) an international treaty that requires porpoise conservation
    (D) the enforcement of rules for porpoise conservation
    (E) the regulation of the tuna industry

19. Which one of the following is NOT described explicitly in the passage?

    (A) Fredson Delacourte's sentiments
    (B) the federal regulations that U.S. fishermen must obey
    (C) the items that won general agreement at the conference
    (D) the relationship between porpoise and yellowfin
    (E) the elements of a solution to the porpoise conservation problem

20. Which one of the following questions is NOT answered by the passage?

    (A) Has the tuna industry finalized a law of the sea?
    (B) Are fishing regulations moral as well as economic issues?
    (C) Has the general public expressed interest in a moral law of the sea?
    (D) Does the porpoise have a value to fishermen?
    (E) Which sea creature seems most human to many non-fishermen?

GO ON TO THE NEXT PAGE ➤

4   4   4   4   4

"A sad spectacle!" exclaimed Thomas Carlyle, contemplating the possibility that millions of planets circle other
line suns. "If they be inhabited, what a scope
(5) for pain and folly; and if they be not inhabited, what a waste of space!" Much more is now known about the universe than in Carlyle's time, but the question of whether ETI (a fashionable new
(10) acronym for Extraterrestrial Intelligence) exists is as open as it ever was. However, one incredible new fact has entered the picture. For the first time in history we have the technology
(15) for maybe answering the question. This mere possibility is so overwhelming in its implications that a new science called "exobiology" has already been named even though its entire subject
(20) matter may not exist.

We do know that our Milky Way galaxy contains more than 200 billion suns, and that there are billions of other galaxies. Are there other planets? Fifty
(25) years ago the two most popular theories about the origin of the solar system each made such planetary systems so unlikely that top astronomers believed that ours was the only one in the galaxy.
(30) After flaws were found in both theories, astronomers returned to a model proposed by Immanuel Kant (later by Laplace) in which solar systems are so likely that most of the Milky Way's stars
(35) must have them. The wobblings of a few nearby suns suggest big planets close to them, but no one really knows.

If solar systems are plentiful, our galaxy could contain billions of planets
(40) earthlike enough to support carbon-based life. Biologists have a strong case for confining life to carbon compounds (silicon and boron are the next best bets), but no one has any notion of how
(45) earthlike a planet must be to permit carbon life to arise. Our two nearest neighbors, Venus and Mars, were probably formed the same time the earth was; yet their atmospheres are
(50) strikingly different from each other and from ours. Even if a planet goes through an early history exactly like our earth's, no one knows the probability that life on its surface can get started. If it does
(55) start, no one knows the probability that

it will evolve anything as intelligent as a fish.

Our probes of Mars have been great disappointments in SETI (Search for
(60) ETI). I can still recall the tingling of my spine when as a boy I read on the first page of H. G. Wells' *War of the Worlds*:

Yet across the gulf of space, minds that are to our minds as ours are to
(65) those of the beasts that perish, intellects vast and cool and unsympathetic, regarded this earth with envious eyes, and slowly and surely drew their plans against us.

(70) Not even Wells guessed how quickly the Martians would vanish from science fiction.

21. From the quotation that opens the passage, we can infer that Thomas Carlyle is

(A) a science fiction writer
(B) a satirist
(C) an astronomer
(D) an exobiologist
(E) a theologian

22. ETI is an acronym for

(A) something fashionable and new
(B) exobiology
(C) a model proposed by Immanuel Kant
(D) Extraterrestrial Intelligence
(E) the situation described in *War of the Worlds*

23. The naming of a new science, exobiology, contradicts the fact that

(A) its subject matter may not exist
(B) the name is probably inappropriate
(C) the name fits no corresponding acronym
(D) carbon-based life is not necessarily biological
(E) there is no literary precedent for the name

GO ON TO THE NEXT PAGE ➤

4　　　　**4**　　　　**4**　　　　**4**　　　　**4**

24. The question "Are there other planets?" refers only to

    (A) planets outside our own solar system
    (B) planets outside our own galaxy
    (C) planets within our own solar system and outside our own galaxy
    (D) planets outside our own solar system and within our own galaxy
    (E) nongalactic planets

25. The passage implies that the intelligence of a fish is

    (A) equal to man's
    (B) equal to that on Venus and Mars
    (C) carbon-based
    (D) small
    (E) confined to water

26. The quotation from H. G. Wells suggests that

    (A) the Martians would vanish from science fiction
    (B) we were being scrutinized by superior aliens
    (C) an intergalactic war would be imminent
    (D) our intellect is comparatively similar to beasts
    (E) it would take a long time for earth to be invaded

27. The primary purpose of this passage is to

    (A) promote increased spending on the space program
    (B) disprove the existence of Martians
    (C) discuss the possibility of ETI
    (D) provide conclusive evidence about ETI
    (E) point out the folly of Carlyle and Wells

STOP

IF YOU FINISH BEFORE TIME IS UP, CHECK YOUR WORK ON THIS SECTION OF THE TEST ONLY.
DO NOT GO ON TO THE NEXT SECTION OF THE TEST UNTIL TIME IS UP FOR THIS SECTION.

SECTION V
TIME — 35 MINUTES
24 QUESTIONS

<u>Directions:</u> In this section you will be given groups of questions based on different sets of conditions. Drawing a simple diagram may be helpful in answering some of the questions. You are to choose the *best* answer and mark the corresponding space on your answer sheet.

<u>Questions 1–6</u>

The eight members of the Political Action Club (numbered 1–8) are either Lawyers or Accountants. Each member is either a Democrat or a Republican. The Club members are arranging the seating for a group portrait. The arrangement will be two rows with four in each row. The front row will consist of numbers 1–4 and the back row will consist of numbers 5–8 as follows:

| 1 | 2 | 3 | 4 |
| 5 | 6 | 7 | 8 |

Each Lawyer must sit adjacent to, in front of, or in back of another Lawyer.
Each Accountant must sit adjacent to, in front of, or in back of another Accountant.
Each Republican must sit adjacent to, in front of, or in back of another Republican.
Each Democrat must sit adjacent to, in front of, or in back of another Democrat.
Members 2 and 8 are Republicans.
Member 3 is an Accountant.
Member 5 is a Democrat.
Member 7 is a Lawyer.

1. If all the Lawyers are Democrats, which one of the following must be true?

   (A) Member 3 is a Republican.
   (B) Member 4 is a Lawyer
   (C) Member 5 is a Lawyer.
   (D) Member 6 is a Democrat.
   (E) Member 7 is a Republican.

2. In addition to member 5, it is possible that the only two Democrats among the remaining seven members are

   (A) members 1 and 7
   (B) members 3 and 6
   (C) members 3 and 7
   (D) members 4 and 6
   (E) members 6 and 7

3. If there are exactly three Accountants and five Lawyers, which one of the following must be true?

   (A) Member 1 is a Lawyer.
   (B) Member 2 is a Lawyer.
   (C) Member 4 is a Lawyer.
   (D) Member 5 is a Lawyer.
   (E) Member 6 is a Lawyer.

4. Which one of the following could be true?

   (A) Members 1 and 4 are two of exactly 4 Lawyers.
   (B) Members 1 and 6 are two of exactly 4 Republicans.
   (C) Members 4 and 6 are two of exactly 4 Accountants.
   (D) Members 4 and 7 are two of exactly 4 Democrats.
   (E) Members 5 and 7 are two of exactly 4 Republicans.

5. What is the maximum number of Democrats in the Club?

   (A) 2
   (B) 3
   (C) 4
   (D) 5
   (E) 6

6. If there are four Republicans and four Democrats in the Club and exactly one of the four Republicans is an Accountant, which one of the following CANNOT be true?

   (A) Member 2 is a Lawyer.
   (B) Member 3 is a Republican.
   (C) Member 4 is an Accountant.
   (D) Member 6 is a Republican.
   (E) Member 6 is a Democrat.

GO ON TO THE NEXT PAGE ➤

5   **5**

Questions 7–13

Eleven people stand single file in a straight line. There are four women, three men, two boys and two girls.

The children are all next to each other.
Three of the women stand next to each other at one end of the line.
No man stands next to another man.

7. If a child is in the sixth place, which one of the following must be true?

   (A) A woman is in the first place.
   (B) A woman is in the second place.
   (C) A woman is in the seventh place.
   (D) A woman is in the eighth place.
   (E) A woman is in the ninth place.

8. Which one of the following must be true?

   (A) A woman is either first or third.
   (B) A woman is either second or tenth.
   (C) A woman is either sixth or seventh.
   (D) A woman is fourth.
   (E) A woman is seventh.

9. All of the following must be true EXCEPT

   (A) if a man is first, a woman is last
   (B) if a child is second, a man is sixth
   (C) if a child is sixth, a woman is tenth
   (D) if a man is fourth, a child is eighth
   (E) if a woman is third, a man is sixth

10. If a girl is second and a boy is third, which one of the following must be true?

    (A) The two boys are next to each other.
    (B) The two boys are not next to each other.
    (C) The two girls are not next to men.
    (D) The two girls are not next to each other.
    (E) A boy is next to a woman.

11. If a boy is eighth, which one of the following could be true?

    (A) A woman is last and a girl is sixth.
    (B) A man is fourth and tenth.
    (C) A woman is sixth and a girl is ninth.
    (D) A man is sixth and a woman is tenth.
    (E) A man is last and a girl is tenth.

12. If a man is fourth, a woman must be

    (A) first and fifth
    (B) second and tenth
    (C) first and second
    (D) first and tenth
    (E) second and fifth

13. If each man is next to at least one woman, which one of the following must be true?

    (A) A man is first.
    (B) A woman is second.
    (C) A woman is third.
    (D) A child is fourth.
    (E) A man is eighth.

GO ON TO THE NEXT PAGE ➤

5   **5**

Questions 14–19

The math club at Union Junior High School consists of three boys—Bill, Clem, and Drew, and four girls—Ann, Ellen, Fran, and Gina. While doing a math project involving measurement, the members arrive at the following information:

    (1) Bill is taller than Ann.
    (2) Drew is shorter than Bill.
    (3) Clem is taller than Drew, but shorter than Ann.
    (4) Ellen is taller than Clem, but shorter than Bill.
    (5) Fran is taller than Ellen.
    (6) Gina is shorter than Ann.

14. If Ann is 5 feet tall, then which one of the following could NOT be true?

    (A) Fran is 4 feet 10 inches tall.
    (B) Ellen is 5 feet 10 inches tall.
    (C) Drew is 5 feet 10 inches tall.
    (D) Clem is 4 feet 10 inches tall.
    (E) Gina is 4 feet 10 inches tall.

15. Which one of the following could NOT be true?

    (A) Drew is shorter than Ann.
    (B) Ellen is 4 feet tall.
    (C) Bill is taller than Fran.
    (D) Fran is shorter than Clem.
    (E) Drew is 4 feet tall.

16. If Ellen is taller than Ann, then which one of the following must be true about Fran?

    (A) Fran is shorter than Gina.
    (B) Fran is taller than Ann.
    (C) Fran is shorter than Clem.
    (D) Fran is taller than Bill.
    (E) Fran is the tallest.

17. Which statement about the math club members is redundant and repeats information obtainable from the other statements?

    (A) (1)
    (B) (2)
    (C) (3)
    (D) (4)
    (E) (5)

18. If Hank joins the group, and if he is shorter than Gina, then which one of the following must be true?

    (A) Hank is taller than Drew.
    (B) Clem is shorter than Hank.
    (C) Hank is shorter than Ellen.
    (D) Hank is taller than Ann.
    (E) Bill is taller than Hank.

19. If Fran and Ann are the same height, then which one of the following must be true?

    (A) Gina is taller than Ellen.
    (B) Ann is taller than Ellen.
    (C) Gina is taller than Fran.
    (D) Gina and Ellen are the same height.
    (E) Fran is taller than Bill.

GO ON TO THE NEXT PAGE ➤

5   **5**

<u>Questions 20–24</u>

In the Game of Bobcat, a player must assign his eight pieces to either the left flank or the right flank. The eight pieces are named the King, the Queen, the Squire, the Cornerman, the Runner, the Goalie, the Boxman, and the Pawn. Assignment to each flank must satisfy the following conditions:

The right flank requires at least four pieces.
The Pawn is always placed on the left flank.
The King and the Boxman cannot be placed on the same flank.
The Runner and the Squire cannot be placed on the same flank.
The King and the Cornerman must be placed on the same flank.

20. Which one of the following could be a complete and accurate list of the pieces placed on the right flank?

   (A) Goalie, King, Runner, Squire
   (B) Cornerman, King, Queen, Squire
   (C) Cornerman, Runner, King, Queen, Squire
   (D) Boxman, Cornerman, King, Squire
   (E) Boxman, Goalie, Runner

21. Which one of the following is a list of all the pieces that could be placed on the left flank at the same time?

   (A) Cornerman, King, Pawn
   (B) Boxman, King, Pawn, Squire
   (C) Goalie, King, Pawn, Runner
   (D) Boxman, Runner, Pawn
   (E) Boxman, Goalie, Queen, Squire

22. If the Boxman is placed on the right flank, then which one of the following pieces must be placed on the left flank?

   (A) Squire
   (B) Runner
   (C) Queen
   (D) Goalie
   (E) Cornerman

23. If the Goalie and the Queen are placed on the same flank, which one of the following pieces must be placed on the right flank?

   (A) Cornerman
   (B) Goalie
   (C) King
   (D) Runner
   (E) Squire

24. If the King and the Cornerman do NOT have to be placed on the same flank, then which one of the following could be a list of all pieces placed on the right flank?

   (A) Boxman, Cornerman, Goalie, Queen, Runner
   (B) Boxman, Cornerman, Goalie, Runner, Squire
   (C) Boxman, Goalie, King, Queen, Runner
   (D) Cornerman, Goalie, King, Queen
   (E) Cornerman, Goalie, Queen, Squire

STOP

END OF MULTIPLE-CHOICE EXAMINATION. IF YOU FINISH BEFORE TIME IS UP, CHECK YOUR WORK ON THIS SECTION ONLY. DO NOT GO BACK TO ANY OTHER SECTION OF THE EXAMINATION.

Writing Sample

Directions: You have 30 minutes to write an essay in response to a given topic. Take a few minutes to plan your work before you begin writing. DO NOT WRITE ON A TOPIC OF YOUR OWN CHOICE. ESSAYS THAT DO NOT ADDRESS THE GIVEN TOPIC ARE UNACCEPTABLE.

   The quality of your writing is more important than the length of your response or the content. Pay attention to organization, appropriate diction, and correct usage. You will not be expected to display any specialized knowledge in your response, nor will you be expected to write a "perfect" essay; law schools understand that you are writing under a time constraint, and will allow for the minor lapses in writing ability that might occur under this circumstance.

   Only the lined area in your booklet will be reproduced for the law schools, so do not write outside this space. *Do not* skip lines or use wide margins. These precautions, along with careful planning and legible handwriting that is not unduly large, will keep you within the allowed space.

Sample Topic

Read the following descriptions of Basil and Nottingham, two finalists for the position of curator at the Museum of Modern Art. *Then, in the space provided, write an argument for hiring either Basil or Nottingham.* The following criteria are relevant to your decision:

- The curator must acquire valuable artworks, design their display, and maintain museum security.
- Acquiring artworks will often require international travel and a talent for negotiating with collectors worldwide.

BASIL was educated at Oxford University, where he studied foreign cultures and languages in preparation for a career in the British diplomatic corps. A sizable family inheritance has allowed him to purchase, over the years, one of the world's largest and most valuable collections of Renaissance sculpture. Those visiting his home marvel at the unobtrusiveness of the sculptures on display there; a London art critic recently noted that "each sculpture seems an integral part of the room in which it is placed." Not one piece of Basil's personal collection has ever been stolen, even though he is often away on foreign travel, and his country home is not equipped with burglar alarms.

NOTTINGHAM's family moved from England to Italy, where his father took a post with the Vatican security force, when Nottingham was only a child. Although he was surrounded by great works by the traditional masters, Nottingham became more interested in experimental artwork—especially painting—and while studying modern art at the University of Rome, he began painting surrealistic landscapes that quickly gained public attention. In the twelve years since his graduation, Nottingham has been recognized as a productive and controversial artist, one whose abstract paintings are representative of the fragmentation and confusion of modern life. Galleries throughout Italy show Nottingham's paintings often, with the artist himself personally supervising every showing.

Answer Key

Section I: Analytical Reasoning

1. **C**	5. **E**	9. **A**	13. **C**	17. **E**	21. **E**
2. **E**	6. **D**	10. **A**	14. **E**	18. **D**	22. **C**
3. **B**	7. **B**	11. **B**	15. **E**	19. **B**	23. **A**
4. **A**	8. **E**	12. **B**	16. **D**	20. **D**	24. **B**

Section II: Logical Reasoning

1. **B**	6. **D**	11. **E**	16. **E**	21. **B**	26. **C**
2. **E**	7. **B**	12. **E**	17. **D**	22. **C**	
3. **A**	8. **B**	13. **D**	18. **C**	23. **D**	
4. **C**	9. **A**	14. **B**	19. **A**	24. **A**	
5. **A**	10. **B**	15. **E**	20. **A**	25. **D**	

Section III: Logical Reasoning

1. **D**	6. **A**	11. **C**	16. **B**	21. **D**
2. **B**	7. **B**	12. **C**	17. **D**	22. **D**
3. **E**	8. **E**	13. **E**	18. **B**	23. **A**
4. **E**	9. **C**	14. **E**	19. **E**	24. **A**
5. **D**	10. **B**	15. **A**	20. **C**	25. **D**

Section IV: Reading Comprehension

1. **D**	6. **D**	11. **D**	16. **C**	21. **B**	26. **B**
2. **B**	7. **D**	12. **B**	17. **D**	22. **D**	27. **C**
3. **D**	8. **C**	13. **B**	18. **B**	23. **A**	
4. **D**	9. **C**	14. **B**	19. **B**	24. **A**	
5. **E**	10. **A**	15. **E**	20. **C**	25. **D**	

Section V: Analytical Reasoning

1. **D**	5. **C**	9. **E**	13. **B**	17. **B**	21. **D**
2. **E**	6. **B**	10. **D**	14. **C**	18. **E**	22. **E**
3. **D**	7. **B**	11. **E**	15. **D**	19. **B**	23. **B**
4. **C**	8. **B**	12. **C**	16. **B**	20. **B**	24. **A**

Model Test Analysis

Doing model exams and understanding the explanations afterwards are of course important in acquainting you with typical LSAT question types and successful approaches to the questions. However, another benefit of carefully analyzing these model tests is to understand the kinds of errors you are making and thus work to minimize them. For instance, if a very high percentage of your incorrect answers is due to "careless error" or "misread problem," then perhaps you are working much too fast and should slow your pace accordingly. If your incorrect answers are due primarily to "lack of knowledge," then a careful rereading and reworking of the appropriate question-type chapter may be in order. Or if you find that you aren't completing a large number of questions because of lack of time you may need to either increase your speed or learn to use the "one-check, two-check" technique more effectively.

This kind of analysis of the model tests will enable you to identify your particular weaknesses and thus remedy them.

Model Test Four Analysis

Section	Total Number of Questions	Number Correct	Number Incorrect	Number Unanswered*
I. Analytical Reasoning	24			
II. Logical Reasoning	26			
III. Logical Reasoning	25			
IV. Reading Comprehension	27			
V. Analytical Reasoning	24			
TOTALS:	126			

*At this stage in your preparation, you should not be leaving any blank answer spaces. At least fill in a guess, as there is no penalty for a wrong answer.

Reasons for Incorrect Answers

You may wish to evaluate the explanations before completing this chart.

Section	Total Number Incorrect	Lack of Knowledge	Misread Problem	Careless Error	Unanswered or Wrong Guess
I. Analytical Reasoning					
II. Logical Reasoning					
III. Logical Reasoning					
IV. Reading Comprehension					
V. Analytical Reasoning					
TOTALS:					

Explanation of Answers

Section I

Answers 1–6

You could have come up with the following diagram:

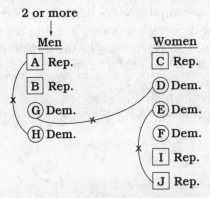

We will use the following more formal chart to actually show you the possibilities for each question:

	Men			Women			
	Rep.	Dem.		Dem.		Rep.	
	B A	H G		D F E		J	I C
Q. 1.	? n	y y		n y y		n	
	y n	y n		y y y		n	
Q. 2.	y n	y y		n n		y	
Q. 3.	n n	y y		n y ?		? y	y
Q. 4.	y y	n n		y y n		y	
Q. 5.	y y	n n		y y n		y	
Q. 6.	y y	n		y n		y y	n

1. **C** There are five Democrats. D and G cannot serve at the same time. Thus H, E, and F must be selected. If H is selected, A cannot be selected. If D is selected and G is not, then B must be selected since there must be two men on the committee. But if G is selected and D is not, then B does not have to be selected.

2. **E** If H is selected then A is not. If G is selected then D is not. If J is selected then E is not. This leaves F, I, and C to fill the other two slots on the committee. If I is not selected, then the other two must be.

3. **B** If A and B cannot be selected, then G and H must be selected since there must be two men on the committee. If G is selected then D cannot be selected. This leaves F, E, J, I, and C to fill the remaining four slots. Since E and J cannot both be selected, the other three must be selected. E or J must be selected, but we do not know which one.

4. **A** If G and H cannot be selected, then A and B must be selected since there must be at least two men on the committee. If J is selected, then E cannot be selected. This leaves D, F, I, and C to fill the other three slots on the committee. Both I and C cannot be selected since this would make five Republicans on the committee.

5. **E** If J is selected then E is not. If D is selected then G is not. Therefore both A and B must be selected since there must be two men on the committee. This leaves F, I, and C to fill the other two slots. Both I and C cannot be selected since that would place five Republicans on the committee. This means only one of them can be selected. This forces F to be selected.

6. **D** If A is selected then H is not. If J is selected then E is not. C cannot be selected since that would make five Republicans on the committee. This leaves G, D, and F to fill the other two slots. Since G and D cannot both be selected, F must be selected.

Answers 7–12

Note: UPPER-case letters denote fixed positions. Lower-case letters denote various possibilities.

7. **B**

1	2	3	4	5
c/d	E	A	B	d/c

Since E, A, and B cannot be 1st or 5th, their places are fixed. Thus, only (B) is true.

8. E

1	2	3	4	5
C	e	a	b	D
	a	e	b	
	a	b	e	

(A) is always true. (B) could be true. (C) could be true. (D) is always true. (E) can't be true. Thus the answer is (E), because if A finishes 4th, B would have to finish 5th.

9. A

1	2	3	4	5
c/d	A	B	E	d/c

Since B finishes ahead of E, we have A, B, and E in fixed positions. Since we do not know the positions of C and D, (C), (D), and (E) are false. (B) is false, since B is 3rd and not 4th. (A) is true.

10. A

1	2	3	4	5
D	a/e	e/a	B	C

Since A finishes ahead of B, B cannot finish 2nd. Thus, B must finish 4th, C finishes 5th, and D finishes 1st.

11. B

1	2	3	4	5	6
c/d	a/e	e/a	F	B	d/c

(A), (C), and (D) are all true from observation. (B) is false since we cannot determine the exact positions of C and D. (E) could be false.

12. B

1	2	3	4	5	6
D	E	A	B	F	C

This is the only arrangement that is possible based on the facts. From this arrangement, we see that B finishes 4th.

Answers 13–18

Drawing the simple diagram below will help answer the questions.

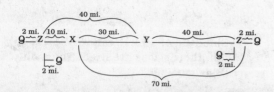

13. C Since Z is 40 miles from Y, and X is 30 miles from Y, Z could be 10 miles from X (left side of diagram).

14. E Q may be either 38 or 42 miles from Y, and either 68 or 8 miles from X. City Q may not be 38 miles from city X.

15. E If city Q is 12 miles from X, Q must be situated at the extreme left side of the diagram above. Therefore Z must be 10 miles from city X.

16. D XQZY may not be a possible order because Q may not come between X and Y.

17. E If a traveler begins at X and ends at Q, he may possibly only travel 8 miles, directly to Q without passing through any other city.

18. D By adding M 5 miles on either side of Y, all of the choices could be true, with the exception of D.

Answers 19–24

19. B If there are 2 essay questions on exam A they would have to be questions 1 and 4, but question 4 cannot be on exam A.

A	B	C
1	3	2
4		

Choice (A) is possible

A	B	C
1	3	2
8	5	4
9	7	6

Choice (C) is possible

A	B	C
1	3	2
5	4	8
7	6	9

Choice (D) is possible

A	B	C
1	3	2
5	4	8
7	6	9

Choice (E) is possible

A	B	C
1	3	2
5	8	4
7	9	6

20. **D** If questions 8 and 9 are on exam C, question 4 cannot be on exam C since questions 4 and 9 cannot be on the same exam. Question 4 cannot be on exam A. Thus, question 4 must be on exam B. This example demonstrates that the other four choices cannot be correct.

A	B	C
		8
		9

A	B	C
2	3	1
5	4	8
7	6	9

21. **E** Choice (A) is incorrect. Using a process of elimination, Question 6 must be on exam C since it cannot be on exam A, and exam B already has 2 short-answer questions. Since question 6 is on exam C, question 1 cannot be on exam C.

A	B	C
	5	6
	7	

Choice (B) is incorrect: Question 6 must be on exam C since it cannot be on exam A, and exam B already has 2 short-answer questions. Since question 6 is on exam C, we cannot put 2 more short-answer questions on exam C.

Choice (C) is incorrect: Since questions 5 and 7 must be on the same exam, there is room for only one more question and it must be an essay question.

Choice (D) is incorrect: Question 5 cannot be on exam A since it must be with question 7 on exam B.

Choice (E) is the correct answer: One possible example is shown to the right.

A	B	C
2	1	4
3	5	6
9	7	8

22. **C** Since question 9 is the only short-answer question on exam B, question 6 must be on exam C since it cannot be on exam A. Questions 5 and 7 can only fit on exam A. Thus, question 8 must be on exam C.

Choice (A) is incorrect since question 7 must be on exam A.

A	B	C
5	9	6
7		8

Choices (B), (D), and (E) are incorrect based on this example.

A	B	C
1	2	4
5	3	6
7	9	8

23. **A** If questions 2 and 7 are on exam C, so is question 5. Since questions 4 and 6 cannot be on exam A, they must be on exam B. Question 9 cannot be with question 4 on exam B, so question 9 must be on exam A.

A	B	C
9	4	2
	6	5
		7

Choice (B) is incorrect since question 1 cannot be on exam B with question 6.

Choices (C), (D), and (E) are incorrect based on this example.

A	B	C
1	3	2
8	4	5
9	6	7

24. **B** If question 3 is on exam A along with question 2, this would force questions 8/9 and questions 5/7 onto exams B and C, not respectively. Thus, there would be 2 short-answer questions on both exams B and C. This implies that the fifth short-answer question, question 6, must be on exam A. This is not possible.

A	B	C
2		
3		

Choices (A), (C), (D), and (E) are incorrect. This example of a possible arrangement shows that the other 4 choices are possible, and therefore incorrect.

A	B	C
2	1	3
5	8	4
7	9	6

Section II

1. **B** The passage states, "Those under . . . 18 . . . account for nearly half of the arrests for the seven major crimes. . . . Yet . . . courts are obliged to treat these young hard-core hoodlums . . ." (A) is a close answer; however, the author is not pointing out that crime has increased, but that violent crime has become more disproportionate.

2. **E** All of the following except (E) are assumed by the author. He would not rely on statistical trend lines if they were not accurate predictors (A). If the years from 1967 to 1976 were abnormal years, his statistics would be suspect (B). He finally makes a statement grouping the laws in most states as handling juveniles in the same manner and leniently (C) and (D). He does not address juveniles and nonviolent crime (E).

3. **A** Since an eland kill requires "at least two and probably three" lions, choice (A) is not at fault. An eland could be killed by three or more lions, a warthog by two or more; the same lion might be involved in all three kills, so only two lions could kill an eland and two warthogs.

4. **C** Although the writer would probably agree with the ideas of choices (A), (B), and (C), the most logical conclusion from the information in the passage is choice (C). If the number of fatalities increases when less than 50 percent of the older population has been inoculated, and the number of those inoculated declines, the number of fatalities should increase. Because we do not know how many (50 percent or more?) were inoculated last year and only that fewer will be inoculated this year, we cannot be sure that "fatalities will increase sharply," choice (D).

5. **A** Because the ridership on the route served by the older buses that are not air-conditioned increased, the larger number of commuters on the other routes may not be due to the new vehicles.

6. **D** (B) and (E) weaken the argument, (A) repeats the argument, and (C) makes no sense, since "average height" is a *single* composite of all heights.

7. **B** Pointing out that "there are too many variables in this type of study" weakens the argument tremendously, because isolating the reason for the growth increase now becomes very difficult. Thus, we could not deduce that modern foods stimulate growth. (D) is close, as it also weakens the argument, but it isn't specific enough. If (D) were "*too* small," then it would be an excellent answer.

8. **B** The information in (B) directly corresponds to the "significant" conclusion in the paragraph's final sentence. (A) is beyond the time scope of the paragraph; (C) is untenable because the final sentence states that accidents are not characteristic of advanced years. There is no evidence in the paragraph which supports (D) or (E).

9. **A** All of the statements except (A) are solidly supported by a comparison of the "cause lists" for 1900, 1910, and 1945. (A) is a conclusion that may be true, but it is not an issue the paragraph raises.

10. **B** The trouble with the conclusion in the original paragraph is there is no demonstration of the cause of the change of taste. But if children who had not been exposed to advertising did not prefer sweetened foods, they would support the notion that the preference is acquired.

11. **E** The passage states that 90 percent of our mind controls 95 percent of our behavior, thus implying that the other 10 percent of our mind controls 5 percent of our behavior. The passage does not state or imply that "dreams, spontaneous recall, and slips of speech constitute about 90 percent of our behavior."

12. **E** The passage states that 90 percent of our mind controls 95 percent of our behavior; therefore, a small part of our mind controls a small part of our behavior, as the other 10 percent of our mind must control 5 percent of our behavior.

13. **D** The passage makes no comment on the majority of a teacher's students.

14. **B** If the workers answered "Yes" to every question, there would be no way to frame a question so the "correct" answer was "No." Regardless of the questions, the answer will be "Yes."

15. **E** (A) is untrue; (B) contradicts the passage. (C) and (D) are not ascertainable from the passage. The author would agree with (E), for self-reported statements cannot be verified.

16. **E** The passage begins with a sentence about the value of on-the-job training, but leaves that topic rather than developing it. The implication of this first sentence is that on-the-job training has just been discussed, thus allowing a transition to consequent topics.

17. **D** This choice summarizes the argument of the paragraph. (A) contradicts the "two-sidedness" of lying that the author explains; (B) and (E) are unsupported conclusions; and (C) is an overstatement because it employs "only."

18. **C** Neither (A) nor (B) is implied, because no comparison is made with other brands of soap. Nor is (D) correct because there is no implication regarding what is economically the best value or price. And though the advertisement states that Cleenup is good for household jobs, it doesn't imply that household chores are its only range. That Cleenup Soap may be used for scouring pots and pans, whitening the sink, and performing other household chores indicates that it can be used for many cleaning jobs (C).

19. **A** The renter's third statement contradicts his second statement.

20. **A** The best choice should be related directly to the claim that "forests will not be consumed so rapidly." Choice (B) is the next best choice, but we cannot know if the speaker is concerned with ecology in general or simply with the preservation of forests. Choices (C) and (D) may be true, but they are not required assumptions for this argument. The speaker may be willing to spend more money to save the forests.

21. **B** The right answer should undermine the case for using safety helmets. If, as choice (B) claims, the cyclist's vision is impaired, accidents are more likely. Choices (A) and (E) do not bear directly enough on the benefits of wearing or not wearing a helmet, whereas choice (D) strengthens the argument.

21. **D** The author sets out to demonstrate this thesis by attacking the validity of the two assumptions made by those who oppose his view and who believe ostentation is either a natural right or an unavoidable impulse in man.

22. **C** (C) is the correct choice, since it contradicts the original statement. (A), (D), and (E) are obviously incorrect; they do not have anything to do with the problem. (B) would tend to strengthen the argument.

23. **D** The fact that Lasch's book is a bestseller has nothing to do with his similarity to Aesop, at least not in the context of this passage. Each of the other choices reinforces or clarifies the comparison.

24. **A** Dr. Graham is not given a full name, and we are not told anything beyond the mention of his evangelical spirit. Therefore, we must conclude that the author is writing to an audience already familiar with the identity and significance of Dr. Graham. Each of the other choices is a possible but not necessary underlying assumption.

25. **D** The author stresses the nice qualities of "folks who cling to the past" (in other words, "the enemies of the future"). (A) contradicts the author's viewpoint and the other choices provide irrelevant or unsubstantiated conclusions.

26. **C** This choice ties reduced nuclear proliferation to arms reduction by the United States and Russia, thus weakening the author's argument that proliferation and arms control are separate issues. (D) strengthens the argument. (A), (B), and (E) are tangential if not irrelevant.

Section III

1. **D** If no bond measure that will bring in large revenues will lose, the argument must be true. The verifying statement can also be expressed with positives instead of the two negatives. Both choices (A) and (B) could be true without assuring the passage of the stadium bond, because bills that do bring profits could also be defeated. Similarly, choice (C) could be true, without assuring the success of the stadium bond. Choice (E) is not relevant.

2. **B** The connective "but" alerts the reader to a contrast, an expression of disapproval. Option (C) is illogical, and (D) and (E) are issues that the passage has not touched upon. Between (A) and (B), (B) is the more likely since the pollution generated on land is 80 percent of the total.

3. **E** (A) is not necessarily true; it could be Wednesday. (B) is not necessarily true; the weather could be bad or it could be Thursday. (C) would be true only if it is Monday, of which we cannot be certain. (D) does not follow; it could be any day. If the band practices in good weather on Tuesdays and the weather is good and the band is not practicing, it cannot be Tuesday.

4. **E** The last sentence, unlike the rest of the paragraph, suggests that the nuclear threat was greater in the past.

5. **D** The passage argues that new construction will flourish if rent controls are abolished. All of the other choices are assumptions the author makes.

6. **A** A shortage of low-cost housing supports the author's claim of a "dire shortage," but (B) does not. If the population is declining (C), the housing shortage should diminish. (D) and (E) contradict the argument that rent control causes the housing shortage or the lack of building new units.

7. **B** The passage is filled with overstatement: "only things," "no concern," "all fields," "unspeakable disaster," and "suicide."

8. **E** If the women taking the tests had studied less math and science, the disparity in grades would be more likely to be due to this difference than to a bias of the test.

9. **C** The pattern is "all the 1 in this 2 are 3; therefore this 2 uses only 3, 1."

10. **B** The situation described makes it impossible for a councilman to continue to be elected. Only by finding an alternative way of funding the railway could a politician avoid defeat.

11. **C** The first paragraph describes the costs, while the second discusses some possible benefits for businesses.

12. **C** The "liabilities" of the legislation are the high costs enumerated in paragraph 1; the "benefits" are those described in the second paragraph.

13. **E** David does not live in an apartment, may or may not be suspicious, and must be thin.

14. **E** Like David, Jane does not live in an apartment, may or may not be suspicious, and is thin.

15. **A** The results of the two different studies both point to the possibility suggested in choice (A).

16. **B** The first sentence presents a benefit of the initiative process, while the second and third sentences criticize initiative campaigns.

17. **D** Dave has not presented high-fiber foods as a cause of weight loss in themselves, but Jane has assumed that he has.

18. **B** The series of questions is based upon the reports of those who claim to have seen UFOs or their inhabitants.

19. **E** The evidence that this author cites *is* relevant to the conclusions. Although this may not be the only evidence to support the author's conclusions, the author is using the observations as a basis for the conclusions. (E) states that the evidence is irrelevant to the conclusions. Thus (E) is false. Choices (A), (B), (C), and (D) are all true with regard to the evidence given.

20. **C** Jack has confused "all" and "only." Compare question 1.

21. **D** If by awarding grants to a wider range of universities the NSF is able to develop new world-class research institutions, there is good reason to do so.

22. **D** The second paragraph questions the economic benefits of the politicization of the awards, but this example supports the case for economic development as a consequence of science centers.

23. **A** (A) follows logically, but we cannot know certainly from the passage if (B), (C), (D), and (E) are true or false.

24. **A** The passage compares banning smoking and banning cars.

25. **D** If restaurants in cities that have banned smoking have not lost money, health reasons would appear to prevail, as the economic arguments no longer apply.

Section IV
Passage 1

1. **D** A conversational tone is mentioned as part of the "natural style" that developed coincidentally with Roosevelt's administration in the 1930s (paragraph 2). Roosevelt's own radio "conversations" would seem to be examples of this natural style. (C) is an irrelevant point; (E) seems unrelated to the limitations of radio; (A) is not supported by a characterization of American politics as propaganda; (B) refers to theatricality, a characteristic largely unrelated to Roosevelt's chats.

2. **B** This is an explicit and repeated point.

3. **D** The author's skepticism is expressed when he says that the Russian films "made the new regime *appear* to be the heir of a glorious revolutionary tradition"; he calls into question the facts by labeling them as merely *apparent*.

4. **D** The author's persistent point, that the style of popular entertainment affects the style of politics, indicates this choice. He associates excessive gestures with early cinema and expressionist theater (paragraph 2); only (D) accounts for at least one of these media. (C) refers to the style of movie *heroes*, a style not necessarily associated with exaggerated gestures.

5. **E** Though choice (A) describes the first paragraph of the passage, the rest is more concerned with the influence of the films upon politics. All other choices are either inaccurate or too specific. The author's repeated comparison of politics and government to popular entertainment (mainly movies) indicates (E).

6. **D** We are told toward the end of the passage that during the 1930s and 1940s the isolated, idolized, one-of-a-kind stars became "more human" and could be imitated. The eventual result of their influence was "the political Mr. Everyman."

7. **D** The author must assume that art imitates life in order to argue that politics imitates phases in film history.

Passage 2

8. **C** The first paragraph cites the stock market crash of 1929 as the "decisive cut in continuity of twentieth-century America."

9. **C** Although the author acknowledges the importance of the stock market crash as an event that makes a "decisive cut" in literary history, he also stresses, "When dates are established, . . . predecessors and successors have a way of making them dissolve," thus suggesting that the crash cannot be isolated as a demarcation point without accounting for the events that led up to it and followed it. (D) and (E) are supported by the passage, but irrelevant to this particular question.

10. **A** In the preceding sentence of the third paragraph, the author states that the Jazz Age ended with the 1929 depression, thus stressing that it was a phenomenon of the 1920s only. Recognizing that "it" stands for "Jazz Age," and refers to the preceding sentence, you must choose (A).

11. **D** The 1960s are mentioned at the end of the second paragraph, just after the author has noted the human tendency to "forget unpleasantness." The '60s may become a happy recollection, we are told, but not until the twenty-first century. This speculation suggests that the author presently regards the '60s as an unhappy time that may be recalled more pleasantly after the passage of a few decades.

12. **B** The Thirties were a period of depression (line 41) while the Twenties were a period of economic boom that lasted until late in 1929. The four other choices are either untrue or irrelevant.

13. **B** In the final paragraph of the passage, the author states that in the 1930s "realism and naturalism are by this time established as dominant modes."

Passage 3

14. **B** The passage is essentially neutral; the author does not take sides or suggest his own program or solution. "Discuss," the most neutral term of the five choices, signals (B) as the appropriate answer.

15. **E** Delacourte's motive is *moral,* and the industry's motive is *economic;* this difference is stressed in the final sentence of the passage.

16. **C** The author is *reporting* information without attempting to slant it subjectively. His impersonal tone should lead you to eliminate (A), (B), and (D), all of them suggesting personal involvement. However, the author is not indifferent (E) to the issue he describes; otherwise, he would not choose to discuss it so extensively.

17. **D** Without explicitly criticizing the tuna industry, the author does contrast fishermen with "compassionate souls" such as Delacourte (final paragraph).

18. **B** The chairman of a "People for Animals" drive would be certain to object to clothing produced through the destruction of animals. Delacourte would probably be in favor of the other choices.

19. **B** Although we are told that U.S. fishermen must conform to federal regulations, those regulations are not mentioned explicitly; we may *infer* that the regulations entail porpoise conservation.

20. **C** The passage gives answers to questions (A), (B), (D), and (E). The opinion of the general public is neither expressed nor implied in the passage.

Passage 4

21. **B** Since the quotation from Carlyle presents life as "pain and folly," the best inference here is that Carlyle is a satirist. Carlyle is a nineteenth-century writer.

22. **D** This is defined in paragraph 1: "ETI (a fashionable new acronym for Extraterrestrial Intelligence)."

23. **A** Paragraph 1 states, "'Exobiology' has already been named even though its entire subject matter may not exist."

24. **A** The first sentence of paragraph 2 mentions both the 200 billion *other* suns in our galaxy and the billions of other galaxies outside our own. The following question, "Are there other planets?" refers directly to planets surrounding these suns and galaxies outside our own solar system.

25. **D** Paragraph 3 discusses the development of ETI and says that even planets which are similar to earth are not certain to develop life as advanced as we know it, perhaps not even life as "intelligent as a fish."

26. **B** The words, "intellects vast and cool and unsympathetic, regarded this earth with envious eyes . . ." suggest that earth was being scrutinized by superior aliens. The quotation also indicates that some sort of plan against us may be imminent ("they drew their plans against us"), but choice (C) is incorrect, as Wells does not necessarily imply an "intergalactic war."

27. **C** The writings of Carlyle and Wells are treated with respect, so (E) should be eliminated. (D) is also incorrect, because the evidence given is incomplete and tentative, not conclusive. (A) and (B) are irrelevant to the purpose of the passage, which is well described by (C).

Section V
Answers 1–6

From the information given, the following chart may be drawn to help you to answer the questions:

1. **D** From the given information:

$$1 \qquad 2_R \qquad 3^A \qquad 4$$
$$5_D \qquad 6 \qquad 7^L \qquad 8_R$$

If all the Lawyers are Democrats, then member 8 must be an Accountant. This means that member 6 must be a Lawyer and, therefore, a Democrat. The following arrangement is required:

$$1 \qquad 2^A_R \qquad 3^A \qquad 4^A_R$$
$$5_D \qquad 6^L_D \qquad 7^L_D \qquad 8^A_R$$

2. **E** From the given information:

$$1 \qquad 2_R \qquad 3^A \qquad 4$$
$$5_D \qquad 6 \qquad 7^L \qquad 8_R$$

If there is a total of exactly three Democrats, members 6 and 7 along with 5 are possible. All other choices leave at least one Democrat isolated.

3. **D** From the given information:

$$1 \qquad 2_R \qquad 3^A \qquad 4$$
$$5_D \qquad 6 \qquad 7^L \qquad 8_R$$

If there are exactly three Accountants and member 5 were an Accountant, either member 3 or 5 would be isolated. Therefore, member 5 must be a Lawyer. Possible pairs of the other two Accountants are 1 and 2, 2 and 6, 2 and 4, 4 and 8.

4. **C** From the given information:

$$1 \qquad 2_R \qquad 3^A \qquad 4$$
$$5_D \qquad 6 \qquad 7^L \qquad 8_R$$

Not (A), since if members 1, 4, and 7 were Lawyers, either member 1 or member 4 would remain isolated with the addition of the 4th Lawyer. Not (B) since if members 1, 2, 6, and 8 are Republicans, member 8 would be isolated. Not (D), since if members 4, 5, and 7 were Democrats, either member 4 or 5 would be isolated. Not (E), since if members 2, 5, 7, and 8 are Republicans, member 2 would be isolated. Choice (C) is possible, since if member 2 is the fourth Accountant, none would be isolated.

5. **C** Two additional Republicans are needed (either members 3 and 4, 3 and 7, or 6 and 7) so that none is isolated. This leaves four members to be Democrats.

6. **B** From the given information:

$$1 \qquad 2_R \qquad 3^A \qquad 4$$
$$5_D \qquad 6 \qquad 7^L \qquad 8_R$$

If there are four Republicans, four Democrats, and exactly one of the Republicans is an Accountant, then the additional Republicans must be either members 3 and 4, 3 and 7, or 6 and 7. If members 3 and 4 are the Republicans, then members 2 and 4 must be Lawyers. This would isolate member 3. If members 3 and 7 were the Republicans, then member 4 must be a Democrat and would be isolated. Therefore, members 6 and 7 must be the other Republicans. Thus member 3 cannot be a Republican. The following configuration results:

$$1_D \qquad 2_R \qquad 3^A_D \qquad 4_D$$
$$5_D \qquad 6_R \qquad 7^L_R \qquad 8_R$$

Answers 7–13

Drawing a simple diagram will help answer the questions. Note, however, that there are several possible diagrams. First, since three of the women are together at one end of the line, these women could be at either the beginning or the end:

W	W	W								
1	2	3	4	5	6	7	8	9	10	11
								W	W	W

Then note that, since a man never stands next to another man, there can only be two possible arrangements of men for each of the above arrangements of women:

W	W	W	M	ʷ⁄ₘ	ᴹ⁄ₘ	ʷ⁄ₘ	ʷ⁄ₘ	ˢ⁄ₘ	ˢ⁄ₘ	M
1	2	3	4	5	6	7	8	9	10	11
M	ʷ⁄ₘ	ᴹ⁄ₘ	ʷ⁄ₘ	ʷ⁄ₘ	ˢ⁄ₘ	ˢ⁄ₘ	M	W	W	W

Now the questions are more easily answered.

7. **B** Note that if a child is in the sixth place (the middle four possible arrangements) then a woman must be in the second place.

8. **B** Since the rules state that three of the women stand next to each other at one end of the line, then a woman must be either second or tenth (second to last).

9. **E** All of the choices must be true except choice (E). If a woman is third, a child could be sixth, as in the second arrangement.

10. **D** If a girl is second and a boy is third, it can only be the fourth arrangement (the bottom arrangement) because that is the only time children are in the second and third positions. Since the other two children are in the fourth and fifth positions, the two girls cannot be next to each other.

11. **E** If a boy is eighth, we may consider both the first and second arrangements. Therefore, a man could be last (in fact, he must be last) and a girl could be tenth.

12. **C** If a man is fourth, we may consider the first and second arrangements. Therefore, women *must* be in the first and second positions.

13. **B** If each man is next to at least one woman, we may rule out the first and fourth arrangements. Therefore, considering the other two arrangements, only that a woman is second must necessarily be true.

Answers 14–19

14. **C** First we draw a diagram to show the height comparisons:

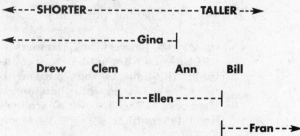

We see Drew is shorter than Ann. Therefore, (C) is false. Also, Fran and Ellen COULD be taller or shorter than Ann.

15. **D** Since Fran is taller than Ellen and Ellen is taller than Clem, Fran is taller than Clem.

16. **B** Since Fran is taller than Ellen, and if Ellen is taller than Ann, then Fran must be taller than Ann.

17. **B** From statement (3) Drew is shorter than Ann. From statement (1) Ann is shorter than Bill. It follows that Drew is shorter than Bill.

18. **E** (A), (B), (C), and (D) are false by inspecting the chart. Only (E) can be deduced.

19. **B** Since Fran is taller than Ellen, Ann must also be taller than Ellen. Since Gina is shorter than Ann, Gina must be shorter than Fran too. No relationship has been established between Gina and Ellen. Since Ann is shorter than Bill, Fran is shorter than Bill.

Answers 20–24

From the initial conditions, the following display can be drawn:

Left P???   Right _ _ _ _???
    KB RS KC

20. **B** From the display and initial conditions the elimination strategy can be applied as follows: Not (A) or (C), since the Runner and the Squire cannot be on the same flank. Not (D), since Boxman and the King cannot be on the same flank. Not (E), since the right flank must have at least four pieces.

21. **D** Using the display and the initial conditions, the elimination strategy can again be applied: Not (A), since this would require the Runner and the Squire to be on the same flank, and that is not permitted. Not (B), since the King and the Boxman cannot be on the same flank. Not (C), since the King and Cornerman must be on the same flank. Not (E), since the left flank must have the Pawn.

22. **E** Filling in the display with the information given in the question makes the reasoning processes easier to follow:

Left P???   Right B _ _ _???
 KB RS KC

The King cannot be on the same flank as the Boxman, so therefore the King must be on the left flank.

Left PK??   Right B _ _ _??
 KB RS KC

Since the King and the Cornerman must be on the same flank, the Cornerman must also be on the left flank.

23. B If the Queen and Goalie were placed on the left flank, then the King and Cornerman would have to be placed on the right flank since they must be together and at most three pieces can be placed on the left flank. The display would now look like this:

Left PQG?   Right K C _ _?
KB RS KC

This would require the Boxman and either the Runner or Squire to be placed on the left flank. That would make five pieces on the left flank, which is not permitted. Therefore, the Queen and Goalie must be on the right flank. So the display above is not possible.

24. **A** The information with the display would now look like this:

Left P???   Right _ _ _ _???
KB RS

Now use the elimination strategy. Not (B) or (D), since the Runner and the Squire would be on the same flank. Not (C) or (E), since the King and Boxman would be on the same flank.

Chapter 10
MODEL TEST FIVE

This chapter contains full-length Model Test Five. It is geared to the format of the LSAT, and it is complete with answers and explanations. It is equivalent to the LSAT in question structure, number of questions, level of difficulty, and time allotments. (The questions used are not taken directly from the LSAT, as those questions are copyrighted and may not be reproduced.)

Model Test Five should be taken under strict test conditions. The test ends with a 30-minute Writing Sample, which is not scored.

Section	Description	Number of Questions	Time Allowed
I.	Analytical Reasoning	24	35 minutes
II.	Reading Comprehension	27	35 minutes
III.	Logical Reasoning	26	35 minutes
IV.	Analytical Reasoning	23	35 minutes
V.	Logical Reasoning	25	35 minutes
	Writing Sample		30 minutes
TOTALS:		125	3 hours 25 minutes

Now please turn to the next page, remove your answer sheet, and begin Model Test Five.

Answer Sheet—Model Test Five

Section 1	Section 2	Section 3	Section 4	Section 5
1. Ⓐ Ⓑ Ⓒ Ⓓ Ⓔ	1. Ⓐ Ⓑ Ⓒ Ⓓ Ⓔ	1. Ⓐ Ⓑ Ⓒ Ⓓ Ⓔ	1. Ⓐ Ⓑ Ⓒ Ⓓ Ⓔ	1. Ⓐ Ⓑ Ⓒ Ⓓ Ⓔ
2. Ⓐ Ⓑ Ⓒ Ⓓ Ⓔ	2. Ⓐ Ⓑ Ⓒ Ⓓ Ⓔ	2. Ⓐ Ⓑ Ⓒ Ⓓ Ⓔ	2. Ⓐ Ⓑ Ⓒ Ⓓ Ⓔ	2. Ⓐ Ⓑ Ⓒ Ⓓ Ⓔ
3. Ⓐ Ⓑ Ⓒ Ⓓ Ⓔ	3. Ⓐ Ⓑ Ⓒ Ⓓ Ⓔ	3. Ⓐ Ⓑ Ⓒ Ⓓ Ⓔ	3. Ⓐ Ⓑ Ⓒ Ⓓ Ⓔ	3. Ⓐ Ⓑ Ⓒ Ⓓ Ⓔ
4. Ⓐ Ⓑ Ⓒ Ⓓ Ⓔ	4. Ⓐ Ⓑ Ⓒ Ⓓ Ⓔ	4. Ⓐ Ⓑ Ⓒ Ⓓ Ⓔ	4. Ⓐ Ⓑ Ⓒ Ⓓ Ⓔ	4. Ⓐ Ⓑ Ⓒ Ⓓ Ⓔ
5. Ⓐ Ⓑ Ⓒ Ⓓ Ⓔ	5. Ⓐ Ⓑ Ⓒ Ⓓ Ⓔ	5. Ⓐ Ⓑ Ⓒ Ⓓ Ⓔ	5. Ⓐ Ⓑ Ⓒ Ⓓ Ⓔ	5. Ⓐ Ⓑ Ⓒ Ⓓ Ⓔ
6. Ⓐ Ⓑ Ⓒ Ⓓ Ⓔ	6. Ⓐ Ⓑ Ⓒ Ⓓ Ⓔ	6. Ⓐ Ⓑ Ⓒ Ⓓ Ⓔ	6. Ⓐ Ⓑ Ⓒ Ⓓ Ⓔ	6. Ⓐ Ⓑ Ⓒ Ⓓ Ⓔ
7. Ⓐ Ⓑ Ⓒ Ⓓ Ⓔ	7. Ⓐ Ⓑ Ⓒ Ⓓ Ⓔ	7. Ⓐ Ⓑ Ⓒ Ⓓ Ⓔ	7. Ⓐ Ⓑ Ⓒ Ⓓ Ⓔ	7. Ⓐ Ⓑ Ⓒ Ⓓ Ⓔ
8. Ⓐ Ⓑ Ⓒ Ⓓ Ⓔ	8. Ⓐ Ⓑ Ⓒ Ⓓ Ⓔ	8. Ⓐ Ⓑ Ⓒ Ⓓ Ⓔ	8. Ⓐ Ⓑ Ⓒ Ⓓ Ⓔ	8. Ⓐ Ⓑ Ⓒ Ⓓ Ⓔ
9. Ⓐ Ⓑ Ⓒ Ⓓ Ⓔ	9. Ⓐ Ⓑ Ⓒ Ⓓ Ⓔ	9. Ⓐ Ⓑ Ⓒ Ⓓ Ⓔ	9. Ⓐ Ⓑ Ⓒ Ⓓ Ⓔ	9. Ⓐ Ⓑ Ⓒ Ⓓ Ⓔ
10. Ⓐ Ⓑ Ⓒ Ⓓ Ⓔ	10. Ⓐ Ⓑ Ⓒ Ⓓ Ⓔ	10. Ⓐ Ⓑ Ⓒ Ⓓ Ⓔ	10. Ⓐ Ⓑ Ⓒ Ⓓ Ⓔ	10. Ⓐ Ⓑ Ⓒ Ⓓ Ⓔ
11. Ⓐ Ⓑ Ⓒ Ⓓ Ⓔ	11. Ⓐ Ⓑ Ⓒ Ⓓ Ⓔ	11. Ⓐ Ⓑ Ⓒ Ⓓ Ⓔ	11. Ⓐ Ⓑ Ⓒ Ⓓ Ⓔ	11. Ⓐ Ⓑ Ⓒ Ⓓ Ⓔ
12. Ⓐ Ⓑ Ⓒ Ⓓ Ⓔ	12. Ⓐ Ⓑ Ⓒ Ⓓ Ⓔ	12. Ⓐ Ⓑ Ⓒ Ⓓ Ⓔ	12. Ⓐ Ⓑ Ⓒ Ⓓ Ⓔ	12. Ⓐ Ⓑ Ⓒ Ⓓ Ⓔ
13. Ⓐ Ⓑ Ⓒ Ⓓ Ⓔ	13. Ⓐ Ⓑ Ⓒ Ⓓ Ⓔ	13. Ⓐ Ⓑ Ⓒ Ⓓ Ⓔ	13. Ⓐ Ⓑ Ⓒ Ⓓ Ⓔ	13. Ⓐ Ⓑ Ⓒ Ⓓ Ⓔ
14. Ⓐ Ⓑ Ⓒ Ⓓ Ⓔ	14. Ⓐ Ⓑ Ⓒ Ⓓ Ⓔ	14. Ⓐ Ⓑ Ⓒ Ⓓ Ⓔ	14. Ⓐ Ⓑ Ⓒ Ⓓ Ⓔ	14. Ⓐ Ⓑ Ⓒ Ⓓ Ⓔ
15. Ⓐ Ⓑ Ⓒ Ⓓ Ⓔ	15. Ⓐ Ⓑ Ⓒ Ⓓ Ⓔ	15. Ⓐ Ⓑ Ⓒ Ⓓ Ⓔ	15. Ⓐ Ⓑ Ⓒ Ⓓ Ⓔ	15. Ⓐ Ⓑ Ⓒ Ⓓ Ⓔ
16. Ⓐ Ⓑ Ⓒ Ⓓ Ⓔ	16. Ⓐ Ⓑ Ⓒ Ⓓ Ⓔ	16. Ⓐ Ⓑ Ⓒ Ⓓ Ⓔ	16. Ⓐ Ⓑ Ⓒ Ⓓ Ⓔ	16. Ⓐ Ⓑ Ⓒ Ⓓ Ⓔ
17. Ⓐ Ⓑ Ⓒ Ⓓ Ⓔ	17. Ⓐ Ⓑ Ⓒ Ⓓ Ⓔ	17. Ⓐ Ⓑ Ⓒ Ⓓ Ⓔ	17. Ⓐ Ⓑ Ⓒ Ⓓ Ⓔ	17. Ⓐ Ⓑ Ⓒ Ⓓ Ⓔ
18. Ⓐ Ⓑ Ⓒ Ⓓ Ⓔ	18. Ⓐ Ⓑ Ⓒ Ⓓ Ⓔ	18. Ⓐ Ⓑ Ⓒ Ⓓ Ⓔ	18. Ⓐ Ⓑ Ⓒ Ⓓ Ⓔ	18. Ⓐ Ⓑ Ⓒ Ⓓ Ⓔ
19. Ⓐ Ⓑ Ⓒ Ⓓ Ⓔ	19. Ⓐ Ⓑ Ⓒ Ⓓ Ⓔ	19. Ⓐ Ⓑ Ⓒ Ⓓ Ⓔ	19. Ⓐ Ⓑ Ⓒ Ⓓ Ⓔ	19. Ⓐ Ⓑ Ⓒ Ⓓ Ⓔ
20. Ⓐ Ⓑ Ⓒ Ⓓ Ⓔ	20. Ⓐ Ⓑ Ⓒ Ⓓ Ⓔ	20. Ⓐ Ⓑ Ⓒ Ⓓ Ⓔ	20. Ⓐ Ⓑ Ⓒ Ⓓ Ⓔ	20. Ⓐ Ⓑ Ⓒ Ⓓ Ⓔ
21. Ⓐ Ⓑ Ⓒ Ⓓ Ⓔ	21. Ⓐ Ⓑ Ⓒ Ⓓ Ⓔ	21. Ⓐ Ⓑ Ⓒ Ⓓ Ⓔ	21. Ⓐ Ⓑ Ⓒ Ⓓ Ⓔ	21. Ⓐ Ⓑ Ⓒ Ⓓ Ⓔ
22. Ⓐ Ⓑ Ⓒ Ⓓ Ⓔ	22. Ⓐ Ⓑ Ⓒ Ⓓ Ⓔ	22. Ⓐ Ⓑ Ⓒ Ⓓ Ⓔ	22. Ⓐ Ⓑ Ⓒ Ⓓ Ⓔ	22. Ⓐ Ⓑ Ⓒ Ⓓ Ⓔ
23. Ⓐ Ⓑ Ⓒ Ⓓ Ⓔ	23. Ⓐ Ⓑ Ⓒ Ⓓ Ⓔ	23. Ⓐ Ⓑ Ⓒ Ⓓ Ⓔ	23. Ⓐ Ⓑ Ⓒ Ⓓ Ⓔ	23. Ⓐ Ⓑ Ⓒ Ⓓ Ⓔ
24. Ⓐ Ⓑ Ⓒ Ⓓ Ⓔ	24. Ⓐ Ⓑ Ⓒ Ⓓ Ⓔ	24. Ⓐ Ⓑ Ⓒ Ⓓ Ⓔ	24. Ⓐ Ⓑ Ⓒ Ⓓ Ⓔ	24. Ⓐ Ⓑ Ⓒ Ⓓ Ⓔ
25. Ⓐ Ⓑ Ⓒ Ⓓ Ⓔ	25. Ⓐ Ⓑ Ⓒ Ⓓ Ⓔ	25. Ⓐ Ⓑ Ⓒ Ⓓ Ⓔ	25. Ⓐ Ⓑ Ⓒ Ⓓ Ⓔ	25. Ⓐ Ⓑ Ⓒ Ⓓ Ⓔ
26. Ⓐ Ⓑ Ⓒ Ⓓ Ⓔ	26. Ⓐ Ⓑ Ⓒ Ⓓ Ⓔ	26. Ⓐ Ⓑ Ⓒ Ⓓ Ⓔ	26. Ⓐ Ⓑ Ⓒ Ⓓ Ⓔ	26. Ⓐ Ⓑ Ⓒ Ⓓ Ⓔ
27. Ⓐ Ⓑ Ⓒ Ⓓ Ⓔ	27. Ⓐ Ⓑ Ⓒ Ⓓ Ⓔ	27. Ⓐ Ⓑ Ⓒ Ⓓ Ⓔ	27. Ⓐ Ⓑ Ⓒ Ⓓ Ⓔ	27. Ⓐ Ⓑ Ⓒ Ⓓ Ⓔ
28. Ⓐ Ⓑ Ⓒ Ⓓ Ⓔ	28. Ⓐ Ⓑ Ⓒ Ⓓ Ⓔ	28. Ⓐ Ⓑ Ⓒ Ⓓ Ⓔ	28. Ⓐ Ⓑ Ⓒ Ⓓ Ⓔ	28. Ⓐ Ⓑ Ⓒ Ⓓ Ⓔ
29. Ⓐ Ⓑ Ⓒ Ⓓ Ⓔ	29. Ⓐ Ⓑ Ⓒ Ⓓ Ⓔ	29. Ⓐ Ⓑ Ⓒ Ⓓ Ⓔ	29. Ⓐ Ⓑ Ⓒ Ⓓ Ⓔ	29. Ⓐ Ⓑ Ⓒ Ⓓ Ⓔ
30. Ⓐ Ⓑ Ⓒ Ⓓ Ⓔ	30. Ⓐ Ⓑ Ⓒ Ⓓ Ⓔ	30. Ⓐ Ⓑ Ⓒ Ⓓ Ⓔ	30. Ⓐ Ⓑ Ⓒ Ⓓ Ⓔ	30. Ⓐ Ⓑ Ⓒ Ⓓ Ⓔ

To remove, cut along dotted rule.

1   1   1   1   1

SECTION I
TIME — 35 MINUTES
24 QUESTIONS

Directions: In this section you will be given groups of questions based on different sets of conditions. Drawing a simple diagram may be helpful in answering some of the questions. You are to choose the *best* answer and mark the corresponding space on your answer sheet.

Questions 1–6

The Westlake Baseball All-Star team is lined up in a single row for a picture. The nine All-Stars consist of players from five different teams. There are three Panthers, two Badgers, two Rockets, one Cobra, and one Viking. The positions in the picture are numbered left to right from 1 through 9.

The Viking is not next to a Rocket.
The two Rockets are separated by exactly three other players.
The three Panthers are located in not more than 5 consecutive positions in the line.
The Cobra is between the two Rockets.
The two Badgers are next to each other in line.

1. If the Viking is not between the two Rockets, and a Rocket is next to a Badger, then what position is NOT possible for the Cobra?

   (A) 2
   (B) 4
   (C) 7
   (D) 8
   (E) 9

2. If the Viking is between the two Rockets and a Panther is first in line, then which one of the following must be true?

   (A) A Panther is 3rd in line.
   (B) The Viking is 6th in line.
   (C) The Cobra is 6th in line.
   (D) A Badger is 7th in line.
   (E) The Viking is 3rd in line.

3. If a Rocket is in position 2, how many possible positions are there for the Viking?

   (A) 1
   (B) 2
   (C) 3
   (D) 4
   (E) 5

4. If the Viking is in position 3 and the Cobra is in position 8, then all of the following must be true EXCEPT that

   (A) a Rocket is in position 5
   (B) a Badger is in position 6
   (C) a Panther is in position 4
   (D) a Rocket is in position 9
   (E) a Panther is next to the Viking

5. If the Viking is next to the Cobra, which one of the following is false?

   (A) The Viking is in an odd-numbered position.
   (B) The three Panthers are not in consecutive positions.
   (C) The Cobra is in an even-numbered position.
   (D) A Badger is either first or last in line.
   (E) A Badger is next to a Viking.

6. If a Badger is next to the Cobra, which one of the following must be true?

   (A) A Panther is in position 4.
   (B) A Badger is in position 6.
   (C) The Cobra is in position 2 or 8.
   (D) A Badger is in position 3 or 7.
   (E) A Rocket is in position 4 or 6.

GO ON TO THE NEXT PAGE ➤

Questions 7–12

Three men, A, B, and C, and three women, X, Y, and Z, are seated equally spaced around a round table.
   X is C's sister.
   B is Z's husband.
   Y is A's mother.
   B is sitting next to X.
   A is sitting next to Y.
   Z is sitting directly across from Y.

7. Which one of the following could be true?

   (A) C sits next to X.
   (B) Z sits next to A.
   (C) Y sits next to B.
   (D) C sits next to Y.
   (E) B sits next to A.

8. If B sits next to his wife, who does C sit directly across from?

   (A) A
   (B) B
   (C) X
   (D) Y
   (E) Z

9. If C sits directly across from his sister, which one of the following must be true?

   (A) C sits next to X.
   (B) X sits next to A's mother.
   (C) A sits next to C's sister.
   (D) Y sits next to Z's husband.
   (E) Z sits next to X.

10. Which one of the following must be true?

   (A) Y sits next to C.
   (B) X sits next to Z.
   (C) B sits next to Y.
   (D) A sits next to C.
   (E) B sits next to Z.

11. If X does not sit directly across from her brother, then C sits directly across from whom?

   (A) A
   (B) B
   (C) X
   (D) Y
   (E) Z

12. How many women have a man sitting to their left?

   (A) 0
   (B) 1
   (C) 2
   (D) 3
   (E) 4

GO ON TO THE NEXT PAGE ➤

1   1   1   1   1

Questions 13–18

Ron, Sharon, and Tom share an office and equipment. Their secretaries are, not necessarily respectively, Fran, George, and Hilda. In the office, there are three computers: a Comstar, a Doufast, and an Excellocalc. The three programs that run on the computers are a spreadsheet, database, and word processing program.

   Not all three computers can run all three programs.
   A program can only be run on one computer at a time.
   Ron and Sharon do their own word processing, but have their secretaries do the spreadsheets and databases.
   George won't use the Excellocalc.
   Hilda uses only the Doufast.
   The Doufast cannot run the database program.
   Fran will not use the Comstar.
   The Comstar cannot run the word processing program.

13. Which computer(s) could Sharon use for her own work?

    (A) Comstar only
    (B) Doufast only
    (C) Excellocalc only
    (D) Doufast or Excellocalc
    (E) Comstar or Doufast

14. Which computer(s) can George use for word processing?

    (A) Comstar
    (B) Doufast
    (C) Excellocalc
    (D) Doufast or Excellocalc
    (E) Comstar or Doufast

15. Which one of the following must be true?

    (A) Sharon does not use the Doufast.
    (B) Fran won't use the database program.
    (C) Ron does not use the Comstar.
    (D) Hilda won't use the spreadsheet program.
    (E) George does not use the Doufast.

16. If Tom's secretary uses the Comstar, which program(s) could they be using?

    (A) word processing
    (B) spreadsheet
    (C) word processing or spreadsheet
    (D) spreadsheet or database
    (E) word processing or database

17. If George is Tom's secretary, which one of the following must be true?

    (A) Ron's secretary cannot use the Doufast.
    (B) Sharon's secretary cannot use the Comstar.
    (C) Ron's secretary cannot use the Excellocalc.
    (D) Sharon's secretary cannot use the Excellocalc.
    (E) Tom's secretary cannot use the Doufast.

18. If the Doufast is upgraded so it can run the database program and Tom's secretary will only use the Excellocalc, which one of the following must be true?

    (A) Hilda can use the Comstar.
    (B) Fran is Tom's secretary.
    (C) Ron's secretary can use the Excellocalc.
    (D) The Doufast cannot run the spreadsheet program.
    (E) Hilda won't use the Doufast.

GO ON TO THE NEXT PAGE ➤

Questions 19–24

A track coach is arranging two relay teams, team X and team Y. Each relay team is composed of four runners, each running one leg of the relay. The eight runners are Aldo, Bryan, Charles, Dominic, Earle, Fred, Gabriel, and Howard. The four positions on each relay team are 1st, 2nd, 3rd, and 4th. The following conditions apply to team organization:

  Earle will only run on team X and only in 2nd or 3rd position.

  Gabriel runs in 2nd position only.

  Howard runs on the same relay team and the leg immediately after the leg run by Dominic.

  Aldo and Earle will not run on the same relay team.

  Fred never runs 4th.

  Bryan runs 4th on relay team X.

19. If Fred runs on relay team Y, which one of the following pairs of runners could run the 1st leg on relay team X?

    (A) Charles or Howard
    (B) Bryan or Dominic
    (C) Gabriel or Howard
    (D) Charles or Dominic
    (E) Charles or Gabriel

20. If Dominic runs 2nd on relay team Y, which one of the following CANNOT be true?

    (A) Earle runs 3rd on relay team X.
    (B) Aldo and Gabriel run on the same relay team.
    (C) Aldo and Fred each run 1st on different relay teams.
    (D) Aldo and Fred run on the same relay team.
    (E) Howard runs 3rd on relay team Y.

21. Which one of the following could be a list of the four runners who could run on the same relay team?

    (A) Aldo, Earle, Fred, Gabriel
    (B) Charles, Dominic, Earle, Fred
    (C) Aldo, Bryan, Charles, Fred
    (D) Aldo, Dominic, Fred, Howard
    (E) Charles, Earle, Fred, Howard

22. Which one of the following could be a list of the ordering of four runners on one of the relay teams?

    (A) 1st—Dominic   2nd—Howard
        3rd—Gabriel   4th—Aldo
    (B) 1st—Aldo   2nd—Charles
        3rd—Earle   4th—Fred
    (C) 1st—Charles   2nd—Howard
        3rd—Dominic   4th—Bryan
    (D) 1st—Charles   2nd—Gabriel
        3rd—Aldo   4th—Fred
    (E) 1st—Charles   2nd—Aldo
        3rd—Dominic   4th—Howard

23. If Howard and Gabriel run on the same relay team, which one of the following must be true?

    (A) Aldo runs 1st on relay team Y.
    (B) Charles runs 2nd on relay team X.
    (C) Earle runs 2nd on relay team X.
    (D) Charles runs 3rd on relay team Y.
    (E) Fred runs 1st on relay team X.

24. If Fred and Howard are on the same relay team, which one of the following must be true?

    (A) Dominic runs 2nd on relay team X.
    (B) Aldo runs 2nd on relay team X.
    (C) Charles runs 1st on relay team X.
    (D) Earle runs 2nd on relay team X.
    (E) Howard runs 3rd on relay team Y.

STOP

IF YOU FINISH BEFORE TIME IS UP, CHECK YOUR WORK ON THIS SECTION OF THE TEST ONLY.
DO NOT GO ON TO THE NEXT SECTION OF THE TEST UNTIL TIME IS UP FOR THIS SECTION.

2   **2**   **2**   **2**   **2**

SECTION II
TIME — 35 MINUTES
27 QUESTIONS

Directions: Read the passages and answer the questions following each passage by blackening the appropriate space on the answer sheet. You may refer back to the passages when answering the questions. Answer all questions on the basis of what is stated or implied.

More than two thousand years ago, Aristotle utilized two major criteria in classifying governments. One was the
line *number of persons* in which governing
(5) authority is vested; the other, the *primary purpose* toward which the exercise of governmental powers is directed.

In terms of the first criterion
(10) Aristotle distinguished three forms of government, viz., government by the one, by the few, and by the many. The second basis of classification, i.e., purpose, led him to differentiate "true"
(15) from "perverted" forms. True forms of government are characterized by the exercise of governmental authority for the benefit of all members of the body politic, whereas *perverted* types are
(20) featured by the use of governing power to promote the special and selfish interests of the ruling personnel. Government by the one for the benefit of all is *kingship* or *royalty;* government
(25) by the one for his private advantage is *tyranny.* Government by the few, if conducted for the purpose of promoting the common welfare, constitutes *aristocracy.* If the few rule in
(30) furtherance of their own selfish interests, the government is an *oligarchy.* The dominant few are likely to be men of property interested in increasing their wealth. Finally,
(35) government by the many (the citizens at large) for the benefit of all was identified as *polity* or *constitutional government,* whereas government by the many, usually the poor or the needy, for the
(40) purpose of promoting their selfish interests, was named *democracy,* a perverted form of government.

Unlike Aristotle, contemporary political scientists usually classify
(45) forms of government without introducing a test of purpose or

motivation with respect to the use of governmental powers. Definitions of
(50) democracy, for instance, seldom include stipulations concerning the objectives to be attained by a government of the democratic type. However, an underlying assumption, even though unstated,
(55) seems to be that democratic processes of government probably will result in promotion of the common welfare.

Aristotle conceived of government by the many, whether of the true or
(60) perverted variety, as involving direct action by the body of qualified citizens in the formulation and adoption of policies. Hamilton and Madison, in their comments about democracy in the
(65) Federalist Papers, revealed a like conception of the nature of democracy. Thus Madison distinguished between a republic (representative government) and pure democracy. In his words a pure
(70) democracy is "a society consisting of a small number of citizens, who assemble and administer the government in person." A distinction is still drawn between direct and indirect democracy,
(75) but emphasis now is placed on the latter form, that is, democracy of the representative variety. Although direct democracy survives in a few small communities, e.g., New England towns
(80) and some of the cantons of Switzerland, representative democracy prevails in communities of large size. Consequently, the term *democracy* as used today almost always signifies a
(85) democratic government of the indirect or representative type.

GO ON TO THE NEXT PAGE ➤

2   **2**   **2**   **2**   **2**

1. According to Aristotle's definitions, a government in which a single hereditary ruler controls political power for the benefit of his family would be termed a(n)

   (A) kingship
   (B) tyranny
   (C) aristocracy
   (D) oligarchy
   (E) polity

2. According to the author's understanding of Aristotle, democracy is a "perverted" form of government because

   (A) the poor comprise a special interest group
   (B) the needs of the poor are sought through perverted behavior
   (C) the poor comprise a larger group than the citizens at large
   (D) the needs of the poor are less pure than those of other groups
   (E) excessive poverty is the prelude to tyranny

3. The author seems to presume that Aristotle

   (A) would have supported the American Revolution
   (B) utilized more than two major criteria in classifying governments
   (C) is the one figure from antiquity whose political analyses are especially relevant to a discussion of modern government
   (D) was studied by Hamilton and Madison
   (E) was a philosopher who scarcely recognized the human potential for democratic government

4. In his discussion of pure democracy, the author is not explicit about

   (A) Madison's conception of pure democracy
   (B) the typical modern definition of democracy
   (C) why pure democracy on a large scale is unwieldy
   (D) the distinction between direct and indirect democracy
   (E) why the views of Hamilton and Madison are similar to those of Aristotle

5. The author says that a modern democracy would regard the promotion of the common welfare as a

   (A) partial result
   (B) probable result
   (C) certain result
   (D) questionable result
   (E) unique result

6. The author's reliance on conceptions of government which are many centuries old suggests his belief that

   (A) governments since antiquity have been obeying Aristotle's classification scheme
   (B) conceptions of government change little through the ages
   (C) political scientists have no need for new definitions
   (D) later political theorists had read Aristotle before formulating their theories
   (E) ancient definitions of government are analogous but not identical to current conceptions

7. The author's primary purpose in this passage is to

   (A) compare American and Greek philosophies
   (B) judge the relative worth of various forms of government
   (C) discuss the relationship of Aristotle's conception to later theory and practice
   (D) praise the foresight of Aristotle
   (E) develop an absolute definition of democracy

GO ON TO THE NEXT PAGE ➤

2　**2**　**2**　**2**　**2**

Under very early common law, all felonies were punishable by death. The perpetrators of the felony were hanged
line whether or not a homicide had been
(5) committed during the felony. Later, however, most felonies were declared to be noncapital offenses. The common law courts, in need of a deterrent to the use of deadly force in the course of
(10) these noncapital felonies, developed the "felony-murder" rule. The first formal statement of the rule stated: "Any killing by one in the commission of a felony is guilty of murder." The killing
(15) was a murder whether intentional or unintentional, accidental or mistaken. The usual requirement of malice was eliminated and the only criminal intent necessary was the intent to commit the
(20) particular underlying felony. All participants in the felony were guilty of murder—actual killer and nonkiller confederates.

Proponents of the rule argued that it
(25) was justified because the felon demonstrated a lack of concern for human life by the commission of a violent and dangerous felony and that the crime was murder either because of
(30) a conclusive presumption of malice or simply by force of statutory definition.

Opponents of the rule describe it as a highly artificial concept and "an enigma wrapped in a riddle." They are quick to
(35) point out that the rule has been abandoned in England where it originated, abolished in India, severely restricted in Canada and a number of other commonwealth countries, is
(40) unknown in continental Europe, and abandoned in Michigan. In reality, the real strength of the opponents' criticism stems from the bizarre and oft times unfair results achieved when the felony-
(45) murder rule is applied mechanically. Defendants have been convicted under the rule where the killing was purely accidental, or the killing took place after the felony during the later flight from
(50) the scene; or a third party killed another (police officer killed a citizen or vice versa; or a victim died of a heart attack 15–20 minutes after the robbery was over; or the person killed was an
(55) accomplice in the felony).

Attacks on the rule have come from all directions with basically the same demand—reevaluate and abandon the archaic legal fiction; restrict and limit
(60) vicarious criminal liability; prosecute killers for murder, not nonkillers; increase punishment for the underlying felony as a real deterrent; and initiate legislative modifications. With the
(65) unstable history of the felony-murder rule, including its abandonment by many jurisdictions in this country, the felony-murder rule is dying a slow but certain death.

8. Which one of the following best states the central idea of the passage?

(A) The felony-murder rule should be abolished.
(B) Some jurisdictions are about to abandon the felony-murder rule.
(C) The felony-murder rule can be unfair.
(D) The felony-murder rule should be abolished by the Supreme Court of the United States.
(E) There are strong arguments to be made both for and against the felony-murder rule.

9. The felony-murder rule was developed in order to

(A) deter felonies
(B) deter murders
(C) deter deadly force in felonies
(D) return death for death
(E) extend the definition of murder to any malicious act resulting in death

GO ON TO THE NEXT PAGE ➤

2 **2** **2** **2** **2**

10. Arguments in favor of the felony-murder rule may include all of the following EXCEPT

   (A) We can infer that anyone undertaking a violent felony does so maliciously.
   (B) We can infer that anyone undertaking a dangerous felony demonstrates an indifference to human life.
   (C) If the punishment for the use of deadly force whether intended or not is the same, criminals will be less likely to use deadly force.
   (D) Because a life has been taken, the crime is murder by force of statutory definition.
   (E) The victim of murder may be an accomplice of the felon.

11. According to the passage, opponents of the felony-murder rule have raised all of the following objections to the statue EXCEPT

   (A) The felony-murder rule results in murder prosecutions of defendants who have not committed murder.
   (B) The felony-murder rule is an archaic law based upon a legal fiction.
   (C) The felony-murder rule is based upon a presumption of malice even if the death is wholly accidental.
   (D) The felony-murder rule deters the use of deadly force in noncapital felonies.
   (E) The felony-murder rule assigns a criminal liability vicariously.

12. In which one of the following situations would the defendant NOT be liable to the charge of murder under the felony-murder rule?

   (A) In escaping from an unsuccessful attempt to rob a bank, the defendant crashes his car, killing an innocent pedestrian in another city.
   (B) A bank security officer, pursuing the defendant after a robbery, falls down a flight of stairs and suffers serious permanent brain and spinal cord injuries.
   (C) The driver of the escape car, who has not entered the bank, crashes the car, killing the armed gunman who committed the robbery.
   (D) A bank teller, locked safely in the bank vault by the robber, has a stroke and dies.
   (E) The driver of a stolen car forces another car off the road, killing a passenger.

13. According to the passage, the decline of support for the felony-murder rule is indicated by the abandoning of the rule in all of the following locations EXCEPT

   (A) continental Europe
   (B) Michigan
   (C) India
   (D) England
   (E) Canada

14. The author believes that the felony-murder rule is

   (A) unconstitutional
   (B) bizarre and unfair
   (C) supported by several hundred years of sound legal tradition
   (D) an unfair equating of intent to commit a felony and intent to commit murder
   (E) a serviceable rule unfairly attacked by the "intelligentsia"

2   **2**   **2**   **2**   **2**

Naturalism differs from realism in several aspects, none of which is clear-cut and definitive. It tends to be more
line doctrinaire in its exposition of
(5) pseudoscientific principles, it is less interested in character and more in the conflict of social forces, and it is concerned to a greater extent with the sordid, the shocking, and the
(10) depressing sides of existence. By these criteria, however, there are naturalistic elements in Dostoevsky; and Galsworthy, Hemingway, and Scott Fitzgerald demonstrate many qualities
(15) of typical realists. Some further suggested qualities of literary naturalism are as follows:

(a) Naturalism is scientific or pseudoscientific in its approach; it
(20) attempts to treat human beings as biological pawns rather than agents of free will. The author does not attempt to judge his characters or to comment on their actions; he merely inserts them
(25) into a crucial situation and then pretends to stand back and watch them with the impassivity of the scientist. Although Zola applied this principle with some success, it has generally
(30) remained a synthetic theory and has only infrequently been applied to actual literary works.

(b) The naturalist attempts to make literature into a document of society. He
(35) writes "novel cycles" purporting to cover every aspect of modern life, or creates characters who are personifications of various social classes. Many naturalists gather
(40) copious data from actual life and include it in their literary works: they write novels around specific occupations such as railroading or textile manufacturing in which they
(45) utilize technical details of the trade for story-interest. This aspect of naturalism represents an attempt to remove literature from the realm of the fine arts into the field of the social sciences.
(50) (c) Because of the above-described documentary nature of naturalism, the technique often involves the conscious suppression of the poetic elements in literature. The prose style is flat,
(55) objective, and bare of imagery; it includes copious details and

explanations, and is wary of highly literary metaphors. Like the pseudoscientific dogma described in (a)
(60) above, this quality is often more theoretical than practical. The best naturalists are those who do not totally abandon the literary traditions of the past. On the other hand some
(65) naturalists are merely writers lacking in the poetic instinct; they avoid a highly literary prose because they have little feeling for style and imagery. Others like Hardy are essentially poets who achieve
(70) highly poetic effects in their prose.

(d) Naturalistic literature tends to be concerned with the less elegant aspects of life; its typical settings are the slum, the sweatshop, the factory, or the farm.
(75) Where the romantic author selects the most pleasant and idealistic elements in his experience, the naturalistic author often seems positively drawn toward the brutal, the sordid, the cruel, and the
(80) degraded. This tendency is in part a reaction against earlier literature, especially against the sentimentalism of the Dumas school where vice is invariably made to appear romantic. The
(85) real motivating forces in a naturalistic novel are not religion, hope, or human idealism; they are alcohol, filth, disease, and the human instinct toward bestiality. It will be seen immediately
(90) that there are important exceptions to this principle. Galsworthy's scenes are middle-class, and Scott Fitzgerald prefers to do his slumming at the Ritz.

15. The purpose of the first paragraph may be best defined as

(A) to define naturalism precisely
(B) to question other definitions of naturalism
(C) to cite examples of naturalistic writers
(D) to offer an introductory definition of naturalism
(E) to define realism

GO ON TO THE NEXT PAGE ➤

2　　　**2**　　　**2**　　　**2**　　　**2**

16. The passage implies that one reason for calling naturalism "pseudoscientific" rather than "scientific" is that

    (A) a scientist would acknowledge the existence of free will
    (B) Zola's theory has been infrequently applied
    (C) biological pawns are not amenable to study
    (D) Zola did not meet with total success
    (E) the author's scientific perspective is a pretense

17. In paragraph (c), the author turns from description to

    (A) documentary
    (B) evaluation
    (C) praise
    (D) disdain
    (E) naturalism

18. We may infer that the naturalist novel is unlikely to contain

    (A) a rural setting
    (B) an acknowledgment of human woes
    (C) a romantic hero
    (D) a social crisis
    (E) an urban setting

19. According to the description of style in the passage, a naturalist author would be likely to avoid which one of the following?

    (A) The sunset was full of reds and yellows.
    (B) His nemesis was iron-willed.
    (C) The community regarded Frank as a tower of strength.
    (D) The president describes the period of military laxity as a "window of vulnerability."
    (E) Marriage is a sad, sober beverage.

20. The passage suggests that the naturalist behaves most like a scientist when he

    (A) gathers details from life
    (B) transforms fact into fiction
    (C) de-emphasizes the importance of character
    (D) writes history or biography rather than actual literary works
    (E) restricts his subject matter

2   **2**   **2**   **2**   **2**

In science as elsewhere, we meet the assumptions of convenience and expedience, such as equations that
(line) assume frictionless machines or
(5) chemicals in a pure state. But by far the most important function of language in the development of scientific understanding and control of the world about us is the use of a kind of
(10) assumption called *hypothesis* at first, *theory* in a more developed state, and *law* when its implications have been extensively corroborated. A hypothesis resembles other assumptions in that it
(15) may be either true or false and may be used as the premise of rational action; otherwise it differs radically as to function and purpose. Hypotheses are employed experimentally in the search
(20) for truth. Without them the so-called scientific method is not possible. The reason for this is not always readily grasped and will now be illustrated in some detail.
(25) Suppose, for example, that you are about to prepare an account of some fairly complex subject, such as the history of marriage. As soon as you have arrived at a clear working definition of
(30) your topic, you begin the collection of data. Now a *datum* is an item of some sort regarded as relevant to your problem. But everything is in some way related to everything else, and since you
(35) cannot possibly consider all the facts related to marriage, you must limit the field of relevance in some practical, arbitrary manner. Let us assume that you are at work on the status of
(40) marriage in modern urban society; perhaps you may attempt to discover to what extent the institution persists because it is biologically useful, economically expedient, socially
(45) convenient, religiously compulsory, or merely psychologically traditional. To proceed thus is to set up a fivefold hypothesis that enables you to gather from the innumerable items cast up by
(50) the sea of experience upon the shores of your observation only the limited number of relevant data—relevant, that is, to one or more of the five factors of your hypothesis. The hypothesis (the
(55) reference of the symbol *hypothesis*) is like a light by means of which we search

for truth; but it is a colored light that may render invisible the very object we seek. That is why, after a fair trial, we
(60) must not hesitate to abandon one color for another. When our hypothesis possesses the proper color and intensity, it will reveal some of the facts as data, which may then be further
(65) studied and verified as signs of truth.

As the evidence in favor of a hypothesis (the thing again, not the word) accumulates to a convincing degree, we frequently symbolize the fact
(70) with the term *theory*. Thus, semantically, a theory is the name of a hypothesis that has outgrown its experimental short pants. With Charles Darwin, *biological evolution* was a
(75) hypothesis; in contemporary science it is a theory that no rational observer, however cautious, hesitates to accept.

When predictions based on the implications of a theory are continually
(80) borne out by observation, the relation symbolized is still further elevated to the status of a *law or natural law.* The abstraction "law" is a dangerous one to employ because it implies that the mind
(85) has finally arrived at the truth, ultimate and eternal. Thus, the eyes of science become myopic and lose the power to discover old errors and discern new truths.

21. The author's primary purpose is to

(A) note the progress in understanding since Darwin's time
(B) define and discuss some basic scientific terms
(C) develop a hypothesis
(D) argue for the value of scientific truth
(E) criticize the scientific method

GO ON TO THE NEXT PAGE ➤

2   **2**   **2**   **2**   **2**

22. We may infer that the author would have difficulty accepting which one of the following statements?

    (A) The discovery of old errors may lead to new truths.
    (B) The Darwinian theory was once a hypothesis.
    (C) The establishment of natural laws is the final goal of science.
    (D) It is sometimes advisable to abandon a hypothesis.
    (E) A hypothesis may be either true or false.

23. On two occasions, the author follows the word "hypothesis" with a parenthetical remark that serves to

    (A) diminish the value of scientific hypotheses
    (B) stress the value of symbolism in science
    (C) demonstrate that the term presents semantic problems
    (D) stress the difference between a hypothesis and a theory
    (E) stress the difference between the term and what it stands for

24. According to the passage, the factor that distinguishes a hypothesis from a theory is the

    (A) passage of time
    (B) goal of the scientist
    (C) method of the scientist
    (D) relevance of the investigation
    (E) convincingness of the evidence

25. The author would agree with which of the following statements?

    (A) Hypotheses and truth are mutually exclusive.
    (B) "Hypothesis," "theory," and "law" are synonymous terms.
    (C) Language hinders the development of scientific understanding.
    (D) Hypotheses are more important for science than are equations.
    (E) Most people understand the importance of hypotheses to the scientific method.

26. We may infer from the passage that a hypothesis is always

    (A) objective
    (B) subjective
    (C) the wrong color
    (D) fivefold
    (E) useful

27. The author assumes that the relationship between hypotheses and the scientific method is

    (A) only a theory
    (B) not commonly understood
    (C) not significant
    (D) a product of evolution
    (E) apparent to most people

STOP

IF YOU FINISH BEFORE TIME IS UP, CHECK YOUR WORK ON THIS SECTION OF THE TEST ONLY.
DO NOT GO ON TO THE NEXT SECTION OF THE TEST UNTIL TIME IS UP FOR THIS SECTION.

3   3   3   3   3

SECTION III
Time — 35 minutes
26 Questions

Directions: In this section you will be given brief statements or passages and will be required to evaluate the reasoning involved. In some instances, more than one choice will appear to be a possible answer. You are to choose the *best* answer. Use common sense and reasonableness in making your selection; then mark the proper space on the answer sheet.

Questions 1–2

Some scientists believe that legal standards for pesticide residues are seriously flawed and were established without adequate health and safety data for produce. Because of the media attention to this issue, it should be no surprise that opinion polls say pesticide residue now tops the list of consumer food worries, beating out cholesterol and calories.

1. Which one of the following would be the most logical completion of the passage above?

   (A) So produce safety has now become the latest battleground in the supermarket wars.
   (B) Farm workers should be concerned with residue standards.
   (C) But consumers should not be worried; opinion polls are often misleading.
   (D) And it is possible that cholesterol standards have been improperly established.
   (E) Media attention to any issue seems to bring unwanted attention and distort the facts.

2. It would be reasonable to conclude from the passage above that

   (A) scientists have been protesting pesticide residue levels for many years
   (B) recommended cholesterol and calorie levels should also be researched
   (C) cholesterol and calories had been the major concern of consumers
   (D) many legal standards are seriously flawed
   (E) most scientists believe that the legal standards for pesticide residue have been adequately researched

3. The politicians cannot be telling the truth about a reduction in taxes. This year my taxes must have been higher than ever, because I was able to save less money than last year or the year before.

All of the following point to an error in reasoning in this passage EXCEPT

   (A) taxes are not the year's only expenses
   (B) this year's earnings may have been smaller than last year's
   (C) politicians are frequently guilty of exaggeration or equivocation
   (D) this year's tax deductions may have been smaller that last year's
   (E) income from invested income may have declined this year due to lower interest rates

4. *Tom:* Sometimes products that are needed by the consumer just don't seem to sell well.
   Stan: That's probably because the product is always sold out.
   Tom: That's ridiculous! How can something that doesn't sell well be sold out!

It can be assumed from Tom's reply that he believes that Stan

   (A) thinks that all products that are in stock don't sell well
   (B) feels that products need to sell well to be sold out
   (C) knows that products that are in demand are always kept in stock
   (D) knows more about consumers than Tom
   (E) is using faulty logic

GO ON TO THE NEXT PAGE ➤

3　　　**3**　　　**3**　　　**3**　　　**3**

5. *Editorial:* Scientists are continually making technological breakthroughs such as developing laser technology. Yet they have not been able to cure the common cold. Once scientists had the proper financial backing from the government, they immediately proceeded to develop laser technology. The proper funding seemed to make all the difference. When our government allocates the necessary financial resources, our scientists will find a cure for the common cold.

In the editorial above, the author does all of the following EXCEPT

(A) fail to consider the significant differences between finding a cure for the common cold and the development of laser technology

(B) explain that there is no significant distinction between developing laser technology and curing the common cold

(C) intimate that the government has not found a cure for the common cold because the government has not allocated sufficient funds to do so

(D) imply that the government has not found a cure for the common cold because there is less desire to do so than there was to develop laser technology

(E) present an analogy between developing laser technology and finding a cure for the common cold

Questions 6–7

Numerous medical studies have been published that associate health risks with the consumption of caffeine. Yet many Americans continue to consume coffee in huge quantities.

6. Which one of the following conclusions does NOT logically follow from the sentences alone?

(A) Therefore, for these Americans, the benefits of coffee apparently outweigh the risks.

(B) Therefore, many Americans may not be aware of the medical studies.

(C) Therefore, some Americans may not accept the studies' conclusions.

(D) Therefore, some Americans continue to risk their health.

(E) Therefore, the amount of caffeine consumed should be determined by the size of the individual.

7. Which one of the following statements would NOT weaken the point of the first sentence?

(A) Most of the medical studies published are based on faulty research.

(B) Many doctors feel that caffeine has many benefits.

(C) Medical research has improved over the past few years.

(D) As a rule, coffee drinkers live longer than those who do not drink coffee.

(E) Ingestion of foods high in caffeine has been shown to hasten the healing of broken bones.

GO ON TO THE NEXT PAGE ➤

3   **3**   **3**   **3**   **3**

Questions 8–9

Hundreds of new self-help books, audio tapes, and video tapes, have been pushed onto the market in the last decade. These self-help methods generally reflect a positive, optimistic approach to modern problems and challenges and are usually based on current research in psychology. The purpose of many of the authors is to offer help to a needy society. Unfortunately, some of those involved in producing self-help materials see the trend and are only in it for the "quick buck."

8. Which one of the following can be inferred from the statements in the passage above?

    (A) An increasing percentage of self-help authors are only in the market for the "quick buck."
    (B) Most of the self-help authors don't care about their product's profits.
    (C) Profits are not the only goal of many self-help authors.
    (D) The trend of self-help authors is toward the "quick buck."
    (E) Self-help authors are positive and optimistic about the sale of their products.

9. Which one of the following statements about the producers of self-help materials is the most logical continuation of the passage above?

    (A) Their products exhibit the same quality of care and workmanship as the majority of self-help products.
    (B) Moreover, their optimism extends not only to the sale of their items, but also to the effectiveness of solving their customers' problems.
    (C) Their involvement includes a close and careful supervision of their excellent self-help products.
    (D) Their products tend to be hastily manufactured and display a disregard for the needs of the consumer.
    (E) Their heartfelt concerns about a needy society may someday be realized.

10. *Nuclear Power Advocate:* Operation of nuclear reactor-driven power plants does not adversely affect small-game hunting within nearby public ranges. The Fertile Crescent Nuclear Facility began operating this year, and the number of squirrels caught nearby set a five-season high.

All of the following statements, if true, are valid objections to the foregoing argument EXCEPT

    (A) radiation from such reactors renders certain species of rodents sterile
    (B) radiation from such reactors reduces the mortality rate among immature squirrels
    (C) factors having nothing to do with the well-being of squirrels may have a marked impact on the number of animals taken in a given season
    (D) radioactivity emanating from power plant reactors interferes with the growth of various forms of vegetation consumed by squirrels
    (E) squirrels are only one of numerous species of small game that may be affected by the presence of a nuclear reactor

11. Williams will be elected to the Retirement Fund Board, and since he will, so will Johnson. In addition, if Johnson and Smith are both elected, then Davidson will be elected. If Davidson is elected, then he will be accused of embezzling retirement funds, found guilty, and sentenced to ten years in prison. Therefore, Davidson will be found guilty of embezzling retirement funds and will be sentenced to ten years in prison.

Which one of the following additional premises must be included among those in the passage above in order for the conclusion to be a logical one?

    (A) Davidson might be elected to the board.
    (B) Smith will be elected to the board.
    (C) Johnson will be elected to the board.
    (D) Williams will be elected to the board.
    (E) Davidson will embezzle funds.

GO ON TO THE NEXT PAGE ➤

3   **3**   **3**   **3**   **3**

Questions 12–13

Speaker: The Federal Safety Commission recently released its study regarding motorbike safety. The study showed some useful statistics. The most noteworthy is that when motorbike operators wearing helmets have accidents, there is a 20 percent chance that they will be seriously injured. However, when motorbike operators who are not wearing helmets have accidents, the chance that they will be seriously injured is 40 percent.

12. From the information above, which one of the following is the best conclusion?

(A) Many more motorbike operators do not wear helmets than do wear helmets.

(B) A motorbike operator not wearing a helmet has a greater chance of having an accident than does an operator who is wearing a helmet.

(C) A motorbike operator not wearing a helmet has a greater chance of having a serious, personal-injury accident than does an operator who wears a helmet.

(D) If a motorbike operator does not wear a helmet, there is a 40 percent chance that the operator will have an accident.

(E) If a motorbike operator has an accident while not wearing a helmet, the chances are greater that the operator will be seriously injured than if the operator had an accident while wearing a helmet.

13. Which one of the following statements must be true in order to conclude that the number of helmeted motorbike operators seriously injured in accidents is greater than the number of nonhelmeted operators seriously injured in accidents?

(A) Three times as many motorbike operators wear helmets as do not wear helmets.

(B) Half as many motorbike operators do not wear helmets as do wear helmets.

(C) There are twice as many accidents involving motorbike operators who were not wearing helmets as there are accidents involving operators who were wearing helmets.

(D) There are four times as many accidents involving motorbike operators wearing helmets as there are accidents involving motorbike operators who are not wearing helmets.

(E) Three times as many motorbike operators wear helmets as do not wear helmets.

3 **3** **3** **3** **3**

14. All commercial buildings constructed within the city of Philadelphia after 1987 have automatic sprinkler systems, and all commercial buildings constructed within the county of Philadelphia after that date have hallway smoke alarms. The city of Philadelphia is within the county of Philadelphia and must abide by all county rules and ordinances.

If the Consolidated Corporation is a commercial business, and if its office building has smoke alarms in all hallways, but does not have an automatic sprinkler system, which one of the following must be true?

(A) Consolidated's office building is not located in the city of Philadelphia.
(B) If Consolidated's office building was constructed in 1988, it is not situated in the city of Philadelphia.
(C) If Consolidated's office building was erected prior to 1987, it is located in the city of Philadelphia.
(D) Consolidated's office building was built prior to 1987; it was constructed in the city of Philadelphia.
(E) If Consolidated's office building was built prior to 1987, it was constructed in the city of Philadelphia.

15. A Broadway show is a greater theatrical pleasure than a high school play because people with a great appreciation of theater invariably select Broadway shows over high school plays. One can identify these people who appreciate theater by their preferences for Broadway shows.

In logically critiquing the statements above, one would most probably point out that the author

(A) contradicts his own reasoning
(B) does not cite any authority in theatrical matters
(C) presupposes the point he intends to establish
(D) draws a generalization from specific evidence
(E) does not distinguish between Broadway and high school theatrical performances

16. Mr. Miko is very good at the sport of Jodo. Therefore, Mr. Miko is a good sport.

The author of the argument above relies upon which one of the following to arrive at a conclusion?

(A) purposely overestimating Mr. Miko's ability in Jodo
(B) generalizing from a particular example
(C) establishing a specific case based upon a general occurrence
(D) establishing a causal relationship
(E) assuming a similarity of meaning between "good at the sport" and "good sport"

17. All Certified Public Accountants are required to have a specified minimal number of hours of auditing experience. Roger, a recent college graduate, has passed all of the required exams and completed all of the necessary course work, but has no auditing experience. Therefore, Roger is not a Certified Public Accountant.

If the information above regarding Roger's auditing experience is not true and Roger has recently started a job as an auditor, the most that could be logically inferred from the passage is that Roger

(A) does not intend to become a Certified Public Accountant
(B) is eligible to become a Certified Public Accountant
(C) will probably become a Certified Public Accountant
(D) would be an excellent Certified Public Accountant
(E) is not qualified to become a Certified Public Accountant

GO ON TO THE NEXT PAGE ➤

18. The greatest danger to a society ruled by a monarchy is the increasing bureaucratization of the ruling process. As the bureaucracy becomes more entrenched, it becomes less responsive to both the ruler and the ruled. There is a threshold beyond which the result is governance by technocracy.

It can be inferred from the foregoing that the author believes that

(A) bureaucracy should be curbed
(B) monarchy is doomed
(C) bureaucracies are more efficient than monarchies
(D) bureaucrats are hostile to those they serve
(E) bureaucracy is a superior form of governance

19. In a recent poll, 93 percent of the 5000 randomly chosen military personnel favored the use of capital punishment. Therefore, it follows that approximately 93 percent of all military personnel favor capital punishment. From this information, it follows that military personnel are more likely to be in favor of capital punishment than people who are not members of the military.

It can be concluded from the statements above that the author most likely makes which one of the following assumptions?

(A) Everyone who is not a member of the military does not favor capital punishment.
(B) Everyone who is a member of the military favors capital punishment.
(C) More than 93 percent of those people not in the military favor capital punishment.
(D) Less than 93 percent of those people not in the military favor capital punishment.
(E) There are more people who are not in the military than people who are in the military.

20. The number of foreign-born students enrolled in the college district increased from 5 percent to 15 percent between 1985 and 1988. Mr. Wong was a member of the district college board between 1985 and 1988. Board member Wong's reelection will bring another rise in the number of foreign students.

Which one of the following statements, if true, would most strengthen the argument above?

(A) Mr. Wong himself is foreign born.
(B) Mr. Wong served on the college board from 1982 to 1983.
(C) Mr. Wong believes that a college education should be available to all.
(D) Board member Wong is the head of the board committee that plays an important role in setting district college admissions policy.
(E) The percentage of students who are foreign-born is less than the percentage of students who are not foreign-born.

GO ON TO THE NEXT PAGE ➤

3   3   3   3   3

Questions 21–22

Within the population of artists, there is not always an even distribution of artistic talent. Recent surveys have indicated that the most productive 5 percent of the artistic community create over half of the artwork sold by that community. As a matter of fact, 15 percent of that community's members creates in excess of 90 percent of the community's sold works.

21. Which one of the following conclusions may be most reasonably inferred from the statements above?

    (A) Overall, the creative output of the artistic community is far less than what it should be.
    (B) A significant number of artists sell their creations.
    (C) Reducing the number of artists would not necessarily cause a decrease in the quantity of artwork sold by the artistic community.
    (D) Eighty-five percent of the members of the artistic community never sell their work.
    (E) An increase in financial support for the arts would result in a needed increase in the creative output of the artistic community.

22. Which one of the following most effectively calls into question the reasoning in this passage?

    (A) Historically, art undergoes significant changes in "style" from one generation to the next.
    (B) Many talented people are not artists.
    (C) Artistic talent is an ambiguous characteristic that may not be measured in terms of sales.
    (D) Many artists who try to sell their work are unsuccessful because they lack talent.
    (E) Most major artists do not achieve high sales until after their deaths.

23. Given that police cars always have a loud siren and flashing lights, and the vehicle following me has a loud siren and flashing lights, it follows that the vehicle following me is a police car.

All of the following statements might reasonably be used to challenge the soundness of the argument used EXCEPT

    (A) ambulances have loud sirens and flashing lights
    (B) automobiles used by the fire department have loud sirens and flashing lights
    (C) given that ostriches have feathers and are flightless, it follows that my featherless and flightless penguin is an ostrich
    (D) given that oysters have shells and are found in the sea, it follows that a lobster is an oyster
    (E) police cars sometimes do not use their sirens

24. The rural community of Potsville has a low crime rate. Urban Los Angeles has a high crime rate. Shady Junction, a small agricultural community, has a high rate of criminal activity. The city of Washington, D.C., has a low rate of criminal activity.

Which one of the following most closely expresses the main point in the passage above?

    (A) Urban communities generally have higher crime rates.
    (B) Crime is rampant in all communities.
    (C) Rural communities generally have higher crime rates.
    (D) Crime is not solely an urban or a rural phenomenon.
    (E) Urban crime is more violent than rural crime.

GO ON TO THE NEXT PAGE ➤

3   **3**   **3**   **3**   **3**

25. *Coach:* Hitting a baseball is certainly one of the most difficult feats in sports. Even the greatest hitters of all time have only been able to hit safely once for every three times at bat. In other words, even great hitters in baseball fail more often than they succeed.

All of the following would logically complete this paragraph EXCEPT

(A) therefore, one does not have to succeed more than fail, to be successful as a hitter in baseball
(B) therefore, success is relative to the situation in life
(C) therefore, one should not give up if one fails on the first try
(D) therefore, without having failed one cannot succeed
(E) therefore, baseball can teach us useful lessons

26. Robert was concerned that he could not find the Maximinima TQ 1000 video camera in stock anywhere. While speaking with him yesterday he explained, "Last month, I finally ordered the Maximinima TQ 1000, the most advanced, state-of-the-art video camera model that has been introduced in years. The Maximinima must be a reliable camera because everybody wants to buy one. With ultra-small size, the Maximinima focuses beautifully, even when the subject is moving."

Which one of the following statements, if true, would weaken Robert's assessment of his camera's reliability?

(A) The Maximinima is not reliable because its small size has nothing to do with how well it focuses.
(B) The Maximinima is not reliable because no one knows if a camera purchased last month will still work after a year.
(C) The Maximinima is not reliable merely because it focuses well on moving subjects.
(D) The Maximinima is not reliable merely because everyone wants to buy one.
(E) The Maximinima is not reliable because it focuses poorly on stationary subjects.

STOP

IF YOU FINISH BEFORE TIME IS UP, CHECK YOUR WORK ON THIS SECTION OF THE TEST ONLY.
DO NOT GO ON TO THE NEXT SECTION OF THE TEST UNTIL TIME IS UP FOR THIS SECTION.

4   **4**   **4**   **4**   **4**

SECTION IV
TIME — 35 MINUTES
23 QUESTIONS

Directions: In this section you will be given groups of questions based on different sets of conditions. Drawing a simple diagram may be helpful in answering some of the questions. You are to choose the *best* answer and mark the corresponding space on your answer sheet.

Questions 1–5

(1) Six people are seated around a circular table. There are no empty seats. Each person is wearing a colored shirt and a colored hat.

(2) Three people are wearing red shirts, two are wearing blue shirts, and one is wearing a green shirt.

(3) Two people are wearing blue hats, two are wearing red hats, and two are wearing green hats.

(4) One person is wearing a matching hat and shirt.

(5) No two people with the same color hats are sitting next to each other.

(6) No two people with the same color shirts are sitting next to each other.

(7) The one person who is wearing the green shirt is sitting between and next to the two people wearing the blue hats.

(8) The two people wearing the blue shirts are wearing the green hats.

1. Which one of the following statements must be true?

   (A) A green hat is worn by a person in a red shirt.
   (B) A blue hat is worn by a person in a blue shirt.
   (C) Both blue hats are worn by people in red shirts.
   (D) The person wearing a matching shirt and hat is wearing blue.
   (E) The person wearing the green shirt is wearing a blue hat.

2. If the green shirt should turn red, then how many of the above conditions would NO LONGER be true?

   (A) 1
   (B) 2
   (C) 3
   (D) 4
   (E) 5

3. If the two blue shirts turned green, then which one of the following must be true?

   (A) Two people would be wearing matching shirts and hats.
   (B) Except for those wearing blue hats, everyone is wearing matching shirts and hats.
   (C) Red and green shirts would alternate around the table.
   (D) A person with a green hat is sitting between and next to two people with blue hats.
   (E) A person with a red shirt is sitting between and next to two people with blue hats.

4. If each person passed his hat two people to the left, how many people would end up with the same color hat they started with?

   (A) one
   (B) two
   (C) three
   (D) four
   (E) five

5. If each person passed his hat three people to the right, then which one of the following would be false?

   (A) Three people would now be wearing matching shirts and hats.
   (B) No one wearing a red shirt would be wearing a blue hat.
   (C) The two people wearing green hats would be wearing red shirts.
   (D) No one wearing a red hat would be wearing a blue shirt.
   (E) No one wearing a blue hat is wearing a blue shirt.

GO ON TO THE NEXT PAGE ➤

4   **4**   **4**   **4**   **4**

Questions 6–11

Seven workers, A, B, C, D, E, F, and G, are to work one day each on a seven-day job. The job can begin on any of the seven days of the week and continues for seven consecutive days including weekends (Saturday and Sunday). The following conditions apply to the scheduling of the workers:

B and F will not work weekends.
C will not work on Tuesday.
D will only work on Monday, Tuesday, or Friday.
If A works on Wednesday, E must work on Sunday.
G must work the day before F works.

6. If the job starts on a Tuesday, which one day will F not be able to work?

   (A) Monday
   (B) Tuesday
   (C) Wednesday
   (D) Thursday
   (E) Friday

7. If the job starts on a Friday, and F works on Tuesday, which one of the following sets of days are available for B to work?

   (A) Wednesday, Thursday, Friday, Saturday
   (B) Wednesday, Friday, Saturday
   (C) Wednesday, Thursday
   (D) Thursday, Friday
   (E) Monday, Wednesday, Thursday

8. If the job starts on a Sunday and G is scheduled for work on Thursday, which one of the following must be true?

   (A) E works on Saturday.
   (B) C and D work on consecutive days.
   (C) B works on Monday or Wednesday.
   (D) D must work on the day after the day that C works.
   (E) G must work on the day after the day that B works.

9. If C does not work on the weekend, and A works on Monday, Tuesday, Wednesday, or Friday, which one of the following CANNOT be true?

   (A) A works on Friday.
   (B) E works on the day after A works.
   (C) C works the first day of the job.
   (D) B works on Friday.
   (E) D works the last day of the job.

10. If D works on the first day of the job and F works on Tuesday, which one of the following could be true?

   (A) If A works the sixth day, then C works on Thursday.
   (B) If D and E work on consecutive days, then A and F work on consecutive days.
   (C) If E works the third day, then B works the last day.
   (D) B works the third day.
   (E) G works the last day.

11. If workers want to work in reverse alphabetical order of their names (G works the first day, F works the second day, E works the third day, and so on), how many different schedules can be established?

   (A) 0
   (B) 1
   (C) 2
   (D) 3
   (E) 4

GO ON TO THE NEXT PAGE ➤

4   **4**   **4**   **4**   **4**

Questions 12–17

Larry's exercise program consists of three aerobic dances, two free weight exercises, and two treadmill routines. Larry performs the aerobic dances (the Bounce, the Glide, the Hop) consecutively, but not necessarily in order; the free weight exercises (the Press, the Curl) consecutively, but not necessarily in order; and the treadmill routines (Speed, Endurance) consecutively, but not necessarily in order. The seven-exercise program is performed subject to the following conditions:

The free weight exercises are not performed first.
The free weight exercises are not performed last.
In the aerobic dances, Larry does the Glide before the Hop.
On the treadmill, Larry does the Speed routine before the Endurance routine.

12. Which one of the following CANNOT be an acceptable list of the exercises Larry performed second, third, and fourth, respectively?

   (A) Bounce, Hop, Press
   (B) Endurance, Press, Curl
   (C) Glide, Bounce, Curl
   (D) Glide, Hop, Curl
   (E) Glide, Hop, Press

13. It is NOT possible that Larry performs the Glide dance

   (A) first
   (B) second
   (C) third
   (D) fifth
   (E) sixth

14. Which one of the following statements CANNOT be true?

   (A) Larry does the Bounce dance first.
   (B) Larry does the Bounce dance second.
   (C) Larry does the Endurance routine second.
   (D) Larry does the Endurance routine third.
   (E) Larry does the Speed routine first.

15. If Larry performed a free weight exercise and performed the Glide dance consecutively, but not necessarily in that order, then which one of the following statements must be FALSE?

   (A) He performed the Bounce dance before the Endurance routine.
   (B) He performed the Bounce dance before the Hop dance.
   (C) He performed the Curl exercise before the Glide dance.
   (D) He performed the Endurance routine before the Press exercise.
   (E) He performed the Hop dance before the Bounce dance.

16. If Larry does the Bounce dance immediately after the Hop dance, then which one of the following statements could be true?

   (A) Larry does the Endurance routine third.
   (B) Larry does the Endurance routine sixth.
   (C) Larry does the Endurance routine seventh.
   (D) Larry does the Glide dance second.
   (E) Larry does the Glide dance third.

17. Which one of the following statements could be true?

   (A) Larry does the Glide dance second.
   (B) Larry does the Glide dance seventh.
   (C) Larry does the Speed routine second.
   (D) Larry does the Speed routine third.
   (E) Larry does the Speed routine fourth.

GO ON TO THE NEXT PAGE ➤

4   **4**   **4**   **4**   **4**

Questions 18–23

Last Chance University offers the following courses for Freshmen Students: Languages (French, German, Italian, Japanese), Sciences (Biology, Chemistry, Physics), and Mathematics (Algebra, Statistics, Trigonometry, Math Analysis). Each Freshman must enroll in exactly five of these courses subject to the following conditions:

Not more than two Math classes may be taken.
If Physics is taken, then Algebra cannot be taken.
If Algebra is taken, then Italian must be taken.
Chemistry may be taken only if both Trigonometry and French are taken.
If German and Biology are taken, then Statistics cannot be taken.
Exactly one language must be taken.

18. Which one of the following could be a list of the five courses taken by a Freshman student at Last Chance University?

    (A) Algebra, Trigonometry, French, Italian, Physics
    (B) Statistics, Trigonometry, Italian, Biology, Physics
    (C) Algebra, Statistics, French, Japanese, Chemistry
    (D) Algebra, Statistics, Trigonometry, French, Chemistry
    (E) Statistics, Trigonometry, German, Biology, Physics

19. If a Freshman at Last Chance University takes Statistics, which one of the following pairs of courses may also be taken?

    (A) Italian, Chemistry
    (B) Algebra, German
    (C) German, Chemistry
    (D) Algebra, French
    (E) Chemistry, Physics

20. Which one of the following could be a list of three of the courses taken by a Freshman at Last Chance University?

    (A) Algebra, French, Biology
    (B) Algebra, Italian, Physics
    (C) Statistics, German, Chemistry
    (D) Statistics, Chemistry, Physics
    (E) Math Analysis, German, Chemistry

21. Other than the language course, which one of the following could be a list of the courses taken by a Freshman at Last Chance University?

    (A) Algebra, Statistics, Biology, Chemistry
    (B) Algebra, Biology, Chemistry, Physics
    (C) Algebra, Math Analysis, Trigonometry, Physics
    (D) Trigonometry, Biology, Chemistry, Physics
    (E) Statistics, Biology, Chemistry, Physics

22. If neither Italian nor Japanese is taken by a Freshman at Last Chance University, which one of the following courses must be taken?

    (A) Physics
    (B) French
    (C) German
    (D) Algebra
    (E) Statistics

23. If a Freshman student at Last Chance University takes Italian, which one of the following pairs of courses must also be taken?

    (A) German, Biology
    (B) Biology, Physics
    (C) Statistics, Chemistry
    (D) Biology, Chemistry
    (E) Algebra, French

STOP

IF YOU FINISH BEFORE TIME IS UP, CHECK YOUR WORK ON THIS SECTION OF THE TEST ONLY.
DO NOT GO ON TO THE NEXT SECTION OF THE TEST UNTIL TIME IS UP FOR THIS SECTION.

5   **5**

SECTION V
TIME — 35 MINUTES
25 QUESTIONS

Directions: In this section you will be given brief statements or passages and will be required to evaluate the reasoning involved. In some instances, more than one choice will appear to be a possible answer. You are to choose the *best* answer. Use common sense and reasonableness in making your selection; then mark the proper space on the answer sheet.

1. *Economist:* The health-care and lost-productivity costs of smoking exceed 15 billion dollars a year. Despite the evidence linking smoking to a number of fatal diseases, 30 percent of the American population still smokes. If we were to tax cigarettes at the high rates imposed in Canada or Great Britain, we could raise badly needed tax money, and greatly reduce the health-care and lost-productivity costs of smoking.

   The argument of the passage would be most weakened if which one of the following were shown to be true?

   (A) Taxes on cigarettes fall more heavily upon the poor than upon the rich.
   (B) Only 15 percent of the population of Canada smokes cigarettes.
   (C) The number of smokers in Canada did not decline when the high taxes on cigarettes were imposed.
   (D) About 25 percent of the population of Great Britain smokes tobacco.
   (E) Taxes on alcoholic beverages in Canada and Great Britain are lower than similar taxes in the United States.

2. *Jane:* I haven't found anyone in the English class who agrees with the professor's interpretation of this poem.
   Dave: No, you're wrong. The three students who got A's on the paper must have agreed with the professor's reading.

   Dave's reply shows that he has interpreted Jane's comment to imply which one of the following?

   (A) Jane has consulted all of the students in the English class.
   (B) Jane has not consulted any of the students who agree with the professor.
   (C) Some students who say they disagree with the professor may change their minds.
   (D) Jane has not consulted all of the students in the English class.
   (E) Some students who say they agree with the professor do not, in fact, believe in his interpretation.

GO ON TO THE NEXT PAGE ➤

5   **5**

Questions 3–4

Advertisement: "You deserve the freedom to choose any doctor and to have no more medical bills. These benefits can be yours when you join Red Shield and go to your choice of one of five thousand Red Shield preferred physicians."

3. This advertisement presupposes as part of its argument that the reader

(A) wishes to choose what doctor she will go to
(B) does not belong to a health maintenance program
(C) belongs to a program which allows the choice of a doctor
(D) pays no medical bills
(E) wishes to reduce her annual medical expenses

4. Which one single word in the advertisement leads to a logical inconsistency to its claim?

(A) deserve
(B) freedom
(C) any
(D) choice
(E) preferred

5. With its large community of conservative former colonists from Algeria and an equally conservative retiree population, Nice is France's only large city sympathetic to the far-right-wing politics of Jean Le Pen. Jacque Medecin, the mayor of Nice for twenty-five years, has said he agrees with 99 percent of Le Pen's ideas, which include hostility to immigration, Arabs, and Jews. Conservatives have been shocked by Medecin's sudden flight to South America with two of his party allies, presumably to avoid prosecution for massive looting of public funds. Medecin claims he is the victim of a Socialist plot.

Which one of the following is most clearly suggested by the information in this passage?

(A) Some right-wing politicians may be guilty of dishonesty.
(B) Some right-wing politicians may deplore racism.
(C) The young are naturally more conservative than the elderly.
(D) Conservatives are likely to be the victims of Socialist plots.
(E) Not all conservatives support the ideas of Jean Le Pen.

6. If Jack were a first baseman for the New York Mets, he would be rich. He is not a first baseman, since he is not rich.

The conclusion above is unsound because the author does not consider the possibility that Jack could be

(A) a rich third baseman
(B) a first baseman for another team
(C) rich for some other reason
(D) a guard for the Boston Celtics
(E) a second baseman for the New York Mets

5 **5** **5** **5**

7. All Italian greyhounds are graceful and fast, but some are nervous. Graceful and fast greyhounds are slender, but nervous greyhounds are unpredictable.

If the statements are true, all of the following must be true EXCEPT

(A) all Italian greyhounds are slender
(B) some greyhounds are nervous
(C) no Italian greyhounds are slow
(D) no Italian greyhounds are predictable
(E) all Italian greyhounds are graceful

8. Researchers have shown that females of a certain species of fish are more attracted to the male of the species when males are fitted with a plastic, swordlike extension of the ends of their tails. The artificial fin makes the males resemble the males of a different species, the swordtail. For some time biologists have wondered how traits like the swordlike tail of the swordtail arise. Do males evolve traits that females later prefer? Or do the traits and preference evolve together? Or do the females have the preference first, and the males evolve to respond to it? The results of the experiment suggest that _____.

Which one of the following is the most logical conclusion of the paragraph?

(A) we still cannot reach even a tentative answer to these questions.
(B) the female's preference arose first and the males adapted to it.
(C) the males' development must come first, and evolutionary pressure causes the females to respond.
(D) the females' and the males' traits and preferences must arise at the same time.
(E) the whole notion of evolutionary development must be in error.

9. Doctors are becoming wary of herbal teas and similar preparations. Many herbs sold in health-food stores or even supermarkets may be toxic. Sales of herbal products are nearly half a billion dollars yearly. And though the majority of herbal products are probably safe, at least twenty-five commonly sold herbs can cause cardiac, gastrointestinal, or nervous system diseases. Some herbs that have been used for thousands of years are neither safe nor effective. The prevailing myth that herbs are "natural" and therefore can do no harm is false. Too few commonly available herbs have been rigorously tested. The same requirements that apply to new drugs should also apply to herbal remedies.

The author of this passage would probably agree with which one of the following statements?

(A) Whole herbs are more effective than their isolated active constituents.
(B) Natural or organic herbs are superior to synthetic drugs.
(C) Harmful plants like cocaine, opium, tobacco, or marijuana should not be regarded as herbs.
(D) Herbs should be classified as foods, not drugs.
(E) Herbs are to be avoided by pregnant or nursing women.

GO ON TO THE NEXT PAGE ➤

10. When we examine the diets of men of the same age and similar background, we see that the smaller the amount of fiber in the diet, the greater the incidence of colon cancer. Therefore, fiber in the diet probably prevents cancer of the colon.

Which one of the following uses reasoning that most closely parallels the reasoning in the argument above?

(A) Studies show that a second child in a family learns to speak at an earlier age than the first child, and also at an earlier age than a third child. Therefore, the second-born child must be more intelligent.

(B) Researchers have shown that shoppers with shopping lists spend less money in supermarkets than shoppers without lists. The same study reported that men are more likely to buy luxury or unnecessary foods than women. Therefore, a woman with a shopping list is likely to spend less in a supermarket than a man without a shopping list.

(C) When one hundred rats are placed in a small cage, a certain percentage will become cannibalistic, and the smaller the cage, the higher the percentage of cannibalism. Overcrowding, therefore, is probably the cause.

(D) Two out of three automobile accidents happen within two miles of the driver's home. Therefore, drivers must be overconfident and more careless when driving on a familiar road.

(E) In certain wilderness areas, more forest fires are caused by acts of nature, such as lightning, than by human acts. But the closer a forest is to a city, the more likely it is that a fire will be caused by human beings. Therefore, the number of fire watchers must be higher nearer urban areas.

GO ON TO THE NEXT PAGE ➤

5 **5** **5** **5** **5**

Questions 11–12

The Yoruba faith considers animal sacrifice during religious ceremonies a source of spiritual power and purity. In Yoruba ceremonies, farm animals, usually chickens, are sacrificed and then consumed. The city has passed an ordinance which forbids any animal sacrifice, and the religious group has challenged the law and vowed to continue the practice. The attorney for the Yorubas argues that denial of the ritual is like forbidding Christians to take communion.

The ban on animal sacrifice was passed in response to complaints about animal remains found in trash containers. Officials attributed the remains to Satanists and to Caribbean and South American communities practicing Santeria, an African animist religion. The Yorubas have pointed out that the remains cannot have come from their ceremonies, where the animal is consumed, and that their animals are killed according to state codes.

11. Which one of the following conclusions should be drawn from the passage above?

(A) This case will be decided in favor of the Yorubas.
(B) This case will be decided in favor of the city ordinance.
(C) If the Yorubas win, the case for animal sacrifice by believers in Santeria will be weakened.
(D) Animal-rights activists are likely to support the Yorubas in this case.
(E) A decision in this case will offend against either religious freedom or animal rights.

12. All of the following arguments might be used in defense of the regulation prohibiting animal sacrifices EXCEPT

(A) even if the Yorubas kill animals humanely, the law is necessary to prevent inhumane killing by other sects
(B) scientific studies have shown that animals feel pain as intensely as humans
(C) not all religious beliefs—polygamy, for example—are tolerated in the United States
(D) animal sacrifices have been a part of religious ceremonies for thousands of years
(E) the sight of animal sacrifice may be traumatic to children

13. After installing an expensive computer-operated drip irrigation system designed to measure moisture and to save up to 20 percent of water usage, Jackson Orchards discovered that its water bill for the month of September was 10 percent higher than last September's bill, before the new system was in use. Jackson Orchards demanded a refund from the irrigation systems company.

Jackson Orchards' demand would be more convincing if which one of the following were true?

(A) The rates charged by the water company were virtually unchanged.
(B) It could demonstrate that the irrigation system was functioning as it should.
(C) The acreage under cultivation was slightly smaller this September than last.
(D) September a year ago was noteworthy for its heavy rains.
(E) None of the farms nearby had any change in their water bills from one September to the other.

GO ON TO THE NEXT PAGE ➤

5 **5** **5** **5**

Questions 14–15

Investors in the bonds of Washington Savings Bank have lost all the money that they invested. Therefore, no savings bank should be permitted to sell new bonds without careful governmental supervision.

14. Which one of the following is an assumption made in the argument above?

   (A) Government insurance does not cover the losses of investors in bonds issued by banks.
   (B) The investors should have been warned by the bank of the possibility of default on the bonds.
   (C) The government will have to make up the losses suffered by the bankrupt savings and loan companies.
   (D) If the bonds of one bank are in default, the bonds of all banks are likely to be in default.
   (E) Government supervision of the Washington Bank could have prevented its issuing bonds that became worthless.

15. Which one of the following arguments most closely resembles the argument above?

   (A) Children exposed to second-hand tobacco smoke in the home are more likely to develop respiratory diseases. Therefore, parents should reduce their smoking in the home.
   (B) Twelve percent of fatal traffic accidents are caused by drivers over 75 years old. Therefore, drivers over 75 should be permitted to drive only after careful state examination.
   (C) Three widely sold brands of herbal tea have been found to contain comfrey, an herb that can be toxic with repeated ingestion. Therefore, these brands of herbal tea should be removed from grocery shelves.
   (D) Two members of the state legislature have pleaded guilty to charges of bribery. Therefore, the laws against bribery must be strengthened.
   (E) A child who does not want to attend school will not do good work in the classroom. Therefore, special classes should be established for weakly motivated students.

GO ON TO THE NEXT PAGE ➤

5

16. *City Planner:* By reading the advertisements in the real estate section of the newspaper, anyone can see that there are far more condominiums for sale than duplex apartment buildings or single-family homes. Builders are beginning to recognize that there is a shortage of homes in the median price range.

Which one of the following would best conclude the passage above?

(A) We should soon see a decline in the high price of condominiums.
(B) Real estate agents are concerned about the lack of movement in the apartment market.
(C) New housing construction will probably concentrate on medium-priced duplex and single-family buildings.
(D) The price of real estate will probably decline if the area is perceived to be overbuilt.
(E) Next year, the number of unsold condominiums should be even larger.

17. The results of the election in Texas show that women can campaign negatively in order to survive mud-slinging primaries, and can win when the opposing party picks a fool as its candidate. But they cannot expect people to vote for them just because they are women. Incumbents still have a huge advantage, and an overwhelming percentage of incumbents are men.

Which one of the following is the most logical conclusion of this paragraph?

(A) So women are still unlikely to win a large number of elective offices.
(B) Therefore, the number of women elected to national and state offices should increase regularly.
(C) If all the women voters supported women candidates, women in office would outnumber men.
(D) Therefore the reelection of office holders should decline in the near future.
(E) So the number of mud-slinging campaigns may be expected to increase.

18. All Japanese gardens inspire contemplation, because they are filled with beautiful plantings.

Of the following, which is the missing premise in the statement above?

(A) All Japanese gardens are beautiful.
(B) Only gardens that inspire contemplation are filled with beautiful plantings.
(C) Beautiful gardens contain beautiful plantings.
(D) Beautiful plantings inspire contemplation.
(E) Only beautiful plantings inspire contemplation.

GO ON TO THE NEXT PAGE ➤

<u>Questions 19–20</u>

Children are not afraid of math and science. They approach these subjects full of questions. For parents who can answer these questions, the danger is explaining too much and preventing the children from learning for themselves and experiencing the pleasures of discovery. Most of us often find ourselves unable to answer such questions as "Why is the sky blue?" What we should do is praise children for their curiosity, and then help them learn where to look for answers. Most libraries stock books geared to introducing math and science to children.

What is most important, however, is the attitude of the adults toward learning. At the turn of the century, it was often the children of Jewish immigrants who excelled in science. Now it is often the Asian children who excel. Both groups have a tradition of respecting education. Obviously children who hear teachers and education praised at home will perform differently in school from children whose parents denigrate education. The attitudes of parents toward education are more important than how much they themselves know.

19. The author of the passage would probably disapprove of

  (A) parents who feel inadequate or embarrassed because they cannot answer their children's questions
  (B) children whose knowledge of math and science is greater than that of their parents
  (C) parents who respond to children's questions with irritation
  (D) immigrant parents with an imperfect knowledge of English
  (E) teaching math and science in elementary schools

20. Which one of the following, if true, would provide the most serious challenge to the argument of this passage?

  (A) Studies show that the earliest appearance of math anxiety is normally in junior high school age students.
  (B) Most children are introduced to science by television rather than by reading.
  (C) Asian-Americans had the highest average score on the mathematics section of the Scholastic Aptitude Test this year.
  (D) The number of males who major in mathematics and science is much greater than the number of females.
  (E) Jewish and Asian parents are more likely to criticize elementary and secondary schools than parents in other ethnic groups.

---

21. Photography is an art because it imposes form upon the chaos of the natural world.

The statement above assumes which of the following?

  (A) Whatever is photographed is art.
  (B) Painting is an art superior to photography.
  (C) Art is the expression of human life.
  (D) Whatever has form is an art.
  (E) The natural world is artistic.

5   **5**

Questions 22–23

Editorial: Should the Forest Service post more warning signs in the areas visited by the public? Advocates say putting up signs would protect the agency from lawsuits and would be easy to do. The Forest Service argues that, by putting up a sign, the agency provides a potential litigant with evidence, if the sign has been removed. Also, almost any location in the wilderness might be dangerous, so the number of signs would equal that of trees. The problem, according to Forest Service spokesmen, is a public unprepared for the woods. People come wearing sandals and shorts, without a map, water, or sunglasses.

22. Which one of the following explains the paradox of using as evidence a sign that has been removed?

   (A) If the sign had never been placed in the forest, the visitor would be unaware of the danger.

   (B) By putting up a sign, the Forest Service gives notice of a hazard.

   (C) Whether or not a victim of an accident has seen a warning sign will be difficult to assess.

   (D) The sign could be placed at the entrance to the forest; then it would not be stolen.

   (E) Not all visitors to the forests understand English, so the signs would have to be in several languages.

23. The case against the Forest Service would be most strengthened if which one of the following were true?

   (A) The Forest Service has only five permanent employees per thousand square miles of forest.

   (B) More than 40 percent of the visitors to the forests are non-English speaking.

   (C) The Forest Service keeps no records of accidents, but private records indicate that fatalities in California forests average fifty per year.

   (D) A high percentage of the accidents in national forests are caused by sudden changes in the weather.

   (E) Studies show that 75 percent of park visitors will follow a rule or warning when they understand it.

---

24. Banning the sale of aerosol spray paints in this city will result in huge losses for paint manufacturers. Not all graffiti are painted with spray paints, and the aerosols' damage to the air is 100 times less than the harm done by automobile exhausts. Therefore the sale of spray paints should not be banned.

Which one of the following, if true, would most seriously weaken the argument in the passage above?

   (A) The cost of graffiti removal outweighs the projected losses of paint manufacturers.

   (B) Industrial air pollution is also 100 times greater than pollution caused by aerosols.

   (C) The quality of the air in the city has improved steadily in the last four years.

   (D) Many serious art critics regard graffiti as a legitimate, artistically significant form of self-expression.

   (E) The banning of spray paints may be the first step in a series of repressive city incursions on personal freedoms.

GO ON TO THE NEXT PAGE ➤

5   **5**

25. All continents have mountain ranges with mountains that are dangerous to climb. Therefore all the world's mountain ranges have mountains dangerous to climbers.

Which one of the following most closely parallels the reasoning in the passage above?

(A) Every bird is warm blooded. Therefore every flying animal is warm blooded.
(B) All the geology books in the library circulate. Therefore all the library books about geology must circulate.
(C) Every atom is made up of electrons. Therefore all things must contain electrons.
(D) Every number is either odd or even. Therefore half of the numbers are odd.
(E) All the television channels on this set are in Spanish. Therefore all the television channels in this city must be in Spanish.

STOP

END OF MULTIPLE-CHOICE EXAMINATION. IF YOU FINISH BEFORE TIME IS UP, CHECK YOUR WORK ON THIS SECTION ONLY. DO NOT GO BACK TO ANY OTHER SECTION OF THE EXAMINATION.

Writing Sample

Directions: You have 30 minutes to write an essay in response to a given topic. Take a few minutes to plan your work before you begin writing. DO NOT WRITE ON A TOPIC OF YOUR OWN CHOICE. ESSAYS THAT DO NOT ADDRESS THE GIVEN TOPIC ARE UNACCEPTABLE.

The quality of your writing is more important than the length of your response or the content. Pay attention to organization, appropriate diction, and correct usage. You will not be expected to display any specialized knowledge in your response, nor will you be expected to write a "perfect" essay; law schools understand that you are writing under a time constraint, and will allow for the minor lapses in writing ability that might occur under this circumstance.

Only the lined area in your booklet will be reproduced for the law schools, so do not write outside this space. *Do not* skip lines or use wide margins. These precautions, along with careful planning and legible handwriting that is not unduly large, will keep you within the allowed space.

Sample Topic

Dolores is a single parent of twelve-year-old twins who attend a private school on scholarship. The head of the purchasing department of a large company located in downtown St. George, Dolores has recently sold the small house she owned in the city and must decide whether to purchase a condominium in the attractively redeveloped harbor area of the city or a house in the suburbs. *In the space provided, write an argument supporting one of the two choices.* The following factors should be taken into consideration:

- Dolores's doctor has urged her to spend more time on her two relaxing hobbies—gardening and bicycling.
- Dolores must significantly increase her yearly savings in order to provide for the twins' college education.

The suburban house that Dolores is considering is sixteen miles from her office. Dolores does not own a car. The house has a large yard and garden. The town is quiet and traffic-free, with stable property values. After making the down payment with the money from the sale of the house she has sold, Dolores will have tax and interest costs of $600 per month. Because the winters in St. George are severe, her yearly heating costs will be an additional $2,000 per year.

The harborfront condominium is located two miles from Dolores's workplace, and the city has bicycle lanes on all of its streets. The down payment on the condominium is equal to that of the house in the suburbs, but the apartment is smaller and has only a small brick patio for outdoor living. Dolores's tenancy costs, including her tax and interest payments, would be $700 per month. Property values in the harbor area of the city have risen sharply in the recent past, but have fallen slightly this year.

Answer Key

Section I: Analytical Reasoning

1. **E**	5. **E**	9. **B**	13. **D**	17. **B**	21. **D**
2. **C**	6. **D**	10. **D**	14. **B**	18. **B**	22. **E**
3. **A**	7. **C**	11. **B**	15. **C**	19. **D**	23. **A**
4. **B**	8. **C**	12. **C**	16. **D**	20. **B**	24. **C**

Section II: Reading Comprehension

1. **B**	6. **E**	11. **D**	16. **E**	21. **B**	26. **B**
2. **A**	7. **C**	12. **B**	17. **B**	22. **C**	27. **B**
3. **C**	8. **A**	13. **E**	18. **C**	23. **E**	
4. **C**	9. **C**	14. **D**	19. **E**	24. **E**	
5. **B**	10. **E**	15. **D**	20. **A**	25. **D**	

Section III: Logical Reasoning

1. **A**	6. **E**	11. **B**	16. **E**	21. **C**	26. **D**
2. **C**	7. **C**	12. **E**	17. **C**	22. **C**	
3. **C**	8. **C**	13. **D**	18. **A**	23. **E**	
4. **E**	9. **D**	14. **B**	19. **D**	24. **D**	
5. **B**	10. **B**	15. **C**	20. **D**	25. **D**	

Section IV: Analytical Reasoning

1. **C**	5. **E**	9. **D**	13. **C**	17. **A**	21. **D**
2. **D**	6. **B**	10. **C**	14. **D**	18. **B**	22. **B**
3. **C**	7. **C**	11. **A**	15. **A**	19. **E**	23. **B**
4. **B**	8. **E**	12. **C**	16. **C**	20. **D**	

Section V: Logical Reasoning

1. **C**	6. **B**	11. **E**	16. **C**	21. **D**
2. **A**	7. **D**	12. **D**	17. **A**	22. **B**
3. **A**	8. **B**	13. **D**	18. **D**	23. **C**
4. **C**	9. **E**	14. **E**	19. **C**	24. **A**
5. **A**	10. **C**	15. **B**	20. **E**	25. **B**

Model Test Analysis

Doing model exams and understanding the explanations afterwards are of course important in acquainting you with typical LSAT question types and successful approaches to the questions. However, another benefit of carefully analyzing these model tests is to understand the kinds of errors you are making and thus work to minimize them. For instance, if a very high percentage of your incorrect answers is due to "careless error" or "misread problem," then perhaps you are working much too fast and should slow your pace accordingly. If your incorrect answers are due primarily to "lack of knowledge," then a careful rereading and reworking of the appropriate question-type chapter may be in order. Or if you find that you aren't completing a large number of questions because of lack of time, you may need to either increase your speed or learn to use the "one-check, two-check" technique more effectively.

This kind of analysis of the model tests will enable you to identify your particular weaknesses and thus remedy them.

Model Test Five Analysis

Section	Total Number of Questions	Number Correct	Number Incorrect	Number Unanswered*
I. Analytical Reasoning	24			
II. Reading Comprehension	27			
III. Logical Reasoning	26			
IV. Analytical Reasoning	23			
V. Logical Reasoning	25			
TOTALS:	125			

*At this stage in your preparation, you should not be leaving any blank answer spaces. At least fill in a guess, as there is no penalty for a wrong answer.

Reasons for Incorrect Answers

You may wish to evaluate the explanations before completing this chart.

Section	Total Number Incorrect	Lack of Knowledge	Misread Problem	Careless Error	Unanswered or Wrong Guess
I. Analytical Reasoning					
II. Reading Comprehension					
III. Logical Reasoning					
IV. Analytical Reasoning					
V. Logical Reasoning					
TOTALS:					

Explanation of Answers

Section I

Answers 1–6

The following notations may be helpful:

```
3   P        P P P (5 places or less)
2   B        B B
2   R        R   R
1   C        R ? C ? R
1   V        V —×— R
```

1. E Since the Cobra must be between the two Rockets, it cannot be on an end.

```
1  2  3  4  5  6  7  8  9
V  B  B  R           R  P     5,6,7
B  B  R           R  P  V     4,5,6
R  C  B  B  R                 2
```

2. C From the information added in the question, you could have constructed the following:

```
1  2  3  4  5  6  7  8  9
P  P  R  P  V  C  R  B  B
```

If the Viking is between the two Rockets along with the Cobra, the remaining slot must be a Panther. Thus, this is the only possible arrangement of the players.

3. A You could have tried these:

```
1  2  3  4  5  6  7  8  9
   R     V     R              (not valid)
   R           R     V        (not valid)
   R           R     V
```

With a Rocket in position 2, and therefore 6, there seem to be three possible positions for the Viking, as illustrated above. BUT, the first two are not valid, since after putting in the Badgers, the Panthers would be spread over more than 5 consecutive positions. Thus, the third arrangement is the only possible one.

4. B You could have constructed the following:

```
1  2  3  4  5  6  7  8  9
   V     R           C  R
```

This is the only possible arrangement of the players. The Badgers can be in either 6 and 7, or 1 and 2. Thus, B could be true, but it could be false. The other choices must be true.

5. E From the information given, you could have set up these possibilities:

```
1  2  3  4  5  6  7  8  9
B  B  P  P  R  P  V  C  R
P  P  R  P  V  C  R  B  B
```
and the reverse of these two
```
R  C  V  P  R  P  P  B  B
B  B  R  C  V  P  R  P  P
```

These are the only arrangements possible.

6. D You could have constructed the following:

```
1  2  3  4  5  6  7  8  9
V  P  P  P  R  B  B  C  R
The Viking may be   R  C  B  B  R
in 1, 2, or 3.
```

These arrangements may be reversed, left to right. One of the Badgers must be in position 7 or 3, making (D) the correct answer. Since the Panthers cannot be split on either side of the Rockets and are not between the Rockets, the Panthers and the Vikings must occupy the four positions on one end of the line or the other. Thus, there must be a Rocket in positions 5 and 9 or in positions 1 and 5.

Answers 7–12

You could have constructed the following diagrams:

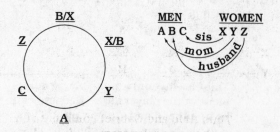

7. **C** From the diagram, we see that Y could sit next to B, depending on the positions of X and B. Thus, (C) could be true. All the other possibilities are always false.

8. **C** If B sits next to Z, then the arrangement is illustrated by those letters to the left of the /. Therefore C sits across from X.

9. **B** If C sits across from X, the arrangement is illustrated by those letters to the left of the /. Thus, X sits next to Y, making (B) true. From the diagram, we see that the other four statements are false.

10. **D** From the diagram, we see that A must sit next to C. The other choices are either always false or sometimes false.

11. **B** If X does not sit across from her brother, then the arrangement is illustrated by those letters to the right of the /. Therefore, C sits across from B.

12. **C** At the table, since there are two of the women sitting next to each other, one of them always has a man to her left. The other woman also has a man to her left. Thus, 2 is the correct number.

Answers 13–18

The following chart proves helpful in organizing the data:

	SS	WP	DB	Com	Dou	Ex	Com	Dou	Ex
R		y	F	n			WP	n	
S		y	G		n	SS			
T			H	n	y	n	DB		n

13. **D** Since Sharon only does her own word processing, she cannot use the Comstar, since it is not used for word processing. The other two are available.

14. **B** The Comstar is not available for word processing. George cannot use the Excellocalc at all. Thus, only the Doufast can be used.

15. **C** Since Ron only does word processing, and the Comstar is not available for word processing, this statement must be true.

16. **D** If Tom's secretary uses the Comstar, they must be using either database or spreadsheet programs, since the Comstar is not available for word processing.

17. **B** If George is Tom's secretary, then Sharon's secretary must be either Fran or Hilda. Neither Fran nor Hilda uses the Comstar. Thus (B) must be true.

18. **B** Since Tom's secretary will only use the Excellocalc, she must be Fran, thus (B) is true. Based on the chart, the other four statements are false.

Answers 19-24

From the information given you could have constructed the following display:

A̶É̶   DH̶

	1	G↓2	3	F̶↓4
X→	___	E?	E?	B
Y→	___	___	___	___

Earle only runs as the 2nd or 3rd runner on relay team X. Bryan runs 4th. Since Aldo and Earle run on different teams, Aldo must run on relay team Y. Since Howard must follow Dominic, Howard cannot run 1st and Dominic cannot run last. A more complete display would look like this:

A̶É̶   DH̶

	H̶1	G↓2	3	F̶D̶4
X→	___	E?	E?	B
Y→	___	___	___	___ ←A

19. D You could eliminate choices (A) and (C) because Howard cannot run 1st. Eliminate choice (E) since Gabriel only runs 2nd, and eliminate choice (B) since Bryan runs 4th. So the only runners that could run 1st on relay team X are Charles, Dominic, and Fred.

20. B If Dominic runs 2nd on relay team Y, then Howard runs 3rd on team Y and Gabriel runs 2nd on relay team X. Your display should look like this:

	1	2	3	4
X→	___	G	E?̶	B
Y→	___	D	H	___ ←A

Thus Aldo and Gabriel could not run on the same relay team.

21. D Dominic and Howard must be on the same team and therefore must be in the answer. This eliminates choices (B) and (E). Aldo and Earle must be on different teams, eliminating choice (A). Aldo and Bryan are on different teams, eliminating (C).

22. E By process of elimination:
Choice (A) is incorrect since Gabriel cannot run 3rd.
Choice (B) is incorrect since Aldo and Earle are not on the same team and Fred cannot run 4th.
Choice (C) is incorrect since Howard must follow Dominic.
Choice (D) is incorrect since Fred cannot run 4th.

23. A If Howard and Gabriel run on the same relay team, so does Dominic. These three runners cannot run on relay team X because there would be no room for Bryan and Earle. Thus Howard and Gabriel must run on relay team Y along with Dominic (who runs in the position immediately before Howard) and Aldo. Since Gabriel must run 2nd, Dominic must be 3rd, Howard 4th, and Aldo 1st. Therefore, choice (A) is correct. The display would look like this:

	1	2	3	4
X→	___	E?	E?	B
Y→	A	G	D	H ←A

24. **C** If Fred and Howard run on the same relay team, so does Dominic. These three runners cannot run on relay team X because there would be no room for Bryan and Earle. Thus Howard and Fred must run on relay team Y along with Dominic (who runs in the position immediately before Howard) and Aldo. Therefore Gabriel is 2nd on relay team X, and Earle is 3rd. Bryan is 4th. Thus Charles must be 1st on relay team X. The display would look like this:

	1	2	3	4
X →	C	G	E	B
Y →	___	___	___	F	← A FDH

Or by process of elimination:
Choice (A) is incorrect since Dominic is on relay team Y.
Choice (B) is incorrect since Aldo is on relay team Y.
Choice (D) is incorrect since Earle is 3rd.
Choice (E) is incorrect since Howard could be 3rd on relay team Y but doesn't have to be.

Section II
Passage 1

1. **B** Aristotle calls a government "by one for his private advantage" tyranny.

2. **A** Aristotle's democracy had the poor "promoting their selfish interests." (D) may be considered, but must be eliminated because no clear relationship exists between "selfish interests" and the *purity* of one's needs.

3. **C** A presumption is the taking of something for granted. By citing Aristotle only, the author seems to presume his singular relevance to modern democracy. (B) and (D) are not matters taken for granted, and (A) and (E) are irrelevant to the passage.

4. **C** By mentioning small countries in which pure democracy is viable, the author implies that large countries cannot administer pure democracy, but he does not detail the difficulties of direct representation on a large scale. Each of the other choices is explicitly mentioned in the paragraph.

5. **B** The common welfare is an "underlying assumption" of modern democracy, says the author, one that "probably will result" (paragraph 3).

6. **E** The author's stress on how "democracy" has changed since Aristotle's time helps us to eliminate (B) and (C). (A) and (D) are neither expressed nor implied. (E) summarizes the belief that motivates the whole discussion.

7. **C** After explaining Aristotle's theory, the author compares it to later conceptions. This overall purpose implies the praise of Aristotle's foresight (D), but the passage as a whole informs much more than it praises.

Passage 2

8. **A** The passage makes the author's support of the abandonment of the felony-murder rule. Options (B) and (C) are true but are not the central idea of the passage. The passage makes no recommendations on Supreme Court actions.

9. **C** The best answer here is to deter the use of deadly force in felonies.

10. **E** Each of choices (A), (B), (C), and (D) can be cited to support the felony-murder rule.

11. **D** All of the arguments except (D), which supports the rule, have been made against the felony-murder rule.

12. **B** Because death does not occur in (B), the felony-murder rule would not apply. It could be used in the other cases.

13. **E** Canada has "restricted" its application, but not yet wholly abandoned the rule.

14. **D** The author uses "bizarre and unfair" to describe the results often achieved by the law, but not to describe the law itself. In the final sentence of the next-to-last paragraph he explicitly objects to the equating of the intent to commit murder with "the mere intent to commit the underlying felony."

Passage 3

15. **D** The paragraph asserts that the differences between realism and naturalism are "not clear-cut." The whole paragraph is an introductory, rather than a "precise" definition of the subject.

16. **E** Paragraph (a) tells us that the author only "pretends" to watch with the "impassivity of the scientist."

17. **B** Halfway through paragraph (c), the author begins generalizing about the "best naturalists," distinguishing them from "mere" naturalists. This section is a mixture of both praise and disdain.

18. **C** Throughout the passage the author stresses the "real life" quality of naturalism. In the final paragraph he explicitly distinguishes between the "romantic" author and the "naturalistic" one, and enumerates factors mentioned in (A), (B), (D), and (E) as aspects of naturalism.

19. **E** Each of the other choices is either factual or a commonplace expression not regarded as literary, or a quite nonliterary use of metaphor (D). (E) compares marriage to a beverage and produces an unusual, highly subjective metaphor that departs from the dispassionate objectivity of the most conservative naturalism.

20. **A** Paragraph (b), which aligns naturalism with social science, stresses the writer's attention to "data from actual life." (C) is generally true of naturalism, but deemphasized character does not receive so close a comparison with scientific research.

Passage 4

21. **B** The passage discusses the terms *hypothesis, theory, law,* and, to a lesser extent, *datum,* all to examine the function of language "in the development of scientific understanding." The second paragraph discusses the method of developing a hypothesis, but does not itself develop one, so (C) is not a good answer.

22. **C** Toward the end of the passage, the author expresses his skepticism about *natural law:* it is a term "dangerous . . . to employ." All other choices are agreeable to the author.

23. **E** The author's parenthetical remarks in paragraphs 2 and 3 emphasize that hypothesis is a *word,* a *symbol,* which stands for (in reference to) an action. He is pointing out the difference between language and what it stands for.

24. **E** In the third paragraph we learn that "As the evidence in favor of a hypothesis . . . accumulates to a convincing degree," it often becomes a theory.

25. **D** All other choices are explicitly refuted in the passage. The author begins the passage by mentioning scientific assumptions such as equations, and then states that the hypothesis is a much more important function.

26. **B** The long second paragraph describing the development of a hypothesis stresses that a hypothesis is a "colored light," that is, subjective and subject to question. The author's claim that a hypothesis may be abandoned suggests that not all hypotheses are useful (E).

27. **B** This is stated at the end of the first paragraph: hypotheses are "not always readily grasped."

Section III

1. **A** Because the passage mentions produce safety and opinion polls, and then leads to a list of consumer food worries, it follows that this could be the latest supermarket battleground.

2. **C** Because the last sentence in the paragraph says "now tops the list of . . . beating out cholesterol and calories," one could reasonably conclude that these last two items were major concerns of consumers.

3. **C** The speaker of this passage may have saved less money because his income was less (B) or (E), his tax deductions were smaller (D), or his expenses besides taxes were larger.

4. **E** Tom's reply shows a disbelief in what he has just heard. Stan's statement doesn't logically follow.

5. **B** The author's argument, that if we can develop laser technology we can cure the common cold, assumes little or no significant distinction between the two challenges. The author, however, does not address this important point.

6. **E** Choice (E) brings in the "size of the individual," which is not an issue in the passage.

7. **C** Statements (A), (B), (D), and (E) would all weaken the claim of the first sentence, but (C) would not.

8. **C** Because the passage states that "the purpose of many of the authors is to offer help to a needy society," it can therefore be inferred that profits are not the *only* goal of many of the authors. Choice (A), an "*increasing* percentage," is not substantiated by the passage.

9. **D** This choice continues the idea that those only in the self-help business for the "quick buck" care little about the needs of the customer. Note the word "hastily" supports the notion of "quick buck."

10. **B** Reducing the mortality rate among squirrels would result in an increase in the squirrel (small game) population. (B) is the only answer that does not point out an ill effect of the reactor—(A), (D)—or a weakness in the argument presented—(C), (E).

11. **B** In order for the conclusion ("Therefore, Davidson will be found guilty . . .") to logically follow, Johnson *and* Smith must be elected for Davidson to be elected. Thereafter Davidson can be accused and found guilty. Therefore (B), "Smith will be elected to the board," must be included in the passage.

12. **E** The only conclusion that can be drawn is that, given an accident, a motorbike operator has less chance for serious injury when wearing a helmet than when not wearing a helmet. Note that there is no relationship given between wearing a helmet and the chance of having an accident.

13. **D** If there are four times as many accidents involving motorbike operators wearing helmets as there are accidents involving operators who are not wearing helmets, and if there is 20 percent chance of serious injury to the former and 40 percent chance to the latter, then helmeted operators will be seriously injured more often (2 out of 10, but 4 times as many, compared to 4 out of 10).

14. **B** If the Consolidated building was constructed in 1988 in the city of Philadelphia, then it would have sprinkler systems. Therefore, it must not be situated in the city of Philadelphia.

15. **C** The author argues that a Broadway show is a greater theatrical experience than a high school play because more people with a greater appreciation elect to attend Broadway shows. This is called circular reasoning, or presupposing a point one later establishes.

16. **E** The author of this argument does not see the difference between "good at the sport" and "good sport."

17. **C** Because it appears that Roger has all of the necessary requirements except auditing experience, when he gains the proper auditing experience he will probably become a Certified Public Accountant.

18. **A** (B) is inappropriate because the argument speaks only of a "danger" and a "threshold beyond which" the monarchy is lost. (C) and (E) are completely contrary to the argument. (D) is inappropriate because the argument does not address bureaucrats or suggest any hostility. (A) is the proper choice because the argument clearly presents bureaucracy as a threat to monarchy.

19. **D** To conclude, based upon the poll, that military personnel favor capital punishment more often than nonmilitary personnel, one must assume that less than 93 percent of the nonmilitary personnel favor capital punishment.

20. **D** That Mr. Wong's committee plays an important role in setting district admissions policy would be a major factor determining the admissions policies from 1985 to 1988. Because there is no reason to doubt that those policies would not continue with Mr. Wong's reelection, (D) is the best answer.

21. **C** Reducing the number of artists would not necessarily decrease the amount of artwork sold, if that reduced number consisted only of artists who never sell their work.

22. **C** Because the author defines "artistic talent" as the number of works sold, an argument challenging that definition must weaken the author's argument.

23. **E** Each of statements (A), (E), and (C) presents additional examples challenging the soundness of the argument. (A) and (B) each introduce the argument that a police car may not be the only vehicle with a loud siren and flashing lights, and that another type of vehicle may exist with those qualities. (C) used birds to suggest that two qualities may be shared by several different items (in this case, ostriches and penguins), much like the police cars and other types of vehicles. (D) uses the same strategy. (E) may be true, but it does not undermine the statement.

24. **D** The passage points out that crime rates can be high or low in rural or urban communities.

25. **D** (A), (B), (C), and (E) are logical conclusions but (D), though it may be true, does not follow from this passage.

26. **D** Robert states that the Maximinima TQ 1000 must be a reliable camera because everyone wants to buy one. Only choice (D) directly addresses this dubious cause-effect statement.

Section IV
Answers 1–5

From the statements we can construct a chart as follows, using statements 2, 3, and 8:

HATS: ___   ___   ___   G   G   ___
SHIRTS: R   R   R   B   B   G

Now, from statement 7 we know that the person wearing the green shirt is not wearing a blue hat. Therefore, we get:

HATS: ___   B   B   G   G   ___
SHIRTS: R   R   R   B   B   G

which leaves the two red hats to complete the chart:

HATS: R   B   B   G   G   R
SHIRTS: R   R   R   B   B   G

Now, placing the people around the table, using first statement 7 and then statement 6, gives:

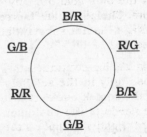

Now all the questions can be easily answered.

1. **C** Only (C) is true.

2. **D** If the green shirt should suddenly turn red, then statements 2, 4, 6, and 7 would no longer be true.

3. **C** If the two blue shirts turned green, then red and green shirts would alternate around the table, thus (C) is true. From the diagram, the other four are false.

4. **B** One of the two people who started with a green hat would still have a green hat, and one of the two people who started with a blue hat would still have a blue hat.

5. **E** The two people wearing blue hats would both be wearing blue shirts, thus (E) is false. All of the other statements are true.

Answers 6–11

6. **B** It is given that G must work the day before the day that F works. Thus, F cannot work on the first day, which is Tuesday.

7. **C** If F works on Tuesday, G must work on Monday. Since D must work on Monday, Tuesday, or Friday, D must work on Friday, since Monday and Tuesday are already scheduled. Weekends are not available for B, so B must work on Wednesday or Thursday.

F	S	S	M	T	W	Th
D	x	x	G	F		

8. **E** Since B will not work weekends, B must work on Monday, Tuesday, or Wednesday. Any of these days is a day before Thursday.

S	M	T	W	Th	F	S
	—	—	—	G	F	

The following is a possible schedule that shows that answer choices (A), (B), (C), and (D) are not necessarily true.

S	M	T	W	Th	F	S
E	D	B	C	G	F	A

9. **D** We are given that B and F do not work weekends. Also, since D works only on Monday, Tuesday, or Friday, D does not work the weekends either. Additionally, if C and A do not work weekends, this leaves only E and G for weekend duty. Since G must work the day before F works, G must work on Sunday, E on Saturday, and F on Monday. The start day is not given, so Wednesday is chosen arbitrarily. Any start day can be used.

W	Th	F	S	S	M	T
			E	G	F	
		A				A
B	B	B				B
C	C	C				
		D				D

Since B and C are the only two workers available for work on Wednesday and Thursday, B and C must work on Wednesday and Thursday (not necessarily respectively). Therefore, answer choice (D) cannot be true.

W	Th	F	S	S	M	T
			E	G	F	
		A				A
B	B					
C	C					
		D				D

From this sample schedule, we see that each of the other answer choices is possible.

10. **C** If D works the first day, the first day must be either Monday, Tuesday, or Friday.

M	T	W	Th	F	S	S
D	F					

T	W	Th	F	S	S	M
D						

F	S	S	M	T	W	Th
D			G	F		

The first chart shows that D cannot work on Monday because if F works on Tuesday, G must work the day before F, or Monday. This is not possible. The second chart shows that D cannot work on Tuesday since F must work Tuesday. This leaves Friday as the start date for D.

F	S	S	M	T	W	Th
D				G	F	
					B	B

Since B cannot work weekends, B must work on Wednesday or Thursday. If E works the third day, which is Sunday, A and C work on Saturday and Wednesday (not necessarily respectively). Thus, answer choice (C) could be true.

F	S	S	M	T	W	Th
D				G	F	
		E				B
	A				A	
	C				C	

Answer choice (A) is incorrect, since if A works the sixth day, which is Wednesday, B, not C, must work on Thursday.

Answer choice (B) is incorrect because if D and E work on consecutive days, E must work on either Saturday or Thursday. If E works on Thursday, B must work on Wednesday and it is therefore not possible for A and F to work on consecutive days.

F	S	S	M	T	W	Th
D				G	F	
					B	E

If E works on Saturday, A cannot work on Wednesday, since if A works on Wednesday, E would have to work on Sunday.

F	S	S	M	T	W	Th
D				G	F	
	E					

Answer choice (D) is incorrect since the third day is a Sunday and B cannot work on weekends.

Answer choice (E) is not correct since G must work on Monday, and Monday is not the last day.

11. **A.** If workers are to work in reverse order of their names, and B and F do not work weekends, the following three schedules are available:

G	F	E	D	C	B	A
W	Th	F	S	S	M	T
Th	F	S	S	M	T	W
S	M	T	W	Th	F	S

Since D will only work on Monday, Tuesday, and Friday, none of these three schedules will work.

Answers 12–17

From the information given you could set up the following display:

G → H	↖↗	S → E
Dance	Free Weight	Treadmill
B G H	P C	S E

— —   —   —   —   —   —

A closer look at the information gives two basic possible setups:

1	2	3	4	5	6	7
Tread	Tread	Free	Free	Dance	Dance	Dance
Dance	Dance	Dance	Free	Free	Tread	Tread

12. **C** Using the display and initial conditions: The Glide must be performed before the Hop. If the Glide is second and the Bounce is third, then the Hop must be fourth. Thus, the Curl cannot be fourth. Also, the dances cannot be second, third, and fourth. They could be first, second, and third or fifth, sixth, and seventh.

13. **C** Because the free weight exercises cannot be performed first or last, they must be either third and fourth or fourth and fifth. If the Glide is third, then the Hop (which comes after the Glide) is either fourth or fifth. This conflicts with the possible positions of the free weight exercises.

14. **D** If Larry does the Endurance routine third, the Speed routine must be done second. This leaves first vacant. This is not permitted. The treadmill routines must be done either first and second or sixth and seventh.

15. **A** Work from the two possible setups and the conditions given in the question:

G
1   2   3   4   5   6   7
Tread Tread Free   Free   Dance Dance Dance

G
Dance Dance Dance Free   Free   Tread Tread

The Glide dance cannot be the last dance performed since the Hop is performed after the Glide. Therefore, if the Glide dance and a free weight exercise are performed consecutively, the dances must be performed fifth, sixth, and seventh, with the Glide being fifth. It follows that the treadmill routines must be done first and second. Thus, the Bounce dance is performed after the Endurance routine, not before.

16. **C** If Larry does the Bounce dance after the Hop, then these two setups are possible (remember the Glide is before the Hop):

                        G   H   B
1   2   3   4   5   6   7
Tread Tread Free   Free   Dance Dance Dance

or

G   H   B
1   2   3   4   5   6   7
Dance Dance Dance Free   Free   Tread Tread

If the Bounce dance is done immediately after the Hop, then the Glide/ Hop/Bounce must be first/second/ third or fifth/sixth/seventh. Thus, Speed/ Endurance must be either first/ second or sixth/seventh. Therefore, Larry could do the Endurance routine seventh.

17. **A** Using the initial conditions and the display, you can see that the Glide is performed before the Hop. Thus, the Glide could be performed first, second, fifth, or sixth. The Speed routine could be done first or sixth.

Answers 18–23

From the initial conditions, you could have made the following simple display:

— — — — —

Languages—F, G, I, J ← 1

Math—A, S, T, M ← 0,1,2

Sciences—B, C, P

P̶A

A →I

C → only if T and F

G and B → S̶

18. **B** Use the elimination strategy while referring to the display. Not (A) or (C), since only one language may be taken. Not (D), since if Algebra is taken, Italian must be taken. Not (E), since Statistics cannot be taken if both German and Biology are taken.

19. **E** Not (A), since Chemistry may be taken only if French is taken and therefore Italian cannot be taken. Not (B), since if Algebra is taken, Italian must be taken and, thus, German cannot be taken. Not (C), since Chemistry may be taken only if French is taken and, therefore, German cannot be taken. Not (D), since if Algebra is taken, Italian must be taken and, thus French cannot be taken.

20. **D** Not (A), since if Algebra is taken, Italian must be taken and, thus, French cannot be taken. Not (B), since if Physics is taken, Algebra cannot be taken. Not (C) or (E), since if Chemistry is taken, French must be taken and German cannot be taken.

21. **D** Not (A), (B), or (E), since if Chemistry is taken, Trigonometry must be taken. Not (C), since a maximum of two math classes may be taken.

22. **B** If neither Italian nor Japanese is taken, then either French or German must be taken. If French is not taken, then Chemistry cannot be taken. If Italian is not taken, then Algebra cannot be taken. This leaves five subjects: German, Statistics, Trigonometry, Biology, and Physics. But if German and Biology are taken, then Statistics cannot be taken. Therefore, French must be taken and not German. Not (A), since the following would be a valid set of courses: Statistics, Trigonometry, French, Biology, Chemistry. Not (D) or (E), since the following would be a valid set of courses: Trigonometry, French, Biology, Chemistry, Physics.

23. **B** If Italian is taken, then not (A) or (E), since a second language may not be taken. Not (C) or (D), since if Chemistry is taken, French must be taken and that would be a second language. Since Italian is taken, French is not, thus Chemistry is not taken either. One math class must be eliminated, since all three cannot be taken. This leaves both Biology and Physics that must be taken.

Section V

1. **C** Though choice (A) may be true, it does not weaken the argument. However, if higher taxes do not reduce the number of smokers, as was the case in Canada, the proposed reductions in health care and lost productivity will not materialize.

2. **A** Jane has said only that she has found none, not that she has spoken to all of the class. Dave has misunderstood.

3. **A** The advertisement assumes a prospective customer who wishes to choose her physician. It makes no assumptions about how much the customer pays now.

4. **C** The first sentence says "choose any doctor," but the second says the doctor will be chosen from the company's "five thousand . . . preferred physicians"—a choice, but not a choice of "any" doctor.

5. **A** Though any of the five choices is possible, the only one supported by the passage is (A). That Medicin, who is sympathetic to right-wing politics, and two colleagues have suddenly fled to South America supports the inference of dishonesty.

6. **B** The logical conclusion from the statements is that, since Jack is not rich, he is not a first baseman for the New York Mets, not that he is not a first baseman. He could be a first baseman for some other team and not be rich.

7. **D** All Italian greyhounds are graceful and fast (C), (E), and graceful and fast greyhounds are slender, so all Italian greyhounds are slender (A). If some graceful and fast Italian greyhounds are nervous, then some greyhounds are nervous (B).

8. **B** In this experiment, the female's preference must already have been present before the artificial fins were added to the males. The evolution of the males presumably has not yet caught up to the female predisposition.

9. **E** The author would probably disagree with choices (A), (B), (C), and (D), but endorse the precaution of (E).

10. **C** The reasoning pattern is as follows: the smaller the x, the greater the y. Therefore the absence of x probably causes y.

11. **E** From the information given, it is not clear how the case will be decided. But any decision will violate the religious rights of the Yorubas or the "rights" of animals.

12. **D** (A), (B), (C), and (E) would support the prohibition, but (D) would oppose it with a historical precedent.

13. **D** If there were heavy rains a year ago, the orchards would use less water and water bills would be lower than normal.

14. **E** The argument assumes that "careful governmental supervision" can prevent default.

15. **B** In each case, the first sentence presents an unhappy event. The second argues for careful oversight (in question 14, "governmental supervision"; here, "state examination").

16. **C** The correct response is based on information from both sentences: the relative scarcity of duplex and single-family homes for sale in the first, the shortage of median-priced homes in the second.

17. **A** If incumbents have an advantage and incumbents are chiefly men, women can win a large number of offices only by unseating the advantaged incumbents—an unlikely event.

18. **D** The logic of the statement is that beautiful plantings inspire contemplation; therefore Japanese gardens, which are filled with beautiful plantings, inspire contemplation.

19. **C** The author would disapprove of parents who discouraged intellectual curiosity in children.

20. **E** The author cites Jewish and Asian parents as examples of those who respect education rather than criticize it.

21. **D** The assumption here is that form is essential to art. Presumably some photographs will not have a formal quality to qualify them as art.

22. **B** The putting up of a warning sign is an admission that a hazard exists. This fact can be used against the Forest Service if the sign has been removed and not replaced.

23. **C** If the number of fatalities in one state is so high, the need for warning signs is underlined.

24. **A** Only choice (A) makes specific use of the details of the argument. Choices (C) and (D) would strengthen the case against banning spray paints.

25. **B** In the passage, "All continents" = "the world" and "mountains . . . dangerous to climb" = "mountains dangerous to climbers." In the correct answer "All the geology books" = "all . . . books about geology," and "circulate" = "circulate."

Chapter 11

MODEL TEST SIX

This chapter contains full-length Model Test Six. It is geared to the format of the LSAT, and it is complete with answers and explanations. It is equivalent to the LSAT in question structure, number of questions, level of difficulty, and time allotments. (The questions used are not taken directly from the LSAT, as those questions are copyrighted and may not be reproduced.)

Model Test Six should be taken under strict test conditions. The test ends with a 30-minute Writing Sample, which is not scored.

Section	Description	Number of Questions	Time Allowed
I.	Logical Reasoning	25	35 minutes
II.	Reading Comprehension	28	35 minutes
III.	Logical Reasoning	25	35 minutes
IV.	Analytical Reasoning	23	35 minutes
V.	Reading Comprehension	28	35 minutes
	Writing Sample		30 minutes
TOTALS:		129	3 hours 25 minutes

Now please turn to the next page, remove your answer sheet, and begin Model Test Six.

Answer Sheet—Model Test Six

Section 1	Section 2	Section 3	Section 4	Section 5
1. Ⓐ Ⓑ Ⓒ Ⓓ Ⓔ	1. Ⓐ Ⓑ Ⓒ Ⓓ Ⓔ	1. Ⓐ Ⓑ Ⓒ Ⓓ Ⓔ	1. Ⓐ Ⓑ Ⓒ Ⓓ Ⓔ	1. Ⓐ Ⓑ Ⓒ Ⓓ Ⓔ
2. Ⓐ Ⓑ Ⓒ Ⓓ Ⓔ	2. Ⓐ Ⓑ Ⓒ Ⓓ Ⓔ	2. Ⓐ Ⓑ Ⓒ Ⓓ Ⓔ	2. Ⓐ Ⓑ Ⓒ Ⓓ Ⓔ	2. Ⓐ Ⓑ Ⓒ Ⓓ Ⓔ
3. Ⓐ Ⓑ Ⓒ Ⓓ Ⓔ	3. Ⓐ Ⓑ Ⓒ Ⓓ Ⓔ	3. Ⓐ Ⓑ Ⓒ Ⓓ Ⓔ	3. Ⓐ Ⓑ Ⓒ Ⓓ Ⓔ	3. Ⓐ Ⓑ Ⓒ Ⓓ Ⓔ
4. Ⓐ Ⓑ Ⓒ Ⓓ Ⓔ	4. Ⓐ Ⓑ Ⓒ Ⓓ Ⓔ	4. Ⓐ Ⓑ Ⓒ Ⓓ Ⓔ	4. Ⓐ Ⓑ Ⓒ Ⓓ Ⓔ	4. Ⓐ Ⓑ Ⓒ Ⓓ Ⓔ
5. Ⓐ Ⓑ Ⓒ Ⓓ Ⓔ	5. Ⓐ Ⓑ Ⓒ Ⓓ Ⓔ	5. Ⓐ Ⓑ Ⓒ Ⓓ Ⓔ	5. Ⓐ Ⓑ Ⓒ Ⓓ Ⓔ	5. Ⓐ Ⓑ Ⓒ Ⓓ Ⓔ
6. Ⓐ Ⓑ Ⓒ Ⓓ Ⓔ	6. Ⓐ Ⓑ Ⓒ Ⓓ Ⓔ	6. Ⓐ Ⓑ Ⓒ Ⓓ Ⓔ	6. Ⓐ Ⓑ Ⓒ Ⓓ Ⓔ	6. Ⓐ Ⓑ Ⓒ Ⓓ Ⓔ
7. Ⓐ Ⓑ Ⓒ Ⓓ Ⓔ	7. Ⓐ Ⓑ Ⓒ Ⓓ Ⓔ	7. Ⓐ Ⓑ Ⓒ Ⓓ Ⓔ	7. Ⓐ Ⓑ Ⓒ Ⓓ Ⓔ	7. Ⓐ Ⓑ Ⓒ Ⓓ Ⓔ
8. Ⓐ Ⓑ Ⓒ Ⓓ Ⓔ	8. Ⓐ Ⓑ Ⓒ Ⓓ Ⓔ	8. Ⓐ Ⓑ Ⓒ Ⓓ Ⓔ	8. Ⓐ Ⓑ Ⓒ Ⓓ Ⓔ	8. Ⓐ Ⓑ Ⓒ Ⓓ Ⓔ
9. Ⓐ Ⓑ Ⓒ Ⓓ Ⓔ	9. Ⓐ Ⓑ Ⓒ Ⓓ Ⓔ	9. Ⓐ Ⓑ Ⓒ Ⓓ Ⓔ	9. Ⓐ Ⓑ Ⓒ Ⓓ Ⓔ	9. Ⓐ Ⓑ Ⓒ Ⓓ Ⓔ
10. Ⓐ Ⓑ Ⓒ Ⓓ Ⓔ	10. Ⓐ Ⓑ Ⓒ Ⓓ Ⓔ	10. Ⓐ Ⓑ Ⓒ Ⓓ Ⓔ	10. Ⓐ Ⓑ Ⓒ Ⓓ Ⓔ	10. Ⓐ Ⓑ Ⓒ Ⓓ Ⓔ
11. Ⓐ Ⓑ Ⓒ Ⓓ Ⓔ	11. Ⓐ Ⓑ Ⓒ Ⓓ Ⓔ	11. Ⓐ Ⓑ Ⓒ Ⓓ Ⓔ	11. Ⓐ Ⓑ Ⓒ Ⓓ Ⓔ	11. Ⓐ Ⓑ Ⓒ Ⓓ Ⓔ
12. Ⓐ Ⓑ Ⓒ Ⓓ Ⓔ	12. Ⓐ Ⓑ Ⓒ Ⓓ Ⓔ	12. Ⓐ Ⓑ Ⓒ Ⓓ Ⓔ	12. Ⓐ Ⓑ Ⓒ Ⓓ Ⓔ	12. Ⓐ Ⓑ Ⓒ Ⓓ Ⓔ
13. Ⓐ Ⓑ Ⓒ Ⓓ Ⓔ	13. Ⓐ Ⓑ Ⓒ Ⓓ Ⓔ	13. Ⓐ Ⓑ Ⓒ Ⓓ Ⓔ	13. Ⓐ Ⓑ Ⓒ Ⓓ Ⓔ	13. Ⓐ Ⓑ Ⓒ Ⓓ Ⓔ
14. Ⓐ Ⓑ Ⓒ Ⓓ Ⓔ	14. Ⓐ Ⓑ Ⓒ Ⓓ Ⓔ	14. Ⓐ Ⓑ Ⓒ Ⓓ Ⓔ	14. Ⓐ Ⓑ Ⓒ Ⓓ Ⓔ	14. Ⓐ Ⓑ Ⓒ Ⓓ Ⓔ
15. Ⓐ Ⓑ Ⓒ Ⓓ Ⓔ	15. Ⓐ Ⓑ Ⓒ Ⓓ Ⓔ	15. Ⓐ Ⓑ Ⓒ Ⓓ Ⓔ	15. Ⓐ Ⓑ Ⓒ Ⓓ Ⓔ	15. Ⓐ Ⓑ Ⓒ Ⓓ Ⓔ
16. Ⓐ Ⓑ Ⓒ Ⓓ Ⓔ	16. Ⓐ Ⓑ Ⓒ Ⓓ Ⓔ	16. Ⓐ Ⓑ Ⓒ Ⓓ Ⓔ	16. Ⓐ Ⓑ Ⓒ Ⓓ Ⓔ	16. Ⓐ Ⓑ Ⓒ Ⓓ Ⓔ
17. Ⓐ Ⓑ Ⓒ Ⓓ Ⓔ	17. Ⓐ Ⓑ Ⓒ Ⓓ Ⓔ	17. Ⓐ Ⓑ Ⓒ Ⓓ Ⓔ	17. Ⓐ Ⓑ Ⓒ Ⓓ Ⓔ	17. Ⓐ Ⓑ Ⓒ Ⓓ Ⓔ
18. Ⓐ Ⓑ Ⓒ Ⓓ Ⓔ	18. Ⓐ Ⓑ Ⓒ Ⓓ Ⓔ	18. Ⓐ Ⓑ Ⓒ Ⓓ Ⓔ	18. Ⓐ Ⓑ Ⓒ Ⓓ Ⓔ	18. Ⓐ Ⓑ Ⓒ Ⓓ Ⓔ
19. Ⓐ Ⓑ Ⓒ Ⓓ Ⓔ	19. Ⓐ Ⓑ Ⓒ Ⓓ Ⓔ	19. Ⓐ Ⓑ Ⓒ Ⓓ Ⓔ	19. Ⓐ Ⓑ Ⓒ Ⓓ Ⓔ	19. Ⓐ Ⓑ Ⓒ Ⓓ Ⓔ
20. Ⓐ Ⓑ Ⓒ Ⓓ Ⓔ	20. Ⓐ Ⓑ Ⓒ Ⓓ Ⓔ	20. Ⓐ Ⓑ Ⓒ Ⓓ Ⓔ	20. Ⓐ Ⓑ Ⓒ Ⓓ Ⓔ	20. Ⓐ Ⓑ Ⓒ Ⓓ Ⓔ
21. Ⓐ Ⓑ Ⓒ Ⓓ Ⓔ	21. Ⓐ Ⓑ Ⓒ Ⓓ Ⓔ	21. Ⓐ Ⓑ Ⓒ Ⓓ Ⓔ	21. Ⓐ Ⓑ Ⓒ Ⓓ Ⓔ	21. Ⓐ Ⓑ Ⓒ Ⓓ Ⓔ
22. Ⓐ Ⓑ Ⓒ Ⓓ Ⓔ	22. Ⓐ Ⓑ Ⓒ Ⓓ Ⓔ	22. Ⓐ Ⓑ Ⓒ Ⓓ Ⓔ	22. Ⓐ Ⓑ Ⓒ Ⓓ Ⓔ	22. Ⓐ Ⓑ Ⓒ Ⓓ Ⓔ
23. Ⓐ Ⓑ Ⓒ Ⓓ Ⓔ	23. Ⓐ Ⓑ Ⓒ Ⓓ Ⓔ	23. Ⓐ Ⓑ Ⓒ Ⓓ Ⓔ	23. Ⓐ Ⓑ Ⓒ Ⓓ Ⓔ	23. Ⓐ Ⓑ Ⓒ Ⓓ Ⓔ
24. Ⓐ Ⓑ Ⓒ Ⓓ Ⓔ	24. Ⓐ Ⓑ Ⓒ Ⓓ Ⓔ	24. Ⓐ Ⓑ Ⓒ Ⓓ Ⓔ	24. Ⓐ Ⓑ Ⓒ Ⓓ Ⓔ	24. Ⓐ Ⓑ Ⓒ Ⓓ Ⓔ
25. Ⓐ Ⓑ Ⓒ Ⓓ Ⓔ	25. Ⓐ Ⓑ Ⓒ Ⓓ Ⓔ	25. Ⓐ Ⓑ Ⓒ Ⓓ Ⓔ	25. Ⓐ Ⓑ Ⓒ Ⓓ Ⓔ	25. Ⓐ Ⓑ Ⓒ Ⓓ Ⓔ
26. Ⓐ Ⓑ Ⓒ Ⓓ Ⓔ	26. Ⓐ Ⓑ Ⓒ Ⓓ Ⓔ	26. Ⓐ Ⓑ Ⓒ Ⓓ Ⓔ	26. Ⓐ Ⓑ Ⓒ Ⓓ Ⓔ	26. Ⓐ Ⓑ Ⓒ Ⓓ Ⓔ
27. Ⓐ Ⓑ Ⓒ Ⓓ Ⓔ	27. Ⓐ Ⓑ Ⓒ Ⓓ Ⓔ	27. Ⓐ Ⓑ Ⓒ Ⓓ Ⓔ	27. Ⓐ Ⓑ Ⓒ Ⓓ Ⓔ	27. Ⓐ Ⓑ Ⓒ Ⓓ Ⓔ
28. Ⓐ Ⓑ Ⓒ Ⓓ Ⓔ	28. Ⓐ Ⓑ Ⓒ Ⓓ Ⓔ	28. Ⓐ Ⓑ Ⓒ Ⓓ Ⓔ	28. Ⓐ Ⓑ Ⓒ Ⓓ Ⓔ	28. Ⓐ Ⓑ Ⓒ Ⓓ Ⓔ
29. Ⓐ Ⓑ Ⓒ Ⓓ Ⓔ	29. Ⓐ Ⓑ Ⓒ Ⓓ Ⓔ	29. Ⓐ Ⓑ Ⓒ Ⓓ Ⓔ	29. Ⓐ Ⓑ Ⓒ Ⓓ Ⓔ	29. Ⓐ Ⓑ Ⓒ Ⓓ Ⓔ
30. Ⓐ Ⓑ Ⓒ Ⓓ Ⓔ	30. Ⓐ Ⓑ Ⓒ Ⓓ Ⓔ	30. Ⓐ Ⓑ Ⓒ Ⓓ Ⓔ	30. Ⓐ Ⓑ Ⓒ Ⓓ Ⓔ	30. Ⓐ Ⓑ Ⓒ Ⓓ Ⓔ

SECTION I
TIME — 35 MINUTES
25 QUESTIONS

Directions: In this section you will be given brief statements or passages and will be required to evaluate the reasoning involved. In some instances, more than one choice will appear to be a possible answer. You are to choose the *best* answer. Use common sense and reasonableness in making your selection; then mark the proper space on the answer sheet.

1. *Political Analyst:* The President's party normally loses seats in the House of Representatives and none in the Senate in the years when there is no presidential election. Johnson lost 47 House seats in 1966, and Nixon lost 12 House seats in 1970. Since the end of World War II, the average loss in the House is 24 seats. In 1990, the Republicans lost only 12 House seats, and so the Congressional election may be regarded as a Republican victory.

The conclusion of this argument is called into doubt by all of the following EXCEPT

(A) the Republicans lost an above-average number of seats in the Senate
(B) the Republicans held fewer seats in the House than usual before the elections
(C) the Republican House losses in this election, added to losses in the House in the presidential election two years before, give them fewer seats than at almost any time since 1946
(D) there were only two Republican Senate seats up for reelection and the Democrats won both
(E) the voter turnout across the country this year was smaller than normal

2. A kindergarten teacher from Solana Beach has won an award for teaching geography. She had her class write to friends or relatives in as many states as possible, and posted the replies on a large classroom map. Her students learned the lessons well. In a competition to locate the states on a blank map, they easily defeated a team from San Marcos High School. The prize was a large collection of materials for teaching geography.

Which one of the following is the most logical concluding sentence for this passage?

(A) These prize materials didn't include workbooks.
(B) Needless to say, these materials are probably more needed at the high school.
(C) It is not surprising that Americans are less likely than Europeans to know much about geography.
(D) Many American educators are concerned about our lack of geographical knowledge.
(E) The kindergarten students located all fifty states without an error.

GO ON TO THE NEXT PAGE ➤

1   1   1   1   1

3. When Mr. Smith attempted to buy the fish of the day at his local supermarket, he discovered there was none left. The store manager explained that the fish of the day had already been sold out.

The store manager's explanation is an example of

(A) failure to generalize from a specific case
(B) euphemism
(C) rephrasing but not explaining a problem
(D) attempting to change the grounds of an argument
(E) using evidence not relevant to a conclusion.

Questions 4–5

Consumer Advocate: The makers of Volvo have spent more than $100,000 for advertisements that apologize for fakery in an earlier ad that showed a reinforced Volvo surviving punishment that destroyed other makes of cars. But the greater cost to the Swedish car company will be the loss of public trust. Company officials say that only one ad is at fault. But prospective customers may be wondering, "If one ad can't be trusted, how about all the others?"

Volvo is not the only advertiser caught trying to hoodwink the public. Every year dozens of fake advertisers are exposed by consumer advocates, Better Business Bureaus, or even the Federal Trade Commission. A cola comparison ad was dropped from television recently when its test results were found unconvincing. The deer in a Canadian travel ad came from a petting zoo. In fact, the history of advertising is a long, nasty story of ads that deceive. Only 8 percent of the consumers responding to a recent survey said they were confident that advertising is truthful.

4. Which one of the following best describes the structure of the argument in this passage?

(A) It moves from the general to the specific.
(B) It replies to anticipated objections of the other side.
(C) It argues from inconsistent points of view.
(D) It relies heavily on the use of analogy.
(E) It moves from a specific example to a conclusion.

5. Which one of the following, if true, would best support the argument of the passage?

(A) Advertisers, or their agencies, insist that hardly any ads are deceptive.
(B) The Federal Trade Commission says that every time they forbid a deceptive practice, advertisers find a new way around it.
(C) The National Advertising Division is a watchdog of advertising for the Better Business Bureau.
(D) The number of convictions on charges of using the mails to defraud declined slightly in the last three years.
(E) Advertisers are now using thirty-minute "infomercials" that combine entertainment and commercial messages.

GO ON TO THE NEXT PAGE ➤

1   1   1   1   1

6. Agriculture presents the biggest problem at the world trade negotiations. Developed nations must agree to reduce farm subsidies and supports as a *quid pro quo* for developing nations to agree to new rules on services and investments. But the European Community has dragged its feet on the farm subsidy issue for years. Germany and France are especially reluctant to agree to any reduction in farm subsidies, no doubt, in part, because the German chancellor faces an election next month. And the European ban on virtually all American meat imports (on the basis of "health inspection standards") is not encouraging.

We can infer from the passage above that

(A) the United States does not support the reduction of farm subsidies
(B) farmers in Germany are a large voting constituency
(C) farm supports and subsidies are common in developing countries
(D) European bans on American meat are based on the known health dangers of American products
(E) French politicians would support the reduction in farm subsidies if they did not face election campaigns

7. According to a leading conservative African-American commentator, preferential admissions policies have not been helpful to African-American students. Their college dropout rate is about 70 percent. What is really needed, he suggests, is an improved public school system. The call for an "ethnic" curriculum comes at a cost to more basic learning. Meanwhile the white middle class that can afford private schools is leaving the public schools, and asking for government help to pay the bills for private education.

Which one of the following statements, if true, could offer the strongest refutation of the argument in the passage above?

(A) The college dropout rate overall is 35 percent.
(B) The call for an "ethnic" curriculum comes not only from African-Americans, but also from Latinos, Asian-Americans, and Native Americans.
(C) Test scores show that the public schools in California have made slow but steady progress in the past four years.
(D) The worker shortage in the years ahead is expected to encompass both blue-collar and white-collar workers.
(E) The society that we construct gives us the education that we deserve.

GO ON TO THE NEXT PAGE ➤

1   1   1   1   1

8. *Editorial:* Super Bowl tickets this year will each cost $150, $25 more than last year, and $50 more than the year before. National Football League spokesmen have pointed out that for $150 the fan will receive a full afternoon's entertainment, four quarters of football, and a half-time show, while people recently paid $1000 for a world-championship boxing match that lasted only seven minutes. Hotel and food prices on the Super Bowl weekend are expected to rise by about 25 percent. The National Football League expects the price rise to continue until the public is no longer stupid enough to pay whatever price is asked. In 1995, the cost per ticket will be $250.

Which one of the following is the best description of the author's attitude toward the price of Super Bowl tickets?

(A) He feels that the increase is inevitable and is not upset.
(B) He is in favor of the increase.
(C) He has no strong feelings in either direction about the increase.
(D) He disapproves of the increase.
(E) He objects to the increase but feels that the game is worth it.

9. *Brian:* "Evolutionists begin by assuming that science excludes the possibility of a creator."
Darrell: "No. Evolutionists attempt to explain the origin of species, not the origin of life."

If Darrell's is the correct view of evolutionary thought, the evolutionists

(A) will not explain where matter came from
(B) would support a view in which the development of life forms is divinely controlled
(C) will support a belief that all the animals were saved by Noah
(D) will deny the existence of the supernatural
(E) will favor Christianity over any of the religions of the East

Questions 10–11

Article: An embargo on the importation of Mexican tuna was recently overturned in an appeals court decision. Environmentalists had won the ban as part of an effort to stop fishing practices that kill dolphins swimming near tuna schools. The decision comes at a time when the administration is trying to adopt a free-trade agreement with Mexico. The government contends that Mexican fishermen have curtailed the dolphin deaths, while the environmentalists charge the government's statistics are inadequate and misleading. The Mexican government claims it has reduced the dolphin kill by 70 percent in recent years. Neither the Mexican nor the U.S. commerce department would connect the embargo to the talks on a free-trade agreement between the two countries.

10. The article implies that

(A) the embargo and the free-trade agreement are connected
(B) the Mexican fisheries have not reduced the number of dolphins killed
(C) the environmentalists had succeeded in having Mexican tuna imported into the United States
(D) the government's statistical support of U.S. tuna fishermen is inadequate
(E) the courts will decide in favor of the environmentalists on this issue

11. From the information presented in the article, an impartial reader should

(A) take sides with the environmentalists
(B) take sides with the U.S. and Mexican governments
(C) be unable to determine which side is right
(D) regard the disagreement as one that can never be settled
(E) regard the disagreement as inappropriate for legal dispute

GO ON TO THE NEXT PAGE ➤

1   1   1   1   1

12. An American defense of a Persian Gulf country is based not on self-interested protection of our oil source but on moral principles that do not permit us to tolerate the invasion of an innocent nation. The Iraqi invasion of Kuwait is just such an action; and if the only Kuwaiti export were tennis balls, we would still defend the country against aggression.

The argument of this paragraph can be described as all of the following EXCEPT

(A) the offering of a moral rather than a materialistic reason for American actions
(B) a condemnation of Iraq as an aggressor
(C) a defense against an accusation of acting on self-interested motives
(D) concealing what is an act of aggression under the guise of a nonaggressive act
(E) using an analogy to support its main point

13. Because the presentation of mothers in the novels of Jane Austen is unflattering and even hostile, many readers have concluded that Jane Austen's attitude to her own mother was disapproving.

Which one of the following, if true, would best support the conclusion above?

(A) The hostile comments about mothers are spoken by characters in the novels of whom the author clearly disapproves.
(B) Jane Austen's presentation of fathers in her novels is equally unflattering.
(C) What an author says in a work of fiction does not necessarily reflect the author's beliefs.
(D) The unfavorable attitude toward mothers is reflected in the ironic comments of the narrator of the novels as well as in the dialogue.
(E) The attitude toward mothers in novels by other writers written in the same period is also disapproving.

Questions 14–15

That a record album was made by unnamed studio musicians rather than by the singers whose names appear on the cover is bad enough. The larger embarrassment to the record industry is that the record was chosen for special honor as the best of the year. The album sold nearly eight million copies, a triumph of marketing since the songs themselves are mediocre and the performances equally pedestrian. Why, then, did it win an award? Because _____.

14. Which one of the following most logically completes the paragraph?

(A) the voters for the awards are sophisticated musicians
(B) all awards for excellence in the arts are folly
(C) in determining awards, sales figures are more important than the quality of the product
(D) the record company was unaware of the deceptions
(E) the record industry is made up of performing artists and business people

15. Which one of the following, if true, would most greatly weaken the argument of the passage?

(A) Last year's winner of record of the year sold fewer than 200,000 copies.
(B) The record company was aware that the singers advertised on the album cover had not made the recording.
(C) Sales of records are now influenced more by television than by radio publicity.
(D) Not all of the workers in the record industry voted for this year's award.
(E) Some reviewers praised the performers and others praised the songs on this year's award-winning album.

GO ON TO THE NEXT PAGE ➤

1   1   1   1   1

16. A Supreme Court decision ruled that a state employee of 61, who retired because of Alzheimer's disease but was barred from disability benefits, was not protected under the Age Discrimination in Employment Act (ADEA). The court limited the application of the act to wages, hiring, and dismissals, not to employee benefits. A proposed new law restoring protection of employee benefits to older workers has been criticized by the president as imposing unfair burdens upon business, and he has threatened to veto it if it is enacted. The American Association of Retired Persons has _____.

Which one of the following best completes the last sentence in the passage above?

(A) criticized the proposed new law as likely to raise the cost of business operations

(B) refused to take a stand on the Supreme Court's decision

(C) supported the Supreme Court's decision as a reasonable interpretation of the ADEA

(D) thrown its support behind the new law, and will lobby for an override of the president's veto

(E) expressed concern that passage of the new law might lead to a reduction in Medicare benefits

17. Anyone can become a financial planner. All you have to do is put up a sign advertising financial planning services, give advice to anyone who asks for it, and collect a fee. Legally, all an "investment advisor" has to do is register with the Securities and Exchange Commission and fill out an information form. Many financial planners lack skill or training, and give bad advice that injures their clients. Some are downright dishonest and either encourage investments in financial products for which the planner receives a fee ("self-dealing"), or run up large fees for unnecessary services, or actually steal from clients.

Which one of the following is the author's main point in this paragraph?

(A) There is insufficient regulation of financial planners.

(B) Some financial planners are dishonest.

(C) To become a financial planner, one must register with the Securities and Exchange Commission.

(D) There should be a required degree and examination for all financial planners.

(E) There are good and bad financial planners, and an investor should choose with care.

GO ON TO THE NEXT PAGE ➤

18. Suzanne discovers that she can play two or three strenuous sets of tennis if she eats a light breakfast and no lunch, but only one set if she has a full meal at either time. She concludes that eating lightly improves her stamina.

Which one of the following most closely resembles the reasoning in the passage above?

(A) David is told that by reducing the fat in his diet he may feel more vigorous in the mornings, but will be more fatigued in the evenings.

(B) Arlene practices golf an hour a day more than Marge and regularly scores better. Arlene concludes that the extra practice makes her the better golfer.

(C) Jean's lawyer tells her that, if she pays her taxes in quarterly payments, she need not pay withholding taxes. She agrees to do so.

(D) Rats that are fed at nine and twelve each day gain more weight than rats that are fed the same total amount of food at a single midafternoon feeding. They also live longer than the rats fed once a day.

(E) Arthur believes that by taking a multivitamin and a vitamin C tablet each day he can reduce the number of colds he has each winter.

Questions 19–20

There is rust between the tines of this fork. This diner must buy cheap utensils. The fork cannot be made of stainless steel.

19. Which one of the following is the best expression of an unstated premise that underlies the reasoning in this passage?

(A) If a diner uses cheap tableware, it will probably save money.

(B) If a utensil is made of stainless steel, it will not rust.

(C) If a utensil is cheap, it will rust quickly.

(D) If there is rust between the tines of a fork, the diner using it must buy cheap tableware.

(E) Nothing that is not made of stainless steel will not rust.

20. Which one of the following could the author logically use to strengthen the argument's conclusion?

(A) Restaurants should not use cheap tableware.

(B) No rusted utensil I have found is made of stainless steel.

(C) Every rusted fork on this table is a cheap utensil.

(D) Cheap utensils are often stolen.

(E) Rusted silverware can be replaced cheaply.

21. Middle-aged American actresses, regardless of their skill, are not trusted to guarantee the box-office success of a film. The audience always wants younger women. While men may be in their forties or fifties, the audiences will not accept women of that age in romantic roles. Middle-aged men often play love scenes with actresses younger than their daughters, while an actress over forty plays a spinster or a nun. Our culture is youth oriented, but with a double standard.

Which one of the following, if true, would most seriously weaken the argument of the passage above?

(A) The largest grossing romantic movie of this year starred a 28-year-old man and a 23-year-old woman.

(B) The most sought-after American actress is paid about 60 percent of the salary of her male co-star.

(C) In European films, actresses continue to appear in romantic roles when they are in their thirties.

(D) The screenplays of two out of three of the year's most successful films were written by women.

(E) The successful film "White Palace" is the love story of an older woman from a blue-collar background and a younger, upper-middle-class man.

GO ON TO THE NEXT PAGE ➤

22. Arthur's explanation of the budget deficit must be the best one because he is the only economist with a Ph.D. who answered the question.

The author of the argument above assumes that

(A) anyone who has a Ph.D. cannot be wrong
(B) any economist who has a Ph.D. is right about economic issues
(C) an economist with a Ph.D. is a better judge of an economic matter than others
(D) an economist with a Ph.D. is a better judge than other economists
(E) any economist with a Ph.D. will usually give the best answer to a question

Questions 23–24

According to conservative grammarians, "hopefully" is a perfectly good English word. It is an adverb, that is, a word used to modify an adjective, verb, or other adverb, and it means "in a hopeful manner." "My horse will win the race," he remarked hopefully. However, the word is not a parenthetical expression that means "I hope," as in "Hopefully, my horse will win the race," he said.

23. The author's argument in this passage includes all of the following EXCEPT

(A) providing an example
(B) explaining the misuse of a word
(C) explaining the proper use of a word
(D) defining a term
(E) drawing an analogy

24. According to the argument of this paragraph, in which one of the following is the word "hopefully" used correctly?

(A) Despite the score of the game after the first half, the coach hopefully encouraged his players.
(B) If we can keep the other team from scoring in the third quarter, hopefully we will score in the fourth.
(C) Hopefully, the other team will begin to make more mistakes, and we can still win this game.
(D) This year my income taxes, hopefully, will be lower than they were last year.
(E) Hopefully, the rain will not start until after we reach home.

25. More than ever before, American TV viewers are watching cable television programs. About 60 percent of American homes are now equipped with cable, and about one quarter of the programs watched are cable programs. Yet some cable networks are already losing their very small share of the audience. They are losing viewers to other cable channels, despite the continuing growth in cable's audience share.

The apparent contradiction of this passage can be explained by the fact that

(A) overall, fewer people are watching any television, network or cable
(B) the monthly fees for cable television deter potential viewers from subscribing to cable channels
(C) video rentals have become increasingly popular and have reduced the number of cable television watchers
(D) only 15 percent of the television shows Americans watch are cable programs, while 85 percent are still network programs
(E) the number of cable channels is increasing more rapidly than the cable television share of the audience

STOP

IF YOU FINISH BEFORE TIME IS UP, CHECK YOUR WORK ON THIS SECTION OF THE TEST ONLY.
DO NOT GO ON TO THE NEXT SECTION OF THE TEST UNTIL TIME IS UP FOR THIS SECTION.

2   **2**   **2**   **2**   **2**

SECTION II
TIME — 35 MINUTES
28 QUESTIONS

Directions: Read the passages and answer the questions following each passage by blackening the appropriate space on the answer sheet. You may refer back to the passages when answering the questions. Answer all questions on the basis of what is stated or implied.

In many ways, the Supreme Court is the worst place to win a human rights case—even when an Earl Warren is
line sitting as Chief Justice. It takes a large
(5) amount of money and a long time to get a case to the Court. Even when a party wins, he may not come out with a clear victory. The decisions are seldom unanimous, and a five-to-four or six-to-
(10) three split tends to weaken the impact of a majority opinion. A Supreme Court decision may have a tremendous effect in the long run, but it seldom brings about immediate major changes.
(15) Most cases do not get to the Supreme Court anyway. This is especially true of human rights disputes, where the parties usually cannot afford to appeal, and their lawyers will never get paid
(20) even if they win because a monetary award seldom goes with a victory on principle. Most disputes never even become lawsuits. People don't tend to go to a lawyer when they think they
(25) have been treated unfairly. They may not know a lawyer they trust; they may not have the money to pay a fee; and they don't think it will help to go to court anyway. This means that for most
(30) people the highest court, the supreme court of the land, is the policeman on the beat, the highway patrolman, the parent, the priest, the landlord, the boss, the creditor, or the voter registrar.
(35) A decision by the Supreme Court guaranteeing human rights has no meaning until these people around the country know about and decide to follow it.
(40) Of course, all the courts and government agencies in the country are required to follow Supreme Court decisions, too. But "the Court's authority—possessed of neither the
(45) purse nor the sword—ultimately rests on sustained public confidence in its moral sanction," as Justice Frankfurter

put it so succinctly. And compliance with Warren Court opinions was
(50) certainly not automatic.
Studying the development of human rights law through the landmark decisions of the Warren Court can lead to increased respect for our legal
(55) system. At the same time it can lead to the opposite conclusion: that the best time to win a human rights case is at the beginning, the best place is where the case starts, the best judge and jury
(60) are the participants, and the best method is without a lawsuit. In other words, the best protectors of human rights are not the courts but rather citizens who know and insist on their
(65) own rights and who act to guarantee the rights of others to freedom, justice, and equality.
Citizens concerned about human rights who were raised during the
(70) Warren Court era came to depend on the Court to right the wrongs created by acts of Congress, executive orders, and lower court decisions, and by the actions of government officials, private
(75) citizens, and groups. The Court did not always fulfill this function, but it did so more often than any previous Supreme Court—and perhaps more often than any Court of the near future. To the
(80) extent it followed and advanced the development of human rights law, it was the Camelot of courts. To the extent it disarmed the people by suggesting reliance on the courts rather than on
(85) their own collective action, it led to disillusionment when Earl Warren stepped down. It is necessary to reassess the opportunities for progress through the judicial system.

GO ON TO THE NEXT PAGE ➤

2   2   2   2   **2**

1. The passage calls the Warren Court the "Camelot of courts" (line 82); this implies that

   (A) it made decisions we usually see only in the movies
   (B) like King Arthur's court, it valued justice and mercy
   (C) Earl Warren was the king and the other justices were knights
   (D) its decisions were mythical
   (E) its decisions were chivalric

2. More often than not, human rights cases

   (A) do not get to the Supreme Court
   (B) are appealed
   (C) result in a split decision
   (D) require high-principled judges
   (E) flounder

3. According to the passage, a human rights case may be won in the Supreme Court, but the winner should NOT expect his victory to bring about

   (A) a unanimous response
   (B) an executive decision
   (C) a clear victory
   (D) immediate major changes
   (E) the approval of the Chief Justice

4. Once the Supreme Court makes a decision, the enforcement of that decision rests largely upon

   (A) a national requirement
   (B) the people's confidence in the Court
   (C) automatic obedience
   (D) the Court's authority
   (E) the support of parents, priests, policemen, and landlords

5. According to the passage, citizens who wish to preserve their human rights must be

   (A) aggressive, knowledgeable, and insistent
   (B) law-abiding and humble
   (C) rich and arrogant
   (D) friends of the Court
   (E) energetic and tenacious

6. The author of this article would probably be the greatest advocate of

   (A) paying jurors a greater amount to serve jury duty
   (B) reviewing more of the Supreme Court decisions
   (C) greater respect for the legal system
   (D) increased compliance with Supreme Court decisions
   (E) decreased reliance on the courts

GO ON TO THE NEXT PAGE ➤

2   **2**   **2**   **2**   **2**

(This passage was written in 1980.)

The exclusionary rule has been continually attacked in recent years as inadequate for its purpose and as a
line "technicality" that allows criminals to
(5) go free since the rule permits exclusion of evidence from a defendant's trial where the evidence was obtained in violation of Fourth Amendment rights against unreasonable searches and
(10) seizures. In a decision of 1961, the Supreme Court held that the exclusionary rule was, in fact, constitutionally required by the Fourth Amendment and not a judicially created
(15) rule of evidence as previously stated in the Wolf decision. This determination of constitutional origin made the exclusionary principle applicable to the states through the due process clause
(20) of the Fourteenth Amendment. The Court relied on the increasing number of states accepting the rule as a matter of law concluding that alternative methods of protecting the Fourth
(25) Amendment's right to be free from unreasonable searches and seizures had been futile. The Court made clear that the purpose of the rule was to deter police abuse of the constitutional right
(30) to be protected from unreasonable searches and seizures by removing any incentive to disregard the guarantee.

A 1974 decision reflects a shift in the Supreme Court's attitude. The precise
(35) issue facing the Court was whether a witness before a grand jury may refuse to answer questions on the ground that they are based on evidence obtained in an illegal search and seizure. The Court
(40) held that the exclusionary rule cannot be invoked by a grand jury witness who is not subject to criminal prosecution. It further concluded that the exclusionary rule was a "judicially created remedy"
(45) rather than a personal constitutional right of the party aggrieved. This conclusion clearly contradicts the 1961 decision, which indicated that the rule was more than just a judicial remedy—it
(50) was a constitutional right applicable to the states.

The immediate ramification is to alter the nature and basis of the rule. It is no longer to be characterized as a personal

(55) right required by the Constitution as a guarantee of protection by the Fourth Amendment. If this conclusion is applicable to future court decisions, it would appear to necessitate an
(60) overruling of the decision of 1961 because the decision of 1974 is contrary to the very heart of that holding. The conspicuous failure of the Court to confront its former decision evidences a
(65) determined effort to reach a different conclusion. This new view evidences the dissatisfaction with the exclusionary rule by the Court and its move toward modification or complete abandonment
(70) of the rule.

In two habeas corpus cases in 1976, it was stated that whereas the states must still apply the exclusionary rule, the responsibility of determining the
(75) constitutionality of the search will fall on the states, rather than the federal courts. Defendants will not be able to challenge the trial court's ruling on the validity of searches in a subsequent
(80) federal habeas corpus proceeding once it has been judged at the state level. It would be an ultimate constitutional disaster to remove the exclusionary rule without some mechanism of police
(85) deterrence. Certainly, no one wants to make the Fourth Amendment a nullity.

7. The primary purpose of the exclusionary rule is to

(A) protect the citizens' rights against any search and seizure
(B) insure that as much relevant evidence as possible is available at trials
(C) deter police from conducting unreasonable searches for evidence
(D) speed up the time spent on criminal trials
(E) encourage the exclusion of irrelevant evidence

GO ON TO THE NEXT PAGE ➤

8. Opponents of the exclusionary rule are likely to cite the following arguments EXCEPT

(A) it permits the guilty to go free on a technicality

(B) it prevents jurors from hearing all the evidence in a case

(C) it encourages law enforcement officers to conceal how evidence was obtained

(D) it protects the criminal but not the law enforcement officer

(E) it protects citizens from unreasonable searches

9. We can infer that the Supreme Court decision in the Wolf case

(A) was handed down after 1961

(B) held the exclusionary rule was not a constitutional right

(C) found the exclusionary rule to be unconstitutional

(D) must extend the exclusionary principle to the states

(E) held the exclusionary rule was not judicially created

10. The phrase "incentive to disregard the guarantee" in line 32 refers to

(A) a felon's temptation to suppress evidence

(B) illegal seizures by law enforcement officers to assure convictions

(C) a state's actions to avoid observing the federal exclusionary rule requirements

(D) rewards given to witnesses in certain criminal prosecutions

(E) the guarantee of freedom from unreasonable search and seizure

11. As a result of the 1974 decision, illegally obtained evidence

(A) could be used against a defendant in a civil trial

(B) could be used against a defendant in a criminal trial

(C) could not be used in questioning a witness

(D) could be used in questioning a witness

(E) was no longer affected by the exclusionary rule

12. The most significant decision of the 1974 case is that

(A) witnesses before a grand jury could be questioned using illegally obtained evidence

(B) witnesses before a grand jury could not be questioned using illegally obtained evidence

(C) the exclusionary rule is not a constitutional right

(D) the exclusionary rule is not a judicially created remedy

(E) the findings in the 1961 decision are reasserted

13. The attitude of the author of this passage to the most recent Supreme Court decisions on the exclusionary rule can best be described as one

(A) of unqualified approval

(B) of qualified approval

(C) of indifference

(D) of disapproval

(E) not expressed in the passage

14. Which one of the following best describes how the passage is organized?

(A) chronologically

(B) by contrasting the specific and the general

(C) by parallel paragraphs

(D) by alternating objective and subjective

(E) anecdotally

GO ON TO THE NEXT PAGE ➤

2   **2**   **2**   **2**   **2**

The United States Supreme Court, in 1977, recognized that establishments selling and exhibiting obscene materials
line are injurious to the public morals and
(5) that the state has the power to regulate such establishments in order to protect the public. Armed with this decision, local prosecutors hoped to take advantage of the relative ease with
(10) which a civil action can be used to abate a public nuisance. For example, in civil proceedings, the plaintiff prosecutor only needs to prove his allegation that the material in question is obscene, and
(15) therefore a public nuisance, by a preponderance of the evidence, rather than beyond a reasonable doubt as is required in criminal proceedings. Furthermore, obtaining an injunction,
(20) even though a temporary one, will halt the display of the questioned material at least until the trial takes place. Also, whenever an equitable remedy, such as an injunction, is sought, a jury is not
(25) required as a matter of right. This is significant because only one person, the judge, must be convinced that the material is obscene, and the job is made easier if the judge is one who adheres to
(30) a broad definition of obscenity.

These substantive and procedural advantages account for the increase in civil nuisance actions to abate the distribution of pornography by closing
(35) down establishments that sell sexually explicit material. However such attempts are limited by the First Amendment prohibition against prior restraints. Inherent in that
(40) amendment's provision for freedom of the press is the aim to avoid "previous restraints of publication" by eliminating any requirement of printing approval by state authorities. In keeping with this
(45) principle, state and federal courts have held that adult bookstores and theaters may be abated as a public nuisance only after all the material sold or exhibited has been determined to be obscene.
(50) In Florida, the state supreme court ruled that a business could be prohibited from selling or exhibiting material if it consists of specifically named books, magazines, or movies
(55) previously judicially determined to be obscene, but the business could not be

closed unless and until all the material sold or shown there was judged to be obscene. It reasoned that closing
(60) bookstores or theaters, even temporarily, before all the material is determined to be obscene is in effect to forbid the sale or exhibition of constitutionally protected books,
(65) magazines, or films, as well as potentially obscene matter. This, the court called an "impermissible prior restraint in violation of the First and Fourteenth Amendments."
(70) Although adult bookstores and theaters cannot be closed by using public nuisance actions, zoning ordinances may be used to regulate their location. The restrictions could
(75) permit such establishments anywhere within the city limits provided certain conditions are met. Such an ordinance was enacted by the city of Detroit and it was upheld by the United States
(80) Supreme Court. The ordinance prohibited adult bookstores, adult motion picture theaters, and adult minitheaters within five hundred feet from a residential dwelling or rooming
(85) unit.

15. Which one of the following titles best summarizes the content of the passage?

(A) Pornography and Zoning
(B) Using Nuisance Ordinances to Control Pornography
(C) Using Zoning Ordinances to Control Pornography
(D) The Prohibition of Using Nuisance Ordinances to Control Pornography
(E) Legal Arguments for Using Nuisance Ordinances to Control Pornography

16. All of the following might be cited as examples of public nuisance EXCEPT

(A) a pickpocket
(B) a pig farm in a residential district
(C) a malicious billboard
(D) a poker parlor
(E) a leaking factory afterburner

GO ON TO THE NEXT PAGE ➤

2 **2** **2** **2** **2**

17. According to the passage, the First Amendment seeks to

    (A) guarantee the freedom of the press to publish whatever it found appropriate
    (B) guarantee the citizens' right to read according to the dictates of conscience
    (C) assure state or federal approval of matter before it is printed
    (D) avoid state or federal approval of matter before it is printed
    (E) protect publishers of so-called obscene materials

18. The advantages of using public nuisance statutes to close a pornographic bookshop would include all of the following EXCEPT

    (A) a burden to prove obscenity only by a preponderance of the evidence
    (B) the halting of display if an injunction is obtained
    (C) the possibility of avoiding a jury in the injunction request
    (D) the need to convince only one person of the obscenity of the material
    (E) the closing of a bookstore may precede the determining that the material on sale is obscene

19. According to the passage, the effect of the Supreme Court's 1977 decision (lines 1–7) was to

    (A) make it possible for prosecutors to use public nuisance laws against establishments exhibiting obscene materials
    (B) increase the number of civil prosecutions of pornographic exhibitors
    (C) decrease the number of prosecutions against pornographic exhibitors
    (D) greatly increase the number of successful closings of pornographic theaters and bookstores
    (E) greatly decrease the number of successful closings of pornographic theaters and bookstores

20. The appeal of an establishment that has exhibited demonstrably obscene material in the past and has been closed after prosecution for public nuisance would

    (A) probably be upheld at all levels
    (B) probably be upheld but only if the federal court also found the material obscene
    (C) result in permission to open under more liberal public nuisance statutes
    (D) probably result in permission to open until all currently displayed materials were found to be obscene
    (E) probably be upheld on the grounds that the exhibition of obscenity is injurious to public morals

21. It is likely to be difficult to close an adult bookshop using public nuisance ordinances because the bookshop

    (A) may change its location
    (B) may close voluntarily
    (C) is permitted to remain open until all the material sold or exhibited has been found to be obscene
    (D) cannot change its books
    (E) can be prohibited from selling specifically named books previously judicially determined to be obscene

22. The advantage of controlling adult theaters and bookstores by zoning regulations rather than by nuisance ordinances is that zoning ordinances

    (A) are less costly to enforce
    (B) are supported by a greater portion of the public
    (C) are not likely to be reversed for impermissible prior restraint
    (D) are more easily amended than public nuisance laws
    (E) can be used to prohibit theaters and bookstores within a thousand feet of someone's home

GO ON TO THE NEXT PAGE ➤

2   **2**   **2**   **2**   **2**

Mary Hamilton, a twenty-eight-year-old black field secretary for the Congress of Racial Equality (CORE),

line participated in a demonstration in
(5) Gadsden, Alabama, in 1963. White police officers arrested her, along with fellow demonstrators. Believing their arrests to be unlawful, the group petitioned the Circuit Court of Etowah
(10) County for release on a writ of habeas corpus (unlawful imprisonment). The hearing on the petition was held on June 25, before Judge Cunningham, a white judge, assisted by white court
(15) clerks and bailiffs.

Black attorneys Charles Conley and Norman Amaker represented the petitioners and white Solicitor Rayburn spoke for the state. Mr. Rayburn
(20) followed the southern establishment practice of addressing each black witness by his or her first name, despite objections from the opposing counsel.

When Mary Hamilton completed her
(25) direct testimony, Solicitor Rayburn began his cross-examination by asking, "What is your name, please?"

"Miss Mary Hamilton."

"Mary, . . . who were you arrested
(30) by?"

"My name is Miss Hamilton. Please address me correctly," she said.

"Who were you arrested by, Mary?" the solicitor asked again, deliberately.
(35) "I will not answer a question—" she began, and Attorney Amaker interjected, "The witness's name is Miss Hamilton."

"—your question until I am addressed correctly," she finished.
(40) "Answer the question," Judge Cunningham ordered.

Miss Hamilton would not be intimidated. "I will not answer them unless I am addressed correctly."
(45) "You are in contempt of court," ruled the judge.

"Your Honor—your Honor—" Attorney Conley began, but the judge paid no attention.
(50) "You are in contempt of this court," he went on, "and you are sentenced to five days in jail and a fifty-dollar fine."

Miss Hamilton was taken to jail then and there, and served the five days.
(55) Since she did not intend to pay the fine, and therefore would be subject to

another twenty days in jail, she was allowed out on bond to appeal the contempt conviction.
(60) On July 25, she petitioned the Alabama Supreme Court to review the contempt citation on two grounds. Her lawyers contended that the solicitor's manner of addressing black witnesses
(65) violated the equal protection clause of the Fourteenth Amendment. Finding no cases on this point, they relied on logic, history, and etiquette. They rejected the state's reliance on Emily Post and Amy
(70) Vanderbilt because their books did not discuss the use of first names in a racial situation. They also reminded the court that Miss Hamilton's contempt conviction violated the due process
(75) clause because she was summarily sentenced without even being given a trial—an opportunity to present a defense to the charge. (Remember the Red Queen in *Alice in Wonderland*—
(80) "sentence first, trial afterward"?) The Alabama Supreme Court found, however, that "the question was a lawful one and the witness invoked no valid legal exemption to support her refusal to
(85) answer it."

The NAACP Legal Defense and Educational Fund then took the case up to the United States Supreme Court for review. The defense lawyers relied on
(90) long-standing principles governing the conduct of prosecuting attorneys: as quasi-judicial officers of the court they are under a duty not to prejudice a party's case through overzealous
(95) prosecution or to detract from the impartiality of courtroom atmosphere. The defense presented historical and sociological proof that the forms of address used by Solicitor Rayburn were
(100) a distinct part of a "racial caste system" that deprived black citizens of equal protection of the laws. They also quoted from novels by Richard Wright, James Baldwin, and Lillian Smith. The United
(105) States Supreme Court handed down a summary decision the same day. Six justices joined in an order reversing Miss Hamilton's contempt citation.

GO ON TO THE NEXT PAGE ➤

2 **2** **2** **2** **2**

23. By objecting to being addressed by her first name, Mary Hamilton implies that such an address is

    (A) illegal
    (B) not appropriate in a southern court
    (C) incorrect and demeaning
    (D) defamatory and criminal
    (E) unfortunate

24. By alluding to *Alice in Wonderland*, the author seems to brand the judge as

    (A) a literary artifact
    (B) an absurd tyrant
    (C) childish
    (D) an intimidating legislator
    (E) an insensitive official

25. We must presume that the author of this passage was either present at the trial or

    (A) given a brief summary of the outcome
    (B) able to secure a transcript of the court proceedings
    (C) able to secure a paraphrase of the court proceedings
    (D) consulted with the judge
    (E) consulted with Mary Hamilton

26. The question raised but left unanswered in this passage is which one of the following?

    (A) Is impartiality possible?
    (B) What did the U.S. Supreme Court decide?
    (C) Is Mary Hamilton still politically active?
    (D) Can a court ruling be made without precedent?
    (E) Are Emily Post and Amy Vanderbilt recognized authorities?

27. By stressing that the judge and the court staff were white, the author implies which one of the following questions?

    (A) Was the court biased against Mary Hamilton?
    (B) Should the legal profession in Alabama be integrated?
    (C) Should Mary Hamilton have been tried in another court?
    (D) Is the race of judges less crucial today?
    (E) Is the race of the judge more important than that of the arresting officers?

28. The author suggests that the judge's response to Miss Hamilton was an effort to

    (A) intimidate the witness
    (B) demonstrate that only the judge should be formally addressed
    (C) cut short the cross examination
    (D) elicit an answer that would help decide the case
    (E) offer a popular ruling

STOP

IF YOU FINISH BEFORE TIME IS UP, CHECK YOUR WORK ON THIS SECTION OF THE TEST ONLY.
DO NOT GO ON TO THE NEXT SECTION OF THE TEST UNTIL TIME IS UP FOR THIS SECTION.

3   **3**   **3**   **3**   **3**

SECTION III
TIME — 35 MINUTES
25 QUESTIONS

Directions: In this section you will be given brief statements or passages and will be required to evaluate the reasoning involved. In some instances, more than one choice will appear to be a possible answer. You are to choose the *best* answer. Use common sense and reasonableness in making your selection; then mark the proper space on the answer sheet.

1. The use of polystyrene for packaging fast food is, fortunately, on the way out. But Carol Wilson has complained in a letter to the editor that paper containers do not keep foods warm or greaseless. She reasons that, because the rocks in landfills biodegrade slowly, we should not worry if plastic cups and hamburger boxes are slow too. And with all the mountain ranges in America, she goes on, there can be no shortage of landfills.

The author's case against Carol Wilson's letter can be strengthened by pointing out all of the following EXCEPT

(A) many areas of the country have no mountain ranges
(B) the use of mountain ranges for landfills would make them unavailable for other uses
(C) Carol Wilson's letter to the editor is a tongue-in-cheek parody of antienvironmentalism
(D) the manufacture of Styrofoam containers releases chemicals that deplete the ozone layer
(E) plastics are manufactured from petroleum products, the supply of which is limited

2. A light rain has fallen on the Concord Turnpike. Seventy-five percent of the 400 yearly traffic accidents on this turnpike take place when the road is wet. Furthermore, two-car collisions are most likely to take place at the evening rush hour between 5 and 6 o'clock in the winter. It is now 5 PM, in January.

In addition to the information above, which of the following would be most useful for determining the probability that there will be a two-car collision on the Concord Turnpike in the next hour?

(A) the percentage of traffic accidents that take place on other roads under the same circumstances
(B) the percentage of wet-road traffic accidents on the turnpike that are two-car collisions
(C) the percentage of evening-rush-hour, winter-traffic accidents that take place on the turnpike when the road is wet
(D) the percentage of rush-hour, winter traffic accidents that take place when the road is not wet
(E) the number of cars involved in traffic accidents on the highways in the month of January

GO ON TO THE NEXT PAGE ➤

3. If you were allowed to enter the United States after 1965, you must have had a polio shot.

The statement above can be logically deduced from which one of the following?

(A) Only if a person were allowed to enter the United States after 1965 could he have had a polio shot.
(B) No one permitted to enter the United States before 1965 had a polio shot.
(C) All people allowed to enter the United States after 1965 have had polio shots.
(D) Before 1965, a polio shot was not required for entry to the United States.
(E) All polio shots have been administered after 1965.

Questions 4–5

A recession is not always bad news for everyone. During hard times, people spend money on repairing broken possessions rather than on buying new ones. Repair services from shoe cobblers to computer technicians are already reporting an increase in business. An increase in repairs can offset a drop in the sales of new items for appliance stores that handle both new sales and repairs.

But there may not be a recession right now. This time of year is usually a busy time in repair shops. And people may be holding onto their money because they fear a recession, not because one is here already. But one businessman claims his sales are always a sure sign. When repairs account for more than 60 percent of his business, the economy is in bad shape.

4. We can infer from the information in the passage

(A) that a recession is bad news for most businesses
(B) that the business of repair shops is likely to thrive in times of economic prosperity
(C) that a recession is now in progress
(D) that, if repair services report an increase in business, there is certainly no recession
(E) that, during a recession, consumers are likely to spend more money

5. The most logical final sentence of the second paragraph would

(A) conclude there is no recession
(B) conclude there is a recession
(C) conclude that we do not yet know whether or not there is a recession
(D) reveal the percentage of repair sales of the businessman
(E) disagree with the businessman's reasoning

---

6. All of Fedmart's customers pay by using Fedmart charge accounts. Only if the O'Haras pay by Fedmart charge will they buy garden tools or rose bushes, but not both and not anything else.

If the O'Haras bought rose bushes, which one of the following must be true?

(A) The O'Haras bought garden tools.
(B) The O'Haras paid by charge account.
(C) The O'Haras paid in cash.
(D) The O'Haras have no charge accounts.
(E) The O'Haras also bought rose food.

3　　**3**　　**3**　　**3**　　**3**

7. In three years, six whales have died at Sea World, including three killer whales. Officials maintain that five of the six died of diseases that could have taken their lives in the wild. The deaths may affect the breeding of killer whales as the Sea World parks have twelve females, but just one male. Since the lone male is not related to any of the females, there is no genetic reason why he cannot mate with them all. The parks have produced five healthy captive-born babies. Breeding is necessary since Sea World's economic success depends on killer whales, and no federal permits to capture the whales have been issued for some time.

Which one of the following, if true, would tend to support the argument that the parks are not depleting the killer whale population?

(A) The transportation of killer whales from one park to another presents a threat to their health.
(B) In the wild, killer whales live longer than killer whales in theme parks.
(C) Three of the killer whales born in captivity died within a year.
(D) Killer whales in captivity are less fertile than those in the wild.
(E) Killer whales in theme parks are protected against diseases common in the wild.

8. *Researcher:* When asked if they would prefer to add ten points to their IQs or three inches to their height, most American men preferred to be taller, while most American women chose the gain in intelligence.

All of the following may be logically inferred from this statement EXCEPT

(A) to be taller is more important to most men than to most women
(B) to be taller is more important to most men than to be more intelligent
(C) to be taller is not as important to most women as to be more intelligent
(D) to be less intelligent is less important to most men than to be taller
(E) to be taller is more important to most men than to be more intelligent is to most women

GO ON TO THE NEXT PAGE ➤

3   **3**   **3**   **3**   **3**

Questions 9–10

Professor Marks: Contrary to popular Western beliefs, the Islamic religion does not forbid women to participate in economic and political life. The Koran has never excluded women from access to education, public office, or employment. The blame lies with social custom and conservative leaders in the male-dominated societies of the Arab world. And despite the prejudices against women in public life, a small number of women have had some success. In Turkey, a woman serves in a Cabinet position, and for a time Benazir Bhutto was Prime Minister of Pakistan.

9. Professor Marks makes her points by using all of the following EXCEPT

  (A) citing a specific case in support of her opinion
  (B) disputing evidence cited by the opposition
  (C) alluding to a popular misconception
  (D) pointing to specific causes of injustice
  (E) referring to spiritual authority

10. If true, which one of the following would not weaken the professor's argument that Arab women can succeed in politics?

  (A) Benazir Bhutto's political power was due more to her being a member of a powerful family than to her gender.
  (B) There are no women in positions of leadership in the Persian Gulf states.
  (C) The female Cabinet member in Turkey is a self-made politician from a modest background.
  (D) Moslem voters in India always strongly opposed Indira Gandhi.
  (E) There are no females in positions of political power in Syria or Iraq.

11. Twenty-five years ago, the poor in America were disproportionately old and female. Now the greater part of those living below the poverty level are young, including children. Women, however, still suffer more than men. The older Americans have taken matters into their hands and promoted legislation that protects them. Laws like Proposition 13 in California and rent controls in New York were intended to allow the elderly to keep their homes after they had retired. But the laws also keep housing out of the reach of younger people with growing families. And now a Republican assemblyman is proposing that senior citizens with no children in the public schools should be exempted from school taxes.

Using the same line of reasoning as the Republican assemblyman, it could be argued that

  (A) the young have a greater need of a tax break than the old
  (B) the greater part of the tax burden already falls upon younger taxpayers
  (C) younger taxpayers should be exempted from taxes that support medical payments to the elderly
  (D) the tax burden should fall more heavily on men than on women
  (E) laws like Proposition 13 and rent controls should be overturned

GO ON TO THE NEXT PAGE ➤

12. A computer analysis of 180,000 drivers shows that women are generally safer drivers than men. Sixteen-year-old girls get fewer traffic tickets than sixteen-year-old boys, and women tend to have fewer accidents at all age levels except at 18, where the sexes are alike and worse than at any other age.

The results of the analysis would be strengthened if all of the following could be shown EXCEPT that

(A) the survey considered how many miles per week both the men and the women drive
(B) equal numbers of men and women were studied
(C) the survey considered drivers in both rural and urban situations
(D) the survey considered drivers of automobiles of similar types
(E) statistics of eighteen-year-old male drivers were compared to those of females of other ages

13. *Editorial:* Does anyone need to be told about the corrupting influence of money on government? The latest revelation comes from internal campaign documents showing that aides and commissioners appointed by the mayor have raised more than a million dollars for her reelection war chest. Much of that money came from business people with contracts with the city. One cannot help asking if there was a *quid pro quo* (something for something).

To make matters worse, these same aides and commissioners were out raising funds on city time, not on their weekends. Unless the voters enact some ethics laws to prohibit officials from activities like these, the practices will continue. And, if anything that has been done is already illegal, the city attorney should prosecute to recover the public resources that have been lost.

All of the following are implied but not explicitly stated by the editorial EXCEPT

(A) business people have contributed to the mayor's campaign funds in order to secure city contracts
(B) the unethical actions of the aides and commissioners are not prohibited by law
(C) if the mayor wins reelection, she will owe favors to business contributors
(D) city aides and commissioners have been fundraising for the mayor rather than doing the jobs for which they are paid
(E) the awarding of city contracts is influenced by the mayor and her staff

GO ON TO THE NEXT PAGE ➤

Questions 14–15

A survey at an eastern state university suggests that most of the large impersonal universities are plagued by dishonest students. A poll of 230 students revealed that 78 percent of them cheated at one time or another and 33 percent admitted cheating regularly. The techniques included copying from other students' exams, using cheat sheets, plagiarizing papers, and stealing tests in advance. Members of fraternities and sororities were more likely to cheat than nonmembers, and the worst offenders were students majoring in economics. That economics majors were the most likely to cheat raised the question whether such dishonesty was "anticipatory socialization for modern American business life."

The motives for cheating were diverse. Competition for entrance into graduate school was the most often cited, but sheer laziness and a preference for partying over studying were common. More than half of the students said their cheating was motivated by a desire for revenge against indifferent professors, large lecture classes, and professors too lazy to make up new examinations each year.

14. The quotation that concludes the first paragraph of the passage implies that

   (A) cheating is commonplace in American business
   (B) economics majors are likely to have to cheat to achieve the grades necessary for admission to American business schools
   (C) American businesspeople anticipate very active social lives
   (D) economics majors who cheat as undergraduates will not be accepted by the American business community
   (E) American businesspeople would question the charge that economics majors are more likely to cheat

15. From the information in the second paragraph we can infer all of the following EXCEPT

   (A) there is less cheating in classes with small enrollments
   (B) premedical and prelaw students are more likely to cheat than students who do not plan on a graduate education
   (C) there will probably be less cheating in the class of a professor who is diligent, well prepared, and well liked by students than in the class of a less able teacher
   (D) both teachers and students may be lazy
   (E) most professors use the same examinations year after year

3   **3**   **3**   **3**   **3**

16. Unlike historians elsewhere, Russian textbook writers cannot revise or rewrite the history books now in print, which are seriously distorted. For more than sixty years, history textbooks have been used to indoctrinate Russian school children, and have contained only statements that supported the views of the leaders in power. But there are now no censors waiting to cut out any offending truth, and historians must start almost from scratch.

In many ways, the old history was easier to write. New historians must separate the truth from the lies, evasions, and half-truths of the books in print. Many sources are still unavailable. Newspapers and magazines are constantly reporting revised versions of history, and every month a famous figure from the past may be rehabilitated or vilified. After a lifetime of caution and self-censorship, historians discover that writing history as it really happened requires a whole new way of thinking.

The author of the passage believes all of the following EXCEPT

(A) Russian historians wrote inaccurate and untrustworthy accounts of historical events

(B) historians in Europe and the United States do not have to deal with many of the problems facing contemporary Russian historians

(C) a Russian history book written in 1950 would reflect the views of the people in power at that time

(D) we now know that Russian men of the past will be reevaluated and rehabilitated

(E) historians of the last sixty years in Russia were subject to self-censorship and state censorship

17. The average value of a share of stock on the American Stock Exchange has increased by 20 percent in the last year. Therefore the value of the shares of bank stocks listed on the American Stock Exchange cannot have gone down in the same period of time.

The reasoning in the passage above is parallel to the reasoning in which one of the following?

(A) The costs of transcontinental flights have declined in each of the last three years. Therefore the cost of railway fare from New York to San Francisco cannot have remained unchanged.

(B) American troops are no longer stationed at air force bases in Great Britain. Therefore American troops are no longer stationed at bases in Europe.

(C) The price of fruits and vegetables has decreased slightly for each of the last six months. Therefore the cost of Winesap and Granny Smith apples cannot have risen in the last two quarters.

(D) Americans watch more television each week than Europeans. Therefore, Americans watch more television each year than Europeans.

(E) The price of unleaded gasoline has remained unchanged for six months. Therefore, the price of leaded gasoline and heating oil cannot have changed for six months.

GO ON TO THE NEXT PAGE ➤

18. The Hemlock Society advocates the legalization of euthanasia in the United States. Its founder, Derek Humphry, believes that, when two doctors have verified that a patient's condition is terminal, the patient should be permitted to put an end to life. In 1984, Holland sanctioned euthanasia by doctors when requested by patients. A physician's-aid-in-dying bill will shortly be voted on in the state of Washington, and the state Medical Association has already opposed the proposal.

All of the following supporting arguments would be reasonable for doctors to use to oppose the passage of the bill described in this paragraph EXCEPT

(A) it is possible that the two doctors making the terminal diagnosis would be wrong

(B) if the bill fails to pass, a doctor who assisted in a suicide could be charged with murder

(C) it is inappropriate for doctors to be participants in the intentional death of a patient

(D) it is possible that a patient who has elected euthanasia will have a change of mind

(E) it is possible that a new cure for a disease believed to be terminal may be found

3   **3**   **3**   **3**   **3**

Questions 19–20

About two thirds of the eligible voters did not cast ballots in the recent election in which all of the members of the House of Representatives were chosen. Once again, the United States placed near the bottom in the scale of eligible voters participating in a national election. All over the country, politicians, educators, and newspaper columnists are expressing horror at the low voter turnout. Because the rich or well-to-do are more likely to vote than the poor, are the poor being disenfranchised? Because older people are more likely to vote than young ones, do the elderly have an unfair influence? The answers to these and questions like them are very surprising.

19. If the electorate was only one third of the total of eligible voters and this third was an accurate cross section of the whole electorate, the election results would

   (A) reflect the will of the whole voting population
   (B) unfairly prevent two thirds of the potential voters from expressing their preference
   (C) probably represent the preference of rich or well-to-do voters
   (D) probably represent the preference of young rather than older voters
   (E) determine the winners of all 100 Senate seats

20. The concern of those who deplore the large number of nonvoters would probably be lessened by all of the following, if true, EXCEPT

   (A) Switzerland, generally regarded as one of the best governed countries in the world, has an even lower percentage of voter turnout than the United States
   (B) two different polls in 1988 found that the nonvoters preferred President Bush over Michael Dukakis by exactly the same margin as the voters
   (C) the demographic differences between voters and nonvoters are narrowing each year because voters in all economic groups have stopped going to the polls
   (D) the same percentage of Asian, Hispanic, African-American, and white voters failed to vote
   (E) of voters over 60, ten percent failed to vote, while ten percent of the voters between 18 and 28 voted in the 1988 election

---

21. *Jane:* I can't afford not to pay a gardener and a maid each ten dollars an hour to take care of my lawn and to do my housework.

Of the following, the most logical interpretation of Jane's comment is that

   (A) Jane's time is worth more than ten dollars an hour
   (B) Jane is compulsively neat
   (C) Jane is indifferent to how much money she spends each week
   (D) most gardeners and maids earn much more than ten dollars an hour
   (E) Jane has no sympathy for the working class

GO ON TO THE NEXT PAGE ➤

3   3   3   3   3

22. Every year about 100,000 fewer fishing licenses are sold in California, so the state is now short of funds to protect wildlife and restock the streams and lakes. The decline in fishing is blamed on drought, pollution, and development. Five years of drought have dried up many trout streams, but the decline in angling began before the drought. Diversion of water supplies to farmers has caused major damage. To reach streams, city dwellers have to travel on overcrowded roads, and even the mountain air may be choked with smog. Once-quiet lakes are now crowded with water-skiers and the shores are lined with condominiums. Tackle shops must now sell video games to survive. Programs that manage and protect fish habitats will have one million dollars less this year, and one fifth of the staff biologists will lose their jobs.

All of the following can be inferred from the information above EXCEPT

(A) the habitats of fish have declined because of human encroachment on wild areas

(B) a primary cause of the decline in fishing in California is the increase in population

(C) as the number of fishermen declines, the quality of the fish habitats can be expected to decline

(D) a primary cause of the decline in fishing in California is the high cost of fishing licenses

(E) if current trends continue, the number of fish in California lakes and streams will decline

23. There were no arrests for currency smuggling at Logan International Airport this month. Therefore, illegal currencies are no longer being smuggled into the United States.

The flawed reasoning of the above is like that of all of the following EXCEPT

(A) The termite inspections revealed no sign of the insects in any of the even-numbered houses on Third Avenue. Therefore, there are no termites in the houses on Third Avenue.

(B) The Save-a-lot Stores are selling boneless chicken breasts for 99 cents a pound. Therefore, all of the supermarkets in the city will have chicken breasts on sale.

(C) There are no weeds in the flower gardens of the Silverlake Park. Therefore, the gardens must have been weeded earlier in the week.

(D) The head of the accounting department has been found guilty of tax evasion. Therefore tax fraud must be widespread among employees of the company.

(E) The captain of the high school cross-country team has agreed to participate in the 10 kilometer run this weekend. Therefore, all of the cross-country teams will run in this race.

GO ON TO THE NEXT PAGE ➤

3   **3**   **3**   **3**   **3**

Questions 24–25

The literary critics of the eighteenth and most of the nineteenth centuries expected a work to instruct and please, and were equally concerned with the art and the moral values of a poem, play, or novel. But in the 1890s, a number of influential critics insisted that the aesthetic pleasure of a work was all-important, and that it was possible for a great work of art to teach no moral lesson at all. More than anything else, this change differentiates the fiction of the eighteenth and the nineteenth centuries from that written in the first 30 years of the twentieth century.

24. Which one of the following is an assumption that this passage makes?

(A) The novels of the eighteenth and nineteenth centuries are less pleasurable than those of the early twentieth century.
(B) The ideas of literary critics are reflected in the literature of their periods.
(C) In the novel, moral values are more important than aesthetic values.
(D) The novels of the eighteenth century and the nineteenth century are essentially the same.
(E) Literature should reflect the social realities of the period in which it is written.

25. If the passage is correct, which one of the following can we infer about the novels of the early twentieth century?

(A) They will be franker in the portrayal of sexuality than the novels of the eighteenth century.
(B) They will be artistically superior to those of the nineteenth century.
(C) Their content will not be determined chiefly by a moral purpose.
(D) Their content will not be influenced by contemporary critical theory.
(E) The greatest works will have no moral purpose.

STOP

IF YOU FINISH BEFORE TIME IS UP, CHECK YOUR WORK ON THIS SECTION OF THE TEST ONLY.
DO NOT GO ON TO THE NEXT SECTION OF THE TEST UNTIL TIME IS UP FOR THIS SECTION.

4   **4**   **4**   **4**   **4**

SECTION IV
Time—35 minutes
23 Questions

<u>Directions:</u> In this section you will be given groups of questions based on different sets of conditions. Drawing a simple diagram may be helpful in answering some of the questions. You are to choose the *best* answer and mark the corresponding space on your answer sheet.

Questions 1–5

On the third Saturday of each month the six members of the Sweeney High School drama club go to the movies together. The club is made up of three boys, Tom, Fred, and Simon, and three girls, Jan, Lynn, and Enola. The members of the drama club always sit in the same row, which has only six seats. The members always follow these seating rules:

No members of the same sex sit next to each other.

No members who are relatives sit next to each other.

Fred has members of the club sitting on each side of him.

Lynn sits between Fred and Simon, and next to each of them.

Enola sits in the first seat and Simon sits in the last seat.

Tom and Lynn are siblings and are the only members of the club who are related.

1. Which one of the following statements must be true?

   (A) Enola sits between Tom and Fred.
   (B) Fred sits between Jan and Lynn, but not next to either one.
   (C) Tom sits next to Enola, and next to Jan.
   (D) Lynn sits next to Fred, but not Simon.
   (E) Jan sits between Tom and Simon, and next to each.

2. Which one of the following must be FALSE?

   (A) Tom sits next to Jan.
   (B) Enola sits next to only one friend.
   (C) Lynn sits next to Tom.
   (D) Fred sits next to Lynn.
   (E) Lynn sits between Enola and Simon.

3. Which one of the following is a possible seating arrangement of the members?

   (A) Enola, Tom, Jan, Fred, Lynn, Simon
   (B) Enola, Fred, Jan, Tom, Lynn, Simon
   (C) Simon, Lynn, Tom, Jan, Fred, Enola
   (D) Simon, Tom, Lynn, Fred, Jan, Enola
   (E) Fred, Lynn, Simon, Enola, Tom, Jan

4. If Enola, Jan, and Tom leave the theater and three new members of the club decided to take their seats following the same seating rules, which one of the following must be true?

   (A) The three new members are all males.
   (B) The three new members are all females.
   (C) Two of the new members are males.
   (D) Two of the new members are females.
   (E) A male new member sits in the first seat.

5. If Enola and Simon do not sit in the end seats, but instead sit next to each other in the two seats in the middle, then which one of the following is a complete and accurate list of the members who could sit next to Tom?

   (A) Enola
   (B) Enola, Jan
   (C) Enola, Jan, Simon
   (D) Enola, Jan, Lynn
   (E) Jan, Lynn, Fred

GO ON TO THE NEXT PAGE ➤

4   **4**   **4**   **4**   **4**

Questions 6–12

There are several clubs available to students at Middlemont High. Many students belong to several different clubs. The names of the clubs are the Actors, Banders, Copycats, Daters, Exercisers, Gumchewers, Jumpers, and Marchers. Membership in the clubs is controlled by the following restrictions:

    All Actors, Banders, and Copycats are Daters.
    All Banders are Actors.
    All Exercisers are Banders.
    All Actors are Gumchewers.
    No Copycats are Banders.
    Some, but not all, Copycats are Actors.

6. Which one of the following must be true?

    (A) All Actors are Exercisers.
    (B) All Gumchewers are Daters.
    (C) Some but not all Exercisers are Actors.
    (D) Some Copycats are Gumchewers.
    (E) All Copycats are Gumchewers.

7. Which one of the following must be FALSE?

    (A) All Actors are Daters.
    (B) All Exercisers are Actors.
    (C) All Gumchewers are Daters.
    (D) No Exercisers are Copycats.
    (E) Some Copycats are Banders.

8. If all Daters are Gumchewers, then

    (A) all Copycats are Gumchewers
    (B) all Gumchewers are Copycats
    (C) all Copycats are Actors
    (D) all Actors are Copycats
    (E) all Daters are Banders

9. If Q is a Copycat, then Q must also be

    (A) an Actor
    (B) a Bander
    (C) a Gumchewer
    (D) a Dater
    (E) an Exerciser

10. Which one of the following statements involving Gumchewers is true?

    (A) If all Copycats are Actors, then all Gumchewers are Actors.
    (B) All Gumchewers are Daters.
    (C) Gumchewers and Banders have nothing in common.
    (D) Some Copycats that are not Gumchewers are Actors.
    (E) Some Gumchewers may not be Daters.

11. If all Jumpers are Banders, then all Jumpers must be

    (A) Actors and Copycats
    (B) Actors and Daters
    (C) Actors and Exercisers
    (D) Copycats and Exercisers
    (E) Copycats and Daters

12. If all Daters are Marchers, then all the following must be Marchers EXCEPT

    (A) Copycats
    (B) Actors
    (C) Gumchewers
    (D) Banders
    (E) Exercisers

GO ON TO THE NEXT PAGE ➤

4　　　4　　　4　　　4　　　4

Questions 13–18

An interior designer is choosing colors for six items in a room. These six items are carpet, drapes, two chairs, and two sofas. The possible colors to choose from are light green, dark green, blue, and yellow. The following restrictions apply to the choices:

Not more than two of the six items are the same color, that is, no color may be used more than twice.

Blue may not be used for the carpet.

Not more than one chair may be blue.

If the drapes are light green, then one of the sofas must be light green and one of the chairs must be dark green.

Both chairs may not be yellow, but either one could be.

If the carpet is yellow, then neither of the sofas can be dark green.

13. If one chair is yellow and the drapes are light green, which one of the following must be true?

    (A) If the carpet is yellow, one sofa is blue.
    (B) If the carpet is dark green, one sofa is dark green.
    (C) Only one item is light green.
    (D) Two items are dark green.
    (E) The carpet cannot be dark green.

14. If one sofa is yellow, the drapes are yellow and the carpet is a different color than either sofa, then what is NOT a possible color combination for the two chairs?

    (A) blue and dark green
    (B) light green and dark green
    (C) blue and light green
    (D) blue and yellow
    (E) light green and light green

15. If the carpet cannot be light green and both chairs are dark green, then which one of the following must be true?

    (A) One of the sofas must be yellow.
    (B) One of the sofas must be dark green.
    (C) The two sofas could be the same color.
    (D) The carpet may be blue.
    (E) If the carpet is yellow, the drapes must be blue.

16. If the carpet and drapes are the same color, which one of the following CANNOT be true?

    (A) Both sofas may be blue.
    (B) Both chairs may be light green.
    (C) Both sofas may be yellow.
    (D) Both sofas may be dark green.
    (E) Both chairs may be dark green.

17. If the two chairs and two sofas are the same color combination pairs, then which one of the following could NOT be that color combination?

    (A) blue and yellow
    (B) light green and yellow
    (C) dark green and yellow
    (D) light green and dark green
    (E) dark green and blue

18. If dark green is not used, which one of the following must be true?

    (A) The sofas are not yellow.
    (B) The drapes are not blue.
    (C) The carpet is not light green.
    (D) The carpet is not yellow.
    (E) The drapes are not light green.

GO ON TO THE NEXT PAGE ➤

4   **4**   **4**   **4**   **4**

Questions 19–23

In a certain culture, people have either blue eyes or green eyes; also, they have either red hair or brown hair.

   All males have either blue eyes or brown hair, or both.

   All females have either green eyes or red hair, or both.

   Male children always retain both of the father's characteristics for eyes and hair.

   All female children retain only one of their father's traits and the other of their mother's traits for eyes and hair.

19. If all the children born of a blue-eyed, brown-haired male each have blue eyes and red hair, then which one of the following must be true?

   (A) Their mother has green eyes.
   (B) None of the children is a girl.
   (C) Their mother has blue eyes.
   (D) They have a red-haired mother.
   (E) They have a brown-haired mother.

20. A blue-eyed, brown-haired male and a blue-eyed, red-haired female marry (first generation) and many years later are blessed with one grandchild. This grandchild (third generation) has red hair and green eyes. Which one of the following must be true?

   (A) The child of the first generation is a male.
   (B) The grandchild is a male.
   (C) If the child of the first generation is female, she has brown hair.
   (D) The grandchild's father has red hair.
   (E) The father from the second generation has green eyes.

21. A blue-eyed, brown-haired male and a green-eyed, red-haired female have a child. All of the following are possible characteristics of the child EXCEPT

   (A) green eyes, brown hair
   (B) red hair, blue eyes
   (C) green eyes, red hair
   (D) blue eyes, brown hair
   (E) all are possible

22. A green-eyed male

   (A) may have red hair
   (B) may have brown hair
   (C) must have red hair
   (D) must have brown hair
   (E) has the same hair color as his mother

23. Two blue-eyed people get married. If their child has red hair, it must be true that

   (A) the child has brown eyes
   (B) the mother has red hair
   (C) the child is a male
   (D) the child is a female
   (E) the father has brown hair

STOP

IF YOU FINISH BEFORE TIME IS UP, CHECK YOUR WORK ON THIS SECTION OF THE TEST ONLY.
DO NOT GO ON TO THE NEXT SECTION OF THE TEST UNTIL TIME IS UP FOR THIS SECTION.

5   **5**

SECTION V
TIME — 35 MINUTES
28 QUESTIONS

Directions: Read the passages and answer the questions following each passage by blackening the appropriate space on the answer sheet. You may refer back to the passages when answering the questions. Answer all questions on the basis of what is stated or implied.

Seventy-five years after the death of Louis XIV, the French Revolution enlarged considerably the dimensions of
(line) the government show, organizing mass
(5) demonstrations with grandiose staging. The national holiday on July 14, 1790, attracted 200,000 people to the Champs de Mars. Robespierre held the main role as president of the Convention. While
(10) choirs intoned a specially composed hymn entitled "Father of the Universe, Supreme Intelligence," he lighted the flame before a statue of Atheism. Then, marching at the head of the column of
(15) members of the Convention, with each member carrying a bouquet of flowers and ears of wheat, he proceeded from the Tuileries Gardens to the Champs de Mars, where a symbolic hillock topped
(20) with the Tree of Freedom had been erected.

The objective of these vast liturgical assemblies? To strike the public imagination, mobilize it, and involve it
(25) in a collective ritual. Later, mass demonstrations in Red Square or Tienanmen Square would be held for the same reason. Participation in such rituals has become an act of allegiance
(30) to official beliefs. Other regimes, like fascism or Nazism, aim at not only raising the consciousness of the people, but at creating a "mass psychology" by using gigantic demonstrations, whether
(35) in Rome or in the stadium at Nuremberg. Here, following Durkheims theory, the demonstration has the double aspect of ceremony-spectacle and diversion. It is diversion also in the
(40) sense of diverting attention away from the true problems and realities. The public lives in a surrealistic atmosphere of festivals and games, like plebeians during the Roman empire.
(45) Other political systems also mix show business and politics in a minor way. American elections are the

occasion for confetti, parades, and majorettes, and each national political
(50) convention has a show business style orchestra. For that matter, political rallies are often held in places generally reserved for sports events like Madison Square Garden in New York, where the
(55) Democratic Convention was held, or the Walnut Street Theater in Philadelphia, where the first Ford-Carter debate was held. And, as with a show, we speak of the "public" to designate the people.
(60) Some refer to what they consider to be the public's taste for theatricalization, arguing that politics must use star system techniques to save it from the public's lack of interest, to adapt it to
(65) "mass culture." From the moment when the television viewer can choose between his president, a film, and a variety show, the president has to become an entertainer to compete
(70) effectively with show business professionals and keep his popularity rating. In short, to compete with stars, political stars have to use their methods and personalize their "performances."

1. The author of this passage would agree that

(A) Durkheim's theory is unrelated to the alignment of politics with show business

(B) the surrealistic atmosphere of festivals and games occurred only in Ancient Rome

(C) politics consistently stresses serious public problems

(D) the theatricality of present-day politics has no historical precedent

(E) a show-business atmosphere has pervaded the politics of democratic as well as totalitarian regimes

GO ON TO THE NEXT PAGE ➤

2. The primary purpose of this passage is to

(A) compare Ancient Rome to modern America
(B) argue that show business and politics have converged throughout history
(C) show that politics diverts attention from real issues
(D) establish Robespierre as the first political "star"
(E) demonstrate that television has sustained the politician celebrity

3. Which one of the following is the most appropriate substitute for "liturgical assemblies" (paragraph 2)?

(A) political circuses
(B) political conventions
(C) spectacles of worship
(D) human dramas
(E) religious holidays

4. The author's attitude toward politicians who are deliberately entertaining would most likely be

(A) sympathetic
(B) skeptical
(C) supportive
(D) unconcerned
(E) hostile

5. The author implies that citizens who are that attracted by entertaining politicians are

(A) too obedient
(B) not facing reality
(C) television addicts
(D) not interested in politics
(E) victims of a totalitarian regime

6. The author strengthens his argument through the use of which one of the following techniques?

(A) the acknowledgment that he might be mistaken
(B) a profusion of references to experts
(C) a profusion of historical facts
(D) an appeal to the "official beliefs" of his readers
(E) the use of specialized terminology

7. Which one of the following would be an additional example of the sort of politics the author describes?

(A) Ronald Reagan's preference for the color red
(B) Nancy Reagan's preference for the color red
(C) Edward Kennedy's New England accent
(D) Rich Little's impersonation of Richard Nixon
(E) Richard Nixon's purchase of a Park Avenue penthouse

GO ON TO THE NEXT PAGE ➤

(This passage was written in 1982.)

On October 30, 1973, a Tuesday
afternoon around two o'clock, radio
station WBAI, NY, NY, owned and
line operated by the Pacifica Foundation,
(5) was conducting a general discussion of
the contemporary society's attitude
toward language. The WBAI host played
a segment of the album "George Carlin,
Occupation: Foole," a twelve-minute
(10) comedy routine entitled "Filthy Words"
in which Carlin related his thoughts
about "the words you couldn't say on
the public . . . airwaves." He proceeded
to list and repeat numerous times a
(15) number of colloquial expressions for
sexual and excretory activities and
organs. In response, the Federal
Communications Commission (FCC)
issued a regulation restricting the
(20) broadcast of "indecent" language to
certain hours of the day. Though a
Court of Appeals reversed the ruling, the
Supreme Court later upheld the FCC.
It can hardly be denied the
(25) proliferation of so-called dirty books
and films has, to date, reached almost a
saturation point. However, the Pacifica
case deals specifically with the mere
use of certain "taboo" words. The real
(30) point of Mr. Carlin's routine was to
illustrate the absurdity of many people's
attitude in regard to the use of these
particular words. Indeed, it is quite
conceivable that many open-minded
(35) parents would not object to their
children being exposed to Carlin's
monologue in hope that their children
might acquire a more objective and
realistic attitude toward these
(40) supposedly "filthy" words.
The concept of channeling such
language to a time of day when children
are less likely to be in the listening
audience would very likely be
(45) interpreted by children as reinforcing
the notion that these words are in fact
dangerous, which can somehow warp
the supple minds of our youth. This
attitude appears to be much less
(50) rational than that of George Carlin, who
was attempting to put in a more realistic
perspective the use of, and reaction to,
this kind of language.

One must not lose sight of the fact
(55) that this case represents a suppression
of the freedom of speech. The Supreme
Court does not acknowledge the
irrefutable fact that children are bound
to be exposed to "dirty words" in a
(60) myriad of ways other than through the
public airwaves. The language used by
Carlin in his monologue is far from
uncommon in the playgrounds and, in
many instances, the homes of America's
(65) children. Ironically, the FCC has
repeatedly refused to impose sanctions
on the depiction of violence on the
public airways, but has been continually
vigilant in attempting to guard against
(70) the use of "indecent" or "obscene"
language. This puzzling attitude seems
to convey the most troublesome
message that it is all right for our
children to be exposed to and
(75) influenced by a seemingly never-ending
barrage of graphic and gratuitous
violence, but heaven forbid if they
should hear a few so-called "dirty
words."

8. When the passage was written, the
Federal Communications Commission
regulation on the use of "indecent"
language had been

(A) referred to Congress
(B) disallowed by two courts
(C) upheld by the Court of Appeals but
not by the Supreme Court
(D) upheld by the Court of Appeals but
reinstated by the Supreme Court
(E) disallowed by the Court of Appeals
but reinstated by the Supreme Court

GO ON TO THE NEXT PAGE ➤

5 **5** **5** **5** **5**

9. According to the Supreme Court decision, a radio station would

   (A) be allowed to broadcast the reading of a James Joyce novel, which included some of the taboo words, at an hour when children would be likely to listen
   (B) not be allowed to broadcast the reading of a D. H. Lawrence novel, which included some of the taboo words, at any hour
   (C) not be allowed to broadcast the reading of a James Joyce novel, which included some of the taboo words, at any hour
   (D) be allowed to broadcast the George Carlin routine at an hour when children are not likely to be listening
   (E) be allowed to broadcast the George Carlin routine at any hour

10. We can infer from the passage that the author's attitude toward the use of taboo words on radio is unlike that of

    (A) George Carlin
    (B) the majority of the Court of Appeals
    (C) the majority of the Supreme Court
    (D) radio station WBAI
    (E) the Pacifica Foundation

11. The author argues that restricting taboo language to odd hours of the broadcast day is likely to

    (A) increase the number of children listening at those hours
    (B) make this language appear more exciting to children
    (C) increase the number of adults listening at those hours
    (D) cut children off from contact with many great works of literature in English
    (E) cut adults off from contact with many great works of literature in English

12. We can infer from the passage that the author would agree with the Supreme Court majority about

    (A) the recent dramatic rise in the number of obscene films
    (B) the absurdity of many people's attitudes to the taboo words
    (C) the need to protect innocent children from exposure to "filth"
    (D) the meaning of freedom of speech
    (E) the indecency of the violence on the public airwaves

13. The author argues that the Supreme Court decision reveals

    (A) that Carlin's belief in the danger of certain words is incorrect
    (B) an irrational fear of the power of language to corrupt
    (C) a move to more liberal attitudes in censorship
    (D) an indifference to serious sexually oriented literature
    (E) a shrewd understanding of adolescent behavior

14. Basic to the author's argument in the passage is the assumption that

    (A) the "filthy" words are harmless
    (B) there should be no restriction on what is broadcast on public airwaves
    (C) the number of "dirty" books and films has reached a saturation point
    (D) what children should be permitted to hear should be determined by children
    (E) forbidden fruits are more alluring because they are forbidden

GO ON TO THE NEXT PAGE ➤

In a sense, no intelligent person in his lifetime can entirely escape at least some informal speculation. In the form
(line) of a dilemma, Aristotle presented this
(5) truth in the fragment of one of his lost treatises, *Protreptikos:* "You say one must philosophize. You say one should not philosophize. Then to prove your contention you must philosophize. In
(10) any case you must philosophize." To abandon philosophy altogether is itself a philosophical decision. In spite of some incurious or inept minds, the human intellect is naturally
(15) philosophical; it has a quenchless thirst for knowledge, not merely for data but for their explorations, justifications, and proofs; it tries to grasp its findings in an ultimate understanding of reality. Man's
(20) search is always for truth; he even proves truth by truth. In a popular sense, every thinking person is philosophizing. Philosophy in the strict, technical sense, however, is quite
(25) different from the popular use of the term. The philosophizing of the common man is superficial, vague, haphazard, unconscious, uncritical, and subjective; but philosophy in the strict
(30) sense is a conscious, precise, critical, objective, and systematic study of all things.

Etymologically, the term "philosophy" derives from two Greek
(35) words: *philia* ("love") and *sophia* ("wisdom"). Originally the term *sophia* designated the carpenter's art, the art of navigation and guessing riddles. Later it meant talent in poetry and excellence in
(40) any art, music in particular. In ancient Greece a wise man was a person characterized by common sense or by great skill and outstanding performance in any art. Not until the time of
(45) Aristotle, though, did the term "philosophy" assume a technical meaning, distinguishing it from other branches of learning.

The main objects of philosophy,
(50) those that best indicate its meaning, are speculation and criticism. Concerning speculation, philosophy looks upon things from the broadest possible perspective; as for criticism, it has the
(55) twofold role of questioning and judging everything that pertains either to the

foundations or to the superstructure of human thinking. [It is interesting to note that the English word "speculation"
(60) comes from the Latin verb *specere* ("to see"), but its immediate origin is in the noun *specula*, indicating a "watch tower" or, metonymically, a "hill." Just as one can see the wide horizon from a
(65) tower or a hilltop, so he obtains through philosophy a broad view of reality.] In short, philosophy is the science of beings in search of their ultimate reasons, causes, and principles. As a
(70) science of beings, philosophy is concerned with everything that is or becomes or is known. Whereas the special sciences are looking for the proximate causes of things, philosophy
(75) searches for the ultimate explanations and causes of being.

15. According to the passage, the very fact that man thinks means that he is

   (A) following in the tradition of the ancient Greeks
   (B) tending toward a strict philosophical practice
   (C) an informal philosopher
   (D) a sage
   (E) beyond the attainment of perfect wisdom

16. Which one of the following was not associated with the term for wisdom by the ancient Greeks?

   (A) fortune-telling
   (B) navigation
   (C) music
   (D) guessing riddles
   (E) poetry

17. According to the passage, one cannot escape philosophizing, because

   (A) Aristotle could not
   (B) antiphilosophy is superficial and vague
   (C) to decide not to philosophize is itself a philosophical decision
   (D) all human beings are intelligent during their lifetimes
   (E) one is obliged to pursue the systematic study of all things

GO ON TO THE NEXT PAGE ➤

18. The author of this passage would probably call philosophy

    (A) the province of the Greeks
    (B) one of the best practical arts
    (C) an essential definition
    (D) a supreme study, encompassing all things
    (E) an indeterminate but highly rewarding pursuit

19. *Philosophos* is derived from which of the following sources?

    (A) Greek
    (B) Phythagoras
    (C) Cicero
    (D) Diogenes
    (E) love and wisdom

20. We can infer that the author of this passage, in addition to philosophy, is a student of

    (A) human history
    (B) political science
    (C) economics
    (D) linguistics
    (E) literary criticism

21. If the word "metonymically," used in the third paragraph (line 63), means using the name of one thing for that of another associated with it, which one of the following is an example of a word used metonymically?

    (A) "hot air" for "pompous speech"
    (B) "the crown" for the Queen of England
    (C) "fast as a greyhound" for "speedy"
    (D) "unctuous" for "fawning"
    (E) "hard times" for "poor economic conditions"

The colonial powers followed a policy of mercantilism, which required their colonies to buy and sell only to them,
line thus enabling the colonial powers to
(5) export more than they imported and build up economic profit. As a result, although some of Africa's resources were developed, the profits went outside the country. Since Africans were
(10) encouraged to raise cash crops and forced to buy more expensive finished products from the mother country, most African nations did not accumulate any capital reserves.
(15) When the African nations became independent, they needed capital to continue development of their resources and to build industries and modernize. They were therefore forced to borrow
(20) heavily from the superpowers and from their former colonial rulers. They also turned to international organizations such as the World Bank. However, they have borrowed so heavily from such
(25) organizations that, with their current economic problems, these organizations are reluctant to lend them more.
Africa's economic problems are a result of many factors. With the capital
(30) from international loans, some gains were made, but often local conditions were not considered. Factories have been built in areas where the climate makes work difficult, both for people
(35) and machines. Dams that were built to supply hydroelectric power sometimes ruin the ecological balance of a region and are therefore harmful to farmers. Also, capital investment in most African
(40) countries has been concentrated in the industrial sectors, and since most of Africa is still rural, these investments haven't given Africans greater purchasing power. Therefore, there is
(45) little domestic market for manufactured products.
Africa also lacks skilled workers. Colonial education was designed to provide lower-level government workers,
(50) and those who can afford higher education today are more interested in law, medicine, and so on—education that provides prestige or entry into politics and government. In addition,
(55) transportation and communication systems in Africa are still inadequate.

Roads are difficult to build and maintain in the tropical climates, and transporting resources to the sites of
(60) manufacturing plants presents a problem.
To achieve progress, people must work together, and this is difficult in African nations where ethnic rivalries
(65) are prevalent. Much of the money from international loans and foreign aid has been squandered in schemes designed to promote national pride (such as huge government buildings, statues, and so
(70) on) or has simply been confiscated by corrupt leaders.
World economic conditions have also affected Africa. During the 1970s many African nations were forced to pay high
(75) prices for petroleum. On the other hand, countries like Nigeria, which export oil, suffered from low oil prices in the 1980s. Prices for many of Africa's cash crops have dropped in the world market.
(80) Africa's heavy debt burden and the export of cash crops create an economic dependency for trade, capital, and food, which is deeply resented by many African peoples and interpreted as
(85) neo-colonialism. The presence of multinational corporations has been encouraged by African nations, even though many Africans resent the foreign ownership and fear a loss of control.
(90) Various attempts at economic development have included the introduction of socialism or mixed economic activities. For example, when Julius Nyerere became president of
(95) Tanzania in the 1960s, he introduced a socialist system called ujamaa, and in 1967 a program of nationalizing industries and plantations and creating cooperative farms began. Villages in
(100) rural areas were formed into cooperatives, schools and clinics were established and new farm machinery and techniques were introduced. But in the 1970s the rising costs of petroleum
(105) products hurt Tanzania, and there were problems with ujamaa. Hit by drought in 1980 to 1984, Tanzania had to appeal for international aid. Nyerere himself was replaced in 1985.
(110) In Nigeria, as well as in several other African nations, a mixed economy is in place. Major Nigerian industries and oil

GO ON TO THE NEXT PAGE ➤

5   **5**

production are nationalized, while small industries and agriculture remain in
(115) private hands. Multinational corporations are required to serve local needs as well as their own interests. While Nigeria has experienced success in industrial and petroleum output,
(120) agricultural production still lags, and food must be imported.

22. Which one of the following would be the best title for this passage?

   (A) African Governments since Independence
   (B) The African Dilemma
   (C) Africa: Moving Forward or Moving Backward?
   (D) Economic Problems in Post-Colonial Africa
   (E) Africa in the World Market

23. According to the passage, economic development in Africa has been hindered by all of the following EXCEPT

   (A) limited natural resources
   (B) lack of capital reserves
   (C) poor utilization of available capital
   (D) limited purchasing power of the majority of Africans
   (E) low prices in the world market for many African exports

24. The author of this passage uses which one of the following methods to present information?

   (A) comparison and contrast
   (B) general statements followed by examples
   (C) specific examples leading to a general conclusion
   (D) presentation of case histories
   (E) analysis of statistics

25. According to the passage, African achievements in economic development

   (A) sometimes resulted in new ethnic rivalries.
   (B) led to the need for more doctors, lawyers, and teachers.
   (C) sometimes created environmental problems.
   (D) significantly reduced the burden of debt.
   (E) adversely affected the market for African exports.

26. To understand why Julius Nyerere was replaced as president of Tanzania, which additional information would probably be most helpful?

   (A) Nyerere's educational background
   (B) the number of cooperatives created in rural vs. urban areas
   (C) specific statistics, such as changes in Tanzania's mortality rate
   (D) more details about the problems with ujamaa
   (E) details about Tanzania's exports vs. imports

27. The main purpose of the last two paragraphs of the passage is to

   (A) provide examples of African attempts to encourage economic development
   (B) describe the results of neo-colonialism in Africa
   (C) illustrate the failure of two African countries to deal with economic problems
   (D) summarize the problems addressed in the rest of the passage
   (E) personalize the general problems in post-colonial Africa

GO ON TO THE NEXT PAGE ➤

5   **5**

28. The best definition of "neo-colonialism" as it is used in this passage (line 85) is

   (A) relying on foreigners to perform high-level jobs and hold political offices.
   (B) being controlled economically and politically by powerful outside countries
   (C) permitting foreign control of branches of multinational corporations
   (D) basing economic and political systems on Western models
   (E) exporting cash crops while importing manufactured goods from major powers

STOP

END OF MULTIPLE-CHOICE EXAMINATION. IF YOU FINISH BEFORE TIME IS UP, CHECK YOUR WORK ON THIS SECTION ONLY. DO NOT GO BACK TO ANY OTHER SECTION OF THE EXAMINATION.

Writing Sample

Directions: You have 30 minutes to write an essay in response to a given topic. Take a few minutes to plan your work before you begin writing. DO NOT WRITE ON A TOPIC OF YOUR OWN CHOICE. ESSAYS THAT DO NOT ADDRESS THE GIVEN TOPIC ARE UNACCEPTABLE.

The quality of your writing is more important than the length of your response or the content. Pay attention to organization, appropriate diction, and correct usage. You will not be expected to display any specialized knowledge in your response, nor will you be expected to write a "perfect" essay; law schools understand that you are writing under a time constraint, and will allow for the minor lapses in writing ability that might occur under this circumstance.

Only the lined area in your booklet will be reproduced for the law schools, so do not write outside this space. *Do not* skip lines or use wide margins. These precautions, along with careful planning and legible handwriting that is not unduly large, will keep you within the allowed space.

Sample Topic

Ralph DeCinces is considering two job offers. Write an argument favoring one offer or the other, taking into account the following factors:

- Ralph has just finished an undergraduate degree in economics and wants to use his knowledge in government service to create programs that reduce inflation and poverty.
- Ralph is interested in running for public office after he gains some practical experience with the machinery of government.

The State Office of Budget and Management has offered Ralph a position as liaison to the Senate Finance Committee. The liaison must be present at all Finance Committee meetings but may only participate when called upon by a Senator. The liaison must be prepared with information from his office that is relevant to the Committee's deliberations and must supply that information from a nonpartisan perspective. In private, informal meetings, Committee members sometimes try to influence the liaison to slant his information in a partisan way. The liaison reviews all Finance legislation before it is discussed by the Committee, in order to be prepared with necessary data.

Wilson County has offered Ralph the position of County Manager. For the last fifteen years, Wilson County has suffered the highest percentage of citizens living in poverty, a situation that has contributed to widespread voter apathy. The County Manager proposes a budget to the County Board of Supervisors each year and administers the County Budget that finally wins approval. Once a budget is approved, the Manager has complete authority to monitor the spending of County funds and must be especially alert to the misuse of funds by any County agency. The former County Manager left his position after an unsuccessful attempt to stop officials in the Public Housing Office from awarding unreasonably lucrative contracts to a local building contractor.

Answer Key

Section I: Logical Reasoning

1. **E**	6. **B**	11. **C**	16. **D**	21. **E**
2. **B**	7. **C**	12. **D**	17. **A**	22. **C**
3. **C**	8. **D**	13. **D**	18. **B**	23. **E**
4. **E**	9. **A**	14. **C**	19. **B**	24. **A**
5. **B**	10. **A**	15. **A**	20. **B**	25. **E**

Section II: Reading Comprehension

1. **B**	6. **E**	11. **D**	16. **A**	21. **C**	26. **B**
2. **A**	7. **C**	12. **C**	17. **D**	22. **C**	27. **A**
3. **D**	8. **E**	13. **D**	18. **E**	23. **C**	28. **A**
4. **B**	9. **B**	14. **A**	19. **B**	24. **B**	
5. **A**	10. **B**	15. **D**	20. **D**	25. **B**	

Section III: Logical Reasoning

1. **C**	6. **B**	11. **C**	16. **D**	21. **A**
2. **B**	7. **E**	12. **E**	17. **C**	22. **D**
3. **C**	8. **E**	13. **D**	18. **B**	23. **C**
4. **A**	9. **B**	14. **A**	19. **A**	24. **B**
5. **D**	10. **C**	15. **E**	20. **E**	25. **C**

Section IV: Analytical Reasoning

1. **C**	5. **B**	9. **D**	13. **A**	17. **D**	21. **C**
2. **C**	6. **D**	10. **E**	14. **D**	18. **E**	22. **D**
3. **A**	7. **E**	11. **B**	15. **C**	19. **D**	23. **B**
4. **D**	8. **A**	12. **C**	16. **D**	20. **E**	

Section V: Reading Comprehension

1. **E**	6. **C**	11. **B**	16. **A**	21. **B**	26. **D**
2. **B**	7. **A**	12. **A**	17. **C**	22. **D**	27. **A**
3. **C**	8. **E**	13. **B**	18. **D**	23. **A**	28. **B**
4. **B**	9. **D**	14. **A**	19. **B**	24. **B**	
5. **B**	10. **C**	15. **C**	20. **D**	25. **C**	

Model Test Analysis

Doing model exams and understanding the explanations afterwards are of course important in acquainting you with typical LSAT question types and successful approaches to the questions. However, another benefit of carefully analyzing these model tests is to understand the kinds of errors you are making and thus work to minimize them. For instance, if a very high percentage of your incorrect answers is due to "careless error" or "misread problem," then perhaps you are working much too fast and should slow your pace accordingly. If your incorrect answers are due primarily to "lack of knowledge," then a careful rereading and reworking of the appropriate question-type chapter may be in order. Or if you find that you aren't completing a large number of questions because of lack of time, you may need to either increase your speed or learn to use the "one-check, two-check" technique more effectively.

This kind of analysis of the model tests will enable you to identify your particular weaknesses and thus remedy them.

Model Test Six Analysis

Section	Total Number of Questions	Number Correct	Number Incorrect	Number Unanswered*
I. Logical Reasoning	25			
II. Reading Comprehension	28			
III. Logical Reasoning	25			
IV. Analytical Reasoning	23			
V. Reading Comprehension	28			
TOTALS:	129			

*At this stage in your preparation, you should not be leaving any blank answer spaces. At least fill in a guess, as there is no penalty for a wrong answer.

Reasons for Incorrect Answers

You may wish to evaluate the explanations before completing this chart.

Section	Total Number Incorrect	Lack of Knowledge	Misread Problem	Careless Error	Unanswered or Wrong Guess
I. Logical Reasoning					
II. Reading Comprehension					
III. Logical Reasoning					
IV. Analytical Reasoning					
V. Reading Comprehension					
TOTALS:					

Explanation of Answers

Section I

1. **E** (A), (B), (C), and (D) would call a Republican "victory" into question. In regard to (B), if the party held fewer seats than usual before the election, there would be fewer to lose and each seat lost would represent a higher percentage of the total. That fewer people voted would not undermine the claim to a victory.

2. **B** The subject of the paragraph has been the kindergarten class and its surprising win over a high school class. (C) and (D) introduce new issues.

3. **C** Phrases like "none left" and "sold out" state the problem but do not explain it.

4. **E** The first paragraph is concerned specifically with the deceptive Volvo ad, and the second with fake advertising and consumer distrust in general.

5. **B** The Federal Trade Commission is, presumably, an objective commentator, and this comment is a grave indictment of advertising.

6. **B** That the Americans are not cited as opposing the move incumbent on developed nations and that they are victims of a questionable European practice suggest that the United States supports the reduction of subsidies. If the German chancellor hesitates to act and faces an upcoming election, we can infer his eagerness not to offend a large voting constituency of farmers. The quotation around "health inspection standards" and the tone of the passage suggest that the author believes this reason for excluding American products is bogus. We have no information on French politicians to infer (E).

7. **C** The passage calls for an improved public school system and suggests the public schools are in decline. But the California test results cited here contradict this view.

8. **D** The passage appears to be a dispassionate account of the rise in prices except for the fourth sentence, where the reference to the public's stupidity reveals the author's disapproval of the rising cost of tickets.

9. **A** Darrell asserts that evolutionists do not explain the origin ("where matter came from") of life, and so take no stand on a creator.

10. **A** The passage never explicitly connects the trade agreement and the embargo, but it twice mentions the trade agreement. The effect is to imply a connection.

11. **C** The passage makes points favorable to both sides of this question, making it very hard to determine a right side and a wrong side.

12. **D** The argument cites "moral principles" and uses the tennis ball analogy to make its point.

13. **D** Choices (A), (C), and (E) would not support the conclusion. Though the narrator is not Jane Austen, the narrator is probably closer to the author than any character in the novels.

14. **C** The paragraph has already revealed the large sales of the record and the skilled marketing of an inferior product.

15. **A** The point of the paragraph is that awards are based on sales. Choice (A) would contradict this idea.

16. **D** A support group for retired persons would logically support a law intended to benefit retired workers.

17. **A** Though choices (B), (C), (D), and (E) are relevant, the purpose of the paragraph as a whole is to call attention to the lack of regulation of financial planners.

18. **B** The original uses a discovery based upon a personal experience. Choices (A), (C), and (D) do not follow this pattern. Choice (E) has no clear cause-and-effect relationship.

19. **B** The reasoning is as follows: this fork is rusted/it cannot be made of stainless steel. The unstated premise between those parts is that, if a utensil is made of stainless steel, it will not rust.

20. **B** (B) would support the conclusion from personal experience. (A), (C), (D), and (E) do not refer to the conclusion of the passage.

21. **E** The film described in choice (E) contradicts the argument of the paragraph.

22. **C** The author assumes the superiority of the explanation of (1) an economist, (2) with a Ph.D., (3) on the budget deficit, but does not assume that the explanation is right. Choice (D) does not specify the subject judged.

23. **E** No analogy is used here, but all the other four choices are employed.

24. **A** Only in (A) is "hopefully" used as an adverb (modifying "encouraged"), meaning "in a hopeful way."

25. **E** The apparent contradiction is resolved if the number of cable channels dividing the audience is growing more rapidly than the cable share, as a whole, of the audience.

Section II

Passage 1

1. **B** Paragraph 5 says that the Warren Court was a Camelot insofar as it advanced human rights; a concern with human rights is consistent with both justice and mercy.

2. **A** "Most [human rights] cases do not get to the Supreme Court anyway" (paragraph 2).

3. **D** "A Supreme Court decision . . . seldom brings about immediate major changes" (paragraph 1).

4. **B** Paragraph 3 says that "the Court's authority . . . ultimately rests on sustained public confidence."

5. **A** Paragraph 4 says that "the best protectors of human rights are . . . citizens who know and insist on their own rights and who act to guarantee the rights of others."

6. **E** The last sentence of the article "It is necessary to reassess the opportunities for progress through the judicial system," sums up the author's feelings about the courts and our judicial system.

Passage 2

7. **C** The rule is intended to deter police abuse of the right to be protected from unreasonable searches and seizures, but not from all searches.

8. **E** The objections in (A), (B), (C), and (D) are plausible, but (E) is an argument in favor of, not against, the rule.

9. **B** The decision of 1961 differs from the earlier Wolf case in its finding that the exclusionary rule is a constitutional right.

10. **B** The incentive that the rule removes is the illegal seizure of evidence by law enforcement. Because this evidence may not be used in the prosecution, the incentive to obtain it no longer exists.

11. **D** The 1974 decision permitted the use of evidence normally excluded in the questioning of a witness before a grand jury. Note the decision did not permit its use against a defendant subject to criminal prosecution.

12. **C** Far more important in the 1974 case is the finding that the exclusionary rule is a judicially created remedy not a constitutional right.

13. **D** The author's comments in the last two paragraphs ("conspicuous failure of the Court to confront . . . constitutional disaster") suggest his disapproval.

14. **A** The passage moves from Wolf (before 1961) to 1961 to 1974 to 1976.

Passage 3

15. **D** Because the point of most of the passage is the objection by higher courts to the use of nuisance ordinances against pornography, option (D) most accurately suggests the content of the passage.

16. **A** Public nuisance is usually anything that is injurious to public health, indecent or offensive to public sensibilities or obstructive to free public passage. A pickpocket would be prosecuted under other laws.

17. **D** The passage speaks of the First Amendment's "aim to avoid previous restraints" by eliminating states' approval of printed matter.

18. **E** According to the first paragraph, (A), (B), (C), and (D) are advantageous. (E) is untrue.

19. **B** The immediate effect of the 1977 decision was to increase the number of civil nuisance actions. But these actions were to be reversed on appeal.

20. **D** The second and third paragraphs suggest that the nuisance laws cannot be used until all currently displayed materials have been found to be obscene.

21. **C** (A) and (B) would result in removal of the store. (D) is untrue; (E) is true but does not logically support the question.

22. **C** The advantage of zoning ordinances is they avoid the problems of prior restraint violations that impair the effectiveness of nuisance regulations.

Passage 4

23. **C** Miss Hamilton's statement, "Please address me correctly" implies that she has been incorrectly addressed. Her later petition indicates the implication of her objection; she cites "equal protection" and "etiquette" in her favor. Both are related to the "demeaning" quality of her court experience.

24. **B** The Red Queen in *Alice* is an absurd tyrant, as you should realize by recognizing that "sentence first, trial afterward" is both absurd and tyrannical.

25. **B** The author's ability to *quote* the court participants indicates that he was either at the hearing or privy to a direct transcript.

26. **B** Only (B) is a question that is both raised and not answered in the passage. Other choices are either questions that are answered or questions that are never raised.

27. **A** (C) is irrelevant to the race of *this* judge and staff; (B) refers to the legal profession in general rather than the officers of the court in particular; (D) should be eliminated because the present racial situation is not addressed; and (E) should be eliminated because the race of the arresting officers is never mentioned.

28. **A** In the midst of recounting the court dialogue, the author says, "Miss Hamilton would not be intimidated," thus suggesting the judge's purpose.

Section III

1. **C** Choices (A), (B), (D), and (E) are all points *against* the argument of the letter. If the letter is ironic, however, there would be no need to make a case against it.

2. **B** The issue is the likelihood of a two-car collision, not simply a traffic accident. Only (B) provides information about two-car collisions.

3. **C** Only (C)—"all . . . have had"—will lead to the conclusion in the statement. The best way to answer questions of this type is to formulate a correct answer before reading the choices given on the test.

4. **A** The correct answer is implied in the first paragraph: "not always bad news," but usually. (B), (D), and (E) are untrue.

5. **D** The second paragraph questions whether or not a recession is in progress. It then introduces a businessman who claims to know the answer, but the paragraph breaks off before giving it. The logical last sentence would reveal what the repair percentage tells us about the possible recession.

6. **B** If they bought rose bushes, they did not buy garden tools or anything else; if they bought roses, they paid by charge account.

7. **E** (E) would help preserve the whales, but (A), (B), (C), and (D), if true, would not.

8. **E** The information in the passage does not compare the degrees of importance to men and to women of height and intelligence. Therefore, though (A, (B), (C), and (D) are logical, (E) is impossible to infer.

9. **B** The passage identifies an opposition, but it does not cite and dispute the evidence proposed by the other side. It does use all the other four techniques.

10. **C** If (C) is true, it shows a woman who has succeeded on her own. (A), (B), (C), and (D) weaken the author's case.

11. **C** The assemblyman's line of reasoning is that a constituency which does not directly benefit from a tax should not have to pay it. By this line of reasoning, younger taxpayers should not have to pay taxes that benefit the old.

12. **E** Choices (A), (B), (C), and (D) present useful definitions of aspects of the survey. In the case of (E), we already know that, at 18, male and female drivers are alike, and worse than at any other age.

13. **D** (A), (B), (C), and (E) are implied but not explicitly stated in the passage. We are not able to infer whether or not the aides have been doing their jobs.

14. **A** The quotation wryly suggests that the dishonesty among economics majors is practice for what they will be doing in business.

15. **E** (A), (B), (C), and (D) are reasonable inferences. We cannot know if "most" professors reuse examinations.

16. **D** The passage says "every month a famous figure from the past may be rehabilitated or vilified."

17. **C** The Winesap and Granny Smith apples of the second sentence in (C) are fruits, while the first sentence refers to fruits and vegetables. Similarly the passage refers to bank stocks listed on the American Exchange in the second sentence, and to the American Exchange in general in the first.

18. **B** (B) is not a reasonable or convincing argument against the bill. Presumably the doctor would not act until after the bill had passed.

19. **A** If the voting third accurately reflected the will of the nonvoting two thirds, the election results would reflect the will of the whole population. The whole Senate is not elected in the same year.

20. **E** (A), (B), (C), and (D) suggest the low voter turnout does not greatly affect the political power of certain groups or the election results. (E) suggests the old have a far larger block of voters than the young.

21. **A** By saying "I can't afford," Jane indicates that the hiring of a maid and a gardener is a financially prudent decision.

22. **D** There is nothing in the passage that would suggest that the cost of a fishing license is too high. (A), (B), (C), and (E) can be inferred; note that the first sentence links the sale of fishing licenses with funds for environmental improvement.

23. **C** The flawed reasoning is a hasty generalization based on a single fact: if Logan Airport is crime-free, so are all others. Choices (A), (B), (D), and (E) have the same kind of errant reasoning. Choice (C) presents an observed effect and its probable cause.

24. **B** The passage describes the works of the eighteenth and nineteenth centuries by describing the views of the critics of these eras. The change it sees in twentieth-century literature is defined by the views of a number of "influential critics." The change it describes in literature is the same change it sees in criticism. The passage makes no judgment on how successful the literature of either period is (A), nor does it take sides with one view or another (C). Though the passage does suggest that the novels of the eighteenth and nineteenth centuries are alike in their difference from those of the twentieth, it does not say they are essentially the same.

25. **C** We should expect the twentieth century novel to be less concerned with "moral values" or a "moral lesson." This does not mean that they will be more or less frank in dealing with sexuality, only that they will be less likely to use it for some moral purpose. (D) and (E) may or may not be true, but there is no reason to infer either from the passage.

Section IV
Answers 1–5

1. **C** From all the information given, the following chart can be constructed:

   $\underline{E} \quad \underline{T} \quad \underline{J} \quad \underline{F} \quad \underline{L} \quad \underline{S}$

   Thus, Tom sits next to Enola and next to Jan.

2. **C** From the chart we can see that Lynn sits next to Fred and Simon, not next to Tom. Note that (E) is still true ("Lynn sits between Enola and Simon") even though Lynn doesn't necessarily sit next to them.

3. **A** From the information given, the friends could sit only in this order: Enola, Tom, Jan, Fred, Lynn, Simon.

4. **D** Since the members who left the theater comprised one male and two females, to follow the same rules the new members must be one male and two females. Choice (E) is not possible because it would put the two females next to each other.

5. **B** If Enola and Simon sit in the two middle seats, and Lynn sits between Fred and Simon, then the seating would look like this:

   $\underline{\quad} \, \underline{\quad} \, \underline{E} \, \underline{S} \, \underline{L} \, \underline{F}$ or $\underline{F} \, \underline{L} \, \underline{S} \, \underline{E} \, \underline{\quad} \, \underline{\quad}$

   In either case, Tom must sit next to Enola and Jan must sit on the other side of Tom. So Tom is between Enola and Jan.

Answers 6–12

The following Venn diagram may be constructed from the information to help you answer the questions:

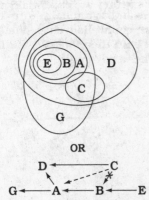

OR

Note that the circles indicate all the possibilities that may exist.

6. **D** If some Cs are As, and all As are Gs, then logically some Cs are Gs. Since all Es are Bs, and all Bs are As, then all Es are Gs.

7. **E** Since no Cs are Bs, then "some Cs are Bs" must be false. Note that (C) *may* be false, but not necessarily *must* be false.

8. **A** If all Ds are Gs, then we can conclude that all As, Bs, and Cs are also Gs. Thus (A) is true. From the diagram, the others are false.

9. **D** Since all Cs are Ds, then, if Q is within C, Q must also be within D.

10. **E** There is no statement that tells us about Gs. Therefore, we can conclude only that (E) is true since it says nothing specific about the Gs. The rest of the choices are false.

11. **B** If all Js are Bs, then all Js must lie within As and Ds.

12. **C** If all Ds are Ms, then all Cs and all As are Ms, since all Cs and all As are Ds.

Answers 13–18

From the information given we could have constructed the following chart:

Carpet	Drapes	Sofa	Sofa	Chair	Chair
~~B~~					~~B~~
				?Y or	?Y

13. **A** If one chair is yellow, and the drapes are light green, then one of the sofas must be light green and one of the chairs must be dark green. Your chart would look like this:

Carpet	Drapes	Sofa	Sofa	Chair	Chair
LG	LG			Y	DG

   If the carpet is yellow then the sofas cannot be dark green. They also cannot be light green or yellow since we have used two of each color. Thus, one sofa must be blue.

14. **D** Since we already have two yellows, (D) is not possible.

15. **C** The chart would now look like this:

Carpet	Drapes	Sofa	Sofa	Chair	Chair
Y	Y	B?	B?	DG	DG

Since the carpet cannot be light green and cannot be blue or dark green, it must be yellow. This does not affect the color of the sofas. It is possible that both sofas are the same color.

16. **D** If the carpet and drapes are the same color, then they cannot be blue or light green. If they were light green, this would force a sofa to be light green also, making three items light green. This leaves yellow and dark green for the carpet and drapes. If the carpet is yellow, the sofas cannot be dark green. If the carpet and drapes are dark green, then no other item can be dark green. Thus the sofas cannot be dark green.

17. **D** If the chair-sofa combinations were light green and dark green, this would force the carpet to be yellow. If the carpet is yellow, then the sofas cannot be dark green. Thus, (D) is false.

18. **E** If the drapes were light green, then one of the chairs must be dark green. Thus choice (E) is the answer.

Answers 19–23

A simple chart may help to answer each question.

19. **D** For this question your chart may look like this:

FATHER
blue eyes
brown hair

MOTHER
?

CHILDREN
blue eyes
red hair

First, note that, if all the children have red hair, then all must be girls, since a boy would take both of the father's characteristics. And the children would thus have to get their red hair from their mother. Statement C is not necessarily true as their red-haired mother could have blue eyes.

20. **E** This is a difficult problem. Your chart should look like this:

1ST GENERATION:	**FATHER**	**MOTHER**	
	blue eyes	blue eyes	
	brown hair	red hair	

2ND GENERATION:	**IF MALE CHILD**	**IF FEMALE CHILD**	**CHILD'S SPOUSE**
	blue eyes	blue eyes	?
	brown hair	red hair	

3RD GENERATION:		**GRANDCHILD**
		green eyes
		red hair

Since the grandchild has red hair and green eyes, she must be a girl. And since she is a girl, she must get one characteristic from each of her parents (the second generation). Therefore, the only person from whom she could get green eyes would be the other spouse of the second generation. The red hair must thus come from the second generation female.

21. **C** Only girls can have both green eyes and red hair. But any girl from a blue-eyed, brown-haired father must have at least one of his characteristics. Therefore, green eyes and red hair are not possible characteristics of his child.

22. **D** Every male must have *at least one* of the following characteristics: blue eyes, brown hair. Therefore, a green-eyed male *must* have brown hair.

23. **B** If two blue-eyed people get married, the female *must* have red hair because all females have *at least one* of the following characteristics: green eyes and/or red hair. Note that the father could also have blue eyes and red hair; therefore, the child could be either a boy or girl.

Section V
Passage 1

1. **E** The passage mentions diverse forms of government, from totalitarian Rome to modern American democracy, in each instance stressing the theatrical nature of political assemblies. The other choices are explicitly contradicted in the passage.

2. **B** Each of the other choices describes a subsidiary point of the passage. In general, the passage demonstrates that, in many governments at many times, politics has been a theatrical enterprise.

3. **C** The author uses "spectacle" at other points in the passage to describe the same sort of assembly he mentions here; we can call the "liturgical assembly" a "spectacle of worship," because the definition of "liturgical" is "connected with public worship."

4. **B** Although the author does not overtly and angrily criticize politics-as-show-business, he certainly calls into question through his descriptions of theatrical frivolity the worth of a politician who is "entertaining." If it seems to you that the author was objective and neutral, your only possible choice would be (D), "unconcerned," which certainly contradicts the author's detailed interest in the phenomenon he describes.

5. **B** In the second paragraph, the author says that the diversion of political entertainment takes attention "away from true problems and realities."

6. **C** Each of the other choices may be eliminated easily, and it is quite obvious that historical facts occur repeatedly throughout the passage.

7. **A** Only (A) is an example of a politician taking part in show business; this example stresses the convergence of politics and show business that is the subject of the whole passage.

Passage 2

8. **E** The FCC regulation was reversed by the Court of Appeals, but this reversal was reversed by the Supreme Court.

9. **D** The FCC regulation prohibits the broadcast of the taboo words at hours when children are likely to be listening, but permits them at some other hours.

10. **C** The author believes that words are not likely to corrupt, the view of George Carlin, the Court of Appeals, and probably of radio station WBAI and the Pacifica Foundation, which broadcasted George Carlin's record. The Supreme Court reversed the decision of the Court of Appeals.

11. **B** The passage suggests the possibility of children being more curious about the words if they are used only at times late at night. The passage makes no mention of literature and no predictions about increased listenership.

12. **A** The author comments explicitly on the number of obscene films. The Court would not endorse option (B) and we can make no inferences about the Court's view of violence.

13. **B** The author refers to the Court's view of language as "much less rational than that of George Carlin."

14. **A** Though the author might agree with options (C) and (E) the assumption that is the basis of his argument in the passage is that the words are harmless.

Passage 3

15. **C** Paragraph 1 states, "In a popular sense, every thinking person is philosophizing." Such informal, popular philosophizing is opposed to "philosophy in the strict, technical sense."

16. **A** Paragraph 2 mentions (B), (C), (D), and (E) as the arts designated by the term for wisdom.

17. **C** The correct answer is a paraphrase of the quotation from Aristotle in paragraph 1.

18. **D** The final paragraph calls philosophy the concern with "everything that is or becomes or is known."

19. **B** Philosophos was chosen as a label by Pythagoras, but the word was *derived* from the Greek words (*philia* + *sophia*) for love and wisdom.

20. **D** The passage discusses the etymology of "philosophy." The author's interest in language appears again in the consideration of the word "speculation" in the third paragraph.

21. **B** The use of "crown" for Queen or "White House" for president are examples of metonymy. The other answers are simply metaphors or definitions.

574 Model Test Six

Passage 4

22. **D** This title addresses the main subject of the paragraph and is more specific than (B). (A) suggests that the passage deals more with governments than with economic problems, while in fact only the last two paragraphs address governmental systems. The passage does not examine the rhetorical question presented in (C), and (E) covers only a minor point.

23. **A** Nowhere in the passage are Africa's limited natural resources cited as a reason for its economic problems; therefore, this is the best answer. Line 14 cites a lack of capital reserves (B); lines 28–38 indicate poor utilization of capital (C); lines 39–44 address the limited purchasing power of the majority of Africans; and lines 72–79 describe Africa's problems in the world market.

24. **B** Paragraphs 3 through 6 provide specific examples of the causes of Africa's economic problems; the first sentence of paragraph 3 is the topic sentence. The author does not present case histories (D) or include any statistics (E). The passage does not end with a general conclusion (C), and nowhere does the author use comparison and contrast to make a point (A).

25. **C** Lines 28–38 cite examples of how local conditions were often not considered when steps were taken to improve Africa's economic potential, and lines 35–38 specifically refer to ecological damage. Although ethnic rivalries are mentioned as hindering development, there is no suggestion that attempts at development caused new rivalries (A). According to the passage, more skilled workers (as opposed to professionals) are needed to support economic development (B). Nothing suggests that achievements have significantly reduced the debt burden, which is cited as a continuing problem (D), and nothing indicates that the market has been adversely affected (E).

26. **D** Lines 105–106 states "there were problems with ujamaa," but no details are provided. Understanding what these problems were and how they affected Tanzanian life would probably be most helpful in understanding why Nyerere was replaced. The second best answer would be (C), but nothing in the passage suggests changes in mortality rate, literacy rate, and so on, whereas problems with ujamaa are specifically mentioned. Both Nyerere's educational background and details about Tanzania's exports are minor points (A and E). (B) is unclear and irrelevant.

27. **A** These two paragraphs briefly mention two countries' attempts to provide a governmental system that encourages economic development. (C) is incorrect, because although both countries encounter setbacks, they attempt to deal with economic problems. (B) doesn't make sense; neither paragraph is concerned with the results of neo-colonialism. Rather than summarizing the problems covered in the rest of the passage (D), these paragraphs provide two examples of attempts to deal with the problems. (E) overstates the purpose of the last two paragraphs; there is no attempt to "personalize" issues or address general problems.

28. **B** Economic dependency on powerful countries suggests that these countries will exert political and economic control reminiscent of true colonialism; therefore, this is the best definition. (C) and (D) are not related to colonial systems, and (A) and (E) are incomplete.

PART FOUR

FINAL TOUCHES

Reviewing the Important Techniques

Chapter 12

A SUMMARY OF STRATEGIES

Directions and Strategies

General Tips

- Use the "one-check, two-check" system, doing the easier questions first, and saving the time-consuming and difficult questions for later.
- Don't leave any blank answer spaces. At least guess on your unanswered questions.
- Eliminate unreasonable or irrelevant answers immediately, marking them out on your question booklet.
- Highlight key words and phrases by marking right in your question booklet. Use the margins to draw diagrams, set up charts, and so on.
- Mark "T" and "F" (for "True" and "False") alongside the Roman numeral statements in "multiple-multiple-choice" questions. Often these will allow you to immediately eliminate incorrect answer choices. This type of question has not appeared recently.
- Watch out for the common mistake—the MISREAD.
- Spend some extra time reviewing Logical Reasoning problems. Remember, Logical Reasoning will comprise two of the four scored sections of your exam.

Review of LSAT Areas

Reading Comprehension

Directions: Read the passages and answer the questions following each passage by blackening the appropriate space on the answer sheet. You may refer to the passages when answering the questions.

Strategies:

- Skim the questions first, marking key words and phrases. (Don't read the answer choices.)
- Skim the passage (optional). Read and mark the first sentence of each paragraph.
- Read actively, marking the passage. In particular, look for answer spots, repeat spots, intuition spots.
- Answer the questions. Skip if necessary. Eliminate weak choices. Don't "read into" the passage.

Analytical Reasoning

<u>Directions:</u> In this section you will be given groups of questions based on different sets of conditions. Drawing a simple diagram may be helpful in answering some of the questions. You are to choose the *best* answer and mark the corresponding space on your answer sheet.

Strategies:

- No formal logic is required.
- Make simple charts or diagrams.
- Fill in as much of the diagram as possible, but don't worry if you cannot complete it.
- Look for the framework of the diagram that would be most effective.
- Apply evidence in both directions, that is, also use what you know is *not* true.
- Use question marks for information that is variable.
- Sometimes looking at the questions can tip off the framework of the diagram that would be most helpful.
- Sometimes no standard chart will apply. Then simply pull out information or use simple notes.

Logical Reasoning

<u>Directions:</u> In this section you will be given brief statements or passages and will be required to evaluate the reasoning involved. In some instances, more than one choice will appear to be a possible answer. You are to choose the *best* answer. Use common sense and reasonableness in making your selection; then mark the proper space on the answer sheet.

Strategies:

- Read the question first; then go back and read the argument or statement. This will give insight into what is going to be asked.
- Watch for items in the answer choices that are irrelevant or not addressed in the given information. Eliminate these immediately.
- Notice the overall tone of the question: Positive or negative? Agreeing with and strengthening the author's argument or criticizing and weakening the statement?
- Watch for important words: *some, all, none, only, one, few, no, could, must, each, except.*

Writing Sample

<u>Directions:</u> You have 30 minutes to write an essay in response to a given topic. Take a few minutes to plan your work before you begin writing. DO NOT WRITE ON A TOPIC OF YOUR OWN CHOICE. ESSAYS THAT DO NOT ADDRESS THE GIVEN TOPIC ARE UNACCEPTABLE.

The quality of your writing is more important than the length of your response or the content. Pay attention to organization, appropriate diction, and correct usage. You will not be expected to display any specialized knowledge in your response, nor will you be expected to write a "perfect" essay; law schools understand that you are writing under a time constraint, and will allow for the minor lapses in writing ability that might occur under this circumstance.

Only the lined area in your booklet will be reproduced for the law schools, so do not write outside this space. *Do not* skip lines or use wide margins. These precautions, along with careful planning and legible handwriting that is not unduly large, will keep you within the allowed space.

Strategies:

- Read statements and biographies or descriptions at least twice, actively.
- Choose your candidate or item.
- Outline your essay.
- Start with a direction. Your first sentence should serve a purpose.
- Support your argument with examples or other specifics.
- Do *not* write a closing paragraph that simply repeats what you have already said.
- Write legibly. Write clearly. Write naturally.
- Proofread and edit your essay.

A Final Checklist

A Few Days before the Test

- Review the test directions and strategies for each area.
- Become familiar with the test site; visit it if necessary.
- Follow your normal daily routine; don't make drastic changes.

The Night before the Test

- Review briefly, but don't cram.
- Get a normal night's sleep; don't go to bed too early or too late.

On the Day of the Test

- Eat a high-protein breakfast, unless you never eat breakfast.
- Arrive on time, equipped with three or four sharpened No. 2 pencils, a good eraser, proper identification, your admission ticket, and a watch.
- Dress comfortably. (You may wish to dress in "layers" so that you can add or remove a sweater or jacket if the room temperature changes.)
- Read the test directions carefully.
- Use the "one-check, two-check" system.
- Read *actively.*
- In Reading Comprehension and Logical Reasoning, remember to look at all choices before marking your answer.
- In Analytical Reasoning, be aware that you may not always need to review all of the choices before marking your answer.
- Before you leave a problem, be sure to take a guess. Try to make it an educated guess by eliminating some choices.
- If there are only a few minutes left for a section, fill in the remaining problems with guesses before time is called.
- Remember: look for problems that you CAN DO and SHOULD GET RIGHT, and DON'T GET STUCK on any one problem.

PART FIVE

ABOUT THE LAW SCHOOLS AND LAW PRACTICE

Chapter 13

OVERVIEW OF ABA-APPROVED LAW SCHOOLS

The following table provides information about the tuition, programs, and academic community at 181 schools that have been approved by the American Bar Association. This is designed to provide a quick overview of the schools.

The information on this table is self-explanatory.

In several sections of the table, a check (✔) indicates "yes" and a blank indicates "no." For example, under Calendar, the possibilities are Fall, Winter, Spring, and Summer. At any given school, you can begin your law studies only at those times indicated by a check.

Since most law schools operate on a semester basis, information about credits and required courses is given in terms of semester hours. If a school operates on the quarter system, the abbreviation *qh* is added.

Similarly, tuition is generally given for a full year. When part-time tuition is given per credit, this refers to semester courses unless the abbreviation *qh* is used.

Where a category does not apply to a school or when information was not available, the cell is left blank.

INSTITUTION	Profile Page	Fee	Deadline	Deadline Financial Aid	Tuition In State FT (PT)	Tuition Out of State FT (PT)	Fall	Winter	Spring	Summer	Day	Evening	Credits for JD	Required Credits for Courses	Transferable Summer Courses	Joint Degree	Graduate Law Degree	Enrolled FT (PT)	Avg Age First Year	% Women	% Minority	Attrition Rate %	Faculty FT (PT)	Volumes	Microforms
American University (Washington College of Law) 4801 Massachusetts Avenue, N.W. Washington, DC 20016-8186 202-274-4101 Fax: 202-274-4107 wcladmit@wcl.american.edu	188		March 1	Check	$23,696 ($16,682)	$23,696 ($16,682)	✓				✓	✓	86	34	✓	✓	✓	873 (448)	24	59	24	1	50 (152)	412,309	1,015,769
Arizona State University (College of Law/Armstrong Hall) Box 877906 Tempe, AZ 85287-7906 602-965-1474 Fax: 602-965-5550 wanda.decrow@asu.edu	190	$40	March 1	Check	$4,938	$12,090	✓		✓	✓	✓		87	40	✓	✓		481	27	49	25	11	37 (21)	351,000	465,411
Baylor University (School of Law) P.O. Box 97288 Waco, TX 76798-7288 254-710-1911 Fax: 254-710-2316 becky-beck@baylor.edu	192		March 1	May 1	$14,719	$14,719	✓				✓		126	79	✓	✓		396	24	40	8	5	21 (33)	114,860	67,835
Boston College (Law School) 885 Centre Street Newton, MA 02459 617-552-4351 Fax: 617-552-2917 bclawadm@bc.edu	194	$65	March 1	March 15	$24,480	$24,480	✓				✓		85	38			✓	828	24	51	18	1	52 (56)	393,179	1,031,218
Boston University (School of Law) 765 Commonwealth Avenue Boston, MA 02215 617-353-3100 bulawadm@bu.edu	196	$50	March 1	March 1	$23,770	$23,770	✓				✓	✓	84	33		✓	✓	892	24	49	23	9	57 (74)	317,000	1,299,800
Brigham Young University (J. Reuben Clark Law School) 342 JRCB Brigham Young University Provo, UT 84602 801-378-4277 Fax: 801-378-5897 wilcock@lawgate.byu.edu	198	$30	Feb 1	March 1	$5,330	$8,000	✓				✓		90	36		✓	✓	452 (5)	26	35	15	1	27 (31)	430,431	137,137
Brooklyn Law School 250 Joralemon Street Brooklyn, NY 11201 718-780-7906 Fax: 718-780-0395 admitq@brooklaw.edu	200	$60	April 1	March 1	$23,340 ($16,625)	$23,340 ($16,625)	✓				✓	✓	86	35	✓	✓	✓	991 (509)	25	49	20	3	67 (97)	486,259	1,103,385

INSTITUTION	Profile Page	APPLICATIONS Fee	Deadline	Deadline Financial Aid	TUITION In State Full Time (Part Time)	TUITION Out of State Full Time (Part Time)	CALENDAR Fall	Winter	Spring	Summer	Day	Evening	Credits for JD	Required Credits for Courses	Transferable Summer Courses	Joint Degree	Graduate Law Degree	ENROLLED Full Time (Part Time)	Avg Age First Year	% Women	% Minority	Attrition Rate %	FACULTY Full Time (Part Time)	LIBRARY Volumes	LIBRARY Microforms
California Western School of Law 225 Cedar Street San Diego, CA 92101-3046 619-525-1401 Fax: 619-615-1401 rbriscoe@cwsl.edu	202	$45	April 1	March 18	$22,200 ($16,200)	$22,200 ($16,200)	✓		✓		✓		89	43	✓	✓		639 (61)	27	52	26	14	42 (45)	257,781	643,130
Campbell University (Norman Adrian Wiggins School of Law) P.O. Box 158 Buies Creek, NC 27506 910-893-1754 Fax: 910-893-1780 culaw@webster.campbell.edu	204	$40	open	open	$17,500	$17,500	✓				✓		90	73		✓		297		50	6		19 (18)	156,000	56,998
Capital University (Law School) 303 East Broad Street Columbus, OH 43215-3200 614-236-6500 Fax: 614-236-6972 admissions@law.capital.edu	206	$35	April 1	April 1	$15,979 ($9,918)	$15,979 ($9,918)	✓				✓	✓	86 sem.	42	✓	✓	✓	389 (346)	27	45	11	10	30 (56)	239,000	35,979
Case Western Reserve University (School of Law) 11075 East Boulevard Cleveland, OH 44106 216-368-3600 Fax: 216-368-6144 lawadmissions@po.cwru.edu or lawmoney@po.cwru.edu	208	$40	April 1	May 1	$21,300 ($888/hr)	$21,300 ($888/hr)	✓				✓		88	33	✓	✓	✓	620 (12)	25	45		3	46 (64)	365,175	419,218
Catholic University of America (Columbus School of Law) Cardinal Station Washington, DC 20064 (202) 319-5151 Fax: (202) 319-6285	210	$55	March 1	March 1	$25,092 ($18,937)	$25,092 ($18,937)	✓				✓	✓	84	33	✓	✓	✓	654 (278)	23	52	22	4	46 (87)	322,816	52,864
Catholic University of Puerto Rico (School of Law) Avenida Las Americas-Station 6 Ponce, PR 00732 809-841-2000	212		Check	Check							✓	✓	94	82		✓	220	(220)	24	50	11	14	(18)	135,000	15,000
Chapman University (School of Law) One University Drive Orange, CA 92866 714-628-2500 Fax: 714-628-2501 misles@chapman.edu	214	$40	open	April 1	$21,600 ($14,850)	$21,600 ($14,850)	✓				✓	✓	88	53 to 54	✓	✓		99 (74)	28	49	26	15	20 (9)	225,945	177,876

No.	School	Fee	Deadline 1	Deadline 2	Resident Tuition	Nonresident Tuition																		
216	City University of New York at Queens College (School of Law) 65-21 Main Street Flushing, NY 11367-1300 718-340-4210 Fax: 718-340-4372 admissions@maclaw.law.cuny.edu	$40	March 15	May 15	$5,700	$8,930	✓	✓	✓	92	70	✓	✓	389	29	59	41	10	38 (12)	250,000	820,000			
218	Cleveland State University (Cleveland-Marshall College of Law) 1801 Euclid Avenue Cleveland, OH 44115 216-687-2304 Fax: 216-687-6881	$35	April 1	March 1	$7,826 ($6,020)	$15,522 ($11,940)	✓	✓	✓	87	34 (plus 2)	✓	✓	481 (305)	27	48	14	10	36 (25)	445,908	57,072			
220	College of William and Mary (William and Mary Law School) P.O. Box 8795 Williamsburg, VA 23187-8795 757-221-3785 Fax: 757-221-3261 lawadm@facstaff.wm.edu	$40	March 1	Feb 15	$9,074	$18,200	✓	✓	✓	90	36	✓	✓	538	25	43	17	2	28 (42)	355,000	840,000			
222	Columbia University (School of Law) 435 West 116th Street New York, NY 10027 212-854-2670 Fax: 212-854-1109	$65	Feb 15	March 1	$27,940	$27,940	✓	✓	✓	83	35	✓	✓	1167	24	46	33		86	993,606	679,900			
224	Cornell University (Law School) Myron Taylor Hall Ithaca, NY 14853 607-255-5141 Fax: 607-255-7193	$65	Feb 1	March 15	$25,500	$25,500	✓	✓	✓	84	36	✓	✓	546	23	47	25	1	45 (11)	473,665	701,091			
226	Creighton University (School of Law) 2500 California Plaza Omaha, NE 68178 402-280-2872 Fax: 402-280-3161 admit@culaw.creighton.edu	$40	May 1	July 1	$16,548 ($555/hr)	$16,548 ($555/hr)	✓	✓	✓	94	39	✓	✓	409 (18)	26	44	9	3	22 (41)	254,585	95,779			
228	De Paul University (College of Law) 25 East Jackson Boulevard Chicago, IL 60604 312-362-6831 lawinfo@wppost.depaul.edu	$40	April 1	March 1	$20,700 ($14,000)	$20,700 ($14,000)	✓	✓	✓	86	37	✓	✓	785 (323)	24	54	20		50 (73)	346,097	902,637			
230	Drake University (Law School) 2507 University Avenue Des Moines, IA 50311 515-271-1990 lawadmit@drake.edu	$40	April 1	March 1	$17,630	$17,630	✓	✓	✓	90	41	✓	✓	338 (18)	26	46	13	6	30 (24)	280,000	90,000			
232	Duke University (School of Law) Science and Towerview Drive, Box 90393 Durham, NC 27708 919-613-7020 Fax: 919-613-7257 admissions@law.duke.edu	$65	Jan 1	March 15	$25,500	$25,500	✓	✓	✓	84	30	✓	✓	680	24	46	26	1	36 (42)	535,000	71,000			

INSTITUTION	Profile Page	APPLICATIONS Fee	APPLICATIONS Deadline	APPLICATIONS Deadline Financial Aid	TUITION In State Full Time (Part Time)	TUITION Out of State Full Time (Part Time)	CALENDAR Fall	CALENDAR Winter	CALENDAR Spring	CALENDAR Summer	PROGRAMS Day	PROGRAMS Evening	PROGRAMS Credits for JD	PROGRAMS Required Credits for Courses	PROGRAMS Transferable Summer Courses	PROGRAMS Joint Degree	PROGRAMS Graduate Law Degree	ENROLLED Full Time (Part Time)	STUDENT BODY Average Age First Year	STUDENT BODY % Women	STUDENT BODY % Minority	STUDENT BODY Attrition Rate %	FACULTY Full Time (Part Time)	LIBRARY Volumes	LIBRARY Microforms
Duquesne University (School of Law) 900 Locust Street, Hanley Hall, Pittsburgh, PA 15282, 412-396-6296, campion@duq.edu	234	$50	April 1	May 31	$15,764 ($12,004)	$15,764 ($12,004)	✓				✓	✓	86	33	✓	✓		377 (314)	27	46	6	2	29 (40)	236,000	210,000
Emory University (School of Law) Gambrell Hall, Atlanta, GA 30322, 404-727-6801, Fax 404-727-2477, jbaley@law.emory.edu	236	$50	March 1	March 1	$23,870	$23,870	✓		✓		✓	✓	88	39	✓	✓	✓	616	24	52	21	3	46 (47)	300,000	71,734
Florida Coastal School of Law 7555 Beach Boulevard, Jacksonville, FL 32216, 904-680-7710, Fax 904-680-7776, admissions@fcsl.edu	238	$50	open		$17,540 ($14,030)	$17,540 ($14,030)	✓				✓	✓	87	56	✓	✓		237 (246)	28	43	23	8	27 (31)	127,829	421,745
Florida State University (College of Law) 425 W. Jefferson St., Tallahassee, FL 32306-1601, 850-644-3787, Fax 850-644-7284, admissions@law.fsu.edu	240	$20	Feb 15	April 1	$4,890	$16,162	✓				✓	✓	88	35	✓	✓	✓	683	25	46	22	3	46 (13)	409,603	842,184
Fordham University (School of Law) 140 West 62nd Street, New York, NY 10023, 212-626-6810	242	$60	March 1	May 1	$24,725 ($18,545)	$24,725 ($18,545)	✓				✓	✓	83	39	✓	✓	✓	1088 (349)	24	46	24	2	64 (200)	543,992	1,044,801
Franklin Pierce Law Center 2 White Street, Concord, NH 03301, 603-228-9217, Fax 603-228-1074, Ladmissions@fplc.edu	244		May 1	open	$17,050		✓				✓	✓	84	39	✓	✓	359		28	36	12	24 / 10	(37)	126,896	447,501
George Mason University (School of Law) 3401 North Fairfax Drive, Arlington, VA 22201-4498, 703-993-8010, Fax 703-993-8260, arichar5@gmu.edu	246		March 1	open	$7,784 ($6,116)	$18,228 ($14,322)	✓				✓	✓	90	41	✓	✓		365 (371)	26	38	10	4	24 (68)	359,000	886,000
George Washington University (Law School) 2000 H Street, N.W., Washington, DC 20052, 202-739-0648, jd@main.nlc.gwu.edu	248	$65	March 1	March 1	$25,635 ($902/hr)	$25,635 ($902/hr)	✓				✓	✓	84	34	✓	✓	✓	1215 (239)	24	45	30	2	67 (170)	519,652	1,096,541

No.	School / Contact	App Fee	Deadline 1	Deadline 2	Tuition 1	Tuition 2	✓	✓ / (b)	✓	✓	Bar	Bar	✓	✓		✓	Enrollment						Faculty	Vol. A	Vol. B
250	**Georgetown University** (Law Center) 600 New Jersey Avenue, N.W. Washington, DC 20001 202-662-9010 admis@law.georgetown.edu	$65	Feb 1	March 1	$25,705 ($18,000)	$25,705 ($18,000)	✓				83	31	✓	✓		✓	1352 (612)	24	49	26		1	87 (92)		2,207,015
252	**Georgia State University** (College of Law) P.O. Box 4037 Atlanta, GA 30302-4037 404-651-2096 Fax: 404-651-2096 cjackson@gsu.edu	$30	March 15	April 1	$3,392 ($142/hr)	$13,568 ($566/hr)	✓				90	43	✓	✓		✓	395 (233)	30	51	15		11	42 (30)	145,617	623,675
254	**Golden Gate University** (School of Law) 536 Mission Street San Francisco, CA 94105-2968 415-442-6630	$40	April 15	March 1	$20,880 ($14,400)	$20,880 ($14,400)	✓				88	54	✓	✓		✓	463 (299)	27	55	18		24	33 (117)	109,831	120,221
256	**Gonzaga University** (School of Law) Box 3528 Spokane, WA 99220-3528 509-323-5532 Fax: 509-323-5710 admissions@lawschool.gonzaga.edu	$40	April 1	Feb 1	$19,350 ($645/hr)	$19,350 ($645/hr)	✓				90	58	✓	✓		✓	439 (19)	28	39	15		10	34 (24)	253,517	596,201
258	**Hamline University** (School of Law) 1536 Hewitt Avenue St. Paul, MN 55104-1284 651-523-2461 Fax: 651-523-3064 lawadme@gw.hamline.edu	$40	May 15		$17,448	$17,448	✓				88	33	✓	✓		✓	442 (46)	27	55	14		3	29 (52)	151,000	87,000
260	**Harvard University** (Harvard Law School) Cambridge, MA 02138 617-495-3109 Fax: 617-495-1110 jdadmiss@law.harvard.edu	$40	Feb 1	check	$25,000		✓	1658			82	30	✓	✓		✓		24	42	28	94	1	(75)	1,920,648	187,600
262	**Hofstra University** (School of Law) 121 Hofstra University Hempstead, NY 11549 516-463-5916 Fax: 516-463-6264 lawpts@hofstra.edu	$60	April 15	June 1	$23,246	$23,246	✓				87	39	✓	✓		✓	900 (2)	25	46	18		4	39 (35)	487,630	1,357,850
264	**Howard University** (Howard University) 2900 Van Ness Street, N.W. Washington, DC 20008 202-806-8008 Fax: 202-806-8162 admissions@law.howard.edu	$60	March 31	April 1	$13,030		✓	412		✓	88	n/av	✓	✓	✓	✓	(3)	25	60	94	33	5	(23)	283,000	54,000
266	**Illinois Institute of Technology** (Chicago-Kent College of Law) 565 West Adams Street Chicago, IL 60661 312-906-5020 admit@kentlaw.edu	$45	April 1	April 15	$21,715 ($15,665)	$21,715 ($15,665)	✓				87	42	✓	✓		✓	796 (347)	25	50	16		5	70 (103)	560,000	687,941
270	**Indiana University at Bloomington** (School of Law) 211 S. Indiana Avenue Bloomington, IN 47405-1001 812-855-4765 Fax: 812-855-0555 lawadmis@indiana.edu	$35	open	March 1	$6,850	$17,568	✓				86	36	✓	✓		✓	608 (4)	24	43	20		3	38 (16)	591,504	1,138,543

INSTITUTION	Profile Page	APPLICATIONS Fee	Deadline	Financial Aid Deadline	TUITION In State Full Time (Part Time)	Out of State Full Time (Part Time)	Fall	Winter	Spring	Summer	Day	Evening	Credits for JD	Required Credits for Courses	Transferable Summer Courses	Joint Degree	Graduate Law Degree	ENROLLED STUDENT BODY Full Time (Part Time)	Average Age First Year	% Women	% Minority	Attrition Rate %	FACULTY Full Time (Part Time)	LIBRARY Volumes	Microforms
Indiana University-Purdue University (Indiana University School of Law-Indianapolis) 735 West New York Street Indianapolis, IN 46202-5194 317-274-2459 Fax: 317-274-3955 khmiller@iupui.edu	268	$35	March 1	March 1	$7,063 ($4,570)	$17,205 ($11,100)	✓				✓	✓	90	37	✓	✓	✓	566 (302)	27	45	13	10	42 (37)	491,716	657,798
Inter-American University of Puerto Rico (School of Law) P.O. Box 70351 San Juan, PR 00936-8351 809-751-1912, ext. 2013	272		Check	Check	$3,250 ($2,590)	$3,250 ($2,590)	✓				✓	✓	92	62	✓	✓	✓	335 (310)	24	47	17	8	20 (16)	160,098	139,963
John Marshall Law School 315 South Plymouth Court Chicago, IL 60604 312-987-1406 Fax: 312-427-5136 admission@jmls.edu	274	$50	March 1	Check	$21,000 ($700/hr)	$700/hr ($700/hr)	✓		✓		✓	✓	90	52	✓	✓	✓	719 (433)	25	43	11	5	56 (138)	353,737	55,710
Lewis and Clark College (Northwestern School of Law) 10015 Southwest Terwilliger Boulevard Portland, OR 97219 503-768-6613 Fax: 503-768-6671 lawadmss@lclark.edu	276	$50	March 15	March 1	$19,180 ($14,386)	$19,180 ($14,386)	✓				✓	✓	86	28-35	✓	✓	✓	491 (181)	25	47	11	14	37 (54)	451,706	254,548
Louisiana State University (Paul M. Hebert Law Center) Baton Rouge, LA 70803 225-388-8646 Fax: 225-388-8647 bloup@lsu.edu	278	$25	Feb 1	April 1	$6,010	$11,851	✓				✓		97	39	✓	✓	✓	644	24	47	11	25	31 (40)	402,195	887,946
Loyola Marymount University (Loyola Law School) 919 S. Albany Street Los Angeles, CA 90015 213-736-1180 admissions@lls.edu	280	$50	Feb 1	March 2	$22,530 ($15,064)	$22,530 ($15,064)	✓				✓	✓	87	49	✓	✓		992 (352)	24	49	38	3	63 (79)	486,509	1,238,076
Loyola University New Orleans (School of Law) 7214 St. Charles Avenue New Orleans, LA 70118 504-861-5575 Fax: 504-861-5772 ladmit@loyno.edu	282		open	Check	$19,685 ($13,335)	✓					✓	90		✓	✓	✓	✓	503 (147)	23	47	23	12	30 (36)	265,089	570,114

																							School
942,152		354,981	29 (149)		5	15	58	25	520 (190)	✓	✓	✓	46	86	✓	✓		✓	$22,990 ($17,244)	$22,990 ($17,244)	March 1	April 1	$50	284	**Loyola University of Chicago (School of Law)** One East Pearson Street Chicago, IL 60611 312-915-7170 Fax: 312-915-7201 law-admissions@luc.edu
			24 (24)		2	8	46	25	420 (65)	✓	✓	✓	34	90	✓	✓		✓	$19,100 ($790/hr)	$19,100 ($790/hr)	April 1	April 1	$40	286	**Marquette University (Law School)** Office of Admissions Sensenbrenner Hall, P.O. Box 1881 Milwaukee, WI 53201-1881 414-288-6767 Fax: 414-288-0676 law.admission@marquette.edu
	292,000		27 (27)		5	12	49	26	415	✓	✓	✓	65	91			✓	$19,250	$19,250	April 1	March 15	$45	288	**Mercer University (Walter F. George School of Law)** 1021 Georgia Ave. Macon, GA 31201 912-301-2605 Fax: 912-301-2989 Sutton_me@mercer.edu
117,794	102,314		25 (40)		14	40	28		547 (149)	✓	✓	✓	56	88	✓	✓		✓	$15,734 ($11,815)	$16,584 ($12,452)	July 2	April 15	$50	290	**Michigan State University (Detroit College of Law)** 316 Law College Bldg. East Lansing, MI 48824-1300 517-432-0222 Fax: 517-432-0098 heatleya@pilot.msu.edu
540,000	253,000		18 (18)	7	9	44	26		372	✓	✓	✓	36	88			✓	$14,370	$14,370		May 1	$25	292	**Mississippi College (School of Law)** 151 E. Griffith Street Jackson, MS 39201 601-925-7150 pevans@mc.edu
645,000	300,000		40 (59)	7	17	54	28		592 (366)	✓	✓		43	84	✓	✓		✓	$15,950 ($11,960)	$15,950 ($11,960)	April 15	March 15	$50	294	**New England School of Law** 154 Stuart Street Boston, MA 02116 617-422-7210 Fax: 617-422-7200 admit@admin.nesl.edu
981,917	463,750		53 (82)	3	24	48	27		920 (476)	✓	✓	✓	38	86	✓	✓		✓	$23,268 ($16,588)	$23,268 ($16,588)	April 15	April 1	$50	296	**New York Law School** 57 Worth Street New York, NY 10013-2960 212-431-2888 Fax: 212-966-1522 admissions@nyls.edu
19,309	997,463		114 (71)		23	50			1328	✓	✓	✓		82	✓	✓		✓	$27,540	$27,540	March 15	Feb 1	$65	298	**New York University (School of Law)** 110 West Third Street New York, NY 10012 212-998-6060 Fax: 212-995-4527
639,314	284,115		23 (9)		53	56			255 (107)	✓	✓	✓	65	88	✓	✓		✓	$11,392 ($11,392)	$2,288 ($2,288)	Feb 1	April 15	$30	300	**North Carolina Central University (School of Law)** 1512 S. Alston Avenue Durham, NC 27707 919-560-6333 Fax: 919-560-6339 jfaucett@wpo.nccu.edu

INSTITUTION	Profile Page	APPLICATIONS Fee	Deadline	Financial Aid Deadline	TUITION In State Full Time (Part Time)	Out of State Full Time (Part Time)	CALENDAR Fall	Day	Evening	PROGRAMS Credits for JD	Required Credits for Courses	Transferable Summer Courses	Joint Degree	Graduate Law Degree	ENROLLED Full Time (Part Time)	STUDENT BODY Average Age First Year	% Women	% Minority	Attrition Rate %	FACULTY Full Time (Part Time)	LIBRARY Volumes	Microforms
Northeastern University (School of Law) 400 Huntington Avenue, Boston, MA 02115; 617-373-2395; Fax: 617-373-8865; pbauer@slaw.neu.edu	302	$65	March 1	March 1	$23,620	$23,620	✓	✓		99	49	✓	✓		591	25	60	25	4	29 (25)	293,243	623,096
Northern Illinois University (College of Law) Swen Parson Hall, De Kalb, IL 60115; 815-753-1420; Fax: 815-753-4501; lawadm@niu.edu	304	$40	May 15	March 1	$5,887	$11,774	✓	✓		90	36		✓		261 (19)	27	40	25	9	27 (10)	210,312	453,961
Northern Kentucky University (Salmon P. Chase College of Law) Louie B. Nunn Hall, Highland Heights, KY 41099; 606-572-6476; Fax: 606-572-6081; brayg@nku.edu	306	$30	March 1	April 1	$7,380 ($4,920)	$19,110 ($12,740)	✓	✓		90	42	✓	✓	✓	185 (173)	28	45	6	19	25 (42)	242,595	856
Northwestern University (School of Law) 357 East Chicago Avenue, Chicago, IL 60611; 312-503-8465; Fax: 312-503-0178; nubwadm@nwu.edu	308	$70	Feb 15	March 15	$26,850	$26,850	✓	✓		86	32		✓	✓	650	25	49	29	1	59 (149)	656,775	195,648
Nova Southeastern University (Shepard Broad Law Center) 3305 College Avenue, Fort Lauderdale, FL 33314-7721; 954-262-6117; Fax: 954-262-3844; admission@nsu.law.nova.edu	310	$50	March 1	March 1	$19,970 ($14,980)	$19,970 ($14,980)	✓	✓	✓	90	44	✓	✓	✓	726 (212)		49	29	8	45 (64)	314,036	137,029
Ohio Northern University (Claude W. Pettit College of Law) 525 South Main Street, Ada, OH 45810; 419-772-2211; Fax: 419-772-1487; g-keener@onu.edu	312			Check	$18,980	$18,980	✓	✓		87	45	✓			283	26	34	18	6	18 (22)	263,747	72,943
Ohio State University (College of Law) 55 West 12th Avenue, John Deaver Drinko Hall, Columbus, OH 43210-1391; 614-292-8810; Fax: 614-292-1383; roboski.1@osu.edu	314		March 15	Check	$8,424		✓	✓		88	38	✓	✓		638	22	44	16	1	(30)	653,399	880,049

School	No.	Fee	Deadline	Deadline	Tuition (Res.)	Tuition (Nonres.)				%84/90	Median age		✓	✓	Enroll (part)						Vol. 1	Vol. 2
Oklahoma City University (School of Law) 2501 North Blackwelder, Oklahoma City, OK 73106-1493 405-521-5354 Fax: 405-521-5802 lawadmit@okcu.edu	316	$35	Aug 1	March 1	$15,900 ($10,600)	$15,900 ($10,600)	✓			90	46	✓	✓		371 (133)	30	41	15	8	31 (17)	271,739	618,909
Pace University (School of Law) 78 North Broadway, White Plains, NY 10603 914-422-4010 Fax: 914-422-4248 adagostino@genesis.law.pace.edu	318	$55	Feb 15	Feb 1	$22,900 ($17,200)	$22,900 ($17,200)	✓			90	40	✓	✓		448 (305)	25	54	19	6	47 (76)	327,913	60,613
Pennsylvania State University (Dickinson School of Law) 150 South College Street, Carlisle, PA 17013 717-240-5207 Fax: 717-241-3503 dsladmit@psu.edu	320	$50	March 1	Feb 15	$15,850	$15,850	✓			88	40	✓	✓		536 (1)	25	42	7	7	35 (57)	425,000	1,017,000
Pepperdine University (School of Law) 24255 Pacific Coast Highway, Malibu, CA 90263 310-456-4631 Fax: 310-317-7668 soladmis@pepperdine.edu	322	$40	March 1	Check	$23,810		✓			88	57	662	✓	✓		23	45	17	34 / 5		252,000	87,000
Quinnipiac College (School of Law) 275 Mt. Carmel Avenue, Hamden, CT 06518-1948 203-287-3400 Fax: 203-287-3339 ladm@quinnipiac.edu	324	$40	open	April 1	$21,200 ($16,150)	$21,200 ($16,150)	✓			86	53	✓	✓		502 (291)	27	47	14	4	38 (25)	344,390	186,502
Regent University (School of Law) 1000 Regent University Drive, Virginia Beach, VA 23464-9800 757-226-4584 Fax: 757-226-4139 lawschool@regent.edu	326	$40	June 1	March 1	$16,480 ($515/hr)	$16,480 ($515/hr)	✓			90	66	✓	✓		413 (78)	27	45	18	7	22 (37)	316,000	900,000
Roger Williams University (School of Law) Ten Metacom Avenue, Bristol, RI 02809-5171 401-254-4555 Fax: 401-254-4516 admissions@rwulaw.rwu.edu	328	$60	May 15	May 15	$20,100 ($15,410)	$2,010 ($15,410)	✓			90	54	✓	✓		231 (163)	28	49	11	12	25 (25)	250,000	891,546
Rutgers University/Camden (School of Law) Fifth and Penn Streets, Camden, NJ 08102 609-225-6102 Fax: 609-225-6537	332	$50	March 1	March 1	$10,106 ($418/hr)	$14,828 ($617/hr)	✓			84	34	✓	✓		604 (145)	26	49	18	4	43 (65)	407,335	630,770
Rutgers University/Newark (School of Law) S.I. Newhouse Center for Law and Justice, 15 Washington St. Newark, NJ 07102 973-353-5557/5554 Fax: 973-353-1445	330		March 1	March 1	$9,100 ($355/hr)	$13,500 ($550/hr)	✓			84	31 to 32	✓	✓		515 (230)	28	46	31	5	49 (34)	412,542	144,376

Institution	Profile Page	Fee	App. Deadline	Financial Aid Deadline	Tuition In State Full Time (Part Time)	Tuition Out of State Full Time (Part Time)	Fall	Winter	Spring	Summer	Day	Evening	Credits for JD	Required Credits for Courses	Transferable Summer Courses	Joint Degree	Graduate Law Degree	Enrolled Full Time (Part Time)	Average Age First Year	% Women	% Minority	Attrition Rate %	Faculty Full Time (Part Time)	Volumes	Microforms
Saint John's University (School of Law) 8000 Utopia Parkway, Jamaica, NY 11439, 718-990-6611/6612, Fax: 718-990-2526, rsvp@sjulaw.stjohns.edu	334		March 1		$22,000 ($16,500)	$22,000 ($16,500)	✓		✓		✓	✓	85	61	✓	✓		691 (276)	23	39	25		59 (37)	432,804	1,148,680
Saint Louis University (School of Law) 3700 Lindell Boulevard, St. Louis, MO 63108, 314-977-2800, admissions@law.slu.edu	336	$55	March 1	April 1	$20,130 ($15,080)	$20,130 ($15,080)	✓				✓	✓	88	36	✓	✓	✓	550 (227)	26	48	13	5	39 (28)	565,677	51,000
Saint Mary's University (School of Law) One Camino Santa Maria, San Antonio, TX 78228-8601, 210-436-3523, Fax: 210-431-4202	338	$45	March 1	March 31	$17,515	$17,515	✓				✓	✓	90	46	✓	✓	✓	764		47	39	2	34 (28)	320,000	633,117
Samford University (Cumberland School of Law) 800 Lakeshore Drive, Birmingham, AL 35229, 205-726-2702, Fax: 205-726-2673, lawadmissions@samford.edu	340	$40	Feb 28	March 1	$18,976	$18,976	✓				✓	✓	86	53	✓	✓	✓	586	24	41	7	2	32 (10)	254,346	471,485
Santa Clara University (School of Law) 500 El Camino Real, Santa Clara, CA 95053, 408-554-4800, Fax: 408-554-7897, lawadmission@scu.edu	342	$50	March 1	Feb 1	$22,000 ($16,000)	$22,000 ($16,000)	✓				✓	✓	90	46	✓	✓	✓	623 (276)	24	51	30	7	34 (26)	262,447	763,854
Seattle University (School of Law) 900 Broadway, Seattle, WA 98122-4340, 206-398-4200, Fax: 206-398-4058, lawadmis@seattleu.edu	344	$50	April 1	March 1	$19,110 ($15,925)	$19,110 ($15,925)	✓			✓	✓	✓	90	44	✓	✓	✓	698 (185)	26	57	23	9	35 (62)	323,466	924,769
Seton Hall University (School of Law) One Newark Center, Newark, NJ 07102-5210, 973-642-8747, Fax: 973-642-8876, admitme@shu.edu	346	$50	April 1	April 15	$20,714 ($750)	$20,714 ($750)	✓				✓	✓	85	44	✓	✓	✓	834 (352)	26	46	15	12	58 (106)	400,039	495,570
South Texas College of Law 1303 San Jacinto Street, Houston, TX 77002-7000, 713-646-1810, Fax: 713-646-2929, acramer@stcl.edu	348	$50	Feb 25	May 1	$15,540 ($10,360)	$15,540 ($10,360)	✓		✓		✓	✓	90	44	✓	✓		850 (370)	27	44	23	12	54 (33)	198,884	1,053,310

#	School	App. fee	Deadline 1	Deadline 2	Tuition (res.)	Tuition (nonres.)		%	%		Enrollment	%	%					
350	**Southern Illinois University (School of Law)** Lesar Law Building, Mail Code 6804, Carbondale, IL 62901-6804, 618-453-8767, Fax: 618-453-8769, lawadmit@siu.edu	$25	March 1	March 1	$4,800	$14,400	✓	90	46	✓	350	27	37	8	7	23 (6)	354,239	157,847
352	**Southern Methodist University (School of Law)** Office of Admissions, P.O. Box 750110, Dallas, TX 75275-0110, 214-768-2550, Fax: 214-768-2549	$50	Feb 1	June 1	$23,000	$23,000	✓	90	37	✓	773 (13)	24	38	13	3	42 (100)	480,000	75,217
354	**Southern University and A & M College (Law Center)** Post Office Box 9294, Baton Rouge, LA 70813, 225-771-5340, Fax: 225-771-2121	$25	March 31	April 15	$3,288	$7,888	✓	96	75	✓	317	27	52	66	10	30 (14)	415,208	7,867
356	**Southwestern University (School of Law)** 675 South Westmoreland Avenue, Los Angeles, CA 90005-3992, 213-738-6717, admissions@swlaw.edu	$50	June 30	June 1	$21,990 ($13,927)	$21,990 ($13,927)	✓	87	52	✓	605 (262)	27	51	36		50 (37)	404,177	934,164
358	**St. Thomas University (School of Law)** 16400 N.W. 32nd Avenue, Miami, FL 33054, 305-623-2310, lamy@stu.edu	$50	April 30	April 15	$20,725	$20,725	✓	90	53	✓	487	27	45	48	25	22 (24)	293,927	990,900
360	**Stanford University (Stanford Law School)** Crown Quadrangle, Stanford, CA 94305-8610, 650-723-4995, law.admissions@forsythe.stanford.edu, law.stanford.edu/	$40	Feb 1		$26,158	$26,158	✓	86	27	✓	545	25	45	32		52	484,858	1,786
362	**State University at Buffalo (Law School)** O'Brian Hall, Buffalo, NY 14260, 716-645-2907, Fax: 716-645-5940, coxublaw@buffalo.edu	$50	March 15	March 1	$8,450	$14,000	✓	87	35	✓	712	25	48	18	2	56 (102)	301,692	1,983,759
364	**Stetson University (College of Law)** 1401 61st Street South, St. Petersburg, FL 33707, 727-562-7802, Fax: 727-343-0136, lawadmit@hermes.law.stetson.edu	$50	March 1	March 1	$20,350	$20,350	✓	88	48	✓	645 (12)	23	55	19	4	42 (40)	356,875	769,000
366	**Suffolk University (Law School)** 120 Tremont Street, Boston, MA 02108-4977, 617-573-8144, Fax: 617-573-1367	$50	March 1	March 3	$21,750 ($16,310)	$21,750 ($16,310)	✓	84	58	✓	997 (711)	26	50	10	8	60 (114)	318,000	801,693

INSTITUTION	Profile Page	APPLICATIONS Fee	APPLICATIONS Deadline	APPLICATIONS Deadline Financial Aid	TUITION In State Full Time (Part Time)	TUITION Out of State Full Time (Part Time)	CALENDAR Fall	CALENDAR Winter	CALENDAR Spring	CALENDAR Summer	PROGRAMS Day	PROGRAMS Evening	PROGRAMS Credits for JD	PROGRAMS Required Credits for Courses	PROGRAMS Transferable Summer Courses	PROGRAMS Joint Degree	PROGRAMS Graduate Law Degree	ENROLLED STUDENT BODY Full Time (Part Time)	ENROLLED Average Age First Year	ENROLLED % Women	ENROLLED % Minority	ENROLLED Attrition Rate %	FACULTY Full Time (Part Time)	LIBRARY Volumes	LIBRARY Microforms
Syracuse University (College of Law) Office of Admissions and Financial Aid, Syracuse, NY 13244-1030, 315-443-1962, Fax: 315-443-9568	368	$50	April 1	March 1	$23,140	$23,140	✓				✓		87	40	✓	✓		763 (3)	24	46	23		47 (43)	377,386	
Temple University (James E. Beasley School of Law) 1719 N. Broad Street, Philadelphia, PA 19122, 215-204-8925, Fax: 215-204-1185, lawadmis@blue.temple.edu	370	$50	March 1	March 1	$9,226 ($7,378)	$15,990 ($12,792)	✓				✓	✓	86	38		✓		789 (319)	26	47	24	4	57 (191)	511,757	671,141
Texas Southern University (Thurgood Marshall School of Law) 3100 Cleburne Avenue, Houston, TX 77004, 713-313-7114, Fax: 713-313-1049, cgardner@tsulaw.edu	372		April 1	Check	$5,144	$9,024	✓				✓		90	70	✓	✓		632	27	46	80	35	34 (19)	229,464	100,536
Texas Tech University (School of Law) 1802 Hartford, Lubbock, TX 79409, 806-742-3985, Fax: 806-742-1629, xydaw@ttacs.ttu.edu	374	$50	Feb 1	March	$6,600	$11,666	✓				✓		90	55	✓	✓		597	25	44	14	15	28 (10)	280,153	492,945
Texas Wesleyan University (School of Law) 1515 Commerce Street, Fort Worth, TX 76102, 817-212-4040, Fax 817-212-4002, law-admissions@law.txwes.edu	376		open	Check	$7,800 ($5,720)	✓				✓	✓	88	50	✓			262 (190)	32	41	19	15	26 (24)	152,556	441,501	
Thomas Jefferson School of Law 2121 San Diego Avenue, San Diego, CA 92110, 619-297-9700, Fax 619-294-4713, adm@tjsl.edu	378	$35	open	Feb 14	$19,950 ($12,400)	$19,950 ($12,400)	✓		✓		✓	✓	88	55	✓			382 (202)		39	22		29 (20)	221,247	121,154
Thomas M. Cooley Law School 300 South Capitol Avenue, Lansing, MI 48901, 517-371-5140, Fax: 517-334-5718, admissions@cooley.edu	380		open	check	$16,500 ($13,200)	$16,500 ($13,200)	✓	✓	✓		✓	✓	90	63	✓			323 (1248)	26	39	16	30	60 (129)	361,885	182,620

Page	School / Contact	App. Fee	Deadline 1	Deadline 2	Tuition A	Tuition B		% 1	% 2		Enrollment					Faculty	Library A	Library B
382	**Touro College** (Jacob D. Fuchsberg Law Center), 300 Nassau Road, Huntington, NY 11743, 631-421-2244 ext. 312, Fax: 631-421-9708, admissions@tourolaw.edu	$50	on a roll	June 1	$20,720 ($16,070)	$20,720 ($16,070)	✓	87	55 to 56	✓	384 (300)	29	49	25	5	37 (30)	380,000	
384	**Tulane University** (Law School), Weinmann Hall, 6329 Freret Street, New Orleans, LA 70118, 504-865-5930, Fax: 504-865-6710, admissions@law.tulane.edu	$50	May 1	Feb 15	$22,664	$22,664	✓	88	31	✓	965 (5)	24	47	25	5	50 (49)	500,000	
386	**Union University** (Albany Law School), 80 New Scotland Avenue, Albany, NY 12208, 518-445-2326, Fax: 518-445-2369, admissions@mail.als.edu	$50	March 15		$19,995 ($14,996)	$19,995 ($14,996)	✓	87	31	✓	646 (42)	26	53	19	10	41 (41)	247,669	1,421,190
388	**University of Akron** (School of Law), Corner Wolf Ledges and University Avenue, Akron, OH 44325-2901, 330-972-7331, Fax: 330-258-2343, lawadmissions@uakron.edu	$35	March 1	May 1	$8,400 ($6,572)	$14,176 ($11,084)	✓	88	44	✓	338 (222)	29	49	13	23	27 (37)	261,818	371,921
390	**University of Alabama** (School of Law), Box 870382, Tuscaloosa, AL 35487-0382, 205-348-5440, Fax: 205-348-3917, admissions@law.ua.edu	$25	March 1	March 1	$4,812	$10,156	✓	90	36	✓	544	24	41	12	2	35 (41)	379,165	97,668
392	**University of Arizona** (James E. Rogers College of Law), Mountain and Speedway, P.O. Box 210176, Tucson, AZ 85721-0176, 520-621-3477, Fax: 520-621-9140, admissions@nt.law.arizona.edu		March 1	Check	$5,014	$10,712	✓	85	39	✓	465	25	48	24	1	33 (33)	380,000	426,000
394	**University of Arkansas** (School of Law), Robert A. Leflar Law Center, Waterman Hall, Fayetteville, AR 72701, 501-575-3102	$40	April 1	April 1	$3,362	$7,779	✓	90	43	✓	372	26	44	10		35 (5)	243,962	43,584
396	**University of Arkansas at Little Rock** (School of Law), 1201 McAlmont Street, Little Rock, AR 72202-5142, 501-324-9439, Fax: 501-324-9433		May 1	March 1	$4,800 ($2,880)	$10,800 ($6,480)	✓	87	48	✓	247 (155)	28	46	10	1	29 (29)	164,039	528,208
398	**University of Baltimore** (School of Law), 1420 North Charles Street, Baltimore, MD 21201-5779, 410-837-4459, Fax: 410-837-4450, lwadmiss@ubmail.ubalt.edu		April 1	Check	$9,027 ($373/hr)	$16,108 ($630/hr)	✓	90	39	✓	602 (302)	28	49	19	2	45 (79)	287,125	561,053

INSTITUTION	Profile Page	Fee	Deadline	Deadline Financial Aid	In State Full Time (Part Time)	Out of State Full Time (Part Time)	Fall	Winter	Spring	Summer	Day	Evening	Credits for JD	Required Credits for Courses	Transferable Summer Courses	Joint Degree	Graduate Law Degree	Full Time (Part Time)	Average Age First Year	% Women	% Minority	Attrition Rate %	Full Time (Part Time)	Volumes	Microforms
University of California (Hastings College of the Law) 200 McAllister Street San Francisco, CA 94102 415-565-4623 Fax: 415-565-4863 admiss@uchastings.edu	400	$40	March 1	March 1	$11,183	$19,953	✓				✓		86	34		✓	✓	1122	25	49	28	5	47 (73)	627,035	1,229,584
University of California at Berkeley (Boalt Hall) 5 Boalt Hall Berkeley, CA 94720 510-642-2274 Fax: 510-643-6222 admissions@law.berkeley.edu	402	$40	Feb 1	March 2	$10,865	$20,669	✓				✓		85	30		✓	✓	845	24	50	31	6	61 (102)	680,000	660,000
University of California at Davis (School of Law) King Hall - 400 Mrak Hall Drive Davis, CA 95616-5201 530-752-6477 lawadmissions@ucdavis.edu	406	$40	Feb 1	March 2	$10,882	$20,266	✓				✓		88	33		✓	✓	511	25	52	24	6	31 (34)	276,361	617,054
University of California at Los Angeles (School of Law) P.O. Box 951445 Los Angeles, CA 90095-1445 310-825-2080 Fax: 310-825-9450 admissions@law.ucla.edu	404		Jan 15	Check	$11,011	$20,815	✓				✓		87	35		✓	✓	957	24	53	37	5	79 (26)	470,789	319,675
University of Chicago (Law School) 1111 East 60th Street Chicago, IL 60637 773-702-9484 Fax: 773-834-0942 admissions@law.uchicago.edu	408	$60		March 1	$26,406	$26,406	✓				✓		105	40	✓		✓	564	24	41	17	1	54 (60)	640,000	61,756
University of Cincinnati (College of Law) P.O. Box 210040 Cincinnati, OH 45221-0040 513-556-6805 Admissions@law.uc.edu	410	$35	April 1	March 1	$8,104	$15,564	✓				✓		90	35		✓		374	25	52	20	1	26 (58)	385,617	673,095
University of Colorado (School of Law) Campus Box 403 Boulder, CO 80309-0403 303-492-7203	412	$45	Feb 15	March 1	$5,917	$17,863	✓				✓		89	43		✓		491	26	51	17	5	40 (30)	383,000	725,704
University of Connecticut (School of Law) 55 Elizabeth Street Hartford, CT 06105 860-570-5159 Fax: 860-570-5153 admit@law.uconn.edu	414	$30	April 1	April 1	$10,630 ($6,678)	$22,420 ($14,076)	✓				✓	✓	86	36	✓	✓	✓		25	44	18	1	52 (74)	471,556	976,556

#	School	App. Fee	Priority Deadline	Final Deadline	Resident Tuition	Nonresident Tuition						Enrollment								
416	**University of Dayton (School of Law)** 300 College Park Dayton, OH 45469-2760 937-229-3555 Fax: 937-229-4194 lawinfo@udayton.edu	$40	May 1	March 1	$19,860	$19,860	✓	87	36	✓	✓	451	26	42	17	6	28 (34)	270,003	640,225
418	**University of Denver (College of Law)** 7039 E. 18th Avenue Denver, CO 80220 303-871-6135 Fax: 303-871-6100	$45	open	Feb 15	$20,026 ($12,920)	$20,026 ($12,920)	✓	90	44	✓	✓	743 (269)	27	55	9	4	38 (35)	274,284	48,685
420	**University of Detroit Mercy (School of Law)** 651 East Jefferson Avenue Detroit, MI 48226 313-596-0264 Fax: 313-596-0280 udmlawao@udmercy.edu	$50	April 15	April 1	$17,360 ($12,400)	$17,360 ($12,400)	✓	90	49	✓	✓	220 (144)	27	52	16	10	19 (20)	307,767	94,430
422	**University of Florida (College of Law)** 325 Holland Hall P.O. Box 117622 Gainesville, FL 32611-7622 352-392-2087 Fax: 352-392-2087 patrick@law.ufl.edu	$20	Feb 1	April 1	$4,836	$16,109	✓	88	34	✓	✓	1145	25	48	26	4	69 (18)	592,000	200,000
424	**University of Georgia (School of Law)** Hirsch Hall, 225 Herty Drive Athens, GA 30602-6012 706-542-7060	$30	March 1		$4,116	$16,464	✓	88	33	✓	✓	640	24	47	11	5	48 (36)	480,005	490,965
426	**University of Hawaii at Manoa (William S. Richardson School of Law)** 2515 Dole Street Honolulu, HI 96822 808-956-7966 Fax: 808-956-3813 lawadm@hawaii.edu		Check	Check	$8,520	$14,940	✓	89	42	✓	✓	245	27	52	72	5	19 (29)	248,838	875,305
428	**University of Houston (Law Center)** Office of Admissions Houston, TX 77204-6391 713-743-1070 Fax: 713-743-2194 admission@www.law.uh.edu	$50	Feb 15	April 1	$6,460 ($4,024)	$11,860 ($7,264)	✓	90	35	✓	✓	762 (227)	25	46	20	3	46 (67)	460,569	911,626
430	**University of Idaho (College of Law)** P.O. Box 442321 Moscow, ID 83844-2321 208-885-6423 Fax: 208-885-5709 adewitt@uidaho.edu	$40	Feb 1	Feb 15	$4,076	$10,076	✓	88	31	✓		295	28	26	4	9	16 (1)	180,892	
432	**University of Illinois (College of Law)** 504 East Pennsylvania Avenue Champaign, IL 61820 217-244-6415 Fax: 217-244-1478	$40	March 15	March 15	$8,024	$18,884	✓	90	34	✓	✓	617	24	40	28	1	45 (33)	565,660	775,212

INSTITUTION	Profile Page	APPLICATIONS Fee	Deadline	Financial Aid Deadline	TUITION In State Full Time (Part Time)	Out of State Full Time (Part Time)	Fall	Winter	Spring	Summer	Day	Evening	Credits for JD	Required Credits for Courses	Transferable Summer Courses	Joint Degree	Graduate Law Degree	ENROLLED Full Time (Part Time)	Average Age First Year	% Women	% Minority	Attrition Rate %	FACULTY Full Time (Part Time)	LIBRARY Volumes	Microforms
University of Iowa (College of Law) 276 Boyd Law Building, Melrose at Byington Street, Iowa City, IA 52242; 319-335-9095 or 319-335-9142; Fax: 319-335-9019; law-admissions@uiowa.edu	434	$30	March 1	on a	$6,822	$17,384	✓			✓	✓		90	35	✓	✓	✓	664	25	43	19	6	52 (29)	642,872	290,909
University of Kansas (School of Law) 205 Green Hall, Lawrence, KS 66045; 785-864-4378; Fax: 785-864-5054; lindeman@law.wpo.ukans.edu	436	$40	March 15	March 1	$6,937	$14,433	✓			✓	✓		90	43 to 45	✓	✓		543	23	41	10	3	34 (7)	325,000	333,169
University of Kentucky (College of Law) 209 Law Building, Lexington, KY 40506-0048; 606-257-7938; dbakert@pop.uky.edu	438	$25	March 1	April 1	$5,560	$14,930	✓				✓		90	34	✓	✓		402	23	45	6	4	28 (20)	408,276	976,440
University of Louisville (Louis D. Brandeis School of Law) University of Louisville Belknap Campus, Wilson W. Wyatt Hall, Louisville, KY 40292; 502-852-6364; Fax: 502-852-0862; charlene.oliva@louisville.edu	440	$30	March 1	June 1	$5,560 ($4,900)	$14,930 ($13,500)	✓				✓	✓	90	44	✓	✓		278 (105)	24	42	12	5	32 (19)	325,639	403
University of Maine (School of Law) 246 Deering Avenue, Portland, ME 04102; 207-780-4341	442	$25	Feb 15	Feb 1	$9,150 ($325/hr)	$17,340 ($578/hr)	✓				✓		89	40		✓		255 (7)	30	44	5	3	17 (4)	300,000	
University of Maryland (School of Law) 515 West Lombard Street, Baltimore, MD 21201; 410-706-3492; Fax: 410-706-4045; admissions@law.umaryland.edu	444	$50	March 1	March 15	$9,982 ($7,432)	$18,254 ($13,634)	✓				✓		85	35 to 38	✓	✓		617 (266)	26	53	26	68	53 (68)	273,129	442,334
University of Memphis (Cecil C. Humphreys School of Law) Campus Box 526513, Memphis, TN 38152-6513; 901-678-2073; Fax: 901-678-5210; uofmlaw@prophet.law.memphis.edu	446	$15	Feb 15	April 1	$4,114 ($3,252)	$10,292 ($8,076)	✓				✓		90	56	✓	✓		421 (22)	26	44	13	10	21 (35)	267,566	502,848
University of Miami (School of Law) P.O. Box 248087, 1311 Miller Drive, Coral Gables, FL 33124-8087; 305-284-2523; admissions@law.miami.edu	448	$50	March 10	March 1	$22,640 ($16,980)	$22,640 ($16,980)	✓				✓	✓	88	73	✓	✓	✓	988 (176)	26	46	32	5	58 (103)	348,552	775,463

School		Fee	Deadline	Deadline	Resident Tuition	Nonresident Tuition									Enrollment							
University of Michigan (Law School), 625 South State Street, Ann Arbor, MI 48109-1215, 313-764-0537	450	$70	Feb 15		$18,930	$24,900	✓			✓	✓	83 min.	37		✓	✓	1067	23	43	23	1	74 (49)	845,328	1,142,830
University of Minnesota (Law School), 229 19th Avenue S., Office of Admissions, Minneapolis, MN 55455, 612-625-3487, Fax 612-626-1874	452	$40	March 1	Feb 1	$9,300	$15,760	✓			✓	✓	88	32		✓	✓	760	25	48	18	4	42	875,000	300,000
University of Mississippi (School of Law), Lamar Hall, Oxford, MS 38677, 601-915-6910, Fax 601-915-1289, bvinson@olemiss.edu	454	$25	March 1	March 1	$4,081	$8,003	✓	✓		✓	✓	90	54 to 57	✓	✓	✓	475 (4)	24	40	12	9	26 (11)	296,871	846,235
University of Missouri-Columbia (School of Law), 103 Hulston Hall, Columbia, MO 65211, 573-882-6042, Fax 573-882-9625, umclawadmissions@missouri.edu	456	$40	March 1	March 1	$9,126	$17,664	✓	✓		✓	✓	89	57		✓	✓	534	23	46	13	5	36 (15)	320,000	444,865
University of Missouri-Kansas City (School of Law), 500 East 52nd Street, Kansas City, MO 64110-2499, 816-235-1644, Fax 816-235-5276, klosterman@umkc.edu	458		open	Check	$9,108 ($355/hr)	$17,645 ($660/hr)	✓	✓		✓	✓	91	52	✓	✓	✓	456 (31)	27	46	7	5	29 (35)	178,058	77,000
University of Montana (School of Law), Missoula, MT 59812, 406-243-2698, lawadmis@selway.umt.edu	460	$60	March 1	March 1	$6,695	$12,298	✓			✓	✓	90	59		✓	✓	234	27	41	7	1	19 (16)	108,599	57,584
University of Nebraska (College of Law), P.O. Box 830902, Lincoln, NE 68583-0902, 402-472-2161, Fax 402-472-5185, lawadm@unlinfo.unl.edu	462	$25	March 1	March 1	$4,086	$10,485	✓	✓		✓	✓	96	45	✓	✓	✓	378 (1)	26	41	8	10	28 (24)	358,016	860,864
University of New Mexico (School of Law), 1117 Stanford Drive N.E., Albuquerque, NM 87131-1431, 505-277-5072, Fax 505-277-9958	464		Feb 15	Check	$4,382	$14,672	✓			✓	✓	86	33		✓	✓	120	25	56	46		32 (27)	300,000	
University of North Carolina at Chapel Hill (School of Law), Campus Box 3380, 101 Van Hecke-Wettach Hall, Chapel Hill, NC 27599-3380, 919-962-5109, Fax 919-843-7939, law_admission@unc.edu	466		Feb 1	Check	$3,602	$15,702	✓	✓		✓	✓	86	33		✓	✓	663	23	49	21	1	44 (35)	447,320	11,302

Institution	Profile Page	Fee	Deadline	Financial Aid Deadline	Tuition In State Full Time (Part Time)	Tuition Out of State Full Time (Part Time)	Fall	Winter	Spring	Summer	Day	Evening	Credits for JD	Required Credits for Courses	Transferable Summer Courses	Joint Degree	Graduate Law Degree	Enrolled Full Time (Part Time)	Average Age First Year	% Women	% Minority	Attrition Rate %	Faculty Full Time (Part Time)	Volumes	Microforms
University of North Dakota (School of Law) Box 9003, Grand Forks, ND 58202, 701-777-2104, Fax: 701-777-2217, linda.kohoutek@thor.law.und.nodak.edu	468		April 1	Check	$4,376	$9,220	✓				✓		90	34	✓	✓		188	26	39	5	6	14 (9)	251,320	129,554
University of Notre Dame (Notre Dame Law School) P.O. Box 959, Notre Dame, IN 46556-0959, 219-631-6626, Fax: 219-631-3980, law.bulletin.1@nd.edu	470	$55	March 1	March 1	$22,630	$22,630	✓				✓		90	52	✓	✓	✓	550	23	40	18	1	27 (33)	501,071	1,340,615
University of Oklahoma (College of Law) 300 Timberdell Road, Norman, OK 73019, 405-325-4726, Fax: 405-325-0502, kmadden@ou.edu	472	$50	March 15	March 1	$4,472	$13,000	✓				✓		90	42		✓		582	24	43	15	4	33 (20)	302,738	80,603
University of Oregon (School of Law, William W. Knight Law Center) 1515 Agate Street, Eugene, OR 97403-1221, 541-346-1553, Fax: 541-346-3984, bmcclure@law.uoregon.edu	474	$65	April 1	Check	$10,898	$14,894	✓				✓		85	37		✓	✓	535	25	48	16	2	32 (11)	177,409	169,187
University of Pennsylvania (Law School) 3400 Chestnut Street, Philadelphia, PA 19104-6204, 215-898-7400, admissions@oyez.law.upenn.edu	476	$50	March 1	March 1	$25,380	$25,380	✓				✓		89	28		✓	✓	754	24	46	22	1	42 (54)	685,675	868,948
University of Pittsburgh (School of Law) 3900 Forbes Avenue, Pittsburgh, PA 15260, 412-648-1412, Fax: 412-648-2647, admissions@law.pitt.edu	478	$50	March 1	March 1	$12,388	$19,362	✓			✓	✓		88	34	✓	✓		685	24	44	10	3	42 (38)	375,000	105,202
University of Puerto Rico (School of Law) P.O. Box 23349, UPR Station, Rio Piedras, PR 00931, 787-764-1655, Fax: 787-764-2675	480		Feb 15	April 1	$2,326 ($1,425)	$2,326 ✓					✓	92	46			✓	(215)	325 (23)	56		5	(29)	35 / 346,360	641,402	
University of Richmond (The T.C. Williams School of Law) University of Richmond, VA 23173, 804-289-8189, admissions@uofrlaw.richmond.edu	482	$35	Jan 15	Feb 25	$19,940 ($995/hr)	$19,940 ($995/hr)	✓			✓	✓		86	38	✓	✓		474 (2)	25	46	19	1	26 (40)	279,403	115,790

#	School	App Fee	Deadline 1	Deadline 2	Tuition (res)	Tuition (nonres)											
484	**University of San Diego** (School of Law) 5998 Alcala Park San Diego, CA 92110 619-260-4528 Fax: 619-260-2218 jdinfo@acusd.edu	$40	Feb 1	March 2	$22,130 ($15,710)	$22,130 ($15,710)	✓	85	48	✓	751 (367)	24	44	23	7	61 (56)	453,301	1,415,092
486	**University of San Francisco** (School of Law) 2130 Fulton Street San Francisco, CA 94117-1080 415-422-6586 Fax: 415-422-6433	$40	April 1	rolling	$22,194 ($792/hr)	$22,194 ($792/hr)	✓	86	48	✓	499 (115)	25	56	28	9	24 (59)	295,317	161,252
488	**University of South Carolina** (School of Law) Main and Greene Streets Columbia, SC 29208 803-777-6605 Fax: 803-777-7751 usclaw@law.law.sc.edu	$25	Feb 15	April 15	$7,548	$15,616	✓	90	46	✓	708	23	44	11	3	43 (26)	330,000	2,718
490	**University of South Dakota** (School of Law) 414 East Clark Street Vermillion, SD 57069-2390 605-677-5443 Fax: 605-677-5417 lawreg@usd.edu	$15	March 1	Check	$3,210	$9,305	✓	90	43	✓	184	27	47	3	7	15 (2)	188,061	11,824
492	**University of Southern California** (Law School) Los Angeles, CA 90089-0071 213-740-7331	$60	Feb 1	Feb 15	$26,092	$26,092	✓	88	31	✓	608	24	48	41	1	46 (40)	366,333	493,817
494	**University of Tennessee** (College of Law) 1505 W. Cumberland Avenue Knoxville, TN 37996-1810 865-974-4131 Fax: 865-974-1572 lawadmit@libra.law.utk.edu	$15	Feb 1	Feb 14	$4,626	$12,932	✓	89	46	✓	484	25	45	13	4	30 (27)	469,108	1,145,172
496	**University of Texas at Austin** (School of Law) 727 East Dean Keeton Street Austin, TX 78705 512-232-1200 Fax: 512-471-6988	$65	Feb 1	March 31	$4,800	$12,600	✓	86	39	✓	1387	25	47	17		75 (73)	936,000	879,118
498	**University of the District of Columbia** (David A. Clarke School of Law) 4200 Connecticut Avenue, N.W. Washington, DC 20008 Null Fax: 202-274-5583 vcanty@law.udc.edu	$35	April 1	May 1	$7,000 ($250/hr)	$14,000 ($500/hr)	✓	90	66	✓	168	29	62	79	15	16 (18)	181,000	90
500	**University of the Pacific** (McGeorge School of Law) 3200 Fifth Avenue Sacramento, CA 95817 916-739-7105 Fax: 916-739-7134 admissionsmcgeorge@uop.edu	$40	May 15	open	$21,656 ($14,396)	$21,656 ($14,396)	✓	88	58	✓	693 (357)	24	49	24	11	44 (59)	436,384	1,189,824
502	**University of Toledo** (College of Law) 2801 West Bancroft Street Toledo, OH 43606-3390 419-530-4131 Fax: 419-530-4345 law.utoledo.edu	$30	June 1	April 1	$6,802 ($5,668)	$14,132 ($11,777)	✓	89	42	✓	374 (147)	26	46	8	8	31 (25)	320,727	117,964

Institution	Profile Page	App Fee	App Deadline	Deadline Financial Aid	Tuition In State Full Time (Part Time)	Tuition Out of State Full Time (Part Time)	Fall	Winter	Spring	Summer	Day	Evening	Credits for JD	Required Credits for Courses	Transferable Summer Courses	Joint Degree	Graduate Law Degree	Enrolled Full Time (Part Time)	Average Age First Year	% Women	% Minority	Attrition Rate %	Faculty Full Time (Part Time)	Volumes	Microforms
University of Tulsa (College of Law), 3120 East Fourth Place, Tulsa, OK 74104-2499, 918-631-2709, Fax: 918-631-3630	504	$30	open	open	$17,000 ($11,400)	$17,000 ($11,400)	✓		✓		✓	✓	88	42	✓	✓	✓	442 (119)	27	35	13	8	37 (34)	280,000	688,772
University of Utah (College of Law), 332 South 1400 East Front, Salt Lake City, UT 84112, 801-581-7479, Fax: 801-581-6897, gormley@law.utah.edu	506	$40	Feb 1	Feb 15	$5,127	$11,439	✓				✓		88	40	✓	✓	✓	369	26	43	14	3	28 (32)	300,000	98,000
University of Virginia (School of Law), 580 Massie Road, Charlottesville, VA 22903-1789, 804-924-7351, Fax: 804-982-2128, lawadmit@virginia.edu	508	$65	Jan 15	Feb 15	$14,201	$20,600	✓				✓		86	27	✓	✓	✓	1090	24	43	15		64 (63)	794,529	1,150,000
University of Washington (School of Law), 1100 Northeast Campus Parkway, Seattle, WA 98105-6617, 206-543-4078	510	$50	Jan 15	Feb 28	$5,500	$13,500	✓				✓		135			✓	✓	520	25	52	29	2	43	506,334	152,681
University of Wisconsin-Madison (Law School), 975 Bascom Mall, Madison, WI 53706, 608-262-5914, Fax: 608-262-5485, Admissions@law.wisc.educ	512		Feb 1	Check	$3,314 ($285/hr)	$14,866 ($767/hr)	✓				✓	✓	90	30 to 31	✓	✓	✓	807 (52)	25	47	23	1	47	475,000	695,000
University of Wyoming (College of Law), P.O. Box 3035, Laramie, WY 82071, 307-766-6416, lawadmis@uwyo.edu	514	$35	March 15	Feb 1	$4,424	$9,692	✓				✓		88	52	✓	✓	✓	235	27	43	4	8	14	134,028	453,081
Valparaiso University (School of Law), Wesemann Hall, Valparaiso, IN 46383-6493, 219-465-7829, Fax: 219-465-7808, heike.spahn@valpo.edu	516	$30	April 15	March	$17,950 ($695)	$17,950 ($695)	✓				✓	✓	90	46	✓	✓	✓	383 (54)	26	47	14	10	27 (37)	283,803	774,186
Vanderbilt University (School of Law), Nashville, TN 37240, 615-322-6452	518	$50	March 1	March 1	$24,350	$24,350	✓				✓		88	34	✓	✓	✓	559	24	45	21	2	36 (40)	207,887	417,126

#	School / Contact	Fee	Deadline	Deadline 2	Tuition (resident)	Tuition (nonresident)
520	**Vermont Law School** P.O. Box 96, Chelsea Street South Royalton, VT 05068-0096 802-763-8303 Fax: 802-763-7071 admiss@vermontlaw.edu		Feb 1	Check	$20,958	
522	**Villanova University** (School of Law) Garey Hall Villanova, PA 19085 610-519-7010	$75	March 1	open	$20,000	
524	**Wake Forest University** (School of Law) P.O. Box 7206, Reynolda Station Winston-Salem, NC 27109 910-758-5437	$60	March 15	May 1	$21,250	$21,250
526	**Washburn University** (School of Law) 1700 College Topeka, KS 66621 785-231-1185 Fax: 785-232-8087 admissions@washburnlaw.edu	$30	March 15	April 1	$7,530 ($251/hr)	$11,340 ($378/hr)
528	**Washington and Lee University** (School of Law) Lewis Hall Lexington, VA 24450 540-463-8504 Fax: 540-463-8586 lawadm@wlu.edu	$40	Feb 1	Feb 15	$17,950	$17,950
530	**Washington University in St. Louis** (School of Law) Box 1120, One Brookings Drive St. Louis, MO 63130 314-935-4525 Fax: 314-935-6959 admiss@walaw.wash.edu	$60	March 1	March 1	$24,240	$24,240
532	**Wayne State University** (Law School) 468 W. Ferry Mall Detroit, MI 48202 313-577-3937 Fax: 313-577-6000 linda.sims@wayne.edu	$20	March 15	April 30	$7,560 ($4,032)	$15,690 ($8,368)
534	**West Virginia University** (College of Law) P.O. Box 6130 Morgantown, WV 26506 304-293-5304 Fax: 304-293-6891 lawaply@wvu.edu		March 1		$5,100 ($235/hr)	$12,200 ($600/hr)
536	**Western New England College** (School of Law) 1215 Wilbraham Road Springfield, MA 01119 413-782-1406 Fax: 413-796-2067 lawadmis@wnec.edu	$45	open	April 1	$19,064 ($14,297)	$19,064 ($14,297)

#	School	A	B	Enrollment	C	D	E	F	G	H (paren)	I	J
520	Vermont	486	84	44		26	48	8	36 / 8	(36)	215,000	95,000
522	Villanova	730	87	44	453 (12)	24	48	15	44 / 1	(75)	450,304	138,811
524	Wake Forest		89	41		24	41	9	2	39 (28)	341,653	800,000
526	Washburn		90	37	411	27	42	15	7	29 (36)	321,470	141,744
528	Washington and Lee		85	37	367	25	42	9	1	33 (18)	372,675	808,493
530	Washington (St. Louis)		85	7	635	24	43	20	7	47 (65)	563,292	847,000
532	Wayne State		86	36	526 (228)	26	48	17	11	35 (33)	569,165	1,088,291
534	West Virginia		93	52	430 (20)	26	46	7		26 (11)	246,532	355,617
536	Western New England		88	46-47	317 (253)	27	51	10	14	27 (38)	360,000	169,000

Institution	Profile Page	Fee	Deadline	Financial Aid Deadline	Tuition In State FT (PT)	Tuition Out of State FT (PT)	Fall	Winter	Spring	Summer	Day	Evening	Credits for JD	Required Credits for Courses	Transferable Summer Courses	Joint Degree	Graduate Law Degree	Enrolled FT (PT)	Avg Age First Year	% Women	% Minority	Attrition Rate %	Faculty FT (PT)	Volumes	Microforms
Western State University (College of Law)	538	$50	open	open	$26,570 ($17,670)	✓	✓	✓	✓	✓	✓	88 units	58	✓	✓		240 (342)		43	30		19 (21)	158,966	370,000	
Whittier College (School of Law)	540	$60	March 15	Check	$21,934 ($13,174)	$21,934 ($13,174)	✓				✓	✓	87	40	✓	✓	✓	383 (277)	26	50	37	5	28 (32)	297,614	122,633
Widener University (School of Law)	542	$50	May 15	Feb 1	$19,500 ($14,620)	$19,500 ($14,620)	✓				✓	✓	87	54	✓	✓	✓	870 (578)	25	47	12	8	75 (91)	314,170	296,560
Willamette University (College of Law)	544	$50	April 1		$18,300	$18,300	✓				✓	✓	88	39	✓	✓	✓	407 (7)	26	45	10	12	21 (6)	285,351	850,015
William Mitchell College of Law	546	$65	June 30	March 16	$18,090 ($13,140)	$18,090 ($13,140)	✓				✓	✓	86	46	✓	✓	✓	501 (518)	29	52	11	2	36 (115)	296,813	132,535
Yale University (Yale Law School)	548	$45	Feb 15	March 15	$26,950		✓				✓		82	19		✓	576		25	45	30	58	(35)	798,200	2,583
Yeshiva University (Benjamin N. Cardozo School of Law)	550	$60	April 1	April 15	$23,936	$23,936	✓	✓	✓	✓	✓		84	38	✓	✓	✓	915	23	48	21	1	46 (92)	440,400	1,095,152

Institution contact details

Western State University (College of Law)
1111 North State College Blvd
Fullerton, CA 92831
714-738-1000, x2909
Fax: 714-526-1062
joel@wsulaw.edu

Whittier College (School of Law)
3333 Harbor Blvd.
Costa Mesa, CA 92626
714-444-4141, ext. 121
Fax: 714-444-0250
info@law.whittier.edu

Widener University (School of Law)
4601 Concord Pike, P.O. Box 7474
and 3800 Vartan Way, Harris
Wilmington, DE 19803
302-477-2162 (DE); 717-541-3903 (HBG)
Fax: 302-477-2224
(DE); 717-541-3999 (HBG)
law.admissions3@law.widener.edu

Willamette University (College of Law)
245 Winter Street S.E.
Salem, OR 97301
503-370-6282
Fax: 503-370-6375
law-admission@willamette.edu

William Mitchell College of Law
875 Summit Avenue
St. Paul, MN 55105-3076
651-290-6476
Fax: 651-290-6414
admissions@wmitchell.edu

Yale University (Yale Law School)
P.O. Box 208329
New Haven, CT 06520-8239
203-432-4995
admissions.law@yale.edu

Yeshiva University (Benjamin N. Cardozo School of Law)
55 Fifth Avenue
New York, NY 10003
212-790-0274
Fax: 212-790-0482
lawinfo@ymail.yu.edu

Chapter 14

YOUR CHANCES OF LAW SCHOOL ADMISSION

A Profile of Recent First-Year Law Students

The table in this section provides basic admissions statistics for the 180 law schools that have been approved by the American Bar Association. All these schools offer the J.D. degree. The information has been compiled from the most recent available information received from schools. If you compare your own GPA and your LSAT percentile with those of students recently admitted, and if you note the number of students who applied and the number who were accepted, you will be able to get an idea of your chances of admission to any given law school.

Bear in mind that many law schools take into account factors other than strictly academic qualifications.

A blank cell on the chart means that information was not available.

LAW SCHOOL	ACADEMIC STATISTICS				ADMISSION STATISTICS		
	Median LSAT Percentile of Enrolled	Median LSAT Score of Enrolled	Lowest LSAT Percentile of Accepted	Median GPA (4.0 scale) of Enrolled	Total Applicants	Applicants Accepted	Applicants Enrolled
American University (Washington College of Law) 4801 Massachusetts Avenue, N.W. Washington, DC 20016-8186 202-274-4101 Fax: 202-274-4107 wcladmit@wcl.american.edu	70	156		3.4	5093	2117	523
Arizona State University (College of Law/Armstrong Hall) Box 877906 Tempe, AZ 85287-7906 602-965-1474 Fax: 602-965-5550 wanda.decrow@asu.edu	74	157		3.4	1815	441	163
Baylor University (School of Law) P.O. Box 97288 Waco, TX 76798-7288 254-710-1911 Fax: 254-710-2316 becky-beck@baylor.edu	82	157	24	3.4	1247	492	161
Boston College (Law School) 885 Centre Street Newton, MA 02459 617-552-4351 Fax: 617-552-2917 bclawadm@bc.edu	88	162		3.5	5446	1445	273
Boston University (School of Law) 765 Commonwealth Avenue Boston, MA 02215 617-353-3100 bulawadm@bu.edu	84	161		3.4	4885	1620	302
Brigham Young University (J. Reuben Clark Law School) 342 JRCB Brigham Young University Provo, UT 84602 801-378-4277 Fax: 801-378-5897 wilcock@lawgate.byu.edu	83	160	23	3.6	663	246	152
Brooklyn Law School 250 Joralemon Street Brooklyn, NY 11201 718-780-7906 Fax: 718-780-0395 admitq@brooklaw.edu	74	157	37	3.3	3158	1442	515
California Western School of Law 225 Cedar Street San Diego, CA 92101-3046 619-525-1401 Fax: 619-615-1401 rbriscoe@cwsl.edu		150	25		1996	1252	275
Campbell University (Norman Adrian Wiggins School of Law) P.O. Box 158 Buies Creek, NC 27506 910-893-1754 Fax: 910-893-1780 culaw@webster.campbell.edu	64	154		3.2	634	209	112

LAW SCHOOL	ACADEMIC STATISTICS				ADMISSION STATISTICS		
	Median LSAT Percentile of Enrolled	Median LSAT Score of Enrolled	Lowest LSAT Percentile of Accepted	Median GPA (4.0 scale) of Enrolled	Total Applicants	Applicants Accepted	Applicants Enrolled
Capital University (Law School) 303 East Broad Street Columbus, OH 43215-3200 614-236-6500 Fax: 614-236-6972 admissions@law.capital.edu	45	150	36	3.1	922	591	259
Case Western Reserve University (School of Law) 11075 East Boulevard Cleveland, OH 44106 216-368-3600 Fax: 216-368-6144 lawadmissions@po.cwru.edu or lawmoney@po.cwru.edu	67	156		3.2	1411	883	213
Catholic University of America (Columbus School of Law) Cardinal Station Washington, DC 20064 (202) 319-5151 Fax: (202) 319-6285		155	23	3.1	2165	1033	314
Catholic University of Puerto Rico (School of Law) Avenida Las Americas-Station 6 Ponce, PR 00732 809-841-2000	13			2.9			
Chapman University (School of Law) One University Drive Orange, CA 92866 714-628-2500 Fax: 714-628-2501 misles@chapman.edu	64	154	26	3	607	266	87
City University of New York (City University of New York School of Law at Queens College) 65-21 Main Street Flushing, NY 11367-1300 718-340-4210 Fax: 718-340-4372 admissions@maclaw.law.cuny.edu					1543	575	175
Cleveland State University (Cleveland-Marshall College of Law) 1801 Euclid Avenue Cleveland, OH 44115 216-687-2304 Fax: 216-687-6881	50	150	5	3	1220	617	254
College of William and Mary (William and Mary Law School) P.O. Box 8795 Williamsburg, VA 23187-8795 757-221-3785 Fax: 757-221-3261 lawadm@facstaff.wm.edu	90	163	41	3.4	2267	718	201
Columbia University (School of Law) 435 West 116th Street New York, NY 10027 212-854-2670 Fax: 212-854-1109	98	169		3.6	6137		367

LAW SCHOOL	ACADEMIC STATISTICS				ADMISSION STATISTICS		
	Median LSAT Percentile of Enrolled	Median LSAT Score of Enrolled	Lowest LSAT Percentile of Accepted	Median GPA (4.0 scale) of Enrolled	Total Applicants	Applicants Accepted	Applicants Enrolled
Cornell University (Law School) Myron Taylor Hall Ithaca, NY 14853 607-255-5141 Fax: 607-255-7193	94	165		3.6	3219		183
Creighton University (School of Law) 2500 California Plaza Omaha, NE 68178 402-280-2872 Fax: 402-280-3161 admit@culaw.creighton.edu	52	151	18	3.1	718	481	159
De Paul University (College of Law) 25 East Jackson Boulevard Chicago, IL 60604 312-362-6831 lawinfo@wppost.depaul.edu	60	154	23	3.2	2074	1274	363
Drake University (Law School) 2507 University Avenue Des Moines, IA 50311 515-271-1990 lawadmit@drake.edu	52	151	8	3.2	639	428	123
Duke University (School of Law) Science and Towerview Drive, Box 90393 Durham, NC 27708 919-613-7020 Fax: 919-613-7257 admissions@law.duke.edu		165		3.5	3418		236
Duquesne University (School of Law) 900 Locust Street, Hanley Hall Pittsburgh, PA 15282 412-396-6296 campion@duq.edu	60			3.2			240
Emory University (School of Law) Gambrell Hall Atlanta, GA 30322 404-727-6801 Fax: 404-727-2477 jbalej@law.emory.edu	87	161	50	3.4	2773	985	190
Florida Coastal School of Law 7555 Beach Boulevard Jacksonville, FL 32216 904-680-7710 Fax: 904-680-7776 admissions@fcsl.edu	50	150	15	2.9	1036	399	195
Florida State University (College of Law) 425 W. Jefferson St. Tallahassee, FL 32306-1601 850-644-3787 Fax: 850-644-7284 admissions@law.fsu.edu	68	155		3.3	1877	726	233
Fordham University (School of Law) 140 West 62nd Street New York, NY 10023 212-626-6810	90	164	30	3.4	4866	1285	463

LAW SCHOOL	ACADEMIC STATISTICS				ADMISSION STATISTICS		
	Median LSAT Percentile of Enrolled	Median LSAT Score of Enrolled	Lowest LSAT Percentile of Accepted	Median GPA (4.0 scale) of Enrolled	Total Applicants	Applicants Accepted	Applicants Enrolled
Franklin Pierce Law Center 2 White Street Concord, NH 03301 603-228-9217 Fax: 603-228-1074 L.admissions@fplc.edu		150	8	3	790	481	128
George Mason University **(School of Law)** 3401 North Fairfax Drive Arlington, VA 22201-4498 703-993-8010 Fax: 703-993-8260 arichar5@gmu.edu	81	159		3.2	2006	667	212
George Washington University **(Law School)** 2000 H Street, N.W. Washington, DC 20052 202-739-0648 jd@main.n/c.gwu.edu	88	162	37	3.5	7126	2048	469
Georgetown University **(Law Center)** 600 New Jersey Avenue, N.W. Washington, DC 20001 202-662-9010 admis@law.georgetown.edu	95	166	50	3.6	7873	2383	601
Georgia State University **(College of Law)** P.O. Box 4037 Atlanta, GA 30302-4037 404-651-2096 Fax: 404-651-2096 cjjackson@gsu.edu	74	157	33	3.2	1705	481	202
Golden Gate University **(School of Law)** 536 Mission Street San Francisco, CA 94105-2968 415-442-6630	48	150		3	1585	923	179
Gonzaga University **(School of Law)** Box 3528 Spokane, WA 99220-3528 509-323-5532 Fax: 509-323-5710 admissions@lawschool.gonzaga.edu	44	149		3.2	826	576	
Hamline University **(School of Law)** 1536 Hewitt Avenue St. Paul, MN 55104-1284 651-523-2461 Fax: 651-523-3064 lawadm@gw.hamline.edu	56	152	11	3.2	671	467	184
Harvard University **(Harvard Law School)** Cambridge, MA 02138 617-495-3109 Fax: 617-495-1110 jdadmiss@law.harvard.edu		170		3.8	5818	845	556
Hofstra University **(School of Law)** 121 Hofstra University Hempstead, NY 11549 516-463-5916 Fax: 516-463-6264 lawpts@hofstra.edu	72	156	12	3.3	1867	823	291

LAW SCHOOL	ACADEMIC STATISTICS				ADMISSION STATISTICS		
	Median LSAT Percentile of Enrolled	Median LSAT Score of Enrolled	Lowest LSAT Percentile of Accepted	Median GPA (4.0 scale) of Enrolled	Total Applicants	Applicants Accepted	Applicants Enrolled
Howard University (Howard University) 2900 Van Ness Street, N.W. Washington, DC 20008 202-806-8008 Fax: 202-806-8162 admissions@law.howard.edu	50	151		2.9	1225	372	140
Illinois Institute of Technology (Chicago-Kent College of Law) 565 West Adams Street Chicago, IL 60661 312-906-5020 admit@kentlaw.edu	64	154	33	3.2	2160	1299	369
Indiana University-Purdue University (Indiana University School of Law-Indianapolis) 735 West New York Street Indianapolis, IN 46202-5194 317-274-2459 Fax: 317-274-3955 khmiller@iupui.edu	62	155	6	3.2	1078	519	263
Indiana University/Bloomington (School of Law) 211 S. Indiana Avenue Bloomington, IN 47405-1001 812-855-4765 Fax: 812-855-0555 lawadmis@indiana.edu	84	160		3.4	1493	692	203
Inter-American University of Puerto Rico (School of Law) P.O. Box 70351 San Juan, PR 00936-8351 809-751-1912, ext. 2013	13		2	3.1			
John Marshall Law School 315 South Plymouth Court Chicago, IL 60604 312-987-1406 Fax: 312-427-5136 admission@jmls.edu		150		3.4	1543	964	255
Lewis and Clark College (Northwestern School of Law) 10015 Southwest Terwilliger Boulevard Portland, OR 97219 503-768-6613 Fax: 503-768-6671 lawadmss@lclark.edu	78	158	21	3.2	1384	839	200
Louisiana State University (Paul M. Hebert Law Center) Baton Rouge, LA 70803 225-388-8646 Fax: 225-388-8647 bloup@lsu.edu	53	153	6	3.3	847	509	247
Loyola Marymount University (Loyola Law School) 919 S. Albany Street Los Angeles, CA 90015 213-736-1180 admissions@lls.edu	75	157	30	3.3	2897	1240	475

LAW SCHOOL	ACADEMIC STATISTICS				ADMISSION STATISTICS		
	Median LSAT Percentile of Enrolled	Median LSAT Score of Enrolled	Lowest LSAT Percentile of Accepted	Median GPA (4.0 scale) of Enrolled	Total Applicants	Applicants Accepted	Applicants Enrolled
Loyola University - New Orleans (School of Law) 7214 St. Charles Avenue New Orleans, LA 70118 504-861-5575 Fax: 504-861-5772 ladmit@loyno.edu	55	152	15	2.9	1321	725	218
Loyola University Chicago (School of Law) One East Pearson Street Chicago, IL 60611 312-915-7170 Fax: 312-915-7201 law-admissions@luc.edu	78	158	40	3.3	2164	924	231
Marquette University (Law School) Office of Admissions, Sensenbrenner Hall, P.O. Box 1881 Milwaukee, WI 53201-1881 414-288-6767 Fax: 414-288-0676 law.admission@marquette.edu	65	154		3.1	811		198
Mercer University (Walter F. George School of Law) 1021 Georgia Ave. Macon, GA 31201 912-301-2605 Fax: 912-301-2989 Sutton_me@mercer.edu		152	25	3.2	958	470	154
Michigan State University (Detroit College of Law) 316 Law College Bldg. East Lansing, MI 48824-1300 517-432-0222 Fax: 517-432-0098 heatleya@pilot.msu.edu	50	152	20	3.1	1052	600	213
Mississippi College (School of Law) 151 E. Griffith Street Jackson, MS 39201 601-925-7150 pevans@mc.edu	50			3	717	401	143
New England School of Law 154 Stuart Street Boston, MA 02116 617-422-7210 Fax: 617-422-7200 admit@admin.nesi.edu					2097	1521	337
New York Law School 57 Worth Street New York, NY 10013-2960 212-431-2888 Fax: 212-966-1522 admissions@nyls.edu		154		3.1	4194	348	470
New York University (School of Law) 110 West Third Street New York, NY 10012 212-998-6060 Fax: 212-995-4527	98	169		3.6	6481		416

LAW SCHOOL	ACADEMIC STATISTICS				ADMISSION STATISTICS		
	Median LSAT Percentile of Enrolled	Median LSAT Score of Enrolled	Lowest LSAT Percentile of Accepted	Median GPA (4.0 scale) of Enrolled	Total Applicants	Applicants Accepted	Applicants Enrolled
North Carolina Central University (School of Law) 1512 S. Alston Avenue Durham, NC 27707 919-560-6333 Fax: 919-560-6339 jfaucett@wpo.nccu.edu	50	148	143	3.1	1080	258	116
Northeastern University (School of Law) 400 Huntington Avenue Boston, MA 02115 617-373-2395 Fax: 617-373-8865 pbauer@slaw.neu.edu	74	157	10	3.2	1922	715	195
Northern Illinois University (College of Law) Swen Parson Hall De Kalb, IL 60115 815-753-1420 Fax: 815-753-4501 lawadm@niu.edu	60	153		3	836	381	99
Northern Kentucky University (Salmon P. Chase College of Law) Louie B. Nunn Hall Highland Heights, KY 41099 606-572-6476 Fax: 606-572-6081 brayg@nku.edu	56	152	18	3.1	620	275	111
Northwestern University (School of Law) 357 East Chicago Avenue Chicago, IL 60611 312-503-8465 Fax: 312-503-0178 nubwadm@nwu.edu	96	167	45	3.5	4103	744	205
Nova Southeastern University (Shepard Broad Law Center) 3305 College Avenue Fort Lauderdale, FL 33314-7721 954-262-6117 Fax: 954-262-3844 admission@nsu.law.nova.edu	37	147	3	2.8	1416	785	334
Ohio Northern University (Claude W. Pettit College of Law) 525 South Main Street Ada, OH 45810 419-772-2211 Fax: 419-772-1487 g-keener@onu.edu			8	2.8	1115	546	108
Ohio State University (College of Law) 55 West 12th Avenue, John Deaver Drinko Hall Columbus, OH 43210-1391 614-292-8810 Fax: 614-292-1383 roboski.1@osu.edu	74	157		3.6	1482	585	214
Oklahoma City University (School of Law) 2501 North Blackwelder Oklahoma City, OK 73106-1493 405-521-5354 Fax: 405-521-5802 lawadmit@okcu.edu	32	145	10	2.9	878	740	190

LAW SCHOOL	ACADEMIC STATISTICS				ADMISSION STATISTICS		
	Median LSAT Percentile of Enrolled	Median LSAT Score of Enrolled	Lowest LSAT Percentile of Accepted	Median GPA (4.0 scale) of Enrolled	Total Applicants	Applicants Accepted	Applicants Enrolled
Pace University (School of Law) 78 North Broadway White Plains, NY 10603 914-422-4010 Fax: 914-422-4248 adagostino@genesis.law.pace.edu	52	151	21	3.2	1795	871	254
Pennsylvania State University (Dickinson School of Law) 150 South College Street Carlisle, PA 17013 717-240-5207 Fax: 717-241-3503 dsladmit@psu.edu	55	152	17	3.2	1320	691	188
Pepperdine University (School of Law) 24255 Pacific Coast Highway Malibu, CA 90263 310-456-4631 Fax: 310-317-7668 soladmis@pepperdine.edu	71	156		3.3	2520	1200	234
Quinnipiac College (School of Law) 275 Mt. Carmel Avenue Hamden, CT 06518-1948 203-287-3400 Fax: 203-287-3339 ladm@quinnipiac.edu		148	9	3	2004	1044	258
Regent University (School of Law) 1000 Regent University Drive Virginia Beach, VA 23464-9800 757-226-4584 Fax: 757-226-4139 lawschool@regent.edu	45	148	18	3.1	565	368	215
Roger Williams University (School of Law) Ten Metacom Avenue Bristol, RI 02809-5171 401-254-4555 Fax: 401-254-4516 admissions@rwulaw.rwu.edu	40	148	8	3	661	396	148
Rutgers University/Newark (School of Law) S.I. Newhouse Center for Law and Justice, 15 Washington St. Newark, NJ 07102 973-353-5557/5554 Fax: 973-353-1445		157		3.3	2335	765	210
Rutgers, The State University of New Jersey (School of Law-Camden) Fifth and Penn Streets Camden, NJ 08102 609-225-6102 Fax: 609-225-6537	74	157	41	3.2	1744	624	206
Saint John's University (School of Law) 8000 Utopia Parkway Jamaica, NY 11439 718-990-6611/6612 Fax: 718-990-2526 rsvp@sjulaw.stjohns.edu	66	154		3	2595	1198	362

LAW SCHOOL	ACADEMIC STATISTICS				ADMISSION STATISTICS		
	Median LSAT Percentile of Enrolled	Median LSAT Score of Enrolled	Lowest LSAT Percentile of Accepted	Median GPA (4.0 scale) of Enrolled	Total Applicants	Applicants Accepted	Applicants Enrolled
Saint Louis University (School of Law) 3700 Lindell Boulevard St. Louis, MO 63108 314-977-2800 admissions@law.slu.edu	64	154	11	3.3	1046	597	250
Saint Mary's University (School of Law) One Camino Santa Maria San Antonio, TX 78228-8601 210-436-3523 Fax: 210-431-4202	46		25	3	1046	603	263
Samford University (Cumberland School of Law) 800 Lakeshore Drive Birmingham, AL 35229 205-726-2702 Fax: 205-726-2673 lawadmissions@samford.edu	52	151	17	3	838	445	190
Santa Clara University (School of Law) 500 El Camino Real Santa Clara, CA 95053 408-554-4800 Fax: 408-554-7897 lawadmission@scu.edu	158	153		3.4	2451	1338	297
Seattle University (School of Law) 900 Broadway Seattle, WA 98122-4340 206-398-4200 Fax: 206-398-4058 lawadmis@seattleu.edu	71	156	15	3.2	1212	769	310
Seton Hall University (School of Law) One Newark Center Newark, NJ 07102-5210 973-642-8747 Fax: 973-642-8876 admitme@shu.edu	65	155	152	3.2	2218	965	384
South Texas College of Law 1303 San Jacinto Street Houston, TX 77002-7000 713-646-1810 Fax: 713-646-2929 acramer@stcl.edu	43	149	15	2.9	1760	1152	515
Southern Illinois University (School of Law) Lesar Law Building, Mail Code 6804 Carbondale, IL 62901-6804 618-453-8767 Fax: 618-453-8769 lawadmit@siu.edu	52	151	26	3.3	669	387	143
Southern Methodist University (School of Law) Office of Admissions, P.O. Box 750110 Dallas, TX 75275-0110 214-768-2550 Fax: 214-768-2549	75	157		3.3			
Southern University and A & M College (Law Center) Post Office Box 9294 Baton Rouge, LA 70813 225-771-5340 Fax: 225-771-2121		146		2.6	589	198	138

LAW SCHOOL	ACADEMIC STATISTICS				ADMISSION STATISTICS		
	Median LSAT Percentile of Enrolled	Median LSAT Score of Enrolled	Lowest LSAT Percentile of Accepted	Median GPA (4.0 scale) of Enrolled	Total Applicants	Applicants Accepted	Applicants Enrolled
Southwestern University (School of Law) 675 South Westmoreland Avenue Los Angeles, CA 90005-3992 213-738-6717 Fax: 213-383-1688 admissions@swlaw.edu	65		29	3.2	1975	1067	353
St. Thomas University (School of Law) 16400 N.W. 32nd Avenue Miami, FL 33054 305-623-2310 lamy@stu.edu	33	145	15	2.7	1524	966	217
Stanford University (Stanford Law School) Crown Quadrangle Stanford, CA 94305-8610 650-723-4985 Fax: 650-723-0838 law.admissions@forsythe.stanford.edu/	96	167		3.7	3824	474	178
State University of New York at Buffalo (University at Buffalo Law School) O'Brian Hall Buffalo, NY 14260 716-645-2907 Fax: 716-645-5940 coxublaw@buffalo.edu	60	153	6	3.2	844	510	232
Stetson University (College of Law) 1401 61st Street South St. Petersburg, FL 33707 727-562-7802 Fax: 727-343-0136 lawadmit@hermes.law.stetson.edu		152		3.4	1943	798	240
Suffolk University (Law School) 120 Tremont Street Boston, MA 02108-4977 617-573-8144 Fax: 617-573-1367	54	153	32	3.2	2100		550
Syracuse University (College of Law) Office of Admissions and Financial Aid Syracuse, NY 13244-1030 315-443-1962 Fax: 315-443-9568	52	151		3.3	1945		265
Temple University (James E. Beasley School of Law) 1719 N. Broad Street Philadelphia, PA 19122 215-204-8925 Fax: 215-204-1185 lawadmis@blue.temple.edu	68	155	21	3.2	2691	1108	343
Texas Southern University (Thurgood Marshall School of Law) 3100 Cleburne Avenue Houston, TX 77004 713-313-7114 Fax: 713-313-1049 cgardner@tsulaw.edu		142		2.7	952	417	322

LAW SCHOOL	ACADEMIC STATISTICS				ADMISSION STATISTICS		
	Median LSAT Percentile of Enrolled	Median LSAT Score of Enrolled	Lowest LSAT Percentile of Accepted	Median GPA (4.0 scale) of Enrolled	Total Applicants	Applicants Accepted	Applicants Enrolled
Texas Tech University (School of Law) 1802 Hartford Lubbock, TX 79409 806-742-3985 Fax: 806-742-1629 xydaw@ttacs.ttu.edu	67	155	17	3.4	1092	536	199
Texas Wesleyan University (School of Law) 1515 Commerce Street Fort Worth, TX 76102 817-212-4040 Fax: 817-212-4002 law-admissions@law.txwes.edu	50	150		3.1	942	238	223
Thomas Jefferson School of Law 2121 San Diego Avenue San Diego, CA 92110 619-297-9700 Fax: 619-294-4713 adm@tjsl.edu		149	9	2.8	1591	1119	243
Thomas M. Cooley Law School 300 South Capitol Avenue Lansing, MI 48901 517-371-5140 Fax: 517-334-5718 admissions@cooley.edu	23	143	6	2.9	2775	2158	769
Touro College (Jacob D. Fuchsberg Law Center) 300 Nassau Road Huntington, NY 11743 631-421-2244 ext. 312 Fax: 631-421-9708 admissions@tourolaw.edu			18		1912	858	219
Tulane University (Law School) Weinmann Hall, 6329 Freret Street New Orleans, LA 70118 504-865-5930 Fax: 504-865-6710 admissions@law.tulane.edu	83	159	25	3.3	2805	1295	323
Union University (Albany Law School) 80 New Scotland Avenue Albany, NY 12208 518-445-2326 Fax: 518-445-2369 admissions@mail.als.edu	47	150	11	3.1	1455	851	254
University of Akron (School of Law) Corner Wolf Ledges and University Avenue Akron, OH 44325-2901 330-972-7331 Fax: 330-258-2343 lawadmissions@uakron.edu	52	151	13	3.2	1149	492	202
University of Alabama (School of Law) Box 870382 Tuscaloosa, AL 35487-0382 205-348-5440 Fax: 205-348-3917 admissions@law.ua.edu	78	158		3.3	621	310	184

LAW SCHOOL	ACADEMIC STATISTICS				ADMISSION STATISTICS		
	Median LSAT Percentile of Enrolled	Median LSAT Score of Enrolled	Lowest LSAT Percentile of Accepted	Median GPA (4.0 scale) of Enrolled	Total Applicants	Applicants Accepted	Applicants Enrolled
University of Arizona **(James E. Rogers College of Law)** Mountain and Speedway P.O. Box 210176 Tucson, AZ 85721-0176 520-621-3477 Fax: 520-621-9140 admissions@nt.law.arizona.edu	85	160	36	3.4	1830	410	150
University of Arkansas **(School of Law)** Robert A. Leflar Law Center, Waterman Hall Fayetteville, AR 72701 501-575-3102		152		3.3	622	338	161
University of Arkansas at Little Rock **(School of Law)** 1201 McAlmont Street Little Rock, AR 72202-5142 501-324-9439 Fax: 501-324-9433	60	153	23	3.3	461	234	109
University of Baltimore **(School of Law)** 1420 North Charles Street Baltimore, MD 21201-5779 410-837-4459 Fax: 410-837-4450 lwadmiss@ubmail.ubalt.edu		149	15	2.9	1473	892	305
University of California **(Hastings College of the Law)** 200 McAllister Street San Francisco, CA 94102 415-565-4623 Fax: 415-565-4863 admiss@uchastings.edu	88	162	23	3.4	3972	1329	416
University of California at Berkeley **(Boalt Hall)** 5 Boalt Hall Berkeley, CA 94720 510-642-2274 Fax: 510-643-6222 admissions@law.berkeley.edu	93	165	37	3.8	4717	867	269
University of California **at Los Angeles** **(School of Law)** P.O. Box 951445 Los Angeles, CA 90095-1445 310-825-2080 Fax: 310-825-9450 admissions@law.ucla.edu	92	164	36	3.7	4721	907	286
University of California, Davis **(School of Law)** King Hall - 400 Mrak Hall Drive Davis, CA 95616-5201 530-752-6477 lawadmissions@ucdavis.edu	81	160	30	3.4	2290	796	161
University of Chicago **(Law School)** 1111 East 60th Street Chicago, IL 60637 773-702-9484 Fax: 773-834-0942 admissions@law.uchicago.edu	97	169		3.7	2972	883	182

	ACADEMIC STATISTICS				ADMISSION STATISTICS		
LAW SCHOOL	Median LSAT Percentile of Enrolled	Median LSAT Score of Enrolled	Lowest LSAT Percentile of Accepted	Median GPA (4.0 scale) of Enrolled	Total Applicants	Applicants Accepted	Applicants Enrolled
University of Cincinnati (College of Law) P.O. Box 210040 Cincinnati, OH 45221-0040 513-556-6805 Admissions@law.uc.edu	84	159	20	3.5	953	416	128
University of Colorado (School of Law) Campus Box 403 Boulder, CO 80309-0403 303-492-7203	86	161	23	3.5	1836	571	168
University of Connecticut (School of Law) 55 Elizabeth Street Hartford, CT 06105 860-570-5159 Fax: 860-570-5153 admit@law.uconn.edu	80	159		3.3	1939	625	184
University of Dayton (School of Law) 300 College Park Dayton, OH 45469-2760 937-229-3555 Fax: 937-229-4194 lawinfo@udayton.edu	56	152	13	3.1	1190	762	167
University of Denver (College of Law) 7039 E. 18th Avenue Denver, CO 80220 303-871-6135 Fax: 303-871-6100	58	154	33	3.2	1751	1161	332
University of Detroit Mercy (School of Law) 651 East Jefferson Avenue Detroit, MI 48226 313-596-0264 Fax: 313-596-0280 udmlawao@udmercy.edu	37	147	15	3	564	312	96
University of Florida (College of Law) 325 Holland Hall P.O. Box 117622 Gainesville, FL 32611-7622 352-392-2087 Fax: 352-392-2087 patrick@law.ufl.edu	75	157		3.5	2328	773	400
University of Georgia (School of Law) Hirsch Hall, 225 Herty Drive Athens, GA 30602-6012 706-542-7060	86	161	20	3.6	1680	532	227
University of Hawaii-Manoa (William S. Richardson School of Law) 2515 Dole Street Honolulu, HI 96822 808-956-7966 Fax: 808-956-3813 lawadm@hawaii.edu	79	159	21	3.4	518	150	77
University of Houston (Law Center) Office of Admissions Houston, TX 77204-6391 713-743-1070 Fax: 713-743-2194 admission@www.law.uh.edu	73	158	18	3.3	2441	881	289

LAW SCHOOL	ACADEMIC STATISTICS				ADMISSION STATISTICS		
	Median LSAT Percentile of Enrolled	Median LSAT Score of Enrolled	Lowest LSAT Percentile of Accepted	Median GPA (4.0 scale) of Enrolled	Total Applicants	Applicants Accepted	Applicants Enrolled
University of Idaho **(College of Law)** P.O. Box 442321 Moscow, ID 83844-2321 208-885-6423 Fax: 208-885-5709 adewitt@uidaho.edu	60	153	23	3.3	479	307	100
University of Illinois **(College of Law)** 504 East Pennsylvania Avenue Champaign, IL 61820 217-244-6415 Fax: 217-244-1478	86	161	33	3.4	1606	609	209
University of Iowa **(College of Law)** 276 Boyd Law Building, Melrose at Byington Street Iowa City, IA 52242 319-335-9095 or 319-335-9142 Fax: 319-335-9019 law-admissions@uiowa.edu	78	158		3.5	1119	537	227
University of Kansas **(School of Law)** 205 Green Hall Lawrence, KS 66045 785-864-4378 Fax: 785-864-5054 lindeman@law.wpo.ukans.edu	69	154	20	3.3			
University of Kentucky **(College of Law)** 209 Law Building Lexington, KY 40506-0048 606-257-7938 dbakert@pop.uky.edu	78	158	33	3.5	843	320	124
University of Louisville **(Louis D. Brandeis School of Law)** University of Louisville Belknap Campus-Wilson W. Wyatt Hall Louisville, KY 40292 502-852-6364 Fax: 502-852-0862 charlene.olivia@louisville.edu	74	157	27	3.4	820	290	125
University of Maine **(School of Law)** 246 Deering Avenue Portland, ME 04102 207-780-4341		154	15	3.1	487	273	77
University of Maryland **(School of Law)** 515 West Lombard Street Baltimore, MD 21201 410-706-3492 Fax: 410-706-4045 admissions@law.umaryland.edu	71	156	10	3.4	2469	984	301
University of Memphis **(Cecil C. Humphreys School of Law)** Campus Box 526513 Memphis, TN 38152-6513 901-678-2073 Fax: 901-678-5210 uofmlaw@profnet.law.memphis.edu	64	154	15	3.2	897	372	139

LAW SCHOOL	ACADEMIC STATISTICS				ADMISSION STATISTICS		
	Median LSAT Percentile of Enrolled	Median LSAT Score of Enrolled	Lowest LSAT Percentile of Accepted	Median GPA (4.0 scale) of Enrolled	Total Applicants	Applicants Accepted	Applicants Enrolled
University of Miami (School of Law) P.O. Box 248087, 1311 Miller Drive Coral Gables, FL 33124-8087 305-284-2523 admissions@law.miami.edu	63	154	13	3.2	2430	1389	435
University of Michigan (Law School) 625 South State Street Ann Arbor, MI 48109-1215 313-764-0537	93	165	40	3.6	3335	1215	343
University of Minnesota (Law School) 229 19th Avenue S., Office of Admissions Minneapolis, MN 55455 612-625-3487 Fax: 612-626-1874	89	162	40	3.6	1773	674	210
University of Mississippi (School of Law) Lamar Hall Oxford, MS 38677 601-915-6910 Fax: 601-915-1289 bvinson@olemiss.edu	60	153	7	3	1122	469	194
University of Missouri-Columbia (School of Law) 103 Hulston Hall Columbia, MO 65211 573-882-6042 Fax: 573-882-9625 umclawadmissions@missouri.edu	62	155	28	3.3	792	445	177
University of Missouri-Kansas City (School of Law) 500 East 52nd Street Kansas City, MO 64110-2499 816-235-1644 Fax: 816-235-5276 klosterman@umkc.edu	52	151	23	3.2	667	386	165
University of Montana (School of Law) Missoula, MT 59812 406-243-2698 lawadmis@selway.umt.edu	60	153	3	3.2	352	235	73
University of Nebraska (College of Law) P.O. Box 830902 Lincoln, NE 68583-0902 402-472-2161 Fax: 402-472-5185 lawadm@unlinfo.unl.edu	60	153	12	4	530	320	133
University of New Mexico (School of Law) 1117 Stanford Drive N.E. Albuquerque, NM 87131-1431 505-277-5072 Fax: 505-277-9958		155		3.2	736	256	120
University of North Carolina at Chapel Hill (School of Law) Campus Box 3380, 101 Van Hecke-Wettach Hall Chapel Hill, NC 27599-3380 919-962-5109 Fax: 919-843-7939 law_admission@unc.edu		160	24	3.6	2481	621	237

LAW SCHOOL	ACADEMIC STATISTICS				ADMISSION STATISTICS		
	Median LSAT Percentile of Enrolled	Median LSAT Score of Enrolled	Lowest LSAT Percentile of Accepted	Median GPA (4.0 scale) of Enrolled	Total Applicants	Applicants Accepted	Applicants Enrolled
University of North Dakota (School of Law) Box 9003 Grand Forks, ND 58202 701-777-2104 Fax: 701-777-2217 linda.kohoutek@thor.law.und.nodak.edu		150	11	3.3	239	129	64
University of Notre Dame (Notre Dame Law School) P.O. Box 959 Notre Dame, IN 46556-0959 219-631-6626 Fax: 219-631-3980 law.bulletin.1@nd.edu	90	163	42	3.4	1869	552	184
University of Oklahoma (College of Law) 300 Timberdell Road Norman, OK 73019 405-325-4726 Fax: 405-325-0502 kmadden@ou.edu	64	154	64	3.4	605	295	187
University of Oregon (School of Law, William W. Knight Law Center) 1515 Agate Street Eugene, OR 97403-1221 541-346-1553 Fax: 541-346-3984 bmcolure@law.uoregon.edu		156	17	3.5	1043	630	177
University of Pennsylvania (Law School) 3400 Chestnut Street Philadelphia, PA 19104-6204 215-898-7400 admissions@oyez.law.upenn.edu	95	166	21	3.6	3422	999	249
University of Pittsburgh (School of Law) 3900 Forbes Avenue Pittsburgh, PA 15260 412-648-1412 Fax: 412-648-2647 admissions@law.pitt.edu	64	154		3.2	1220	765	263
University of Puerto Rico (School of Law) P.O. Box 23349, UPR Station Rio Piedras, PR 00931 787-764-1655 Fax: 787-764-2675	34	146	4	3.6	719	180	168
University of Richmond (The T.C. Williams School of Law) University of Richmond, VA 23173 804-289-8189 admissions@uofrlaw.richmond.edu	74	157		3.2	1246	543	156
University of San Diego (School of Law) 5998 Alcala Park San Diego, CA 92110 619-260-4528 Fax: 619-260-2218 jdinfo@acusd.edu	84	160		3.2	2935		334

LAW SCHOOL	ACADEMIC STATISTICS				ADMISSION STATISTICS		
	Median LSAT Percentile of Enrolled	Median LSAT Score of Enrolled	Lowest LSAT Percentile of Accepted	Median GPA (4.0 scale) of Enrolled	Total Applicants	Applicants Accepted	Applicants Enrolled
University of San Francisco (School of Law) 2130 Fulton Street San Francisco, CA 94117-1080 415-422-6586 Fax: 415-422-6433	68	155		3.2	2445	1148	228
University of South Carolina (School of Law) Main and Greene Streets Columbia, SC 29208 803-777-6605 Fax: 803-777-7751 usclaw@law.law.sc.edu	75	155		3.2	1195	425	223
University of South Dakota (School of Law) 414 East Clark Street Vermillion, SD 57069-2390 605-677-5443 Fax: 605-677-5417 lawreq@usd.edu	56	152	5	3.3	239	116	45
University of Southern California (Law School) Los Angeles, CA 90089-0071 213-740-7331	92	164		3.5	3878	869	199
University of Tennessee (College of Law) 1505 W. Cumberland Avenue Knoxville, TN 37996-1810 865-974-4131 Fax: 865-974-1572 lawadmit@libra.law.utk.edu	70	156	20	3.5	1049	387	168
University of Texas at Austin (School of Law) 727 East Dean Keeton Street Austin, TX 78705 512-232-1200 Fax: 512-471-6988	88		30		3284	1088	483
University of the District of Columbia (David A. Clarke School of Law) 4200 Connecticut Avenue, N.W. Washington, DC 20008 Null Fax: 202-274-5583 vcanty@law.udc.edu	23	143	2	2.7	362	141	88
University of the Pacific (McGeorge School of Law) 3200 Fifth Avenue Sacramento, CA 95817 916-739-7105 Fax: 916-739-7134 admissionsmcgeorge@uop.edu	48	150	30	3	1680	1174	364
University of Toledo (College of Law) 2801 West Bancroft Street Toledo, OH 43606-3390 419-530-4131 Fax: 419-530-4345 law.utoledo.edu	52	152	15	3.2	633	427	190

LAW SCHOOL	ACADEMIC STATISTICS				ADMISSION STATISTICS		
	Median LSAT Percentile of Enrolled	Median LSAT Score of Enrolled	Lowest LSAT Percentile of Accepted	Median GPA (4.0 scale) of Enrolled	Total Applicants	Applicants Accepted	Applicants Enrolled
University of Tulsa (College of Law) 3120 East Fourth Place Tulsa, OK 74104-2499 918-631-2709 Fax: 918-631-3630	50	149	25	3.1	844	518	181
University of Utah (College of Law) 332 South 1400 East Front Salt Lake City, UT 84112 801-581-7479 Fax: 801-581-6897 gormleyl@law.utah.edu	84	159	32	3.5	805	304	125
University of Virginia (School of Law) 580 Massie Road Charlottesville, VA 22903-1789 804-924-7351 Fax: 804-982-2128 lawadmit@virginia.edu	93	165		3.7	3368	975	353
University of Washington (School of Law) 1100 Northeast Campus Parkway Seattle, WA 98105-6617 206-543-4078	88	162	28	3.5	1770	470	170
University of Wisconsin-Madison (Law School) 975 Bascom Mall Madison, WI 53706 608-262-5914 Fax: 608-262-5485 Admissions@law.wisc.educ		158		3.4	1639	708	310
University of Wyoming (College of Law) P.O. Box 3035 Laramie, WY 82071 307-766-6416 lawadmis@uwyo.edu	55	152	29	3.3	379	249	83
Valparaiso University (School of Law) Wesemann Hall Valparaiso, IN 46383-6493 219-465-7829 Fax: 219-465-7808 heike.spahn@valpo.edu	52	151	17	3.1	734	532	166
Vanderbilt University (School of Law) 131 21st Avenue South Nashville, TN 37203 615-322-6452	88	162	29	3.6	2387	760	182
Vermont Law School P.O. Box 96, Chelsea Street South Royalton, VT 05068-0096 802-763-8303 Fax: 802-763-7071 admiss@vermontlaw.edu	52	151	7	3	781	574	179
Villanova University (School of Law) Garey Hall Villanova, PA 19085 610-519-7010	67	157	50	3.4	1511	858	249

LAW SCHOOL	ACADEMIC STATISTICS				ADMISSION STATISTICS		
	Median LSAT Percentile of Enrolled	Median LSAT Score of Enrolled	Lowest LSAT Percentile of Accepted	Median GPA (4.0 scale) of Enrolled	Total Applicants	Applicants Accepted	Applicants Enrolled
Wake Forest University (School of Law) P.O. Box 7206, Reynolda Station Winston-Salem, NC 27109 910-758-5437	86	160	26	3.3	1391	580	163
Washburn University (School of Law) 1700 College Topeka, KS 66621 785-231-1185 Fax: 785-232-8087 admissions@washburnlaw.edu		149		3.1	543	353	141
Washington and Lee University (School of Law) Lewis Hall Lexington, VA 24450 540-463-8504 Fax: 540-463-8586 lawadm@wlu.edu	92	164	26	3.4	1282	488	120
Washington University in St. Louis (School of Law) Box 1120, One Brookings Drive St. Louis, MO 63130 314-935-4525 Fax: 314-935-6959 admiss@walaw.wash.edu	83	161	31	3.4	1961	813	212
Wayne State University (Law School) 468 W. Ferry Mall Detroit, MI 48202 313-577-3937 Fax: 313-577-6000 linda.sims@wayne.edu	65	154		3.2	910	464	213
West Virginia University (College of Law) P.O. Box 6130 Morgantown, WV 26506 304-293-5304 Fax: 304-293-6891 lawaply@wvu.edu	68	156		3.3	515	260	155
Western New England College (School of Law) 1215 Wilbraham Road Springfield, MA 01119 413-782-1406 Fax: 413-796-2067 lawadmis@wnec.edu		148	3	3	962	640	175
Western State University (College of Law) 1111 North State College Blvd Fullerton, CA 92831 714-738-1000, x2909 Fax: 714-526-1062 joel@wsulaw.edu		145		2.9	838	503	214
Whittier College (School of Law) 3333 Harbor Blvd. Costa Mesa, CA 92626 714-444-4141, ext. 121 Fax: 714-444-0250 info@law.whittier.edu		150	8	3	1427	822	233

LAW SCHOOL	ACADEMIC STATISTICS				ADMISSION STATISTICS		
	Median LSAT Percentile of Enrolled	Median LSAT Score of Enrolled	Lowest LSAT Percentile of Accepted	Median GPA (4.0 scale) of Enrolled	Total Applicants	Applicants Accepted	Applicants Enrolled
Widener University (School of Law) 4601 Concord Pike, P.O. Box 7474 and 3800 Vartan Way, Harris Wilmington, DE 19803 302-477-2162 (DE); 717-541-3903 (HBG) Fax: 302-477-2224 (DE); 717-541-3999 (HBG) law.admissions@law.widener.edu	32	147	4	3	1963	1237	520
Willamette University (College of Law) 245 Winter Street S.E. Salem, OR 97301 503-370-6282 Fax: 503-370-6375 law-admission@willamette.edu	64	154		3.2	720	491	150
William Mitchell College of Law 875 Summit Avenue St. Paul, MN 55105-3076 651-290-6476 Fax: 651-290-6414 admissions@wmitchell.edu	56	152	13	3.2	972	638	352
Yale University (Yale Law School) P.O. Box 208329 New Haven, CT 06520-8239 203-432-4995 admissions.law@yale.edu	99	171	71	3.9	3173	259	183
Yeshiva University (Benjamin N. Cardozo School of Law) 55 Fifth Avenue New York, NY 10003 212-790-0274 Fax: 212-790-0482 lawinfo@ymail.yu.edu		157		3.4	2506	1086	347

The following documentation applies if you purchased *How to Prepare for the LSAT, 10th Edition,* book with CD-ROM. Please disregard this information if your version does not contain the CD-ROM.

SOFTWARE DOCUMENTATION
This book/disk package should contain one Windows CD. It is recommended that you read the following documentation and instructions before you begin working with the computer program.

System Requirements
PC: Windows 3.1 or higher, 486 processor or higher, at least 4MB RAM (8MB or higher recommended), 6MB available hard-disk space, VGA compatible graphics adapter (640 × 480, 256 colors or higher recommended), and VGA or SVGA monitor.

Installation Instructions
To install Barron's LSAT software to your computer, do the following:
1. Boot the computer in the normal way. Start Windows. (Be sure that you are using Microsoft Windows 3.1 or higher.)
2. Insert the Windows CD into your computer's CD-ROM drive.
3. From the Windows File Manager, click on the "D" drive (if your CD drive is designated as "D"). Then, double-click on the "setup.exe" icon. Win 95: Click "Start" on the task bar and choose "Run."
4. You will see a "Barron's LSAT Setup" window. Click on "Next" to proceed with the installation. Win 95: Enter "d:\setup" (if your CD drive is designated as "D") and choose "OK."
5. You will now be asked to select the directory in which Barron's LSAT software will be installed. The default directory is C:\LSAT. If you wish to use a different directory, click on "browse" and enter it in the space provided. When you are ready, click on "OK." Click "Next" if you use the default directory.
6. The files needed to run Barron's LSAT software will now be copied to the computer's hard disk drive and the directory you selected. A screen message will inform you when the installation process is complete.
7. Once the files have been copied, a Program Manager group and the program icons will be created.

Technical Support
For further assistance call 626-568-3219 between 9 A.M. and 5 P.M. (Pacific Standard Time). Or you may fax your questions to 626-568-3267. You may also send your questions to the E-mail address below.

> E-mail: techsupport@barronseduc.com